MICROECONOMICS

CANADA IN THE GLOBAL ENVIRONMENT

THIRD EDITION

MICROECONOMICS

CANADA IN THE GLOBAL ENVIRONMENT
THIRD EDITION

MICHAEL PARKIN ◆ ROBIN BADE

✥ ADDISON-WESLEY PUBLISHERS LIMITED

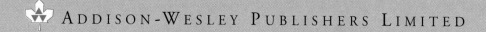

DON MILLS, ONTARIO • READING, MASSACHUSETTS • MENLO PARK, CALIFORNIA
NEW YORK • WOKINGHAM, ENGLAND • AMSTERDAM • BONN
SYDNEY • SINGAPORE • TOKYO • MADRID • SAN JUAN • PARIS • SEOUL
MILAN • MEXICO CITY • TAIPEI

Canadian Cataloguing in Publication Data

Parkin, Michael, 1939–
    Microeconomics: Canada in the global environment

3rd ed.
Includes index.
ISBN 0-201-42956-X

1. Microeconomics.   2. Canada – Economic conditions
– 1991 –   I. Bade, Robin.   II. Title.

HB172.P37   1997   338.5   C97-930131-9

Executive Editor:	Joseph Gladstone
Managing Editor:	Linda Scott
Acquisitions Editor:	Dawn Lee
Editorial Team:	Pam Erlichman
	Gail Copeland
	Suzanne Schaan
	Louise MacKenzie
Design, Cover Design, and Desktopping:	Anthony Leung
Production Team:	Melanie van Rensburg
	Roberta Dick
	Sharon Latta Paterson
Art Development:	Richard Parkin, RWP Graphics

ISBN 0-201-42956-X

A B C D E -DON- 01 00 99 98 97

About the Authors

Michael Parkin was educated at the University of Leicester. Currently in the Department of Economics at the University of Western Ontario, Professor Parkin has held faculty appointments at the Universities of Sheffield, Leicester, Essex, and Manchester, and has lectured extensively throughout Canada, the United States, Europe, Australia, and Japan. He has served as managing editor of the *Canadian Journal of Economics* and on the editorial boards of the *American Economic Review* and the *Journal of Monetary Economics*. Professor Parkin's research on macroeconomics, monetary economics, and international economics has resulted in 160 publications in the *American Economic Review*, the *Journal of Political Economy*, the *Review of Economic Studies*, the *Journal of Monetary Economics*, the *Journal of Money, Credit and Banking*, and dozens of other journals and edited volumes. In 1997-1998, Michael Parkin is the President of the Canadian Economics Association.

Robin Bade earned degrees in mathematics and economics at the University of Queensland and her Ph.D. at the Australian National University. She has held faculty appointments in the business school at the University of Edinburgh and Bond University and in the economics departments at the University of Manitoba, the University of Toronto, and the University of Western Ontario. Her research on international capital flows appears in the *International Economic Review* and the *Economic Record*.

Professor Parkin and Dr. Bade are joint authors of *Modern Macroeconomics* (Prentice-Hall), an intermediate text, and have collaborated on many research and textbook writing projects. They are both experienced and dedicated teachers of introductory economics.

Preface

To change the way students see the world—this is our purpose in teaching economics, and it has remained our goal in preparing the third edition of this text. There is no greater satisfaction for a teacher than to share the joy of students who have begun to understand the powerful lessons of the economic way of thinking. But these lessons are hard to learn. Every day in our classrooms, we relive the challenges of gaining the insights that economics provides and recall our own early struggles to master this discipline. In preparing this edition, we have been privileged to draw on the experiences of our own students at the University of Western Ontario and also of the many teachers and students who have used the two previous editions across Canada and other editions around the world. ◆ The principles of economics course is constantly evolving, and the past few years have seen some major shifts of emphasis in both microeconomics and macroeconomics. Today's principles course springs from today's issues—the slowdown in productivity growth, the information revolution, the emerging market economies of Central Europe and Asia, and the expansion of global trade and investment. In microeconomics, we want to place more emphasis on the core principles of opportunity cost, substitution, and choice and the power of the market to enable people to specialize and gain from trade. In macroeconomics, we more and more recognize the value of teaching long-run fundamentals as a basis for understanding these issues and as a springboard to understanding short-run economic fluctuations. This book allows you to place an early emphasis on long-run fundamentals. And for the first time, it allows you to teach the theory of long-run economic growth, including new growth theory, using the familiar tools of supply and demand.

The Third Edition Approach

THIS EDITION HAS BEEN CRAFTED TO MEET three overriding goals:

- Focus on the core principles
- Explain the issues and problems of the 1990s
- Create a flexible teaching and learning tool

Focus on Core Principles

The core principles of choice and opportunity cost, marginal analysis, substitution and incentives, and the power of the competitive process focus the micro chapters. The tools of demand and supply are thoroughly explained and repeatedly used throughout both the micro and macro chapters. New ideas, such as dynamic comparative advantage, game theory and its applications, the modern theory of the firm, information, public choice, new growth theory, and real business cycle theory, also appear in this book. But they are described and explained by using the core principles—new ideas are explained by using familiar ideas and tools.

Explain the Issues and Problems of the 1990s

The core principles and tools are not merely explained. They are *used* to help students understand the issues that confront them in today's world. Among the issues that are explored, some at length, are the environment, widening income gaps, the productivity growth slowdown, budget deficits, restraining inflation, watching for the next recession, avoiding protectionism, and the long-term growth of output and incomes.

Flexible Teaching and Learning Tool

One of the most exciting facts about economics is that its teachers hold strong views about what to teach and how to teach, yet they do not all hold the *same* view. This fact poses a special challenge to textbook authors, especially in the macro part of our subject. To be useful in a wide range of situations and to appeal to a diversity of teachers, a book must be flexi-

ble. This book can be used to teach all the traditional macro sequences, which place the main emphasis on short-term fluctuations in output, prices, and unemployment. It can support a course with a Keynesian emphasis or one with a monetarist emphasis. This book can also be used to teach a principles of macroeconomics course that places an early emphasis on supply-side issues and the long-term growth of output and incomes.

To signal that the chapters can be used not only in the order in which they are printed but in several others, the flexibility guide on p. xvi shows the main alternative possibilities.

Level and Viewpoint   The presence of modern topics does not translate into "high level," nor does it translate into "bias."

But this book does have a point of view. It is that economics is a serious, lively, and evolving science that seeks to develop a body of theory that can explain the economic world around us and that pursues its task by building, testing, and rejecting economic models. In some areas it has succeeded at its task, but in others it has some way to go and controversy persists. Where matters are settled, we present what is known; where controversy persists, we present the alternative viewpoints. This positive approach to economics is especially valuable for students as they prepare to function in a world in which simple ideologies have become irrelevant and in which familiar patterns in the economic landscape have shifted and blurred.

Always recalling our own early struggles with economics, we place the student at centre stage and write for the student foremost. We are conscious that many students find economics hard. As a result, our goal has been to make the material as accessible as possible. We use a style and language that make for an easy read and that don't intimidate.

Each chapter opens with a clear statement of learning objectives, a vignette that connects with the student's world and seeks to grab attention, and a preview of where we are heading. Once in the chapter, we do not reduce economics to a set of recipes to be memorized. Instead, we encourage the student to try to understand each concept. To accomplish this goal, we illustrate every principle with examples that have been selected both to hold the student's interest and to bring the subject to life. And to encourage a sense of enthusiasm and confidence in the student, as soon as we have explained a new principle, we put it to work and use it to illuminate a current real-world problem or issue.

Changes in the Third Edition

THE STRUCTURE OF THE MICROECONOMICS PRE-
sentation remains consistent with the first two editions, but it reflects the central goals of the revision:
to focus on core concepts, to explain current issues,
and to be leaner and simpler.

Chapter 1 is substantially new and is organized
around the themes of "how economists think" and
"what economists do." Chapter 3 uses lively new
examples to illustrate the core concepts of scarcity,
choice, opportunity cost, comparative advantage, and
the gains from trade.

The core demand and supply chapter (Chapter
4) has been refined and strengthened and Chapter 5
has a new example and illustration of the connection
between elasticity and total revenue, as well as new
international elasticity comparisons.

Chapter 9 explains why agency relationships arise
and how they lead to different types of business organization. Chapter 10 has a simplified explanation of
long-run average cost curves and of the relationship
between the shapes of the product curves and cost
curves. Chapter 11 gets to the point of the competitive model more quickly and has an improved explanation of competition and efficiency. Chapter 12 has
a new expanded explanation of price discrimination.
Chapter 13 has a more streamlined coverage of the
game theory approach to oligopoly.

We have reorganized and extended the chapters on
markets and government—again, consistent with our
focus on core principles. Chapter 18 previews the entire
range of government and public choice issues and combines material on public goods and public choice found
in Chapters 19 and 20 of the second edition. Chapter
19 (Chapter 18 in the second edition) discusses
inequality and redistribution. Chapter 20 on competition policy (Chapter 21 in the second edition) includes
new cases and examples, such as Bell Canada and
Smith and Coles bookstores. Chapter 21, a new chapter on externalities, gives an extensive discussion of the
economics of the environment and of knowledge.

The macroeconomics revision is extensive. The
organization has been revised and substantial
amounts of new material have been added.

Chapter 22 shows the macro landscape. It
describes its origins and rebirth in the Great
Depression; the issues it explores, both current and
historical and in Canada and around the world; and
the policy challenges it faces.

Chapter 23 has a new and streamlined treatment
of the circular flow and an expanded evaluation of the
uses of GDP along with international comparisons.

Chapter 24 has been thoroughly revised to give a
focused and streamlined introduction to the aggregate demand–aggregate supply model. And Chapter
25, which draws heavily on material from Chapters
25 and 26 in the second edition, presents the
Keynesian aggregate expenditure model and the mul-
tiplier in a single chapter. *Chapters 24 and 25 may be
studied in either order* and have been written especially to make either sequencing work well.

Policy issues come early in Chapter 26, a new
chapter on the budget and fiscal policy, and in
Chapters 27 and 28, on money and monetary policy.
Chapter 29 (an optional chapter) on the interactions
of fiscal and monetary policy is shorter and simpler.

Chapter 30 (an optional chapter) derives the
long-run and short-run aggregate supply curves and
Chapter 31, which is mostly new, uses demand and
supply to explain the trends in employment, unemployment, and real wage rates. This chapter can be
studied any time after Chapter 22. Chapter 32 (a
new optional chapter) gives a thorough treatment of
capital markets and the fundamentals driving real
interest rates.

Chapter 33, an entirely new chapter, makes economic growth and growth theory accessible to the
principles student. It describes the growth of the
Canadian and world economies and the sources of
the productivity growth slowdown. The entire block
of chapters on aggregate supply (Chapters 30 through
32) and Chapter 33 on long-term growth can be
studied *before* the chapters on aggregate demand topics (Chapters 25 through 29). This flexibility allows
teachers to structure a course that has a long-run
focus and that places short-term fluctuations in a
long-term perspective.

The next block of chapters covers policy problems. Chapter 34 is a new treatment of business cycle
and includes real business cycle theory. Chapter 35 is
a simpler and clearer coverage of inflation. And
Chapter 36 gives a big picture treatment of macro
policy. It shows how fiscal and monetary policy have
been used and it explains how policy can influence
long-term growth and the external balance.

Chapter 37 on international trade now includes
a section that evaluates the arguments for protection,
and Chapter 38 on the exchange rate is entirely
rewritten to present a simpler and much more accessible treatment of exchange rate determination and
the sources of exchange rate fluctuations.

Features That Enhance the Learning Process

THIS THIRD EDITION, LIKE ITS PREDECESSORS, IS packed with special features designed to enhance the learning process.

The Art Program: Showing the Economic Action

The first and second editions of this book set new standards with their highly successful and innovative art programs. Our goal has always been to show clearly where the economic action is. The figures and diagrams in this book continue to generate enormously positive feedback, confirming our view that graphical analysis is the most important tool for teaching and learning economics. But it is a tool that gives many students much difficulty. Because many students find graphs hard to work with, the art has been designed both to be visually attractive and engaging and to communicate economic principles unambiguously and clearly. In the third edition, the crystal clear style of the data-based art that reveals the data and trends has been retained. In addition, diagrams that illustrate economic processes now consistently distinguish among key economic players (firms, households, governments, and markets).

We observe a consistent protocol in style, notation, and use of colour, which includes

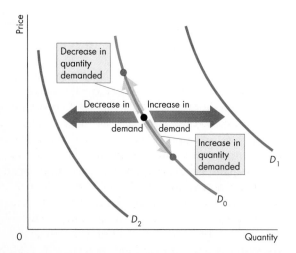

- Highlighting shifted curves, points of equilibrium, and the most important features in red
- Using arrows in conjunction with colour to lend directional movement to what are usually static presentations
- Pairing graphs with data tables from which the curves have been plotted
- Using colour consistently to underscore the content and referring to such use of colour in the text and captions
- Labelling key pieces of information in graphs with boxed notes
- Rendering each piece electronically so that precision is achieved

The entire art program has been developed with the study and review needs of the student in mind. It has the following features:

- Marking the most important figures and tables with an icon ◇ and listing them at the end of the chapter under key figures and tables
- Using complete, informative captions that encapsulate major points in the graph so that students can preview or review the chapter by skimming through the art

Interviews: Leading Economists Lend a Hand

Live interviews with famous economists are another popular feature in the previous editions. We continue the tradition and present nine—all new—interviews with economists who have contributed significantly to advancing thinking and practice in our discipline. One of the interviews is with a recent Nobel Laureate: Douglass North. The interviews encourage students to participate in the conversations as the economists discuss their areas of specialization, their unique contributions to economics, and their general insights that are relevant to beginning students.

The interviews appear as part openers and because they discuss topics that are introduced formally in the subsequent chapters, students can use them to preview some of the ideas they are about to encounter. A more careful reading afterward will give students a fuller appreciation of the discussion. Finally, the whole series of interviews can be approached as an informal symposium on the subject matter of economics as it is practised today.

Reading Between the Lines: News Articles for Critical Thinking

Another widely acclaimed feature of the previous editions is "Reading Between the Lines." This feature is designed to help students build critical thinking skills and use economic principles to interpret daily news events and their coverage in the media. We use stories from *The Economist, The Globe and Mail, The Financial Post*, and other Canadian newspapers coast to coast. All the "Reading Between the Lines" in this edition are new and were selected to appeal to students. Some of the "Reading Between the Lines" entitled "Policy Watch" deal with current political debates on topics such as slow economic growth, jobs and unemployment, inflation, the Bank of Canada's policy, and international trade policy. They have a series of "You're the Voter" questions that encourage critical policy evaluation and student participation in the political process by writing about their ideas and economic reasoning in e-mail messages to members of parliament. This activity is facilitated by providing a direct link from the Parkin-Bade home page to Parliamentary Internet Parlementaire at http://www.parl.gc.ca/. The detailed table of contents identifies the chapters with a "Policy Watch" feature with an icon ✛.

Economics in History

The "Economics in History" feature helps students trace the evolution of path-breaking economic ideas and recognize the universality of their application, not only to the past but also to the present. For example, Adam Smith's powerful ideas about the division of labour apply to the creation of a computer chip as well as to the pin factory of the eighteenth century.

Learning Aids: Pedagogy That Leads to Active Learning

The careful pedagogical plan has been refined to ensure that this book complements and reinforces classroom learning. Each chapter contains the following pedagogical elements:

Objectives   A list of learning objectives that enable students to see exactly where the chapter is going and to set their goals before they begin the chapter. The goals are linked directly to the chapter's major heads.

Chapter Openers   Intriguing puzzles, paradoxes, or metaphors frame questions that are unravelled and resolved as the chapter progresses.

Highlighted In-Text Reviews   Frequent, succinct summaries for review that have a list format.

Key Terms   Highlighted terms within the text form the first part of a three-tiered review of vocabulary. These terms are repeated with page references in the chapter summary and in the end-of-book glossary.

Key Figures and Tables   The most important figures and tables are identified with an icon ✧ and listed in the summary at the end of each chapter.

End-of-Chapter Study Material   Chapters close with a summary, lists of key terms, figures, and tables (with page references), and questions and problems. We have worked hard to create truly effective end-of-chapter questions, critical thinking issues, which are new to this edition, and problems. Each chapter has questions based on "Reading Between the Lines" as well as current policy topics. The problems have been revised to include many new ones and many that use diagrams. Problems identified by an icon ↺ are linked to our *Economics in Action* software package.

In many critical thinking questions and problems, identified with an icon ▦, we send the student to sites such as Statistics Canada, the Department of Finance, the Bank of Canada, and the Parkin-Bade home page on the World Wide Web. Our hope is to encourage the student to keep up-to-date and gain confidence using the web to access information.

Flexibility: Navigating the Principles Course

One semester or term is a short amount of time to accomplish the goals of the principles course. Our wants exceed our resources and we must make choices. To facilitate these choices, a text must be flexible and contain much optional material. The table on p. xvi explains which chapters form the core, which are applications, and which are optional. There is much variety in how we approach microeconomics at the principles level. Therefore a text must be flexible enough to support a number of different teaching styles and course organizations. Notes on the table on p. xvi indicate how the chapters can be organized to support several different courses.

The Teaching and Learning Package

ADDISON-WESLEY'S EDITORS, THE SUPPLEMENTS' authors, and we have worked closely together to ensure that our integrated text and supplements package provides students and teachers with a seamless learning and teaching experience. The authors of the supplements are outstanding economists and teachers who have brought their own human capital (and that of their students) to the job of ensuring that the supplements are of the highest quality and value. The package contains three broad components:

- Tools to enhance learning
- Tools to enhance teaching
- Tools for the electronic classroom

Tools to Enhance Learning

Study Guide   Available in microeconomics and macroeconomics split versions, the all new third edition Study Guide was prepared by Avi J. Cohen of York University and Harvey B. King of the University of Regina. Carefully coordinated with the main text, and the Test Bank, each chapter of the Study Guide contains:

- Key concepts that give the student a one- or two-page summary of the key definitions, concepts, and material of the chapter
- Helpful hints that help the student to avoid common mistakes and to understand the most important concept
- Self-test that helps the student practise exam-style questions

The self-test contains true/false/uncertain questions (that ask students to explain their answers), multiple-choice questions, short answer questions, and problems (graphical, numerical, analytical, and policy-oriented ones). The Study Guide gives complete answers, including brief explanations, to all questions and page references to the text for the multiple-choice and true/false/uncertain questions. All multiple-choice questions, and ones similar to them, are in the Test Bank.

The Study Guide has a Part Overview that corresponds with each Part of the textbook. The Part Overview contains a Problem and, new to the third edition, a Midterm Examination. The problem allows the student to test his or her cumulative understanding by integrating concepts from the chapters in the Part. Each problem is policy oriented and helps the student to apply what he or she has learned to real-world situations. Each midterm examination simulates a midterm test by presenting a selection of questions similar to those in the Test Bank. The midterm examination allows the student to check his or her understanding of the course to date and to see how prepared he or she is for the real midterm. The Study Guide gives the answers to the problem and the midterm examination.

Several elements of the Study Guide are geared to building critical thinking: True/false/uncertain questions, multiple-choice answers, critical thinking questions in the short answer problems, and the part overview problems. Other elements are geared to make studying economics a bit easier. The key concepts are a study aid; the helpful hints focus on ways to better understand the principles or to avoid common pitfalls; the multiple-choice questions are plentiful and include an explanation of why the answer to each question is correct; the part overview midterm examination allows the student to simulate an exam.

Economics in Action Interactive Software   The second edition supplements package included truly interactive software to support student mastery of economic principles. Students across the country and around the world have used this path-breaking and widely acclaimed computer learning tool to increase their success in the principles course. *Economics in Action* is a truly interactive learning tool.

Economics in Action Release 2.0 that accompanies the third edition is a thoroughly revised and expanded tool. It contains the original material updated and more closely coordinated with the text than its predecessor. It also includes an entirely new Excel (™Microsoft) spreadsheet data and graphing tool. This tool parallels the Variable Graphing utility of *Economics in Action* and enables users to create their own datasets and to print data and graphs.

Students will have fun working the tutorials, answering questions that give instant feedback, and testing themselves ahead of their midterm exams. One of our students told us that using *EIA* is like having a private professor in your dorm room! And students will find the real-world data both illuminating and useful for projects. The new release of the software has the following features:

- Step-by-step, graph-based tutorials that put the student in a business situation and actively engage the student by exploring economic concepts
- A graphing tool that allows the student to graph real-world economic data for Canada, the United State, twelve European countries, Japan, and Australia
- A Quiz that shows the student how to work out the answers to multiple-choice questions
- A self-testing facility that simulates a multiple-choice test setting and gathers results
- A problem-solving tool that allows students to solve homework problems from the text

NoteTaker   NoteTaker, formerly Graphpad, contains reproductions of all key figures in the textbook along with space for making notes. NoteTaker eliminates the tedious copying of graphs during lectures and allows the student more time to focus on understanding the material presented.

Tools to Enhance Teaching

Computerized Test Bank   Thoroughly revised test items were prepared by Harvey B. King of the University of Regina to accurately reflect the content and terminology of the third edition. The Test Bank includes 5,000 multiple-choice questions, of which 25 percent are new to this edition. All questions have been reviewed carefully for accuracy. The Test Bank includes all the multiple-choice questions in the Study Guide plus a set of questions that parallel those in the Study Guide. These questions are identified in the Test Bank.

Testing software is available to qualified adopters in an intuitive, easy-to-use Windows format. Tests and exams can be constructed with a few clicks of the mouse. This software gives instructors the ability to view graphs on the screen, add questions, edit questions, scramble question order and answer options, export to a word processor, and more. A print version is available on request (contact your Addison-Wesley sales consultant).

Instructor's Manual   A truly innovative Instructor's Manual has been prepared by Avi J. Cohen of York University and Susan Cohen of Digital Learning Inc.

Many of us today face the difficult challenge of teaching larger classes with fewer resources.

Responding to this trend and unique to this third edition of the Instructor's Manual are new teaching strategies for large class sizes. These strategies include tips on how to use teaching assistants effectively, how to minimize cheating on exams, and how to solve other large-class problems.

This Instructor's Manual also shows professors how to integrate the components of the Parkin-Bade package to create a comprehensive and engaging learning experience for their students.

One of the most innovative features of the Instructor's Manual is "Integrating Technology into Teaching." A full set of PowerPoint Lectures, including key textbook figures, accompanies the Instructor's Manual. "Integrating Technology into Teaching" provides step-by-step guidance on how to use the other computer-based learning tools such as *Economics in Action*, Internet resources, and the Parkin-Bade home page on the World Wide Web.

Solutions Manual   A Solutions Manual that contains the detailed solutions to all the problems at the end of the chapters has been prepared by Robin Bade and Jeannie Gillmore. This manual is available in electronic form. A print version is available to adopters of the textbook on request and to obtain it in this form, contact your Addison-Wesley sales consultant.

Acetates   Key figures from the text are rendered in full colour on the acetates. Several figures include overlays that make it easy to walk through the figure as you lecture. The acetates are enlarged and simplified to be more legible in large classrooms. They are available to qualified adopters of the textbook and may be obtained by contacting your Addison-Wesley sales consultant.

Tools for the Electronic Classroom

Electronic Lecture Support   A complete lecture framework in Microsoft PowerPoint is available for Macintosh and Windows. Prepared by Avi and Susan Cohen, this lecture support system is organized by chapter and includes key figures from the text in addition to speaking notes. Some of the PowerPoint slides simulate the overlays in the full-colour acetates. The PowerPoint Lectures and the viewer are available to adopters of the textbook free of charge.

Economics in Action Software   Instructors can use *Economics in Action* interactive software in the classroom. Its full-screen display option makes it possible to use its many analytical graphs as "electronic transparencies" and to do live graph manipulation and curve-shifting in lectures. Its real-world data sets and Variable Graphing utility enable time-series graphs and scatter diagrams to be made and displayed in the classroom. Additionally, *Economics in Action* is a helpful review tool for instructors to use with their students or assign to their students to help reinforce economic principles before tests or exams.

Parkin-Bade on the World Wide Web   Our lives as teachers, researchers, students, and just plain citizens have been transformed during the past year by the explosive emergence of an industry whose growth rate surpasses all others—the World Wide Web.

You can find many places in this book where we suggest that students visit a web site to obtain data or other information to work a problem or evaluate an opinion. We also provide a brief account of three of the most significant sites for Canadian macroeconomic policy data and information—the Bank of Canada, the Department of Finance, and Statistics Canada—in a Note to Chapter 36 (see pp. 895-896).

Because of the rapid technological changes taking place in this area, and because we intend to be at the forefront in utilizing these developments in the principles of economics course, we are not, at the time of writing, ready to reveal the full details of the Internet resources that we will have available in the fall of 1997 and beyond. Future announcements by Addison-Wesley will provide more details.

But we can say that the Parkin-Bade home page on the World Wide Web will become a must visit site for all teachers and students of the principles of economics. You will find much there to help your teaching and learning and to keep you current with economic developments in Canada and the world economy.

Whether you are a teacher or a student, you can reach all our Internet services at http://www.aw.com/canada/. Select 'Colleges and Universities' and then Economics.

Finally, if you have questions, comments, or suggestions for improvement, you can submit them via e-mail to Michael Parkin, whose address is parkin@sscl.uwo.ca or Robin Bade, whose address is bade@rogers.wave.com.

Acknowledgments

THE ENDEAVOUR OF CREATING A PRINCIPLES TEXT involves the creative collaboration and contribution of many people. Although the extent of our debts cannot be fully acknowledged, it is nevertheless a joy to record our gratitude to the many people who have helped, some without realizing just how helpful they were.

We thank those of our current and former colleagues at the University of Western Ontario who have taught us a great deal that can be found in these pages: Jim Davies, Jeremy Greenwood, Ig Horstmann, Peter Howit, Greg Huffman, David Laidler, Phil Reny, Chris Robinson, John Whalley, and Ron Wonnacott. We also thank Doug McTaggart of Bond University and Christopher Findlay of the University of Adelaide, co-authors of the Australian edition. Their suggestions arising from their adaptation of the first two editions have been extremely helpful in preparing this edition.

It is a special pleasure to acknowledge our debt and express our thanks to the several thousand students whom we have been privileged to teach. The instant feedback that comes from the look of puzzlement or enlightenment has taught us, more than anything else, how to teach economics.

Producing a text such as this is a team effort, and the members of the Addison-Wesley Canada "Parkin-Bade Team" are full co-producers of this book. We are especially grateful to Tony Vander Woude, President of Addison-Wesley Canada, and Allan Reynolds, Executive Vice-President and Chief Operating Officer, for their deep support for this project, to John More, Director and Vice-President of the College Division, for his overall direction of the project, to Joseph Gladstone, Executive Editor, Linda Scott, Managing Editor, and Dawn Lee, Acquisitions Editor, for their meticulous attention to details and for getting the book out on time. To publish a book of this magnitude and complexity requires the dedication and commitment of many other outstanding people. We acknowledge with gratitude and admiration the extraordinary efforts of Melanie van Rensburg, Anthony Leung, Roberta Dick, Sharon Latta Patterson, and Suzanne Schaan.

We also thank Jeannie Gillmore for helping us to find good news articles for the "Reading Between the Lines" features and for reading every line and letter of the final page proofs and helping to make this book as error-free as possible. Our thanks also to Jane McAndrew and to Christine Bies for helping us track down references and sources.

This edition has some common parentage with its U.S counterpart and we want to thank our U.S. editors who have contributed to this edition. We are especially grateful to the Senior Economics Editor at Addison-Wesley-Longman, Denise Clinton. She started working with us midway through the third edition revision and coaxed us to a thorough rethink of the structure of the macro principles course. This book contains much that would not be here without her insights and encouragement. We have been fortunate to work with a sequence of extraordinary editors. Marilyn Freedman was Senior Development Editor on two editions and we thank her again for her personal and professional commitment to this project. We also thank Lena Buonanno, who helped us to find extraordinarily helpful reviewers.

Throughout the revision process, we have been helped in innumerable ways by our supplements' authors, Avi Cohen and Harvey King. They have been constant and instantly available sources of inspiration and constructive criticism. We are enormously grateful to them. Robin wants to say a special thank you to Harvey for his trans-Pacific e-mail 'conversations' when we were working in the Australian morning and he in the Saskatchewan evening during the summer of 1996.

We thank Richard Parkin, who has provided outstanding support in creating the electronic art files and has contributed many ideas that have improved the figures in this book. We also thank Catherine Baum for providing the index and Ann Parkin for introducing us to many successful young people on Bay Street who have used our book in its earlier editions.

The empirical test of this book's value continues to be made in the classroom and we would appreciate hearing from you, our reader, about how we can continue to improve it in future editions.

Robin Bade and Michael Parkin
London, Ontario
January 1997

Reviewers

WE WOULD LIKE TO EXPRESS APPRECIATION FOR THE valuable advice and encouragement received from teachers across Canada during the creation and revisions of this book. We particularly wish to thank: **Syed Ahmed**, Red Deer College; **Benjamin Amoah**, University of Guelph; **Torben Andersen**, Red Deer College; **Syed Ashan**, Concordia University; **Andy Baziliauskas**, University of Winnipeg; **Karl Bennett**, University of Waterloo; **Ronald Bodkin**, University of Ottawa; **Paul Booth**, University of Alberta; **John Boyd**, University of British Columbia; **John Brander**, University of New Brunswick; **Emanuel Carvalho**, University of Waterloo; **Francois Casas**, University of Toronto; **Robert Cherneff**, University of Victoria; **Louis Christofides**, University of Guelph; **George Churchman**, University of Manitoba; **Avi Cohen**, York University; **Michael Hare**, University of Toronto; **Kam Hon Chu**, Memorial University; **Douglas Curtis**, Trent University; **Mohammed Dore**, Brock University; **Byron Eastman**, Laurentian Universtiy; **Brian Ferguson**, University of Guelph; **Len Fitzpatrick** Carleton University; **Peter Fortura**, Algonquin College; **Donald Garrie**, Georgian College; **David M. Gray**, University of Ottawa; **Rod Hill**, University of New Brunswick; **Susan Kamp**, University of Alberta; **Peter Kennedy**, Simon Fraser University; **Harvey King**, Universtiy of Regina; **Patricia Koss**, Concordia University; **Robert Kunimoto**, Mt. Royal College; **David Johnson**, Wilfrid Laurier University; **Eva Lau**, University of Waterloo; **Scott Lynch**, Memorial University; **Dan MacKay**, SIAST; **Keith MacKinnon**, York University; **Raimo Martalla**, Malaspina University College; **Dennis McGuire**, Okanagan University College; **David Murrell**, University of New Brunswick, Fredricton; **Robin Neill**, Carleton University; **A. Gyasi Nimarko**, Vanier College; **Sonia Novkovic**, Saint Mary's University; **John O'Brien**, Concordia University; **Arnold Paus-Jennessen**, University of Saskatchewan; **Don Reddick**, Kwantlen University College; **E. Riser**, Memorial University; **Nick Rowe**, Carleton University; **Michael Rushton**, University of Regina; **Balbir Sahni**, Concordia University; **Brian Scarfe**, University of Regina; **Marlyce Searcy**, SIAST Palliser; **Judith Skuce**, Georgian College; **Peter Sinclair**, Wilfrid Laurier University; **Stan Shedd**, University of Calgary; **Ian Skaith**, Fanshawe College; **George Slasor**, University of Toronto; **Bertram Somers**, Concordia University; **Bruce Wilkinson**, University of Alberta; **Russell Uhler**, University of British Columbia.

Microeconomics Flexibility Chart

Core	Policy	Optional

Core

1. What Is Economics?

3. Production, Growth, and Trade

4. Demand and Supply

5. Elasticity

7. Utility and Demand

Some teachers like to cover this material before Chapter 4. Some like to skip it. Both are possible.

9. Organizing Production

This chapter may be skipped.

10. Output and Costs

11. Competition

12. Monopoly

13. Monopolistic Competition and Oligopoly

14. Pricing and Allocating Factors of Production

This chapter gives an overview of factor markets. Chapters 15 and 16, which are optional, give a deeper account of the topic.

37. Trading with the World

Policy

6. Markets in Action

A unique chapter that gives extensive applications of demand and supply.

18. Market Failure and Public Choice

A general introduction to the role of government in the economy and the positive theory of government.

19. Inequality and Redistribution

20. Competition Policy

21. Externalities, the Environment, and Knowledge

Optional

2. Making and Using Graphs

Good chapter for students with fear of graphs.

8. Possibilities, Preferences, and Choices

Easy-to-teach coverage of indifference curves. Strictly optional.

15. Labour Markets

16. Capital and Natural Resource Markets

17. Uncertainty and Information

To the Student

WE WANT YOU TO DO WELL IN YOUR ECONOMICS course, to enjoy it, and to develop a deeper understanding of the economic world around you. With our colleagues Avi Cohen and Harvey King, we have written a book and supporting teaching and learning package that are designed to accomplish these goals.

Here's what we think *you* must do to achieve these same goals:

- Allocate at least four hours a week to economics in addition to your lecture and class time. Work steadily week by week. Cramming does not work.

- Read your textbook *before* each lecture and make good notes.

- Don't skip any lectures. Right after the lecture, modify your notes to incorporate the things your teacher emphasizes.

- Work *all* the questions and about a half of the problems at the end of the chapter.

- Work *all* the review material in the Study Guide.

- Work the Quiz section in *Economics in Action* and, if you need further help, the Tutorial section too.

- Test yourself by using the evaluation section of *Economics in Action.*

In our experience (and we have taught this course for sixty person years to some 15,000 students!), if you follow these steps, you will do well, you will have fun, and you might even get hooked on economics.

The Economics Major

If you find economics interesting and plan to study it further, you must decide whether to major in economics or to major in a related subject such as business. Over the past several years, more and more students have chosen business rather than economics as their major. We respect the choices people make. But we do believe that an economics major is a good choice, even for a student who knows that he or she is going to pursue a career in business (see page 819 of our interview with Finance Minister Paul Martin).

A degree in economics does three things for you especially well. First, it gives you the best training available in how to formulate and solve a decision problem.

The economic way of thinking gives insights into how to approach a decision, how to figure out the factors that are relevant to its solution, and how to use tools and techniques that find the best outcome available.

Second, an economics degree gives you lots of opportunities to develop your conceptual skills. People who can imagine the untried and then figure out how to move from an idea to a product are the most valuable economic resource that exists, and they command high returns for their efforts. Economics does not provide a checklist of new ideas. The essence of new ideas is their novelty. But it does equip you with a way of thinking about and exploiting new ideas that is not tied to the past. It liberates the mind to approach new ideas in new ways.

Third, an economics degree keeps doors open. In today's world, and more so in tomorrow's, an undergraduate degree is not sufficient for a truly rewarding career. The payoff from a postgraduate professional degree is on the average more than sufficient to justify the investment in it. In fact, for most of us, it is the highest yielding investment we will ever make. But in what field will you do post-graduate work? A great strength of an undergraduate degree in economics is that it prepares you well for a wide range of paths into professions, ranging from accounting, finance, banking, business and law to urban planning, and even to medicine. The insights of economics are relevant in all areas of life.

Economics and Math

Economics is a mathematical subject. Your principles course, and this book, are not very mathematical. But in second year and beyond, you can't do well in economics and avoid mathematics. And a good background in math is vital for any decently educated person today. So if you have the ability and inclination, it will pay to take some math courses alongside your principles of economics course.

Do I Need a Computer?

Yes! You need a computer. By the time you graduate, at the bare minimum, you must be familiar with wordprocessing, spreadsheets, and Internet applications. You do not absolutely have to have a computer to do your principles of economics course, but it will help a lot and will also help you move along the path to full computer literacy. So bite the bullet and buy one if you possibly can.

Brief Contents

part 1 Introduction

Summary, Review Questions, Critical Thinking, and
Problems appear at the end of each chapter.

Contents

part 3 Markets for Factors of Production

part 4 Markets and Government

part I

Introduction

Douglass North, who teaches economics and economic history at Washington University in St. Louis, was born in Cambridge, Massachusetts, in 1920. He was an undergraduate and graduate student at the University of California, Berkeley, where he earned his Ph.D. in 1952. Professor North has pioneered the study of economic institutions such as stable government, the rule of law, and private property rights and the role these institutions play in fostering economic development and sustained income growth. He has used his ideas to explain why the United States and Western Europe have evolved from low-income agricultural societies 200 years ago into high-income complex societies today. In 1993, Professor North was awarded the Nobel Prize for

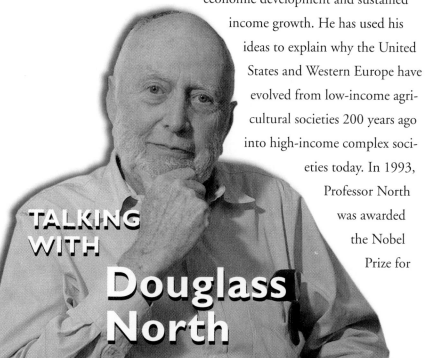

TALKING WITH Douglass North

Economic Science for this work. Robin Bade and Michael Parkin talked with Professor North about his work and its relevance to today's—and tomorrow's—world.

Professor North, what attracted you to economics?

I grew up during the Great Depression of the 1930s. While I went to college in 1938, I was a concerned young man, and I became a Marxist because a Marxist had answers, or at least avowed to have answers, to the economic concerns that were so prevalent during the Depression. If the market economy of capitalism was replaced by the planned economy of socialism, the Depression and other economic ills could, we then believed, be cured.

As a student at the University of California at Berkeley, I looked for courses that were directed to researching and understanding why some countries are rich and others are poor. Economic history seemed to me to be most related to this area.

When I graduated from college I was going to be a lawyer. However, World War II broke out, and I spent four years in the Merchant Marines. During those four years, I just took a whole slew of books and read and read. You don't have much else to do when you're going around the world at ten miles an hour. I decided that I wanted to save the world—like any good Marxist wanted to—and I decided that the way to save it was to understand what made economies work badly or work well. And I've been pursuing that utopian goal ever since.

How did you abandon your Marxist beginning? Was there a sudden revelation or was it a gradual process?
Converting from Marxism was a very slow process. My first teaching job was at the University of Washington in Seattle in 1950. I used to play chess every day with my colleague, Donald Gordon. He was a good economist, and over three years of playing chess every day and talking economics, I gradually evolved away from Marxism and became a mainstream economist.

What are the key economic principles that guide your work—the principles and perspectives the economist brings to a study of long-term historical processes?
There are two. The first is the importance of transactions costs—the costs that people incur in order to do business with each other.

Economics attempts to understand how societies cope with the problem of scarcity—with the fact that people's wants always outstrip their limited resources. Traditionally, economists have focused on how resources are allocated at a moment of time—what determines today's allocation of spending between high schools and hospitals, computers and cars. Economic history deals with how societies evolve over time and tries to discover why some societies become wealthy while others remain poor. I became convinced that the economic way of reasoning underlying the economic principles is the right way to understand how societies evolve over time. But this conviction led me on a long trail.

Back in the days when I was learning economics, economic theories were based on the *assumption* that people could specialize and exchange their products in markets that function efficiently. They ignored transaction costs—the costs that people incur when they do business with each other and the costs that governments and firms incur to make markets work. So the first problem was to think about how exchange takes place in the face of large transactions costs.

And the second principle?
The second principle is that transactions costs depend crucially on the way that human beings structure the economic order—on their institutions. And this fact gave me my second problem, to think about how institutions evolve to make markets work better over time.

When an economist talks about economic institutions, what exactly is he or she talking about? What are these institutions?
Institutions are rules of the society that structure the interaction among people. Institutions are made up of formal rules, like constitutions and statute law, and common rules and regulations. But they're also more than that. They are the informal ways by which people deal with each other every day, which you could think of as norms of behaviour.

Institutions are the framework within which all of human interaction—political, social, and economic—takes place. And so, understanding how those work, why they work well in some circumstances, and why they work badly in others is the key, really, to the wealth of nations. Some examples of economic institutions include antitrust laws, patent laws, and bankruptcy laws.

The institutions that have evolved in the United States have brought economic development and prosperity while those that evolved in the former Soviet Union and that to some degree still prevail in Russia and other Eastern European countries have brought stagnation and poverty. Can economists explain the radically different institutional evolution of the United States and Eastern Europe?
This question is at the very heart of what economic history should be about and in part is about. How did a country's economy get to where it is today? Why did countries, such as the former Soviet Union, evolve differently? A lot of my research, including my work in U.S. economic history, attempts to research and understand the incremental process of institutional change.

> *In order to have efficient markets, a country needs to structure a set of rules and regulations to provide incentives for people to do productive and creative things ...*

The United States first inherited a set of institutions—among them common law and property rights—from Great Britain. These institutions made Britain the leading nation in the world by the end of the eighteenth century. The United States took Britain's institutions over, modified them, and elaborated on them. The result has been two and a half centuries of economic growth. Much of the rest of the world, and Russia in particular, evolved institutions that didn't work very well.

In the evolution of Britain and the United States, the governments evolved a set of rules that provided a lot of freedom and latitude for people to make contracts and agreements among themselves. These rules produced economic efficiency on an unparalleled scale and led to sustained economic growth, which is the foundation of successful economies.

Third World countries and Eastern Europe chose different economic paths. Communism, for example, was an institution that did not provide sustained economic growth.

The goal of research in economic development and economic history is to understand exactly what it was that led to this very differential process of change between countries like the United States, Britain, and Russia.

Are there lessons in the economic histories of the United States and Western Europe from which Eastern Europe can learn?
How to make countries change is a very complicated process. Countries need to develop efficient markets. Increases in productivity underlie a country's economic growth. In order to achieve productivity increases, investment is required in a number of areas including human capital, physical capital, technological knowledge, and research and development.

What is unique to every country is how to get from one kind of an economy to another. The first step is to start from where people are. The degree to which you can change at any moment of time is a function of the perceptions and knowledge and ideas that people have at a moment of time, as well as the existing institutions.

The economic growth of a country depends on its institutions. People can specialize, develop their human skills, and create profitable businesses only if they live under a framework of laws and property rights and have a

system of courts that enforce those property rights. Ultimately, and this is the most difficult of all things, you've got to have political stability which will perpetuate institutions conducive to economic development and income growth.

How do you explain the economic success of China and economic failure of Russia?
China had political authoritarianism at the top, and those authorities have either deliberately or accidentally loosened control in the provinces. The result has made for a very lucrative combination of local communist party officials teaming up with entrepreneurs, who got their capital and sometimes their training from the governments of Hong Kong and Taiwan, being let loose to pursue business ventures. And that's a unique situation. This certainly doesn't appear likely to happen in the former Soviet Union.

I think the biggest economic lessons are from Asia, the very successful countries of South Korea, Taiwan, and so on. They're interesting because they've shown that sometimes a proper dose of government can accelerate the process of creating efficient markets. Clearly, it teaches an impor-

> *... the biggest economic lessons are from Asia, the very successful countries of South Korea, Taiwan, and so on.*

tant lesson: In order to have efficient markets, a country needs to structure a set of rules and regulations to provide incentives for people to do productive and creative things and to produce better-quality goods at lower cost. And that takes a market with a set of rules that provides incentives for people to do that. It doesn't happen automatically. What Asia has shown us is that sometimes governments can in fact hasten the evolution of efficient markets.

Can you identify some of the key stages in which the U.S. government played a critical role in nurturing development of the rule of law, property rights, and the market economy?
The United States inherited economic and political rules from Great Britain. These rules provided the basis for efficient property rights and for the transfer of land, which was the biggest asset during the colonial period. Not only did

the United States create an efficient economic market, but it also created effective political markets. The Constitution of the United States was established, 11 years after that country's independence from Britain, to address growing trade and economic developments. It established a set of very efficient economic rules for the operation of the country. The Senate and House of Representatives were established and given power to, among other things, collect taxes, regulate commerce with other nations, regulate the value of money, and establish rules of bankruptcy.

How would you characterize the changes that are taking place in today's global and national economy?
I look at economic revolutions as changes in knowledge that fundamentally changed the whole economic social organization of societies. The origin and development of agriculture were the first economic revolution. This economic revolution probably occurred in the eighth millennium B.C. Agriculture completely altered the pace of economic and all other kinds of human change. Human beings settled down into villages and towns. This eventually led to the growth of exchange and to the whole basis for civilization. Agriculture enormously increased productivity potential and the potential for human progress.

The next real fundamental economic change was the application of science to technology. I would say there's never been a time in human history in which there's been as dramatic a setting of change as we're seeing in the world we live in today. I think it's extraordinary. It's a very exciting world to live in, particularly for an economic historian. I have argued that something happened in the

nineteenth century, which I call the Second Economic Revolution: there was a systematic wedding of science to technology that led to the development of the disciplines of physics, chemistry, genetics, and biology. This revolution has completely changed the way in which all of modern economic activity takes place and the way that human beings live and interact.

The personal and social implications of that revolution are enormous. As a result of this revolution, we live packed together in huge cities, many of which are plagued by crime on a scale that frightens us, and we depend for

our economic well-being on millions of people we do not know. Many people have benefited from the advances in technology and enjoy unimagined high living standards, while many others have been left behind and are not sharing in the prosperity that the second economic revolution has created. So, combined with the prosperity of this economic revolution, we've created a set of social, political, and

economic problems that we haven't figured out how to solve. And they may overwhelm us down the road.

What is your advice to a student who is just setting out to become an economist? How should the student approach his or her work? What are the things to study?
You should find excitement and challenge in the things you do and pursue them. At a university, this means that you ought to bug your professors. You should be continually trying to get a lot out of them. I think most university students don't get out of school what they

could. Both in and out of class, you should ask questions and pursue the answers to those questions. I think that's terribly important.

I think the most important thing in the world is to have a creative, stimulating, exciting life. Everybody can do that in their own way, depending on their own curiosities, interests, and talents. Find out what things excite you, and pursue them all your life.

I think the most important thing in the world is to have a creative, stimulating, exciting life. ... Find out what things excite you, and pursue them all your life.

Chapter

1

What Is Economics?

After studying this chapter, you will be able to:

- Identify the kinds of questions that economics seeks to answer

- Explain why all economic questions arise from scarcity

- Explain why scarcity forces people to make choices and face costs

- Explain how economists think and describe what they do

- Describe the functions and the components of the economy

Twenty years ago almost no one watched a movie at home. But what was once a luxury enjoyed by only the wealthiest Canadians is today an event enjoyed by millions. Why? Because advances in video and communications technologies have slashed the cost of home movies. The technologies that are transforming our homes are revolutionizing our farms, mines, factories, and assembly lines.

Economic Questions

Video cameras guide robots that pick fruit, mine coal, make steel, and assemble cars. As a result, millions of old jobs have gone, and millions of new jobs have been created. These facts raise the first set of economic questions:

How does technological change affect the goods people consume and the jobs they do both here in Canada and around the world?

Movie stars, pop singers, news anchors, outstanding sports men and women, lawyers, doctors, and the chief executive officers of big companies earn large incomes. Gas pump attendants, supermarket check-out clerks, and day-care workers earn just a few dollars an hour. On the average, men earn more than women. These facts raise a second set of economic questions:

What determines people's incomes? Why are women paid less than men, often when they do jobs that seem similar?

Over the years, the scope of government has expanded. At the time of Confederation, the main business of government was to provide law and order. Today governments provide social insurance, health care, education, and equalization payments to the provinces as well as national defence. They also regulate food and drug production, nuclear energy, and agriculture. Also, over the years, we've become more aware of our fragile environment. Chemicals called CFCs (chlorofluorocarbons), used in a wide variety of products from coolants in refrigerators and air conditioners to plastic phones and cleaning solvents for computer circuits, are believed to damage the atmosphere's protective ozone layer. Burning fossil fuels—coal and oil—adds carbon dioxide and other gases to the atmosphere, which prevents infrared radiation from escaping and might result in what has been called the "greenhouse effect." These facts raise a third set of economic questions:

What is the government's role in economic life? Can government help us to protect our environment and be as effective as private enterprise at producing goods and services?

Since the late 1970s, China has been undergoing a dramatic economic transformation. Incomes in that country have grown at more than 10 percent a year— doubling every 7 years. In some cities—such as Shanghai —incomes have grown by more than 20 percent in some years. And China is not alone. Rapid income growth has occurred in Hong Kong, India, Indonesia, Malaysia, Singapore, South Korea, Taiwan, and Thailand. Incomes continue to grow in the rich countries of the world—Canada and the United States, Japan, Western Europe, and Australia and New Zealand—but the pace of expansion in these countries has slowed compared with the 1960s. In stark contrast to the growth miracles, Russian incomes shrank by an alarming 12 percent in 1993. Incomes also shrank in the Czech Republic and Hungary. These facts raise a fourth set of economic questions:

Why do incomes grow at an incredibly rapid rate in some countries, grow at a slower rate in other countries, and even fall in a few countries?

During the Great Depression—the early 1930s— unemployment afflicted almost one-fifth of the work force in the industrial world. The Great Depression was a period of extreme hardship. But high unemployment is not unusual. For the past several years, unemployment has been around or above 10 percent in Canada, the United Kingdom, France, and Italy. In Canada, when the average unemployment rate is 10 percent—as it was approaching in 1996—the unemployment rate among young people (15 to 24 year olds) is close to 16 percent and for young people in Newfoundland it is 20 percent. These facts raise a fifth set of economic questions:

What causes unemployment and why are some countries and groups more severely affected than others? Why are there so few good jobs for young Canadians, and even fewer jobs for young Canadians in Atlantic Canada?

In 1993, the cost of living in Brazil rose by 2,500 percent. This meant that on the Copacabana beach, a pineapple that cost 15 cruzeiros on January 1 cost 390 cruzeiros by the end of the year. In that same year, prices in Russia rose by almost 1,000 percent. In contrast, prices in Canada increased by only 2 percent. But in the late 1970s, prices in Canada were rising by more than 10 percent a year. These facts raise a sixth set of economic questions:

Why do prices rise and why do some countries sometimes experience rapid price increases while others have stable prices?

In the 1960s, almost all the cars and trucks on the highways of North America were Fords, Chevrolets, and Chryslers. In 1996, more than one-fifth of the cars were imported. And cars are not exceptional. We now import most of our television sets, clothing, and computers.

Governments impose taxes (called tariffs) on imports and also restrict the quantities of some goods that might be imported. They also enter into agreements with other governments such as the North American Free Trade Agreement (NAFTA) between Canada, the United States, and Mexico. These facts raise a seventh set of economic questions:

What determines the amount of trade between nations, and how do international trade agreements affect jobs and prosperity in Canada and other countries?

◆ These seven questions give you a sense of what economics is about. But they don't tell you what economics *is*. They don't tell you how to identify an *economic* question and distinguish it from a noneconomic question. Nor do they tell you how economists think about economic questions and seek answers to them. How do economists identify *economic* questions? And how do they think about economic issues?

How Economists Think

ECONOMISTS, AS INDIVIDUALS, ARE LIKE EVERYONE else. They have their own private objectives and agendas and have opinions about all sorts of economic and noneconomic issues. You have perhaps already thought that the seven economic questions are very political. They are. They have an enormous influence on the quality of human life and they generate fierce argument and debate.

Economists, as professionals, try to stand clear of the emotion, and to approach their work with the detachment, rigor, and objectivity of a scientist. The first step in this process is to identify the fundamental problem from which all economic questions stem. That fundamental problem—*the* economic problem—is the fact that we have limited resources but unlimited wants.

Scarcity

When wants exceed the resources available to satisfy them, there is **scarcity**. Scarcity is everywhere. People want good health and long life, material comfort, security, physical and mental recreation, and knowledge. None of these wants is completely satisfied for everyone; and everyone has some unsatisfied wants. Although many Canadians have all the material comfort they want, many others do not. No one feels entirely satisfied with her or his state of health and expected length of life. No one feels entirely secure, even in this post–Cold War era, and no one has enough time for sport, travel, vacations, movies, theatre, reading, and other leisure pursuits.

Scarcity is not *poverty*. The poor and the rich face scarcity. A child wants a 75¢ can of soft drink and a 50¢ pack of gum but has only $1.00 in her pocket. She experiences scarcity. A wealthy student wants to go to a party on Saturday night but also wants to spend that same night catching up on late assignments. He experiences scarcity. Even parrots face scarcity—there just aren't enough crackers to go around.

Choice and Opportunity Cost

Faced with scarcity, people must make *choices*. When we cannot have everything we want, we choose

Not only do I want a cracker—we all want a cracker!

Drawing by Modell; ©1985 The New Yorker Magazine, Inc.

among the available alternatives. The concepts of scarcity and choice give a definition of economics. **Economics** is the study of how people make *choices* to cope with *scarcity*. Because scarcity forces choice, economics is sometimes called the *science of choice*— the science that explains the choices that people make and predicts how choices change as circumstances change.

Choosing more of one thing means having less of something else. Expressed another way, in making choices, we face costs. Whatever we choose to do, we could have chosen to do something else instead. There is no such thing as a free lunch. This popular phrase is not just a clever throwaway line. It expresses in a vivid way the central idea of economics that every choice involves a cost.

Economists use the term *opportunity cost* to emphasize that making choices in the face of scarcity implies a cost. The **opportunity cost** of any action is the best alternative forgone. The best action that you choose *not* to do—the forgone alternative—is the cost of the action that you choose to do.

Opportunity cost is the *best* alternative forgone. It is not *all* the *possible* alternatives forgone. An example will make this clear. Your economics lecture is at 8:30 on a Monday morning. You contemplate *two* alternatives to attending the lecture: staying in bed for an hour or going jogging for an hour. You can't stay in bed *and* go jogging for that same hour. The opportunity cost of attending the lecture is not the cost of an hour in bed *and* the cost of jogging for an hour. If these are the only alternatives you contemplate, then you have to decide which one you would do if you did not go to the lecture. The opportunity cost of attending a lecture for a jogger is a forgone hour of exercise; the opportunity cost of attending a lecture for a late sleeper is a forgone hour in bed.

Money Cost Versus Real Cost   We often express cost in terms of money. But this is just a convenient unit and is not a measure of opportunity cost. For example, the $40 spent on a book is not available for spending on four $10 CDs. So if four CDs are the best alternative forgone, the opportunity cost of a book is four CDs.

It is especially vital to look behind the money costs when the amount that money will buy changes. For example, a book that today costs $40, cost $25 in 1987. You can't conclude from this fact that the opportunity cost of a book has increased. To calculate the change in the opportunity cost of a book, you need to know the money cost of the alternative forgone in 1987 and today. If in 1987 a CD cost $25, the opportunity cost of a book has indeed increased—from one CD in 1987 to four CDs today. Why? Because book prices have increased and CD prices have decreased.

The key points are that it is fine to express opportunity cost in money units so long as you remember that this is just a convenient measure and that you can't compare opportunity costs in money units between different times when the value of money has changed.

Time Cost   The opportunity cost of a good or service includes the value of the time spent obtaining it. If it takes an hour to visit your dentist, the value of that hour must be added to the amount you paid your dentist. We can convert time into a money cost by using a person's hourly wage rate. If you take an hour off work to visit your dentist, the opportunity cost of that visit (expressed in units of money) is the amount that you paid to your dentist plus the wages that you lost by not being at work. Again, it's important to keep reminding yourself that the opportunity cost is not the money itself but the goods and services that you would have bought with the money.

External Cost   Not all of the opportunity costs that you incur are the result of your own choices. Sometimes others make choices that impose opportunity costs on you. For example, when someone smokes at a table next to you in a restaurant, you bear a cost. Also your own choices can impose opportunity costs on others. For example, when you enjoy a cold drink from your refrigerator, part of its opportunity cost, borne by others, is the increased carbon dioxide in the atmosphere resulting from burning coal to generate the electricity that powers your refrigerator.

Marginal Analysis

Marginal analysis is a fundamental idea that permeates economics. The core of the idea is that people make choices in small steps—or *at the margin.* They decide whether to do a little bit more or a little bit less of an activity. To make such a decision, they compare the cost of a little bit more of the activity with its benefit. For example, to decide when to stop reading this book, you compare the cost of sticking with it for another five minutes with the benefit you expect (hope) it will bring. When you get to the point at which the cost of another five minutes reading exceeds the benefit, you quit.

The cost of a small increase in an activity is called **marginal cost**.[1] For example, suppose your personal computer has 2 megabytes of memory and you are thinking about increasing its memory to 3 megabytes. The marginal cost of increasing your computer's memory is the cost of the additional megabyte of memory you are thinking about installing.

The benefit that arises from a small increase in an activity is called **marginal benefit**. For example, marginal benefit is the benefit you will get from one additional megabyte of memory in your computer, not the benefit you'll get from all 3 megabytes that you will have if you add one more megabyte. The reason is that you already have the benefit from 2 megabytes, so you don't count the benefit of these 2 megabytes as resulting from the decision you are now making.

To make your decision about computer memory, you compare the marginal cost of 1 megabyte with its marginal benefit. If the marginal benefit exceeds the marginal cost, you buy the extra memory. If the marginal cost exceeds the marginal benefit, you stick with what you've got.

When the marginal benefit of an action exceeds the marginal cost, taking the action adds to total benefit by more than it adds to total cost. When the marginal cost of an action exceeds the marginal benefit, not taking the action adds to total benefit by more than it adds to total cost. By evaluating marginal costs and marginal benefits, people are able to use their scarce resources in the way that makes them as well off as possible.

---

[1] The term *marginal cost* has a narrower technical definition: the cost of increasing output by one unit. This technical use of the term is just a special case of its more general meaning used here.

Substitution and Incentives

When opportunity costs change, people change their actions. Another central principle of economics, called the **principle of substitution**, is that when the opportunity cost of an activity increases, people substitute other activities in its place. Every activity has a *substitute*. Skiing is a substitute for skating; surfing is a substitute for skin diving; drinking Coke is a substitute for drinking Pepsi; studying economics is a substitute for taking dance training. A substitute might be similar to the original—Pepsi and Coke—or quite different—economics and dance.

If the opportunity cost of Coke increases, some people will substitute Pepsi for Coke; if the opportunity cost of studying economics increases (by a really large amount), some people will substitute dance for economics. The closer the substitutes, the greater is the degree of switching that takes place when the opportunity cost changes.

Substituting away from more costly activities towards less costly ones is responding to incentives. An **incentive** is an inducement to take a particular action. The inducement may be a reward—a carrot—or a penalty—a stick. Changes in opportunity costs—in marginal costs—and changes in marginal benefits change the incentives that people face and lead to changes in their actions. For example, long-distance phone companies give their customers an incentive to make calls in the evenings and at weekends by offering lower prices at those times. Ski resorts cut prices during the summer to create an incentive that encourages people to use winter vacation facilities all year. Electric power utilities charge higher prices to industrial users at peak times.

Whenever some unusual event disrupts the normal state of affairs, the economist always asks: How will opportunity costs change and what substitutions will arise from the changed incentives? For example, a frost kills Florida's orange crop and sends the price of orange juice through the roof. This increase in price, with all other prices unchanged, increases the opportunity cost of orange juice and gives people an incentive to drink less orange juice and substitute other fruit juices in its place. Or a bumper broccoli crop in Canada sends the price of broccoli tumbling. This decrease in price, with all other prices unchanged, decreases the opportunity cost of broccoli and gives people an incentive to eat more broccoli as a substitute for cauliflower and other vegetables.

Competition and Second Round Effects

Scarcity leads to *competition*. Each individual tries to obtain as many goods and services as possible by competing with other individuals. This competition takes many forms. For example, producers compete with each other for market share and seek the highest profit available. People compete with each other for jobs and seek the highest wages available (for a given amount of work effort). Shoppers compete with each other for bargains and seek the lowest prices available. And students compete with each other for concert tickets, parking spaces, and places in heavily demanded courses.

The effects of an economic disturbance are usually spread out over time. The immediate effects are the substitutions that people make in response to changes in incentives. But these effects lead to second round effects that ripple through the economy and in some cases have effects that are quite different from the initial or first round effects. Consider, for example, the effect of a Florida frost. The first round effect of a Florida frost is an increase in the price of orange juice and a substitution of other fruit juices (say apple juice) for orange juice. The second round effects are the consequences of the increased competition for scarce apples. Juice drinkers compete with apple eaters for the available apples and the price of apples increases. People now search for yet other substitutes—guava juice perhaps. As these second round effects play out, a long chain of substitutions and price changes take place, all triggered by a simple frost in Florida.

Economists try to predict second round effects by considering all the main substitutions that are likely as people compete with each other for the available resources. Trying to predict the number of vacant parking spaces on a busy day in Montreal or New York City is a good example of the importance of the effects of competition and of the distinction between first round and second round effects. The first round effect of a shopper going home is a vacant parking space. But the first round effect is short-lived. Competition for parking spaces results in vacant spaces being filled almost immediately. So, taking account of competition and second round effects, you predict that there are rarely any vacant parking spaces!

"And now a traffic update: A parking space has just become available on Sixty-fifth Street between Second and Third. Hold it! A bulletin has just been handed to me. That space has been taken."

Drawing by H. Martin; ©1987 The New Yorker Magazine, Inc.

REVIEW

The economic way of thinking is based on five core ideas:

■ All economic problems arise from scarcity, and scarcity forces people to make choices and evaluate opportunity cost.

■ Opportunity cost is the *best* alternative forgone, not the money cost, and includes time cost and external cost.

■ Decisions are made by comparing marginal benefit and marginal cost.

■ When the opportunity cost of an activity increases, the incentive to substitute an alternative activity increases.

■ Competition creates ripples along the chain of substitution—second round effects—that dominate the first round effects.

You've examined the types of questions that economists try to answer. You've also seen something of the way economists think and have learned the five core ideas that guide that thinking. Your next task is to move beyond ideas to actions and to study the things that economists *do*.

What Economists Do

ECONOMISTS WORK ON A WIDE ARRAY OF problems and the questions at the start of this chapter are just a small sample of what is covered. Economic questions can be divided into two big groups: microeconomic questions and macroeconomic questions.

Microeconomics and Macroeconomics

Microeconomics is the study of the decisions of people and businesses and the interaction of those decisions in markets. The goal of microeconomics is to explain the prices and quantities of individual goods and services. Microeconomics also studies the effects of government regulation and taxes on the prices and quantities of individual goods and services. For example, microeconomics studies the forces that determine the prices of cars and the quantities of cars produced and sold. It also studies the effects of regulations and taxes on the prices and quantities of cars.

Macroeconomics is the study of the national economy and the global economy and the way that economic aggregates grow and fluctuate. The goal of macroeconomics is to explain *average* prices and the *total* employment, income, and production. Macroeconomics also studies the effects of government actions—taxes, spending, and the deficit—on total jobs and incomes. For example, macroeconomics studies the forces that determine the average cost of living in Canada, the total value of the nation's production, and the effects of the federal budget on these variables.

Although microeconomics and macroeconomics have their own separate focus, they use a common set of tools and ideas. Some problems have both a microeconomic and a macroeconomic dimension. An example is the invention of video games and the growth of the market in multimedia products. Microeconomics seeks to explain the prices and quantities of games, while macroeconomics explains the effects on the total amount of spending and jobs in the economy as a whole.

Economists not only work on a wide range of questions. They also approach their work in a variety of ways. The different approaches can be summarized under two broad heads:

- Economic science
- Economic policy

Economic science is the attempt to *understand* the economic world, and economic policy is the attempt to *improve* it. Another way of putting the distinctions is this: Science makes *predictions*, while policy offers *prescriptions*. Policy and science overlap in many ways, and policy cannot get very far without science—it is not possible to make something work better without first understanding it. Let's take a closer look at these two approaches that economists take to their work.

Economic Science

Economics is a social science (along with political science, psychology, and sociology) and a major task of economists is to discover how the economic world works. In the pursuit of this goal, economists (like all other scientists) distinguish between two types of statements. Statements about

1. What *is*
2. What *ought* to be

Statements about what *is* are called *positive* statements. They say what is currently believed about the way the world operates. A positive statement might be right or wrong. And a positive statement can be tested by checking it against the facts. Statements about what *ought* to be are called *normative* statements. These statements depend on values and cannot be tested.

To see the distinction between positive and normative statements, consider the controversy over global warming. Some scientists believe that centuries of the burning of coal and oil are increasing the carbon dioxide content of the earth's atmosphere and leading to higher temperatures that eventually will have devastating consequences for life on this planet. "Our planet is warming because of an increased carbon dioxide buildup in the atmosphere" is a positive statement. It can (in principle and with sufficient data) be tested. "We ought to cut back on our use of carbon-based fuels such as coal and oil" is a normative statement. You might agree with or disagree with this statement, but you can't test it. It is based on values. Health care provides an economic example of the distinction. "Universal health care cuts the amount of work-time lost to illness" is a positive statement. "Every Canadian should have equal access to health care" is a normative statement.

It is the task of economic science to discover and catalogue positive statements that are consistent with what we observe in the world and that enable us to understand how the economic world works. This task is a large one and it can be broken into three steps:

- Observation and measurement
- Model building
- Testing models

Observation and Measurement Economists keep track of the amounts and locations of natural resources and human resources, of people's wages and work hours, of the prices and quantities of different goods and services produced, of interest rates and the amounts borrowed and lent, of taxes and government spending, and of the quantities of goods and services bought from and sold to other countries. This list gives a flavour of the array of things that economists can observe and measure.

Model Building The second step towards understanding the economic world is to build an economic model. An **economic model** is a description of some aspect of the economic world that includes only those features of the world that are needed for the purpose at hand. What a model includes and what it leaves out results from *assumptions* about what is essential and what is inessential detail.

You can see how ignoring detail is useful—even essential—to our understanding by thinking about a model that you use every time you need a book from your school library. That model is the library catalogue and floor plan. This model guides you to the locations of the books. The catalogue doesn't tell you whether the book you want is red or blue. And the floor plan doesn't tell you where the telephone cables run. These details don't affect your search for a book.

An economic model tells us how a number of variables are determined by a number of other variables. For example, a model of the economic effects of the recent large nickle discovery in Newfoundland might tell us the effects of the discovery on the number of jobs, the number of houses and apartments, rents, and prices and incomes in the vicinity. The model might also tell us the effects of the discovery on future revenue of the Newfoundland government.

Testing Models A model's predictions might correspond to or be in conflict with the facts. By comparing the model's predictions with the facts, we are able to test and develop an economic model. An **economic theory** is a generalization that summarizes what we think we understand about the economic choices that people make and the performance of industries and entire economies. It is a bridge between an economic model and the real economy.

A theory is created by a process of building and testing models. For example, you have a theory that if you follow the library floor plan (a model) you will get to the second floor stacks (reality). When you follow the floor plan, you are testing your theory. Suppose the floor plan doesn't show that the second floor stacks can only be reached by taking the north elevator. When you take the south elevator and hit a dead-end, you have tested your theory. This particular theory must be rejected. But you can develop a new theory, based on a model that does include the essential assumption about the solid wall between the south elevator and the second floor stacks.

Figure 1.1 illustrates the process of developing theories by building and testing models. We begin by building a model. The model's implications are used to generate predictions about the world. These predictions and their test form the basis of a theory. When predictions are in conflict with the facts, either a theory is discarded in favour of a superior alternative or we return to the model-building stage, modifying our assumptions and creating a new model.

While Fig. 1.1 shows the logical structure of the search for new knowledge, it does not describe the actual processes followed. In practice, scientific discovery is a human activity marked by stabs in the dark, blind alleys, flashes of insight, and, occasionally, revolutionary new views. Also, some models are discarded even when they fit the facts, and others are clung to even when they fail. Albert Einstein, the great physicist, put it well when he said:

> Creating a new theory is not like destroying an old barn and erecting a skyscraper in its place. It is rather like climbing a mountain, gaining new and wider views, discovering new connections between our starting point and its rich environment. But the point from which we started still exists and can be seen, although it appears smaller and forms a tiny part of our broad view gained by the mastery of the obstacles on our adventurous way up.[2]

[2]These words are attributed to Einstein in a letter by Oliver Sacks to *The Listener*, 88 (2279), November 30, 1972, 756.

FIGURE 1.1
How Economic Theories Are Developed

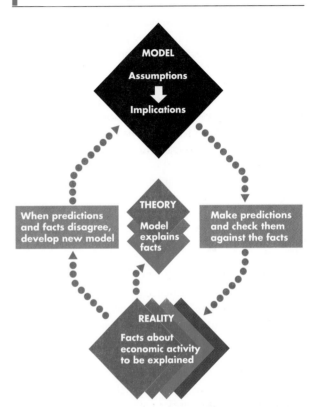

Economists develop economic theories by building and testing economic models. An economic model is based on *assumptions* about what is essential and what can be ignored and the *implications* of those assumptions. The implications of a model form the basis of *predictions* about the world. Economists test these predictions by checking them against the facts. If the predictions are in conflict with the facts, the model-building process begins again with new assumptions. It is only when predictions are in agreement with the facts that a useful theory has been developed.

Economics is a young science and a long way from having achieved its goal of explaining and understanding economic activity. Its birth can be dated fairly precisely to 1776 and the publication of Adam Smith's *The Wealth of Nations* (see *Economics in History*, pp. 64–65). In the closing years of the twentieth century, economics has managed to discover a sizeable number of useful generalizations. In many areas, however, we are still going around the circle—

changing assumptions, performing new logical deductions, generating new predictions, and getting wrong answers yet again. The gradual accumulation of correct answers gives most practitioners some faith that their methods will, eventually, provide useable answers to the big economic questions.

But progress in economics comes slowly and economists must be careful how they proceed. Let's look at some of the obstacles to progress in economics.

Unscrambling Cause and Effect   It is difficult in economics to isolate forces and identify what is a cause and what is the effect. The logical tool that is used by all scientists for identifying cause and effect is *ceteris paribus*. **Ceteris paribus** is a Latin term that means "other things being equal" or "if all other relevant things remain the same." All successful attempts to understand the world use this device. By changing one factor at a time and holding all the other relevant factors constant, we isolate the factor of interest and are able to investigate its effects in the clearest possible way.

Economic models (like the models in all other sciences) enable the influence of one factor at a time to be isolated in the imaginary world of the model. Indeed, one of the strengths of model building is that it enables us to imagine what would happen if only one factor changed. But *ceteris paribus* can be a problem in economics when we try to test a model.

In the laboratory sciences, such as chemistry and physics, experiments are performed that actually hold all the relevant factors constant except for the one under investigation. In the nonexperimental sciences such as economics (and astronomy), we usually observe the outcomes of the *simultaneous* operation of several—perhaps many—factors. As a result, it is hard to sort out the effects of each individual factor and to compare the effects with what a model predicts. To cope with this problem, economists take three complementary approaches.

First, they look for pairs of events in which other things were equal (or similar). An example might be to study the effects of unemployment insurance on the unemployment rate by comparing Canada and the United States on the presumption that the people in the two economies are sufficiently similar. Second, economists have developed statistical tools—called *econometrics*—that unscramble the separate factors that simultaneously influence economic behaviour. Third, economists are beginning to design experiments that are undertaken in economic laboratories.

This relatively new and exciting approach puts real subjects (usually students) in a decision-making situation and varies their incentives in some way to discover how they respond to one factor at a time.

Economists work hard to avoid *fallacies*—errors of reasoning that lead to a wrong conclusion. But two fallacies are common, and you need to be on your guard to avoid them. They are the

- Fallacy of composition
- *Post hoc* fallacy

Fallacy of Composition   The fallacy of composition is the (false) statement that what is true of the parts is true of the whole, or what is true of the whole is true of the parts. For one tuna fishing firm (a part), using bigger nets and boats enables more tuna to be caught. But if all the tuna fishing firms (the whole) use bigger nets and boats, eventually over-fishing will result and everyone will catch fewer tuna.

The fallacy of composition arises mainly in macroeconomics and it stems from the fact that the parts interact with each other to produce an outcome for the whole that might differ from the intent of the parts. A firm lays off some workers to cut costs and improve its profits. If all firms take similar actions, incomes fall and so does spending. The firm sells less and its profits don't improve.

Post Hoc Fallacy   Another Latin phrase—*post hoc ergo propter hoc*—means "after this, therefore because of this." The *post hoc* fallacy is the error of reasoning from timing to cause and effect. You see a flash of lightning and some seconds later hear a clap of thunder. But the lightning did not *cause* the thunder. The flash and the clap were the *simultaneous* effect of—were *caused* by—an electrical disturbance in the atmosphere.

Unravelling cause and effect is extremely difficult in economics. And just looking at the timing of events often doesn't help. For example, the stock market booms and some months later the economy expands—jobs and incomes grow. Did the stock market boom cause the economy to expand? Possibly, but perhaps businesses started to plan the expansion of production because a new technology that lowered costs had become available. As knowledge of the plans spread, the stock market reacted to *anticipate* the economic expansion. To disentangle cause and effect, economists use economic models, data, and to the extent that they can, perform experiments.

We've now looked at the way in which econo-mists try to understand the world—economic sci-ence. Let's study economic policy to see how econo-mists try to contribute to improving economic performance.

Economic Policy

Economic policy is the attempt to devise government actions and to design institutions that might improve economic performance. Economists play two distinct roles in the formulation of economic policy.

First, they try to predict the consequence of alter-native policies. For example, economists who work on health-care reform try to predict the cost and ben-efits and effectiveness of alternative ways of financing and organizing the health-care industry. Economists who work on environmental issues attempt to predict the cost and quality of urban air resulting from changes in auto emission standards. And macroecon-omists try to predict the effects of interest rate changes on the stock market and employment.

Second, economists evaluate alternative policies on the scale of better to worse. To do this, economists must state the policy *objectives*. Provided there is clar-ity and openness about the policy objectives, this type of policy analysis can be as objective and scientific as the development of economic theories. And over the years, by responding to the societies of which they are a part and interpreting sentiments expressed in the political arena, economists have developed criteria for judging social and political outcomes on the better-to-worse scale. Four objectives of policy have emerged:

- Efficiency
- Equity
- Growth
- Stability

Efficiency   When **economic efficiency** has been achieved, production costs are as low as possible and consumers want the combination of goods and ser-vices that is being produced. Three distinct condi-tions produce economic efficiency. They are efficient production, efficient consumption, and efficient exchange.

Efficient production is achieved when each firm produces its output at the least possible cost. Cost includes costs borne by the firm and costs borne by others—*external* costs. Efficient consumption is

achieved when everyone buys the goods and services that make them as well off as possible, by their own evaluations. And efficient exchange is achieved when everyone specializes to earn a living by doing the job that gives them the maximum possible economic benefit. When economic efficiency is achieved, it is not possible to make one person better off without at the same time making someone else worse off.

Equity   **Equity** is economic justice or fairness. An efficient economy is not necessarily an equitable or just one. Economic efficiency could bring very large incomes to a few people and very low incomes to the vast majority. Such a situation would be regarded as inequitable by the majority but possibly not by every-one. Economists have succeeded in arriving at a widely accepted definition of efficiency, but attaining the same degree of consensus on a definition of equi-ty or economic justice is elusive. Equity remains a matter on which reasonable people disagree.

Growth   **Economic growth** is the increase in incomes and production per person. It results from the ongoing advance of technology, the accumulation of ever larger quantities of productive equipment and ever rising standards of education. Poor societies are transformed into rich ones by economic growth. But economic growth has a cost. It uses up exhaustible natural resources. And it sometimes destroys natural vegetation and damages the environment. But these are not inevitable drawbacks of economic growth and the richest countries are the ones that devote the greatest efforts to enriching and protecting the envi-ronment.

Economic growth can be encouraged or discour-aged by the policies that governments adopt. For example, tax incentives for research and development might stimulate growth while tax penalties that encourage resource conservation might retard it. In reaching policy conclusions, economists must take a view about the desirable growth rate and the effects of the policies being considered on growth.

Stability   **Economic stability** is the absence of wide fluctuations in the economic growth rate, the level of employment, and average prices. Almost the whole of macroeconomics has developed to under-stand these problems, and many macroeconomists specialize in designing policies to tame an unstable economy.

Agreement and Disagreement

Economists have a reputation for being a divided lot. Perhaps you've heard the joke: "If you laid all the economists in the world end to end, they still wouldn't reach agreement." There is a hint of truth in the joke, but only a hint. The fact is that there is a remarkable consensus among economists on a wide range of issues. Table 1.1 gives a flavour of this consensus.

Some disagreements are about what is possible—*positive* matters—and some are about what is desirable—*normative* matters. Disagreements on positive issues arise when the available evidence is insufficient for a clear conclusion to be reached, and disagree-

ments on normative issues arise from differences in values or priorities. It is hardly surprising that economists have such disagreements since they are just a reflection of similar disagreements in the larger society of which they are members.

You now know the types of questions that economists try to answer and that all economic questions and economic activity arise from scarcity. You know something about the way economists think and about the work they do. In the chapters that follow, you are going to study economic activity and discover how the Canadian economy and the global economy work. But before we do that, we need to stand back and take an overview of our economy.

TABLE 1.1

Agreement and Disagreement Among Economists

	Percentage of economists who	
Positive propositions	**Agree**	**Disagree**
Rent ceilings cut the availability of housing	93	7
A tax cut can help to achieve full employment	90	9
A minimum wage increases unemployment of young workers	79	21
Big firms are likely to collude	71	28
Lower unemployment brings higher inflation	59	39
Lower marginal income tax rates increase work effort	55	44
A lower capital gains tax would promote economic growth	49	50
Normative propositions		
The distribution of income should be more equal	73	27
Laws should be enforced more vigorously to curtail monopoly power	72	28
The level of government spending should be reduced	55	45
Positive propositions about economic efficiency		
Tariff and import quotas usually reduce economic well-being	93	7
A large federal budget has an adverse effect on the economy	84	16
Cash payments benefit welfare recipients more than transfers-in-kind of equal value	84	15
Pollution taxes are more efficient than pollution limits	78	21

Source: Richard M. Alston, J. R. Kearl, and Michael B. Vaughan, "Is There a Consensus Among Economists?" *American Economic Review,* 82 (May 1992), pp. 203–209.

The Economy: An Overview

THE ECONOMY IS A MECHANISM THAT ALLOCATES scarce resources among alternative uses. This mechanism achieves five things:

- What
- How
- When
- Where
- Who

1. *What* goods and services will be produced and in *what* quantities? Will more cable companies offer pay-per-view service or will more movie theatres be built? Will young professionals vacation in Europe or live in large houses? Will more high-performance sports cars or more trucks and station wagons be made?

2. *How* will the various goods and services be produced? Will a supermarket operate with three check-out lines and clerks using laser scanners or six check-out lines and clerks keying in prices by hand? Will workers weld station wagons by hand or will robots do the job? Will farmers keep track of their livestock feeding schedules and inventories by using paper and pencil records or personal computers? Will credit card companies use computers or clerks to read charge slips?

3. *When* will the various goods and services be produced? Will a supermarket operate 24 hours a day and 7 days a week, or just 8 hours a day for 6 days a week? Will a car factory close for the summer and lay off its workers? Will there be a surge of house building in the spring, bringing higher wages and longer hours for construction workers? Will crude oil be used now or saved for later?

4. *Where* will the various goods and services be produced? Will American Express process its charge slips and accounts in Toronto, or will it hire less costly labour in Barbados and transfer its records by satellite? Will Honda make its cars in Japan and then ship them to Canada, or will it open a factory in Ontario and export cars from Canada to Japan? Will General Motors build railway engines in London, Ontario, or will it close its operations there and open a new assembly plant in Beijing?

5. *Who* will consume the various goods and services? The distribution of economic benefits depends on the distribution of income. People with high incomes are able to consume more goods and services than people with low incomes. Who gets to consume what thus depends on income. Will the ski instructor consume more than the lawyer's secretary? Will the people of Hong Kong consume more than the people of Ethiopia?

To understand how an economy works, we must identify its components and see how they interact with each other. Figure 1.2 shows a picture of an economy. This picture is of a *closed economy*—an economy that has no links to other economies. We can gain a lot of insight by studying a closed-economy model. In reality, the only closed economy is the economy of the entire world—the global economy. During the 1980s, the global economy became a highly integrated mechanism for allocating scarce resources and deciding *what, how, when, where* the various goods and services will be produced and *who* will consume them.

The economy shown in Fig. 1.2 contains two types of components:

- Decision makers
- Markets

Decision Makers and Choices

Decision makers are the economic actors. They make the choices. Figure 1.2 identifies three types of decision maker:

1. Households
2. Firms
3. Governments

A *household* is any group of people living together as a decision-making unit. Every individual in the economy belongs to a household. Some households consist of a single person, while others consist either of families or of groups of unrelated individuals, such as two or three students sharing an apartment. Each household has unlimited wants and limited resources.

FIGURE 1.2

A Picture of an Economy

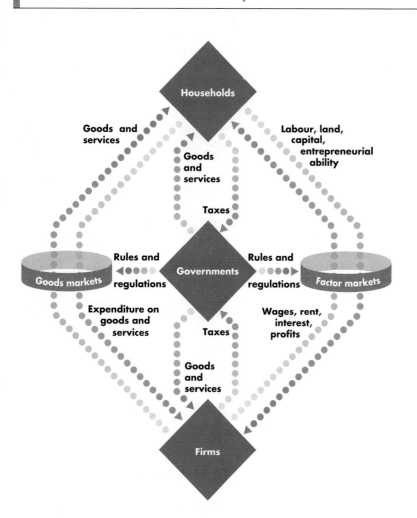

Households, firms, and governments make economic decisions. Households decide how much of their labour, land, and capital, and entrepreneurial ability to sell or rent in exchange for wages, rent, interest, and profits. They also decide how much of their income to spend on the various types of goods and services available. Firms decide how much labour, land, and capital to hire and how much of the various types of goods and services to produce. Governments decide which goods and services they will provide and the taxes that households and firms will pay.

These decisions by households, firms, and governments are coordinated in markets—the goods markets and factor markets—that are regulated by rules that governments establish and enforce. In these markets, prices constantly adjust to keep buying and selling plans consistent.

A *firm* is an organization that uses resources to produce goods and services. All producers are called firms, no matter how big they are or what they produce. Car makers, farmers, banks, and insurance companies are all firms.

A *government* is a many-layered organization that sets laws and rules, operates a law-enforcement mechanism (courts and police forces), taxes households and firms, and provides public services such as national defence, public health, transportation, and education. By changing laws and rules, taxes, and spending, governments try to influence the choices that households and firms make.

Markets

In ordinary speech, the word *market* means a place where people buy and sell goods such as fish, meat, fruits, and vegetables. In economics, *market* has a more general meaning. A **market** is any arrangement that enables buyers and sellers to get information and to do business with each other. An example is the market in which oil is bought and sold—the world oil market. The world oil market is not a place. It is the network of oil producers, oil users, wholesalers, and brokers who buy and sell. In the world oil market, decision makers do not meet physically. They make deals throughout the world by telephone, fax, and direct computer link.

Figure 1.2 identifies two types of market: goods markets and factor markets. *Goods markets* are those in which goods and services are bought and sold. *Factor markets* are those in which factors of production are bought and sold.

Factors of production are the economy's productive resources. They are classified under four headings:

1. Labour
2. Land
3. Capital
4. Entrepreneurial ability

Labour is the time and effort that people devote to producing goods and services. It is rewarded with wages. **Land** is all the natural resources used to produce goods and services. The return to land is rent. **Capital** is all the equipment, buildings, tools, and other manufactured goods used to produce other goods and services. The return to capital is interest. **Entrepreneurial ability** is a special type of human resource that organizes the other three factors of production, makes business decisions, innovates, and bears business risk. Entrepreneurship is rewarded with profit.

Households and firms make decisions that result in the transactions in the goods markets and factor markets shown in Fig. 1.2. Households decide how much of their labour, land, and capital to sell or rent in factor markets. They receive incomes in the form of wages, rent, interest, and profit. Households also decide how to spend their incomes on goods and services produced by firms.

Firms decide the quantities of factors of production to hire, how to use them to produce goods and services, what goods and services to produce, and in what quantities. They sell their output in goods markets.

The flows resulting from these decisions by households and firms are shown in Fig. 1.2. The red flows are the factors of production that go from households to firms and the goods and services that go from firms to households. The green flows in the opposite direction are the payments made in exchange for these items.

A public choice process determines the rules and regulations imposed by governments, the taxes governments raise, and the goods and services they provide. These public choices by governments are also shown in Fig. 1.2.

Coordinating Decisions

Perhaps the most striking thing about the choices made by households, firms, and governments is that they surely must come into conflict with each other. For example, households choose how much work to do and what type of work to specialize in, but firms choose the type and quantity of labour to employ in the production of various goods and services. In other words, households choose the types and quantities of labour to sell, and firms choose the types and quantities of labour to buy. Similarly, in markets for goods and services, households choose the types and quantities of goods and services to buy, while firms choose the types and quantities to sell.

How is it possible for the millions of individual decisions made by households, firms, and governments to be consistent with each other? What makes households want to sell the same types and quantities of labour that firms want to buy? What happens if the number of households wanting to work as airline pilots exceeds the number that airlines want to hire? How do firms know what to produce so that households will buy their output? What happens if firms want to sell more hamburgers than households want to buy?

Markets Coordinate Decisions   Markets coordinate individual decisions through price adjustments. To see how, think about the market for hamburgers in your local area. Suppose that at the current price, the quantity of hamburgers being offered for sale is less than the quantity that people would like to buy. Some people who want to buy hamburgers are not able to do so. To make the choices of buyers and sellers compatible, buyers must scale down their appetites and more hamburgers must be offered for sale. An increase in the price of hamburgers produces this outcome. Because there is a shortage of hamburgers, their price rises. And the higher price encourages producers to offer more hamburgers for sale. It also curbs the appetite for hamburgers and changes some lunch plans. Fewer people buy hamburgers and more buy hot dogs (or some other alternative to hamburgers). More hamburgers (and more hot dogs) are offered for sale.

Now imagine the opposite situation. At the current price, more hamburgers are available than people want to buy. In this case, to make the choices of buyers and sellers compatible, more hamburgers must be bought and fewer must be offered for sale. A fall in the price of hamburgers achieves this outcome.

Because there is a surplus of hamburgers, the price falls. And the lower price discourages the production of hamburgers and encourages consumption. Decisions to produce and sell and to buy and consume are continuously adjusted and kept in balance with each other by price adjustments.

Sometimes prices get stuck or fixed. For example, the government might impose a rent ceiling or a minimum wage that prevents the price changes that would make the plans of buyers and sellers consistent. Other mechanisms then begin to operate. One possibility is that customers wait in line and get served on a first-come-first-served basis. Another is that inventories operate as a temporary safety valve. If the price is fixed too low, firms sell more than they would like and their inventories shrink. If the price is fixed too high, firms sell less than they would like and their inventories pile up. Waiting lines and inventory changes are only a temporary solution to inconsistent buying and selling plans. Eventually, a price adjustment is needed.

We've seen how decisions coordinated in markets determine *what* gets produced—in the example, how many hamburgers are produced. Decisions coordinated in markets also determine *how* goods and services are produced. For example, hamburger producers can use gas, electric power, or charcoal to cook their hamburgers. Which fuel is used depends in part on the flavour that the producer wants to achieve. It also depends on the cost of the different fuels. If a fuel becomes very expensive, as did oil in the 1970s, less of it is used and more of other fuels are used. By substituting one fuel for another as the costs of the different fuels change, the market solves the question of how to produce.

Market-coordinated decisions also determine *when* goods and services are produced. If consumer spending on fast food falls temporarily and prices drop below the level that covers the wage bill and other expenses, hamburger and hot dog producers close down and lay off their workers. If consumer spending rises and fast food prices rise, firms respond by producing more hamburgers and hot dogs.

And the market-coordinated decisions also determine *where* goods and services are produced. If the cost of making beef patties rises in Canada and falls in Mexico, McDonald's and other fast food firms switch their production of patties to the low-cost source.

Finally, market-coordinated decisions determine *who* consumes the goods and services produced. Those skills, talents, and resources that are rare but highly valued command a high price and their owners receive a large share of the economy's output. Those skills, talents, and resources that are common and less highly valued command a low price and their owners receive a small share of the economy's output.

Alternative Coordination Mechanisms The market is one of two alternative coordination mechanisms. The other is a command mechanism. A *command mechanism* is a method of determining *what, how, when,* and *where* goods and services are produced and *who* consumes them, using an hierarchical organization structure in which people carry out the instructions given to them. The best example of an hierarchical organization structure is the military. Commanders make decisions requiring actions that are passed down a chain of command. Soldiers and marines on the front line take the actions they are ordered to take.

An economy that relies on a command mechanism is called a *command economy*. Examples of command economies in today's world are becoming rare and only North Korea falls squarely into this category. Before they embarked on programs of reform in the late 1980s, the Soviet Union and other countries of Eastern Europe also had command economies.

An economy that uses a market coordinating mechanism is called a *market economy*. But most real-world economies use both markets and commands to coordinate economic activity. An economy that relies on both markets and command mechanisms is called a *mixed economy*.

The Canadian economy relies extensively on the market as a mechanism for coordinating the decisions of individual households and firms. But the Canadian economy also uses command mechanisms. The economy of the armed forces is a command economy. Command mechanisms are also employed in other government organizations and within large firms. There is also a command element in our legal system. By enacting laws and establishing regulations and agencies to monitor the market economy, governments influence the economic decisions of households and firms and change our economic course.

Thus Canada depends mainly on the market mechanism, but also partly on a command mechanism, so the Canadian economy is a mixed economy.

International Linkages

We've just looked at a closed economy—one that has no links with any other economy—and noted that the only closed economy is the entire world. A national economy like the Canadian economy is an *open economy*. It has economic links with other economies.

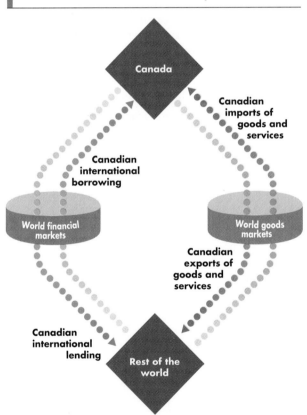

FIGURE 1.3
The Global Economy

The figure shows the economic links between Canada and the rest of the world. The Canadian economy buys and sells goods and services in world goods markets. What Canada buys from the rest of the world are Canada's imports, and what Canada sells to the rest of the world are Canada's exports.

The Canadian economy also borrows from and lends to the rest of the world. And Canadian firms set up businesses in other countries and foreign firms set up businesses in Canada. These transactions take place through the world's financial markets.

Figure 1.3 illustrates the economic links between the Canadian economy and the rest of the world. Firms in the open Canadian economy sell some of their production to the rest of the world. These sales are Canada's exports of goods and services. Also, firms, households, and governments in Canada buy goods and services from firms in other countries. These purchases are Canada's imports of goods and services. These export and import transactions take place in world goods markets and are illustrated in the figure.

The total values of exports and imports are not necessarily equal to each other. When Canadian exports exceed Canadian imports, we have a surplus. When Canadian imports exceed Canadian exports, we have a deficit. A country with a surplus lends to the rest of the world and a country with a deficit borrows from the rest of the world. These international lending and borrowing transactions take place on the world financial markets; they are illustrated in Fig. 1.3.

The volume of international transactions is large. In 1996, Canadian businesses sold 30 percent of their production to other countries and Canadian imports were more than 30 percent of total spending. Total world exports (and imports) approached $10 trillion in 1996, which is larger than the total value of all the goods and services produced in the United States. And in 1995, international transactions on world financial markets exceeded $10 trillion, 136 percent of all the goods and services produced in the United States.

R E V I E W

■ An economy is a mechanism that determines what is produced, how, when, and where it is produced, and for whom it is produced.

■ Choices made by households, firms, and governments are coordinated through markets for goods and services and factors of production.

■ Choices are sometimes coordinated by command mechanisms.

◆ In the next chapter, we will study some of the tools that economists use to describe economic performance and to build economic models. Then, in Chapter 3, we will build an economic model and use that model to sharpen our understanding of opportunity cost and to study the way in which people make choices about what to produce.

SUMMARY

Key Points

How Economists Think Economists see all economic questions as arising from scarcity—from the fact that wants exceed resources. Economists study the ways people cope with scarcity. Scarcity forces people to make choices and face opportunity costs. The opportunity cost of an action is the best alternative action that could have been undertaken in its place. Two fundamental ideas permeate economics: the margin and substitution. People make decisions at the margin. They evaluate actions in incremental steps. All actions have substitutes. The higher the opportunity cost of an action, the greater is the incentive for people to seek a substitute—an alternative—action. Scarcity forces people to compete for scarce resources. (pp. 8–11)

What Economists Do Economists work on microeconomics—the study of the decisions of individual households and firms—and macroeconomics—the study of the economy as a whole and the way it fluctuates and expands over time. Economists try to understand the economic world by doing economic science and to improve economic performance by studying economic policy. Economists develop theories by building and testing economic models. Economists find it hard to disentangle cause and effect because their observations of the real world are the outcomes of simultaneous changes in many factors. To cope with this problem, economists use the *ceteris paribus* (other things remaining the same) assumption and develop statistical and experimental methods for isolating each factor. Economists avoid the fallacy of composition and the *post hoc* fallacy. In conducting economic policy analysis, economists use four policy objectives: efficiency, equity, growth, and stability. Economists have many disagreements, but they do agree on a wide range of questions. (pp. 11–16)

The Economy: An Overview People have unlimited wants but limited resources or factors of production—labour, land, capital, and entrepreneurial ability. The economy is a mechanism that allocates scarce resources among competing uses, determining what, how, when, and where goods and services will be produced, and who will consume them. The economy's two key components are decision makers and markets. Economic decision makers are households, firms, and governments. Households decide how much of their labour, land, and capital to sell or rent and how much of each good and service to buy. Firms decide what factors of production to hire and which goods and services to produce. Governments decide what goods and services to provide to households and firms and how much to raise in taxes. The decisions of households, firms, and governments are coordinated through markets in which prices adjust to keep buying plans and selling plans consistent. Alternatively, coordination can be achieved by a command mechanism. The Canadian economy relies on both market and command mechanisms and is a mixed economy. National economies are interlinked in the global economy. Countries exchange goods and services (exports and imports) and undertake international borrowing and lending. (pp. 17–21)

Key Figure

Figure 1.2 A Picture of an Economy, 18

Key Terms

Capital, 19
Ceteris paribus, 14
Economic efficiency, 15
Economic growth, 15
Economic model, 12
Economic stability, 15
Economic theory, 13
Economics, 8
Entrepreneurial ability, 19
Equity, 15
Factors of production, 19
Incentive, 10
Labour, 19
Land, 19
Macroeconomics, 11
Marginal benefit, 9
Marginal cost, 9
Market, 18
Microeconomics, 11
Opportunity cost, 8
Principle of substitution, 10
Scarcity, 8

R E V I E W Q U E S T I O N S

1. What is economics?
2. Give some examples, different from those in the chapter, of the questions that economics tries to answer.
3. What is scarcity and how is it different from poverty?
4. Why does scarcity force people to make choices?
5. Why does scarcity force people to face costs?
6. What is *opportunity cost*?
7. Why does the money we spend on something not tell us its opportunity cost?
8. Why is the time taken to do something part of its opportunity cost?
9. What is *marginal* cost and why is it the relevant cost for making a decision?
10. What is an external cost?
11. What is the *principle of substitution*?
12. What is an *incentive* and how do people respond to incentives?
13. Why does scarcity imply competition?
14. Why does competition lead to second round effects that determine the consequences of an economic disturbance?
15. Distinguish between microeconomics and macroeconomics.
16. Distinguish between positive and normative statements and list three examples of each type of statement.
17. What is an economic model?
18. What does *ceteris paribus* mean?
19. What is the fallacy of composition? Give an example.
20. What is the *post hoc* fallacy? Give an example.
21. Explain the difference between economic theory and economic policy.
22. What are the four main goals of economic policy?
23. Name the main economic decision makers.
24. List the economic decisions made by households, firms, and governments.
25. What is a market?
26. What is a command mechanism?
27. How does the market determine what, how, when, and where things will be produced and who will consume them?

C R I T I C A L T H I N K I N G

1. Economists often remark, "There's no such thing as a free lunch!" Explain what economists mean by this statement.
2. "Every decision has an opportunity cost." Can you think of one example that would make this statement incorrect?
3. Explain why or why not we could eliminate scarcity by taking some of what rich people own and giving it to poor people so that everyone would be equal.
4. Is free speech really free for society? Explain your answer.
5. A proposal to cut pollution in Toronto is: Owners of cars that are older than five years should have their cars checked when they renew their licences to see if they meet emission standards. The cost will be $25 an inspection.

   a. What is the opportunity cost of people driving older cars in Toronto?
   b. Is all the opportunity cost of driving older cars borne by drivers?
   c. Is the cost of having an old car checked part of the opportunity cost of driving one?

6. The former Soviet Union did not use the market mechanism to coordinate buying plans of households and selling plans of firms. Instead, prices of basic goods were fixed and the coordination of buying and selling plans was achieved by buyers waiting in line for hours. What can you say about the opportunity costs of basic goods in the former Soviet Union compared with those in Canada?

P R O B L E M S

1. You plan to go to school this summer. If you do you won't be able to take your usual job that pays $6,000 for the summer and you won't be able to live at home for free. The cost of your tuition will be $2,000, textbooks $200, and living expenses $1,400. What is the opportunity cost of going to summer school?

2. On Valentine's Day, Bernie and Catherine exchanged gifts: Bernie sent Catherine red roses and Catherine bought Bernie a box of chocolates. They each spent $15. They also spent $50 on dinner and split the cost evenly. Did either Bernie or Catherine incur any opportunity costs? If so, what were they? Explain your answer.

3. Nancy asks Beth to be her maid of honour at her wedding. Beth accepts. Which of the following are part of her opportunity cost of being Nancy's maid of honour? Explain why they are or are not.
   a. The $200 she spent on a new outfit for the occasion
   b. The $50 she spent on a party for Nancy's friends
   c. The money she spent on a haircut a week before the wedding
   d. The weekend visit she missed for her grandmother's 75th birthday—the same weekend as the wedding
   e. The $10 she spent on lunch on the way to the wedding

4. The local mall has free parking, but the mall is always very busy and it usually takes 30 minutes to find a parking space. Today when you found a vacant spot, Harry also wanted it. Is parking really free at this mall? If not, what did it cost you to park today? When you parked your car today did you impose any costs on Harry? Explain your answers.

5. Which of the following statements are positive and which are normative?

   a. A cut in wages will reduce the number of people willing to work.
   b. High interest rates prohibit many young people from buying their first home.
   c. No family ought to pay more than 25 percent of its income in taxes.
   d. The government should reduce the number of men in the military and increase the number of women.
   e. The government ought to stop overspending.
   f. The government ought to behave in such a way as to ensure that resources are used efficiently.

6. You have been hired by Soundtrend, a company that makes and markets tapes, records, and compact discs (CDs). Your employer is going to start selling these products in a new region that has a population of 10 million people. A survey has indicated that 50 percent of people buy only popular music, 10 percent buy only classical music, and no one buys both types of music. Another survey suggests that the average income of a pop music fan is $10,000 a year and that of a classical fan is $50,000 a year. Based on a third survey, it appears that, on the average, people with low incomes spend one-quarter of 1 percent of their income on tapes, records, and CDs, while people with high incomes spend 2 percent of their income on these products.

   Build a model to enable Soundtrend to predict how much will be spent on pop music and classical music in this region in one year. In doing so
   a. List your assumptions.
   b. What are the predictions of your model?
   c. Highlight the potential sources of errors in your predictions.

Making and Using Graphs

After studying this chapter, you will be able to:

- Make and interpret a scatter diagram, a time-series graph, and a cross-section graph

- Distinguish between linear and nonlinear relationships and between relationships that have a maximum and a minimum

- Define and calculate the slope of a line

- Graph relationships among more than two variables

Three Kinds of Lies

Benjamin Disraeli, British prime minister in the late nineteenth century, is reputed to have said that there are three kinds of lies: lies, damned lies, and statistics. One of the most powerful ways of conveying statistical information is in the form of a graph. And like statistics, graphs can lie. But the right graph does not lie. It reveals a relationship that would otherwise be obscure. ◆ Graphs are a modern invention. They first appeared in the late eighteenth century, long after the discovery of logarithms and calculus. But today, in the age of the personal computer and video display, graphs have become as important as words and numbers. How do economists use graphs? What types of graphs do they use? What do graphs reveal and what can they hide? ◆ The seven big questions that you studied in Chapter 1—the questions that economics tries to answer—are difficult ones. They involve relationships among a large number of variables. Virtually nothing in economics has a single cause. Instead, a large number of variables interact with each other. It is often said that in economics, everything depends on everything else. Changes in the quantity of ice cream consumed are caused by changes in the price of ice cream, the temperature, and many other factors. How can we make and interpret graphs of relationships among several variables?

◈ In this chapter, you are going to look at the kinds of graphs that are used in economics. You are going to learn how to make them and read them. You are also going to learn how to calculate the strength of the effect of one variable on another. There are no graphs or techniques used in this book that are more complicated than those explained and described in this chapter. If you are already familiar with graphs, you may want to skip (or skim) this chapter. Whether you study it or give it a quick pass, you can use this chapter as a handy reference and return to it whenever you feel that you need extra help understanding the graphs that you encounter in your study of economics.

Graphing Data

GRAPHS REPRESENT A QUANTITY AS A DISTANCE on a line. Figure 2.1 gives two examples. Part (a) shows temperature, measured in degrees Celsius, as the distance on a scale. Movements from left to right show increases in temperature. Movements from right to left show decreases in temperature. The point marked zero represents zero degrees Celsius. To the right of zero, the temperatures are positive. To the left of zero, the temperatures are negative (as indicated by the minus sign in front of the numbers).

Figure 2.1(b) provides another example. This time altitude, or height, is measured in thousands of metres above sea level. The point marked zero represents sea level. Points to the right of zero represent heights above sea level. Points to the left of zero (indicated by a minus sign) represent depths below sea level. There are no rigid rules about the scale for a graph. The scale is determined by the range of the variable being graphed and the space available for the graph.

The two graphs in Fig. 2.1 show just a single variable. Marking a point on either of the two scales indicates a particular temperature or a particular height. Thus point *a* represents 100°C, the boiling point of water. Point *b* represents 6,194 metres, the height of Mount McKinley, the highest mountain in North America.

Graphing a single variable does not usually reveal much. Graphs become powerful when they show how two variables are related to each other.

Two-Variable Graphs

To construct a two-variable graph, we set two scales perpendicular to each other. Figure 2.2 shows how this looks for temperature and height. Temperature is shown as it was before but height is now shown by movements up and down a vertical scale.

The two scale lines in Fig. 2.2 are called *axes*. The horizontal line is called the *x-axis* and the vertical line

FIGURE **2.2**

Graphing Two Variables

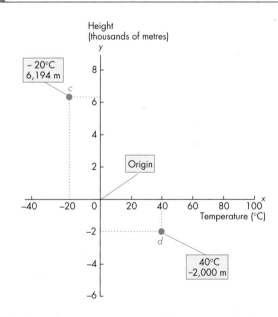

The relationship between two variables is graphed by drawing two axes perpendicular to each other. Height is measured here on the *y*-axis, and temperature is measured on the *x*-axis. Point *c* represents the top of Mount McKinley, 6,194 metres above sea level (measured on the *y*-axis) with a temperature of –20°C (measured on the *x*-axis). Point *d* represents the inside temperature of a submarine, 40°C, exploring the depths of an ocean, 2,000 metres below sea level.

FIGURE **2.1**

Graphing a Single Variable

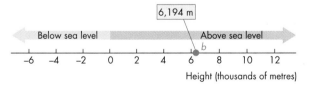

(a) Temperature

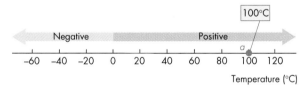

(b) Height

All graphs have a scale that measures a quantity as a distance. The two scales here measure temperature and height. Numbers to the right of zero are positive. Numbers to the left of zero are negative.

is called the *y-axis*. The letters *x* and *y* appear on the axes of Fig. 2.2. Each axis has a zero point shared by the two axes. The zero point, common to both axes, is called the *origin*.

To show something in a two-variable graph, we need two pieces of information. For example, Mount McKinley is 6,194 metres high and, on a particular day, the temperature at its peak is –20°C. We show this information in Fig. 2.2 by marking the height of the mountain on the *y*-axis at 6,194 metres and the temperature on the *x*-axis at –20°C. We can identify the values of the two variables that appear on the axes by marking point *c*.

Two lines, called *coordinates*, can be drawn from point *c*. The line running from *c* to the vertical axis is the *x*-coordinate, because its length is the same as the value marked off on the *x*-axis. Similarly, the line running from *c* to the horizontal axis is the *y*-coordinate, because its length is the same as the value marked off on the *y*-axis.

Figure 2.2 also illustrates that at the depths of an ocean, the inside temperature of a submarine 2,000 metres *below* sea level is a sweltering 40°C. This information is shown by point *d*.

Economists use graphs similar to the one in Fig. 2.2 to reveal and describe the relationships among economic variables. The main types of graph used in economics are

- Scatter diagrams
- Time-series graphs
- Cross-section graphs

Let's look at each of these types of graph.

Scatter Diagrams

A scatter diagram plots the value of one economic variable against the value of another variable. Such a graph is used to reveal whether a relationship exists between two economic variables. It is also used to describe a relationship.

The Relationship Between Consumption and Income   Figure 2.3 shows a scatter diagram of the relationship between average consumption and average income. The *x*-axis measures average income, and the *y*-axis measures average consumption. Each point shows consumption per person (on the average) and income per person (on the average) in Canada in a given year between 1985 and 1995. The points for all

eleven years are "scattered" within the graph. Each point is labelled with a two-digit number that shows us its year. For example, the point marked 88 shows us that in 1988, consumption per person was $13,200 and income per person was $18,400.

This graph shows us that a relationship exists between average income and average consumption. The dots form a pattern that shows us that when income increases, consumption also increases.

Breaks in the Axes   Each axis in Fig. 2.3 has a break in it, as shown by the small gaps. The breaks

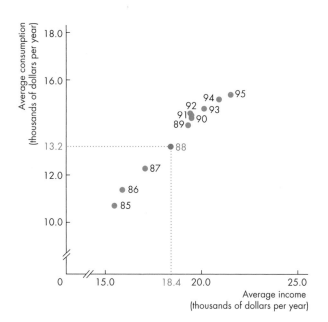

FIGURE   2.3

A Scatter Diagram

A scatter diagram shows the relationship between two variables. This scatter diagram shows the relationship between average consumption and average income during the years 1985 to 1995. Each point shows the values of the two variables in a specific year and the year is identified by the two-digit number. For example, in 1988 average consumption was $13,200 and average income was $18,400. The pattern formed by the points shows that as average income increases, so does average consumption.

indicate that there are jumps from the origin, 0, to the first values recorded. The breaks are used because in the period covered by the graph, consumption was never less than $10,000 and income was never less than $15,000. With no breaks in the axes of this graph, there would be a lot of empty space, all the points would be crowded into the top right corner, and we would not be able to see whether a relationship existed between these two variables. By breaking the axes we are able to bring the relationship into view. In effect, we use a zoom lens to bring the relationship into the centre of the graph and magnify it so that it fills the graph.

The range of the variables plotted on the axes of a graph are an important feature of a graph, and it is a good idea to get into the habit of always looking closely at the values and the labels on the axes before you start to interpret a graph.

Other Relationships Figure 2.4 shows two other scatter diagrams. Part (a) shows the relationship between the number of households owning a VCR and the average price of a VCR. The pattern formed by the points shows us that as the price of a VCR falls, a larger percentage of households own one.

Part (b) looks at inflation and unemployment in Canada. The pattern formed by the points in this graph does not reveal a clear relationship between the two variables. The graph shows us, by its lack of a distinct pattern, that there is no relationship between inflation and unemployment.

A scatter diagram enables us to see the relationship between two economic variables. But it does not give us a clear picture of how those variables evolve over time. To see the evolution of economic variables, we use a time-series graph.

FIGURE 2.4

More Scatter Diagrams

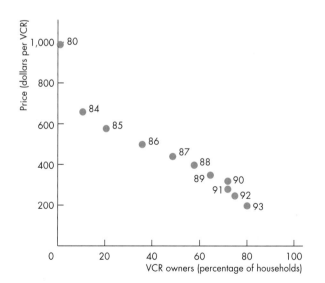

(a) VCR ownership and price

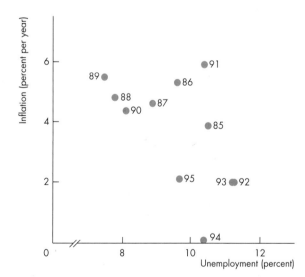

(b) Unemployment and inflation

Part (a) is a scatter diagram that plots the price of a VCR against VCR ownership for 1980 and each year from 1984 to 1993. This graph shows that as the price of a VCR has fallen, the percentage of households owning one has increased.

Part (b) is a scatter diagram that plots the inflation rate against the unemployment rate. This graph shows that inflation and unemployment are not closely related.

Time-Series Graphs

A time-series graph measures time (for example, months or years) on the *x*-axis and the variable or variables in which we are interested on the *y*-axis. Figure 2.5 shows a time-series graph. Time is measured in years on the *x*-axis. The variable that we are interested in—the price of coffee—is measured on the *y*-axis. This time-series graph conveys an enormous amount of information quickly and easily:

1. It shows us the *level* of the price of coffee—when it is *high* and *low*. When the line is a long way from the *x*-axis, the price is high. When the line is close to the *x*-axis, the price is low.

2. It shows us how the price *changes*—whether it *rises* or *falls*. When the line slopes upward, as in 1976, the price is rising. When the line slopes downward, as in 1980, the price is falling.

3. It shows us the *speed* with which the price is *changing*—whether it is rising or falling *quickly* or *slowly*. If the line rises or falls very steeply, then the price is changing quickly. If the line is not steep, the price is rising or falling slowly. For example, the price rose very quickly between 1976 and 1977. The price went up again in 1982 but more slowly. Similarly, when the price was falling in 1978, it fell quickly but during the mid-1960s, it fell more slowly.

A time-series graph also reveals whether there is a trend. A trend is a general tendency for a variable to rise or fall. You can see that the price of coffee had a general tendency to fall from the mid-1970s to the early 1990s. That is, although there were ups and downs in the price, there was a general tendency for it to fall.

A time-series graph also lets us compare different periods quickly. Figure 2.5 shows that the 1970s were different from the 1980s. The price of coffee fluctuated more violently in the 1970s than it did in the 1980s. This graph conveys a wealth of information, and it does so in much less space than we have used to describe only some of its features.

Comparing Two Time-Series Sometimes we want to use a time-series graph to compare two different variables. For example, suppose you want to know if the government's budget balance fluctuates with the unemployment rate. You can examine the government's budget balance and the unemployment rate by drawing a graph of each of them on the same time scale. But we can measure the government's budget balance either as a surplus or as a deficit (a deficit is a negative surplus).

Figure 2.6(a) plots the budget balance as a surplus. The scale of the unemployment rate is on the left side of the figure, and the scale of the government's budget surplus is on the right. The orange line shows unemployment and the blue line shows the government's budget surplus. You will probably agree that it is pretty hard work figuring out from Fig. 2.6(a) just what the relationship is between the unemployment rate and the government's budget.

In Fig. 2.6(b) the scale for the government's budget balance is measured as a deficit. That is, we flip

FIGURE 2.5
A Time-Series Graph

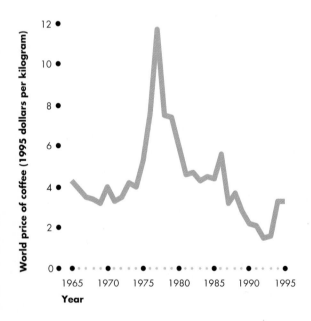

A time-series graph plots the level of a variable on the *y*-axis against time (for example, day, week, month, or year) on the *x*-axis. This graph shows the world price of coffee (in 1995 dollars per kilogram) each year from 1965 to 1995. It shows us when the price of coffee was *high* and when it was *low*, when the price *increased* and when it *decreased*, when it changed *quickly* and when it changed *slowly*.

the right side scale over. In part (a), the budget surplus is negative, so in part (b) that negative surplus becomes a positive deficit. You can now "see" more clearly the relationship between these two variables.

Cross-Section Graphs

A cross-section graph shows the values of an economic variable for different groups in a population at a point in time. Figure 2.7 is an example of a cross-section graph. It shows unemployment rate across ten metropolitan cities in Canada in January 1993. This graph uses bars rather than dots and lines and the length of each bar indicates the percentage of the labour force in the city that was unemployed. Figure 2.7 enables you to compare the unemployment rate in these ten cities. And you can do so much more quickly and clearly than by looking at a list of numbers.

FIGURE 2.6
Time-Series Relationships

(a) Unemployment and budget surplus

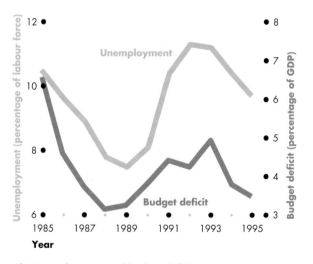

(b) Unemployment and budget deficit

These two graphs show the unemployment rate and the balance of the government's budget. The unemployment line is identical in the two parts. Part (a) shows the budget surplus—taxes *minus* spending—on the right scale. It is hard to see a relationship between the budget surplus and unemployment. Part (b) shows the budget as a deficit—spending *minus* taxes. It inverts the scale of part (a). With the scale for the budget balance inverted, the graph reveals a tendency for unemployment and the budget deficit to move together.

FIGURE 2.7
A Cross-Section Graph

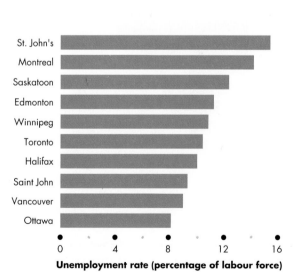

A cross-section graph shows the level of a variable across the members of a population. This graph shows the unemployment rate in each of ten cities in Canada.

Misleading Graphs

All types of graphs—time-series graphs, scatter diagrams, and cross-section graphs—can mislead. And a cross-section graph gives a good example. Figure 2.8 dramatizes a point of view rather than revealing the facts. A quick glance at this graph gives the impression that the unemployment rate in Toronto is about one-half the unemployment rate in St. John's. But a closer look reveals that the scale on the axis has been increased and unemployment rates between zero and 7 percent chopped off the graph. If, when you look at a graph, you make it a habit to look first at the numbers on the axes, you will not be misled, even if the intention of the graph is to mislead you. You can often see misleading graphs in the media. Keep your eyes open for such graphs in the newspapers and magazines you read and learn how to avoid being misled by them.

FIGURE 2.8
A Misleading Graph

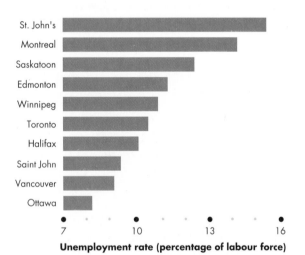

Unemployment rate (percentage of labour force)

A graph can mislead when it distorts the scale on one of its axes. Here, the scale measuring the unemployment rate has been stretched by chopping off the unemployment rates between zero and 7 percent. The result is that the comparison of unemployment rates across the cities is distorted. Unemployment rates in the lower unemployment rate cities are made to look much smaller than they are compared with those in the highest unemployment rate cities.

Now that we have seen how we can use graphs in economics to show economic data and relationships between variables, let us examine how economists use graphs in a more abstract way in economic models.

Graphs Used in Economic Models

THE GRAPHS USED IN ECONOMICS ARE not always designed to show data. Another use of graphs is to show the relationships among the variables in an economic model. Although you will encounter many different kinds of graphs in economics, there are some patterns. And once you have learned to recognize them, they will instantly convey to you the meaning of a graph. There are graphs that show each of the following:

- Variables that go up and down together
- Variables that move in opposite directions
- Variables that have a maximum or a minimum
- Variables that are unrelated

Let's look at these four cases.

Variables That Go Up and Down Together

Figure. 2.9 shows graphs of relationships between two variables that move up and down together. A relationship between two variables that move in the same direction is called a positive relationship or a direct relationship. Such a relationship is shown by a line that slopes upward. In the figure, there are three types of relationship, one straight line and two curved lines. A relationship shown by a straight line is called a linear relationship. But all the lines in these three graphs are called curves. Any line on a graph—no matter whether it is straight or curved—is called a *curve*.

Fig. 2.9(a) shows a linear relationship between the number of kilometres travelled in 5 hours and speed. For example, point *a* shows us that we will travel 200 kilometres in 5 hours if our speed is 40 kilometres an hour. If we double our speed to 80 kilometres an hour, we will travel 400 kilometres in 5 hours. That is, when the speed doubles and the travelling time remains the same, the distance travelled doubles.

Part (b) shows the relationship between distance sprinted and exhaustion (exhaustion being measured

FIGURE 2.9
Positive (Direct) Relationships

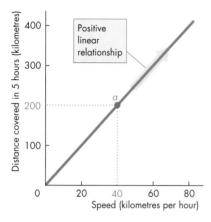

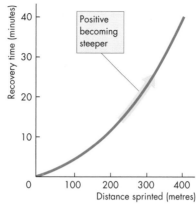

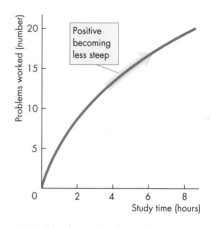

(a) Positive linear relationship   **(b) Positive becoming steeper**   **(c) Positive becoming less steep**

Each part of this figure shows a positive (direct) relationship between two variables. That is, as the value of the variable measured on the x-axis increases, so does the value of the variable measured on the y-axis. Part (a) shows a linear relationship—as the two variables increase together we move along a straight line. Part (b) shows a positive relationship such that as the two variables increase together we move along a curve that becomes steeper. Part (c) shows a positive relationship such that as the two variables increase together we move along a curve that becomes flatter.

---

by the time it takes the heart rate to return to normal). This relationship is an upward-sloping one shown by a curved line that starts out fairly flat but then becomes steeper as we move along the curve away from the origin. As the distance sprinted doubles, the recovery time more than doubles.

Part (c) shows the relationship between the number of problems worked by a student and the amount of study time. This relationship is shown by an upward-sloping curved line that starts out fairly steep but then becomes flatter as we move away from the origin. As the study time doubles, the number of problems solved increases but it does not double.

Variables That Move in Opposite Directions

Figure 2.10 shows relationships between things that move in opposite directions. A relationship between variables that move in opposite directions is called a negative relationship or an inverse relationship.

Part (a) shows the relationship between the num-

ber of hours available for playing squash and the number of hours for playing tennis. One extra hour spent playing tennis means one hour less playing squash and vice versa. This relationship is negative and linear.

Part (b) shows the relationship between the cost per kilometre travelled and the length of a journey. The longer the journey, the lower is the cost per kilometre. But as the journey length increases, the cost per kilometre decreases; and the fall in the cost is smaller, the longer is the journey. This feature of the relationship is shown by the fact that the curve slopes downward, starting out steep at a short journey length and then becoming flatter as the journey length increases.

Part (c) shows the relationship between the amount of leisure time and the number of problems worked by a student. Increasing leisure time produces an increasingly large reduction in the number of problems worked. This relationship is a negative one that starts out with a gentle slope at a small number of leisure hours and becomes steeper as the number of leisure hours increases.

FIGURE 2.10

Negative (Inverse) Relationships

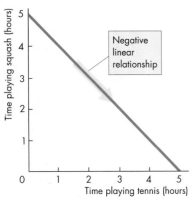

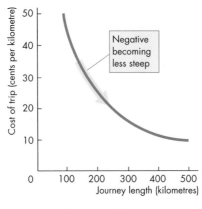

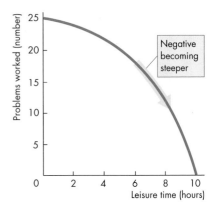

(a) Negative linear relationship **(b) Negative becoming less steep** **(c) Negative becoming steeper**

Each part of this figure shows a negative (inverse) relationship between two variables. Part (a) shows a linear relationship—as one variable increases and the other variable decreases, we travel along a straight line. Part (b) shows a negative relation-ship such that as the journey length increases the curve becomes flatter. Part (c) shows a negative relationship such that as the leisure time increases the curve becomes steeper.

Variables That Have a Maximum or a Minimum

Many relationships in economic models have a maximum or a minimum. For example, firms try to make the maximum possible profit and to produce at the lowest possible cost. Figure 2.11 shows relationships that have a maximum or a minimum.

Part (a) shows the relationship between rainfall and wheat yield. When there is no rainfall, wheat will not grow, so the yield is zero. As the rainfall increases up to 10 days a month, the wheat yield also increases. With 10 rainy days each month, the wheat yield reaches its maximum at 2 tonnes a hectare (point *a*). Rain in excess of 10 days a month starts to lower the yield of wheat. If every day is rainy, the wheat suffers from a lack of sunshine and the yield falls back almost to zero. This relationship starts out sloping upward, reaches a maximum, and then slopes downward.

Part (b) shows the reverse case—a relationship that begins sloping downward, falls to a minimum, and then slopes upward. An example of such a relationship is the gasoline cost per kilometre as the speed varies. At low speeds, the car is creeping along.

The number of kilometres per litre is low, so the gasoline cost per kilometre is high. At very high speeds, the car is travelling faster than its most efficient speed and, again, the number of kilometres per litre is low and the gasoline cost per kilometre is high. At a speed of 100 kilometres an hour, the gasoline cost per kilometre travelled is at its minimum (point *b*). This relationship starts out sloping downward, reaches a minimum, and then slopes upward.

Variables That Are Unrelated

There are many situations in which one variable is unrelated to another. No matter what happens to the value of one variable, the other variable remains constant. Figure 2.12 shows the independence between two variables. In Fig. 2.12(a), your grade in economics is shown on the *y*-axis against the price of bananas on the *x*-axis. Your grade (75 percent in this example) is unrelated to the price of bananas. The relationship between these two variables is shown by a horizontal straight line. This line neither slopes upward or downward. In part (b), the output of French wine is

FIGURE 2.11

Maximum and Minimum Points

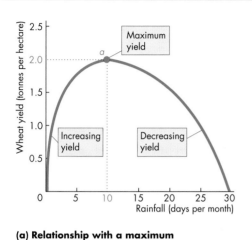

(a) Relationship with a maximum

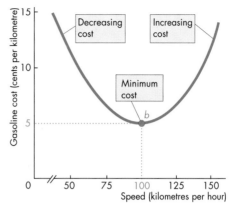

(b) Relationship with a minimum

Part (a) shows a relationship that has a maximum point, *a*. The curve slopes upward as it rises to its maximum point, is flat at its maximum, and then slopes downward. Part (b) shows a relationship with a minimum point, *b*. The curve slopes downward as it falls to its minimum, is flat at its minimum, and then slopes upward.

shown on the *x*-axis and the number of rainy days a month is shown on the *y*-axis. Again, the output of French wine (15 billion litres a year in this example) is unrelated to the number of rainy days in Ontario. The relationship between these two variables is shown by a vertical straight line.

Figures 2.9 through 2.12 show ten different shapes of graphs that we will encounter in economic models. In describing these graphs, we have talked about the slopes of curves. The concept of slope is an intuitive one. But it is also a precise technical concept. Let's look more closely at the concept of slope.

FIGURE 2.12

Variables That Are Unrelated

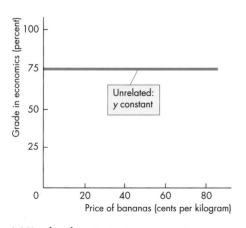

(a) Unrelated: *y* constant

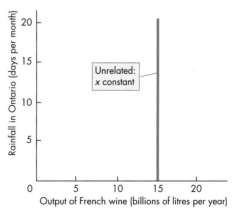

(b) Unrelated: *x* constant

This figure shows how we can graph two variables that are unrelated to each other. In part (a), a student's grade in economics is plotted at 75 percent regardless of the price of bananas on the *x*-axis. The curve is horizontal. In part (b), the output of the vineyards of France does not vary with the rainfall in Ontario. The curve is vertical .

The Slope of a Relationship

WE CAN MEASURE THE INFLUENCE OF ONE VARI-
able on another by the slope of the relationship. The
slope of a relationship is the change in the value of
the variable measured on the *y*-axis divided by the
change in the value of the variable measured on the
x-axis. We use the Greek letter Δ (delta) to represent
"change in." Thus Δ*y* means the change in the value
of the variable measured on the *y*-axis, and Δ*x* means
the change in the value of the variable measured on
the *x*-axis. Therefore the slope of the relationship is

$$\Delta y \, / \, \Delta x.$$

If a large change in the variable measured on the
y-axis (Δ*y*) is associated with a small change in the
variable measured on the *x*-axis (Δ*x*), the slope is
large and the curve is steep. If a small change in the
variable measured on the *y*-axis (Δ*y*) is associated with
a large change in the variable measured on the *x*-axis
(Δ*x*), the slope is small and the curve is flat.

We can make the idea of slope sharper by doing
some calculations.

The Slope of a Straight Line

The slope of a straight line is the same regardless of
where on the line you calculate it. Thus the slope of a
straight line is constant. Let's calculate the slopes of
the lines in Fig. 2.13. In part (a), when *x* increases

FIGURE 2.13

The Slope of a Straight Line

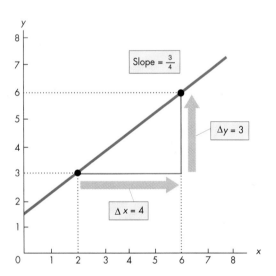

(a) Positive slope

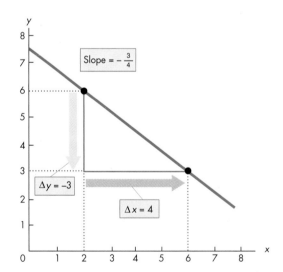

(b) Negative slope

To calculate the slope of a straight line, we divide the change
in the value of the variable measured on the *y*-axis (Δ*y*) by the
change in the value of the variable measured on the *x*-axis
(Δ*x*).

Part (a) shows the calculation of a positive slope. When *x*
increases from 2 to 6, Δ*x* equals 4. That change in *x* brings

about an increase in *y* from 3 to 6, so Δ*y* equals 3. The slope
(Δ*y*/Δ*x*) equals 3/4.

Part (b) shows the calculation of a negative slope. When *x*
increases from 2 to 6, Δ*x* equals 4. That increase in *x* brings
about a decrease in *y* from 6 to 3, so Δ*y* equals −3. The slope
(Δ*y*/Δ*x*) equals −3/4.

from 2 to 6, y increases from 3 to 6. The change in x is +4—that is, Δx is 4. The change in y is +3—that is, Δy is 3. The slope of that line is

$$\frac{\Delta y}{\Delta x} = \frac{3}{4}.$$

In part (b), when x increases from 2 to 6, y decreases from 6 to 3. The change in y is *minus* 3—that is Δy is −3. The change in x is *plus* 4—that is Δx is 4. The slope of the curve is

$$\frac{\Delta y}{\Delta x} = \frac{-3}{4}.$$

Notice that the two slopes have the same magnitude (3/4), but the slope of the line in part (a) is positive (+3/+4 = 3/4), while that in part (b) is negative

(−3/+4 = −3/4). The slope of a positive relationship is positive; the slope of a negative relationship is negative.

The Slope of a Curved Line

The slope of a curved line is not constant. It depends on where on the line we calculate it. There are two ways to calculate the slope of a curved line: at a point on the curve or across an arc of the curve. Let's look at them.

Slope at a Point   To calculate the slope at a point on a curve, you need to construct a straight line that has the same slope as the curve at the point in question. Figure 2.14(a) shows how this is done. Suppose you want to calculate the slope of the curve at point a.

FIGURE 2.14

The Slope of a Curve

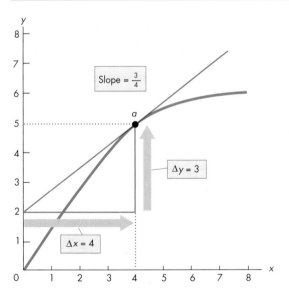

(a) Slope at a point

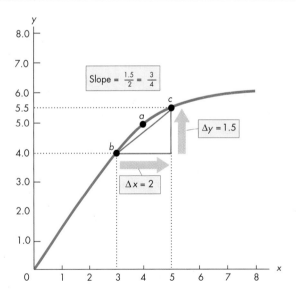

(b) Slope across an arc

To calculate the slope of the curve at point a, draw the red line that just touches the curve at a—the tangent. The slope of this straight line is calculated by dividing the change in y by the change in x along the line. When x increases from 0 to 4, Δx equals 4. That change in x is associated with an increase in y from 2 to 5, so Δy equals 3. The slope of the red line is 3/4. So the slope of the curve at point a is 3/4.

To calculate the average slope of the curve along the arc bc, draw a straight line from b to c in part (b). The slope of the line bc is calculated by dividing the change in y by the change in x. In moving from b to c, Δx equals 2, and Δy equals 1.5. The slope of the line bc is 1.5 divided by 2, or 3/4. So the slope of the curve across the arc bc is 3/4.

Place a ruler on the graph so that it touches point *a* and no other point on the curve, then draw a straight line along the edge of the ruler. The straight red line in part (a) is this line and it is the tangent to the curve at point *a*. If the ruler touches the curve only at point *a*, then the slope of the curve at point *a* must be the same as the slope of the edge of the ruler. If the curve and the ruler do not have the same slope, the line along the edge of the ruler will cut the curve instead of just touching it.

Having found a straight line with the same slope as the curve at point *a*, you can calculate the slope of the curve at point *a* by calculating the slope of the straight line. Along the straight line, as *x* increases from 0 to 4 ($\Delta x = 4$) *y* increases from 2 to 5 ($\Delta y = 3$). Therefore the slope of the line is

$$\frac{\Delta y}{\Delta x} = \frac{3}{4}.$$

Thus the slope of the curve at point *a* is 3/4.

Slope Across an Arc Calculating a slope across an arc is similar to calculating an average slope. An arc of a curve is a piece of a curve. In Fig. 2.14(b), we are looking at the same curve as in part (a) but instead of calculating the slope at point *a*, we calculate the slope across the arc from *b* to *c*. Moving along the arc from *b* to *c*, *x* increases from 3 to 5 and *y* increases from 4 to 5.5. The change in *x* is 2 ($\Delta x = 2$) and the change in *y* is 1.5 ($\Delta y = 1.5$). Therefore the slope of the line is

$$\frac{\Delta y}{\Delta x} = \frac{1.5}{2} = \frac{3}{4}.$$

Thus the slope of the curve across the arc *bc* is 3/4.

This calculation gives us the slope of the curve between points *b* and *c*. The actual slope calculated is the slope of the straight line from point *b* to point *c*. This slope approximates the average slope of the curve along the arc *bc*. In this particular example, the slope of the arc *bc* is identical to the slope of the curve at point *a* in part (a). But the calculation of the slope of a curve does not always work out so neatly. You might have some fun constructing counterexamples.

Graphing Relationships Among More Than Two Variables

WE HAVE SEEN THAT WE CAN GRAPH A SINGLE VARIable as a point on a straight line and we can graph the relationship between two variables as a point formed by the *x*- and *y*-coordinates in a two-dimensional graph. You may be thinking that although a two-dimensional graph is informative, most of the things in which you are likely to be interested involve relationships among many variables, not just two. For example, the amount of ice cream consumed depends on the price of ice cream and the temperature. If ice cream is expensive and the temperature is low, people eat much less ice cream than when ice cream is inexpensive and the temperature is high. For any given price of ice cream, the quantity consumed varies with the temperature, and for any given temperature, the quantity of ice cream consumed varies with its price.

Figure 2.15 shows the relationship between three variables. The table shows the number of litres of ice cream consumed each day at various temperatures and ice cream prices. How can we graph these numbers?

To graph a relationship that involves more than two variables, we consider what happens if all but two of the variables are held constant. When we hold other things constant, we are using the *ceteris paribus* assumption that is described in Chapter 1, p. 14. An example is shown in Fig. 2.15(a). There, you can see what happens to the quantity of ice cream consumed when the price of ice cream varies while the temperature is held constant. The line labelled 21°C shows the relationship between ice cream consumption and the price of ice cream when the temperature stays at 21°C. The numbers used to plot that line are those in the third column of the table in Fig. 2.15. For example, when the temperature is 21°C, 10 litres are consumed when the price is 60¢ a scoop and 18 litres are consumed when the price is 30¢. The curve labelled 32°C shows the consumption of ice cream when the price varies and the temperature is 32°C.

We can also show the relationship between ice cream consumption and temperature when the price of ice cream is held constant, as shown in Fig. 2.15(b). The curve labelled 60¢ shows how the consumption of ice cream varies with the temperature when ice cream costs 60¢, and a second curve shows

FIGURE **2.15**

Graphing a Relationship Among Three Variables

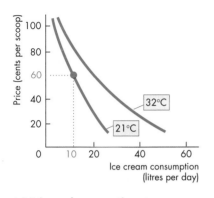

(a) Price and consumption at a given temperature

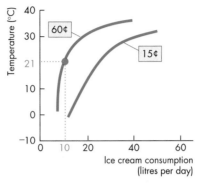

(b) Temperature and consumption at a given price

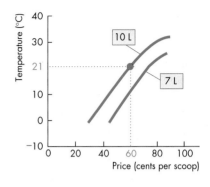

(c) Temperature and price at a given consumption

Price (cents per scoop)	**Ice cream consumption** (litres per day)			
	–1°C	**10°C**	**21°C**	**32°C**
15	12	18	25	50
30	10	12	18	37
45	7	10	13	27
60	5	7	10	20
75	3	5	7	14
90	2	3	5	10
105	1	2	3	6

The quantity of ice cream consumed depends on its price and the temperature. The table gives some hypothetical numbers that tell us how many litres of ice cream are consumed each day at different prices and different temperatures. For example, if the price is 45¢ per scoop and the temperature is 10°C, 10 litres of ice cream are consumed. In order to graph a relationship among three variables, the value of one variable is held constant.

Part (a) shows the relationship between price and consumption, holding temperature constant. One curve holds temperature constant at 32°C and the other at 21°C. Part (b) shows the relationship between temperature and consumption, with the price held constant. One curve holds the price at 60¢ and the other at 15¢. Part (c) shows the relationship between temperature and price, with consumption held constant. One curve holds consumption at 10 litres and the other at 7 litres.

the relationship when ice cream costs 15¢. For example, at 60¢ a scoop, 10 litres are consumed when the temperature is 21°C and 20 litres when the temperature is 32°C.

Figure 2.15(c) shows the combinations of temperature and price that result in a constant consumption of ice cream. One curve shows the combination that results in 10 litres a day being consumed, and the other shows the combination that results in 7 litres a day being consumed. A high price and a high tem-

perature lead to the same consumption as a lower price and a lower temperature. For example, 10 litres are consumed at 32°C and 90¢ per scoop, at 21°C and 60¢ per scoop, and at 10°C and 45¢ per scoop.

◆ With what you have learned about graphs, you can move forward with your study of economics. There are no graphs in this book that are more complicated than those that have been explained here.

S U M M A R Y

Key Points

Graphing Data   Three types of graph used to show economic data are scatter diagrams, time-series graphs, and cross-section graphs. Each graph reveals the nature of the relationship between variables. But a graph can mislead if its scale is distorted. (pp. 27–32)

Graphs Used in Economic Models   Five types of graph used to show relationships among variables in economic models are: positive (an upward-sloping curve), negative (a downward-sloping curve), positive and then negative (a maximum), negative and then positive (a minimum), and unrelated (a horizontal or vertical curve). (pp. 32–35)

The Slope of a Relationship   The slope of a relationship is calculated as the change in the value of the variable measured on the y-axis divided by the change in the value of the variable measured on the x-axis— $\Delta y / \Delta x$. A straight line has a constant slope, but a curved line has a varying slope. To calculate the slope of a curved line, we calculate the slope at a point or across an arc. (pp. 36–38)

Graphing Relationships Among More Than Two Variables   To graph a relationship among more than two variables, we hold constant the values of all the variables except two. We then plot the value of one of the variables against the value of another. (pp. 38–39)

Key Figures

Key Terms

R E V I E W   Q U E S T I O N S

1. What are the three types of graph used to show economic data?
2. Give an example of a scatter diagram.
3. Give an example of a time-series graph.
4. Give an example of a cross-section graph.
5. List three things that a time-series graph shows quickly and easily.
6. What do we mean by trend?
7. How can a graph mislead?
8. Draw some graphs to show the relationships between two variables:

   a.   That move in the same direction
   b.   That move in opposite directions
   c.   That have a maximum
   d.   That have a minimum

9. Which of the relationships in question 8 is a positive relationship and which a negative relationship?
10. What is the definition of the slope of a curve?
11. What are the two ways of calculating the slope of a curved line?
12. How do we graph relationships among more than two variables?

P R O B L E M S

1. The inflation rate in Canada and the interest rate on Government of Canada treasury bills between 1974 and 1995 were as follows:

Year	Inflation rate (percent per year)	Interest rate (percent per year)
1974	11.0	7.9
1975	9.0	7.4
1976	8.0	8.9
1977	5.9	7.4
1978	5.7	8.6
1979	9.1	11.6
1980	9.6	12.7
1981	10.8	17.8
1982	8.7	13.8
1983	5.0	9.3
1984	3.1	11.1
1985	2.6	9.5
1986	2.4	9.0
1987	4.7	8.2
1988	4.6	9.4
1989	4.8	12.0
1990	3.1	12.8
1991	2.7	8.9
1992	1.4	6.5
1993	1.1	4.9
1994	0.6	5.4
1995	1.8	7.0

a. Draw a time-series graph of the inflation rate and use your graph to answer the following questions:
   (i) In which year was inflation highest?
   (ii) In which year was inflation lowest?
   (iii) In which years did inflation increase?
   (iv) In which years did inflation decrease?
   (v) In which year did inflation increase most?
   (vi) In which year did inflation decrease most?
   (vii) What have been the main trends in inflation?

b. Draw a scatter diagram showing the relationship between inflation and the interest rate.

c. Does a relationship exist between inflation and the interest rate? If so, what kind of a relationship?

2. Use the following information to draw a graph showing the relationship between two variables x and y.

x	0	1	2	3	4	5	6	7	8
y	0	1	4	9	16	25	36	49	64

a. Is the relationship between x and y positive or negative?

b. Does the slope of the relationship rise or fall as the value of x rises?

3. Using the data in problem 2,
   a. Calculate the slope of the relationship between x and y when x equals 4.
   b. Calculate the slope of the arc when x rises from 3 to 4.
   c. Calculate the slope of the arc when x rises from 4 to 5.
   d. Calculate the slope of the arc when x rises from 3 to 5.
   e. What do you notice that is interesting about your answers to (b), (c), and (d) compared with your answer to (a)?

4. The table gives data on the price of a balloon ride, the temperature, and the rides taken per day.

Price (dollars per ride)	Balloon rides (number per day)		
	10°C	20°C	30°C
5.00	32	40	60
10.00	27	32	48
15.00	18	27	32
20.00	10	18	27

Draw a graph to show the relationship between
a. The price and the number of rides taken, holding temperature constant.
b. The number of balloon rides taken and the temperature, holding the price constant.
c. The temperature and the price, holding the number of balloon rides constant.

3

Production, Growth, and Trade

After studying this chapter, you will be able to:

- Define the production possibility frontier

- Define production efficiency

- Calculate opportunity cost

- Explain how economic growth expands production possibilities but does not provide free gifts

- Explain comparative advantage

- Explain why people specialize and how they gain from trade

Making the Most of It

We live in a style that surprises our grandparents and would have astonished our great grandparents. Most of us live in more spacious homes than they did. We eat more, grow taller, and are even born larger than they were. Video games, cellular phones, gene splices, personal computers, and fax machines did not exist even twenty years ago. But today it is hard to imagine life without them. Economic growth has made us richer than our grandparents. But it has not liberated us from scarcity. Why not? Why, despite our immense wealth, must we still make choices and face costs? Why are there no "free lunches"? ◆ We see an incredible amount of specialization and trade in the world. Each one of us specializes in a particular job—as a lawyer, a car maker, a homemaker. We have become so specialized that one farm worker can feed 100 people. Less than one-sixth of the Canadian labour force is employed in manufacturing. More than half of the labour force is employed in wholesale and retail trade, banking and finance, government, and other services. Why do we specialize? How do we benefit from specialization and trade? ◆ Over many centuries, institutions and social arrangements have evolved that we take for granted. One of them is markets. Another is property rights and a political and legal system that protects them. Yet another is money. Why have these arrangements evolved? And how do they extend our ability to specialize and increase production?

◆ These are the questions that we tackle in this chapter. We begin by studying the limits to production and the concept of efficiency. We next learn how to measure opportunity cost. We also discover how we can increase production by specializing and trading with each other.

The Production Possibility Frontier

PRODUCTION IS THE CONVERSION OF LABOUR, land, and capital into goods and services. We defined the factors of production in Chapter 1, but let's briefly recall what they are.

Labour is the time and effort that people devote to producing goods and services. It includes the physical and mental activities of the many thousands of people who make cars and cola, gum and glue, wallpaper and watering cans. *Land* is the gifts of nature that are used to produce goods and services. It includes the air, the water, and the land surface, as well as the minerals that lie beneath the surface of the earth. *Capital* is the goods that have been produced and can now themselves be used in the production of other goods and services. Examples include the highway system, the fine buildings of great cities, dams and power projects, airports and airplanes, car production lines, shirt factories, and cookie shops.

A special kind of capital is called human capital. **Human capital** is the skill and knowledge of people, which arise from their education and on-the-job training. You are getting human capital right now as you work on your economics course and other subjects. And your human capital will continue to grow when you get a full-time job and become better at it. Human capital improves the *quality* of labour.

Land, labour, and capital are organized by a fourth factor of production, *entrepreneurial ability*. Entrepreneurs come up with new ideas about what, how, when, and where to produce, make key business decisions, and bear the risks that arise from their decisions.

Goods and services are all the valuable things that people produce. Goods are tangible—cars, spoons, VCRs, and bread. Services are intangible—haircuts, amusement park rides, and telephone calls. There are two types of goods: capital goods and consumption goods. *Capital goods* are goods that are used to produce other goods. Examples of capital goods are buildings, computers, automobile assembly lines, and telephones. *Consumption goods* are goods that are bought by households. Some consumption goods are *durable*, such as shoes and shirts, and some are *nondurable*, such as dill pickles and toothpaste. *Consumption* is the process of using goods and services.

The quantities of goods and services that can be produced are limited by the available resources and by technology. That limit is described by the production possibility frontier. The **production possibility frontier** (*PPF*) marks the boundary between those combinations of goods and services that can be produced and those that cannot.

To study the production possibility frontier, we will consider just two goods at a time. They could be any two goods. In focusing on two goods, we hold the quantities produced of all the other goods constant—we use the *ceteris paribus* assumption. By this device, we look at a *model* of the economy—a model in which everything remains the same except the production of the two goods that we are (currently) interested in.

Let's begin by looking at the production possibility frontier for a single firm—one that produces denim jeans.

A Firm's Production Possibility Frontier

Mark's Jeans, Inc. employs 50 workers (labour). It has a small site (land), and it has a building that contains cutting and sewing machines (capital). Mark is the entrepreneur, and he uses these given amounts of labour, land, and capital to produce two types of jeans, baggy and Western cut. Mark's resources can produce a maximum of 5,000 jeans a week, in any combination of baggy and Western cut.

Figure 3.1 illustrates Mark's production possibilities. With his fixed quantities of labour, land, and capital, the maximum quantity of jeans he can produce is 5,000 a week. If he uses all his resources to produce baggys, he can produce no Western cuts. This combination of jeans, 5,000 baggys and no Western cuts, is one of Mark's *production possibilities*—shown in the table as possibility *a*. But there are other possibilities, and some of these are also shown in the table. For example, a second possibility is *b*. In this case, Mark uses one-fifth of his resources to produce Western cuts and the rest to produce baggys. He produces 1,000 Western cuts and 4,000 baggys a week—and he continues to produce a total of 5,000 jeans a week. The pattern continues to possibility *f*, in which Mark devotes all his resources to producing Western cuts. In this case, he produces 5,000 Western cuts a week and no baggys.

FIGURE 3.1
Production Possibility Frontier for Jeans

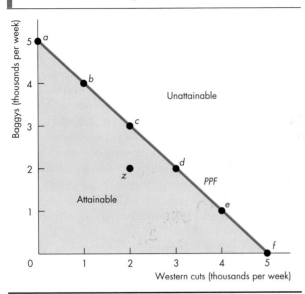

The table lists six points on Mark's production possibility frontier for Western cuts and baggys. Row *a* tells us that if he produces no Western cuts, the maximum quantity of baggys that he can produce is 5,000 a week. The rows of the table are graphed as points *a, b, c, d, e,* and *f* in the figure. The line passing through these points is Mark's *production possibility frontier* (*PPF*). It separates what Mark can attain from what he cannot attain. Mark can produce at any point inside the orange area or on the frontier. Points *outside* the frontier are unattainable. Points *inside* the frontier such as point z are *inefficient* because resources are being wasted or misallocated. At such points, it is possible for Mark to use his resources to produce more of either or both kinds of jeans.

Possibility	Western cuts (thousands per week)		Baggys (thousands per week)
a	0	and	5
b	1	and	4
c	2	and	3
d	3	and	2
e	4	and	1
f	5	and	0

The numbers in the table are plotted in the graph shown in Fig. 3.1. Thousands of Western cuts are measured on the horizontal axis, and thousands of baggys on the vertical axis. Points *a, b, c, d, e,* and *f* represent the numbers in the corresponding row of the table.

Mark does not have to produce jeans in batches of 1,000 as in the table. He could produce 1 Western cut and 4,999 baggys a week or any other combination that totals 5,000. All the other feasible allocations of Mark's resources enable him to produce the combinations of baggys and Western cuts described by the line that joins points *a, b, c, d, e,* and *f.* This line shows Mark's production possibility frontier for baggys and Western cuts, given his fixed resources. He can produce at any point on the frontier or at any point inside it, within the orange area. These are his attainable points. Points outside the frontier are unattainable. To produce at points beyond the frontier, Mark would need more resources. But more resources are not available to him—he can't attain points outside the frontier.

Production Efficiency

Production efficiency is achieved when it is not possible to produce more of one good without producing less of some other good. Production efficiency occurs only at points *on* the production possibility frontier. Possible production points *inside* the frontier, such as point *z,* are *inefficient.* They are points at which resources are being either wasted or misallocated. Resources are *wasted* when they are idle but could be working. For example, Mark might not run all his sewing machines all the time. Resources are *misallocated* when they are assigned to inappropriate tasks. For example, Mark might assign a skilled cutter to sewing and a skilled sewer to cutting. This would be like assigning a pitcher to batting and a batter to pitching. Each works hard, but the team does not perform as well as it could. The allocation would be inefficient.

If Mark is producing inefficiently at a point such as *z,* he can use his resources more efficiently and produce more jeans of either or both types. Mark will strive to avoid waste and try to produce at a point on the production possibility frontier—he will try to produce efficiently.

Although Mark will try to be efficient, he must choose among the many efficient points along his *PPF.* And in choosing among the efficient points, he faces opportunity cost. Let's explore Mark's opportunity costs.

A Firm's Opportunity Cost of Production

The *opportunity cost* of an action is the best alternative forgone. Of all the things you choose not to do—the alternatives forgone—the best one is the opportunity cost of the action you choose. The concept of opportunity cost can be made precise by using the production possibility frontier. Along the frontier, Mark is producing only two goods so it is easy to work out the best alternative forgone. Given Mark's current resources and technology, he can produce more Western cuts only if he produces fewer baggys. Thus the opportunity cost of producing an additional Western cut is the quantity of baggys forgone. Similarly, the opportunity cost of producing an additional baggy is the quantity of Western cuts forgone. For example, at point *c* in Fig. 3.1, Mark produces fewer Western cuts and more baggys than at point *d*. If he chooses point *d* over point *c*, the additional 1,000 Western cuts *cost* 1,000 baggys. One Western cut costs 1 baggy—and 1 baggy costs 1 Western cut.

In this example, the opportunity costs of producing more of either type of jeans are the same. They are also constant, regardless of how many of each type is produced. That is, at any point on the *PPF* in Fig. 3.1, 1 Western cut costs 1 baggy. These opportunity costs are constant because the resources used to produce jeans are equally productive regardless of the type of jeans produced.

Opportunity Costs Are Inescapable

The lesson we've learned by studying a model of a denim jeans factory is a fundamental one: We face trade-offs. A **trade-off** is a constraint that entails giving up one thing to get something else. For Mark, the trade-off is between baggys and Western cuts, and his production possibility frontier defines the terms of the trade-off. With your fixed financial resources, you must make a trade-off between going to the movies and buying magazines.

Trade-offs arise in every imaginable real-world situation. At any given point in time, the world has a fixed amount of labour, land, capital, and entrepreneurial ability. By using the available technologies, these resources can be employed to produce goods and services. But there is a limit to what goods and

services can be produced. This limit defines the boundary between what is attainable and what is not attainable. This boundary is the real-world economy's production possibility frontier, and it defines the trade-off we must make. On the frontier, producing more of any one good or service requires producing less of some other goods or services.

For example, a political party that promises better welfare and better education is making a trade-off. By devoting more resources to these activities, fewer resources are available for defence or for private consumption. The opportunity cost of better welfare and educational services is less of other goods and services.

An environmental lobby group is making a trade-off when it campaigns for less logging and greater conservation of endangered wildlife. By devoting more resources to wildlife protection, fewer resources are available for making the paper products that come from the forests.

On a smaller scale but equally important, each time you decide to rent a video you make a trade-off. You decide not to use your limited income to buy pop, or popcorn, or some other good. The opportunity cost of renting one more video is having less of something else.

R E V I E W

- The production possibility frontier (*PPF*) is the boundary between attainable and unattainable levels of production.
- Points on the *PPF* and inside it are attainable, and points outside the *PPF* are unattainable.
- Points *on* the *PPF* are *efficient*, and points *inside* it are *inefficient*.
- Choosing among efficient points on the *PPF* involves a *trade-off* and an *opportunity cost*.
- The opportunity cost of producing an additional unit of one good is the decrease in the number of units of another good that can be produced.

Along the production possibility frontier for jeans, Mark's opportunity costs are constant. But constant opportunity costs are unusual. Generally, the opportunity cost of producing a good increases as the quantity of that good produced increases. Let's look at this more general case.

Increasing Opportunity Cost

ALMOST ALL THE AVAILABLE LABOUR, LAND, AND capital is *relatively* more productive in some activities than in others. Some people are creative and good at making entertaining movies while others are well coordinated and good at performing challenging physical tasks. Some land is good for farming, while other land is good for building shopping malls. Most capital (tools, machines, and buildings) is custom designed to do a small range of jobs—cutting and sewing machines, automobile assembly lines, or schools.

When each worker, each plot of land, and each piece of capital is allocated to the task in which it is relatively most productive, the economy is at a point on its production possibility frontier. But there are many points on the frontier. And as the economy moves along its *PPF* and produces more of one good or service and less of some others, factors of production must be assigned to tasks for which they are an increasingly poor match. Let's consider a contemporary example of the age-old *trade-off* between military expenditure and private consumption (sometimes called the guns and butter trade-off). Our guns will be missiles, and our butter will be video games.

Missiles Versus Video Games

The economy's production possibility frontier for missiles and video games shows the limits to the production of these two goods, given the total resources available to produce them. Figure 3.2 shows this production possibility frontier.

Suppose that in a year, 4,000 games and 2,000 missiles are produced—point *e* in Fig. 3.2 and possibility *e* in the table. The figure shows other production possibilities. For example, in a tense international situation, we might stop producing games and put all the creative people who devise games and all the programmers, assembly-line workers, computers, buildings, and other resources used to produce games into the defence industry to produce missiles. This case is shown as point *a* in the figure and possibility *a* in the table. The quantity of missiles produced increases to 4,000 a year and games production dries up. Alternatively, we might close down the missile program and switch the resources into producing games. In this case, 5,000 games are produced—point *g*.

FIGURE 3.2

Production Possibility Frontier for Missiles and Video Games

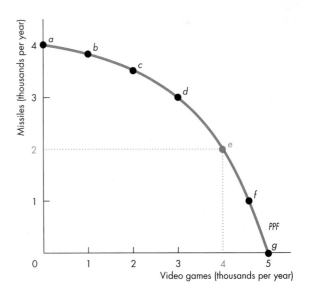

Possibility	Games (thousands per year)		Missiles (thousands per year)
a	0.0	and	4.0
b	1.0	and	3.8
c	2.0	and	3.5
d	3.0	and	3.0
e	4.0	and	2.0
f	4.6	and	1.0
g	5.0	and	0.0

The production possibility frontier for missiles and video games, *PPF*, is bowed outward because resources are not equally productive in all activities. Production is at point e—2,000 missiles and 4,000 games a year. If the economy moves from e to f, a small increase in the quantity of games produced is achieved at the cost of a large decrease in the quantity of missiles produced. If the economy moves back from f to e, a relatively large increase in the quantity of missiles is achieved at the cost of a small decrease in the quantity of games produced.

The Bowed-Out Frontier

Pay attention to the shape of the production possibility frontier in Fig. 3.2. When a large quantity of missiles and a small quantity of games are produced—between points *a* and *d*—the frontier has a gentle slope. When a large quantity of games and a small quantity of missiles is produced—between points *e* and *f*—the frontier is steep. The whole frontier bows outward.

These features of the production possibility frontier reflect the fact that not all resources are equally productive in all activities. Game inventors and programmers can work on missiles, so if they switch from making games to building missiles—moving along the frontier from *e* towards *a*—the production of missiles increases. But these people are not as good at building missiles as the original defence workers. So for a small increase in the quantity of missiles produced, the production of games falls a lot.

Similarly, defence workers can produce games, but they are not as good at that activity as the people currently making games. So when defence workers switch to producing games, the quantity of games produced increases by only a small amount and the quantity of missiles produced falls a lot.

Measuring Opportunity Cost

We can measure the opportunity cost of missiles and of games by using the production possibility frontier in Fig. 3.2. To do so, we calculate how many missiles must be given up to get more games and how many games must be given up to get more missiles.

If all the available resources are used to produce missiles, 4,000 missiles and no games are produced. If we decide to produce 1,000 games, what is the opportunity cost of these 1,000 games? It is the number of missiles that we have to give up. Fig. 3.2 shows that to produce 1,000 games, we move from *a* to *b* and the quantity of missiles decreases by 200 to 3,800 a year. So the opportunity cost of the first 1,000 games is 200 missiles. If we decide to produce an additional 1,000 games, how many missiles must we give up? This time, we move from *b* to *c* and the quantity of missiles decreases by 300.

Figure 3.3(a) illustrates these opportunity costs. The first two rows of table (a) set out the opportu-

nity costs that we have just calculated. The table also lists the opportunity costs of producing an additional 1,000 games by moving along the production possibility frontier of Fig. 3.2 from *c* to *d*, from *d* to *e*, and from *e* to *g*. To be sure that you understand how to calculate the opportunity cost, you might want to work out another example on your own. Calculate the opportunity cost of moving from *e* to *g*.

We've just worked out the opportunity cost of games. We can use the same idea to calculate the opportunity cost of missiles. If all the resources are used to produce games, we produce 5,000 a year and have no missiles. If we decide to produce 1,000 missiles, how many games must we give up? Again, you can work out the answer by using the information in Fig. 3.2. To build 1,000 missiles, we move from *g* to *f* and the quantity of games decreases by 400 to 4,600 a year. So the opportunity cost of the first 1,000 missiles is 400 games. If we decide to build an additional 1,000 missiles a year, how many games must we give up? This time, we move from *f* to *e* and the quantity of games decreases by 600.

Figure 3.3(b) illustrates these opportunity costs. The first two rows of the table (b) show the opportunity costs that we have just calculated. The table also lists the opportunity costs of producing an additional 1,000 missiles by moving along the production possibility frontier from *e* to *d* and from *d* to *a*. You might want to work out another example on your own to be sure that you understand what is going on. Calculate the opportunity cost of moving from *d* to *a*.

Opportunity Cost Is a Ratio

The opportunity cost of producing one additional unit of a good is a ratio. It is the decrease in the quantity produced of one good divided by the increase in the quantity produced of another good as we move along the production possibility frontier. For example, in Fig. 3.3, the opportunity cost of 1 of the first 1,000 missiles is the decrease in the quantity of games, 400, divided by the increase in the quantity of missiles, 1,000. That is, the opportunity cost of 1 missile is 0.4 games.

Because opportunity cost is a ratio, the opportunity cost of producing good *X* (the quantity of units of good *Y* forgone) is always equal to the

FIGURE 3.3

Increasing Opportunity Cost

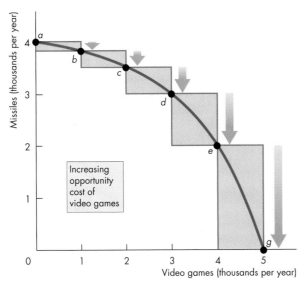

(a) Opportunity cost of video games

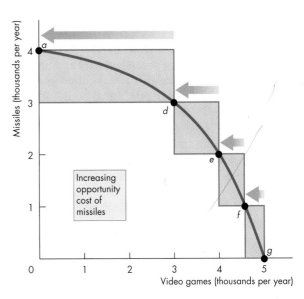

(b) Opportunity cost of missiles

(a) As the production of games increases:
First 1,000 games cost 200 missiles
Second 1,000 games cost 300 missiles
Third 1,000 games cost 500 missiles
Fourth 1,000 games cost 1,000 missiles
Fifth 1,000 games cost 2,000 missiles

(b) As the production of missiles increases:
First 1,000 missiles cost 400 games
Second 1,000 missiles cost 600 games
Third 1,000 missiles cost 1,000 games
Fourth 1,000 missiles cost 3,000 games

The tables record the opportunity costs of games and missiles, and the graphs illustrate the opportunity costs by the bars and arrows.

In part (a), the opportunity cost of games increases from 200 missiles for the first 1,000 games to 2,000 missiles for the fifth 1,000 games. In part (b), the opportunity cost of missiles increases from 400 games for the first 1,000 missiles to 3,000 games for the fourth 1,000 missiles.

inverse of the opportunity cost of producing good Y (the number of units of good X forgone). Let's check this proposition by returning once more to Fig. 3.3. To increase the production of games from 4,600 to 5,000, an increase of 400, the quantity of missiles must decrease from 1,000 to zero. The opportunity cost of the extra 400 games is 1,000 missiles, or 2.5 missiles per game. Similarly, an extra 1,000 missiles cost 400 games, so the opportunity cost of 1 missile is 0.4 games and the opportunity cost of 1 game is 2.5 missiles (1/0.4 = 2.5).

Increasing Opportunity Costs Are Everywhere

Increasing opportunity cost and the bowed-out production possibility frontier are two different ways of expressing the same idea: Resources are not equally productive in all activities. Just about every activity that you can think of is one with *increasing* opportunity cost. Two examples are producing food and producing health care. We allocate the most skilful farmers and the most fertile land to producing food. And we allocate the best doctors and less fertile land to producing health care. If we shift fertile land and tractors away from farming and ask farmers to become hospital porters, the production of food drops drastically and the increase in the production of health-care services is small. The opportunity cost of a unit of health-care services rises. Similarly, if we shift our resources away from health care towards farming, we must use more doctors and nurses as farmers and more hospitals as hydroponic tomato factories. The decrease in the production of health-care services is large, but the increase in food production is small. The opportunity cost of producing a unit of food rises.

This example is extreme and unlikely, but these same considerations apply to any pair of goods that you can imagine: housing and diamonds, wheelchairs and golf carts, pet food and breakfast cereals. Given our limited resources, producing more of one thing always means producing less of something else, and because resources are not equally productive in all activities, the more of anything that we produce, the higher is its opportunity cost.

R E V I E W

- The *PPF* is bowed outward, and the opportunity cost of producing a good increases as more of it is produced.
- The bowed-out frontier and increasing opportunity cost arise from the fact that resources are not equally productive in all activities, and the resources most suitable for any given activity are the first to be used.

We've seen how the production possibility frontier shows the limits to production. And we've seen how we can use the production possibility frontier to measure opportunity cost. Our next task is to study the forces that make our production possibilities grow.

Economic Growth

THE PRODUCTION POSSIBILITY FRONTIER THAT defines the boundary between what is attainable and what is unattainable is not static. It is constantly changing. Sometimes the production possibility frontier shifts *inward*, reducing our production possibilities. For example, when droughts or other extreme climatic conditions occur, productivity decreases, and the production possibility frontier shifts inward. At other times, the frontier shifts *outward*. For example, when excellent growing and harvesting conditions occur, productivity increases, and the production possibility frontier shifts outward.

Over the years, our production possibilities have expanded enormously. The expansion of our production possibilities is called **economic growth**. As a consequence of economic growth, we can now produce much more than we could a hundred years ago and quite a bit more than even ten years ago. By 2000, if the same pace of growth continues, our production possibilities will be even greater. By pushing out the frontier, can we avoid the constraints imposed on us by our limited resources? Can we avoid opportunity costs? Is the economists' quip about there being no free lunches wrong?

The Cost of Shifting the Frontier

We are going to discover that, although we can and do shift the production possibility frontier outward over time, we cannot have economic growth without incurring costs. The faster we push the *PPF* outward, the more goods and services we will have in the future but the less we can consume today. Let's investigate the costs of growth by examining why economies grow and how the choice between the future and the present is made.

The two key factors that influence economic growth are technological progress and capital accumulation. **Technological progress** is the development of new and better ways to produce goods and services and the development of new goods. **Capital accumulation** is the growth of capital resources. As a consequence of technological progress and capital accumulation, we have an enormous quantity of cars and airplanes that enable us to produce more transportation than when we only had horses and carriages; we have satellites that make transcontinental communications possible on a scale much larger than that produced by the earlier cable technology. But to develop new technologies and to accumulate capital, we must bear an opportunity cost. That opportunity cost is a decrease in the quantity of consumption goods and services available because resources are switched from producing goods and services and from research and development to making new machines and other forms of capital. To understand these opportunity costs, let's return to Mark's denim jeans factory.

Technological Change and Capital Accumulation

Given its resources, Mark's factory can produce 5,000 jeans a week. But Mark and his workers do not have to produce jeans. They can do other activities instead. For example, they can spend some of their time installing cutting and sewing machines.

Suppose that Mark spends part of his working time keeping abreast of the latest developments in jeans-making technology. One day, he discovers a recent *technological change* that he can use in his factory. To implement his idea, he must get some of his workers to stop making jeans and to work on installing some computer-controlled cutting and sewing machines that use the new technology—*capital accumulation*.

But Mark's workers are not equally productive in all activities. Some workers are relatively more productive at making jeans, and others are relatively more productive at installing machines.

In assigning workers to tasks, Mark strives to be efficient. So the workers he assigns to installing machines are those who are relatively more productive in that activity. But the more workers he assigns to installing machines, the less suitable they are for that task, and the more suitable they are for making jeans. So to increase the number of machines installed, jeans production decreases by an increasing amount. Mark's *PPF* for jeans and machines is bowed outward like that for video games and missiles.

Mark's production possibilities for jeans and machines are shown in Fig. 3.4. His production possibility frontier initially is the blue curve *abc*. If Mark devotes no resources to installing machines, he produces at point *a*. If he devotes one-fifth of his capacity to installing machines, he produces 4,000 jeans and installs 1 machine at point *b*. If he produces no

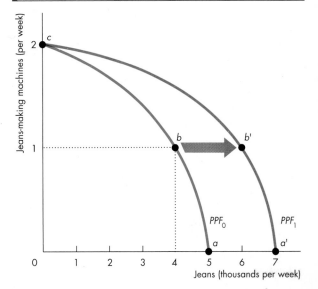

FIGURE 3.4

Economic Growth in a Jeans Factory

If Mark devotes all his resources to producing jeans, he installs no new machines and he produces 5,000 jeans a week (point *a*). If he devotes sufficient resources to installing 1 new machine, his jeans production falls to 4,000 a week (point *b*). But when the new machine is in place, Mark can increase his production to a point on the red *PPF*. For example, if he returns to using all his resources to produce jeans, he can produce at point *a'* (7,000 a week). If he continues to devote resources to installing 1 additional machine, he can produce at point *b'* (6,000 jeans a week). So by installing machines, Mark can shift his *PPF* outward. But he cannot avoid opportunity cost. To shift the frontier outward and increase his *future* production possibilities, Mark must decrease his *current* production of jeans.

jeans, he installs 2 machines at point *c*.

If Mark produces at point *a* in Fig. 3.4, his production possibilities remain stuck on the blue production possibility frontier. But if he moves to point *b* in Fig. 3.4 and installs 1 machine, he increases his future production possibilities. An increase in the number of machines enables Mark to produce more jeans. As a consequence, Mark's production possibilities expand and he experiences economic growth.

The amount by which Mark's production possibilities expand depends on how much of his resources he devotes to technological change and capital accumulation. If he devotes no resources to this activity, the frontier remains at *abc*—the original blue curve. If he cuts the current production of jeans and installs 1 machine (point *b*), then his frontier moves out in the future to the position shown by the red curve in Fig. 3.4. The fewer resources he devotes to current production of jeans and the more resources he devotes to installing machines, the greater is the expansion of his production possibilities.

But economic growth is not free for Mark. To make it happen, he devotes more resources to installing new machines and less to producing jeans. There is no free lunch. Scarcity still remains, so economic growth is not a magic formula for abolishing scarcity. On the new production possibility frontier, Mark continues to face opportunity costs.

The ideas about economic growth that we have explored in the setting of a denim jeans factory also apply to individual households and to nations. Let's see why.

The Economic Growth of Households

To expand its production possibilities, a family must forgo current consumption and devote resources to accumulating capital. It can accumulate claims to the income from real capital or it can accumulate human capital. For example, by forgoing current consumption and undertaking full-time schooling, members of a household can increase their human capital, increase their earning potential, and increase their future consumption.

The Economic Growth of Nations

If as a nation we devote all our resources to producing food, clothing, housing, vacations, and other consumer goods and no resources to research, development, and the accumulation of capital, we will have no more capital and no better technologies in the future than we have at present. Our production possibilities in the future will be the same as today. To expand our production possibilities in the future, we must produce fewer consumption goods today. The resources that we free up today enable us to accumulate capital and to

develop better technologies for producing consumption goods in the future. The decrease in the output of

FIGURE 3.5
Economic Growth in Canada and Hong Kong

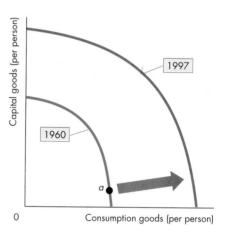

(a) Canada

(b) Hong Kong

In 1960, the production possibilities per person in Canada, part (a), were much larger than those in Hong Kong, part (b). But Hong Kong devotes more than one-third of its resources to accumulating capital, while Canada devotes only one-fifth—point *a* in each part of the figure. Hong Kong's more rapid capital accumulation results in its production possibility frontier shifting out more quickly than does that of Canada. By 1997, the two production possibilities per person were similar.

consumption goods today is the opportunity cost of economic growth and the attainment of more consumption goods in the future.

The experiences of Canada and some East Asian economies, such as Hong Kong's, provide striking examples of the effects of choices on the rate of economic growth. In 1960, the production possibilities per person in Canada were more than four times those in Hong Kong (see Fig. 3.5). Canada devotes one-fifth of its resources to accumulating capital and the other four-fifths to consumption. In 1960, Canada was at point *a* in Fig. 3.5(a). But Hong Kong devotes more than one-third of its resources to accumulating capital and less than two-thirds to consumption. In 1960, Hong Kong was at point *a* in Fig. 3.5(b). Since 1960, both countries have experienced economic growth, but growth in Hong Kong has been much more rapid than in Canada. Because Hong Kong devotes a bigger fraction of its resources to accumulating capital, its production possibilities have expanded more quickly. By 1997, the production possibilities per person in Canada and in Hong Kong were similar.

If Hong Kong's production possibilities per person continue to grow as quickly as they have during the past few decades, Hong Kong will possibly overtake Canada in the near future. If Hong Kong continues to devote such a large proportion of its resources to accumulating capital (at point *b* on its 1997 production possibility frontier), it will most likely continue to grow more rapidly than Canada, and its frontier will move out beyond our own. But if Hong Kong increases its consumption and decreases its capital accumulation (moving to point *c* on its 1997 production possibility frontier), then its rate of economic expansion will slow down to match that of our own.

Hong Kong has been the fastest-growing East Asian economy, but others such as Singapore, Taiwan, South Korea, and China have performed similarly to Hong Kong and they too are gaining on Canada.

R E V I E W

- Economic growth results from technological change and capital accumulation.
- The opportunity cost of faster economic growth is a decrease in current consumption.
- By decreasing current consumption, we can devote more resources to developing new technologies and accumulating capital and speed up the rate of economic growth.

Gains from Trade

PEOPLE CAN PRODUCE FOR THEMSELVES ALL THE goods that they consume or they can concentrate on producing one good (or perhaps a few goods) and then trade with others—exchange some of their own products for the products of others. Concentrating on the production of only one good or a few goods is called *specialization*. We are going to discover how people gain by specializing in the production of the good in which they have a *comparative advantage* and trading with each other. You will see that everyone gains from specialization and exchange. Even people who are less productive than others can gain. Let's explore these ideas further by learning about comparative advantage.

Comparative Advantage

A person has a **comparative advantage** in an activity if that person can perform the activity at a lower opportunity cost than anyone else. Differences in opportunity costs arise from differences in individual abilities and from differences in the characteristics of other resources.

No one excels at everything. One person is an outstanding pitcher but a poor catcher; another person is a brilliant lawyer but a poor teacher. In almost all human endeavours, what one person does easily, someone else finds difficult. The same principle applies to land and capital. One plot of land is fertile but has no mineral deposits; another plot of land has outstanding views but is infertile. One machine has great precision but is difficult to operate; another machine is fast but often breaks down.

Although no one excels at everything, some people excel and can outperform others in many activities. But such a person does not have a *comparative* advantage in every activity. Robertson Davies, for example, was a better actor than most people. But he was an even better writer of fiction. His *comparative* advantage was writing.

Differences in individual abilities and differences in the quality of other resources mean that there are differences in individual opportunity costs of producing various goods. Such differences give rise to comparative advantage. Let's take a closer look at the idea of comparative advantage by returning again to Mark's denim jeans factory.

We've seen that Mark can produce jeans or install machines. But he can also modify his machines and produce other goods. Suppose that one of these goods is denim skirts. And suppose that Mark's production possibility frontier for jeans and skirts is shown in Fig. 3.6(a). As we already know from Fig. 3.1, if Mark uses all his resources to make jeans, he can produce 5,000 a week. The *PPF* in Fig. 3.6(a) tells us that if he uses all his resources to make skirts, he can produce 10,000 skirts a week. But to produce skirts, Mark must decrease his production of jeans. For each 1,000 skirts produced, he must decrease his production of jeans by 500. Mark's opportunity cost of producing 1 skirt is 0.5 jeans.

Similarly, if Mark wants to increase his production of jeans, he must decrease his production of skirts. For each 1,000 additional jeans produced, he must decrease his production of skirts by 2,000. So Mark's opportunity cost of producing 1 pair of jeans is 2 skirts.

Another factory, operated by Marjorie, can also produce skirts and jeans. But Marjorie's factory has machines that are custom made for skirt production rather than for jeans production. Also, Marjorie's work force is more accustomed to making skirts. Marjorie's factory can produce 25,000 skirts a week or 2,000 jeans a week.

This difference between the two factories means that Marjorie's production possibility frontier— shown in Fig. 3.6(b)—is different from Mark's. If Marjorie uses all her resources to make skirts, she can produce 25,000 a week. If she uses all her resources to make jeans, she can produce 2,000 a week. To produce jeans, Marjorie must decrease her production of skirts. For each 1,000 additional jeans produced, she must decrease her production of skirts by 12,500. Marjorie's opportunity cost of producing 1 pair of jeans is 12.5 skirts.

Similarly, if Marjorie wants to increase her production of skirts, she must decrease her production of jeans. For each 1,000 additional skirts produced, she must decrease her production of jeans by 80. So Marjorie's opportunity cost of producing 1 skirt is 0.08 jeans.

Mark and Marjorie can be *diversified* and produce both jeans and skirts. Suppose, for example, that Mark and Marjorie each produce the same quantities of skirts and jeans—1,400 jeans and 7,100 skirts. That is, they each produce at point *a* on their respective production possibility frontiers. Their total production is 2,800 jeans and 14,200 skirts.

In which of the two goods does Marjorie have a comparative advantage? Recall that comparative advantage is a situation in which one person's opportunity cost of producing a good is less than another person's opportunity cost of producing that same good. Marjorie has a comparative advantage in producing skirts.

You can see her comparative advantage by looking at the production possibility frontiers for Marjorie and Mark in Fig. 3.6. Marjorie's production possibility frontier is steeper than Mark's. To produce one more skirt, Marjorie gives up fewer jeans than Mark. Hence Marjorie's opportunity cost of a skirt is less than Mark's. This means that Marjorie has a comparative advantage in producing skirts.

Mark's comparative advantage is in producing jeans. His production possibility frontier is flatter than Marjorie's. This means that Mark gives up fewer skirts to produce one more pair of jeans than Marjorie does. Mark's opportunity cost of producing a pair of jeans is less than Marjorie's, so Mark has a comparative advantage in jeans production.

Achieving the Gains from Trade

If Mark, who has a comparative advantage in jeans production, puts all his resources into that activity, he can produce 5,000 jeans a week—point *b* on his *PPF*. If Marjorie, who has a comparative advantage in skirts production, puts all her resources into that activity, she can produce 25,000 skirts a week—point *b* on her *PPF*. By specializing, Mark and Marjorie together can produce 5,000 jeans and 25,000 skirts a week.

To achieve the gains from specialization, Mark and Marjorie must trade with each other. Suppose they agree to the following deal: Each week, Marjorie produces 25,000 skirts, Mark produces 5,000 jeans, and Marjorie supplies Mark with 12,500 skirts in exchange for 2,500 jeans. With this deal in place, Mark and Marjorie move along the red "Trade line" to point *c*. At this point, each has 12,500 skirts and 2,500 jeans—an additional 1,100 jeans and an additional 5,400 skirts. These are the gains from specialization and trade, and both the parties to the trade share the gains.

Marjorie, who can produce jeans at an opportunity cost of 12.5 skirts per pair can buy jeans from Mark for a price of 5 skirts per pair. Mark, who can produce skirts at an opportunity cost of 0.5 jeans per

FIGURE 3.6

The Gains from Specialization and Trade

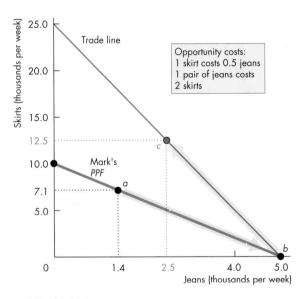

(a) Mark's factory

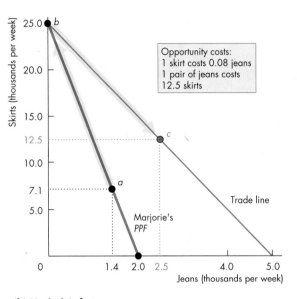

(b) Marjorie's factory

Mark (part a) and Marjorie (part b) each produce at point *a* on their respective *PPF*. For Mark, the opportunity cost of 1 pair of jeans is 2 skirts and the opportunity cost of 1 skirt is 0.5 jeans. For Marjorie the opportunity cost of 1 pair of jeans is 12.5 skirts—higher than Mark's—and the opportunity cost of 1 skirt is 0.08 jeans—lower than Mark's. Marjorie has a comparative advantage in skirts, and Mark has a comparative advantage in jeans.

If Marjorie specializes in skirts and Mark specializes in jeans, they each produce at point *b* on their respective *PPF*. They then exchange skirts for jeans along the red "Trade line." Marjorie buys jeans from Mark for less than her opportunity cost of producing them, and Mark buys skirts from Marjorie for less than his opportunity cost of producing them. They each go to point *c*—a point *outside* his or her *PPF*—where each has 2,500 jeans and 12,500 skirts per week.

skirt can buy skirts from Marjorie at a price of 0.2 jeans per skirt. Marjorie gets her jeans more cheaply, and Mark gets his skirts more cheaply. By specialization and trade, Mark and Marjorie get quantities of skirts and jeans that are *outside* their individual production possibility frontiers.

Absolute Advantage

We've seen that Mark has a comparative advantage in producing jeans and Marjorie has a comparative

advantage in producing skirts. We've also seen that Mark can produce a larger quantity of jeans than Marjorie and that Marjorie can produce a larger quantity of skirts than Mark. Neither Mark nor Marjorie can produce more of *both* goods than the other.

If by using the same quantities of inputs, one person can produce more of *both* goods than someone else can, that person is said to have an **absolute advantage** in the production of both goods. In our example, neither Mark nor Marjorie has an absolute advantage in producing both goods.

It is tempting to suppose that when a person (or country) has an absolute advantage, it is not possible to benefit from specialization and trade. But this line of reasoning is wrong. To see why, let's look again at the case of Mark and Marjorie. Suppose that Marjorie invents and patents a production process that makes her *four* times as productive as she was before. With her new technology, Marjorie can produce 100,000 skirts a week (4 times the original 25,000) if she puts all her resources into that activity. Alternatively, she can produce 8,000 jeans (4 times the original 2,000) if she puts all her resources into that activity. Notice that Marjorie now has an absolute advantage in producing both goods.

We have already worked out that the gains from specialization arise when each person specializes in producing the good in which he or she has a *comparative* advantage. Recall that a person has a comparative advantage in producing a particular good if that person can produce the good at a *lower opportunity cost* than anyone else. Mark's opportunity costs remain exactly the same as they were before. But what has happened to Marjorie's opportunity costs now that she has become four times as productive?

You can work out Marjorie's opportunity costs by doing exactly the same calculation that you've done before. And you can see that her opportunity costs have not changed. Marjorie can produce four times as much of *both* goods as before. But to increase the production of jeans by 1,000 along her new production possibility frontier, she must decrease her production of skirts by 12,500, so her opportunity cost of 1 pair of jeans is still 12.5 skirts. And to increase her production of skirts by 1,000, she must decrease her production of jeans by 80, so her opportunity cost of 1 skirt is still 0.08 jeans.

When Marjorie becomes four times as productive as before, each unit of her resources produces more output, but her opportunity costs remain the same. To produce one more pair of jeans costs the same in terms of the quantity of skirts forgone as it did previously. Since neither Marjorie's nor Mark's opportunity costs have changed, Marjorie continues to have a comparative advantage in producing skirts, and Mark continues to have a comparative advantage in producing jeans. Mark can buy skirts from Marjorie at a lower price than his own opportunity cost of producing them. And Marjorie can buy jeans from Mark for a lower price than her opportunity cost of producing them. So they can both continue to gain by specialization and trade.

The key point to recognize is that it is *not* possible for *anyone*, even someone who has an absolute advantage, to have a comparative advantage in everything. So gains from specialization and trade are always available.

Dynamic Comparative Advantage

Comparative advantage is not a static concept. At any given point in time, the resources available and the technologies in use determine the comparative advantages that individuals and nations have. But as technological change and capital accumulation shift the production possibility frontiers outward, so comparative advantages change. Also, people get better at doing what they do repeatedly. Just by repeatedly producing a particular good or service, people can become more productive in that activity, a phenomenon called **learning-by-doing**. For example, the more often you play a video game, the better you become at it. Learning-by-doing is the basis of *dynamic* comparative advantage. **Dynamic comparative advantage** is a comparative advantage that a person (or country) possesses as a result of having specialized in a particular activity and, as a result of learning-by-doing, having become the producer with the lowest opportunity cost.

Dynamic comparative advantage applies to individuals, firms, and countries. Some people have a steep learning curve—they initially do not seem to be very different from anyone else, but through practice and hard work they become outstanding in some activity. Bombardier, the Canadian maker of train and transit equipment, has pursued dynamic comparative advantage. As Bombardier's labour force and management have gained experience in building high speed trains, they have successively lowered costs and strengthened their comparative advantage.

Singapore, South Korea, Hong Kong, and Taiwan are examples of countries that have pursued dynamic comparative advantage vigorously. They have developed industries in which initially they might not have had a comparative advantage and, through learning-by-doing, have become low opportunity cost producers of high-technology products. An example is the decision to develop a genetic engineering industry in Singapore. Singapore probably did not have a comparative advantage in genetic engineering initially. But it might develop one as its scientists and production workers become more skilled in this activity.

R E V I E W

■ Production increases if people specialize in the activity in which they have a comparative advantage.

■ A person has a comparative advantage in producing a good if that person's opportunity cost of producing the good is lower than everyone else's.

■ Differences in opportunity cost are the source of gains from specialization and trade.

■ If by using the same inputs, a person can produce more of all goods than someone else, then that person has an absolute advantage.

■ Even persons with an absolute advantage gain by specializing in the activities in which they have a comparative advantage and trading.

■ Dynamic comparative advantage can result from learning-by-doing.

The Evolution of Trading Arrangements

INDIVIDUALS AND COUNTRIES CAN GAIN BY specializing in the production of those goods and services in which they have a comparative advantage and trading—see *Economics in History*, pp. 64–65. But to reap the gains from trade from billions of people specializing in millions of different activities, trade must be organized. And to organize trade, social arrangements have evolved. The most important of these arrangements are

■ Markets
■ Property rights
■ Money

Markets

We defined a *market* in Chapter 1 as any arrangement that enables buyers and sellers to get information and to do business with each other. Markets might be physical locations, such as a wholesale meat or fish market. Or they might be electronic links, such as the world oil market.

But all markets share a common feature. They link the producers and the consumers of goods and services together. Sometimes those links are direct—as in the market for haircuts—and sometimes they are indirect and involve many layers of producers of services and traders—as in the market for milk.

Markets work by pooling an enormous amount of information about buyers' and sellers' plans and summarizing this information in just one number: a price. The price moves in response to the decisions of the buyers and sellers. It rises when there is a shortage and it falls when there is a relative abundance. The price sends a signal to buyers and sellers. Each potential buyer or seller knows her or his own opportunity cost of producing a good or service. By comparing this opportunity cost with the market price, each person can decide whether to become a buyer or a seller. Someone who can produce a good (or service) at an opportunity cost that is less than the market price can gain from producing and selling that good (or service). Someone who can produce a good at an opportunity cost that is greater than the market price can gain by buying the good rather than producing it.

Markets are one of the social arrangements that enable people to specialize and gain from the increased production that results from specialization. But markets would not work very smoothly without property rights and money.

Property Rights

Property rights are social arrangements that govern the ownership, use, and disposal of factors of production and goods and services. *Real property* includes land and buildings—the things we call property in ordinary speech—and durable goods such as plant and equipment. *Financial property* includes stocks and bonds and money in the bank. *Intellectual property* is the intangible product of creative effort. This type of property includes books, music, computer programs, and inventions of all kinds and is protected by copyrights and patents.

With no property rights, or with weakly enforced property rights, the incentive to specialize and produce the goods in which each person has a comparative advantage is weakened and some of the potential gains from specialization and trade are lost. If people can take possession of whatever they have the ability to obtain for themselves—steal—then a good deal of time, energy, and resources must be devoted not to production, but to protecting possessions.

Establishing property rights is one of the greatest challenges facing Russia and other Eastern European nations as they seek to develop market economies. And in countries where property rights are well established, such as Canada, upholding intellectual property rights is proving a challenge in the face of modern technologies that make it relatively easy to copy audio and video material, computer programs, and books.

Money

Markets and property rights enable people to specialize and trade their output. But *how* do they trade? There are two possible ways:

- Barter
- Monetary exchange

Barter   **Barter** is the direct exchange of one good or service for another. This method of trading severely limits the amount of exchange that takes place. Imagine that you have oranges, but you want to get apples. You look for someone with apples who wants oranges. Economists call this a *double coincidence of wants*—when person A wants to sell exactly what person B wants to buy, and person B wants to sell exactly what person A wants to buy. As the term implies, such occurrences are coincidences and do not arise frequently. Another way of trading by barter is to undertake a sequence of exchanges. Failing to find someone with apples who wants oranges, you might trade oranges for plums, plums for pomegranates, pomegranates for pineapples, and then eventually pineapples for apples.

Although it is a cumbersome way to do business, quite a large amount of barter does take place. For example, when British rock star Rod Stewart played in Budapest, Hungary, in 1986, he received part of his $30,000 compensation in Hungarian sound equipment, electrical cable, and the use of a forklift truck. And before the recent changes in Eastern Europe, hairdressers in Warsaw, Poland, obtained their barbershop equipment from England in exchange for hair clippings that they supplied to London wigmakers. Today, Australian meat processors swap cans of meat for Russian salmon, crab meat, and scallops; Australian wool growers swap wool for Russian electrical motors.

Although barter does occur, it is inefficient. Fortunately, a better alternative has evolved.

Monetary Exchange   *Monetary exchange* is a system of trading in which a commodity or token that we call *money* serves as the means of payment and the medium of exchange. Money lowers the cost of making a transaction and makes millions of transactions possible that otherwise would not be worth undertaking. Imagine the chain of barter transactions you'd have to go through every day to get your coffee, Coke, textbooks, professor's time, video, and all the other goods and services you consume. In a monetary exchange system, you exchange your time and effort for money and use that money to buy the goods and services you consume, cutting out the incredible hassle you'd face each day in a world of barter.

Metals such as gold, silver, and copper have long served as money. Most commonly, they serve as money by being stamped as coins. Primitive societies have traditionally used commodities such as seashells as money. Prisoners of war in German camps in World War II used cigarettes as money. Using cigarettes as a medium of exchange should not be confused with barter. When cigarettes play the role of money, smokers and nonsmokers buy and sell goods by using cigarettes as a means of payment.

In modern societies, governments provide paper money. The banking system also provides money in the form of chequing accounts. Chequing accounts can be used for settling debts simply by writing an instruction—writing a cheque—to the bank requesting that funds be transferred to another bank account. Electronic links between bank accounts, which are now becoming more widespread, enable direct transfers between different accounts without any cheques being written.

◆ You have now begun to see how economists go about the job of trying to answer economic questions. The fact of scarcity and the associated concept of opportunity cost allow us to understand why people specialize, why they trade with each other, and why they have developed social arrangements such as markets, property rights, and money. One simple fact, scarcity, and its direct implications, choice and opportunity cost, explain so much! Examples abound of how Canadians are discovering new activities in which they have a comparative advantage. *Reading Between the Lines* on pp. 60–61 looks at one of these, microwave telecommunications. In this news article, you can see the lessons you've learned in this chapter at work in the world.

Key Points

The Production Possibility Frontier   The production possibility frontier is the boundary between production levels that are attainable and those that are not attainable when all available resources are being used to their limit. Production can take place at any point on or inside the production possibility frontier, but it is not possible to produce outside the frontier. Points on the production possibility frontier are efficient and points inside the frontier are inefficient. Along the production possibility frontier, the opportunity cost of producing more of one good is the amount of the other good that must be given up. Opportunity cost is inescapable and confronts people with trade-offs. (pp. 44–46)

Increasing Opportunity Cost   Opportunity cost is measured as the decrease in the quantity of one good divided by the increase in the quantity of the other good as we move along the production possibility frontier. As the quantity produced of a good increases, so does the opportunity cost of producing it. Equivalently, the production possibility frontier is bowed outward. The production possibility frontier is bowed outward and opportunity cost increases because resources are not equally productive in all activities. As the economy moves along its *PPF,* producing more of one good and less of another, factors of production are assigned to tasks for which they are an increasingly poor match and so the opportunity cost increases. (pp. 47–50)

Economic Growth   The production possibility frontier shifts outward over time because of the choices we make about the accumulation of knowledge and capital. The opportunity cost of economic growth (of more goods and services in the future) is consuming fewer goods and services in the present. (pp. 50–53)

Gains from Trade   Production can be increased if people specialize in the activity at which they have a comparative advantage. Each person produces the good for which her or his opportunity cost is less than everyone else's, and goods produced at the low-est possible opportunity cost are exchanged—traded. Comparative advantage changes over time, and dynamic comparative advantage arises from learning-by-doing. (pp. 53–57)

The Evolution of Trading Arrangements
Exchange in the real world involves the specialization of billions of people in millions of different activities. To enable individuals and societies to specialize and trade, markets, property rights, and money have evolved. These social arrangements enable people to reap the gains from specialization and trade. (pp. 57–58)

Key Figures

Key Terms

Policy
WATCH

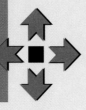

Canada Specializes and Exchanges

Essence of
THE STORY

■ St. Laurent-based SR Telecom Inc., which makes microwave telephone systems, had sales of $140 million in 1995, 97 percent of which were exports.

■ SR Telecom sells to 77 countries in Asia, Europe, the Middle East, Africa, and Latin America.

■ As countries in emerging markets modernize and extend telephone services, SR Telecom's potential market is huge.

■ In this decade alone, total spending on new telephone services around the world is expected to be $700 billion.

■ SR Telecom with the other Canadian exporters shipped a total of $209.2 billion worth of goods abroad in the first 10 months of 1995—up 18.4 percent over the same period a year earlier.

MONTREAL GAZETTE, JANUARY 20, 1996

Trading up

BY PETER HADEKEL

Canada's export business is booming and few companies are doing it better than St. Laurent-based SR Telecom Inc.

The maker of rural-based microwave telephone systems rang up over $140 million in sales in 1995 with exports accounting for an astonishing 97 per cent of the total.

Selling abroad is not just a virtue, it's a necessity for SR Telecom, says Mike Morris, vice-president (technical and industrial liaison). Because there's a limited market for the company's products at home, "we have to look outside Canada if we wish to grow."

Companies like SR Telecom helped the country produce what should be a record-breaking trade performance in 1995. Through the first 10 months of the year, Canada shipped $209.2 billion worth of goods abroad—up 18.4 per cent over the same period a year earlier. ...

SR Telecom... got its start in the North American market and now sells its telephone systems in 77 countries. More than 45 per cent of its business is in Asia and it sells widely in Europe, the Middle East, Africa and Latin America.

Recent export sales have included an $80-million contract in Saudi Arabia and an $81-million deal in Thailand.

Competing against international giants such as Alcatel, NEC and AT&T, SR Telecom has been successful because it essentially founded and developed the technology now widely used in the industry. Its microwave radio systems allow affordable quality telephone services to be provided in rural or isolated regions. As countries in emerging markets begin to modernize and extend basic telephone service, the potential market is huge.

In this decade alone, nations are expected to spend $700 billion adding new telephone services around the world, according to one industry estimate.

Economic

A N A L Y S I S

■ Canadians specialize in producing the goods and services at which they have a comparative advantage.

■ One item at which Canadians have a comparative advantage is paper and pulp. This item is one of Canada's biggest exports.

■ But in recent years, Canadians have developed a comparative advantage in electronic equipment, especially telecommunications equipment.

■ Figure 1 shows Canada's exports of telecommunications equipment alongside those of paper and pulp.

■ You can see that in 1980, paper and pulp exports were about four times those of telecommunications equipment but by 1994, the two items were very similar in magnitude.

■ Figure 2 shows how Canadians gain from trade in telecommunications equipment. Canada's production possibilities curve is the blue *PPF*. And Canada's trade line is the red line.

■ The *PPF* shows Canada's trade-off between producing telecommunications equipment and all other goods and services.

■ With no trade, Canada might produce at point *a*, where it produces *A* of other goods and services and *B* of telecommunications equipment.

■ But if Canada puts more resources into telecommunications equipment, it can move around its *PPF* to point *b*. Here, production is *C* of other goods and services and *D* of telecommunications equipment.

■ By exporting telecommunications equipment and importing other goods and services, Canadians can consume at point *c*, where they have *B* of telecommunications equipment and *E* of other goods and services.

■ At point *c*, Canadians consume the same quantity of telecommunications equipment as with no trade but more other goods and services.

■ Canadians gain from specialization and exchange with the rest of the world.

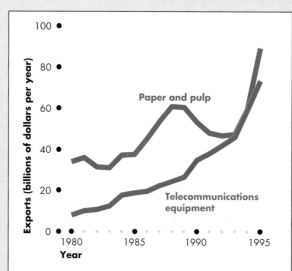

Figure 1 Canadian exports

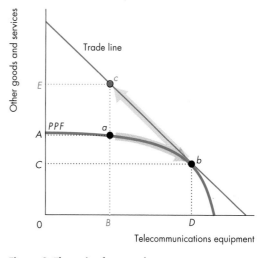

Figure 2 The gains from trade

You're

THE VOTER

■ Some people say that Canada should prevent foreign goods and services from freely entering Canada because foreign labour is too cheap and Canadians cannot compete. How do you respond? Why?

R E V I E W   Q U E S T I O N S

1. How does the production possibility frontier illustrate scarcity?
2. How does the production possibility frontier illustrate production efficiency?
3. How does the production possibility frontier illustrate opportunity cost?
4. Why does the production possibility frontier bow outward for most goods?
5. Why does opportunity cost generally increase as the quantity produced of a good increases?
6. What shifts the production possibility frontier outward and what shifts it inward?
7. Explain how our choices influence the pace of economic growth.
8. What is the opportunity cost of economic growth?
9. Why do people gain as a result of specialization and trade?
10. What are the gains from specialization and trade? How do they arise?
11. What is the difference between comparative advantage and absolute advantage?
12. Why do social arrangements such as markets, property rights and money become necessary?

C R I T I C A L   T H I N K I N G

1. Study *Reading Between the Lines* on pp. 60–61 and then
   a. Describe the growth of Canada's exports of telecommunications equipment and paper and pulp products.
   b. Explain why Canadian exports of telecommunications equipment have grown so quickly in recent years.
   c. Explain why Canadians gain when companies such as SR Telecom produce goods for export.
2. Do the countries that buy Canadian telephone equipment also gain? Explain exactly what and how they gain or lose.
3. Canada's traditional exports have been timber and pulp products. What would be the main effects of Canada trying to export more of these products and less telecommunications equipment?
4. What effect do you think the growth in Canada's exports has on the level of production in Canada? Does it matter what we export?
5. Explain why economic growth does not eliminate scarcity.
6. Why do people specialize in a profession or trade? What are the benefits from specialization?
7. Why does everyone gain from specialization and trade? Why don't only the most productive people gain?

P R O B L E M S

1. Suppose that Leisureland produces only two goods—food and sunscreen. The table gives its production possibilities:

Food (kilograms per month)		Sunscreen (litres per month)
300	and	0
200	and	50
100	and	100
0	and	150

a. Draw a graph of Leisureland's production possibility frontier.
b. What are the opportunity costs of producing food and sunscreen in Leisureland? List them at each output given in the table.
c. Why are the opportunity costs the same at each output level?

2. Busyland produces only food and sunscreen, and its production possibilities are

Food (kilograms per month)		Sunscreen (litres per month)
150	and	0
100	and	100
50	and	200
0	and	300

a. Draw a graph of Busyland's production possibility frontier.
b. What are the opportunity costs of producing food and sunscreen in Busyland? List them at each output given in the table.

3. In problems 1 and 2, Leisureland produces and consumes 50 kilograms of food and 125 litres of sunscreen per month. Busyland produces and consumes 150 kilograms of food per month and no sunscreen. Now the countries specialize and trade with each other.
a. What good does Leisureland export, and what good does it import?
b. What good does Busyland export, and what good does it import?
c. What is the maximum quantity of food and sunscreen that the two countries can produce if each country specializes in the activity in which it has a comparative advantage?

4. Suppose that Busyland acquires new technology and becomes three times as productive as in problem 2.
a. Show, on a graph, the effect of the increased productivity on Busyland's production possibility frontier.
b. Has the new technology changed Busyland's opportunity costs of producing food and sunscreen?
c. Does Busyland now have an absolute advantage in producing both goods?
d. Can Busyland gain from specialization and trade with Leisureland? If so, what will it produce?
e. What are the total gains from trade? What do these gains depend on?

5. Andy and Bob work at Mario's Pizza Palace. In an eight-hour day, Andy can make 240 pizzas or 100 ice cream sundaes, and Bob can make 80 pizzas or 80 ice cream sundaes. Who does Mario assign to make the ice cream sundaes? Who makes the pizzas? Explain your answer.

6. Wendell enjoys playing tennis but the more time he spends on tennis, the lower is his grade in economics. The figure shows the trade-off he faces:

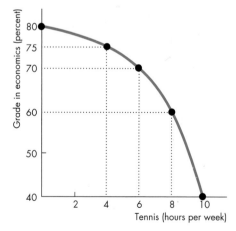

Calculate the opportunity cost of 2 hours of tennis if Wendell increases the time he plays tennis from
a. 4 to 6 hours a week.
b. 6 to 8 hours a week.
c. 8 to 10 hours a week.

7. In problem 6, what is the relationship between the time Wendell spends playing tennis and the opportunity cost of an hour of tennis?

"*It is not from the benevolence of the butcher, the brewer, or the baker that we expect our dinner, but from their regard to their own interest.*"

ADAM SMITH, *THE WEALTH OF NATIONS*

Understanding the Sources of Economic Wealth

THE ISSUES AND IDEAS

Why do some nations become wealthy and others remain poor? Adam Smith was one of the first to try to answer this question. At the time that Smith was pondering this question, between 1760 and 1830, an "industrial revolution" was taking place. During these years, new technologies were invented and applied to the manufacture of cotton and wool, iron, transportation, and agriculture.

Smith wanted to understand the sources of economic wealth, and he brought his acute powers of observation and abstraction to bear on this question. His answer:

■ The division of labour
■ Free domestic and international markets

Smith identified the division of labour as the source of "the greatest improvement in the productive powers of labour." The division of labour became even more productive when it was applied to creating new technologies. Scientists and engineers, trained in extremely narrow fields, became specialists at inventing. Their powerful skills accelerated the advance of technology, so that by the 1820s, machines could make consumer goods faster and more accurately than any craftsman could. And by the 1850s, machines could make other machines that labour alone could never have made.

But, said Smith, the fruits of the division of labour are limited by the extent of the market. To make the market as large as possible, there must be no impediments to free trade both within a country and among countries. Smith argued that when each person makes the best possible economic choice, that choice leads as if by "an invisible hand" to the best outcome for society as a whole.

THEN ...

ADAM SMITH *speculated that one person, working hard, using the hand tools available in the 1770s, might possibly make 20 pins a day. Yet, he observed, by using those same hand tools but breaking the process into a number of individually small operations in which people specialize—by the* division of labour—*ten people could make a staggering 48,000 pins a day. One draws out the wire, another straightens it, a third cuts it, a fourth points it, a fifth grinds it. Three specialists make the head, and a fourth attaches it. Finally, the pin is polished and packaged. But a large market is needed to support the division of labour: one factory employing ten workers would need to sell more than 15 million pins a year.*

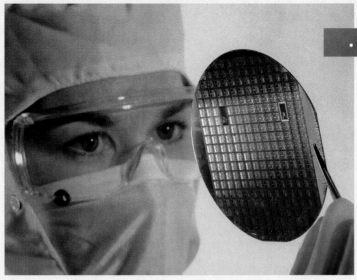

MEMORY CHIPS give your computer its instant recall ability, logic chips provide its number-crunching power, and custom chips make your camera idiot-proof. The computer chip is an extraordinary example of the productivity of the division of labour. Designers lay out a chip's intricate circuits. Printers and cameras transfer an image of the design to glass plates that work like stencils. Workers prepare silicon wafers on which the circuits will be printed. Some slice the wafers, others polish them, others bake them, and yet others coat them with a light-sensitive chemical. Machines transfer a copy of the circuit onto the wafer. Chemicals then etch the design onto the wafer. A further series of processes deposit atoms that act as transistors and aluminum that connects the transistors. Finally, a diamond saw or laser separates the hundreds of chips on the wafer. Every stage in the process of creating a computer chip, from its conception to its final separation from the wafer, uses other computer chips. And like the pin of the 1770s, the computer chip of the 1990s needs a large market—a global market—to support the huge quantities in which chips are produced.

THE ECONOMIST: ADAM SMITH

Adam Smith was a giant of a scholar who made extraordinary contributions in ethics and jurisprudence as well as economics. Born in 1723 in Kirkcaldy, a small fishing town near Edinburgh, Scotland, he was the only child of the town's customs officer (who died before Adam was born).

His first academic appointment, at age 28, was as Professor of Logic at the University of Glasgow. He subsequently became tutor to a wealthy Scottish duke, whom he accompanied on a two-year grand European tour, following which he received a pension of £300 a year—ten times the average income at that time.

With the financial security of his pension, Smith devoted ten years to writing *An Inquiry into the Nature and Causes of **The Wealth of Nations**.* This book, published in 1776, established economics as a science. Many people had written on economic issues before Adam Smith, but it was he who made economics a science. Smith's account was so broad and authoritative that no subsequent writer on economics could advance ideas without tracing their connections with those of Smith's ideas.

Chapter

4

Demand and Supply

After studying this chapter, you will be able to:

- Distinguish between a money price and a relative price

- Explain the main influences on demand

- Explain the main influences on supply

- Explain how prices are determined by demand and supply

- Explain how quantities bought and sold are determined

- Explain why some prices fall, some rise, and some fluctuate

- Make predictions about price changes using the demand and supply model

Slide, Rocket, and Roller Coaster

Slide, rocket, and roller coaster—rides at Canada's Wonderland? No. Commonly used descriptions of the behaviour of prices. ◆ CD players have taken a price slide. In 1983, when they first became available, their price tag was around $800—$1,100 in today's money. Now you can buy one for less than $200, and during the time that CD players have been with us, the quantity bought has increased steadily. Why has there been a slide in the price of CD players? And why hasn't the increase in the quantity bought kept their price high? ◆ Occasionally, a price will rocket upward. But a price rocket, like a satellite-launching rocket, has a limited life. It eventually runs out of fuel. One spectacular price rocket occurred in 1993 and 1994 when the price of coffee shot skyward from from $1.30 a kilogram in 1993 to $4.60 a kilogram in 1994. Why did the price of coffee rise so spectacularly? ◆ Over longer periods, the price of coffee along with the prices of bananas, corn, wheat, and other agricultural commodities rise and fall like a roller coaster ride. Why does the price of bananas roller-coaster even when people's taste for them hardly changes at all? ◆ Although prices may slide, rocket, and roll, many of the things we buy have remarkably steady prices. The price of the audiocassette tapes that we play in a Walkman is an example. But despite their steady price, the number of tapes bought has increased each year. Why do firms sell more tapes, even though they're not able to get higher prices for them, and why do people buy more tapes even though their price is no lower than it was a decade ago?

◇ We will discover the answers to these and similar questions by studying the theory of demand and supply. The central aim of this theory is to explain prices and quantities. But first, we're going to take a closer look at the concept of price. Just what do we mean by price?

Opportunity Cost and Price

ECONOMIC ACTIONS ARISE FROM SCARCITY—WANTS exceed the resources available to satisfy them. Faced with *scarcity*, people must make choices. And in making choices, people are confronted with *opportunity costs*. Choices are influenced by opportunity costs. If the opportunity cost of a good or service increases, people look for less costly substitutes—the *principle of substitution*—and decrease their purchases of the more costly item.

We are going to build on these fundamental ideas and principles and study both the way people respond to *prices* and the forces that determine prices. But before we do that, we need to understand the relationship between opportunity cost and price.

The *opportunity cost* of an action is the best alternative forgone. When you buy a cup of coffee, you forgo something. If the best thing forgone is some gum, then the opportunity cost of buying a cup of coffee is a *quantity* of gum forgone. To calculate this quantity, we need to know the prices of the two goods.

The *price* of an object is the number of dollars that must be given up in exchange for it. Economists refer to this everyday idea of price as the *money price*. If the money price of coffee is $1 a cup and the money price of gum is 50¢ a pack, then the opportunity cost of one cup of coffee is two packs of gum. To calculate this opportunity cost, we divide the price of a cup of coffee by the price of a pack of gum and find the *ratio* of one price to the other. The ratio of one price to another is called a **relative price** and a *relative price is an opportunity cost*. It is the price of good *X* divided by the price of good *Y* and it tells us how many units of good *Y* must be given up to get one more unit of good *X*.

There are trillions of relative prices—coffee to gum, coffee to Coke, coffee to everything else, gum to Coke, gum to everything else, Coke to everything else—and we need a convenient way of expressing relative prices. The normal way of expressing a relative price is in terms of a "basket" of all goods and services rather than in terms of one particular good or service. That is, we divide the money price of a good by the price of a "basket" of all goods (called a *price index*). The resulting relative price tells us the opportunity cost of an item in terms of how much of the "basket" of all goods must be given up to buy it.

Figure 4.1 gives an example of the distinction between a money price and a relative price. The green line shows the money price of wheat and tells us that the money price has fluctuated but has tended to rise. The red line shows the relative price of wheat measured in 1995 dollars. This curve tells us about the opportunity cost of wheat. It shows what the price would have been each year if prices *on the average* had been the same as they were in 1995. The relative price of wheat peaked in 1974 and has tended to fall since that year.

The theory of demand and supply that we are about to study determines *relative prices*, and the word "price" means *relative* price. When we predict that a price will fall, we do not mean that its *money* price will fall—although it might. We mean that its *relative* price will fall. That is, its price will fall *relative* to the average price of other goods and services.

Let's now begin our study of demand and supply, starting with demand.

FIGURE 4.1
The Price of Wheat

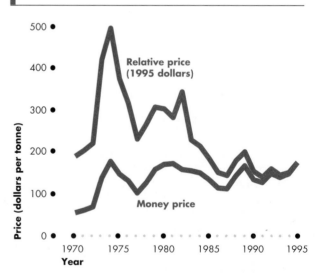

The money price of wheat—the number of dollars that must be given up for a tonne of wheat—has fluctuated between $50 and $175. But the *relative* price or *opportunity cost* of wheat, expressed in 1995 dollars, has fluctuated between $175 and $500 and has tended to decrease. This a fact is obscured by the behaviour of the money price of wheat.

Source: International Monetary Fund, *International Financial Statistics Yearbook, 1995,* Washington, DC.

Demand

IF YOU DEMAND SOMETHING, THEN YOU HAVE made a definite plan to buy it. Demands are different from wants. *Wants* are the unlimited desires or wishes that people have for goods and services. How many times have you thought that you would like something "if only you could afford it" or "if it weren't so expensive"? Scarcity guarantees that many—perhaps most—of our wants will never be satisfied. Demand reflects a decision about which wants we plan to satisfy.

The **quantity demanded** of a good or service is the amount that consumers plan to buy during a given time period at a particular price. The quantity demanded is not necessarily the same amount as the quantity actually bought. Sometimes the quantity demanded is greater than the amount of goods available, so the quantity bought is less than the quantity demanded.

The quantity demanded is measured as an amount per unit of time. For example, suppose a person consumes one cup of coffee a day. The quantity of coffee demanded by that person can be expressed as 1 cup per day or 7 cups per week or 365 cups per year. Without a time dimension, we cannot tell whether a particular quantity demanded is large or small.

What Determines Buying Plans?

The amount of any particular good or service that consumers plan to buy depends on many factors. The main ones are

- The price of the good
- The prices of related goods
- Income
- Expected future prices
- Population
- Preferences

Let's first focus on the relationship between the quantity demanded and the price of a good. To study this relationship, we hold constant all other influences on consumers' planned purchases. We can then ask: How does the quantity demanded of the good vary as its price varies?

The Law of Demand

The law of demand states

Other things remaining the same, the higher the price of a good, the smaller is the quantity demanded.

Why does a higher price reduce the quantity demanded? There are two reasons:[1]

- Substitution effect
- Income effect

Substitution Effect   When the price of a good rises, other things remaining the same, its price rises relative to the prices of all other goods. Equivalently, its opportunity cost increases. Although each good is unique, it has substitutes—other goods that serve almost as well. As the opportunity cost of a good increases, relative to the opportunity costs of its substitutes, people buy less of that good and more of its substitutes.

Income Effect   When the price of a good rises, other things remaining the same, the price rises relative to people's incomes. Faced with a higher price and an unchanged income, the quantities demanded of at least some goods and services must be decreased. Normally the good whose price has increased will be one of the goods bought in a smaller quantity.

To see the substitution effect and the income effect at work, think about blank audiocassette tapes, which we'll refer to as "tapes." Many different goods provide a similar service to a tape; for example, a compact disc, a prerecorded tape, a radio or television broadcast, and a live concert. Tapes sell for about $3 each.

If the price of a tape doubles to $6 while income and the prices of all the other goods remain constant, the quantity of tapes demanded decreases. People substitute compact discs and prerecorded tapes for blank tapes, and faced with tighter budgets, they buy fewer tapes as well as less of other goods and services.

---

[1] We can derive the downward-sloping demand curve from a *marginal analysis* of consumers' choices. One way to study these choices is based on the idea of *diminishing marginal utility* (the more of a good you consume, the less benefit you derive from one extra unit), which is explained in Chapter 7. Another way is based on a model of the substitution effect and income effect, which is explained in Chapter 8.

If the price of a tape falls to $1 while income and the prices of all the other goods remain constant, the quantity of tapes demanded increases. People now substitute blank tapes for compact discs and prerecorded tapes and, with a budget that has some slack from the lower price of a tape, buy more tapes as well as more of other goods and services.

Demand Schedule and Demand Curve

The table in Fig. 4.2 sets out the demand schedule for tapes. A *demand schedule* lists the quantities demanded at each different price, when all the other influences on consumers' planned purchases—such as the prices of related goods, income, expected future prices, population, and preferences—remain the same. For example, if the price of a tape is $1, the quantity demanded is 9 million tapes a week. If the price of a tape is $5, the quantity demanded is 2 million tapes a week. The other rows of the table show us the quantities demanded at prices of $2, $3, and $4.

Figure 4.2 shows the demand curve for tapes. A **demand curve** shows the relationship between the quantity demanded of a good and its price, all other influences on consumers' planned purchases remaining the same. It is a graph of a demand schedule. By convention, the quantity demanded is measured on the horizontal axis, and the price is measured on the vertical axis. The points on the demand curve labelled *a* through *e* represent the rows of the demand schedule. For example, point *a* on the graph represents a quantity demanded of 9 million tapes a week at a price of $1 a tape. Point *e* represents a quantity demanded of 2 million tapes a week at a price of $5 a tape.

Willingness and Ability to Pay   Another way of looking at the demand curve is as a willingness-and-ability-to-pay curve. It tells us the highest price that someone is willing and able to pay for the last unit bought. If a large quantity is bought, that price is low; if a small quantity is bought, that price is high. In Fig. 4.2, if 9 million tapes are bought each week, the highest price that someone is willing to pay for the 9 millionth tape is $1. But if only 2 million tapes are bought each week, someone is willing to pay $5 for the last tape bought.

FIGURE 4.2

The Demand Curve

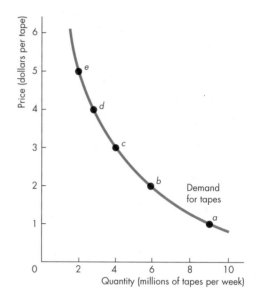

	Price (dollars per tape)	Quantity (millions of tapes per week)
a	1	9
b	2	6
c	3	4
d	4	3
e	5	2

The table shows a demand schedule listing the quantity of tapes demanded at each price if all other influences on buyers' plans remain the same. At a price of $1 a tape, 9 million tapes a week are demanded; at a price of $3 a tape, 4 million tapes a week are demanded. The demand curve shows the relationship between quantity demanded and price, everything else remaining the same. The demand curve slopes downward: As price decreases, the quantity demanded increases.

The demand curve can be read in two ways. For a given price, it tells us the quantity that people plan to buy. For example, at a price of $3 a tape, the quantity demanded is 4 million tapes a week. For a given quantity, the demand curve tells us the maximum price that consumers are willing to pay for the last tape bought. For example, the maximum price that consumers will pay for the 6 millionth tape is $2.

A Change in Demand

The term **demand** refers to the entire relationship between the quantity demanded and the price of a good, other things remaining the same. The demand for tapes is described by both the demand schedule and the demand curve in Fig. 4.2. To construct a demand schedule and demand curve, we hold constant all the other influences on consumers' buying plans. What are the effects of each of those other influences?

1. Prices of Related Goods The quantity of tapes that consumers plan to buy depends in part on the prices of related goods and services that fall into two categories: substitutes and complements.

A **substitute** is a good that can be used in place of another good. For example, a bus ride substitutes for a train ride; a hamburger substitutes for a hot dog; a pear substitutes for an apple. As we have noted, tapes have many substitutes—prerecorded tapes, compact discs, radio and television broadcasts, and live concerts. If the price of one of these substitutes increases, people economize on its use and buy more tapes. For example, if the price of a compact disc rises, more tapes are bought and there is more taping of other people's discs—the demand for tapes increases.

A **complement** is a good used in conjunction with another good. Some examples of complements are hamburgers and french fries, party snacks and drinks, spaghetti and meat sauce, running shoes and jogging pants. Tapes also have complements: Walkmans, tape recorders, and stereo tape decks. If the price of one of these complements increases, people buy fewer tapes. For example, if the price of a Walkman rises, fewer Walkmans are bought and, as a consequence, fewer tapes are bought—the demand for tapes decreases.

2. Income Another influence on demand is consumer income. Other things remaining the same, when income increases, consumers buy more of most goods, and when income decreases, they buy less of most goods. Although an increase in income leads to an increase in the demand for *most* goods, it does not lead to an increase in the demand for *all* goods. **Normal goods** are those for which demand increases as income increases. **Inferior goods** are those for which demand decreases as income increases. An example of an inferior good is public transportation. The biggest users of public transportation are people with low incomes. As incomes increase, the demand for public transportation declines as more expensive, but more convenient, private transportation is substituted for it.

3. Expected Future Prices If the price of a good is expected to rise in the future and if the good can be stored, the opportunity cost of obtaining the good for future use is lower now than it will be when the price has increased. So people retime their purchases—substitute over time. They buy more of the good before its expected price rises (and less after), so the current demand for the good increases.

For example, suppose that Florida is hit by a severe frost that damages the season's orange crop. You expect the price of orange juice to soar. So, anticipating the higher price, you fill your freezer with enough frozen orange juice to get you through the next six months. Your current demand for orange juice has increased (and your future demand has decreased).

Similarly, if the price of a good is expected to fall in the future, the opportunity cost of the good in the present is high relative to what is expected. So again, people retime their purchases. They buy less of the good before its price is expected to fall (and more after), so the current demand for the good decreases.

Computer prices are constantly falling, and this fact poses a dilemma. Will you buy a new computer now, in time for the start of the school year, or will you wait until the price has fallen some more? Because people expect computer prices to keep falling, the current demand for computers is less (the future demand is greater) than it otherwise would be.

4. Population Demand also depends on the size and the age structure of the population. Other things remaining the same, the larger the population, the greater is the demand for all goods and services, and the smaller the population, the smaller is the demand for all goods and services. For example, the demand for car parking spaces or movies or tapes or just about anything you can imagine is much greater in Toronto than it is in Thunder Bay.

Also, other things remaining the same, the larger the proportion of the population in a given age group, the greater is the demand for the types of goods and services used by that age group. For example, in 1995, there were about 1.9 million 20 to 24 year olds in Canada compared with 2.3 million in 1985. As a result, the demand for college places decreased between 1985 and 1995. During the same period, the number of people living in Canada aged 85 years and over increased. As a result, the demand for nursing home services increased.

5. Preferences Finally, demand depends on preferences. *Preferences* are an individual's attitudes towards goods and services. For example, a rock music fanatic has a much greater taste for tapes than does a tone-deaf workaholic. As a consequence, even if they have the same incomes, their demands for tapes will be very different.

Table 4.1 summarizes the influences on demand and the direction of those influences.

Movement Along Versus a Shift of the Demand Curve

Changes in the factors that influence buyers' plans cause either a movement along the demand curve or a shift of the demand curve.

Movement Along the Demand Curve If the price of a good changes but everything else remains

the same, there is a movement along the demand curve. For example, if the price of a tape changes from $3 to $5, the result is a movement along the demand curve, from point *c* to point *e* in Fig. 4.2. The negative slope of the demand curve reveals that a decrease in the price of a good or service increases the quantity demanded—the law of demand.

A Shift of the Demand Curve If the price of a good remains constant but some other influence on buyers' plans changes, there is a change in demand for that good. We illustrate a change in demand as a shift of the demand curve. For example, a fall in the price of the Walkman—a complement of tapes—increases the demand for tapes. We illustrate this increase in demand for tapes with a new demand schedule and a new demand curve. If the price of the Walkman falls, consumers buy more tapes regardless of whether the price of a tape is high or low. That is what a shift of the demand curve shows. It shows that more tapes are bought at each and every price.

Figure 4.3 illustrates such a shift. The table sets out the original demand schedule when the price of a Walkman is $200 and the new demand schedule when the price of a Walkman is $50. These numbers record the change in demand. The graph illustrates the corresponding shift of the demand curve. When the price of the Walkman falls, the demand curve for tapes shifts rightward.

A Change in Demand Versus a Change in Quantity Demanded A point on the demand curve shows the quantity demanded at a given price. A movement along the demand curve shows a **change in the quantity demanded**. The entire demand curve shows demand, so a shift of the demand curve shows a **change in demand**.

Figure 4.4 illustrates and summarizes these distinctions. If the price of a good falls when everything else remains the same, the quantity demanded of that good increases and there is a movement down the demand curve D_0. If the price rises when everything else remains the same, the quantity demanded decreases and there is a movement up the demand curve D_0.

When any other influence on buyers' planned purchases changes, the demand curve shifts and there is a *change* (an increase or a decrease) *in demand*. A rise in income (for a normal good), in population, in the price of a substitute, or in the expected future price of the good or a fall in the price of a comple-

---

TABLE 4.1
The Demand for Tapes

THE LAW OF DEMAND

The quantity of tapes demanded

Decreases if:	*Increases if:*
■ The price of a tape rises	■ The price of a tape falls

CHANGES IN DEMAND

The demand for tapes

Decreases if:	*Increases if:*
■ The price of a substitute falls	■ The price of a substitute rises
■ The price of a complement rises	■ The price of a complement falls
■ Income falls*	■ Income rises*
■ The price of a tape is expected to fall in the future	■ The price of a tape is expected to rise in the future
■ The population decreases	■ The population increases

*A tape is a normal good.

FIGURE 4.3

An Increase in Demand

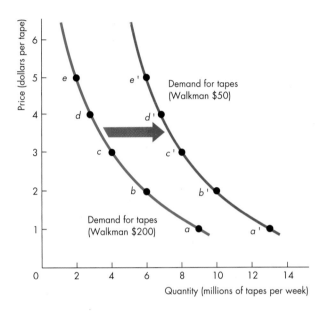

FIGURE 4.4

A Change in the Quantity Demanded Versus a Change in Demand

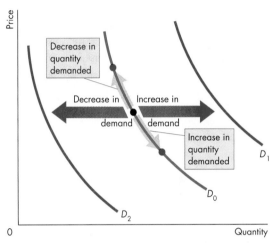

When the price of the good changes, there is a movement along the demand curve and *a change in the quantity demanded* of the good. For example, if the demand curve is D_0, a rise in the price of the good produces a decrease in the quantity demanded and a fall in the price of the good produces an increase in the quantity demanded. The blue arrows on demand curve D_0 represent these movements along the demand curve.

If some other influence on buying plans changes that increases the quantity that people plan to buy, the demand curve shifts rightward (from D_0 to D_1) and *demand increases*. If some other influence on buying plans changes that reduces the quantity people plan to buy, the demand curve shifts leftward (from D_0 to D_2) and *demand decreases*.

Original demand schedule (Walkman $200)		New demand schedule (Walkman $50)	
Price (dollars per tape)	**Quantity** (millions of tapes per week)	**Price** (dollars per tape)	**Quantity** (millions of tapes per week)
a 1	9	a' 1	13
b 2	6	b' 2	10
c 3	4	c' 3	8
d 4	3	d' 4	7
e 5	2	e' 5	6

A change in any influence on buyers' plans other than the price of the good itself results in a new demand schedule and a shift of the demand curve. A change in the price of a Walkman changes the demand for tapes. At a price of $3 a tape (row c of table), 4 million tapes a week are demanded when the Walkman costs $200 and 8 million tapes a week are demanded when the Walkman costs only $50. A *fall* in the price of a Walkman *increases* the demand for tapes because the Walkman is a complement of tapes. When demand *increases*, the demand curve shifts *rightward*, as shown by the shift arrow and the resulting red curve.

ment shifts the demand curve rightward (to the red demand curve D_1). This represents an *increase in demand.* A fall in income (for a normal good), in population, in the price of a substitute, or in the expected future price of the good or a rise in the price of a complement shifts the demand curve leftward (to the red demand curve D_2). This represents a *decrease in demand.* (For an inferior good, the effects of changes in income are in the direction opposite to those described above.)

■ The *quantity demanded* is the amount of a good that consumers plan to buy during a given period of time at a particular price. Other things remaining the same, the quantity demanded increases as price decreases.

■ *Demand* is the relationship between price and quantity demanded, other things remaining the same.

■ When the price of the good changes and all other influences on buying plans remain the same, *the quantity demanded changes* and there is a *movement along the demand curve*.

■ When any influence on buying plans other than the price of the good changes, *demand changes* and *the demand curve shifts*.

Supply

WHEN SOMEONE HAS A SUPPLY OF A GOOD OR service, they have a definite plan to sell. The amount of a good or service that producers plan to sell during a given time period at a particular price is called the **quantity supplied**. The quantity supplied is not necessarily the same as the quantity actually sold. If consumers do not want to buy the quantity producers plan to sell, the sales plans will be frustrated. Like quantity demanded, the quantity supplied is expressed as an amount per unit of time.

What Determines Selling Plans?

The amount that producers plan to sell of any particular good or service depends on many factors. The main ones are

■ The price of the good
■ The prices of factors of production
■ The prices of other goods produced
■ Expected future prices
■ The number of suppliers
■ Technology

Let's first look at the relationship between the price of a good and the quantity supplied. To study this relationship, we hold constant all the other influences on the quantity supplied. We ask: How does the quantity supplied of a good vary as its price varies?

The Law of Supply

The law of supply states

Other things remaining the same, the higher the price of a good, the greater is the quantity supplied.

Why does a higher price lead to a greater quantity supplied? It does so because the opportunity cost of supplying an additional unit of the good increases as the quantity produced increases. So the higher the price of a good, the more willing are the producers to incur a higher opportunity cost of an increase in production.

Supply Schedule and Supply Curve

The table in Fig. 4.5 sets out the supply schedule for tapes. A *supply schedule* lists the quantities supplied at each different price, when all other influences on the amount producers plan to sell are held constant. For example, if the price of a tape is $1, no tapes are supplied. If the price of a tape is $4, 5 million tapes are supplied each week.

Figure 4.5 illustrates the supply curve for tapes. A **supply curve** shows the relationship between the quantity supplied and the price of a good, everything else remaining the same. It is a graph of a supply schedule. The points on the supply curve labelled *a* through *e* represent the rows of the supply schedule. For example, point *d* represents a quantity supplied of 5 million tapes a week at a price of $4 a tape.

Minimum Supply Price   Just as the demand curve has two interpretations, so too does the supply curve. It shows the quantity that producers plan to sell at each possible price. The supply curve also shows the minimum price at which producers are willing to supply the last unit. For producers to be willing to supply the 3 millionth tape each week, the price must be at least $2 a tape. For producers to be willing to supply the 5 millionth tape each week, they must get at least $4 a tape.

A Change in Supply

The term **supply** refers to the entire relationship between the quantity supplied of a good and its price, other things remaining the same. The supply of tapes is described by both the supply schedule and the supply curve in Fig. 4.5. To construct a supply schedule and supply curve, we hold constant all the other influences on suppliers' plans. Let's now consider these other influences.

FIGURE 4.5

The Supply Curve

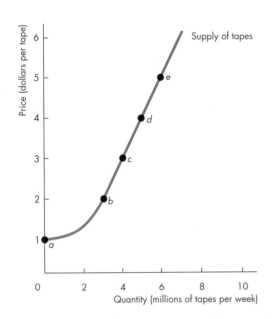

	Price (dollars per tape)	Quantity (millions of tapes per week)
a	1	0
b	2	3
c	3	4
d	4	5
e	5	6

The table shows the supply schedule of tapes. For example, at $2 a tape, 3 million tapes a week are supplied; at $5 a tape, 6 million tapes a week are supplied. The supply curve shows the relationship between the quantity supplied and price, everything else remaining the same. The supply curve usually slopes upward: As the price of a good increases, so does the quantity supplied.

A supply curve can be read in two ways. For a given price, it tells us the quantity that producers plan to sell. For example, at a price of $3 a tape, producers plan to sell 4 million tapes a week. The supply curve also tells us the minimum price at which a given quantity will be offered for sale. For example, the minimum price that will bring forth a quantity supplied of 4 million tapes a week is $3 a tape.

1. Prices of Factors of Production   The prices of the factors of production used to produce a good influence its supply. For example, an increase in the prices of the labour and the capital equipment used to produce tapes increases the cost of producing tapes, so the supply of tapes decreases.

2. Prices of Other Goods   The supply of a good can be influenced by the prices of other goods. For example, if an automobile assembly line can produce either sports cars or sedans, the quantity of sedans produced will depend on the price of sports cars and the quantity of sports cars produced will depend on the price of sedans. These two goods are *substitutes in production*. An increase in the price of a substitute in production lowers the supply of the good. Goods can also be complements in production. *Complements in production* arise when two things are, of necessity, produced together. For example, extracting chemicals from coal produces coke, coal tar, and nylon. An increase in the price of any one of these by-products of coal increases the supply of the other by-products.

Blank tapes have no obvious complements in production, but they do have substitutes in production: prerecorded tapes. Suppliers of tapes can produce blank tapes and prerecorded tapes. An increase in the price of prerecorded tapes encourages producers to use their equipment to produce more prerecorded tapes and so the supply of blank tapes decreases.

3. Expected Future Prices   If the price of a good is expected to rise in the future, and if the good can be stored, the return from selling the good in the future is higher than it is in the present. So producers substitute over time. They offer a smaller quantity for sale before the expected price rise (and a greater quantity later), so the current supply of the good decreases. Similarly, if the price of a good is expected to fall in the future, the return from selling it in the present is high relative to what is expected. So again, producers substitute over time. They offer to sell more of the good before its price is expected to fall (and less later), so the current supply of the good increases.

4. The Number of Suppliers   Other things remaining the same, the larger the number of firms supplying a good, the larger is the supply of the good.

5. Technology   New technologies that enable producers to use less of each factor of production or cheaper factors of production lower the cost of production and increase supply. For example, the development of a new technology for tape production by Sony and Minnesota Mining and Manufacturing (3M) has lowered the cost of producing tapes and increased their supply. Over the long term, changes in technology are the most important influence on supply.

Table 4.2 summarizes the influences on supply and the directions of those influences.

Movement Along Versus a Shift of the Supply Curve

Changes in the factors that influence producers' planned sales cause either a movement along the supply curve or a shift in the supply curve.

Movement Along the Supply Curve   If the price of a good changes but everything else influencing suppliers' planned sales remains constant, there is a movement along the supply curve. For example, if the price of tapes increases from $3 to $5 a tape, there will be a movement along the supply curve from point *c* (4 million tapes a week) to point *e* (6 million tapes a week) in Fig. 4.5. The positive slope of the supply curve reveals that an increase in the price of a good or service increases the quantity supplied—the law of supply.

A Shift of the Supply Curve   If the price of a good remains the same but another influence on suppliers' planned sales changes, supply changes and there is a shift of the supply curve. For example, as we have already noted, technological advances lower the cost of producing tapes and increase their supply. As a result, the supply schedule changes. The table in Fig. 4.6 provides some hypothetical numbers that illustrate such a change. The table contains two supply schedules: the original, based on old technology, and one based on new technology. With the new technology, more tapes are supplied at each price. The graph in Fig. 4.6 illustrates the resulting shift of the supply curve. When tape-producing technology improves, the supply curve of tapes shifts rightward, as shown by the shift arrow and the red supply curve.

A Change in Supply Versus a Change in Quantity Supplied   A point on the supply curve shows the quantity supplied at a given price. A movement along the supply curve shows a **change in the quantity supplied**. The entire supply curve shows supply. A

TABLE 4.2
The Supply of Tapes

THE LAW OF SUPPLY

The quantity of tapes supplied

Decreases if:	*Increases if:*
■ The price of a tape falls	■ The price of a tape rises

CHANGES IN SUPPLY

The supply of tapes

Decreases if:	*Increases if:*
■ The price of a factor of production used to produce tapes increases	■ The price of a factor of production used to produce tapes decreases
■ The price of a substitute in production rises	■ The price of a substitute in production falls
■ The price of a complement in production falls	■ The price of a complement in production rises
■ The price of a tape is expected to rise in the future	■ The price of a tape is expected to fall in the future
■ The number of firms supplying tapes decreases	■ The number of firms supplying tapes increases
	■ More efficient technologies for producing tapes are discovered

shift of the supply curve shows a **change in supply**.

Figure 4.7 illustrates and summarizes these distinctions. If the price of a good falls and everything else remains the same, the quantity supplied of that good decreases and there is a movement down the supply curve S_0. If the price of a good rises and everything else remains the same, the quantity supplied increases and there is a movement up the supply curve S_0. When any other influence on sellers changes, the supply curve shifts and there is a *change in supply*. If the supply curve is S_0 and there is, say, a technological change that reduces the amounts of the factors of production needed to produce the good, then supply increases and the supply curve shifts to the red supply curve S_1. If production costs rise, supply decreases and the supply curve shifts to the red supply curve S_2.

FIGURE 4.6

An Increase in Supply

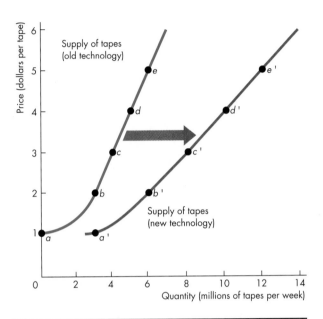

Original supply schedule (old technology)			New supply schedule (new technology)		
	Price (dollars per tape)	**Quantity** (millions of tapes per week)		**Price** (dollars per tape)	**Quantity** (millions of tapes per week)
a	1	0	a'	1	3
b	2	3	b'	2	6
c	3	4	c'	3	8
d	4	5	d'	4	10
e	5	6	e'	5	12

A change in any influence on producers' selling plans other than the price of the good itself results in a new supply schedule and a shift of the supply curve. For example, if Sony and 3M invent a new, cost-saving technology for producing tapes, the supply of tapes changes.

At a price of $3 a tape (row *c* of table), 4 million tapes a week are supplied when the producers use the old technology, and 8 million tapes a week are supplied with the new technology. An advance in technology *increases* the supply of tapes and the supply curve shifts *rightward*, as shown by the shift arrow and the resulting red curve.

FIGURE 4.7

A Change in the Quantity Supplied Versus a Change in Supply

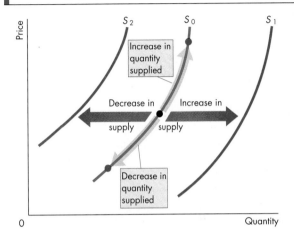

If the supply curve is S_0, a rise in the price of the good *increases the quantity supplied*, and a fall in the price *decreases the quantity supplied*. The blue arrows on curve S_0 represent these movements along the supply curve. If some other influence on supply changes that increases the quantity that producers plan to sell, the supply curve shifts rightward (from S_0 to S_1) and *there is an increase in supply*. If some other influence on supply changes that decreases the quantity that producers plan to sell, the supply curve shifts leftward (from S_0 to S_2) and there is a *decrease in supply*.

R E V I E W

- The *quantity supplied* is the amount of a good that producers plan to sell in a given period at a particular price. Other things remaining the same, the quantity supplied increases as price increases.
- *Supply* is the relationship between quantity supplied and price, other things remaining the same.
- When the price of the good changes, other things remaining the same, *the quantity supplied changes* and there is a *movement along the supply curve.*
- Changes in influences on selling plans other than the price *change supply* and *shift the supply curve.*

Let's now bring demand and supply together and see how prices and quantities are determined.

Price Determination

WE HAVE SEEN THAT WHEN THE PRICE OF A GOOD rises, the quantity demanded decreases and the quantity supplied increases. We are now going to see how adjustments in price coordinate the choices of buyers and sellers.

Price as a Regulator

The price of a good regulates the quantities demanded and supplied. If the price is too high, the quantity supplied exceeds the quantity demanded. If the price is too low, the quantity demanded exceeds the quantity supplied. There is one price, and only one price, at which the quantity demanded equals the quantity supplied. Let's work out what that price is.

The table in Fig. 4.8 shows the demand schedule (from Fig. 4.2) and the supply schedule (from Fig. 4.5). If the price of a tape is $1, the quantity demanded is 9 million tapes a week, but no tapes are supplied. The quantity demanded exceeds the quantity supplied by 9 million tapes a week. In other words, at a price of $1 a tape, there is a shortage of 9 million tapes a week. This shortage is shown in the final column of the table. At a price of $2 a tape, there is still a shortage, but only of 3 million tapes a week. If the price of a tape is $5, the quantity supplied exceeds the quantity demanded. The quantity supplied is 6 million tapes a week, but the quantity demanded is only 2 million. There is a surplus of 4 million tapes a week. The only price at which there is neither a shortage nor a surplus is $3 a tape. At that price the quantity demanded is equal to the quantity supplied—4 million tapes a week.

Figure 4.8 shows the market for tapes. The demand curve (of Fig. 4.2) and the supply curve (of Fig. 4.5) intersect when the price is $3 a tape. At that price, the quantity demanded and supplied is 4 million tapes a week. At each price *above* $3 a tape, the quantity supplied exceeds the quantity demanded. There is a surplus of tapes. For example, at $4 a tape the surplus is 2 million tapes a week, as shown by the blue arrow in the figure. At each price *below* $3 a tape, the quantity demanded exceeds the quantity supplied. There is a shortage of tapes. For example, at $2 a tape, the shortage is 3 million tapes a week, as shown by the red arrow in the figure.

FIGURE 4.8

Equilibrium

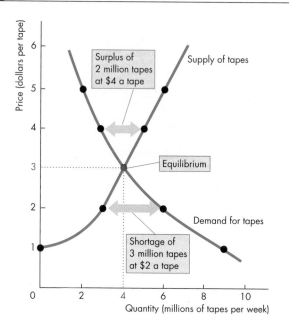

The table lists the quantities demanded and quantities supplied as well as the shortage or surplus of tapes at each price. If the price is $2 a tape, 6 million tapes a week are demanded and 3 million are supplied. There is a shortage of 3 million tapes a week, and the price rises. If the price is $4 a tape, 3 million tapes a week are demanded but 5 million are supplied. There is a surplus of 2 million tapes a week, and the price falls. If the price is $3 a tape, 4 million tapes a week are demanded and 4 million are supplied. There is neither a shortage nor a surplus. Neither buyers nor sellers have any incentive to change the price. The price at which the quantity demanded equals the quantity supplied is the equilibrium price.

Price (dollars per tape)	Quantity demanded	Quantity supplied	Shortage (–) or surplus (+)
	(millions of tapes per week)		
1	9	0	–9
2	6	3	–3
3	4	4	0
4	3	5	+2
5	2	6	+4

Equilibrium

An *equilibrium* is a situation in which opposing forces balance each other. Equilibrium in a market occurs when the price is such that the opposing forces of the plans of buyers and sellers balance each other. The **equilibrium price** is the price at which the quantity demanded equals the quantity supplied. The **equilibrium quantity** is the quantity bought and sold at the equilibrium price.

To see why equilibrium occurs where the quantity demanded equals the quantity supplied, we need to see how buyers and sellers behave if there is a shortage or surplus.

A Shortage Forces the Price Up Suppose the price of a tape is $2. Consumers plan to buy 6 million tapes a week and producers plan to sell 3 million tapes a week. Consumers can't force producers to sell, so the quantity actually offered for sale is 3 million tapes a week. In this situation, powerful forces operate to increase the price and move it towards the equilibrium price. Some people, unable to find the tapes they planned to buy, offer to pay more. And some producers, noticing lines of unsatisfied consumers, move their prices up. As buyers try to outbid one another, and as producers push their prices up, the price rises towards its equilibrium. The rising price reduces the shortage because it decreases the quantity demanded and increases the quantity supplied. When the price has increased to the point at which there is no longer a shortage, the forces moving the price stop operating and the price comes to rest at its equilibrium.

A Surplus Forces the Price Down Suppose the price of a tape is $4. Producers plan to sell 5 million tapes a week and consumers plan to buy 3 million tapes a week. Producers cannot force consumers to buy, so the quantity actually bought is 3 million tapes a week. In this situation, powerful forces operate to lower the price and move it towards the equilibrium price. Some producers, unable to sell the quantities of tapes they planned to sell, cut their prices. In addition, some producers cut production. And some buyers, noticing shelves of unsold tapes, offer to buy for a lower price. As producers try to undercut one another and as buyers make lower price offers, the price falls towards its equilibrium. The falling price reduces the surplus because it increases the quantity demanded and decreases the quantity supplied.

When the price has decreased to the point at which there is no longer a surplus, the forces moving the price stop operating and the price comes to rest at its equilibrium.

The Best Deal Available for Buyers and Sellers
Both situations we have just examined result in price changes. In the first case, the price starts out at $2 and is bid upward. In the second case, the price starts out at $4 and producers undercut each other. In both cases, prices change until they hit the price of $3 a tape. At that price, the quantity demanded and the quantity supplied are equal and neither buyers nor sellers can do business at a better price. Consumers pay the highest price they are willing to pay for the last unit bought, and producers receive the lowest price at which they are willing to supply the last unit sold.

When people freely make bids and offers and when buyers seek the lowest price and sellers seek the highest price, the price at which trade takes place is the equilibrium price—the quantity demanded equals the quantity supplied.

R E V I E W

■ The *equilibrium price* is the price at which buyers' and sellers' plans match each other—the price at which the quantity demanded equals the quantity supplied.

■ At prices below the equilibrium, there is a shortage and the price rises.

■ At prices above the equilibrium, there is a surplus and the price falls.

■ Only at the equilibrium price are there no forces acting on the price to make it change.

The theory of demand and supply that you have just studied is now a central part of economics. But that was not always so. Only 100 years ago, the best economists of the day were quite confused about matters that even students in introductory courses can get right—see *Economics in History* on pp. 94–95. You'll discover in the rest of this chapter that the theory of demand and supply helps us to understand and make predictions about changes in prices—including the price slides, rockets, and roller coasters described in the chapter opener.

Predicting Changes in Price and Quantity

THE THEORY WE HAVE JUST STUDIED PROVIDES us with a powerful way of analysing influences on prices and the quantities bought and sold. According to the theory, a change in price stems from either a change in demand or a change in supply or a change in both demand and supply. Let's look first at the effects of a change in demand.

A Change in Demand

What happens to the price and quantity of tapes if demand for tapes increases? We can answer this question with a specific example. If the price of a Walkman falls from $200 to $50, the demand for tapes increases as is shown in the table in Fig. 4.9. (Recall that tapes and Walkmans are complements and that when the price of a complement falls the demand for the good increases.) The original demand schedule and the new one are set out in the first three columns of the table. The table also shows the supply schedule for tapes.

The original equilibrium price is $3 a tape. At that price, 4 million tapes a week are demanded and supplied. When demand increases, the price that makes the quantity demanded equal the quantity supplied is $5 a tape. At this price, 6 million tapes are bought and sold each week. When demand increases, both the price and the quantity increase.

Figure 4.9 shows these changes. The figure shows the original demand for and supply of tapes. The original equilibrium price is $3 a tape and the quantity is 4 million tapes a week. When demand increases, the demand curve shifts rightward. The equilibrium price rises to $5 a tape and the quantity supplied increases to 6 million tapes a week, as is highlighted in the figure. The quantity supplied increases but there is *no change in supply*. That is, the supply curve does not shift.

The exercise that we've just conducted can easily be reversed. If we start at a price of $5 a tape, with 6 million tapes a week being bought and sold, we can then work out what happens if demand decreases to its original level. You can see that the decrease in demand lowers the equilibrium price to $3 a tape and decreases the equilibrium quantity to 4 million tapes a week. Such a decrease in demand

FIGURE 4.9

The Effects of a Change in Demand

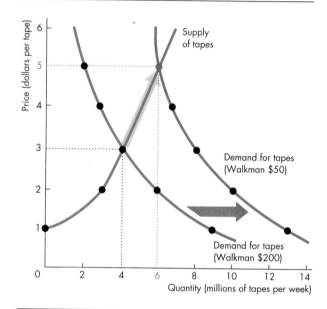

Price	Quantity demanded (millions of tapes per week)		Quantity supplied
(dollars per tape)	Walkman $200	Walkman $50	(millions of tapes per week)
1	9	13	0
2	6	10	3
3	4	8	4
4	3	7	5
5	2	6	6

With the price of a Walkman at $200, the demand for tapes is the blue curve. The equilibrium price is $3 a tape and the equilibrium quantity is 4 million tapes a week. When the price of a Walkman falls from $200 to $50, the demand for tapes increases and the demand curve shifts rightward to become the red curve. At $3 a tape, there is now a shortage of 4 million tapes a week.

The price of a tape rises to a new equilibrium of $5 a tape. As the price rises to $5, the quantity supplied increases—shown by the blue arrow on the supply curve—to the new equilibrium quantity of 6 million tapes a week. Following an increase in demand, the quantity supplied increases but supply does not change—the supply curve does not shift.

might arise from a decrease in the price of compact discs or of CD players. (CDs and CD players are substitutes for tapes.)

We can now make our first two predictions, other things remaining the same:

- When demand increases, both the price and the quantity increase.
- When demand decreases, both the price and the quantity decrease.

A Change in Supply

Suppose that Sony and 3M introduce a new cost-saving technology in their tape-production plants. The new technology changes the supply. The new supply schedule (the same one that was shown in Fig. 4.6) is presented in the table in Fig. 4.10. What is the new equilibrium price and quantity? The answer is highlighted in the table: The price falls to $2 a tape, and the quantity increases to to 6 million tapes a week. You can see why by looking at the quantities demanded and supplied at the old price of $3 a tape. The quantity supplied at that price is 8 million tapes a week and there is a surplus of tapes. The price falls. Only when the price is $2 a tape does the quantity supplied equal the quantity demanded.

Figure 4.10 illustrates the effect of an increase in supply. It shows the demand curve for tapes and the original and new supply curves. The initial equilibrium price is $3 a tape, and the original quantity is 4 million tapes a week. When the supply increases, the supply curve shifts rightward. The equilibrium price falls to $2 a tape, and the quantity demanded increases to 6 million tapes a week, highlighted in the figure. The quantity demanded increases, but there is *no change in demand*—the demand curve does not shift. The equilibrium quantity is 6 million tapes a week.

The exercise that we've just conducted can be reversed. If we start out at a price of $2 a tape with 6 million tapes a week being bought and sold, we can work out what happens if supply decreases to its original level. The decrease in supply shifts the supply curve leftward. The equilibrium price rises to $3 a tape, the quantity demanded decreases, but there is no change in demand. The equilibrium quantity decreases to 4 million tapes a week. Such a decrease in supply might arise from an increase in the cost of labour or raw materials.

FIGURE 4.10

The Effects of a Change in Supply

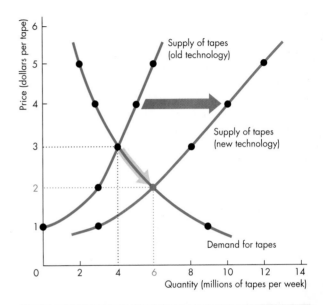

Price	Quantity demanded	Quantity supplied (millions of tapes per week)	
(dollars per tape)	(millions of tapes per week)	Old technology	New technology
1	9	0	3
2	6	3	6
3	4	4	8
4	3	5	10
5	2	6	12

With the old technology, the supply of tapes is shown by the blue supply curve. The equilibrium price is $3 a tape and the equilibrium quantity is 4 million tapes a week. When the new technology is adopted, the supply of tapes increases and the supply curve shifts rightward to become the red curve.

At $3 a tape, there is now a surplus of 4 million tapes a week. The price of a tape falls to a new equilibrium of $2 a tape. As the price falls to $2, the quantity demanded increases—shown by the blue arrow on the demand curve—to the new equilibrium quantity of 6 million tapes a week. Following an increase in supply, the quantity demanded increases but demand does not change—the demand curve does not shift.

We can now make two more predictions, other things remaining the same:

- When supply increases, the quantity increases and the price falls.
- When supply decreases, the quantity decreases and the price rises.

A Change in Both Supply and Demand

In the above exercises, either demand or supply changed, but only one at a time. In each of these cases, we can predict the direction of change of the price and the quantity. But if demand and supply change together, we cannot always say what will happen to both the price and the quantity. We'll look at two cases in which both demand and supply change. First, we'll see what happens when they both change in the same direction—both demand and supply increase (or decrease) together. Then we'll look at the case in which they move in opposite directions—demand decreases and supply increases or demand increases and supply decreases.

Demand and Supply Change in the Same Direction   We've seen that an increase in the demand for tapes increases the price of tapes and increases the quantity bought and sold. And we've seen that an increase in the supply of tapes lowers the price of tapes and increases the quantity bought and sold. Let's now examine what happens when both of these changes occur together.

The table in Fig. 4.11 brings together the numbers that describe the original quantities demanded and supplied and the new quantities demanded and supplied after the fall in the price of the Walkman and the improved tape-production technology. These same numbers are illustrated in the graph. The original (blue) demand and supply curves intersect at a price of $3 a tape and a quantity of 4 million tapes a week. The new (red) supply and demand curves also intersect at a price of $3 a tape but at a quantity of 8 million tapes a week.

An increase in either demand or supply increases the quantity. Therefore when both demand and supply increase, so does quantity.

An increase in demand increases the price and an increase in supply lowers the price, so we can't say for sure which way the price will change when demand

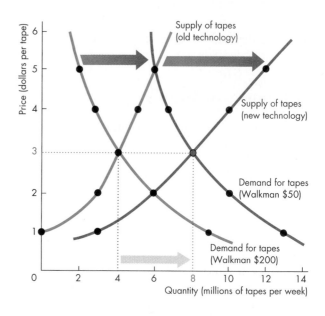

FIGURE 4.11

The Effects of an Increase in Both Demand and Supply

	Original quantities (millions of tapes per week)		**New quantities** (millions of tapes per week)	
Price (dollars per tape)	**Quantity demanded** (Walkman $200)	**Quantity supplied** (old technology)	**Quantity demanded** (Walkman $50)	**Quantity supplied** (new technology)
1	9	0	13	3
2	6	3	10	6
3	4	4	8	8
4	3	5	7	10
5	2	6	6	12

When a Walkman costs $200, and the old technology is used to produce tapes, the price of a tape is $3 and the quantity bought and sold is 4 million tapes a week. A fall in the price of a Walkman increases the demand for tapes, and improved technology increases the supply of tapes. The new supply curve intersects the new demand curve at $3 a tape, the same price as before, but the quantity increases to 8 million tapes a week. These increases in demand and supply increase the quantity but leave the price unchanged.

and supply increase together. In this example, the increases in demand and supply are such that the rise in price brought about by an increase in demand is offset by the fall in price brought about by an increase in supply—so the price does not change. But notice that if demand had increased by slightly more than that shown in the figure, the price would have risen. If supply had increased by slightly more than that shown in the figure, the price would have fallen.

We can now make two more predictions:

■ When *both* demand and supply increase, the quantity increases and the price increases, decreases, or remains constant.
■ When *both* demand and supply decrease, the quantity decreases and the price increases, decreases, or remains constant.

Demand and Supply Change in Opposite Directions Let's now see what happens when demand and supply change together but move in *opposite* directions. We'll look yet again at the market for tapes, but this time supply increases and demand decreases. An improved production technology increases the supply of tapes as before. But now the price of CD players falls. A CD player is a *substitute* for tapes. With CD players now cheaper, more people buy them and switch from buying tapes to buying CDs. The demand for tapes decreases.

The table in Fig. 4.12 describes the original and new demand and supply schedules and these schedules are shown as the original (blue) and new (red) demand and supply curves in the graph. The original demand and supply curves intersect at a price of $5 a tape and a quantity of 6 million tapes a week. The new supply and demand curves intersect at a price of $2 a tape and at the original quantity of 6 million tapes a week.

A decrease in demand or an increase in supply lowers the price. Therefore when both a decrease in demand and an increase in supply occur together, the price falls.

A decrease in demand decreases the quantity, and an increase in supply increases the quantity, so we can't say for sure which way the quantity will change when demand decreases and supply increases at the same time. In this example, the decrease in demand and the increase in supply are such that the increase in quantity, brought about by an increase in supply, is offset by the decrease in quantity, brought about by a decrease in demand—so the quantity does not

FIGURE 4.12

The Effects of a Decrease in Demand and an Increase in Supply

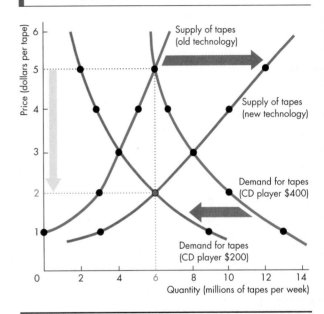

	Original quantities (millions of tapes per week)		New quantities (millions of tapes per week)	
Price (dollars per tape)	**Quantity demanded** (CD player $400)	**Quantity supplied** (old technology)	**Quantity demanded** (CD player $200)	**Quantity supplied** (new technology)
1	13	0	9	3
2	10	3	6	6
3	8	4	4	8
4	7	5	3	10
5	**6**	**6**	**2**	**12**

When the price of a CD player is $400 and the old technology is used to produce tapes, the price of a tape is $5 and the quantity is 6 million tapes a week. A fall in the price of a CD player decreases the demand for tapes, and improved technology increases the supply of tapes. The new supply curve intersects the new demand curve at $2 a tape, a lower price, but in this case the quantity remains constant at 6 million tapes a week. This decrease in demand and increase in supply lowers the price but leaves the quantity unchanged.

change. But notice that if demand had decreased by slightly more than that shown in the figure, the quantity would have decreased. And if supply had increased by slightly more than that shown in the figure, the quantity would have increased.

We can now make two more predictions:

■ When demand decreases and supply increases, the price falls and the quantity increases, decreases, or remains constant.

■ When demand increases and supply decreases, the price rises and the quantity increases, decreases, or remains constant.

CD Players, Coffee, and Bananas

At the beginning of this chapter, we looked at some facts about prices and quantities of CD players, coffee, and bananas. Let's use the theory of demand and supply that we have just studied to explain the movements in the prices and the quantities of those goods.

A Price Slide: CD Players   Figure 4.13(a) shows the market for CD players. In 1983, when CD players were first manufactured, very few firms made them and the supply was small. The supply curve was S_0. In 1983, there weren't many titles on CDs and the demand for CD players was small. The demand curve was D_0. The quantities supplied and demanded in 1983 were equal at Q_0, and the price of a CD player was $1,100 (1994 dollars).

As the technology for making CD players improved and as more and more factories began to produce CD players, the supply increased by a large amount and the supply curve shifted rightward from S_0 to S_1. At the same time, increases in incomes, a decrease in the price of a CD, and an increase in the number of titles on CDs increased the demand for CD players. But the increase in demand was much smaller than the increase in supply. The demand curve shifted rightward from D_0 to D_1. With the new demand curve D_1 and new supply curve S_1, the equilibrium price of a CD player fell to $170 and the quantity increased to Q_1.

The large increase in supply combined with a smaller increase in demand resulted in an increase in the quantity of CD players and a dramatic fall in the price. Figure 4.13(a) shows the CD player price slide.

A Price Rocket: Coffee   Figure 4.13(b) shows the market for coffee. In the second quarter of 1993, the supply curve for coffee was S_0 and the demand for coffee was D_0. The price of coffee was $1.30 a kilogram and the quantity was Q_0.

Serious back-to-back frosts in Brazil damaged coffee plants and severely cut the harvest. As a result, the supply of coffee decreased. This decrease in supply shifted the supply curve leftward from S_0 to S_1. At the same time that the supply of coffee decreased, the demand for coffee increased. The increase in demand was not large, but higher incomes and a larger population brought some increase in demand. The demand curve shifted rightward from D_0 to D_1. The combined effect of a large decrease in supply and a small increase in demand was a rapid rise in price from $1.30 a kilogram in the second quarter of 1993 to $4.60 a kilogram in the third quarter of 1994. The quantity decreased from Q_0 to Q_1. Figure 4.13(b) shows the coffee price rocket.

A Price Roller Coaster: Bananas   Figure 4.13(c) shows the market for bananas. The demand for bananas—curve D—does not change much over the years. But the supply of bananas, which depends mainly on the weather, fluctuates between S_0 and S_1. With good growing conditions, the supply curve is S_1. With bad growing conditions, supply decreases and the supply curve is S_0. As a consequence of fluctuations in supply, the quantity fluctuates between Q_0 and Q_1. The price of bananas fluctuates between 44 cents a kilogram (1995 cents), the minimum price, and 73 cents a kilogram, the maximum price. Figure 4.13(c) shows the banana price roller coaster.

◆ By using the theory of demand and supply, you can explain past fluctuations in prices and quantities and also make predictions about future fluctuations. But you will want to do more than predict whether prices are going to rise or fall. In your study of microeconomics, you will learn to predict *by how much* they will change. In your study of macroeconomics, you will learn to explain fluctuations in the economy as a whole. In fact, the theory of demand and supply can help answer almost every economic question. Two further examples of the kinds of questions you can tackle with these tools can be found in *Reading Between the Lines* on pp. 86–89. Study these stories to gain a deeper understanding of how the forces of demand and supply shape today's world.

FIGURE 4.13

FIGURE 4.13

Price Slide, Rocket, and Roller Coaster

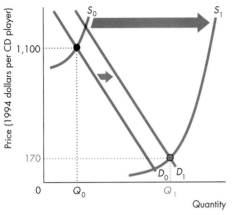

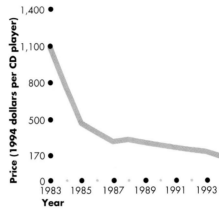

A large increase in the supply of CD players, from S_0 to S_1, combined with a small increase in demand, from D_0 to D_1, resulted in an increase in the number of CD players bought and sold from Q_0 to Q_1. The average price of a CD player fell from $1,100 in 1983 to $170 in 1994—a price slide.

(a) Price slide: CD players

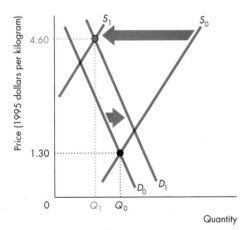

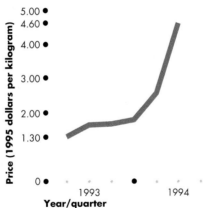

A large decrease in the supply of coffee, from S_0 to S_1, combined with a small increase in the demand, resulted in a decrease in the quantity, from Q_0 to Q_1, and a rise in the price of coffee from $1.30 a kilogram in the second quarter of 1993 to $4.60 a kilogram in the third quarter of 1994—a price rocket.

(b) Price rocket: coffee

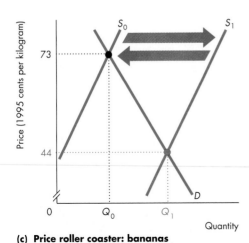

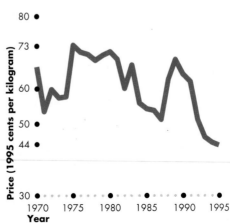

The demand for bananas remains constant at D. But supply fluctuates between S_0 and S_1. As a result, the price of bananas has fluctuated between 44 cents a kilogram and 73 cents a kilogram—a roller coaster.

(c) Price roller coaster: bananas

Policy
WATCH

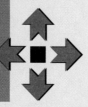

Demand and Supply in Action

Essence of THE STORY

■ In Manitoba, the maximum allowable milk prices are set by the Manitoba Milk Prices Review Commission.

■ From Feb. 1, 1996, dairy farmers in Manitoba received 3.3 cents more per litre. Allowing for increases in other costs, the price to the consumer was expected to rise 4 cents a litre (a 2 to 3 percent rise).

■ The main cause of higher milk prices was higher cattle feed prices.

■ The higher feed prices were the result of a shortage of grains around the world.

WINNIPEG FREE PRESS, FEBRUARY 2, 1996

Milk prices set to rise

BY WANDA CHOW

Manitoba consumers can expect milk prices to jump as much as four cents a litre in the next few weeks, mainly as a result of the rising cost to feed dairy cattle.

Effective Feb. 1, dairy farmers will receive 3.3 cents more per litre. After increases in processing costs, that will translate into a maximum four-cents-a-litre or two to three per cent increase for consumers, said Daryl Kraft, chairman of the Manitoba Milk Prices Review Commission, which sets the maximum allowable prices.

But social advocates and at least one Winnipeg grocer think that's too much.

Joe Cantor said many of his customers are low-income earners or people on social assistance.

An average family of four could be looking at another $10 a month after the increase, Cantor said.

"It's not a healthy situation."

However, even with the increase, dairy farmers will only be recovering their costs, said James Wade, general manager of the Manitoba Milk Producers.

The increase is "a welcome adjustment for producers who have been dealing with increased costs for the last six months," he said. "The increased costs have not been reflected in milk prices until now."

Feed bills have increased "enormously" for dairy farmers since last August, by as much as 20 to 25 per cent for some.

The average farmer will receive about $4,200 a year more with the increase, all of which will go to cover costs.

Other contributing factors to the price hike include a decrease in what farmers can recover for dairy cattle that are no longer as productive and an increase in the cost of replacement cattle.

The jump in feed prices comes from the shortage of grains around the world, said Kraft, who is also a professor of agricultural economics at the University of Manitoba.

Economic

A N A L Y S I S

■ Figure 1 shows the market for milk in Manitoba. The demand curve is D. Initially, the supply curve is S_0, and the equilibrium price is $1.25 a litre.

■ A rise in the price of cattle feed increases the cost of producing milk and decreases the supply of milk. The supply curve shifts leftward to S_1.

■ If the price remains constant at $1.25 a litre, there is a shortage of milk. The quantity demanded is Q_0 and the quantity supplied is Q_2.

■ To prevent a shortage, the Manitoba Milk Prices Review Commission approves a price rise to $1.29 a litre.

■ When the price rises, there is a decrease in the quantity of milk demanded—as shown by the arrow along the demand curve—and an increase in the quantity of milk supplied—as shown by the arrow along the supply curve.

■ The market is again in equilibrium in Fig. 1. The quantity of milk bought and sold is Q_1.

■ Figure 2 shows the events in the market for cattle feed. These events are similar to those in the market for milk. The demand curve is D. Initially, the supply curve is S_0, and the equilibrium price is $200 a tonne.

■ In 1995–1996, world grain production decreased. Drought was one cause and continued political problems kept Russian production low.

■ The decrease in grain production decreased the supply of cattle feed and the supply curve shifted leftward to S_1.

■ With the smaller supply, the price increased to $215 a tonne.

■ When the price rises, there is a decrease in the quantity of cattle feed demanded and an increase in the quantity supplied.

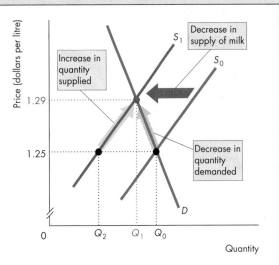

Figure 1 Manitoba milk market

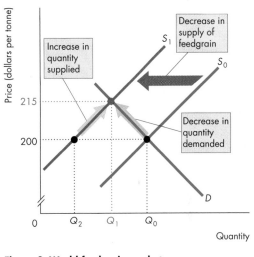

Figure 2 World feedgrain market

You're

THE VOTER

■ Does Manitoba need a Milk Prices Review Commission?

■ Why can't market forces be relied upon to find the right price for milk?

■ What would happen if the Milk Prices Review Commission did not approve a price rise?

■ Would you vote for or against a proposal to abolish the Milk Prices Review Commission?

Demand and Supply: Price of Pagers

THE BOSTON GLOBE, MAY 6, 1994

At your beep and call

BY MICHAEL PUTZEL

WASHINGTON—Don't look now, but somebody's trying to get your attention.

Spurred by better, cheaper technology and a price war that has brought the cost down to consumer levels, all sorts of people are using beepers these days.

The Bugaboo Creek Family Steak House in Seekonk, Mass., is among a growing number of busy restaurants that hand pagers to customers when they arrive and then beep them when their tables are ready.

Kid Klubhouse, a day-care center in Tigard, Ore., loans a pager to each parent who drops a child off in the morning and beeps the parent for advice if there's a problem with the child during the day.

And get this one: A dairy farmer in Japan calls his cows in at milking time every evening by dialing the number for his lead bovine, who has a vibrating pager strapped to her neck and knows to head for the barn when she feels the tickle. I don't have the farmer's name, but people in the industry swear this is a true story. ...

The manufacturer has recently introduced two new lines aimed at the nonbusiness user, which is where the action is in this growth industry. Pagers—the preferred term since many of them don't "beep" anymore—now come in hot colors like "Bimini Blue" and "Totally Teal." And there is an increasing array of features, from musical signaling to automatic relaying of news bulletins. ...

On the horizon is a Seiko watch that goes on sale later this year with a built-in pager that has limited text messages and reports sports and winning lottery numbers. Two-way pagers that will let you reply to a beeped message are in development, to be announced soon.

With the purchase price of cellular phones falling even faster than pagers, it might seem reasonable to expect wireless telephones to replace beepers. But an analyst who specializes in watching developments in wireless technology said there is no indication that is going to happen in the foreseeable future, and studies show continued growth of pager sales at about 25 percent a year. ...

Reprinted with permission.

Essence of THE STORY

- Technological advances have lowered the prices of pagers, which are being used in novel ways.

- Some examples: a busy restaurant provides pagers on which it beeps its customers when their tables are ready; a day-care centre loans pagers to parents and beeps them if there's a problem with a child; and a Japanese farmer beeps his cows at milking time.

- New lines of pagers are being aimed at the non-business user.

- The purchase price of cellular phones is falling even faster than pagers, but pager sales are growing at 25 percent a year and are showing no signs of slowing down.

Economic

ANALYSIS

■ Figure 1 shows the market for pagers. The demand curve is D and initially, the supply curve is S_0. The price of a pager is $300, and 1 million pagers a year are bought.

■ The lower the price of a pager, other things remaining the same, the more uses people find for pagers—calling diners to the table at a restaurant, alerting parents to problems at a day-care centre, even calling cows for milking.

■ As technology has advanced and as new firms have entered the pager market, supply has increased and the supply curve in Fig. 1 has shifted rightward to S_1.

■ If this were the only change in the market for pagers, the price of a pager would have fallen to $200 in this example, and there would have been an increase in the quantity of pagers demanded—shown by a movement along the demand curve—to 7 million a year.

■ But another change has influenced the market for pagers. Technological

advances have increased the supply and decreased the prices of all forms of wireless communication, including the cellular telephone, which is a *substitute* for a pager.

■ The fall in the price of a cellular telephone (a substitute for a pager) has decreased the demand for pagers. The leftward shift of the demand curve from D_0 to D_1 in Fig. 2 illustrates this decrease in demand.

■ The decrease in the demand for pagers has lowered the price even farther, to $100 in this example, and brought a decrease in the quantity supplied—shown by the movement along the supply curve in Fig. 2.

■ Because the supply of pagers has increased and the demand for pagers has decreased, the price of a pager has fallen.

■ But because the increase in the quantity demanded in Fig. 1 is larger than the decrease in the quantity supplied in Fig. 2, the quantity of pagers bought has increased.

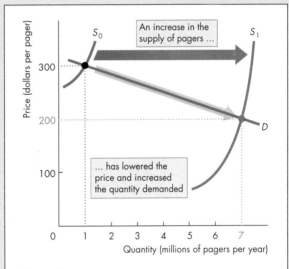

Figure 1

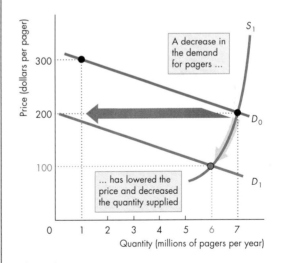

Figure 2

S U M M A R Y

Key Points

Opportunity Cost and Price   Opportunity cost is a relative price, which can be measured as the money price of one good or service divided by the price (index) of a "basket" of other goods and services. The theory of demand and supply explains how relative prices are determined. (p. 68)

Demand   The quantity demanded of a good or service is the amount that consumers plan to buy in a given period at a particular price. Other things remaining the same, the higher the price of a good, the smaller is the quantity demanded of that good. A change in price of a good brings a change in the quantity demanded, which is shown by a movement along the demand curve. A change in any influence on buying plans other than the price changes demand, which is shown by a shift of the demand curve. The demand curve shifts rightward for an increase in demand and leftward for a decrease in demand. (pp. 69–74)

Supply   The quantity supplied of a good or service is the amount that producers plan to sell in a given period at a particular price. Other things remaining the same, the higher the price of a good, the greater is the quantity supplied of that good. A change in the price of a good brings a change in the quantity supplied, which is shown by a movement along the supply curve. A change in any influence on selling plans other than the price changes supply, which is shown by a shift of the supply curve. The supply curve shifts rightward for an increase in supply and leftward for a decrease in supply. (pp. 74–77)

Price Determination   The higher the price, the greater is the quantity supplied and the smaller is the quantity demanded. At the equilibrium price, the quantity demanded equals the quantity supplied. At prices above equilibrium, there is a surplus—the quantity demanded is less than the quantity supplied—and the price falls. At prices bellow equilibrium, there is a shortage—the quantity supplied is less than the quantity demanded—and the price rises. (pp. 78–79)

Predicting Changes in Price and Quantity   An increase in demand leads to a rise in price and to an increase in quantity. A decrease in demand leads to a fall in price and to a decrease in quantity. An increase in supply leads to an increase in quantity and to a fall in price. A decrease in supply leads to a decrease in quantity and a rise in price. (pp. 80–85)

Key Figures and Tables

Key Terms

R E V I E W   Q U E S T I O N S

1. Distinguish between a money price and a relative price. Which is an opportunity cost and why?

2. Define the quantity demanded of a good or service.

3. Define the quantity supplied of a good or service.

4. List the main factors that influence the amount that consumers plan to buy and say whether an increase in the factor increases or decreases consumers' planned purchases.

5. List the main factors that influence the quantity that producers plan to sell and say whether an increase in that factor increases or decreases firms' planned sales.

6. State the law of demand and the law of supply.

7. If a fixed amount of a good is available, what does the demand curve tell us about the price that consumers are willing to pay for that fixed quantity?

8. If consumers are only willing to buy a certain fixed quantity, what does the supply curve tell us about the price at which firms will supply that quantity?

9. Distinguish between
   a. A change in demand and a change in the quantity demanded.
   b. A change in supply and a change in the quantity supplied.

10. Why is the price at which the quantity demanded equals the quantity supplied the equilibrium price?

11. What is the effect on the price of a tape and the quantity of tapes sold if
   a. The price of CDs increases?
   b. The price of a Walkman increases?
   c. The supply of CD players increases?
   d. Consumers' incomes increase and firms producing tapes switch to new cost-saving technology?
   e. The prices of the factors of production used to make tapes increase?

C R I T I C A L   T H I N K I N G

1. Study the market for milk in Manitoba (*Reading Between the Lines*, pp. 86–87), and then
   a. Explain why the supply of milk decreased.
   b. Draw a demand–supply diagram to explain what happened to the price of milk and the quantity of milk bought and sold.
   c. Explain what happened to the demand for milk and the quantity of milk demanded.
   d. Explain what happened in the world feed-grain market.

2. Study the market for pagers (*Reading Between the Lines,* pp. 88–89), and then
   a. Describe the changes in the price of a pager and to the quantity sold.
   b. By drawing a demand–supply diagram, explain the changes in the price and quantity of pagers.

3. Why, despite the steady price of audiocassettes, has the number of tapes bought increased each year? Why do firms sell more tapes, even though they're not able to get higher prices for them, and why do people buy more tapes, even though their price is no lower than it was a decade ago?

4. The government of Canada has reduced the B.C. fishing fleet by 50 percent. What effects do you think such a policy will have on the price of B.C. salmon and the quantity of B.C. salmon bought and sold?

5. During the Gulf War, the United Nations imposed a ban on imports of oil from Iraq. Did this ban create a shortage of oil? Explain your answer.

6. In response to global warming, many countries have decided to reduce the amount of coal that they burn. What effect will this decision have on the price of coal and the quantity of coal bought and sold?

P R O B L E M S

1. Suppose that one of the following events occurs:
   a. The price of gasoline rises.
   b. The price of gasoline falls.
   c. All speed limits on highways are abolished.
   d. A new fuel-effective engine that runs on cheap alcohol is invented.
   e. The population doubles.
   f. Robotic production plants lower the cost of producing cars.
   g. A new law bans car imports from Japan.
   h. The rates for auto insurance double.
   i. The minimum age for drivers is increased.
   j. A massive supply of high-grade oil is discovered in Mexico.
   k. The environmental lobby succeeds in closing down all nuclear power stations.
   l. The price of cars rises.
   m. The price of cars falls.
   n. The summer temperature is 10 degrees lower than normal.

   State which of the above events will produce
   (i) A movement along the demand curve for gasoline.
   (ii) A shift of the demand curve for gasoline rightward.
   (iii) A shift of the demand curve for gasoline leftward.
   (iv) A movement along the supply curve of gasoline.
   (v) A shift of the supply curve of gasoline rightward.
   (vi) A shift of the supply curve of gasoline leftward.
   (vii) A movement along the demand curve for cars.
   (viii) A movement along the supply curve of cars.
   (ix) A shift of the demand curve for cars rightward.
   (x) A shift of the demand curve for cars leftward.
   (xi) A shift of the supply curve of cars rightward.
   (xii) A shift of the supply curve of cars leftward.
   (xiii) An increase in the price of gasoline.
   (xiv) A decrease in the equilibrium quantity of oil.

2. The figure illustrates the market for pizza.

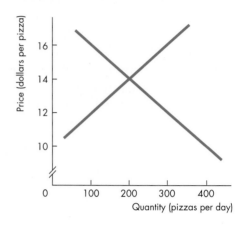

   a. Label the curves.
   b. What is the equilibrium price of a pizza?
   c. What is the quantity of pizza bought and sold?
   d. Describe the pizza market when the price of a pizza is $12.
   e. Describe the pizza market when the price of a pizza is $15.

3. The demand and supply schedules for gum are as follows:

Price	Quantity demanded	Quantity supplied
(cents per pack)	(millions of packs per week)	
10	200	0
20	180	30
30	160	60
40	140	90
50	120	120
60	100	140
70	80	160
80	60	180
90	40	200

   a. What is the equilibrium price of gum?
   b. What is the equilibrium quantity of gum?

   Suppose that a huge fire destroys one-half of the gum-producing factories. Supply decreases to one-half of the amount shown in the above supply schedule.
   c. What is the new equilibrium price of gum?

    d. What is the new equilibrium quantity of gum?

    e. Has there been a shift in or a movement along the supply curve of gum?

    f. Has there been a shift in or a movement along the demand curve for gum?

    g. As the gum factories destroyed by fire are rebuilt and gradually resume gum production what will happen to

        (i)   The price of gum?

        (ii) The quantity of gum bought?

        (iii) The demand curve for gum?

        (iv) The supply curve of gum?

4. Suppose the demand and supply schedules for gum are those in problem 3. An increase in the teenage population increases the demand for gum by 40 million packs per week.

    a. Write out the new demand schedule for gum.

    b. What is the new equilibrium quantity of gum?

    c. What is the new equilibrium price of gum?

    d. Has there been a shift in or a movement along the demand curve for gum?

    f. Has there been a shift in or a movement along the supply curve of gum?

5. Suppose the demand and supply schedules for gum are those in problem 3. An increase in the teenage population increases the demand for gum by 40 million packs per week, and simultaneously the fire described in problem 3 occurs, wiping out one-half of the gum-producing factories.

    a. Draw a graph of the original and new demand and supply curves.

    b. What is the new equilibrium quantity of gum?

    c. What is the new equilibrium price of gum?

6. Fill in the following table by inserting in each column an up arrow ↑ for an increase, and a down arrow ↓ for a decrease, and a question mark ? for indeterminate (can increase or decrease depending on the size of the change in demand and supply). Hint: To fill in the table, draw a separate demand and supply diagram for each case.

	Increase in demand	No change in demand	Decrease in demand
Increase in supply	P Q	P Q	P Q
No change in supply	P Q	P — Q —	P Q
Decrease in supply	P Q	P Q	P Q

" ... if any accident should move the scale of production from its equilibrium position, there will be instantly brought into play forces tending to push it back; just as, if a stone hanging by a string is displaced from its equilibrium position, the force of gravity will at once tend to bring it back ...; "

ALFRED MARSHALL, *PRINCIPLES OF ECONOMICS*

Discovering the Laws of Demand and Supply

THE ISSUES AND IDEAS

How are prices determined? Antoine-Augustin Cournot was the first to answer this question by using demand and supply, in the 1830s. But it was the development and expansion of the railways during the 1850s that gave the newly emerging theory its first practical applications. Railways in the 1850s were as close to the cutting edge of technology as airlines are today. And just as in the airline industry today, competition among the railways was fierce.

In England, Dionysius Lardner used demand and supply to show railway companies how they could increase their profits by cutting rates on long-distance business on which competition was fiercest, and by raising them on short-haul business on which they had less to fear from other transportation suppliers.

The principles that were first worked out by Lardner in the 1850s are used by economists today to calculate the freight rates and passenger fares that will give airlines the largest possible profit. And the rates that result have a lot in common with the railway rates of the nineteenth century. The airlines have local routes that feed like the spokes of a wheel into a hub on which there is little competition and on which they charge high fares (per kilometre), and they have long-distance routes between hubs on which they compete fiercely with other airlines and on which fares per kilometre are lowest.

In France, Jules Dupuit worked out how to use demand theory to calculate the value of railway bridges. His work was the forerunner of what is today called *cost-benefit analysis*. Working with the very same principles invented by Dupuit, economists today calculate the costs and benefits of highways and airports, of dams and power stations.

THEN ...

DUPUIT USED the law of demand to determine whether a bridge or canal would be valued enough by its users to justify the cost of building it. Lardner first worked out the relationship between the cost of production and supply and used demand and supply theory to explain the costs, prices, and profits of railway operations. He also used the theory to discover ways of increasing revenue by raising rates on short-haul business and lowering them on long-distance freight.

TODAY, USING the same principles devised by Dupuit, economists calculate whether the benefits of expanding airports and air traffic control facilities are sufficient to cover their costs, and airline companies use the principles developed by Lardner to set their prices and to decide when to offer "seat sales." Like the railways before them, the airlines charge a high price per kilometre on short flights, for which they face little competition and a low price per kilometre on long flights, for which competition is fierce.

Antoine-Augustin Cournot

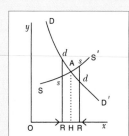

THE ECONOMISTS: ANTOINE-AUGUSTIN COURNOT AND ALFRED MARSHALL

Antoine-Augustin Cournot (1801–1877), professor of mathematics at the University of Lyon, France, drew the first demand curve in the 1830s. The first practical application of demand theory, by Jules Dupuit (1804–1866), a French engineer/economist, was the calculation of the benefits from building a bridge—and, given that a bridge had been built, of the correct toll to charge for its use.

The laws of demand and supply and the connection between the costs of production and supply were first worked out by Dionysius Lardner (1793–1859), an Irish professor of philosophy at the University of London. Known satirically among scientists of the day as "Dionysius Diddler," Lardner worked on an amazing range of problems from astronomy to railway engineering to economics. A colourful character, he would have been a regular guest of TV talk shows if they had been around in the 1850s. Lardner visited the École des Ponts et Chaussées (the School of Bridges and Roads) in Paris and must have learned a great deal from Dupuit, who was doing his major work on economics at the time.

Many others had a hand in refining the theory of demand and supply, but the first thorough and complete statement of the theory as we know it today was that of Alfred Marshall (1842–1924), professor of political economy at the University of Cambridge who, in 1890, published a monumental treatise—*Principles of Economics*—a work that became the textbook on economics for almost half a century. Marshall was an outstanding mathematician, but he kept mathematics and even diagrams in the background. His own supply and demand diagram (reproduced here at its original size) appears only in a footnote.

Alfred Marshall

The equation that describes a downward sloping demand curve is

$$P = a - bQ_D,$$

where P is the price and Q_D is the quantity demanded. If the price is a, buyers are not willing to buy the good. As the price falls, the quantity demanded increases. Equivalently, the demand equation tells us the maximum price that buyers are willing to pay for a given quantity. As the quantity increases, the maximum price that buyers are willing to pay falls.

The equation that describes an upward sloping supply curve is

$$P = c + dQ_S,$$

where Q_S the quantity supplied. If the price is c, sellers are not willing to supply the good. As the price rises, the quantity supplied increases. Equivalently, the supply equation tells us the minimum price at which sellers are willing to supply a given quantity. As the quantity increases, the minimum price that sellers are willing to accept rises.

Price adjusts to achieve an equilibrium. In equilibrium, the quantity demanded equals the quantity supplied. That is,

$$Q_D = Q_S.$$

To find the equilibrium price (P^*) and equilibrium quantity (Q^*) set

$$Q_D = Q_S = Q^*.$$

Then

$$P^* = a - bQ^*$$

$$P^* = c + dQ^*.$$

Solve these two equation for Q^*:

$$c + dQ^* = a - bQ^*$$

$$bQ^* + dQ^* = a - c$$

$$(b + d)Q^* = a - c$$

$$Q^* = \frac{a - c}{b + d}.$$

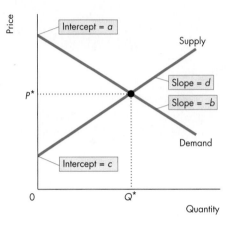

To find the equilibrium price (P^*) substitute $\dfrac{a - c}{b + d}$ for Q^* in either the demand equation or the supply equation. Using the demand equation,

$$P^* = a - b\left(\frac{a - c}{b + d}\right)$$

$$P^* = \frac{a(b + d) - b(a - c)}{b + d}$$

$$P^* = \frac{ad + bc}{b + d}.$$

We can now see how changes in demand and supply lead to changes in the price and quantity. When

- Demand increases, a increases and both P^* and Q^* increase.
- Demand decreases, a decreases and both P^* and Q^* decrease.
- Supply increases, c decreases, P^* decreases and Q^* increases.
- Supply decreases, c increases, P^* increases and Q^* decreases.

Elasticity

After studying this chapter, you will be able to:

■ Define and calculate the price elasticity of demand

■ Explain what determines the elasticity of demand

■ Use elasticity to determine whether a price change will increase or decrease total revenue

■ Define and calculate other elasticities of demand

■ Define and calculate the elasticity of supply

The Pricing Dilemma

You are the chief economic strategist for La Belle Pizza and you want to increase its revenue. But you have a dilemma. You know that to increase the price of a pizza, you must restrict its supply. You also know that to sell more pizza, you must lower its price. What will you recommend: raise the price or lower the price? Which action will increase La Belle Pizza's revenue? ◆ As La Belle Pizza's economic strategist, you need to know a lot about the demand for pizza. For example, as people's incomes grow, how will that growth translate into an increase in demand for pizza? What about the substitutes for pizza? Will entrepreneurs create new varieties of fast food? Will a health craze drive people away from pizza? ◆ La Belle Pizza is not the only producer with a dilemma. A bumper grape crop is good news for wine consumers. It lowers the price of wine. But is it good news for grape growers? Do they get more revenue? Or does the lower price more than wipe out their gains from larger quantities sold? ◆ The government also faces a dilemma. Looking for greater tax revenue to balance its budget, it decides to increase the tax rates on tobacco and alcohol. Do the higher tax rates bring in more tax revenue? Or do people switch to substitutes for tobacco and alcohol on such a large scale that the higher tax rate brings in less tax revenue?

◇ In this chapter, you will learn how to tackle questions such as the ones just posed. You will learn how we can measure in a precise way the responsiveness of the quantities bought and sold to changes in prices and other influences on buyers or sellers.

Elasticity of Demand

L LET'S BEGIN BY LOOKING A BIT MORE CLOSELY AT your task as La Belle Pizza's economic strategist. You are trying to decide whether to advise a cut in production that decreases supply and shifts the supply curve leftward. To make this decision, you need to know how the quantity of pizza demanded responds to a change in price. You also need some way to measure that response.

The Responsiveness of the Quantity Demanded to Price

To understand the importance of the responsiveness of the quantity demanded of pizza to a change in its price, let's compare two possible scenarios for La Belle Pizza that are shown in Fig. 5.1. In both parts of the figure, the supply curves are identical, but the demand curves differ.

The supply curve S_0 in each part of the figure shows the initial supply. In both cases, it intersects the demand curve at a price of $10 a pizza and a quantity of 40 pizzas a day. Suppose that you contemplate a decrease in supply that shifts the supply curve from S_0 to S_1. In part (a), the new supply curve S_1 intersects the demand curve D_a at a price of $30 a pizza and a quantity of 23 pizzas a day. In part (b), with demand curve D_b, the same shift of the supply curve increases the price to $15 a pizza and decreases the quantity to 15 pizzas a day. You can see that in part (a) the price increases by more and the quantity decreases by less than it does in part (b). What happens to La Belle's total revenue in these two cases?

The **total revenue** from the sale of a good equals the price of the good multiplied by the quantity sold. For example, when the price of a pizza is $10 and 40 pizzas a day are sold, total revenue is $400 a day. This amount is equal to the buyer's expenditure on the good.

An increase in price has two opposing effects on total revenue. It increases the revenue on each unit sold (blue area). But an increase in price also leads to a decrease in the quantity sold, which decreases revenue (red area). Either of these two opposing effects could be larger. In case (a), the first effect is larger (blue area exceeds red area), so total revenue increases. In case (b), the second effect is larger (red area exceeds blue area), so total revenue decreases.

FIGURE 5.1

Demand, Supply, and Total Revenue

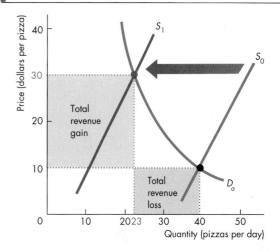

(a) More total revenue

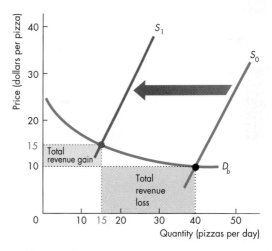

(b) Less total revenue

If supply is cut from S_0 to S_1, the price rises and the quantity decreases. In part (a), total revenue—the quantity multiplied by price—increases from $400 to $690 a day. The increase in total revenue from a higher price (blue area) exceeds the decrease in total revenue from the smaller quantity sold (red area). In part (b), total revenue decreases from $400 to $225 a day. The increase in total revenue from a higher price (blue area) is less than the decrease in total revenue from the smaller quantity sold (red area). These two different responses of total revenue arise from different responses of the quantity demanded to a change in price.

Slope Depends on Units of Measurement

The difference between these two cases is the responsiveness of the quantity demanded to a change in price. Demand curve D_a is steeper than demand curve D_b. But we can't compare two demand curves simply by their slopes, because the slope of a demand curve depends on the units in which we measure the price and quantity. Also, we often need to compare the demand curves for different goods and services. For example, when deciding by how much to change tax rates, the government needs to compare the demand for pizza and the demand for tobacco. Which is more responsive to price? Which can be taxed at a higher rate without decreasing the tax revenue? Comparing the slope of the demand curve for pizza with the slope of the demand curve for tobacco has no meaning since pizzas are measured by the number and tobacco is measured in kilograms—completely unrelated units.

To overcome these problems, we need a measure of responsiveness that is independent of the units of measurement of prices and quantities. Elasticity is such a measure.

Elasticity: A Units-Free Measure

The **price elasticity of demand** is a units-free measure of the responsiveness of the quantity demanded of a good to a change in its price, other things remaining the same. It is calculated by using the formula

$$\text{Price elasticity of demand} = \frac{\text{Percentage change in quantity demanded}}{\text{Percentage change in price}}.$$

Elasticity is a units-free measure because the percentage change in a variable is independent of the units in which the variable is measured. For example, if we measure a price in dollars, an increase from $1.00 to $1.50 is a $0.50 increase. If we measure a price in cents, an increase from 100¢ to 150¢ is a 50¢ increase. The first increase is 0.5 of a unit and the second increase is 50 units, but they are both 50 percent increases.

Minus Sign and Elasticity The demand curve slopes downward, so when the price of a good *increases,* the quantity demanded *decreases.* Because a *positive* price change results in a *negative* change in the quantity demanded, the price elasticity of

demand is a negative number. But it is the magnitude, or *absolute value,* of the price elasticity of demand that tells us how responsive—how elastic— demand is. To compare elasticities, we use the magnitude of the price elasticity of demand and ignore the minus sign.

Calculating Elasticity

To calculate the elasticity of demand, we need to know the quantities demanded at different prices, all the other influences on consumers' buying plans remaining the same. Let's assume that we have the relevant data on prices and quantities demanded of pizza and calculate the elasticity of demand for pizza.

Figure 5.2 zooms in on the demand curve for pizza and shows how the quantity demanded responds to a small change in price. Initially the price is $9.50 a pizza and 41 pizzas a day are sold—the original point in the figure. Then the price increases to $10.50 a pizza and the quantity demanded decreases to 39 pizzas a day—the new point in the figure. When the price increases by $1 a pizza, the quantity demanded decreases by 2 pizzas a day.

To calculate the elasticity of demand, we express the changes in price and quantity demanded as percentages of the *average price* and the *average quantity.* By using the average price and average quantity, we calculate the elasticity at a point on the demand curve midway between the original point and the new point. The original price is $9.50 and the new price is $10.50, so the average price is $10.00. The $1 price increase is 10 percent of the average price. That is,

$$\Delta P/P_{ave} = 10\%.$$

The original quantity demanded is 41 pizzas and the new quantity demanded is 39 pizzas, so the average quantity demanded is 40 pizzas. The 2 pizza decrease in the quantity demanded is 5 percent of the average quantity. That is,

$$\Delta Q/Q_{ave} = 5\%.$$

So the price elasticity of demand, which is the percentage change in the quantity demanded (5 percent) divided by the percentage change in price (10 percent) is 0.5. That is,

$$\begin{aligned}\text{Price elasticity of demand} &= \frac{\%\Delta Q}{\%\Delta P} \\ &= \frac{5\%}{10\%} = 0.5.\end{aligned}$$

FIGURE 5.2

Calculating the Elasticity of Demand

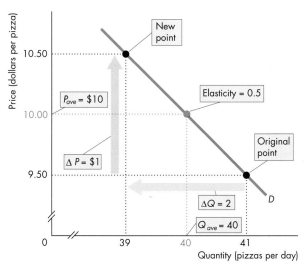

The elasticity of demand is calculated by using the formula*

$$\text{Price elasticity of demand} = \frac{\text{Percentage change in quantity demanded}}{\text{Percentage change in price}}$$

$$= \frac{\%\Delta Q}{\%\Delta P}$$

$$= \frac{\dfrac{\Delta Q}{Q_{ave}}}{\dfrac{\Delta P}{P_{ave}}}$$

$$= \frac{\dfrac{2}{40}}{\dfrac{1}{10}} = 0.5.$$

This calculation measures the elasticity at an average price of $10 a pizza and an average quantity of 40 pizzas.

*In the formula, the Greek letter delta (Δ) stands for "change in" and %Δ stands for "percentage change in."

Average Price and Quantity We use the *average* price and *average* quantity to avoid having two values for the elasticity of demand, depending on whether the price increases or decreases. A price increase of $1 is 10.5 percent of $9.50, and 2 pizzas is 4.9 percent of 41 pizzas. If we use these numbers to calculate the elasticity, we get 0.47. A price decrease of $1 is 9.5 percent of $10.50, and 2 pizzas is 5.1 percent of 39 pizzas. Using these numbers to calculate the elasticity,

we get 0.54. By using the average price and average quantity demanded, the elasticity is 0.5 regardless of whether the price increases or decreases.

Percentages and Proportions Elasticity is the ratio of the *percentage* change in the quantity demanded to the percentage change in the price. It is also, equivalently, the proportionate change in the quantity demanded divided by the proportionate change in the price. The proportionate change in price is $\Delta P/P_{ave}$, and the proportionate change in quantity demanded is $\Delta Q/Q_{ave}$. The percentage changes are the proportionate changes multiplied by 100. So when we divide one percentage change by another, the 100s cancel and the result is the same as we get by using the proportionate changes.

Inelastic and Elastic Demand

Figure 5.3 shows three demand curves that cover the entire range of possible elasticities of demand. In Fig. 5.3(a), the quantity demanded is constant regardless of the price. If the quantity demanded remains constant when the price changes, then the elasticity of demand is zero and the good is said to have a **perfectly inelastic demand**. One good that has a very low elasticity of demand (perhaps zero over some price range) is insulin. Insulin is of such importance to some people with diabetes that they will buy the quantity that keeps them healthy at almost any price. And even at low prices, they have no reason to buy a larger quantity.

If the percentage change in the quantity demanded is less than the percentage change in price, then the magnitude of the elasticity of demand is between zero and 1 and the good is said to have an **inelastic demand**. The demand curve in Fig. 5.3(a) is an example of an inelastic demand.

If the percentage change in the quantity demanded exceeds the percentage change in price, then the magnitude of the elasticity is greater than 1 and the good is said to have an **elastic demand**. The dividing line between inelastic and elastic demand is the case in which the percentage change in the quantity demanded equals the percentage change in price. In this case, the elasticity of demand is 1 and the good is said to have a **unit elastic demand**. The demand curve in Fig. 5.3(b) is an example of a unit elastic demand.

If the quantity demanded is infinitely responsive to a price change, then the magnitude of the elasticity

FIGURE 5.3

Inelastic and Elastic Demand

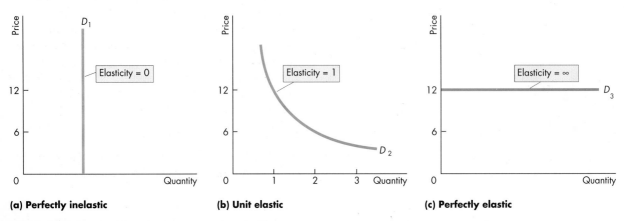

(a) Perfectly inelastic **(b) Unit elastic** **(c) Perfectly elastic**

Each demand illustrated here has a constant elasticity. The demand curve in part (a) is for a good that has a zero price elasticity of demand. The demand curve in part (b) is for a

good with a unit elasticity of demand. The demand curve in part (c) is for a good with an infinite elasticity of demand.

of demand is infinity and the good is said to have a **perfectly elastic demand**. The demand curve in Fig. 5.3(c) is an example of a perfectly elastic demand. An example of a good that has a very high elasticity of demand (almost infinite) is marker pens from the campus bookstore and from the convenience store next door. If the two stores offer pens for the same price, some people buy from one and some from the other. But if the bookstore increases the price of pens, even by a small amount, while the shop next door maintains the lower price, the quantity of pens demanded from the bookstore will fall to zero. Marker pens from the two stores are perfect substitutes for each other.

Elasticity Along a Straight-Line Demand Curve

Elasticity is not the same as slope, but the two are related. To understand how they are related, let's look at elasticity along a straight-line demand curve—a demand curve that has a constant slope.

Figure 5.4 illustrates the calculation of elasticity along a straight-line demand curve. Let's calculate the elasticity of demand at an average price of $40 a pizza and an average quantity of 4 pizzas a day. To do so,

imagine that the price rises from $30 a pizza to $50 a pizza. The change in the price is $20 and the average price is $40 (average of $30 and $50), which means that the proportionate change in price is

$$\frac{\Delta P}{P_{ave}} = \frac{20}{40}.$$

At a price of $30 a pizza, the quantity demanded is 8 pizzas a day. At a price of $50 a pizza, the quantity demanded is zero. So the change in the quantity demanded is 8 pizzas a day and the average quantity is 4 pizzas a day (the average of 8 and zero), so the proportionate change in the quantity demanded is

$$\frac{\Delta Q}{Q_{ave}} = \frac{8}{4}.$$

Dividing the proportionate change in the quantity demanded by the proportionate change in the price gives

$$\frac{\Delta Q/Q_{ave}}{\Delta P/P_{ave}} = \frac{8/4}{20/40} = 4.$$

By using this same method, we can calculate the elasticity of demand at any price and quantity along the demand curve. Because the demand curve is a straight line, a $20 price change brings a change in

FIGURE 5.4

Elasticity Along a Straight-Line Demand Curve ◆

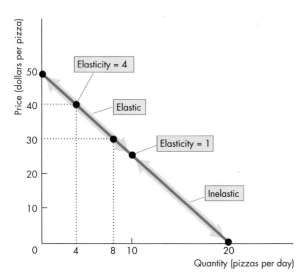

On a straight-line demand curve, elasticity decreases as the price falls and the quantity demanded increases. Demand is unit elastic at the midpoint of the demand curve (elasticity is 1). Above the midpoint, demand is elastic; and below the midpoint, demand is inelastic.

the quantity of 8 pizzas at every average price. So in the elasticity formula, $\Delta Q = 8$ and $\Delta P = 20$ regardless of average quantity and average price. But the lower the average price, the greater is the average quantity demanded. So the lower the average price, the less elastic is demand.

Check this proposition by calculating the elasticity of demand at the midpoint of the demand curve, where the price is $25 a pizza and the quantity demanded is 10 pizzas a day. The proportionate change in price is $20 ÷ $25 = 0.8, and the proportionate change in the quantity demanded is 8 ÷ 10 = 0.8, so the elasticity of demand is 1. On a straight-line demand curve, the price elasticity is always 1 at the midpoint. Above the midpoint, demand is elastic (the price elasticity exceeds 1), and below the midpoint, demand is inelastic (the price elasticity is less than 1).

Demand is perfectly elastic (infinity) where the quantity demanded is zero and perfectly inelastic (zero) where the price is zero.

The Factors That Influence the Elasticity of Demand

Actual values of elasticities of demand have been estimated from the average spending patterns of consumers, and some examples are set out in Table 5.1. You can see that these real-world elasticities of demand range from 1.52 for metals, the most elastic in the table, to 0.12 for food, the least elastic in the table. What makes the demand for some goods elastic and the demand for others inelastic? Elasticity depends on three main factors:

- The closeness of substitutes
- The proportion of income spent on the good
- The time elapsed since a price change

Closeness of Substitutes The closer the substitutes for a good or service, the more elastic is the demand for it. For example, metals have good substitutes such as plastics, so the demand for metals is elastic. In contrast, oil has substitutes but none that are very close (imagine a steam-driven, coal-fuelled car or a nuclear-powered jetliner). As a result, the demand for oil is inelastic.

In everyday language we call some goods, such as food and housing, *necessities* and other goods, such as exotic vacations, *luxuries.* Necessities are goods that have poor substitutes and that are crucial for our well-being, so generally, they have inelastic demands. Luxuries are goods that usually have many substitutes and so have elastic demands.

The degree of substitutability between two goods also depends on how narrowly (or broadly) we define them. For example, even though oil does not have a close substitute, different types of oil are close substitutes for each. Saudi Arabian Light, a particular type of oil is a close substitute for Alaskan North Slope, another particular type of oil. If you happen to be the economic advisor to Saudi Arabia, you will not contemplate a unilateral price increase. Even though Saudi Arabian Light has some unique characteristics, other oil can easily substitute for it, and most buyers will be very sensitive to its price relative to the prices of other types of oil. So the demand for Saudi Arabian Light is highly elastic.

This example, which distinguishes between oil in general and different types of oil, applies to many other goods and services. The elasticity of demand for meat in general is small, but the elasticity of demand for beef, lamb, or chicken is large. The elasticity of demand for personal computers is small, but the elasticity of demand for a Compaq, Dell, or IBM is large.

TABLE 5.1

Some Real-World Price Elasticities of Demand

Good or Service	Elasticity
Elastic Demand	
Metals	1.52
Electrical engineering products	1.39
Mechanical engineering products	1.30
Furniture	1.26
Motor vehicles	1.14
Instrument engineering products	1.10
Professional services	1.09
Transportation services	1.03
Inelastic Demand	
Gas, electricity, and water	0.92
Oil	0.91
Chemicals	0.89
Beverages (all types)	0.78
Clothing	0.64
Tobacco	0.61
Banking and insurance services	0.56
Housing services	0.55
Agricultural and fish products	0.42
Books, magazines, and newspapers	0.34
Food	0.12

Sources: Ahsan Mansur and John Whalley, "Numerical Specification of Applied General Equilibrium Models: Estimation, Calibration, and Data," in *Applied General Equilibrium Analysis*, eds. Herbert E. Scarf and John B. Shoven (New York: Cambridge University Press, 1984), 109, and Henri Theil, Ching-Fan Chung, and James L. Seale, Jr., *Advances in Econometrics, Supplement 1, 1989, International Evidence on Consumption Patterns* (Greenwich, CT: JAI Press Inc., 1989).

Proportion of Income Spent on the Good

Other things remaining the same, the higher the proportion of income spent on a good, the more elastic is the demand for it. If only a small fraction of income is spent on a good, then a change in its price has little impact on the consumer's overall budget. But a small rise in the price of a good that is a large part of a consumer's budget induces the consumer to make a radical reappraisal of expenditures.

To appreciate the importance of the proportion of income spent on a good, consider your own elasticity of demand for textbooks and chewing gum. If the price of textbooks doubles (increases 100 percent), there will be a big decrease in the quantity of textbooks bought. There will be an increase in sharing and in illegal photocopying. If the price of chewing gum doubles, also a 100 percent increase, there will be almost no change in the quantity of gum demanded. Why the difference? Textbooks take a large proportion of your budget, while gum takes only a tiny portion. You don't like either price increase, but you hardly notice the effects of the increased price of gum, while the increased price of textbooks puts your budget under severe strain.

Figure 5.5 shows the proportion of income spent on food and the price elasticity of demand for food in 20 countries. This figure confirms the general tendency we have just described. The larger proportion of income spent on food, the more price elastic is the demand for food. For example, in Tanzania, a poor African nation where average incomes are 3.3 percent of incomes in the United States and where 62 percent of income is spent on food, the price elasticity of demand for food is 0.77. In contrast, in the United States where 12 percent of income is spent on food, the elasticity of demand for food is 0.12. These numbers confirm that in a country that spends a large proportion of income on food, an increase in the price of food forces people to make a bigger adjustment to the quantity of food bought than in a country in which a small proportion of income is spent on food.

Time Elapsed Since a Price Change   The greater the time lapse since a price change, the more elastic is demand. When a price changes, consumers often continue to buy similar quantities of a good for a while. But given enough time, they find acceptable and less costly substitutes. As this process of substitution occurs, the quantity purchased of an item that has become more expensive gradually declines.

To describe the effect of time on demand, we distinguish between two time frames:

1. Short-run demand
2. Long-run demand

Short-run demand describes the response of buyers to a change in the price of a good *before* sufficient time has elapsed for all the possible substitutions to be made. Long-run demand describes the

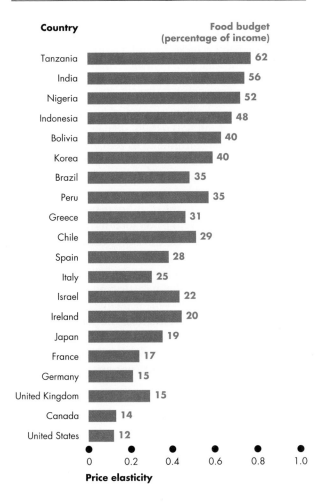

FIGURE 5.5

Price Elasticities in 20 Countries

As income increases and the proportion of income spent on food decreases, the demand for food becomes less elastic.

Source: Henri Theil, Ching-Fan Chung, and James L. Seale, Jr., *Advances in Econometrics, Supplement 1, 1989, International Evidence on Consumption Patterns* (Greenwich, CT: JAI Press Inc., 1989).

during 1973 and 1974. The higher price of oil led to sharp increases in the costs of home heating and gasoline. Initially, consumers maintained consumption at more or less their original levels. Then, gradually, buyers responded to higher oil and gasoline prices by using their existing capital—furnaces and gas guzzlers—in a way that economized on the more expensive fuel. But there were severe limits in the extent to which people felt it worthwhile to cut back on their consumption of the now much more costly fuel. Thermostats could be turned down but that imposed costs—costs of discomfort. Drivers could lower their average speed and economize on gasoline. But that also imposed costs—costs of increases in travel time and forgone trips. So the short-run buyer response in the face of this sharp price increase was a relatively small decrease in the consumption of oil. Demand was inelastic.

But with a longer time to respond to the higher price of oil, many more options became available. And as these additional options were used, the quantity of oil demanded decreased further—demand became more elastic. People bought more energy-efficient capital. As yet more time elapsed, technological advances made even more economies on fuel possible. Furnaces and electric power generators became more fuel efficient. Cars became smaller, on the average, and car and airplane engines became more fuel efficient.

Elasticity, Total Revenue, and Expenditure

This chapter began with a dilemma. How can a producer of pizza (or anything else) increase total revenue: by decreasing production to increase price or by lowering price to sell a larger quantity? We can now answer this question by using the concept of the price elasticity of demand.

The change in a producer's total revenue (and in the total expenditure of the buyers) depends on the extent to which the quantity sold changes as the price changes—the elasticity of demand. If demand is elastic, a 1 percent price cut increases the quantity sold by more than 1 percent and total revenue increases. If demand is unit elastic, a 1 percent price cut increases the quantity sold by 1 percent and total revenue does not change. And if demand is inelastic, a 1 percent price cut increases the quantity sold by less than 1 percent and total revenue decreases.

response of buyers to a change in price *after* sufficient time has elapsed for all the possible substitutions to be made.

An example of a long-lasting price increase was the fourfold rise in the price of oil that occurred

FIGURE 5.6

Elasticity and Total Revenue

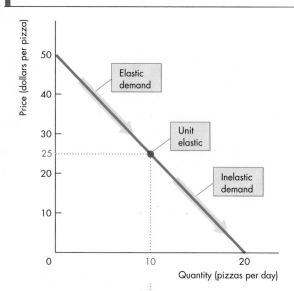

(a) Demand

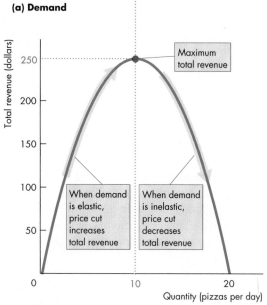

(b) Total revenue

When demand is elastic, in the price range from $50 to $25, a decrease in price (part a) brings an increase in total revenue (part b). When demand is inelastic, in the price range from $25 to zero, a decrease in price (part a) brings a decrease in total revenue (part b). When demand is unit elastic, at a price of $25 (part a), total revenue is at a maximum (part b).

Total Revenue Test We can use this relationship between elasticity and total revenue to estimate elasticity using a total revenue test. The **total revenue test** is a method of estimating the price elasticity of demand by observing the change in total revenue that results from a price change (with all other influences on the quantity sold remaining unchanged). If a price cut increases total revenue, demand is elastic; if a price cut decreases total revenue, demand is inelastic; and if a price cut leaves total revenue unchanged, demand is unit elastic.

Figure 5.6 shows the connection between the elasticity of demand and total revenue. Part (a) shows the same demand curve that you studied in Fig. 5.4. Over the price range from $50 to $25, demand is elastic. Over the price range from $25 to zero, demand is inelastic. At a price of $25, demand is unit elastic.

Figure 5.6(b) shows total revenue. At a price of $50, the quantity sold is zero so total revenue is also zero. At a price of zero, the quantity demanded is 20 pizzas a day, but at a zero price, total revenue is again zero. A price cut in the elastic range brings an increase in total revenue—the percentage increase in the quantity demanded is greater than the percentage decrease in price. A price cut in the inelastic range brings a decrease in total revenue—the percentage increase in the quantity demanded is less than the percentage decrease in price. At the point of unit elasticity, total revenue is a maximum. A small price change either side of $25 keeps total revenue constant.

R E V I E W

- Elasticity of demand measures the responsiveness of the quantity demanded of a good or service to a change in its price.
- The elasticity of demand is the percentage change in the quantity demanded of a good divided by the percentage change in its price.
- The elasticity of demand for a good is determined by the closeness of substitutes for it, the proportion of income spent on it, and the time lapse since its price changed.
- A price cut increases total revenue if demand is elastic, decreases total revenue if demand is inelastic, and does not change total revenue if demand is unit elastic.

So far, we've studied the most widely used elasticity—the *price* elasticity of demand. But there are some other useful elasticity of demand concepts. Let's look at them.

More Elasticities of Demand

BUYING PLANS ARE INFLUENCED BY MANY factors other than price. Among these other factors are incomes and the prices of other goods. We can calculate an elasticity of demand for each of these other factors as well as for price. Let's examine some of these additional elasticities.

Cross Elasticity of Demand

The quantity of any good that consumers plan to buy depends on the prices of its substitutes and complements. We measure these influences by using the concept of the cross elasticity of demand. The **cross elasticity of demand** is a measure of the responsiveness of the demand for a good to a change in the price of a substitute or complement, other things remaining the same. It is calculated by using the formula

$$\text{Cross elasticity of demand} = \frac{\text{Percentage change in quantity demanded}}{\text{Percentage change in the price of a substitute or complement}}.$$

The cross elasticity of demand is positive for a substitute and negative for a complement. Figure 5.7 makes it clear why. When the price of a burger—a substitute for pizza—rises, the demand for pizza increases and the demand curve for pizza shifts rightward from D_0 to D_1. Because an increase in the price of a burger brings an increase in the demand for pizza, the quantity demanded increases and the cross elasticity of demand for pizza with respect to the price of a burger is positive. When the price of a Coke—a complement of pizza—rises, the demand for pizza decreases and the demand curve for pizza shifts leftward from D_0 to D_2. Because an increase in the price of a Coke brings a decrease in the demand for pizza, the quantity demanded decreases and the cross elasticity of demand for pizza with respect to the price of a Coke is negative.

Income Elasticity of Demand

As income grows, how does the demand for a particular good change? The answer depends on the

FIGURE 5.7

Cross Elasticity of Demand

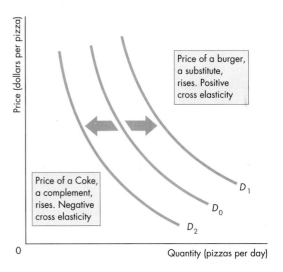

Price of a burger, a substitute, rises. Positive cross elasticity

Price of a Coke, a complement, rises. Negative cross elasticity

When the price of a burger, a substitute for pizza, increases, the demand for pizza increases and the demand curve for pizza shifts rightward from D_0 to D_1. The cross elasticity of the demand for pizza with respect to the price of a burger is *positive*. When the price of a Coke, a complement of pizza, increases, the demand for pizza decreases and the demand curve for pizza shifts leftward from D_0 to D_2. The cross elasticity of the demand for pizza with respect to the price of a Coke is *negative*.

income elasticity of demand for the good. The **income elasticity of demand** is a measure of the responsiveness of demand to a change in income, other things remaining the same. It is calculated by using the formula

$$\text{Income elasticity of demand} = \frac{\text{Percentage change in quantity demanded}}{\text{Percentage change in income}}.$$

Income elasticities of demand can be positive or negative and fall into three interesting ranges:

1. Greater than 1 (*normal* good, income elastic)
2. Between zero and 1 (*normal* good, income inelastic)
3. Less than zero (*inferior* good)

Figure 5.8 illustrates these three cases. Part (a) shows an income elasticity of demand that is greater than 1. As income increases, the quantity demanded increases, but the quantity demanded increases faster than income. Examples of goods in this category are ocean cruises, custom clothing, international travel, jewellery, and works of art.

Part (b) shows an income elasticity of demand that is between zero and 1. In this case, the quantity demanded increases as income increases, but income increases faster than the quantity demanded. Examples of goods in this category are food, clothing, furniture, newspapers, and magazines.

Part (c) shows an income elasticity of demand that eventually becomes negative. In this case, the quantity demanded increases as income increases until the quantity demanded reaches a maximum at income *m*. Beyond that point, as income continues to increase, the quantity demanded declines. The elasticity of demand is positive but less than 1 up to income *m*. Beyond income *m*, the income elasticity of demand is negative. Examples of goods in this category are one-speed bicycles, small motorcycles, potatoes, and rice. Low-income consumers buy most of these goods. At low income levels, the demand for such goods increases as income increases. But as income increases above point *m*, consumers replace these goods with superior alternatives. For example, a small car replaces the motorcycle: fruit, vegetables, and meat begin to appear in a diet that was heavy in rice or potatoes.

Goods whose income elasticities of demand are positive are called *normal goods*. Goods whose income elasticities of demand are negative are called *inferior goods*. They are "inferior" in the sense that they are replaced with "superior" but more expensive goods.

Real-World Income Elasticities of Demand

Table 5.2 shows estimates of some income elasticities of demand. Necessities such as food and clothing are income inelastic, while luxuries such as airline and foreign travel are income elastic.

What is a necessity and a luxury depends on the level of income. For people with a low income, food and clothing can be luxuries. So the *level* of income

---

FIGURE 5.8
Income Elasticity of Demand

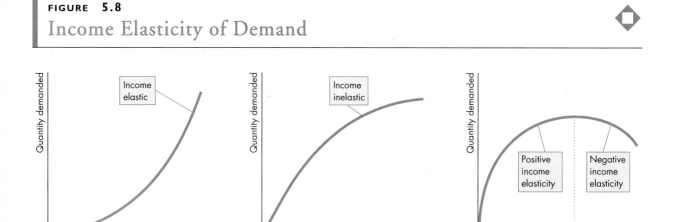

(a) Elasticity greater than 1   **(b) Elasticity between zero and 1**   **(c) Elasticity less than 1 and becomes negative**

Income elasticity of demand has three ranges of values. In part (a), income elasticity of demand is greater than 1. In this case, as income increases, the quantity demanded increases but by a bigger percentage than the increase in income. In part (b), income elasticity of demand is between zero and 1. In this case, as income increases, the quantity demanded increases but by a smaller percentage than the increase in income. In part (c), the income elasticity of demand is positive at low incomes but becomes negative as income increases above level *m*. Maximum consumption of this good occurs at the income *m*.

TABLE 5.2
Some Real-World Income Elasticities of Demand

Good or Service	Elasticity
Elastic Demand	
Airline travel	5.82
Movies	3.41
Foreign travel	3.08
Housing services	2.45
Electricity	1.94
Restaurant meals	1.61
Local buses and trains	1.38
Gasoline and oil	1.36
Haircutting	1.36
Cars	1.07
Unit Elastic Demand	
Dentists' services	1.00
Inelastic Demand	
Shoes and other footwear	0.94
Tobacco	0.86
Shoe repairs	0.72
Alcoholic beverages	0.62
Furniture	0.53
Clothing	0.51
Newspapers and magazines	0.38
Telephone	0.32
Food	0.14

Sources: H. S. Houthakker and Lester D. Taylor, *Consumer Demand in the United States* (Cambridge, Mass.: Harvard University Press, 1970) , and Henri Theil, Ching-Fan Chung, and James L. Seale, Jr., *Advances in Econometrics, Supplement 1, 1989, International Evidence on Consumption Patterns* (Greenwich, CT: JAI Press Inc., 1989).

FIGURE 5.9
Income Elasticities in 20 Countries

As income increases, the income elasticity of demand for food decreases. For low-income consumers, a larger percentage of any increase in income is spent on food than for high-income consumers.

Source: Henri Theil, Ching-Fan Chung, and James L. Seale, Jr., *Advances in Econometrics, Supplement 1, 1989, International Evidence on Consumption Patterns* (Greenwich, CT: JAI Press Inc., 1989).

has a big effect on income elasticities of demand. Figure 5.9 shows this effect on the income elasticity of demand for food in 20 countries. In countries with low incomes, such as Tanzania and India, the income elasticity of demand for food is high whereas in countries with high incomes, such as Canada and the United States, it is low. A 10 percent increase in income leads to an increase in the demand for food of 7.5 percent in India and only 1.5 percent in Canada and the United States. These numbers confirm that necessities have a lower income elasticity of demand than do luxuries.

Elasticity of Supply

IN 1994, THE NORTH AMERICAN AUTO INDUSTRY expanded and increased its demand for steel. There was a *change in demand* for steel. Both car producers and steel producers were very interested in the likely changes in the price of steel that this increase in demand would bring. A change in demand shifts the demand curve and leads to a *movement along the supply curve.* To predict the changes in price and quantity, we need to know how responsive the quantity supplied is to the price of a good. That is, we need to know the elasticity of supply.

The **elasticity of supply** measures the responsiveness of the quantity supplied of a good to a change in its price. It is calculated by using the formula

$$\text{Elasticity of supply} = \frac{\text{Percentage change in quantity supplied}}{\text{Percentage change in price}}.$$

There are two interesting cases of the elasticity of supply. If the quantity supplied is fixed regardless of the price, the supply curve is vertical and the elasticity of supply is zero. Supply is perfectly inelastic. If there is a price at which suppliers are willing to sell any quantity demanded, the supply curve is horizontal and the elasticity of supply is infinite. Supply is perfectly elastic.

The magnitude of the elasticity of supply depends on

■ Factor substitution possibilities
■ Time frame for the supply decision

Factor Substitution Possibilities

Some goods and services are produced by using unique or rare factors of production. These items have a low, and perhaps zero, elasticity of supply. Other goods and services are produced by using factors of production that are more common and that can be allocated to a wide variety of alternative tasks. Such items have a high elasticity of supply.

A Van Gogh painting has been produced by a unique type of labour—Van Gogh's. No other factor of production can be substituted for this labour. There is just one of each painting, so its supply curve is vertical and its elasticity of supply is zero. At the

other extreme, wheat can be grown on land that is almost equally good for growing corn. So it is just as easy to grow wheat or corn, and the opportunity cost of wheat in terms of forgone corn is almost constant. As a result, the supply curve of wheat is almost horizontal and its elasticity of supply is very large. Similarly, when a good is produced in many different countries (for example, sugar and beef), the supply of the good is highly elastic.

The supply of most goods and services lies between the two extremes. The quantity produced can be increased but only by incurring higher cost. If a higher price is offered, the quantity supplied increases. Such goods and services have an elasticity of supply between zero and infinity.

Elasticity of Supply and the Time Frame for Supply Decisions

To study the influence of the length of time elapsed since a price change, we distinguish three time frames of supply:

■ Momentary supply
■ Long-run supply
■ Short-run supply

Momentary Supply When the price of a good rises or falls, the *momentary supply curve* shows the response of the quantity supplied immediately following a price change.

Some goods, such as fruits and vegetables, have a perfectly inelastic momentary supply—a vertical supply curve. The quantities supplied depend on crop planting decisions made earlier. In the case of oranges, for example, planting decisions have to be made many years in advance of the crop being available. A change in the price today does not lead to a change in the quantity supplied today.

Other goods, such as long-distance phone calls, have an elastic momentary supply. When many people simultaneously make a call, there is a big surge in the demand for cable, computer switching, and satellite time, and the quantity bought increases (up to the physical limits of the telephone system) but the price remains constant. Long-distance carriers monitor fluctuations in demand and re-route calls to ensure that the quantity supplied equals the quantity demanded without raising the price.

Long-Run Supply   The *long-run supply curve* shows the response of the quantity supplied to a change in price after all the technologically possible ways of adjusting supply have been exploited. In the case of oranges, the long run is the time it takes new plantings to grow to full maturity—about 15 years. In some cases, the long-run adjustment occurs only after a completely new production plant has been built and workers have been trained to operate it—typically a process that might take several years.

Short-Run Supply   The *short-run supply curve* shows how the quantity supplied responds to a price change when only *some* of the technologically possible adjustments to production have been made. The first adjustment usually made is in the amount of labour employed. To increase output in the short run, firms work their labour force overtime and perhaps hire additional workers. To decrease their output in the short run, firms lay off workers or reduce their hours of work. With the passage of time, firms can make additional adjustments, perhaps training additional workers or buying additional tools and other equipment. The short-run response to a price change, unlike the momentary and long-run responses, is not a unique response but a sequence of adjustments.

Three Supply Curves   Figure 5.10 shows three supply curves that correspond to the three time frames. They are the supply curves in the world market for oranges on a given day in which the price is $2 a kilogram and the quantity of oranges grown is 3 million kilograms. Each supply curve passes through that point. Momentary supply is perfectly inelastic, as shown by the blue curve *MS*. As time passes, the quantity supplied becomes more responsive to price, as shown by the purple short-run supply curve, *SS*. As yet more time passes, the supply curve becomes the red long-run curve *LS*, the most elastic of the three supplies.

The momentary supply curve is vertical because, on a given day, no matter what the price of oranges, producers cannot change their output. They have picked, packed, and shipped their crop to market and the quantity available for that day is fixed. The short-run supply curve slopes upward because producers can take actions quite quickly to change the quantity supplied in response to a price change. They can, for example, stop picking and leave oranges to rot on the tree if the price falls by a large amount. Or they can use more fertilizers and improved irrigation to

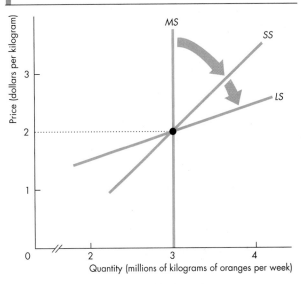

FIGURE 5.10

Supply: Momentary, Short-Run, and Long-Run

The momentary supply curve, *MS*, shows how quantity supplied responds to a price change the moment that it occurs. The blue momentary supply curve shown here is perfectly inelastic. The purple short-run supply curve, *SS*, shows how the quantity supplied responds to a price change after some adjustments to production have been made. The red long-run supply curve, *LS*, shows how the quantity supplied responds to a price change when all the technologically possible adjustments to the production process have been made.

increase the yields of their existing trees if the price rises. In the long run, they can plant more trees and increase the quantity supplied even more in response to a given price rise.

◆ You have now learned how to calculate and use the concept of elasticity. *Reading Between the Lines* on pp. 112–113 shows you a practical application of elasticity in the market for patented drugs. And all the different kinds of elasticities you've just studied are defined and summarized in Table 5.3 on p. 114.

In the next chapter, we are going to use what you have learned to study some real-world markets—markets in action.

Policy
WATCH

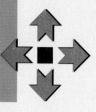

Elasticity in Action

Essence of
THE STORY

■ Prices of patented drugs fell 1.75 percent in 1995.

■ The decrease compares with the overall increase of 2.14 percent in the Consumer Price Index (CPI), which measures a basket of goods and services regularly purchased by consumers.

■ When prices declined in 1995, the quantities sold increased by 14.8 percent.

■ In 1994, prices of patented drugs dropped 0.42 percent, when the CPI rose 0.19 percent and expenditures on drugs increased by 3.8 percent. (Expenditures cover unregulated drug prices as well as dispensing fees and wholesale costs.)

GLOBE AND MAIL, June 20, 1996

Patented drug prices drop for second consecutive year

By Marian Stinson

TORONTO—Prices of patented drugs fell in 1995 for the second successive year, the first two-year decline since the federal government began monitoring prices and extending the patent protection of drug companies in 1987.

Prices fell 1.75 per cent last year, according to the annual report of the Patented Medicine Prices Review Board, the federal watchdog that regulates prices. The decrease compares with the overall increase of 2.14 per cent in the consumer price index, which measures a basket of goods and services regularly purchased by consumers.

In 1994, prices of patented drugs dropped 0.42 per cent, when the CPI rose 0.19 per cent.

Since the board was established in 1987, prices have increased by an annual average of 1.6 per cent. Between 1983 and 1987, drug prices climbed by an annual average of 7.5 per cent, which is twice the rate of increase in the CPI.

The board can force manufacturers of patented drugs to keep price increases within the rate of inflation. ...

In 1995, 69 companies sold patented medicines in Canada, down from 73 a year earlier because of mergers within the industry last year.

The agency said it saved consumers $32.7 million last year through enforcement of drug price guidelines.

Although prices fell in 1994, expenditures on drugs rose 3.8 per cent. The agency regulates manufacturers' prices of patented medicines, which accounts for 44 per cent of all drug sales. As well, expenditures cover dispensing fees and wholesale costs, which are not covered by the federal price monitor.

Although prices declined last year, the quantities sold climbed 14.8 per cent, the largest increase since 1988.

Economic

A N A L Y S I S

■ The following table summarizes the information in the news article in the form of index numbers for the money price, quantity, and expenditure:

Year	Money Price	Quantity	Expenditure	CPI
1993	10.00	10.00	100.0	100.00
1994	9.96	10.42	103.8	100.19
1995	9.79	11.97	117.1	102.33

■ Money prices fell by 0.42 percent in 1994 and by 1.75 percent in 1995.

■ Expenditure increased by 3.8 percent in 1994 and the quantity increased by 14.8 percent in 1995. The other numbers for quantity and expenditure are found from the fact that price multiplied by quantity equals expenditure.

■ The Consumer Price Index (CPI) rose 0.19 percent in 1994 and 2.14 percent in 1995.

■ To calculate the elasticity of demand, we use the formula:

Price elasticity of demand =

$$\frac{\text{Percentage change in quantity demand}}{\text{Percentage change in price}}$$

■ We can use these numbers to estimate the elasticity of demand for patented drugs.

■ *Price* in demand analysis means *relative price* (see p. 68).

■ To calculate the relative price of patented drugs, P, divide the money price by the CPI. The resulting numbers for P along with the values for quantity (Q) and expenditure (PQ) are as follows:

Year	P	Q	PQ
1993	10.00	10.00	100.0
1994	9.94	10.42	103.6
1995	9.56	11.97	114.4

■ The figure illustrates and the table below summarizes the elasticity calculations.

■ In 1993–1994, the estimated elasticity is 6.83 and in 1994–1995, it is 3.55.

■ Probably both of these estimates overstate the elasticity. But these are the estimates implied by the numbers in the news article.

■ As the figure shows, with an elasticity greater than one, demand is elastic and as the price falls, the quantity demanded increases and total expenditure increases.

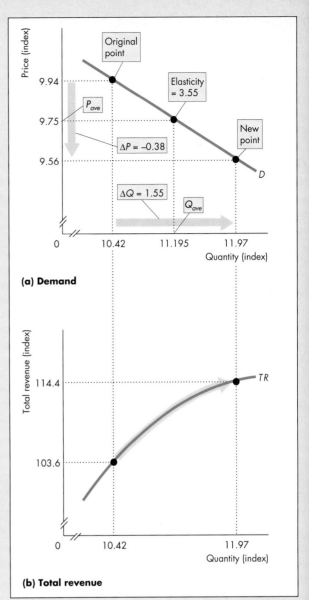

(a) Demand

(b) Total revenue

Year	ΔP	P_{ave}	ΔQ	Q_{ave}	Elasticity
1993–1994	−0.06	9.97	0.42	10.21	−6.83
1994–1995	−0.38	9.75	1.55	11.195	−3.55

You're

THE VOTER

■ What are the pros and cons of a government agency controlling the prices of patented drugs?

■ If this matter became an election issue, on which side would you vote?

TABLE 5.3

A Compact Glossary of Elasticities

PRICE ELASTICITIES OF DEMAND

A relationship is described as	When its magnitude is	Which means that
Perfectly elastic or infinitely elastic	Infinity	The smallest possible increase in price causes an infinitely large decrease in the quantity demanded*
Elastic	Less than infinity but greater than 1	The percentage decrease in the quantity demanded exceeds the percentage increase in price
Unit elastic	1	The percentage decrease in the quantity demanded equals the percentage increase in price
Inelastic	Greater than zero but less than 1	The percentage decrease in the quantity demanded is less than the percentage increase in price
Perfectly inelastic or completely inelastic	Zero	The quantity demanded is the same at all prices

CROSS ELASTICITIES OF DEMAND

A relationship is described as	When its value is	Which means that
Perfect substitutes	Infinity	The smallest possible increase in the price of one good causes an infinitely large increase in the quantity demanded of the other good
Substitutes	Positive, less than infinity	If the price of one good increases, the quantity demanded of the other good also increases
Independent	Zero	The quantity demanded of one good remains constant regardless of the price of the other good
Complements	Less than zero (negative)	The quantity demanded of one good decreases when the price of the other good increases

INCOME ELASTICITIES OF DEMAND

A relationship is described as	When its value is	Which means that
Income elastic (normal good)	Greater than 1	The percentage increase in the quantity demanded is greater than the percentage increase in income
Income inelastic (normal good)	Less than 1 but greater than zero	The percentage increase in the quantity demanded is less than the percentage increase in income
Negative income elastic (inferior good)	Less than zero	When income increases, quantity demanded decreases

ELASTICITIES OF SUPPLY

A relationship is described as	When its value is	Which means that
Perfectly elastic	Infinity	The smallest possible increase in price causes an infinitely large increase in the quantity supplied
Elastic	Less than infinity but greater than 1	The percentage increase in the quantity supplied exceeds the percentage increase in the price
Inelastic	Greater than zero but less than 1	The percentage increase in the quantity supplied is less than the percentage increase in the price
Perfectly inelastic	Zero	The quantity supplied is the same at all prices

*In each description, the directions of change may be reversed. For example, in this case: The smallest possible *decrease* in price causes an infinitely large *increase* in the quantity demanded.

S U M M A R Y

Key Points

Elasticity of Demand   The elasticity of demand is calculated as the percentage change in the quantity demanded divided by the percentage change in price. The larger the magnitude of the elasticity of demand, the greater is the responsiveness of the quantity demanded to a given change in price. When the percentage change in the quantity demanded is smaller than the percentage change in price, demand is inelastic. When the percentage change in the quantity demanded equals the percentage change in price, demand is unit elastic. And when the percentage change in the quantity demanded is larger than the percentage change in price, demand is elastic.

Elasticity depends on how easily one good serves as a substitute for another, the proportion of income spent on the good, and the length of time that has elapsed since the price change.

If demand is elastic, a decrease in price leads to an increase in total revenue. If demand is unit elastic, a decrease in price leaves total revenue unchanged. And if demand is inelastic, a decrease in price leads to a decrease in total revenue. (pp. 99–106)

More Elasticities of Demand   The cross elasticity of demand is calculated as the percentage change in the quantity demanded of one good divided by the percentage change in the price of another good. The cross elasticity of demand with respect to the price of a substitute is positive and with respect to the price of a complement is negative.

The income elasticity of demand is calculated as the percentage change in the quantity demanded divided by the percentage change in income. The larger the income elasticity of demand, the greater is the responsiveness of demand to a given change in income. When income elasticity is between zero and 1, demand is income inelastic and as income increases the percentage of income spent on the good decreases. When income elasticity is greater than 1, demand is income elastic and as income increases the percentage of income spent on the good also increases. When income elasticity is less than zero, demand decreases as income increases (and the good is an inferior good). (pp. 107–109)

Elasticity of Supply   The elasticity of supply measures the responsiveness of the quantity supplied of a good to a change in its price. Elasticity of supply is calculated as the percentage change in the quantity supplied of a good divided by the percentage change in its price. Supply elasticities are usually positive and range between zero (vertical supply curve) and infinity (horizontal supply curve).

Supply decisions have three time frames: momentary, long run, and short run. Momentary supply refers to the response of suppliers to a price change at the instant that the price changes. Long-run supply refers to the response of suppliers to a price change when all the technologically feasible adjustments in production have been made. Short-run supply refers to the response of suppliers to a price change after some adjustments in production have been made. (pp. 110–111)

Key Figures and Table

Key Terms

R E V I E W   Q U E S T I O N S

1. Define the price elasticity of demand.
2. Why is elasticity a more useful measure of responsiveness than slope?
3. Draw a graph and describe the shape of a demand curve that represents a good that has an elasticity of demand equal to
   a. Infinity.
   b. Zero.
   c. Unity.
4. Which item in each of the following pairs has the larger elasticity of demand:
   a. *People* magazine or magazines?
   b. Vacations or vacations in Florida?
   c. Broccoli or vegetables?
5. What three factors determine the size of the elasticity of demand?
6. What do we mean by short-run demand and long-run demand?
7. Explain why the short-run demand curve is usually less elastic than the long-run demand curve.
8. What is the connection between elasticity and total revenue? If the elasticity of demand for dental work is 1, by how much does a 10 percent increase in the price of dental work change total revenue?
9. Define the cross elasticity of demand. Is the cross elasticity of demand positive or negative?
10. Define the income elasticity of demand.

11. Give an example of a good whose income elasticity of demand is
    a. Greater than 1.
    b. Positive but less than 1.
    c. Less than zero.
12. State the sign (positive or negative) of the following elasticities:
    a. The cross elasticity of demand for ice cream with respect to the price of frozen yogurt.
    b. The cross elasticity of demand for corn ready to be popped with respect to the price of popcorn machines.
    c. The income elasticity of demand for Caribbean cruises.
    d. The income elasticity of demand for toothpaste.
    e. The elasticity of supply of Irish salmon.
13. Define the elasticity of supply. Is the elasticity of supply positive or negative?
14. Give an example of a good whose elasticity of supply is
    a. Zero.
    b. Greater than zero but less than infinity.
    c. Infinity.
15. What do we mean by momentary, short-run, and long-run supply?
16. Why is momentary supply perfectly inelastic for many goods?
17. Why is long-run supply more elastic than short-run supply?

C R I T I C A L   T H I N K I N G

1. Study *Reading Between the Lines* on pp. 112–113 and then answer the following questions.
   a. What happened to the prices, quantities, and expenditures on patented drugs during 1994 and 1995?
   b. How can we use the information in the news article to estimate the elasticity of demand for patented drugs?
   c. Why might our estimate of the elasticity of demand be wrong? Is it more likely that we have underestimated or overestimated its value?
   d. What are the implications of our estimated elasticity of demand for future expenditures on drugs?
2. Under what conditions would grape growers receive more revenue from a bumper harvest?
3. What is the elasticity of demand for tobacco and alcohol if a higher tax brings in more tax revenue for the government?
4. How would you use the concept of elasticity to determine whether a good is a normal good or an inferior good? What information would you need to make this determination?

P R O B L E M S

1. The figure shows the demand for videotape rentals.

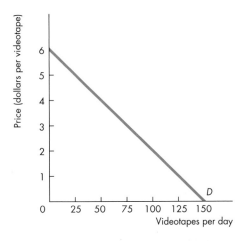

a. At what prices is the elasticity of demand equal to 1, greater than 1, and less than 1?
b. At what price is total revenue maximized?
c. Calculate the elasticity of demand for a rise in rental price from $4 to $5.

2. The following schedule gives the world demand for oil:

Price (dollars per barrel)	Quantity demanded (millions of barrels per day)
10	60
20	50
30	40
40	30
50	20

a. If the price rises from $20 to $30 a barrel, will the total revenue from oil sales increase or decrease?
b. What will happen to total revenue if the price rises to $40 a barrel?
c. What is the price that will achieve the highest total revenue?
d. What quantity of oil will be sold at the price that answers problem 2(c)?
e. Calculate the price elasticity of demand for price changes of $10 a barrel at average prices of $15, $25, $35, and $45 a barrel.
f. What is the elasticity of demand at the price that maximizes total revenue?

3. If a 10 percent increase in the price of chicken decreases the quantity of chicken demanded by 5 percent and increases the quantity of pork by 8 percent, calculate the cross elasticity of demand between chicken and pork.

4. Last year, Lee's income increased from $9,000 to $11,000. Lee increased his consumption of peanut butter from 2 to 4 jars a month and decreased his consumption of macaroni and cheese from 12 packets to 8 packets a month. Calculate the income elasticity of demand for
a. Peanut butter.
b. Macaroni and cheese.

5. The following table gives some data on the demand for long-distance telephone calls:

Price (cents per minute)	Quantity demanded (millions of minutes per day)	
	Short run	Long run
10	700	1,000
20	500	500
30	300	0

At a price of 20¢ a minute, is the demand for calls more elastic in the short run or the long run?

6. In problem 5, does total expenditure on calls increase or decrease as the price of a call decreases from 20¢ a minute to 10¢ a minute?

7. The following table gives some data on the supply of long-distance phone calls:

Price (cents per minute)	Quantity supplied (millions of minutes per day)	
	Short run	Long run
10	300	0
20	500	500
30	700	1,000

At a price of 20¢ a minute, calculate the elasticity of
a. Short-run supply.
b. Long-run supply.

8. In problem 7, which supply is more elastic and why? Compare the elasticities when the price is 15¢ a minute and when it is 25¢ a minute.

Chapter 6

Markets in Action

After studying
this chapter,
you will be
able to:

- Explain the short-run and long-run effects
  of a change in supply on price and the
  quantity bought and sold

- Explain the short-run and long-run effects
  of a change in demand on price and the
  quantity bought and sold

- Explain the effects of price controls

- Explain how sales taxes affect prices

- Explain how making a product illegal
  affects its price and the quantity consumed

- Explain how inventories and speculation
  limit fluctuations in farm prices

- Explain how farm marketing boards
  influence prices and quantities produced

In 1906, San Francisco suffered a devastating earthquake that destroyed more than half the city's homes, but killed very few people. How did the San Francisco housing market cope with this enormous shock? What happened to rents and to the quantity of housing services available? Did rents have to be controlled to keep housing affordable? ◆ Almost every day, new machines are invented that save labour and increase productivity. How do labour markets cope with the consequences of technological change? Does a decreasing demand for labour drive wages lower and lower? Is it necessary to have minimum wage laws to prevent wages from falling? ◆ Almost everything we buy is taxed. How do taxes affect the prices and quantities of the things we buy? Do prices increase by the full amount of the tax so that we, the buyers, pay all of the tax? Or does the seller bear part of the tax? ◆ Trading in items such as drugs, automatic firearms, and enriched uranium is prohibited. How does the prohibition of trade affect the actual amounts of prohibited goods consumed? And how does it affect the prices paid by those who trade illegally? ◆ In 1988, grain yields were extremely low as crops were devastated by drought. But in 1991, yields were high. How do farm prices and revenues react to such output fluctuations? How do the actions of speculators and official agencies influence farm revenues?

Turbulent Times

◆ In this chapter, we use the theory of demand and supply (of Chapter 4) and the concept of elasticity (of Chapter 5) to answer questions such as those just posed. We're going to begin by studying how a market responds to a severe supply shock.

Housing Markets and Rent Ceilings

TO SEE HOW AN UNREGULATED MARKET COPES with a supply shock, let's transport ourselves to San Francisco in April 1906, as the city is suffering from a massive earthquake and fire. You can sense the enormity of San Francisco's problems by reading some headlines from the *New York Times* on the first days of the crisis. On April 19, 1906:

Over 500 Dead, $200,000,000 Lost in San Francisco Earthquake
Nearly Half the City Is in Ruins and 50,000 Are Homeless

On April 20, 1906:

Army of Homeless Fleeing from Devastated City
200,000 Without Shelter and Facing Famine

And again on April 21, 1906:

San Francisco's New Peril; Gale Drives Fire Ferryward
Fighting Famine and Disease Among the 200,000 Refugees
San Francisco Multitudes Camped Out Shelterless and in Want

The commander of federal troops in charge of the emergency described the magnitude of the problem:

> Not a hotel of note or importance was left standing. The great apartment houses had vanished ... two hundred-and-twenty-five thousand people were ... homeless.[1]

Almost overnight, more than half the people in a city of 400,000 had lost their homes. Temporary shelters and camps alleviated some of the problem, but it was also necessary to utilize the apartment buildings and houses left standing. As a consequence, they had to accommodate 40 percent more people than they had prior to the earthquake.

The *San Francisco Chronicle* was not published for more than a month after the earthquake. When the newspaper reappeared on May 24, 1906, the city's housing shortage—what would seem like a major news item that would still be of grave importance—was not mentioned. Milton Friedman and George Stigler describe the situation:

> *There is not a single mention of a housing shortage!* The classified advertisements listed sixty-four offers of flats and houses for rent, and nineteen of houses for sale, against five advertisements of flats or houses wanted. Then and thereafter a considerable number of all types of accommodation except hotel rooms were offered for rent.[2]

How did San Francisco cope with such a devastating reduction in the supply of housing?

The Market Response to a Decrease in Supply

Figure 6.1 shows the market for housing in San Francisco. The demand curve for housing is *D*. There are two supply curves: the short-run supply curve, which is labelled *SS,* and the long-run supply curve, which is labelled *LS.* The short-run supply curve shows how the quantity of housing supplied varies as the price (rent) varies, while the number of houses and apartment buildings remains constant. This supply response arises from a variation in the intensity with which existing buildings are used. The quantity of housing supplied increases if families decide to rent out rooms that they previously used themselves, and the quantity supplied decreases if families decide to use rooms they previously rented out to others.

The long-run supply curve shows how the quantity supplied varies after enough time has elapsed for new apartment buildings and houses to be erected or existing buildings to be destroyed. The long-run supply curve is shown as being perfectly elastic. We do not actually know that the long-run supply curve is perfectly elastic, but it is a reasonable assumption. It implies that the cost of building an apartment is pretty much the same regardless of whether there are 50,000 or 150,000 apartments in existence.

The equilibrium price (rent) and quantity are determined at the point of intersection of the *short-run* supply curve and the demand curve. Before the earthquake, the equilibrium rent is $16 a month and the quantity is 100,000 units of housing.[3] In addition (for

---

[1] Reported in Milton Friedman and George J. Stigler, "Roofs or Ceilings? The Current Housing Problem," in *Popular Essays on Current Problems*, vol. 1, no. 2 (New York: Foundation for Economic Education, 1946), 3–159.

[2] *Ibid.*, 3.

[3] These numbers are close to the actual monthly rent and quantity of housing in San Francisco in 1906. (Average monthly incomes were about $46 in 1906.)

FIGURE 6.1

The San Francisco Housing Market in 1906

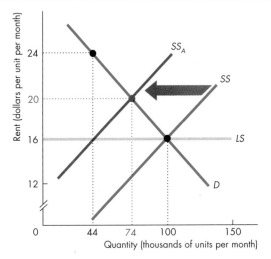

(a) After earthquake

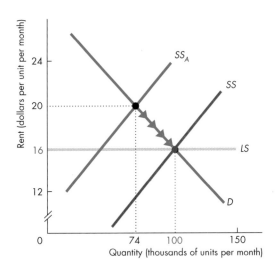

(b) Long-run adjustment

Part (a) shows that before the earthquake 100,000 housing units were rented each month at $16 a month. After the earthquake, the short-run supply curve shifts from SS to SS_A. The rent rises to $20 a month, and the quantity of housing falls to 74,000 units.

With rents at $20 a month, there is profit in building new apartments and houses. As the building program proceeds, the short-run supply curve shifts rightward (part b). Rents gradually fall to $16 a month, and the quantity of housing increases gradually to 100,000 units—as shown by the arrowed line.

simplicity), the housing market is assumed to be on its long-run supply curve, *LS*. Let's now look at the situation immediately after the earthquake.

Figure 6.1(a) reflects the new situation. The destruction of buildings decreases the supply of housing and shifts the short-run supply curve *SS* leftward to *SS_A*. If people use the remaining housing units with the same intensity as before the earthquake and if the rent remains at $16 a month, only 44,000 units of housing are available. But rents do not remain at $16 a month. With only 44,000 units of housing available, the maximum rent that someone is willing to pay for the last available apartment is $24 a month. So to get an apartment, a higher rent than $16 is offered. As people try to outbid each other for the available apartments, rents rise. In Fig. 6.1(a), they rise to $20 a month. And as the rent rises, people economize on their use of space and make spare rooms, attics, and basements available to others. The quantity of housing supplied increases to 74,000 units.

The response we've just seen takes place in the short run. What happens in the long run?

Long-Run Adjustments

With sufficient time for new apartment buildings and houses to be constructed, supply will increase. The long-run supply curve tells us that in the long-run, housing will be supplied at a rent of $16 a month. Because the current rent of $20 a month is higher than the long-run supply price of housing, there will be a rush to build and supply new apartments and houses. As time passes, more apartments and houses are built, and the short-run supply curve gradually shifts rightward.

Figure 6.1(b) illustrates the long-run adjustment. As more housing is built, the short-run supply curve shifts rightward and intersects the demand curve at lower rents and higher quantities. The market equilibrium follows the arrows down the demand curve. The process ends when there is no further profit in building new housing units. Such a situation occurs at the original rent of $16 a month and the original quantity of 100,000 units of housing.

The analysis of the short-run and long-run response of a housing market that we've just studied applies to a wide range of other markets. And it applies regardless of whether the initial shock is to supply (as it is here) or demand.

A Regulated Housing Market

We've just seen how a housing market responds to a decrease in supply. And we've seen that a key part of the adjustment process is a rise in rents. Suppose the government passes a law to stop rents from rising. Such a law is called a price ceiling. A **price ceiling** is a regulation making it illegal to charge a price higher than a specified level. When a price ceiling is applied to rents in housing markets it is called a **rent ceiling**. How does a rent ceiling affect the way the housing market works?

The effect of a price (rent) ceiling depends on whether it is imposed at a level that is above or below the equilibrium price (rent). A price ceiling set above the equilibrium price has no effect. The reason is that the price ceiling does not constrain the market forces. The force of the law and the market forces are not in conflict. But a price ceiling below the equilibrium price has powerful effects on a market. The reason is that it attempts to prevent the price from regulating the quantities demanded and supplied. The force of the law and the market forces are in conflict, and one (or both) of these forces must yield to some degree. Let's study the effects of a price ceiling set below the equilibrium price by returning to San Francisco.

What would have happened in San Francisco if a rent ceiling of $16 a month—the rent before the earthquake—had been imposed? This question and some answers are illustrated in Fig. 6.2. If a rent ceiling holds the rent at $16 a month, then the quantity of housing supplied is 44,000 units and the quantity demanded is 100,000 units. So there is a shortage of 56,000 units of housing.

When the quantity demanded exceeds the quantity supplied, what determines the quantity actually bought and sold? The answer is the smaller quantity—the quantity supplied. Suppliers cannot be forced to offer housing for rent, and at a monthly rent of $16, they are willing to offer only 44,000 units.

So the immediate effect of a rent ceiling of $16 a month is that only 44,000 units of housing are available and a demand for a further 56,000 units is unsatisfied. But the story does not end here. Somehow, the 44,000 units of available housing must be allocated among the people demanding 100,000 units. How is this allocation achieved?

In an unregulated market, the shortage would drive the rent up, as shown in Fig. 6.1(a), and the price mechanism would regulate the quantities demanded and supplied and allocate the scarce housing resources. As long as one person was willing to

FIGURE 6.2

A Rent Ceiling

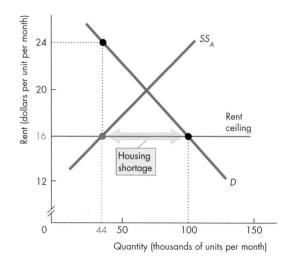

If there had been a rent ceiling of $16 a month, then the quantity of housing supplied after the earthquake would have been stuck at 44,000 units. People would willingly have paid $24 a month for the 44,000th unit. Because the last unit of housing available is worth more than the regulated rent, frustrated buyers will spend time searching for housing and frustrated buyers and sellers will make deals in a black market.

pay a higher price than another person's minimum supply price, the price would rise and the quantity of housing available would increase. When a rent ceiling tries to block this market mechanism by making rent increases illegal, two developments occur. They are

- Search activity
- Black markets

Search Activity

When the quantity demanded exceeds the quantity supplied, many suppliers have nothing to sell and many demanders have nothing to buy. So unsatisfied demanders devote time and other resources searching for a supplier. The time spent looking for someone with whom to do business is called **search activity**. Even in markets where prices adjust freely to keep the quantities demanded and supplied equal, search activity takes place. But when price is regulated, search activity increases.

Search activity is costly. It uses time and other resources such as telephones, cars, and gasoline that could be used in other productive ways. Frustrated would-be renters scan the newspapers, not for housing ads but for death notices! Any information about newly available housing is useful. And they race to be first on the scene when news of a possible supplier breaks. The *total cost* of housing is equal to the rent—the regulated price—plus the cost of the time and other resources spent searching—an unregulated price. So rent ceilings might control the rent portion of the cost of housing, but they do not control the total cost. And the total cost may well be *higher* than the unregulated market price.

Black Markets

A **black market** is an illegal trading arrangement in which buyers and sellers do business at a price higher than the legally imposed price ceiling. There are many examples of markets, in addition to housing markets, that are regulated in some way and in which economic forces result in black market trading. For example, ticket scalping is banned, but this method of allocating scarce tickets for big games and rock concerts is common.

In regulated housing markets, a black market usually takes the form of a buyer and a seller colluding to avoid the rent ceiling. They have a written agreement that uses the regulated rent but have an unwritten side-deal that changes the actual rent. The level of the black market rent depends mainly on how tightly the government polices its rent ceiling regulations, the chances of being caught violating them, and the scale of the penalties imposed for violations.

At one extreme, the chance of being caught violating a rent ceiling is small. In this case, the black market will function similarly to an unregulated market, and the black market rent and quantity traded will be close to the unregulated equilibrium. At the other extreme, where policing is highly effective and where large penalties are imposed on violators, the rent ceiling will restrict the quantity traded. In the San Francisco example, with strict enforcement of the rent ceiling, the quantity of housing available is restricted to 44,000 units. A small number of people will offer housing for sale at $24 a month—the highest price that a buyer is willing to pay—and the government will detect and punish some of these black market traders.

Rent Ceilings in Practice

New York, Paris, and Toronto are just three of the many great cities that have rent ceilings, and rent ceilings have had their most devastating effects in New York. There have been times when landlords in the Harlem and Bronx districts of New York have abandoned unprofitable housing units at a rate of several thousand a month, leaving entire city blocks occupied only by rats and drug dealers. In Paris, rent-controlled apartments are handed down from one generation to the next. Would-be renters scan the obituary columns for clues about possible vacancies.

Frustrated renters and landlords constantly seek ways of increasing rents and evading the controls. One common way is for a new tenant to pay the landlord a high price for worthless fittings—$2,000 for threadbare drapes—or "key money" to change the locks.

There is a good deal of evidence that rent ceilings do not help the poorest people but instead benefit the middle- and higher-income groups. In Toronto, it is not uncommon for a low-income, single mother to pay $800 a month for a basement apartment, while a wealthy lawyer pays $600 a month for a spacious and comfortable rent-controlled apartment. If the goal of rent ceilings is to help the poor, they do not achieve that goal. The effects of rent ceilings have led Assar Lindbeck, chairman of the economic science Nobel Prize committee to claim that rent ceilings are the most effective means yet invented for destroying cities, even more effective than the hydrogen bomb.

REVIEW

- A decrease in the supply of housing increases equilibrium rents.
- In the short run, higher rents result in a decrease in the quantity of housing demanded and an increase in the quantity supplied as existing houses and apartments are used more intensively.
- In the long run, higher rents stimulate building. The supply of housing increases and rents fall.
- Rent ceilings limit the ability of the housing market to respond to change and can result in a permanent housing shortage.

We next look at the effects of a price floor—a minimum price. To do so, we'll study the labour market.

The Labour Market and Minimum Wages

FOR MOST OF US, THE LABOUR MARKET IS THE most important market in which we participate. It is the interaction of demand and supply in the labour market that influences the jobs we get and the wages we earn. Firms decide how much labour to demand and households decide how much labour to supply. The wage rate balances the quantities demanded and the quantities supplied and determines the level of employment. But the labour market is constantly being bombarded by shocks, and wages and employment prospects are constantly changing. The most pervasive source of these shocks is the advance of technology.

Labour-saving technology is constantly being invented. As a result, the demand for certain types of labour, usually the least skilled types, is constantly decreasing. How does the labour market cope with this continuous decrease in the demand for low-skilled labour? Doesn't it mean that the wages of the low-skilled are constantly falling? Let's find out.

Figure 6.3 shows the market for low-skilled labour. Labour is demanded by firms and, other things remaining the same, the lower the wage rate, the greater is the quantity of labour demanded. The demand curve for labour, *D* in part (a), shows this relationship between the wage rate and the quantity of labour demanded. Labour is supplied by households and, other things remaining the same, the higher the wage rate, the greater is the quantity of labour supplied. But the longer the period of adjustment, the greater is the elasticity of supply of labour. Thus there are two supply curves, a short-run supply curve *SS* and a long-run supply curve *LS*.

The short-run supply curve shows how the hours of labour supplied by a given number of workers change as the wage rate changes. To get workers to work longer hours, firms must offer higher wages, so the short-run supply curve slopes upward.

The long-run supply curve shows the relationship between the quantity of labour supplied and the wage rate after enough time has passed for people to acquire new skills and find new types of jobs. The number of people in the low-skilled labour market depends on the wage rate in this market compared with other opportunities. If the wage rate is high enough, people will enter this market. If the wage rate is too low, people will leave it. Some will seek training to enter the higher-skilled labour markets, and others will leave the labour force and work at home or retire.

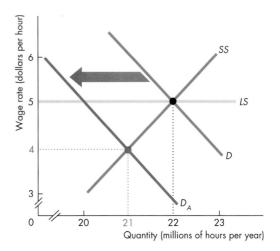

(a) After invention

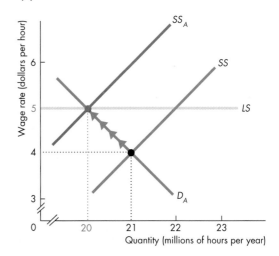

(b) Long-run adjustment

Part (a) shows the immediate effect of a labour-saving invention on the market for low-skilled labour. Initially, the wage rate is $5 an hour and 22 million hours of labour a year are employed. A labour-saving invention shifts the demand curve from *D* to D_A. The wage rate falls to $4 an hour, and employment decreases to 21 million hours a year. With the lower wage, some workers leave this market, and the short-run supply curve starts to shift gradually to SS_A (part b). The wage rate gradually increases, and the employment level decreases. In the long run, the wage rate returns to $5 an hour and employment decreases to 20 million hours a year.

Because people can freely enter and leave the low-skilled labour market, the long-run supply curve is highly elastic. In Fig. 6.3, for simplicity, the long-run supply curve is assumed to be perfectly elastic (horizontal). The low-skilled labour market is in equilibrium at a wage rate of $5 an hour and 22 million hours of labour are employed.

What happens if a labour-saving invention decreases the demand for low-skilled labour? Figure 6.3(a) shows the short-run effects of such a change. The demand curve before the new technology is introduced is *D*. After the introduction of the new technology, the demand curve shifts leftward to D_A. The wage rate falls to $4 an hour, and the quantity of labour employed decreases to 21 million hours. This short-run effect on wages and employment is not the end of the story.

People who are now earning only $4 an hour look around for other opportunities. They see many other jobs (in markets for other types of skills) that pay wages above $4 an hour. One by one, workers decide to go back to school or they take jobs that pay less but offer on-the-job training. As a result, the short-run supply curve begins to shift leftward.

Figure 6.3(b) shows the long-run adjustment. As the short-run supply curve shifts leftward, it intersects the demand curve D_A at higher wage rates and lower levels of employment. In the long run, the short-run supply curve must shift all the way to SS_A. At this point, the wage has returned to $5 an hour, and employment has decreased to 20 million hours a year.

Sometimes, the adjustment process that we've just described takes place quickly. At other times, it is a long drawn-out affair. If the adjustment process is long and drawn out, wages remain low for a long period. In such a situation, the government is tempted to intervene in the labour market by legislating a minimum wage to protect the lowest-paid workers.

The Minimum Wage

A **minimum wage law** is a regulation that makes hiring labour below a specified wage illegal. If the minimum wage is set *below* the equilibrium wage, it has no effect. The law and the market forces are not in conflict. But if a minimum wage is set *above* the equilibrium wage, the minimum wage is in conflict with the market forces and does have some effects on the labour market. Let's study these effects by returning to the market for low-skilled labour.

Suppose that when the wage falls to $4 an hour (in Fig. 6.3a) the government imposes a minimum wage of $5 an hour. What are the effects of this law? Figure 6.4 shows the minimum wage as the horizontal red line labelled "Minimum wage." At the minimum wage, only 20 million hours of labour are demanded (point *a*) but 22 million hours of labour are supplied (point *b*), so 2 million hours of available labour go unemployed.

What are the workers doing with their unemployed hours? They are searching for work. With only 20 million hours of labour employed, there are many people willing to supply their labour for wage rates much lower than the minimum wage. In fact, the 20 millionth hour of labour will be supplied for as little as $3. How do we know that there are people willing to work for as little as $3 an hour?

FIGURE   6.4

Minimum Wage and Unemployment

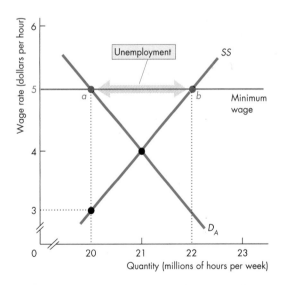

The demand curve for labour is D_A, and the supply curve is SS. In an unregulated market, the wage rate is $4 an hour, and 21 million hours of labour a year are employed. If a minimum wage of $5 an hour is imposed, only 20 million hours are hired but 22 million hours are available. This results in unemployment—*ab*—of 2 million hours a year. With only 20 million hours being demanded, some workers will willingly supply that 20 millionth hour for $3. These frustrated unemployed workers will spend time and other resources looking for a job.

Look again at Fig. 6.4. As you can see, when only 20 million hours of work are available, the lowest wage at which workers are willing to supply that 20 millionth hour—read off from the supply curve—is $3 an hour. Someone who manages to find a job will earn $5 an hour—$2 an hour more than the lowest wage rate at which someone is willing to work. Therefore it pays the unemployed to spend time and effort looking for work. Even though only 20 million hours of labour actually get employed, each person spends time and effort searching for one of the scarce jobs.

The Minimum Wage in Reality

Regulations and laws governing labour markets are matters under the jurisdiction of the provinces, and each province has its own minimum wage regulation. Economists do not agree on the effects of the minimum wage or on how much unemployment it causes. But they do agree that minimum wages bite hardest on the low-skilled. Because there is a preponderance of low-skilled workers among the young—they have had less opportunity to obtain work experience and acquire skills—we would expect the minimum wage to cause more unemployment among young workers than among older workers. And that is exactly what happens. The unemployment rate for teenagers is more than twice the average. Although there are many factors other than the minimum wage influencing unemployment among young people, it is almost certainly the case that part of the higher unemployment among the young arises from the impact of minimum wage laws.

R E V I E W

- A decrease in the demand for low-skilled labour lowers the equilibrium wage.
- In the short run, lower wages result in a decrease in the quantity of low-skilled labour supplied and bring forth an increase in the quantity demanded.
- In the long run, lower wages encourage some people to leave the labour force and others to train and obtain skills. The supply of low-skilled labour decreases and wages rise.
- Minimum wage regulations limit the ability of the labour market to respond to change and result in persistent unemployment.

Next we study the effects of taxes.

Taxes

LAST YEAR, THE FEDERAL, PROVINCIAL, AND municipal governments raised more than $100 billion—an average of more than $3,000 per person—by taxing the goods and services that we buy. These taxes include the sales tax and special taxes on gasoline, alcoholic beverages, and tobacco. When you buy a good or service that is taxed, you pay the price tag amount *plus* an additional amount, the *tax*. What are the effects of taxes on the prices and quantities of goods bought and sold? Do the prices of the goods and services you buy increase by the full amount of the tax? Because the sales tax is added to the price of a good or service, isn't it obvious that you, the consumer, pay the entire tax? Isn't the price higher than it otherwise would be by an amount equal to the tax? It can be, but usually it isn't. And it is even possible that you actually pay none of the tax, forcing the seller to pay it for you. Let's see how we can make sense of these apparently absurd statements.

Who Pays the Sales Tax?

To study the effect of the sales tax, we need to start by looking at a market in which there is no such tax. We'll then introduce a sales tax and see the changes it brings.

Figure 6.5 shows the market for CD players. The demand curve is *D*, and the supply curve is *S*. The equilibrium price of a CD player is $100, and the quantity is 5,000 players a week.

Suppose the government puts a $10 tax on CD players. What are the effects of this tax on the price and quantity in the market for CD players? To answer this question, we need to work out what happens to demand and supply in the market for CD players.

When a good is taxed, it has two prices: a price that excludes the tax and a price that includes it. Consumers respond only to the price that includes the tax. Producers respond only to the price they receive—the price that excludes the tax. The tax is like a wedge between these two prices.

Let's think of the price on the vertical axis of Fig. 6.5 as the price paid by the consumer that *includes* the tax. When a tax is imposed, there is no change in demand—the demand curve does not shift. Regardless of whether the price includes some tax or not, it is the total price including the tax that influences the quantity demanded.

FIGURE 6.5

The Sales Tax

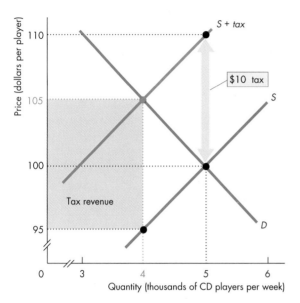

The demand curve for CD players is *D*, and the supply curve is *S*. With no sales tax, the price is $100 a player and 5,000 players a week are bought and sold. Then a sales tax of $10 a player is imposed. The price on the vertical axis is the price *including* the tax. The demand curve does not change, but the supply decreases and the supply curve shifts leftward. The curve *S + tax* shows the terms on which sellers will make CD players available. The vertical distance between the supply curve *S* and the new supply curve *S + tax* equals the tax—$10 a player.

The new equilibrium is at a price of $105 with 4,000 CD players a week bought and sold. The sales tax increases the price by less than the tax, decreases the price received by the supplier, and decreases the quantity bought and sold. It brings in revenue to the government equal to the blue area.

But the supply curve *does* shift. When a sales tax is imposed on a good, it is offered for sale at a higher price than in a no-tax situation. Supply of the good decreases and the supply curve shifts leftward to *S + tax*. To determine the position of this new supply curve, we add the tax to the minimum price that suppliers are willing to accept for each quantity sold. For example, with no tax, suppliers are willing to sell 4,000 players a week for $95 a player. So with a $10 tax, they will supply 4,000 players a week for $105—a price that includes the tax. Similarly, with no tax, suppliers

are willing to sell 5,000 players a week at a price of $100, so they will supply this quantity for $110 including the tax. The new supply curve *S + tax* lies to the left of the original curve—supply has decreased—and the vertical distance between the original supply curve *S* and the new supply curve *S + tax* equals the tax. The curve *S + tax* describes the terms on which the good is available to buyers.

A new equilibrium is determined where the new supply curve intersects the demand curve—at a price of $105 and a quantity of 4,000 CD players a week. The $10 sales tax has increased the price paid by the consumer by only $5 ($105 versus $100), which is less than the $10 tax. And it has decreased the price received by the supplier by $5 ($95 versus $100). The $10 tax paid is made up of the higher price to the buyer and the lower price to the seller.

The tax brings in tax revenue to the government equal to the tax per item multiplied by the items sold. It is illustrated by the blue area in Fig. 6.5. The $10 tax on CD players brings in a tax revenue of $40,000 a week.

In this example, the buyer and the seller split the tax equally; the buyer pays $5 a player and so does the seller. This equal sharing of the tax is a special case and does not usually occur. But some split of the tax between the buyer and seller is usual. Cases in which either the buyer or seller pays the entire tax can, however, occur. Let's look at these.

Tax Division and Elasticity of Demand

The division of the burden of a tax between buyers and sellers also depends on the elasticity of demand. Again, there are two extreme cases:

- Perfectly inelastic demand—buyer pays.
- Perfectly elastic demand—seller pays.

Perfectly Inelastic Demand   Figure 6.6(a) shows the market for insulin, a vital daily medication of diabetics. The quantity demanded is 100,000 doses a day, regardless of the price. That is, a person with diabetes would sacrifice all other goods and services rather than not consume the insulin dose that provides good health and survival. The demand for insulin reflects this fact and is perfectly inelastic. It is shown by the vertical curve D_I. The supply curve of insulin is *S*. With no tax, the price is $2 a dose, and the 100,000 doses a day that keep the population with diabetes healthy are bought.

FIGURE 6.6

Sales Tax and the Elasticity of Demand

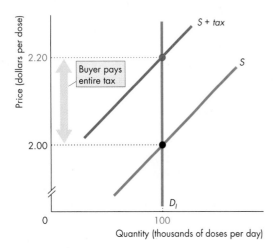

(a) Inelastic demand

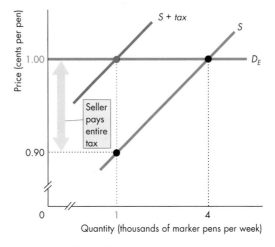

(b) Elastic demand

Part (a) shows the market for insulin. The demand for insulin is perfectly inelastic. With no tax, the price is $2 a dose and 100,000 doses a day are bought. A sales tax of 20¢ a dose increases the price at which sellers are willing to make insulin available and shifts the supply curve to S + tax. The price rises to $2.20 a dose, but the quantity bought does not change. Buyers pay the entire tax.

Part (b) shows the market for pink marker pens. The demand for pink marker pens is perfectly elastic. With no tax, the price of a pink marker pen is $1 and 4,000 a week are bought. A sales tax of 10¢ a pink pen shifts the supply curve to S + tax. The price remains at $1 a pen, and the quantity of pink markers sold decreases to 1,000 a week. Suppliers pay the entire tax.

If insulin is taxed at 20¢ a dose, we must add the tax to the minimum price at which the drug companies are willing to sell insulin to determine the terms on which it will be available to consumers. The result is a new supply curve S + tax. The price rises to $2.20 a dose, but the quantity does not change. The buyer pays the entire sales tax of 20¢ a dose.

Perfectly Elastic Demand   Figure 6.6(b) shows the market for pink marker pens. Aside from a few pink freaks, no one cares whether they use a pink, blue, yellow, or green marker pen. If pink markers are less expensive than the others, everyone will use pink. If pink markers are more expensive than the others, no one will use them. The demand for pink marker pens is perfectly elastic at the price of other coloured marker pens—$1 a pen in Fig. 6.6(b). The demand curve for pink markers is the horizontal curve D_E. The supply curve is S. With no tax; the price of a pink marker is $1 and 4,000 a week are bought.

If a sales tax of 10¢ a pen is levied on pink, and only pink, marker pens, we must add the tax to the minimum price at which suppliers are willing to sell them to determine the terms on which pink marker pens will be available to consumers. The new supply curve is S + tax. The price remains at $1 a pen, and the quantity of pink markers decreases to 1,000 a week. The 10¢ sales tax has left the price paid by the consumer unchanged, but decreased the amount received by the supplier by the full amount of the sales tax—10¢ a pen. As a result, sellers decrease the quantity offered for sale.

We've seen that when demand is perfectly inelastic, the buyer pays the entire tax and when demand is perfectly elastic, the seller pays it. In the usual case, where demand is neither perfectly inelastic or perfectly elastic, the tax is split between the buyer and the seller. But the division depends on the elasticity of demand. The more inelastic the demand, the larger is the portion of the tax paid by the buyer.

FIGURE 6.7

Sales Tax and the Elasticity of Supply

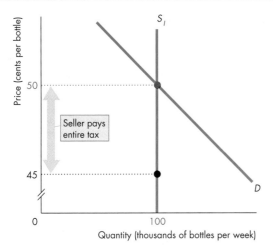

(a) Inelastic supply

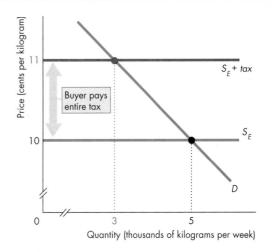

(b) Elastic supply

Part (a) shows the market for water from a mineral spring. Supply is perfectly inelastic. With no tax, the price is 50¢ a bottle. The sales tax of 5¢ decreases the price received by sellers, but the price paid by buyers remains at 50¢ a bottle and the number of bottles bought remains the same. Suppliers pay the entire tax.

Part (b) shows the market for sand. Supply is perfectly elastic. With no tax, the price is 10¢ a kilogram and 5,000 kilograms a week are bought. The sales tax of 1¢ a kilogram increases the minimum price at which sellers are willing to supply to 11¢ a kilogram. The supply curve shifts to S_E + *tax*. The price increases to 11¢ a kilogram, and the quantity decreases to 3,000 kilograms a week. Buyers pay the entire tax.

Tax Division and Elasticity of Supply

The division of the burden of a tax between buyers and sellers depends, in part, on the elasticity of supply. There are two extreme cases:

■ Perfectly inelastic supply—seller pays.
■ Perfectly elastic supply—buyer pays.

Perfectly Inelastic Supply   Figure 6.7(a) shows the market for water from a mineral spring that flows at a constant rate that can't be controlled. The quantity supplied is 100,000 bottles a week, regardless of the price. The supply is perfectly inelastic and the supply curve is S_I. The demand curve for the water from this spring is D. With no tax, the price is 50¢ a bottle and the 100,000 bottles that flow from the spring are bought at that price.

Suppose this spring water is taxed at 5¢ a bottle. Even if the price received by the spring owners fell by the full amount of the tax, they would still produce the same quantity—100,000 bottles a week. Consumers, on the other hand, are willing to buy the 100,000 bottles available each week only if the price is 50¢ a bottle. So the price remains at 50¢ a bottle, and the suppliers pay the entire tax. The sales tax of 5¢ a bottle reduces the price received by suppliers to 45¢ a bottle.

Perfectly Elastic Supply   Figure 6.7(b) shows the market for sand from which computer-chip makers extract silicon. A virtually unlimited quantity of this sand is available, and its owners are willing to supply any quantity at a price of 10¢ a kilogram. The supply is perfectly elastic and the supply curve is S_E. The demand curve for sand is D. With no tax, the price is 10¢ a kilogram and 5,000 kilograms a week are bought at that price.

If this sand is taxed at 1¢ a kilogram, we must add the tax to the minimum price at which the suppliers are willing to sell the sand to determine the terms on which this sand will be available to computer-chip makers. Because with no tax the suppliers of sand are willing to supply any quantity at 10¢ a kilogram, with the 1¢ tax they are willing to supply any quantity at 11¢ a kilogram along the curve S_E + *tax*. That is, when supply is perfectly elastic, the tax shifts the supply curve upwards by the amount of the tax. A new equilibrium is determined where the new supply curve intersects the demand curve—at a price of 11¢ a kilogram and a quantity of 3,000 kilograms a week. The sales tax has increased the price paid by computer-chip makers by the full amount of the tax—1¢ a kilogram—and has decreased the quantity sold.

We've seen that when supply is perfectly inelastic, the seller pays the entire tax and when supply is perfectly elastic, the buyer pays it. In the usual case, where supply is neither perfectly inelastic nor perfectly elastic, the tax is split between the seller and the buyer. But the division depends on the elasticity of supply. The more elastic the supply, the larger is the portion of the tax paid by the buyer.

Sales Taxes in Practice

We've looked at the range of possible effects of a sales tax by studying the extreme cases. In practice, supply and demand are rarely perfectly elastic or perfectly inelastic. They lie somewhere in between, like in the first example we studied. But some items tend towards one of the extremes. For example, a heavily taxed item such as alcohol, tobacco, or gasoline has a low elasticity of demand. Consequently, the buyer pays most of the tax. Also, because demand is inelastic, the quantity bought does not decrease much and the government collects a large tax revenue.

It is unusual to tax an item heavily if its demand is elastic. A good or service that has an elastic demand is usually a good or service that has close substitutes. If a tax is levied on such a good or service, people will reduce their purchases of the taxed good and increase their purchases of an untaxed substitute. That is, the quantity of the taxed good bought decreases by a large amount and the government will not collect much tax revenue. This explains why the items that are taxed are those that have inelastic demands and why buyers pay most of the taxes.

R E V I E W

- The effect of the sales tax depends on the elasticities of supply and demand.
- For a given supply, the less elastic the demand, the larger is the price increase, the smaller is the quantity decrease, and the larger is the portion of the tax paid by the buyer.
- For a given demand, the more elastic the supply, the larger is the price increase, the larger is the quantity decrease, and the larger is the portion of the tax paid by the buyer.

Taxes are just one method used to change prices and quantities. Another is to prohibit trade in a good.

Markets for Prohibited Goods

THE MARKETS FOR MANY GOODS AND SERVICES are regulated, and buying and selling some goods is prohibited—the goods and services are illegal. The best known examples of such goods are drugs such as marijuana, cocaine, and heroin.

Despite the fact that these drugs are illegal, trade in them is a multibillion dollar business. This trade can be understood by using the same economic model and principles that explain trade in legal goods and services.

As you study the market for drugs, remember that economics tries to answer questions about how the economic world works. It neither condones nor condemns the activities it seeks to explain. As a well-informed citizen, you have an opinion about drugs and about public policy towards them. What you learn about the economics of markets for illegal goods is one input into developing your opinion. But it is not a substitute for your moral judgments and does not help you to develop those judgments. What follows is a value-free analysis of how markets for prohibited goods work and not an argument about how they ought to be regulated and controlled.

To study the market for prohibited goods, we're first going to examine the prices and quantities that would prevail if these goods were not prohibited. Next, we'll see how prohibition works. Then we'll see how a tax might limit the consumption of these goods.

A Free Market for Drugs

Figure 6.8 shows a market for drugs. The demand curve, D, shows that other things remaining the same, the lower the price of drugs, the larger is the quantity of drugs demanded. And the supply curve, S, shows that, other things remaining the same, the lower the price of drugs, the smaller is the quantity supplied. If drugs were not prohibited, the quantity bought and sold would be Q_c and the price would be P_c.

Prohibition on Drugs

When a good is prohibited, the cost of trading in the good increases. By how much the cost increases and on whom the cost falls depend on the penalties for violating the law and the effectiveness with which the law is enforced. The larger the penalties for violation and the more effective the policing, the higher are the costs. Penalties may be imposed on sellers, buyers, or both.

Penalties on Sellers   Drug dealers in Canada face large penalties if their activities are detected. For example, a marijuana dealer could pay a $200,000 fine and serve a 15-year prison term. A heroin dealer could pay a $500,000 fine and serve a 20-year prison term. These penalties are part of the cost of supplying illegal drugs and they bring a decrease in supply—a leftward shift in the supply curve. To determine the new supply curve, we add the cost of breaking the law to the minimum price that drug dealers are willing to accept. In Fig. 6.8, the cost of breaking the law by selling drugs (CBL) is added to the minimum price that dealers will accept and the supply curve shifts leftward to $S + CBL$. If penalties are imposed only on sellers, the market moves from point c to point a. The price increases and the quantity bought decreases.

Penalties on Buyers   In Canada, it is illegal to *possess* drugs such as marijuana, cocaine, and heroin. For example, possession of marijuana can bring a prison term of 1 year and possession of heroin can bring a prison term of 2 years. Penalties for possession fall on buyers and the cost of breaking the law must be subtracted from the value of the good to determine the maximum price buyers are willing to pay. Demand decreases and the demand curve shifts leftward. In Fig. 6.8, the demand curve shifts to $D - CBL$. If penalties are imposed only on buyers, the market

FIGURE   6.8

The Market for a Prohibited Good

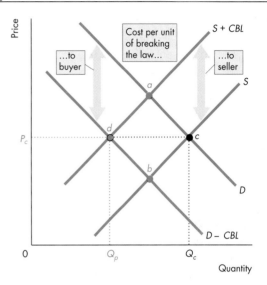

The demand curve for drugs is D and the supply curve is S. With no prohibition on drugs, the quantity consumed is Q_c at a price of P_c—point c. If selling drugs is illegal, the cost of breaking the law by selling drugs (CBL) is added to the other costs, and supply decreases to $S + CBL$. The price rises and the quantity consumed decreases—point a. If buying drugs is illegal, the cost of breaking the law is subtracted from the maximum price that buyers are willing to pay, and demand decreases to $D - CBL$. The price falls and the quantity consumed decreases—point b. If both buying and selling are illegal, both the supply and demand curves shift and the quantity consumed decreases even more, but (in this example) the price remains at its unregulated level—point d.

moves from point c to point b. The price and the quantity bought decrease.

Penalties on Both Sellers and Buyers   If penalties are imposed on sellers *and* buyers, both supply and demand decrease and both the supply curve and demand curve shift. In Fig. 6.8, the costs of breaking the law are the same for both buyers and sellers, so both curves shift leftward by the same amounts. The market moves to point d. The price remains at the competitive market price but the quantity bought decreases to Q_p.

The larger the penalty and greater the degree of law enforcement, the larger is the decrease in demand and/or supply and the greater the shift of the demand and/or supply curve. If the penalties are heavier on sellers, the price will rise above P_c, and if the penalties are heavier on buyers, the price will fall below P_c. In Canada, the penalties on sellers are much larger than those on buyers. As a result, the decrease in supply is much larger than the decrease in demand. The quantity of drugs traded decreases and the price increases, compared with an unregulated market.

With high enough penalties and effective law enforcement, it is possible to decrease demand and/or supply to the point at which the quantity bought is zero. But in reality, such an outcome is unusual. It does not happen in the case of illegal drugs. The key reason is the high cost of law enforcement and insufficient resources for the police to achieve effective enforcement. Because of this situation, some people suggest that drugs (and other illegal goods) should be legalized and sold openly but also be taxed at a high rate in the same way that legal drugs such as alcohol are taxed. How would such an arrangement work?

Legalizing and Taxing Drugs

Figure 6.9 shows what happens if drugs are legalized and taxed. With no tax, the quantity of drugs is Q_c and the price is P_c. Now suppose that drugs are taxed at a rate chosen to make the quantity bought the same as with a prohibition. The tax added to the supply price shifts the supply curve to $S + tax$. Equilibrium occurs at a quantity of Q_p. The price paid by consumers increases to P_b and the price received by suppliers decreases to P_s. The government collects a tax revenue equal to the blue area in the figure.

Illegal Trading to Evade the Tax   It is likely that an extremely high tax rate would be needed to cut drug consumption to the level prevailing with a prohibition. It is also likely that many drug dealers and consumers would try to cover up their activities to evade the tax. If they did act in this way, they would face the cost of breaking the law—the tax law. If the penalty for tax law violation is as severe and as effectively policed as drug-dealing laws, the analysis we've already conducted applies also to this case. The quantity of drugs consumed would depend on the penalties for law breaking and on the way in which the penalties are assigned to buyers and sellers. When

FIGURE 6.9

Legalizing and Taxing Drugs

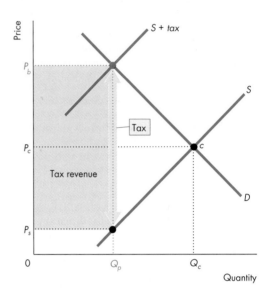

Drugs are legalized but taxed at a high rate. The tax added to the supply price shifts the supply curve from S to $S + tax$. The quantity bought decreases to Q_p, the price paid by consumers increases to P_b, and the price received by suppliers decreases to P_s. The government collects a tax revenue equal to the blue area.

penalties are imposed, the quantity consumed decreases, and the tax revenue would be less than the blue area in Fig. 6.9.

Some Pros and Cons of Taxes Versus Prohibition
So which works more effectively, prohibition or taxing? The comparison we've just made suggests that the two methods can be made to be equivalent if the taxes and penalties are set at the appropriate levels. But there are some other differences.

In favour of taxes and against prohibition is the fact that the tax revenue can be used to make law enforcement more effective. It can also be used to run a more effective education campaign against drugs. In favour of prohibition and against taxes is the fact that a prohibition sends a signal that may influence preferences, decreasing the demand for drugs. Also, some people intensely dislike the idea of the government profiting from trade in harmful substances.

Stabilizing Farm Revenue

FARM OUTPUT FLUCTUATES A GREAT DEAL BECAUSE of fluctuations in the weather. How do changes in farm output affect farm prices and farm revenues? And how might farm revenues be stabilized? The answers to these questions depend on how the markets for agricultural products are organized. We'll begin by looking at an unregulated agricultural market.

An Unregulated Agricultural Market

Figure 6.10 illustrates the market for wheat. In both parts, the demand curve for wheat is *D*. Once farmers have harvested their crop, they have no control over the quantity supplied, and supply is inelastic along a *momentary supply curve.* In normal climate conditions, the momentary supply curve is MS_0 (in both parts of the figure).

The price is determined at the point of intersection of the momentary supply curve and the demand curve. In normal conditions, the price is $200 a tonne. The quantity of wheat produced is 20 million tonnes, and farm revenue is $4 billion. Suppose the opportunity cost to farmers of producing wheat is also $4 billion. Then in normal conditions, farmers just cover their opportunity cost.

FIGURE 6.10

Harvests, Farm Prices, and Farm Revenue

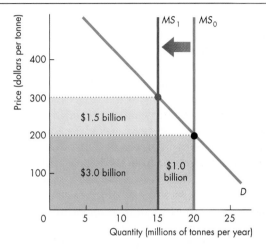

(a) Poor harvest: revenue increases

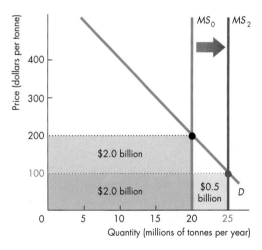

(b) Bumper harvest: revenue decreases

The demand curve for wheat is *D*. In normal times, the supply curve is MS_0, and 20 million tonnes are sold for $200 a tonne. In part (a), a poor growing season decreases supply to MS_1. The price rises to $300 a tonne, and farm revenue *increases* from $4.0 billion to $4.5 billion—the $1.5 billion increase in revenue from the higher price (light blue area) exceeds the $1.0 billion decrease in revenue from the smaller quantity (red area). In part (b), a bumper harvest increases supply to MS_2. The price falls to $100 a tonne, and farm revenue *decreases* to $2.5 billion—the $2.0 billion decrease in revenue from the lower price (red area) exceeds the $0.5 billion increase in revenue from the increase in the quantity sold (light blue area).

Poor Harvest   Suppose there is a bad growing season resulting in a poor harvest. What happens to the price of wheat and the revenue of farmers? These questions are answered in Fig. 6.10(a). Supply decreases and the momentary supply curve shifts leftward to MS_1 where 15 million tonnes of wheat are produced. With a decrease in supply, the price increases to $300 a tonne.

What happens to total farm revenue? It *increases* to $4.5 billion. A decrease in supply has brought an increase in price and an increase in farm revenue. The reason is the demand for wheat is *inelastic*. The percentage decrease in the quantity demanded is less than the percentage increase in price. You can verify this fact by noticing in Fig. 6.10(a) that the $1.5 billion increase in revenue from the higher price (light blue area) exceeds the $1.0 billion decrease in revenue from the smaller quantity (red area). Farmers are now making a profit in excess of their opportunity cost.

Although total farm revenue increases when there is a poor harvest, some farmers, whose entire crop is wiped out, suffer a fall in revenue. Others whose crop is unaffected make an enormous gain.

Bumper Harvest   Figure 6.10(b) shows what happens in the opposite situation when there is a bumper harvest. Now, supply increases to 25 million tonnes and the momentary supply curve shifts rightward to MS_2. With the increased quantity supplied, the price falls to $100 a tonne. Farm revenues also decline—to $2.5 billion. They do so because the demand for wheat is inelastic. To see this fact, notice in Fig. 6.10(b) that the $2.0 billion decrease in revenue from the lower price (red area) exceeds the $0.5 billion increase in revenue from the increase in the quantity sold (light blue area).

Elasticity of Demand   In the example we've just worked through, demand is inelastic. If demand is elastic, the price fluctuations go in the same directions as those we've worked out, but revenues fluctuate in the opposite directions. Bumper harvests increase revenue and poor harvests decrease it. But the demand for most agricultural products is inelastic, and the case we've studied is the relevant one.

Because farm prices fluctuate, institutions have evolved to stabilize them. There are two types of institutions:

- Speculative markets in inventories
- Farm marketing boards

Speculative Markets in Inventories

Many goods, including a wide variety of agricultural products, can be stored. These inventories provide a cushion between production and consumption. If production decreases, goods can be sold from inventory; if production increases, goods can be put into inventory.

In a market that has inventories, we must distinguish production from supply. The quantity produced is not the same as the quantity supplied. The quantity supplied exceeds the quantity produced when goods are sold from inventory. And the quantity supplied is less than the quantity produced when goods are put into inventory. The supply curve, therefore, depends on the behaviour of inventory holders.

The Behaviour of Inventory Holders   Inventory holders speculate. They hope to buy at a low price and sell at a high price. That is, they hope to buy goods and put them into inventory when the price is low, and sell them from inventory when the price is high. They make a profit or incur a loss equal to their selling price minus their buying price and minus the cost of storage.[4]

But how do inventory holders know when to buy and when to sell? How do they know if the price is high or low? To decide whether a price is high or low, inventory holders make their best forecast of future prices. If the current price is above its expected future level, they sell goods from inventory. If the current price is below its expected future level, they buy goods to put into inventory. This behaviour by inventory holders makes the supply curve perfectly elastic at the future price expected by inventory holders.

Let's work out what happens to price and quantity in a market in which inventories are held when production fluctuates. Let's look again at the wheat market.

Fluctuations in Production   In Fig. 6.11 the demand curve for wheat is D. Inventory holders expect the future price to be $200 a tonne. The supply curve is S—supply is perfectly elastic at the price expected by inventory holders. Production fluctuates between Q_1 and Q_2.

---

[4] We will suppose that the cost of storage is so small that we can ignore it. This assumption, though not essential, enables us to see more sharply the effects of inventory holders' decisions on prices.

FIGURE 6.11
How Inventories Limit Price Changes

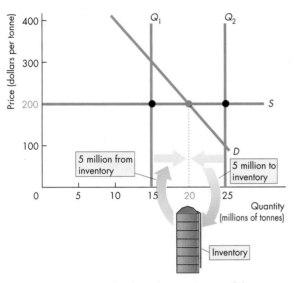

Inventory holders supply wheat from inventory if the price rises above $200 a tonne and take wheat into inventory if the price falls below $200 a tonne, making supply perfectly elastic along the supply curve S. When production decreases to Q_1, 5 million tonnes are supplied from inventory; when production increases to Q_2, 5 million tonnes are added to inventory. The price remains at $200 a tonne.

When production fluctuates and there are no inventories, the price and the quantity fluctuate. Price falls when production increases and rises when production decreases. We saw this result in Fig. 6.10. But if there are inventories, the price does not fluctuate. When production is low, at Q_1 or 15 million tonnes, inventory holders sell 5 million tonnes from inventory and the quantity bought by consumers is 20 million tonnes. The price remains at $200 a tonne. When production is high, at Q_2 or 25 million tonnes, inventory holders buy 5 million tonnes and consumers continue to buy 20 million tonnes. Again, the price remains at $200 a tonne.

Inventories reduce price fluctuations. In Fig. 6.11, the price fluctuations are entirely eliminated. When there are costs of carrying inventories and when inventories become almost depleted, some price fluctuations do occur, but these fluctuations are smaller than those occurring in a market without inventories.

Farm Revenue   Even if inventory speculation succeeds in stabilizing prices, it does not stabilize farm revenue. With the price stabilized, farm revenue fluctuates as production fluctuates. But bumper harvests now bring larger revenues than poor harvests. The reason is that now farmers, in effect, face a perfectly elastic demand curve for their output.

Farm Marketing Boards

In every country, the government intervenes in agricultural markets. The most extensive intervention in agricultural markets is in the European Union. But it also occurs in Canada and the United States, where intervention is designed to stabilize the prices of many agricultural products, such as grains, milk, eggs, tobacco, rice, peanuts, cotton, and poultry meats. In Canada, more than 100 farm marketing boards operate and influence more than one-half of total farm sales. A **farm marketing board** is a regulatory agency that intervenes in agricultural markets to stabilize the prices of many agricultural products. Farm marketing boards are often supported by government funds. How do agricultural markets work when a stabilization program is in place? The answer depends on which type of intervention takes place.

There are three types of intervention:

■ Price floor
■ Quota
■ Subsidy

Price Floor   A price floor operates in an agricultural market in much the same way that it operates in other markets. Earlier in this chapter we examined a price floor in the labour market when we studied the effect of minimum wages. The principles are the same in the case of agricultural markets.

Figure 6.12 shows how a price floor works in the market for skim milk powder. The competitive equilibrium price of skim milk powder is $3 a tonne, and 16 million tonnes are produced and bought. If the Canadian Dairy Commission imposes a price floor of $4 a tonne, then the price increases to $4 a tonne and the quantity demanded decreases to 14 million tonnes. The quantity supplied increases to 18 million tonnes. Farmers produce a surplus of 4 million tonnes.

This method of supporting the price of an agricultural product will fail unless there is some method of taking up the surplus produced. If farmers are left to find a market for their surplus, then

FIGURE 6.12

A Price Floor

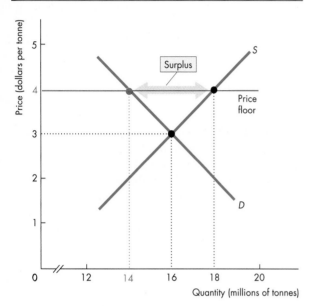

The competitive equilibrium price is $3 a tonne and the equilibrium quantity produced and bought is 16 million tonnes. A price floor of $4 a tonne increases the price to $4 a tonne, decreases the quantity sold to 14 million tonnes, and increases the quantity produced to 18 million tonnes. The price floor creates a surplus of 4 million tonnes. If the Canadian Dairy Commission does not buy the surplus and allows farmers to find their own market, the price will return to its competitive level of $3 a tonne.

FIGURE 6.13

A Wheat Quota

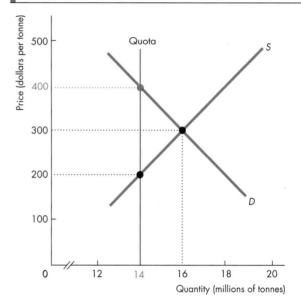

The competitive equilibrium price is $300 a tonne and the equilibrium quantity produced and bought is 16 million tonnes. A quota is set at 14 million tonnes. As a result, the price rises to $400 a tonne and the quantity sold decreases to 14 million tonnes. Producers are willing to supply 14 million tonnes at $200 a tonne, so they will want to increase the quantity that they supply. If the marketing board cannot control the quantity produced, then the quantity produced will increase and the price will fall to its competitive level of $300 a tonne.

the price will fall below the price floor to the competitive price—$3 a tonne. If, on the other hand, the Canadian Dairy Commission purchases the surplus at the support price, then the price will remain at the price floor. If the marketing board systematically buys more than it sells, then it will end up with a large inventory. Such has been the outcome in the European Union where stabilization agencies have mountains of butter and lakes of wine! The cost of buying and storing the inventory falls on taxpayers, and the main gainers from the support price are the large, efficient farms.

Quota   A **quota** is a restriction on the quantity of a good that a farm is permitted to produce. If farm

production is restricted by a quota, then the supply curve becomes perfectly inelastic at the quota quantity. Figure 6.13 illustrates how a quota works in the market for wheat.

The competitive price is $300 a tonne and the competitive quantity is 16 million tonnes. The Canadian Wheat Board then imposes quotas that restrict total production to 14 million tonnes. The supply curve becomes the vertical line labelled "Quota." With output restricted by the quota, the quantity produced is now 14 million tonnes and the price increases to $400 a tonne.

But this might not be the end of the story. Farmers are willing to produce wheat at $200 a tonne, so at a market price of $400 a tonne, they will

FIGURE 6.14

A Milk Subsidy

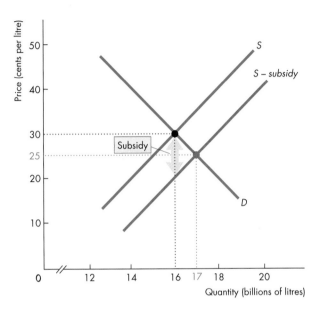

The competitive equilibrium price is 30¢ a litre and the equilibrium quantity produced and bought is 16 billion litres. The Canadian Dairy Commission introduces a subsidy of 10¢ a litre. As a result, producers are now willing to supply each quantity at 10¢ a litre less. The supply curve shifts rightward such that the vertical distance between the supply curve S and the supply curve S – subsidy is 10¢ a litre. The price falls to 25¢ a litre, and the quantity produced and sold increases to 17 billion litres. Producers receive 35¢ a litre, which is the market price of 25¢ a litre plus the subsidy of 10¢ a litre. The total subsidy is $1.7 billion, which taxpayers will have to pay.

want to increase their output. If the Canadian Wheat Board does not prevent quotas from being exceeded, a gradual increase in the quantity of wheat supplied will eventually restore the competitive equilibrium.

Subsidy   A **subsidy** is a payment made by the government to the producer. A subsidy is like a tax—a payment made by a producer to the government—but it goes in the reverse direction. Therefore a subsidy works in a similar way to a tax, but instead of adding something to the price paid by the consumer, a subsidy lowers the price to below what it would be in the absence of a subsidy.

Figure 6.14 illustrates how a subsidy works in the market for milk. The competitive equilibrium is at 30¢ a litre with 16 billion litres produced and bought. The Canadian Dairy Commission then offers a subsidy of 10¢ a litre. The subsidy increases the supply of milk and shifts the supply curve rightward. The magnitude of the shift depends on the size of the subsidy. In this case, farmers are willing to sell each litre for 10¢ less than they would be willing to accept in the absence of a subsidy. The equilibrium price falls to 25¢ a litre, and the quantity produced and bought increases to 17 billion litres. Farmers receive 35¢ a litre, which is the market price of 25¢ a litre plus the subsidy of 10¢ a litre. Thus farmers gain, but taxpayers pay the subsidy. The total subsidy paid is $1.7 billion, which is the 10¢ a litre subsidy multiplied by the 17 billion litres of milk produced. This method of agricultural support lowers the price paid by consumers of the subsidized good but it can impose major costs on all taxpayers.

R E V I E W

- The demand for most farm products is inelastic.
- With no inventories, a poor harvest (a decrease in supply) increases price and increases farm revenue and a bumper harvest (an increase in supply) decreases price and decreases farm revenue.
- Inventory holders speculate by trying to buy at a low price and sell at a high price. Successful speculation reduces price fluctuations.
- Farm marketing boards also limit price fluctuations by setting a price floor or a quota, or by paying a subsidy.

◆ We've now completed our study of demand and supply and its applications. You've seen how the demand–supply model enables us to make predictions about prices and quantities bought and sold and also how it enables us to understand a wide variety of real-world events. The issues that we've studied in this chapter enable you to make an informed contribution to many of the current policy debates. One such debate, about which you're going to hear a lot during the next few years, concerns the Canada Pension Plan. The tools you have studied here help you to make sense of some of the issues in that debate, as you can see in *Reading Between the Lines* on pp. 138–139.

Policy
WATCH

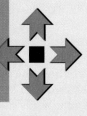

Taxes in the Labour Market

Essence of
THE STORY

- The federal and provincial governments proposed to double Canada Pension Plan (CPP) premiums by 2004 and nearly triple them by 2025.

- The governments say higher premiums are fair and force working baby boomers to pay more for their own pensions.

- But the Canadian Youth Foundation says higher CPP premiums will hurt today's youth who will have to support retired baby boomers.

- The Foundation predicts that higher CPP premiums will raise the youth unemployment rate, which is close to 15 percent.

- It wants CPP premiums to rise as a worker ages and receives a higher income.

TORONTO STAR, MAY 22, 1996

Expect higher rate of youth unemployment if pension plan premiums rise, report says

BY SHAWN McCARTHY

OTTAWA—Government plans to drive up Canada Pension Plan premiums will hurt the very people they are intended to help— today's youth who will have to support retired baby boomers, a youth-oriented research group says.

The Canadian Youth Foundation—a non-profit, independent organization—argues the CPP should be fundamentally overhauled to make it fairer to post-baby boomers.

"We know that, in an inter-generation way, today's young workers and future workers are going to get a heck of a lot less out of the system than their elders," Michael Grant, the foundation's research director, said in an interview. ...

Grant said yesterday there are serious problems with a proposal to raise premiums quickly in order to offset the need for even steeper rates when the large baby-boomer generation has retired.

Ottawa and the provinces have proposed to double CPP premiums over the next eight years, although that increase could be offset by cutting benefits.

Premiums are now expected to nearly triple by 2025.

Governments argue imposing higher premiums is the most fair approach because it forces working baby boomers to pay more for their own pensions.

But Grant said he worries about the impact rising CPP premiums would have on youth unemployment, now hovering above 15 per cent.

"We think there is a direct relationship between an increase in the tax on labor and the burden that is passed on to youth in terms of unemployment," he said. "Payroll taxes fall disproportionately on youth."

As a result, the foundation argues CPP premiums should be assessed on a sliding scale—rising as a worker ages to reflect the typical pattern of rising incomes and the tendency of middle-aged people to save more for their retirement.

Economic

A N A L Y S I S

■ The Canadian population is aging. A "baby-boom" generation born during the late 1940s and early 1950s will retire between 2010 and 2020.

■ By 2025, a smaller proportion of Canadian workers will be supporting a larger proportion of retired Canadians.

■ To anticipate this situation, the federal and provincial governments plan to increase CPP contributions.

■ These contributions are a form of tax on employment. They are paid both by employers and workers.

■ We can study the effects of such a tax by examining its effects on demand and supply in the labour market.

■ Figure 1 shows a labour market with no taxes. The demand curve is D and the supply curve is S. The equilibrium wage rate is $5 an hour and 20 million hours of labour a year are employed.

■ Figure 2 shows what happens when both the employer and worker must pay a tax. In this example, the tax is $1 an hour on both the employer and the worker.

■ The tax on the employer, called a payroll tax, decreases the demand for labour. The demand curve shifts leftward from D_0 to D_1. The reason is that because the employer must pay a tax of $1 an hour, he or she is now willing to hire a given amount of labour only if the wage rate is $1 *less* than before.

■ The tax on the worker decreases the supply of labour. The supply curve shifts leftward from S_0 to S_1. The reason is that because the worker must pay a tax of $1 an hour, he or she is now willing to work a given amount of time only if the wage rate is $1 *more* than before.

■ The new equilibrium level of employment is 15 million hours a year. In this example, the wage rate is unchanged (but you can easily change the example to make the wage rate either rise or fall).

■ Whether the fall in employment is large or small depends on the elasticities of demand and supply in ways that are explained on pp. 126–130 of this chapter.

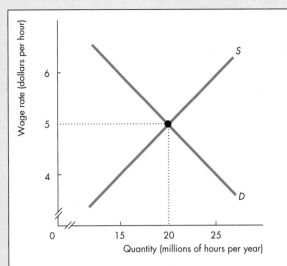

Figure 1 A labour market with no taxes

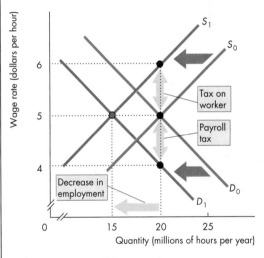

Figure 2 Taxes in a labour market

You're

THE VOTER

■ Should CPP premiums be increased?

■ Or instead, should tax incentives be strengthened to encourage people to save more for their retirement by contributing to private pension plans?

■ Explain how you would vote on this issue and give detailed reasons.

S U M M A R Y

Key Points

Housing Markets and Rent Ceilings A decrease in the supply of housing decreases short-run supply and raises rents. Higher rents increase the quantity of housing supplied in the short run and stimulate building activity, which increases supply in the long run. Rents fall as supply increases. If a rent ceiling prevents rents from rising, there is no inducement to increase the quantity supplied in the short run or the long run. The quantity of housing is less than what it would be in an unregulated market. People spend time searching for housing and the cost of housing, including the value of the time spent searching, exceeds that in an unregulated market. (pp. 120–123)

The Labour Market and Minimum Wages A decrease in the demand for low-skilled labour lowers the wage and reduces employment. The lower wage encourages people with low skill to acquire skills. As they do so, the short-run supply of low-skilled labour decreases and the wage rises. If the government imposes a minimum wage above the equilibrium wage, a decrease in the demand for labour results in unemployment. Minimum wages bite hardest on young workers. (pp. 124–126)

Taxes When a good or service is taxed, usually the price increases and the quantity bought decreases, but the price increases by less than the tax. The tax is paid partly by the buyer and partly by the seller. The portion of the tax paid by the buyer and by the seller depends on the elasticity of demand and the elasticity of supply. The less elastic the demand and the more elastic the supply, the greater is the price increase, the smaller is the quantity decrease, and the larger is the portion of the tax paid by the buyer. (pp. 126–130)

Markets for Prohibited Goods Penalties on sellers of an illegal good increase the cost of selling the good and decrease its supply. Penalties on buyers decrease their willingness to pay and decrease the demand for the good. The higher the penalties and the more effective the law enforcement, the smaller is the quantity bought. The price is higher or lower than the unregulated price, depending on whether penalties on sellers or buyers are

higher. A tax on drugs can achieve the same outcome as penalties. But prohibiting drugs sends a signal that might influence preferences and decrease the demand for drugs. (pp. 130–133)

Stabilizing Farm Revenue Farm revenues fluctuate because crop yields vary as climatic conditions fluctuate. The demand for most farm products is inelastic, so a decrease in supply increases the price and increases farm revenues, while an increase in supply decreases the price and decreases farm revenues. Inventory holders and official agencies act to stabilize farm prices and revenues. Inventory holders buy at a low price and sell at a high price. As a result, supply is perfectly elastic at the future price expected by inventory holders. When production is low, inventory holders sell from inventory, preventing the price from rising. When production is high, inventory holders buy, preventing the price from falling. Farm marketing boards set price floors above the equilibrium price that create persistent surpluses, set quotas that restrict supply and increase the price, or subsidize production that increases supply, lowers the market price, and increases farm revenues. (pp. 133–137)

Key Figures

Key Terms

R E V I E W   Q U E S T I O N S

1. Describe what happens to the rent and to the quantity of housing available if the supply of housing unexpectedly decreases. Trace the rent and the quantity of housing rented over time.

2. In the situation described in question 1, how will things be different if a rent ceiling is imposed?

3. Describe what happens to the price and quantity in a market in which there is an increase in supply. Trace the price and quantity over time.

4. Describe what happens to the price and quantity in a market in which there is an increase in demand. Trace the price and quantity over time.

5. Describe what happens to the wage rate and quantity of labour employed when there is an increase in demand for labour. Trace the evolution of the wage rate and employment over time.

6. Why does a minimum wage create unemployment?

7. When a government regulation prevents a price from changing, what forces come into operation to achieve an equilibrium?

8. How does the imposition of the sales tax on a good influence the supply of and demand for that good? How does the sales tax influence the price of the good and the quantity bought?

9. When a sales tax is imposed on a good or service with a perfectly elastic demand, who pays the tax?

10. When a sales tax is imposed on a good or service with a perfectly elastic supply, who pays the tax?

11. How does a prohibition of the sale of a good affect the demand for and supply of the good? How does the prohibition affect the price of the good and the quantity bought?

12. How does a prohibition of the consumption of a good affect the demand for and supply of the good? How does the prohibition affect the price of the good and the quantity bought?

13. Explain the alternative ways in which the consumption of harmful drugs can be controlled. What are the arguments for and against each method?

14. Why do farm revenues fluctuate?

15. Do farm revenues increase or decrease when there is a bumper crop? Why?

16. Explain why speculation can stabilize the price of a storable commodity, but why it does not stabilize the revenues of the producers of such a commodity.

17. How can farm prices be stabilized? Is such stabilization profitable?

C R I T I C A L   T H I N K I N G

1. Study *Reading Between the Lines* on pp. 138–139 on the effects of Canada Pension Plan (CPP) premiums on the labour market and then answer the following questions. Explain all your answers.
   a. Do CPP premiums affect the demand for labour or the supply of labour or both?
   b. Do CPP premiums affect all types of labour equally or do they have a bigger impact on some types of labour?
   c. What does the news article predict will happen to the unemployment rate if CPP premiums are increased?
   d. How does the elasticity of demand for labour and the elasticity of supply of labour influence the effects of an increase in the CPP premium on wages, employment, and unemployment?

2. Rent ceilings exist in many Canadian cities. What impact do you think rent ceilings have on the rent that students have to pay for rented accommodation and the amount and qualtity of rented accommodation available?

3. For years, the provinces increased the tax on cigarettes. Recently, Quebec and Ontario cut this tax. What will be the change in the price of cigarettes, the quantity of cigarettes sold, and provincial tax revenue? Who will gain from the tax cut—buyers or sellers of cigarettes?

4. Some grain growers in Western Canada would like to sell their grain on the world market. Under Canadian law, such action is prohibited. The Wheat Board is the sole seller of these grains. What would be the change in the farmers' revenue if the law was changed and they were allowed to market their own grain?

P R O B L E M S

1. The figure illustrates the market for rental housing in your town:

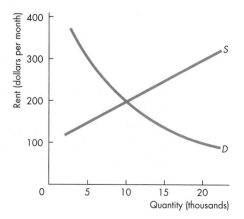

a.   What is the equilibrium rent?
b.   What is the equilibrium quantity of rented housing?

2. Now suppose that a rent ceiling of $150 a month is imposed in the housing market described in problem 1.
a.   What is the quantity of housing rented?
b.   What is the shortage of housing?
c.   What is the maximum price that demanders will be willing to pay for the last unit available?

3. The demand for and supply of teenage labour are:

Wage rate (dollars per hour)	Quantity demanded	Quantity supplied
	(hours per month)	
2	3,000	1,000
3	2,500	1,500
4	2,000	2,000
5	1,500	2,500
6	1,000	3,000

a.   What is the equilibrium wage rate?
b.   What is the level of employment?
c.   What is the level of unemployment?
d.   If the government imposes a minimum wage of $3 an hour for teenagers, how many hours do teenagers work?
e.   If the government imposes a minimum wage of $5 an hour for teenagers, what are the employment and unemployment levels?

f.   If there is a minimum wage of $5 an hour and demand increases by 500 hours, what is the level of unemployment?

4. The following table illustrates three supply curves for train travel:

Price (cents per passenger kilometre)	Quantity supplied (billions of passenger kilometres)		
	Momentary	Short-run	Long-run
20	500	350	200
30	500	400	300
40	500	450	400
50	500	500	500
60	500	550	600
70	500	600	700
80	500	650	800
90	500	700	900

a.   If the price is 50¢ a passenger kilometre, what is the quantity supplied in
(i)   The long run?
(ii)   The short run?
b.   Suppose that the price is initially 50¢, but that it then rises to 70¢. What will be the quantity supplied
(i)   Immediately following the price rise?
(ii)   In the short run?
(iii)   In the long run?

5. Suppose that the supply of train travel is the same as in problem 4. The following table gives two demand schedules—original and new:

Price (cents per passenger kilometre)	Quantity demanded (billions of passenger kilometres)	
	Original	New
20	5,000	5,300
30	2,000	2,300
40	1,000	1,300
50	500	800
60	400	700
70	300	600
80	200	500
90	100	400

a. What are the original equilibrium price and quantity?

b. After the increase in demand has occurred, what are

   (i)   The momentary equilibrium price and quantity?

   (ii)   The short-run equilibrium price and quantity?

   (iii) The long-run equilibrium price and quantity?

6. The short-run and long-run demand for train travel are:

Price	Quantity demanded (billions of passenger kilometres)	
(cents per passenger kilometre)	Short-run	Long-run
20	650	5,000
30	600	2,000
40	550	1,000
50	500	500
60	450	400
70	400	300
80	350	200
90	300	100

The supply of train travel is the same as in problem 4.

a. What are the long-run equilibrium price and quantity of train travel?

b. Floods destroy one-fifth of the trains and train tracks. Supply falls by 100 billion passenger kilometres. What happens to the price and the quantity of train travel in

   (i)   The short run?

   (ii)   The long run?

7. The following are the demand and supply schedules for chocolate brownies.

Price (cents per brownie)	Quantity demanded	Quantity supplied
	(millions per day)	
50	5	3
60	4	4
70	3	5
80	2	6
90	1	7

a. With no tax on brownies, what is their price and how many are produced and consumed?

b. If a tax of 20¢ a brownie is introduced, what happens to the price of a brownie and the number produced and consumed?

c. How much tax does the government collect and who pays it?

8. Calculate the elasticity of demand in Fig. 6.10 when the price of wheat is $300 a tonne. Does its magnitude imply that farm revenues fluctuate in the same direction as price fluctuations or in the opposite direction?

9. On Turtle Island, the government is considering ways of stabilizing farm prices and farm revenues. Currently the egg market is competitive, and the demand for and supply of eggs are

Price (dollars per dozen)	Quantity demanded	Quantity supplied
	(dozens per week)	
1.20	3,000	500
1.30	2,750	1,500
1.40	2,500	2,500
1.50	2,250	3,500
1.60	2,000	4,500
1.70	1,750	5,500
1.80	1,500	6,500

a. Calculate the competitive equilibrium price and quantity bought and sold.

b. The government introduces a floor price of $1.50 a dozen. Calculate the market price, the quantity of eggs bought and sold, and farm revenues. Calculate the surplus of eggs.

c. Calculate the amount the government must spend on eggs to maintain the floor price.

10. In the egg market in problem 9, the government imposes a quota of 1,500 dozen eggs a week.

a. What is the price that consumers of eggs pay?

b. What is the revenue that egg producers get?

part 2

Markets for Goods and Services

Alice Nakamura is the Francis Winspear Professor of Business at the University of Alberta, where she has spent her entire professional career. Born in Boston, Massachusetts, in 1945, she was an undergraduate at the University of Wisconsin and a graduate student at Johns Hopkins University, where she earned her Ph.D. in 1972. She is a past president of the Canadian Economics Association and a prolific author of books and articles on an astonishingly wide array of

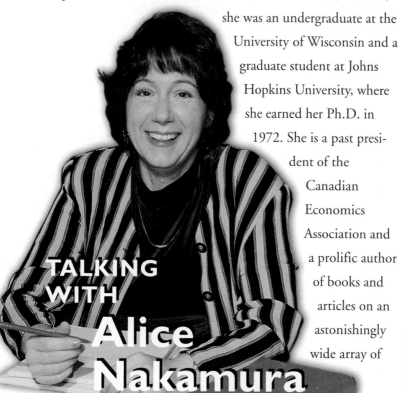

TALKING WITH Alice Nakamura

issues including the role of women in the labour market and the comparative behaviour of American and Japanese firms. She has also made contributions to econometrics (the application of statistical and mathematical tools to economics). Robin Bade and Michael Parkin talked with Alice Nakamura about her work and about how markets work and how they help people cope with the fundamental economic problem of scarcity.

What attracted you to economics?

As Paul Davenport said in his citation for the honorary doctorate that the University of Western Ontario bestowed on me June 10, 1996, I was "born into economics." Those students who study econometrics and learn about the Cochrane-Orcutt iterative technique, read the literature on trade elasticities, or discover the evolving literature on microsimulation modelling will find references to the work of my father, Guy H. Orcutt— work that I grew up hearing him talk about at home. While I understood little of the technical aspects of his research before taking college-level courses in economics, I came to believe that improving our understanding of human economic behaviour and institutions is one of the main ways in which significant improvements in the human condition can be achieved.

My choice of economics as a profession was also shaped by external events. My college years coincided with the Vietnam war years. The issues that the war brought to public prominence underlined the key role of economic behaviour in everything from U.S. and allied involvement in the war to the racial composition of the U.S. combat forces to the role of women in the domestic economy. The combination of current affairs and beliefs instilled in me by my parents ultimately led me to give up my initial career choice of music and the piano for the study of economics.

> *I came to believe that improving our understanding of human economic behaviour and institutions is one of the main ways in which significant improvements in the human condition can be achieved.*

Most of your work, even when it deals with policy issues, uses rigorous mathematical and statistical methods. Can economics be done without mathematics or is a good grounding in math essential for an economist today?

I am currently striving to upgrade my own knowledge of mathematics. This is a powerful analytical tool and mode for expression for both conceptual and empirical research in economics, though I am not one who supports the use of mathematical deduction from asserted axioms of economic behaviour as a substitute for the direct observation and analysis of real-life economic activity.

You've studied an astonishingly wide array of topics. What do you regard as the most important issue that your work has shed light on?

My published research is mostly in the areas of econometric methodology, empirical labour economics, microeconomics studies of firm behaviour, microsimulation modelling, and the study of price and productivity indexes, though I do also have papers in other areas such as forensic economics and public finance: a seemingly unrelated array of topics. However,

almost all of my research is actually linked in one way or another to core interests in the determinants of employment and earnings. For instance, my work with my husband, Masao Nakamura, on specification error testing is econometric methodology research that was motivated by problems we were struggling with in our empirical research on the determinants of the employment and earnings of married women.

I believe that the main substantive contributions of my research to date are the results from joint research with my husband that establish that the labour market behaviour of married women, with respect to both the wage elasticity of hours of work and continuity over time for those who had been working full year, is quite similar to that of men. These results are so accepted by now that many younger economists probably do not recognize these as "findings." However, at the point in time when we published our first papers on that topic, the established view was that the wage elasticity was positive and large for women, but small and perhaps negative for men, and that the employment behaviour of married

women was predominately intermittent in contrast to the continuity of work effort for men. Those prevailing views affected public policy concerning labour relations regulations, the treatment of women under transfer programs such as employment insurance, public and employer education and training investments in women versus men, the design of tax policies, and many other important areas. The prevailing views were so strongly entrenched that we had considerable difficulty publishing our initial research on this topic, though this was also why journals ultimately accepted the papers. (Findings that break new ground are both a curse and boon when it comes to publication.)

Are women being treated appropriately by the market economy of the 1990s?

I feel a great deal of progress has been made since I was in college in the areas of education, training, and employment opportunities for women, though there are clearly areas in which there is still room for improvement.

To me, there is also an urgent need for accompanying progress on ensuring that the needs of children for nurturing and material support are adequately met. Large numbers of married women with small children are now working full time. Perhaps it is partly due to the erosion of earnings and job security for working men—both real and perceived—that relatively few families seem to be responding to the increased employment opportunities for women by opting for work patterns for fathers that allow substantially more time for parenting and other "home production" activities. Rather, it appears that family inputs into child rearing have been and are continuing to be reduced, on average. Nor have these reductions been fully counterbalanced by increases in market and public sector services for children.

The situation of children has been further complicated by the fact that the growth in employment and earnings opportunities for women has gone together with widespread changes in family structure that lead to increases in the proportions of children growing up with lone mothers or in family units that do not include their biological fathers. Women are still less likely to work, less likely to work full time, and less likely to earn as much per hour as men, and the changes in family structure mean fewer children are in family units with male earners committed to their material support.

I do not feel that efforts to end the remaining vestiges of discrimination against women in our labour markets should be put on hold till the associated problems of ensuring that the needs of children are met can be solved, but I would like to see a greater public emphasis on the child-related problems.

Why are there so few women in economics?
When I was in college, it was still widely believed that women did not have the type of minds needed for careers in mathematics, and hence also in economics because of the central role of mathematics in modern economics.

I believe many women decided not to take economics courses because they believed they would do poorly, and that those women like myself who did take the courses gave up more readily than would otherwise have been the case when they encountered material that proved difficult to understand. I believe this is part of the explanation for why there are few

> *There has been an increase in both the number and prominence of women in the economics profession over the course of my professional life, and I expect these trends to continue.*

"senior" women faculty in economics who have made truly substantial contributions to the profession. Poor initial job opportunities for the women of my vintage who *did* do well in their graduate studies and poor access to mentoring and professional networks, is surely another part of the explanation.

What trends do we see in the number and prominence of women in the economics profession?
There has been an increase in both the number and prominence of women in the economics profession over the course of my professional life, and I expect these trends to continue.

What are the most important features of the working markets that we do not understand and that will repay further research?
I feel there are many important issues having to do with the allocation of resources and productive activities among the private sector (with its price-based market allocation mechanisms); the public sector (with its electoral-based allocation mechanisms); the nonprofit, nongovernment sector (NGOs

with their self-designated, internal resource allocation mechanisms); and families (household production units).

I feel there is an urgent need for research on factors affecting employment levels and wages— everything from macro studies of how interest rates and trade and tax policies have, or could, alter employment outcomes to micro studies of how firms make hiring and remuneration decisions and how individuals make their choices about labour supply.

What should a student just embarking on a career in business or economics study today?
Ideally, those pursuing a career in business need solid preparation in both the "tools" of the business world, such as accounting and the use of computers for common business applications, and an area of applied specialization, such as marketing or human resource management, business information systems, business law, or international finance. Practical knowledge in the area where a student intends to seek employment, including relevant summer or co-op job experiences, also helps greatly.

Utility and Demand

After studying this chapter, you will be able to:

■ Explain the limits to consumers' spending

■ Define total utility and marginal utility

■ Explain the marginal utility theory of consumer choice

■ Use marginal utility theory to predict the effects of changing prices

■ Use marginal utility theory to predict the effects of changing income

■ Define and calculate consumer surplus

■ Explain the paradox of value

We need water to live. We don't need diamonds for much besides decoration.

If the benefits of water far outweigh the benefits of diamonds, why, then, does

Water, Water, Everywhere

water cost practically nothing while diamonds are terribly expensive? ◆ When OPEC restricted its sale of oil in 1973, it created a dramatic rise in price, but people continued to use almost as much oil as they had before.

Our demand for oil was price inelastic. But why? ◆ When the CD player was

introduced in 1983, it cost more than $1,000, and consumers didn't buy very

many of them. Since then, the price has decreased dramatically, and people are

buying them in enormous quantities. Our demand for CD players is price elas-

tic. What makes the demand for some things price elastic while the demand for

others is price inelastic? ◆ Over the past 50 years, there have been dramatic

changes in the way we spend our incomes. Spending on cars has increased from

5 percent of expenditure during the 1940s to more than 15 percent of expendi-

ture today. Spending on food has fallen from 30 percent of expenditure during

the 1940s to less than 20 percent of expenditure today. Why, as incomes rise,

does the proportion of income spent on some goods rise and on others fall?

◈ In the preceding three chapters, you saw that demand has a major effect on

prices. You are now going to look behind the market demand curve at the forces

that shape a person's demand. You are going to learn how people make their

buying decisions and how those decisions lead to the law of demand. You are

also going to gain some new insights into the forces that determine prices. You

will learn why, for example, the prices of some things, such as diamonds and

water, are so out of proportion to their total benefits.

Household Consumption Choices

A HOUSEHOLD'S CONSUMPTION CHOICES ARE determined by many factors, but we can summarize all of these factors under two concepts:

- Budget constraint
- Preferences

Budget Constraint

A household's consumption choices are constrained by its income and by the prices of the goods and services it buys. The household has a given amount of income to spend and cannot influence the prices of the goods and services it buys.

The limits to a household's consumption choices are described by its *budget line*. To make the concept of the household's budget line as clear as possible, we'll consider the example of Lisa's household. Lisa has an income of $30 a month to spend. She buys two goods—movies and pop. Movies cost $6 each; pop costs $3 for a six-pack. If Lisa spends all of her income, she will reach the limits to her consumption of movies and pop.

Figure 7.1 illustrates Lisa's possible consumption levels of movies and pop. Rows *a* through *f* in the table show six possible ways of allocating $30 to these two goods. For example, Lisa can see 2 movies for $12 and buy 6 six-packs for $18 (row *c*). The same possibilities are presented by the dots *a* through *f* in the figure. The line passing through these points is Lisa's budget line.

Lisa's budget line is a constraint on her choices. It marks the boundary between what is affordable and what is unaffordable. She can afford all the points on the line and inside it. She cannot afford points outside the line. The constraint on her consumption depends on prices and on her income, and the constraint changes when prices and her income change.

Preferences

How does Lisa divide her $30 between these two goods? The answer depends on her likes and dislikes—her *preferences*. Economists use the concept of utility to describe preferences. The benefit or satisfaction that a person gets from the consumption of a good or service is called **utility**. But what exactly is utility and in what units can we measure it? Utility is an abstract concept and its units are arbitrary.

Consumption Possibilities

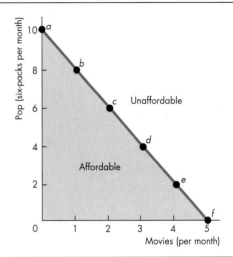

| Possibility | Movies | | Pop | |
	Quantity	Expenditure (dollars)	Six-packs	Expenditure (dollars)
a	0	0	10	30
b	1	6	8	24
c	2	12	6	18
d	3	18	4	12
e	4	24	2	6
f	5	30	0	0

Rows *a* through *f* in the table show six possible ways of allocating $30 to movies and pop. For example, Lisa can buy 2 movies and 6 six-packs (row *c*). The combination in each row costs $30. These possibilities are points *a* through *f* in the figure. The line through those points is a boundary between what Lisa can afford and cannot afford. Her choices must lie along the line *af* or inside the orange area.

Temperature—An Analogy   Temperature is an abstract concept and the units of temperature are arbitrary. You know when you feel hot and you know when you feel cold. But you can't *observe* temperature. You can observe water turning to steam if it is hot enough or turning to ice if it is cold enough. You can construct an instrument, called a thermometer, that can help you to predict when such changes will occur. The scale on the thermometer is what we call temperature. But the units in which we measure temperature are arbitrary. For example, we can accurately predict that when a Celsius thermometer shows a temperature of 0°, water will turn to ice. But the units of measurement do not matter because this same event also occurs when a Fahrenheit thermometer shows a temperature of 32°.

The concept of utility helps us make predictions about consumption choices in much the same way that the concept of temperature helps us make predictions about physical phenomena. It has to be admitted, though, that the marginal utility theory is not as precise as the theory that enables us to predict when water will turn to ice or steam.

Let's now see how we can use the concept of utility to describe preferences.

Total Utility

Total utility is the total benefit or satisfaction that a person gets from the consumption of goods and services. Total utility depends on the person's level of consumption—more consumption generally gives more total utility. Table 7.1 shows Lisa's total utility from movies and pop. If she sees no movies, she gets no utility from movies. If she sees 1 movie in a month, she gets 50 units of utility. As the number of movies she sees in a month increases, her total utility increases; if she sees 10 movies a month, she gets 250 units of total utility. The other part of the table shows Lisa's total utility from pop. If she drinks no pop, she gets no utility from pop. As the amount of pop she drinks increases, her total utility increases.

Marginal Utility

Marginal utility is the change in total utility resulting from a one-unit increase in the quantity of a good consumed. The table in Fig. 7.2 shows the calculation of Lisa's marginal utility of movies. When her consumption of movies increases from 4 to 5 movies a month, her total utility from movies increases from 150 units to 175 units. Thus for Lisa, the marginal utility of seeing a fifth movie each month is 25 units. Notice that marginal utility appears midway between the quantities of consumption. It does so because it is the *change* in consumption from 4 to 5 movies that produces the *marginal* utility of 25 units. The table displays calculations of marginal utility for each level of movie consumption.

TABLE 7.1

Lisa's Total Utility from Movies and Pop

Movies		Pop	
Quantity per month	Total utility	Six-packs per month	Total utility
0	0	0	0
1	50	1	75
2	88	2	117
3	121	3	153
4	150	4	181
5	175	5	206
6	196	6	225
7	214	7	243
8	229	8	260
9	241	9	276
10	250	10	291
11	256	11	305
12	259	12	318
13	261	13	330
14	262	14	341

Figure 7.2(a) illustrates the total utility that Lisa gets from movies. The more movies Lisa sees in a month, the more total utility she gets. Part (b) illustrates her marginal utility. This graph tells us that as Lisa sees more movies, the marginal utility that Lisa gets from watching movies decreases. For example, her marginal utility decreases from 50 units for the first movie to 38 units from the second and 33 units from the third. We call this decrease in marginal utility as the quantity of a good consumed increases the principle of **diminishing marginal utility**.

Marginal utility is positive but diminishes as the consumption of a good increases. Why does marginal utility have these two features? In Lisa's case, she likes movies, and the more she sees the better. That's why marginal utility is positive. The benefit that Lisa gets from the last movie seen is its marginal utility. To see why marginal utility diminishes, think about how you'd feel in the following two situations: In one,

FIGURE 7.2
Total Utility and Marginal Utility

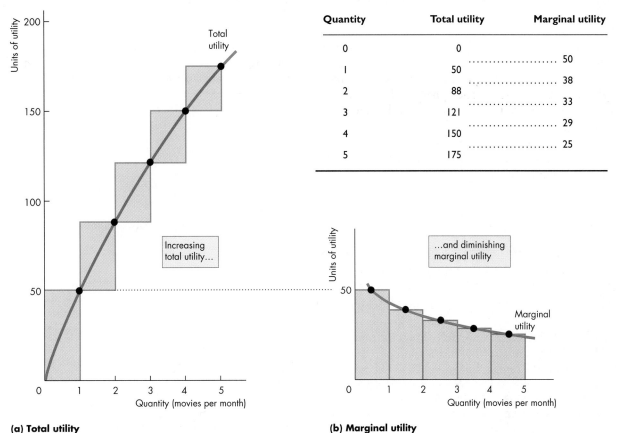

Quantity	Total utility	Marginal utility
0	0	
		50
1	50	
		38
2	88	
		33
3	121	
		29
4	150	
		25
5	175	

(a) Total utility

(b) Marginal utility

The table shows that as Lisa sees more movies, her total utility from movies increases. The table also shows her marginal utility—the change in utility resulting from the last movie seen. Marginal utility declines as consumption increases. The figure graphs Lisa's total utility and marginal utility from

movies. Part (a) shows her total utility. It also shows as a bar the extra utility she gains from each additional movie—her marginal utility. Part (b) shows how Lisa's marginal utility from movies diminishes by placing the bars shown in part (a) side by side as a series of declining steps.

you've just been studying for 29 evenings in a row. An opportunity arises to see a movie. The utility you get from that movie is the marginal utility from seeing one movie in a month. In the second situation, you've been on a movie binge. For the past 29 nights, you have not even looked at an assignment or studied for a test. You are up to your eyeballs in movies. You are happy enough to go to a movie on yet one more night. But the thrill that you get out of that thirtieth movie in 30 days is not very large. It is the marginal utility of the thirtieth movie in a month.

R E V I E W

- Consumption possibilities are limited by the consumer's income and the prices of goods.
- Consumers' preferences can be described by using the concept of utility, and marginal utility theory assumes that the greater the quantity of a good consumed, the larger is total utility, and as the quantity of a good consumed increases, the marginal utility from that good decreases.

Maximizing Utility

A household's income and the prices that it faces limit the utility that it can obtain. The key assumption of marginal utility theory is that, taking into consideration the income available for spending and the prices they face, households consume the quantities of goods and services that maximize total utility. The assumption of utility maximization is a way of expressing the fundamental economic problem. People's wants exceed the resources available to satisfy those wants, so they must make hard choices. In making choices, they try to get the maximum attainable benefit—they try to maximize total utility.

Let's see how Lisa allocates $30 a month between movies and pop to maximize her total utility. We'll continue to assume that movies cost $6 each and pop costs $3 a six-pack.

The Utility-Maximizing Choice

The most direct way of calculating how Lisa spends her income to maximize her total utility is by making a table like Table 7.2. This table shows the same affordable combinations of movies and pop that you can find on her budget line in Fig. 7.1. The table records three things: first, the number of movies seen and the total utility derived from them (the left side of the table); second, the number of six-packs of pop consumed and the total utility derived from them (the right side of the table); and third, the total utility derived from both movies and pop (the centre column of the table).

The first row of Table 7.2 records the situation if Lisa watches no movies and buys 10 six-packs. In this case, she gets no utility from movies and 291 units of total utility from pop. Her total utility from movies and pop (the centre column) is 291 units. The rest of the table is constructed in the same way.

The consumption of movies and pop that maximizes Lisa's total utility is highlighted in the table. When Lisa consumes 2 movies and 6 six-packs of pop, she gets 313 units of total utility. This is the best Lisa can do given that she has only $30 to spend and given the prices of movies and six-packs. If she buys 8 six-packs of pop, she can see only 1 movie and gets 310 units of total utility, 3 less than the maximum attainable. If she sees 3 movies and drinks only 4 six-packs, she gets 302 units of total utility, 11 less than the maximum attainable.

TABLE 7.2
Lisa's Utility-Maximizing Combinations

Movies		Total utility from movies and pop	Pop	
Quantity per month	Total utility		Total utility	Six-packs per month
0	0	291	291	10
1	50	310	260	8
2	88	313	225	6
3	121	302	181	4
4	150	267	117	2
5	175	175	0	0

We've just described a consumer equilibrium. A **consumer equilibrium** is a situation in which a consumer has allocated his or her income in the way that, given the prices of goods and services, maximizes his or her total utility.

In finding Lisa's consumer equilibrium, we measured her *total* utility from the consumption of movies and pop. There is a better way of determining a consumer equilibrium, which does not involve measuring total utility at all. Let's look at this alternative.

Equalizing Marginal Utility per Dollar Spent

Another way to find out the allocation that maximizes a consumer's total utility is to make the marginal utility per dollar spent on each good equal for all goods. The **marginal utility per dollar spent** is the marginal utility obtained from the last unit of a good consumed divided by the price of the good. For example, Lisa's marginal utility from seeing the first movie is 50 units of utility. The price of a movie is $6, which means that the marginal utility per dollar spent on movies is 50 units divided by $6, or 8.33 units of utility per dollar.

Total utility is maximized when all the consumer's income is spent and when the marginal utility per dollar spent is equal for all goods.

Lisa maximizes total utility when she spends all her income and consumes movies and pop such that

$$\frac{\text{Marginal utility from movies}}{\text{Price of a movie}} = \frac{\text{Marginal utility from pop}}{\text{Price of pop}}.$$

Call all the marginal utility from movies MU_m, the marginal utility from pop MU_p, the price of a movie P_m, and the price of pop P_p. Then Lisa's utility is maximized when she spends all her income and when

$$\frac{MU_m}{P_m} = \frac{MU_p}{P_p}.$$

Let's use this formula to find Lisa's utility-maximizing allocation of her income.

Table 7.3 sets out Lisa's marginal utilities per dollar spent for both movies and pop. For example, in row *b*, Lisa's marginal utility from movies is 50 units, and since movies cost $6 each, her marginal utility per dollar spent on movies is 8.33 units per dollar (50 units divided by $6). Each row exhausts Lisa's income of $30. You can see that Lisa's marginal utility per dollar spent on each good, like marginal utility itself, decreases as more of the good is consumed.

Total utility is maximized when the marginal utility per dollar spent on movies is equal to the marginal utility per dollar spent on pop—possibility *c*—when Lisa consumes 2 movies and 6 six-packs.

TABLE 7.3

Equalizing Marginal Utilities per Dollar Spent

		Movies ($6 each)			Pop ($3 per six-pack)	
	Quantity	Marginal utility	Marginal utility per dollar spent	Six-packs	Marginal utility	Marginal utility per dollar spent
a	0	0		10	15	5.00
b	1	50	8.33	8	17	5.67
c	2	38	6.33	6	19	6.33
d	3	33	5.50	4	28	9.33
e	4	29	4.83	2	42	14.00
f	5	25	4.17	0	0	

Figure 7.3 shows why the rule "equalize marginal utility per dollar spent on all goods" works. Suppose that instead of consuming 2 movies and 6 six-packs (possibility *c*), Lisa consumes 1 movie and 8 six-packs (possibility *b*). She then gets 8.33 units of utility from the last dollar spent on movies and 5.67 units from the last dollar spent on pop. Lisa can increase her total utility by buying less pop and seeing more movies. If she spends a dollar less on pop and a dollar more on movies, her total utility from pop decreases by 5.67 units and her total utility from movies increases by 8.33 units. Lisa's total utility increases by 2.66 units.

FIGURE 7.3

Equalizing Marginal Utilities per Dollar Spent

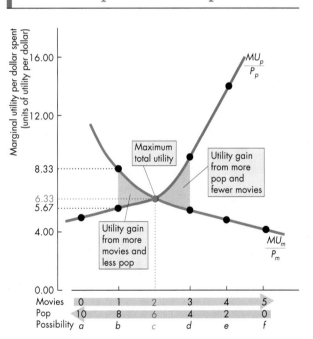

If Lisa consumes 1 movie and 8 six-packs of pop (possibility *b*), she gets 8.33 units of utility from the last dollar spent on movies and 5.67 units of utility from the last dollar spent on pop. She can get more total utility by seeing one more movie. If she consumes 4 six-packs and 3 movies (possibility *d*), she gets 5.50 units of utility from the last dollar spent on movies and 9.33 units of utility from the last dollar spent on pop. She can get more total utility by seeing one less movie. When Lisa's marginal utility per dollar spent on both goods is equal, her total utility is maximized.

Or, suppose that Lisa consumes 3 movies and 4 six-packs (possibility *d*). In this situation, her marginal utility from the last dollar spent on movies is less than her marginal utility from the last dollar spent on pop. Lisa can now increase her total utility by spending less on movies and more on pop.

The Power of Marginal Analysis   The method we've just used to maximize Lisa's utility is an example of the power of *marginal analysis.* By comparing the marginal gain from having more of one good with the marginal loss from having less of another good, Lisa is able to ensure that she gets the maximum attainable utility.

In the example, Lisa consumes at the point at which the marginal utility per dollar spent on movies and pop are equal. Because we buy goods and services in indivisible lumps, the numbers don't always work out so precisely. But the basic approach always works. The rule to follow is very simple: If the marginal utility per dollar spent on movies exceeds the marginal utility per dollar spent on pop, buy more movies and less pop; if the marginal utility per dollar spent on pop exceeds the marginal utility per dollar spent on movies, buy more pop and fewer movies.

More generally, if the marginal gain from an action exceeds the marginal loss, take the action. You will meet this principle time and again in your study of economics. And you will find yourself using it every time you make your own economic choices.

Units of Utility   In calculating the utility-maximizing allocation of income in Table 7.3 and Fig. 7.3, we have not used the concept of total utility at all. All the calculations have been performed using marginal utility and price. By making the marginal utility per dollar spent equal for both goods, we know that Lisa has maximized her total utility.

This way of viewing maximum utility is important; it means that the units in which utility is measured do not matter. We could double or halve all the numbers measuring utility, or multiply them by any other positive number, or square them, or take their square roots. None of these transformations of the units used to measure utility makes any difference to the outcome. It is in this respect that utility is analogous to temperature. Our prediction about the freezing of water does not depend on the temperature scale; our prediction about maximizing utility does not depend on the units of utility.

R E V I E W

■ A consumer chooses the quantities of goods and services that maximize total utility.

■ The consumer does so by spending all available income and by making the marginal utility per dollar spent on each good equal.

■ When marginal utilities per dollar spent are equal for all goods, a consumer cannot reallocate spending to get more total utility.

Predictions of Marginal Utility Theory

LET'S NOW USE MARGINAL UTILITY THEORY TO make some predictions. What happens to Lisa's consumption of movies and pop when their prices change and when her income changes?

A Fall in the Price of Movies

To determine the effect of a change in price on consumption requires three steps. First, determine the combinations of movies and pop that just exhaust the income at the new prices. Second, calculate the new marginal utilities per dollar spent. Third, determine the combinations that make the marginal utility per dollar spent on each good equal.

Table 7.4 shows the combinations of movies and pop that exactly exhaust Lisa's $30 of income when movies cost $3 each and pop costs $3 a six-pack. Her preferences do not change when prices change, so her marginal utility schedule remains the same as that in Table 7.3. But now we divide her marginal utility from movies by $3, the new price of a movie, to get the marginal utility per dollar spent on movies.

To find how Lisa responds to a fall in the price of a movie compare her new utility-maximizing allocation (Table 7.4) with her original allocation (Table 7.3). Lisa sees more movies (up from 2 to 5 a month) and drinks less pop (down from 6 to 5 six-packs a month). That is, Lisa substitutes movies for pop. Figure 7.4 illustrates these effects. In part (a), a fall in the price of movies produces a movement along Lisa's demand curve for movies, and in part (b), it shifts her demand curve for pop.

TABLE 7.4
How a Change in Price of Movies Affects Lisa's Choices

Movies ($3 each)		Pop ($3 per six-pack)	
Quantity	Marginal utility per dollar spent	Six-packs	Marginal utility per dollar spent
0		10	5.00
1	16.67	9	5.33
2	12.67	8	5.67
3	11.00	7	6.00
4	9.67	6	6.33
5	8.33	5	8.33
6	7.00	4	9.33
7	6.00	3	12.00
8	5.00	2	14.00
9	4.00	1	25.00
10	3.00	0	

A Rise in the Price of Pop

Table 7.5 shows the combinations of movies and pop that exactly exhaust Lisa's $30 of income when movies cost $3 each and pop costs $6 a six-pack. Now we divide her marginal utility from pop by $6, the new price of a six-pack, to get the marginal utility per dollar spent on pop.

The effect of the rise in the price of pop on Lisa's consumption is seen by comparing her new utility-maximizing allocation (Table 7.5) with her previous allocation (Table 7.4). Lisa responds to a rise in the price of pop by drinking less pop (down from 5 to 2 six-packs a month) and seeing more movies (up from 5 to 6 a month). That is, Lisa substitutes movies for pop when the price of pop rises. Figure 7.5 illustrates these effects. In part (a), a rise in the price of pop produces a movement along Lisa's demand curve for pop, and in part (b), the rise in the price of pop shifts her demand curve for movies.

FIGURE 7.4
A Fall in the Price of Movies

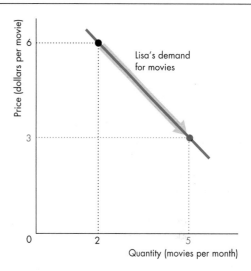

(a) Movies

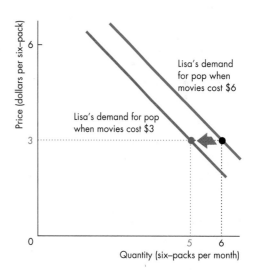

(b) Pop

When the price of a movie falls and the price of pop remains constant, the quantity of movies demanded by Lisa increases, and in part (a), Lisa moves along her demand curve for movies. Also, Lisa's demand for pop decreases, and in part (b), her demand curve for pop shifts leftward.

TABLE 7.5

How a Change in Price of Pop Affects Lisa's Choices

Movies ($3 each)		Pop ($6 per six-pack)	
Quantity	Marginal utility per dollar spent	Six-packs	Marginal utility per dollar spent
0		5	4.17
2	12.67	4	4.67
4	9.67	3	6.00
6	7.00	2	7.00
8	5.00	1	12.50
10	3.00	0	

Marginal utility theory predicts these two results:

- When the price of a good rises, the quantity demanded of that good decreases.
- If the price of one good rises, the demand for another good that can serve as a substitute increases.

Does this sound familiar? It should. These predictions of marginal utility theory correspond to the assumptions that we made about consumer demand in Chapter 4. There we *assumed* that the demand curve for a good sloped downward, and we *assumed* that a rise in the price of a substitute of a good increased the demand for the good.

We have now seen that marginal utility theory predicts how the quantities of goods and services that people demand respond to price changes. The theory helps us to understand both the shape and the position of the demand curve. It also helps us to understand how the demand curve for one good shifts when the price of another good changes. Marginal utility theory also helps us to understand one further thing about demand—how it changes when income changes. Let's study the effects of a change in income on consumption.

FIGURE 7.5

A Rise in the Price of Pop

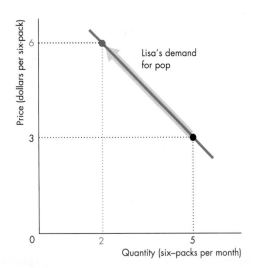

(a) Pop

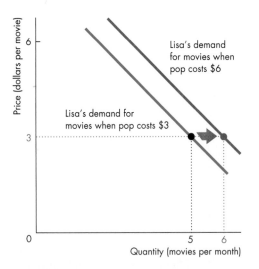

(b) Movies

When the price of pop rises and the price of a movie remains constant, the quantity of pop demanded by Lisa decreases, and in part (a), Lisa moves along her demand curve for pop. Also,

Lisa's demand for movies increases, and in part (b), her demand curve for movies shifts rightward.

A Rise in Income

Let's suppose that Lisa's income increases to $42 a month and that movies cost $3 each and a six-pack costs $3. We saw, in Table 7.4, that with these prices and with an income of $30 a month, Lisa consumes 5 movies and 5 six-packs a month. We want to compare this consumption of movies and pop with Lisa's consumption at an income of $42. The calculations for the comparison are shown in Table 7.6. With $42, Lisa can buy 14 movies a month and no pop or 14 six-packs a month and no movies or any combination of the two goods as shown in the rows of the table. We calculate the marginal utility per dollar spent in exactly the same way as we did before and find the quantities at which the marginal utilities per dollar spent on movies and on pop are equal. With an income of $42, the marginal utility per dollar spent on each good is equal when Lisa watches 7 movies and drinks 7 six-packs of pop a month.

By comparing this situation with that in Table 7.4, we see that with an additional $12 a month, Lisa consumes 2 more six-packs and 2 more movies. This response arises from Lisa's preferences, as described by her marginal utilities. Different preferences produce different quantitative responses. A higher income always brings a larger consumption of a *normal good* and a smaller consumption of an *inferior good*. For Lisa, pop and movies are normal goods. When her income increases, Lisa buys more of both goods.

You have now completed your study of the marginal utility theory of a household's consumption decisions. Table 7.7 summarizes the key assumptions, implication, and predictions of the theory.

TABLE 7.6

Lisa's Choices with an Income of $42 a Month

Movies ($3 each)		Pop ($3 per six-pack)	
Quantity	Marginal utility per dollar spent	Six-packs	Marginal utility per dollar spent
0		14	3.67
1	16.67	13	4.00
2	12.67	12	4.33
3	11.00	11	4.67
4	9.67	10	5.00
5	**8.33**	9	5.33
6	7.00	8	5.67
7	6.00	7	6.00
8	5.00	6	6.33
9	4.00	**5**	**8.33**
10	3.00	4	9.33
11	2.00	3	12.00
12	1.00	2	14.00
13	0.67	1	25.00
14	0.33	0	

TABLE 7.7

Marginal Utility Theory

Assumptions

- A consumer derives utility from the goods consumed.

- Each additional unit of consumption yields additional total utility; marginal utility is positive.

- As the quantity of a good consumed increases, marginal utility decreases.

- A consumer's aim is to maximize total utility.

Implication

Utility is maximized when all the available income is spent and when the marginal utility per dollar spent is equal for all goods.

Predictions

- Other things remaining the same, the higher the price of a good, the lower is the quantity bought (the law of demand).

- The higher the price of a good, the greater is the consumption of substitutes for that good.

- The higher the consumer's income, the greater is the quantity demanded of normal goods.

Individual Demand and Market Demand

One purpose of marginal utility theory is to explain both how an individual household spends its income and an individual household's demand. But the main purpose of the theory is to explain market demand. Let's look at the connection between the individual demand and market demand.

The relationship between the quantity demanded of a good by a single individual and its price is called *individual demand.* And the relationship between the total quantity demanded of a good and its price is called **market demand**.

Figure 7.6 illustrates the relationship between individual demand and market demand. In this example, Lisa and Chuck are the only people. The market demand is the total demand of Lisa and Chuck. At $3 a movie, Lisa demands 5 movies a month and Chuck demands 2, so the total quantity demanded by the market is 7 movies a month. Lisa's demand curve for movies in part (a) and Chuck's in part (b) sum *horizontally* to give the market demand curve in part (c).

The market demand curve is the horizontal sum of the individual demand curves and is formed by adding the quantities demanded by each individual at each price.

Because marginal utility theory predicts that individual demand curves slope downward, it also predicts that market demand curves slope downward.

FIGURE 7.6

Individual and Market Demand Curves

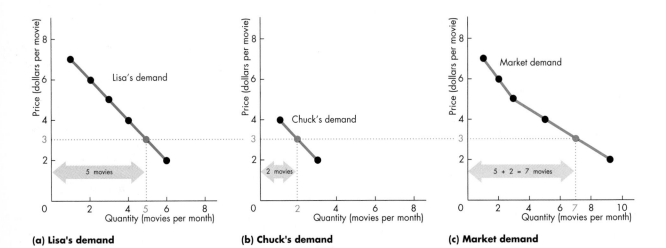

(a) Lisa's demand

(b) Chuck's demand

(c) Market demand

Price	Quantity of movies demanded		
(dollars per movie)	Lisa	Chuck	Market
7	1	0	1
6	2	0	2
5	3	0	3
4	4	1	5
3	5	2	7
2	6	3	9

The table and diagram illustrate how the quantity of movies demanded varies as the price of a movie varies. In the table, the market demand is the sum of the individual demands. For example, at a price of $3, Lisa demands 5 movies and Chuck demands 2 movies, so the total quantity demanded in the market is 7 movies. In the diagram, the market demand curve is the horizontal sum of the individual demand curves. Thus when the price is $3, the market demand curve shows that the quantity demanded is 7 movies, the sum of the quantities demanded by Lisa and Chuck.

Marginal Utility and the Real World

Marginal utility theory can be used to answer a wide range of questions about the real world. The theory can be used to interpret some of the facts set out at the beginning of this chapter—for example, why the demand for CD players is price elastic and the demand for oil is price inelastic. Elasticities of demand are determined by preferences. The feature of our preferences that determine elasticity is the step size with which marginal utility declines—the steepness of the marginal utility steps in Fig. 7.2(b).

Goods differ in the rate at which marginal utility diminishes as consumption increases. For example, it seems likely that the marginal utility of hot chili diminishes more rapidly than the marginal utility of chicken. For chicken, it takes a large change in the quantity bought to bring about a small change in marginal utility. So when the price of chicken changes by a small amount, there must be a large change in the quantity of chicken demanded to restore consumer equilibrium. The demand for chicken is elastic. For hot chili, a small change in the quantity bought brings about a large change in marginal utility. So when the price of chili changes, a small change in the quantity of chili demanded restores consumer equilibrium. The demand for chili is inelastic.

But the marginal utility theory can do much more than explain *consumption* choices. It can be used to explain *all* household choices such as the allocation of time between work in the home, office, or factory and leisure. It is even used by economic demographers to predict the number of children people will have!

R E V I E W

- When the price of a good falls and the prices of other goods and the consumer's income remain the same, the consumer increases consumption of the good whose price has fallen and decreases demands for other goods.
- These changes result in a movement along the demand curve for the good whose price has changed and a shift in the demand curves for other goods whose prices have remained constant.
- When a consumer's income increases, the consumer can afford to buy more of all goods and the quantity bought increases for all *normal* goods.

Criticisms of Marginal Utility Theory

MARGINAL UTILITY THEORY HELPS US TO understand the choices people make and to predict how those choices change in response to price and income changes. But there are some criticisms of this theory. Let's look at them.

Utility Can't Be Observed

Agreed—we can't observe utility. But we do not need to observe it to use it. We can and do observe the quantities of goods and services that people consume, the prices of those goods and services, and people's incomes. Our goal is to understand the consumption choices that people make and to predict the effects of changes in prices and incomes on these choices. To make such predictions, we *assume* that people derive utility from their consumption, that more consumption yields more utility, that marginal utility diminishes, and that people attempt to maximize total utility. From these assumptions, we make predictions about the directions of change in consumption when prices and incomes change. As we've already seen, the actual numbers we use to express utility do not matter. Consumers maximize total utility by making the marginal utility per dollar spent on each good equal. As long as we use the same scale to express utility for all goods, we'll get the same answer regardless of the units on our scale. In this regard, utility is similar to temperature—water freezes when it's cold enough, and that occurs independently of the temperature scale used.

"People Aren't That Smart"

Some critics maintain that marginal utility theory must be wrong because it assumes that people are supercomputers—or at least rocket scientists. It implies, such critics say, that people look at the marginal utility of every good at every different quantity they might consume, divide those numbers by the prices of the goods, and then find the quantities at which the marginal utility per dollar spent is the same for each good.

This criticism of marginal utility theory confuses the actions of people in the real world with those of people in a model economy. A model economy is no more an actual economy than a model railway is an actual railway. The people in the model economy perform the calculations that we have just described. People in the real world simply decide which is the best deal available. In doing so, they implicitly do the calculations that economists do explicitly. We observe people's consumption choices, not their mental gymnastics. Marginal utility theory says that the consumption patterns we observe in the real world are similar to those implied by a model economy in which people do compute the quantities of goods that maximize total utility. We test how closely the model economy resembles reality by checking the predictions of the model against observed consumption choices.

Marginal utility theory also has some broader implications that provide an interesting way of testing its usefulness. Let's examine two of these.

Implications of Marginal Utility Theory

WE ALL LOVE BARGAINS—PAYING LESS FOR something than its usual price. One implication of the marginal utility theory is that we almost *always* get a bargain when we buy something. That is, we place a higher total value on the things we buy than the amount that it costs us. Let's see why.

Consumer Surplus and the Gains from Trade

People can gain by specializing in the production of the things in which they have a comparative advantage and then trading with each other. These gains are explored in Chapter 3, pp. 53–55. Marginal utility theory gives us a way of measuring the value to consumers of the gains from trade.

When Lisa buys movies and pop, she exchanges her income for them. Does Lisa profit from this exchange? Are the dollars she has to give up worth more or less than the movies and pop are worth to her? As we are about to discover, the principle of diminishing marginal utility guarantees that Lisa, and everyone else, gets more value from the things they buy than the amount of money they give up in exchange.

Calculating Consumer Surplus

The **value** a consumer places on a good is the maximum amount that the person would be willing to pay for it. The amount actually paid for a good is its price. **Consumer surplus** is the value of a good minus its price. When people can buy any chosen quantity of a good at a given price, diminishing marginal utility guarantees that a consumer always makes some consumer surplus. To understand why, let's look again at Lisa's consumption choices.

Figure 7.7(a) shows Lisa's demand curve for movies. If Lisa were able to watch only 1 movie a month, she would be willing to pay $7 to see it. She would be willing to pay $6 to see a second movie, $5 to see a third, and so on.

Luckily for Lisa, she has to pay only $3 for each movie she sees—the market price of a movie. Although she values the first movie she sees in a month at $7, she pays only $3, which is $4 less than she would be willing to pay. The second movie she sees in a month is worth $6 to her. The difference between the value she places on the movie and what she has to pay is $3. The third movie she sees in a month is worth $5 to her, which is $2 more than she has to pay for it, and the fourth movie is worth $4, which is $1 more than she has to pay for it. Figure 7.7(a) highlights the difference between the value she places on the first, second, third, and fourth movies and the price she pays ($3). These differences are a gain to Lisa. The total amount that Lisa is willing to pay for the 5 movies that she sees is $25 (the sum of $7, $6, $5, $4, and $3). She actually pays $15 (5 movies multiplied by $3). The extra value she receives from the movies is therefore $10. This amount is the value of Lisa's consumer surplus. From watching 5 movies a month, she gets $10 worth of value in excess of what she has to spend to see them.

Suppose there are a million consumers similar, but not quite identical, to Lisa. Some are willing to pay $8 for the first movie. At $7.99, even more movies are demanded. And as the price falls a penny at a time, the quantity of movies demanded increases. For the market as a whole, the consumer surplus is the entire area under the demand curve and above the market price line as shown in Fig. 7.7(b). In this case, the consumer surplus can be calculated as the area of the triangle. That area equals the base (5 million movies) multiplied by the height ($5 a movie— $8 minus $3) divided by 2 and equals $12.5 million.

Let's now look at another implication of the marginal utility theory.

FIGURE 7.7
Consumer Surplus

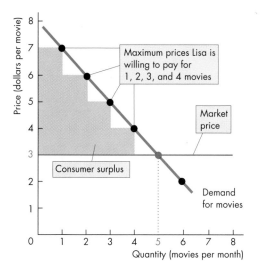

(a) Lisa

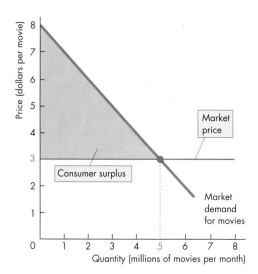

(b) Market

In part (a), Lisa is willing to pay $7 for the first movie, $6 for the second, $5 for the third, $4 for the fourth, and $3 for the fifth. The actual price of a movie is $3, so she sees 5 movies and pays $3 for each. Lisa has a consumer surplus on the first four movies equal to $10 ($4 + $3 + $2 + $1). In part (b), the entire market has a consumer surplus shown by the green triangle. Its value is $12.5 million (the area of the triangle is equal to its base—5 million movies a month—multiplied by its height—$5 a movie—divided by 2).

The Paradox of Value

For centuries, philosophers have been puzzled by a paradox that we raised at the start of this chapter. Water, which is essential to life itself, costs little, but diamonds, which are useless compared to water, are expensive. Why? Adam Smith tried to solve the paradox. But not until the theory of marginal utility had been developed could anyone give a satisfactory answer.

You can solve this puzzle by distinguishing between *total* utility and *marginal* utility. The total utility that we get from water is enormous. But remember, the more we consume of something, the smaller is its marginal utility. We use so much water that the marginal utility—the benefit we get from one more glass of water—diminishes to a tiny value. Diamonds, on the other hand, have a small total utility relative to water, but because we buy few diamonds, they have a high marginal utility.

When a household has maximized total utility, it has allocated its budgets in the way that makes the marginal utility per dollar spent equal for all goods. That is, the marginal utility from a good divided by the price of the good is equal for all goods. This equality of marginal utilities per dollar spent holds true for diamonds and water: Diamonds have a high price and a high marginal utility. Water has a low price and a low marginal utility. When the high marginal utility of diamonds is divided by the high price of diamonds, the result is a number that equals the low marginal utility of water divided by the low price of water. The marginal utility per dollar spent is the same for diamonds as for water.

◆ We've now completed our study of the marginal utility theory of consumption. We've used that theory to examine how Lisa allocates her income between the two goods that she consumes—movies and pop. We've also seen how the theory can be used to resolve the paradox of value. Furthermore, we've seen how the theory can be used to explain our real-world consumption choices. *Reading Between the Lines* on pp. 162–163 shows you one more real-world application—to the market for new age drinks.

In the next chapter, we study an alternative theory of household behaviour. To help you see the connection between the marginal utility theory and the alternative theory, we'll continue with the same example. We'll meet Lisa again and discover another way of understanding how she gets the most out of her $30 a month.

The Utility of New Products

GLOBE AND MAIL, JULY 29, 1996

New age drinks lose sparkle

BY ANN GIBBON

A few decades ago, if you wanted to quench your thirst with something non-alcoholic, there wasn't much beyond soda pop or fruit juice.

Clearly Canadian Beverage Corp. helped change all that. In 1988, the Vancouver-based company burst onto the scene with sparkling fruit-flavoured water in clear glass bottles.

Astute marketing helped it redefine the industry and shape a new category: "alternative beverages" or "new age drinks." Exotic sounding concoctions such as kiwi lime and grapefruit spring water and raspberry-flavoured iced tea brought bored tastebuds back from the dead.

Other companies soon poured in, including smaller companies along with the majors like Coca-Cola, which launched Fruitopia drinks.

But the bubbles have gone out of the sector. In most cases, sales have been flat and shares in some companies have tumbled dramatically.

"This particular industry has hit its peak and is declining," said Hellen Berry, vice-president of marketing and research for New York-based Beverage Marketing Corp. She was referring to the entire North American market, with sales of about $5.5 billion (U.S.). "Consumers have moved on to other things." ...

President Peter van Stolk [of Urban Juice and Soda Co.] appreciates that the shelf life of new age beverages can be rather short, just like the attention span of the sector's market—generally people in their twenties.

He compares the new age beverage sector with the fashion industry: "It's subject to trends. And like anything, people get bored with a brand."

To that end, he said he changes his labels regularly. And because he believes each product has a limited life-span, he has been careful never to name a product after his company's name.

Reprinted with permission from *The Globe and Mail.*

Essence of THE STORY

■ In 1988, Clearly Canadian Beverage Corp., a Vancouver-based company, introduced a new category of "alternative beverages" or "new age drinks"—sparkling fruit-flavoured water sold in a clear glass bottle.

■ Other companies, small and large, entered this new market, which reached sales of $5.5 billion (U.S.) a year throughout Canada and the United States.

■ By 1996, sales of "new age drinks" had peaked and were beginning to fall as consumers, mainly people in their twenties, moved on to other things.

Economic

A N A L Y S I S

■ In 1988, a new style drink was created that generated more marginal utility per drink than traditional drinks such as pop.

■ Figure 1 shows some hypothetical marginal utility numbers. The blue bars show the marginal utility of pop and the red bars show the marginal utility of the new drink. In this example, the marginal utility of the new drink ($MU_{new\ age}$) is twice that of pop (MU_{pop}).

■ To maximize utility, a consumer allocates his or her budget to make the marginal utility per dollar spent equal for all goods. So each consumer achieves

$$\frac{MU_{pop}}{Price_{pop}} = \frac{MU_{new\ age}}{Price_{new\ age}}$$

■ If in 1988, a bottle of pop cost $1 and a bottle of new age drink cost $2, the consumer in Fig. 1 would drink an equal number of bottles of each type of drink a week. (The total number of bottles would depend on the consumer's income and on the marginal utility of other goods.)

■ Figure 2 shows what has happened in the market for new age drinks since 1988. Based on consumers' marginal utility schedules, the demand for new age drinks is D.

■ In 1988, the supply of new age drinks was S_0, so the price was $2 a bottle and 1 billion bottles a year were sold.

■ Over the years, many more firms have entered the new age drinks market and the supply curve has shifted rightward to S_1. The price has gradually fallen to $1 a bottle.

■ As the price has fallen, the quantity demanded has increased.

■ Total industry revenue has also increased. In 1988, it was $2 billion (1 billion bottles at $2 a bottle) and by 1995 it was $5.5 billion (5.5 billion bottles at $1 a bottle).

■ It is also possible that the introduction of the 1990s new age drinks (for example, sports drinks) have decreased the marginal utility of the 1980s drinks and decreased the demand for the 1990s drinks.

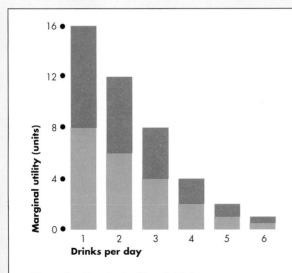

Figure 1   Marginal utility of drinks

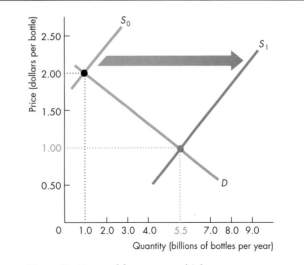

Figure 2   Demand for new age drinks

S U M M A R Y

Key Points

Household Consumption Choices   A household's consumption choices are determined by the constraints it faces and by its preferences. A household is constrained by its income and by the prices of the goods it wants to buy. A household's preferences are described by the marginal utility from the goods consumed. Marginal utility declines as consumption increases. This assumption is the basis of marginal utility theory. Marginal utility theory assumes that people buy the combination that is affordable and that maximizes total utility. (pp. 149–151)

Maximizing Utility   The consumer's goal is to maximize total utility, given the income available to be spent and the prices of the goods and services bought. Total utility is maximized when all the available income is spent and when the marginal utility per dollar spent on each good is equal. (pp. 152–154)

Predictions of Marginal Utility Theory   Marginal utility theory predicts that, other things remaining the same, the higher the price of a good, the smaller is the quantity demanded of that good—the law of demand. The relationship between the price of the good and the quantity demanded by an individual household is called individual demand. Market demand is the sum of all individual demands, and the market demand curve is found by summing horizontally all the individual demand curves. Because individual demand curves slope downward, so do the market demand curves. (pp. 154–159)

Criticisms of Marginal Utility Theory   Utility cannot be observed. But utility does not need to be observed to be used. Marginal utility theory predicts that the ratio of marginal utility to price is equal for all goods. Any arbitrary units can be used to represent utility.

Consumers aren't as smart as marginal utility theory implies. But the theory doesn't predict thought processes of consumers. It predicts their actions by assuming that they spend their income in what seems to them to be the best possible way. (pp. 159–160)

Implications of Marginal Utility Theory   Marginal utility theory implies that we usually get more value for our expenditure than the money we spend. We benefit from consumer surplus, which is equal to the maximum amount that we are willing to pay for a good minus the price that we actually pay.

Marginal utility theory resolves the paradox of value. Value is determined by marginal utility, not total utility. Water, which we consume in large amounts, has a high total utility but a low marginal utility, while diamonds, which we consume in small amounts, have a low total utility and a high marginal utility. (pp. 160–161)

Key Figures and Table

Key Terms

R E V I E W   Q U E S T I O N S

1. What is a household's budget constraint?
2. What determines a household's consumption possibilities?
3. What do we mean by utility?
4. Distinguish between total utility and marginal utility.
5. How does marginal utility from a good change as the household
   a. Increases the amount of the good it consumes?
   b. Decreases the amount of the good it consumes?
6. Susan is a consumer. When is Susan's total utility maximized?
   a. When she has spent all her income.
   b. When she has spent all her income, and marginal utility is equal for all goods.
   c. When she has spent all her income, and the marginal utility per dollar spent is equal for all goods.

   Explain your answers.
7. What does the term "marginal utility per dollar spent" mean?
8. Explain what happens to the marginal utility per dollar spent on a good as
   a. More dollars are spent on the good.
   b. Fewer dollars are spent on the good.
9. What does marginal utility theory predict about the effect of a change in price on the quantity of a good consumed?
10. What does marginal utility theory predict about the effect of a change in the price of one good on the consumption of another good?
11. What does marginal utility theory predict about the effect of a change in income on consumption of a good?
12. What is the relationship between individual demand and market demand?
13. How do we construct a market demand curve from individual demand curves?
14. How would you answer someone who says that marginal utility theory is useless because utility cannot be observed?
15. How would you respond to someone who tells you that marginal utility theory is useless because people are not smart enough to compute a consumer equilibrium in which the marginal utility per dollar spent is equal for all goods?
16. What is the value a consumer places on a good?
17. What is consumer surplus? How is consumer surplus calculated?
18. What is the paradox of value? How does marginal utility theory resolve it?

C R I T I C A L   T H I N K I N G

1. Study *Reading Between the Lines* on pp. 162–163 and then
   a. Summarize the main points of the news article.
   b. Explain how we can interpret the trends described in the article by using marginal utility theory.
2. What can we infer about the elasticity of demand for new age drinks from the information provided in the news article?
3. What predictions can you make about the likely course of revenue from the sale of new age drinks?
4. Are new age drinks a good item to tax from the point of view of the government?
5. Explain why the percentage of income spent on food has decreased while the percentage of income spent on cars has increased since the 1940s.
6. Some provincial governments have recently cut the tax on cigarettes and as a result the price of a pack of cigarettes has decreased. How will smokers adjust their expenditure on cigarettes and other goods? Use marginal utility theory to explain your answer.
7. The City of Toronto recently proposed a ban on smoking in bars. What effect will such a ban have on the utility of smokers? How will smokers adjust their expenditure in bars and on other goods? Use marginal utility theory to explain your answer.

P R O B L E M S

1. Calculate Lisa's marginal utility from pop from the numbers given in Table 7.1. Draw two graphs, one of her total utility and the other of her marginal utility from pop. Make your graphs look similar to those in Fig. 7.2.

2. Max enjoys windsurfing and snorkeling. He obtains the following utility from each of these sports:

Half-hours per month	Utility from windsurfing	Utility from snorkeling
1	60	20
2	110	38
3	150	53
4	180	64
5	200	70
6	206	75
7	211	79
8	215	82
9	218	84

   a. Draw graphs showing Max's utility from windsurfing and from snorkeling.
   b. Compare the two utility graphs. Can you say anything about Max's preferences?
   c. Draw graphs showing Max's marginal utility from windsurfing and from snorkeling.
   d. Compare the two marginal utility graphs. Can you say anything about Max's preferences?

3. Max has $35 to spend. Equipment for windsurfing rents for $10 an hour, while snorkeling equipment rents for $5 an hour. By using this information, together with that given in problem 2, how long will Max choose to windsurf and snorkel?

4. Max's sister gives him $20 to spend on his leisure pursuits, so he now has $55 to spend. How long will Max now windsurf and snorkel?

5. If Max has only $55 to spend and the rent on windsurfing equipment decreases to $5 an hour, how will Max now spend his time windsurfing and snorkeling?

6. Does Max's demand curve for windsurfing slope downward or upward?

7. Max takes a Club Med holiday, the cost of which includes unlimited sports activities. There is no extra charge for any equipment. Max decides to spend a total of three hours each day on windsurfing and snorkeling. How does Max allocate his three hours between windsurfing and snorkeling?

8. Shirley's and Dan's demand schedules for yogurt are:

Price (cents per carton)	Quantity demanded (cartons per week)	
	By Shirley	By Dan
10	12	6
30	9	5
50	6	4
70	3	3
90	1	2

   If Shirley and Dan are the only two individuals, show that the market demand curve is the horizontal sum of Shirley's and Dan's demand curves.

9. The figure illustrates Sara's demand for windsurfing.

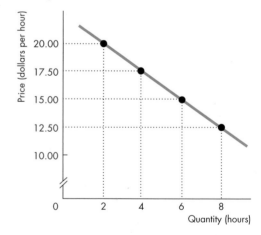

   What is Sara's consumer surplus if
   a. Windsurfing costs $17.50 an hour?
   b. Windsurfing costs $12.50 an hour?

Possibilities, Preferences, and Choices

After studying
this chapter,
you will be
able to:

- Calculate and graph a household's budget line

- Work out how the budget line changes when prices or income change

- Make a map of preferences by using indifference curves

- Explain the choices that households make

- Predict the effects of price and income changes on consumption choices

Subterranean Movements

Like the continents floating on the earth's mantle, our spending patterns change steadily over time. On such subterranean movements, business empires rise and fall. Goods such as home videos and microwave popcorn now appear on our shopping lists while 78 rpm phonograph records and horse-drawn carriages have disappeared. Miniskirts appear, disappear, and reappear in cycles of fashion.

◆ But the glittering surface of our consumption obscures deeper and slower changes in how we spend. In the last few years, we've seen a proliferation of gourmet food shops and designer clothing boutiques. Yet we spend a smaller percentage of our income today on food and clothing than we did in 1950. At the same time, the percentage of our income spent on housing, transportation, and recreation has grown steadily. Why does consumer spending change over the years? How do people react to changes in income and changes in the prices of the things they buy? ◆ Similar subterranean movements govern the way we spend our time. For example, the average workweek has fallen steadily from 70 hours a week in the nineteenth century to 35 hours a week today. Although the average workweek is now much shorter than it once was, far more people now have jobs. This change has been especially dramatic for women who are much more likely to work outside the home than they were in previous generations. Why has the average workweek declined? And why do more women work?

◈ We're going to study a model of choice that predicts the effects of changes in prices and incomes on what people buy, how much work they do, and how much they borrow and lend.

Consumption Possibilities

CONSUMPTION CHOICES ARE LIMITED BY INCOME and by prices. A household has a given amount of income to spend and cannot influence the prices of the goods and services it buys. It takes prices as given. The limits to a household's consumption choices are described by its **budget line**.

To make the concept of the household's budget line clear, we'll consider a concrete example—the household of Lisa.[1] Lisa has an income of $30 a month to spend. She buys two goods—movies and pop. Movies cost $6 each; pop costs $3 for a six-pack. If Lisa spends all of her income, she will reach the limits to her consumption of movies and pop.

In Fig. 8.1, each row of the table shows an affordable way for Lisa to consume movies and pop. Row *a* says that she can buy 10 six-packs of pop and see no movies. You can see that this combination of movies and pop exhausts her monthly income of $30. Row *f* says that Lisa can watch 5 movies and drink no pop—another combination that exhausts the $30 available. Each of the other rows in the table also exhausts Lisa's income. (Check that each of the other rows costs exactly $30.) The numbers in the table define Lisa's consumption possibilities. We can graph Lisa's consumption possibilities as points *a* through *f* in Fig. 8.1.

Divisible and Indivisible Goods   Some goods—called divisible goods—can be bought in any quantity desired. Examples are gasoline and electricity. We can best understand the model of household choice we're about to study if we suppose that all goods and services are divisible. For example, Lisa can consume a half a movie a month *on the average* by seeing one movie every two months. When we think of goods as being divisible, the consumption possibilities are not just the points *a* through *f* shown in Fig. 8.1, but those points plus all the intermediate points that form the line running from *a* to *f*. Such a line is a budget line.

Lisa's budget line is a constraint on her choices. It marks the boundary between what is affordable and

---

[1]If you have read the preceding chapter on marginal utility theory, you have already met Lisa. This tale of her thirst for pop and zeal for movies will sound familiar to you—up to a point. But in this chapter, we're going to use a different method for representing preferences—one that does not require us to resort to the idea of utility.

FIGURE   8.1

The Budget Line

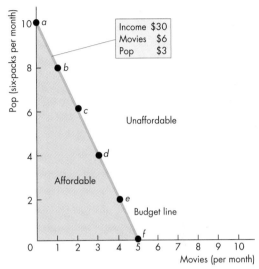

Consumption possibility	Movies (per month)	Pop (six-packs per month)
a	0	10
b	1	8
c	2	6
d	3	4
e	4	2
f	5	0

Lisa's budget line shows the boundary between what she can and cannot afford. Each row of the table lists Lisa's affordable combinations of movies and pop when her income is $30, the price of pop is $3 a six-pack, and the price of a movie is $6. For example, row *a* tells us that Lisa exhausts her $30 income when she buys 10 six-packs and sees no movies. The figure graphs Lisa's budget line. Points *a* through *f* on the graph represent the rows of the table. For divisible goods, the budget line is the continuous line *af*. To calculate the equation for Lisa's budget line, start from the fact that expenditure equals income:

$$\$3 \times Q_p + \$6 \times Q_m = \$30.$$

Divide by $3 to obtain

$$Q_p + 2Q_m = 10.$$

Subtract $2Q_m$ from both sides to obtain

$$Q_p = 10 - 2Q_m.$$

what is unaffordable. She can afford all the points on the line and inside it. She cannot afford points outside the line. The constraint on her consumption depends on prices and her income, and the constraint changes when prices or her income change. Let's see how by studying an equation that describes her consumption possibilities.

The Budget Equation

We can describe the budget line by using a *budget equation*. The budget equation starts with the fact that

$$\text{Expenditure} = \text{Income}.$$

In Lisa's case, expenditure and income equal $30 a week.

Expenditure is equal to the sum of the price of each good multiplied by the quantity bought. For Lisa,

$$\text{Expenditure} = \text{Price of pop} \times \text{Quantity of pop}$$
$$+ \text{Price of movie} \times \text{Quantity of movies}.$$

Call the price of pop P_p, the quantity of pop Q_p, the price of a movie P_m, the quantity of movies Q_m, and income y. Using these symbols, Lisa's budget equation is

$$P_p Q_p + P_m Q_m = y.$$

Or, using the prices Lisa faces, $3 for a six-pack and $6 for a movie, and Lisa's income, $30, we get

$$\$3 \times Q_p + \$6 \times Q_m = \$30.$$

Lisa can choose any quantities of pop (Q_p) and movies (Q_m) that satisfy this equation. To express the relationship between these quantities, we rearrange the equation so that it describes Lisa's budget line. To do so, divide both sides of the equation by the price of pop (P_p) to get

$$Q_p + \frac{P_m}{P_p} \times Q_m = \frac{y}{P_p}.$$

Now subtract the term $\frac{P_m}{P_p} \times Q_m$ from both sides of this equation to give

$$Q_p = \frac{y}{P_p} - \frac{P_m}{P_p} \times Q_m.$$

For Lisa, income (y) is $30, the price of a movie (P_m) is $6, and the price of a six-pack (P_p) is $3. So Lisa

must choose the quantities of movies and pop to satisfy the equation

$$Q_p = \frac{\$30}{\$3} - \frac{\$6}{\$3} \times Q_m,$$

or

$$Q_p = 10 - 2 Q_m.$$

This equation tells us how Lisa's consumption of pop (Q_p) varies as her consumption of movies (Q_m) varies. To interpret the equation, go back to the budget line of Fig. 8.1 and check that the equation you've just derived delivers that budget line. Begin by setting Q_m, the quantity of movies, equal to zero. In this case, the budget equation tells us that Q_p, the quantity of pop, is y/P_p, which is $30/$3, or 10 six-packs. This combination of Q_m and Q_p is the same as that shown in row *a* of the table in Fig. 8.1. Setting Q_m equal to 5 makes Q_p equal to zero (row *f* of the table in Fig. 8.1). Check that you can derive the other rows.

The budget equation contains two variables chosen by the household (Q_m and Q_p) and two variables (y/P_p and P_m/P_p) that the household takes as given. Let's look more closely at these variables.

Real Income A household's **real income** is the maximum quantity of a good that the household can afford to buy. In the budget equation, real income is y/P_p. This quantity is the maximum number of six-packs that Lisa can buy and is Lisa's real income in terms of pop. It is equal to her money income divided by the price of pop. Lisa's income is $30 and the price of pop is $3 a six-pack, so her real income in terms of pop is 10 six-packs. In Fig. 8.1, real income is the point at which the budget line intersects the *y*-axis.

Relative Price A **relative price** is the price of one good divided by the price of another good. In Lisa's budget equation, the variable (P_m/P_p) is the relative price of a movie in terms of pop. For Lisa, P_m is $6 a movie and P_p is $3 a six-pack, so P_m/P_p is equal to 2 six-packs per movie. That is, to see one more movie, Lisa must give up 2 six-packs.

You've just calculated Lisa's opportunity cost of a movie. Recall that the opportunity cost of an action is the best alternative forgone. For Lisa to see 1 more movie a month, she must forgo 2 six-packs. You've also calculated Lisa's opportunity cost of pop. For Lisa to consume 2 more six-packs a month, she must give up seeing 1 movie. So her opportunity cost of 2 six-packs is 1 movie.

The relative price of a movie in terms of pop is the magnitude of the slope of Lisa's budget line. To calculate the slope of the budget line, recall the formula for slope (Chapter 2): Slope equals the change in the variable measured on the *y*-axis divided by the change in the variable measured on the *x*-axis as we move along the line. In Lisa's case (Fig. 8.1), the variable measured on the *y*-axis is the quantity of pop and the variable measured on the *x*-axis is the quantity of movies. Along Lisa's budget line, as pop decreases from 10 to 0 six-packs, movies increase from 0 to 5. Therefore the magnitude of the slope of the budget line is 10 six-packs divided by 5 movies, or 2 six-packs per movie. The magnitude of this slope is exactly the same as the relative price we've just calculated. It is also the opportunity cost of a movie.

A Change in Prices When prices change, so does the budget line. The lower the price of the good measured on the horizontal axis, other things remaining the same, the flatter is the budget line. For example, if the price of a movie falls from $6 to $3, real income in terms of pop does not change but the relative price of a movie falls. The budget line rotates outward and becomes flatter as shown in Fig. 8.2(a). The higher the price of the good measured on the horizontal axis, other things remaining the same, the steeper is the budget line. For example, if the price of a movie rises from $6 to $12, the relative price of a movie increases. The budget line rotates inward and becomes steeper as shown in Fig. 8.2(a).

A Change in Income A change in *money income* changes real income but does not change relative prices. The budget line shifts, but its slope does not change. The bigger a consumer's money income, the bigger is real income and the farther to the right is the budget line. The smaller a consumer's money income, the smaller is real income and the farther to the left is the budget line. The effect of a change in income on Lisa's budget line is shown in Fig. 8.2(b). The initial budget line is the same one that we began with in Fig. 8.1 when Lisa's income is $30. A new budget line shows how much Lisa can consume if her income falls to $15 a month. The new budget line is parallel to the old one but closer to the origin. The two budget lines are parallel—have the same slope—because the relative price is the same in both cases. The new budget line is closer to the origin than the initial one because Lisa's real income has decreased.

FIGURE 8.2

Changes in Prices and Income

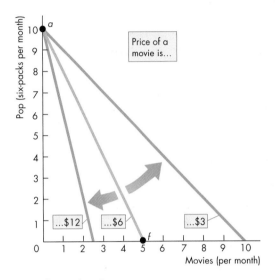

(a) A change in price

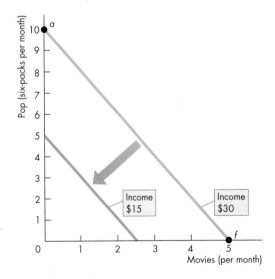

(b) A change in income

In part (a), the price of a movie changes. A fall in the price from $6 to $3 rotates the budget line outward and makes it flatter. A rise in the price from $6 to $12 rotates the budget line inward and makes it steeper.

In part (b), income falls from $30 to $15 while the prices of movies and pop remain constant. The budget line shifts leftward, but its slope does not change.

R E V I E W

- The budget line describes the limits to a household's consumption, which depends on its income and the prices of the goods that it buys.
- The position of the budget line depends on real income, and its slope depends on the relative price.
- A change in the price of one good changes the relative price and changes the slope of the budget line. If the price of the good measured on the horizontal axis rises, the budget line becomes steeper.
- A change in money income changes real income and shifts the budget line, but its slope does not change. An increase in money income shifts the budget line outward.

We've studied the limits to what a household can consume. Let's now see how we can describe the household's preferences.

Preferences and Indifference Curves

PREFERENCES ARE A PERSON'S LIKES AND DISLIKES. A key assumption about preferences is that they do not depend on prices or income. The things you like and dislike do not depend on what you can afford. When a price changes or when your income changes, you make a new choice, but the preferences that guide that choice don't change. We are going to discover a very neat idea—that of drawing a map of a person's preferences.

A preference map is based on the intuitively appealing assumption that people can sort all the possible combinations of goods they might consume into three groups: preferred, not preferred, and indifferent. To make this idea more concrete, let's ask Lisa to tell us how she ranks various combinations of movies and pop. Figure 8.3 illustrates part of her answer.

Lisa tells us that she currently consumes 2 movies and 6 six-packs a month at point *c* in Fig. 8.3. She then lists all the combinations of movies and pop that she regards as equally acceptable to her as her current consumption. When we plot the combinations of movies and pop that Lisa tells us she likes just as much as the combination at point *c*, we get the green curve

FIGURE 8.3
Mapping Preferences

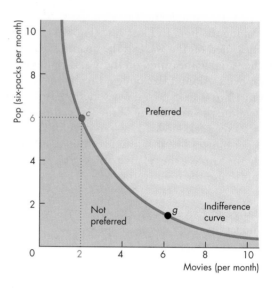

If Lisa drinks 6 six-packs of pop and sees 2 movies a month, she consumes at point *c*. Lisa can compare all other possible combinations of pop and movies to point *c* and rank them on the scale preferred to point *c*, not preferred to point *c*, or indifferent. The boundary between points that she prefers to point *c* and those that she does not prefer to point *c* is an indifference curve. Lisa is indifferent between points such as *g* and *c* on the indifference curve. She prefers any point above the indifference curve (yellow area) to any point on it, and she prefers any point on the indifference curve to any point below it (grey area).

in Fig. 8.3. This curve is the key element in a map of preferences and is called an indifference curve.

An **indifference curve** is a line that shows combinations of goods among which a consumer is *indifferent*. The indifference curve in Fig. 8.3 tells us that Lisa is just as happy to consume 2 movies and 6 six-packs a month at point *c* as to consume the combination of movies and pop at point *g* or at any other point along the curve.

Lisa goes on to tell us that starting from any combination of movies and pop, she prefers to have more movies and no less pop, or more pop and no fewer movies. We can interpret Lisa as saying that the indifference curve defines the boundary between combinations of goods that she prefers and combinations that she does not prefer to those on the indifference curve. Lisa prefers any combination in the yellow area above the indifference curve to any combination along the indifference curve. And she prefers any combination on the indifference curve to any combination in the grey area below the indifference curve.

The indifference curve shown in Fig. 8.3 is just one of a whole family of such curves. This indifference curve appears again in Fig. 8.4. It is labelled I_1 and passes through points c and g. Two other indifference curves are I_0 and I_2. Lisa prefers any point on indifference curve I_2 to any point on indifference curve I_1, and she prefers any point on I_1 to any point on I_0. We refer to I_2 as being a higher indifference curve than I_1 and I_1 as being higher than I_0.

Indifference curves never intersect. To see why, consider indifference curves I_1 and I_2 in Fig. 8.4. We know that Lisa prefers point j to point c. We also know that Lisa prefers any point on indifference curve I_2 to any point on indifference curve I_1. If these indifference curves did intersect, Lisa would be indifferent between the combination of goods at the intersection point and combinations c and j. But we know that Lisa prefers j to c, so there cannot be an intersection point. Hence the indifference curves never intersect.

A preference map consists of a series of indifference curves. The indifference curves shown in Fig. 8.4 are only a part of Lisa's preference map. Her entire map consists of an infinite number of indifference curves; each one slopes downward, and they do not intersect. They resemble the contour lines on a map that measures the height of a mountain. An indifference curve joins points representing combinations of goods among which a consumer is indifferent in much the same way that contour lines on a map join points of equal height above sea level. By looking at the shape of the contour lines on a map, we can draw conclusions about the terrain. In the same way, by looking at the shape of a person's indifference curves, we can draw conclusions about preferences. But interpreting a preference map requires a bit of work. It also requires some way of describing the shape of the indifference curves. In the next two sections, we'll learn how to "read" a preference map.

FIGURE 8.4
A Preference Map

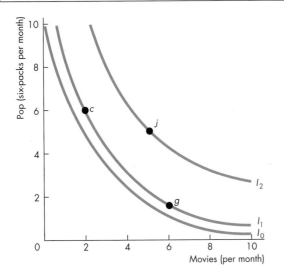

A preference map consists of an infinite number of indifference curves. Here, we show just three—I_0, I_1, and I_2—that are part of Lisa's preference map. Each indifference curve shows points among which Lisa is indifferent. For example, she is indifferent between point c and point g on indifference curve I_1. But she prefers any point on a higher indifference curve to any point on a lower indifference curve. For example, Lisa prefers point j to point c or g, so she prefers any point on indifference curve I_2 to any point on indifference curve I_1.

Marginal Rate of Substitution

The **marginal rate of substitution** (*MRS*) is the rate at which a person will give up good y (the good measured on the y-axis) to get more of good x (the good measured on the x-axis) and at the same time remain indifferent (remain on the same indifference curve). The marginal rate of substitution is measured from the slope of an indifference curve. If the indifference curve is steep, the marginal rate of substitution is high. The person is willing to give up a large quantity of good y in exchange for a small quantity of good x while remaining indifferent. If the indifference curve is flat, the marginal rate of substitution is low. The person is willing to give up only a small amount of good y in exchange for a large amount of good x to remain indifferent.

Figure 8.5 shows you how to calculate the marginal rate of substitution. The curve labelled I_1 is one of Lisa's indifference curves. Suppose that Lisa drinks 6 six-packs and watches 2 movies at point c in the figure. Her marginal rate of substitution is calculated by measuring the magnitude of the slope of the indifference curve at point *c*. To measure this magnitude, place a straight line against, or tangent to, the indifference curve at point *c*. The slope of that line is the change in the quantity of pop divided by the change in the quantity of movies as we move along the straight line. As the quantity of pop decreases by 10 six-packs, the quantity of movies increases by 5. So at point *c* Lisa is willing to give up pop for movies at the rate of 2 six-packs per movie. Her marginal rate of substitution is 2.

Now, suppose that Lisa consumes 6 movies and $1^1/_2$ six-packs at point *g* in Fig. 8.5. What is her marginal rate of substitution at this point? The answer is found by calculating the magnitude of the slope of the indifference curve at point *g*. That slope is the

same as the slope of the tangent to the indifference curve at point *g*. Here, as the quantity of pop decreases by $4^1/_2$ six-packs, the quantity of movies increases by 9. So at point *g*, Lisa is willing to give up pop for movies at the rate of $^1/_2$ six-pack per movie. Her marginal rate of substitution is $^1/_2$.

Notice that if Lisa drinks a lot of pop and does not see many movies (point *c*), her marginal rate of substitution is large. If she sees a lot of movies and does not drink much pop (point *g*), her marginal rate of substitution is small. This feature of the marginal rate of substitution is the central assumption of the theory of consumer behaviour and is referred to as the diminishing marginal rate of substitution. **Diminishing marginal rate of substitution** is a general tendency for the marginal rate of substitution to diminish as the consumer moves along an indifference curve, increasing consumption of good *x* and decreasing consumption of good *y*.

Your Own Diminishing Marginal Rate of Substitution   You might be able to appreciate why we assume the principle of a diminishing marginal rate of substitution by thinking about your own preferences for movies and pop. Suppose you consume 10 six-packs of pop a week and see no movies. How many six-packs are you willing to give up in exchange for seeing 1 movie a week? Your answer to this question is your marginal rate of substitution between pop and movies when you consume no movies. For example, if you are willing to give up 4 six-packs to see 1 movie, your marginal rate of substitution of pop for movies is 4. Now suppose that you consume 6 six-packs and see 1 movie a week. How many six-packs are you now willing to give up to see 2 movies a week? Your answer to this question is your marginal rate of substitution when you consume 1 movie a week. If your answer is a smaller number than when you see no movies, your preferences display a diminishing marginal rate of substitution between pop and movies. The greater the number of movies you see, the smaller is the quantity of pop you are willing to give up to see one additional movie.

The shape of the indifference curves incorporates the principle of the diminishing marginal rate of substitution because the curves are bowed towards the origin. The tightness of the bend of an indifference curve tells us how willing a person is to substitute one good for another while remaining indifferent. Let's look at some examples that will clarify this point.

FIGURE   8.5

The Marginal Rate of Substitution

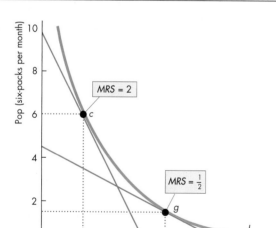

The magnitude of the slope of an indifference curve is called the marginal rate of substitution (*MRS*). The marginal rate of substitution tells us how much of one good a person is willing to give up to gain more of another good while remaining indifferent—that is, staying on the same indifference curve. The red line at point *c* tells us that Lisa is willing to give up 10 six-packs to see 5 movies. Her marginal rate of substitution at point *c* is 10 divided by 5, which equals 2. The red line at point *g* tells us that Lisa is willing to give up 4 1/2 six-packs to see 9 movies. Her marginal rate of substitution at point *g* is 4 1/2 divided by 9, which equals 1/2.

Degree of Substitutability

Most of us would not regard movies and pop as being close substitutes for each other. We probably have some fairly clear ideas about how many movies we want to see each month and how many cans of pop we want to drink. Nevertheless, to some degree, we are willing to substitute between these two goods. No matter how big a pop freak you are, there is surely some increase in the number of movies you can see that will compensate you for being deprived of a can of pop. Similarly, no matter how addicted you are to the movies, surely some number of cans of pop will compensate you for being deprived of seeing one movie. A person's indifference curves for movies and pop might look something like those shown in Fig. 8.6(a).

Close Substitutes   Some goods substitute so easily for each other that most of us do not even notice which we are consuming. A good example concerns different brands of personal computers. Dell, Compaq, and Toshiba are all clones of the IBM

PC—but most of us can't tell the difference between the clones and the IBM. The same holds true for marker pens. Most of us don't care whether we use a marker pen from the campus bookstore or the local supermarket. When two goods are perfect substitutes for each other, their indifference curves are straight lines that slope downward, as Fig. 8.6(b) illustrates. The marginal rate of substitution is constant.

Complements   Some goods cannot substitute for each other at all. Instead they are complements. The complements in Fig. 8.6(c) are left and right running shoes. Indifference curves of perfect complements are L-shaped. One left running shoe and one right running shoe are as good as one left shoe and two right ones. Two of each is preferred to one of each, but two of one and one of the other is no better than one of each.

The extreme cases of perfect substitutes and perfect complements shown here don't often happen in reality. They do, however, illustrate that the shape of the indifference curve shows the degree of substitutability between two goods. The more perfectly substitutable

---

FIGURE   8.6
The Degree of Substitutability

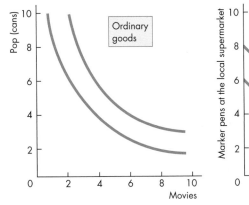

(a) Ordinary goods

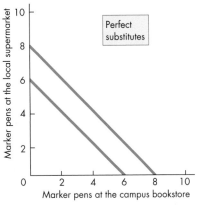

(b) Perfect substitutes

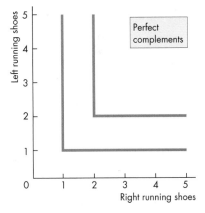

(c) Perfect complements

The shape of the indifference curves reveals the degree of substitutability between two goods. Part (a) shows the indifference curves for two ordinary goods: movies and pop. To consume less pop and remain indifferent, one must see more movies. The number of movies that compensates for a reduction in pop increases as less pop is consumed. Part (b) shows the indifference curves for two perfect substitutes. For the consumer to remain indifferent, one fewer marker pen from the local supermarket must be replaced by one extra marker pen from the campus bookstore. Part (c) shows two perfect complements—goods that cannot be substituted for each other at all. Having two left running shoes with one right running shoe is no better than having one of each. But having two of each is preferred to having one of each.

"With the pork I'd recommend an Alsatian white or a Coke."

Drawing by Weber; © 1988 The New Yorker Magazine, Inc.

the two goods, the more nearly are their indifference curves straight lines and the less quickly does the marginal rate of substitution fall. Poor substitutes for each other have tightly curved indifference curves, approaching the shape of those shown in Fig. 8.6(c).

As you can see in the cartoon, according to the waiter's preferences, Coke and Alsatian white wine are perfect substitutes for each other and are each complements with pork. We hope the customers agree with him.

R E V I E W

- A person's preferences can be represented by a preference map that consists of a series of indifference curves.

- For most goods, indifference curves slope downward and bow towards the origin. They never intersect.

- The magnitude of the slope of an indifference curve is called the marginal rate of substitution.

- The marginal rate of substitution diminishes as a person consumes less of the good measured on the *y*-axis and more of the good measured on the *x*-axis.

The two components of the model of household choice are now in place: the budget line and the preference map. We will now use these components to work out the consumer's choice.

The Household's Consumption Choice

WE ARE NOW GOING TO BRING LISA'S BUDGET line and indifference curves together and discover her best affordable choice of movies and pop. What are the quantities of movies and pop that Lisa *chooses* to buy? In Fig. 8.7 you can see her budget line from Fig. 8.1 and her indifference curves from Fig. 8.4. First focus on point h on indifference curve I_0. Point h is on Lisa's budget line, so we know that she can afford it. But does she *choose* this combination of movies and pop over all the other affordable combinations? No, she does not. To see why not, consider point c, where she consumes 2 movies and 6 six-packs. Point c is also on Lisa's budget line, so we know she can afford to consume at this point. But point c is on indifference curve I_1, a higher indifference curve than

---

FIGURE 8.7

The Best Affordable Point

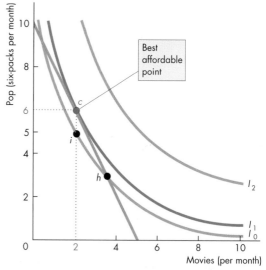

Lisa's best affordable point is c. At that point, she is on her budget line and also on the highest attainable indifference curve. At a point such as h, Lisa is willing to give up more movies in exchange for 1 six-pack than she has to. She can move to point i, which is just as good as point h, and have some unspent income. She can spend that income and move to point c, a point that she prefers to point i.

I_0. Therefore we know that Lisa prefers point c to point h.

Is there any affordable point that Lisa prefers to point c? There is not. All Lisa's other affordable consumption points—all the other points on or below her budget line—lie on indifference curves that are below I_1. Indifference curve I_1 is the highest indifference curve on which Lisa can afford to consume.

Let's look more closely at Lisa's best affordable choice.

Properties of the Best Affordable Point

The best affordable point—point c in this example—has two properties. It is

- On the budget line
- On the highest attainable indifference curve

On the Budget Line The best affordable point is *on* the budget line. If Lisa chooses a point inside the budget line, she will have an affordable point on the budget line at which she can consume more of both goods. Lisa prefers that point to the one inside the budget line. The best affordable point cannot be outside the budget line because Lisa cannot afford such a point.

On the Highest Attainable Indifference Curve The chosen point is on the highest attainable indifference curve. At this point, the indifference curve has the same slope as the budget line. Stated another way, the marginal rate of substitution between the two goods (the magnitude of the slope of the indifference curve) equals their relative price (the magnitude of the slope of the budget line).

To see why this condition describes the best affordable point, consider point h in Fig. 8.7, which Lisa regards as inferior to point c. At point h, Lisa's marginal rate of substitution is less than the relative price—indifference curve I_0 is flatter than Lisa's budget line. As Lisa gives up movies for pop and moves up indifference curve I_0, she moves inside her budget line and has some money left over. She can move to point i, for example, where she consumes 2 movies and 5 six-packs and has $3 to spare. She is indifferent between the combination of goods at point i and the combination at point h. But she prefers point c to point i, since at c she has more pop than at i and sees the same number of movies.

By moving along her budget line from point h towards point c, Lisa passes through a number of indifference curves (not shown in the figure) located between indifference curves I_0 and I_1. All of these indifference curves are higher than I_0 and therefore any point on them is preferred to point h. Once Lisa gets to point c, she has reached the highest attainable indifference curve. If she keeps moving along the budget line, she will start to encounter indifference curves that are lower than I_1.

R E V I E W

- Affordable combinations of goods lie on or inside the consumer's budget line.
- The consumer's preferences are described by indifference curves.
- The consumer's best affordable allocation of income occurs when all income is spent (on the budget line) and when the marginal rate of substitution (the magnitude of the slope of the indifference curve) equals the relative price (the magnitude of the slope of the budget line).

We will now use this model of household choice to make some predictions about changes in consumption patterns when income and prices change.

Predicting Consumer Behaviour

LET'S START BY LOOKING AT THE EFFECT OF A change in price. By studying the effect of a change in price on a consumer's choice, other things held constant, we can derive a consumer's demand curve.

A Change in Price

The effect of a change in price on the quantity of a good consumed is called the **price effect**. We will use Fig. 8.8(a) to work out the price effect of a fall in the price of a movie. We start with movies costing $6 each, pop costing $3 a six-pack, and with Lisa's income at $30 a month. In this situation, she consumes at point c, where her budget line is tangent to her highest attainable indifference curve, I_1. She consumes 6 six-packs and sees 2 movies a month.

FIGURE 8.8

Price Effect and Demand Curve

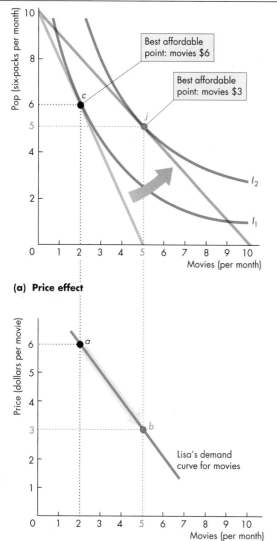

(a) Price effect

(b) Demand curve

Initially, Lisa consumes at point *c* (part a). If the price of a movie falls from $6 to $3, she consumes at point *j*. The increase in movies from 2 to 5 per month and the decrease in pop from 6 to 5 six-packs is the price effect.

Part (b) shows Lisa's demand curve for movies. When the price of a movie is $6, she sees 2 movies a month, at point *a*. When the price of a movie falls to $3, she sees 5 a month, at point *b*. Lisa's demand curve traces out her best affordable quantity of movies as the price of a movie varies.

Now suppose that the price of a movie falls to $3. We've already seen how a change in price (in Fig. 8.2a) affects the budget line. With a lower price of a movie, the budget line rotates outward and becomes flatter. The new budget line is the dark orange one in Fig. 8.8(a). Lisa's best affordable point is *j*, where she consumes 5 movies and 5 six-packs of pop. As you can see, Lisa drinks less pop and sees more movies now that movies cost less. She reduces her pop consumption from 6 to 5 six-packs and increases the number of movies she sees from 2 to 5 a month. Lisa substitutes movies for pop when the price of a movie falls and the price of pop and her income remain constant.

The Demand Curve

A demand curve graphs the relationship between the quantity demanded of a good and its price, when all other influences on buying plans remain the same. In Chapter 4, we asserted that the demand curve slopes downward and that it shifts when the consumer's income changes or when the price of another good changes. We can now derive a demand curve from a consumer's budget line and indifference curves. By doing so, we can see that the law of demand and the downward-sloping demand curve are consequences of the consumer choosing his or her best affordable combination of goods.

Let's derive Lisa's demand curve for movies. We do so by lowering the price of a movie and finding her best affordable point at different prices. We just did this for two movie prices in Fig. 8.8(a). Figure 8.8(b) highlights these two prices and two points that lie on Lisa's demand curve for movies. When the price of a movie is $6, Lisa sees 2 movies a month at point *a*. When the price falls to $3, she increases the number of movies she sees to 5 a month at point *b*. The entire demand curve is made up of these two points plus all the other points that tell us Lisa's best affordable consumption of movies at each movie price—more than $6, between $6 and $3, and less than $3—given the price of pop and Lisa's income. As you can see, Lisa's demand curve for movies slopes downward—the lower the price of a movie, the more movies she watches each month. This is the law of demand.

Next, let's examine how Lisa adjusts her consumption when her income changes.

A Change in Income

The effect of a change in income on consumption is called the **income effect**. Let's work out the income effect by examining how consumption changes when income changes and prices remain constant. Figure 8.9(a) shows the income effect when Lisa's income falls. With an income of $30 and with a movie costing $3 and pop $3 a six-pack, she consumes at point *j*—5 movies and 5 six-packs. If her income falls to $21 and the prices of movies and pop remain the same, she consumes at point *k*—consuming 4 movies and 3 six-packs. Thus when Lisa's income falls, she consumes less of both goods. For Lisa, movies and pop are normal goods.

The Demand Curve and the Income Effect   A change in income leads to a shift in the demand curve, as shown in Fig. 8.9(b). With an income of $30, Lisa's demand curve is D_0, the same as in Fig. 8.8. But when her income falls to $21, she plans to see fewer movies at each price, so her demand curve shifts leftward to D_1.

Substitution Effect and Income Effect

We've now worked out the effects of a change in the price of a movie and the effects of a change in Lisa's income on her consumption of movies and pop. We've discovered that when her income increases, she increases her consumption of both goods. Movies and pop are *normal goods*. When the price of a movie falls, Lisa increases her consumption of movies and decreases her consumption of pop. A fall in the price of a normal good leads to an increase in the consumption of that good. To see why these changes occur, we separate the price effect into two parts. One part is called the substitution effect; the other part is called the income effect.

Figure 8.10 illustrates the price effect and its separation into a substitution effect and an income effect. Part (a) shows the price effect that you've already worked out in Fig. 8.8. Let's see how that price effect comes about, first by isolating the substitution effect.

Substitution Effect   The **substitution effect** is the effect of a change in price on the quantities consumed when the consumer (hypothetically) remains

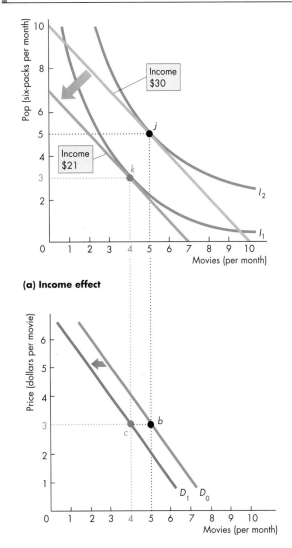

FIGURE   8.9

Income Effect and Change in Demand

(a) Income effect

(b) Demand curve

A change in income shifts the budget line and changes the best affordable point and changes consumption. In part (a), when Lisa's income decreases from $30 to $21, she consumes less of both movies and pop. In part (b), Lisa's demand curve for movies when her income is $30 is D_0. When Lisa's income decreases to $21, her demand curve for movies shifts leftward to D_1. Lisa's demand for movies decreases because at each price she now sees fewer movies.

FIGURE 8.10

Price Effect, Substitution Effect, and Income Effect

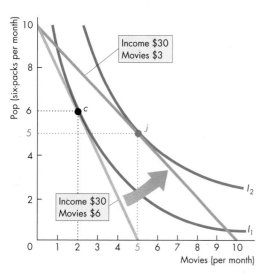

(a) Price effect

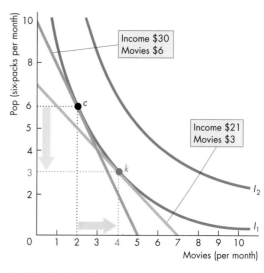

(b) Substitution effect

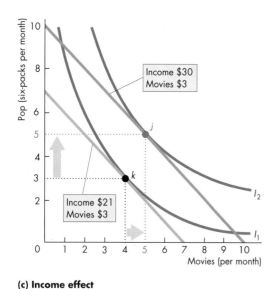

(c) Income effect

The price effect can be separated into a substitution effect and an income effect. Part (a) shows the price effect and it is the same as Fig. 8.8(a).

To calculate the substitution effect (part b), when the price of a movie falls, imagine that Lisa's income decreases so that her best affordable point remains on her original indifference curve I_1. The substitution effect of the price change is the move from *c* to *k*.

To calculate the income effect (part c), reverse Lisa's imaginary income cut while holding prices constant at their new level. The increase in income shifts the budget line outward and the quantities of movies and pop consumed increase. The income effect of the price change is the move from *k* to *j*.

indifferent between the original and the new combinations of goods consumed. To work out Lisa's substitution effect, we have to imagine that when the price of a movie falls, Lisa's income also decreases by an amount that is just enough to leave her on the same indifference curve as before.

Figure 8.10(b) illustrates the substitution effect. When the price of a movie falls from $6 to $3, let's suppose (hypothetically) that Lisa's income decreases to $21. What's special about $21? It is the income that is just enough, at the new price of a movie, to keep Lisa's best affordable point on the *same* indifference curve as her original consumption point *c*. Lisa's budget line in this situation is the light orange line shown in Fig. 8.10(b). With the new price of a movie and the new lower income, Lisa's best affordable point is *k* on indifference curve I_1. The move from *c* to *k* isolates the substitution effect of the price change. The substitution effect of the fall in the price of a movie is an increase in the consumption of movies from 2 to 4 and a decrease in the consumption of pop. The direction of the substitution effect never varies: When the relative price of a good falls, the consumer substitutes more of that good for the other good.

Income Effect   To calculate the substitution effect, we gave Lisa a $9 pay cut. Now let's give Lisa her $9 back. The $9 increase in income shifts Lisa's budget line outward, as shown in Fig. 8.10(c). The slope of the budget line does not change because both prices remain constant. This change in Lisa's budget line is similar to the one illustrated in Fig. 8.9 where we study the effect of income on consumption. As Lisa's budget line shifts outward, her consumption possibilities expand and her best affordable point becomes *j* on indifference curve I_2. The move from *k* to *j* isolates the income effect of the price change. In this example, as Lisa's income increases, she increases her consumption of both movies and pop. For Lisa, movies and pop are normal goods.

Price Effect   Figure 8.10 shows how the price effect in part (a) is broken into two effects, the substitution effect in part (b) and the income effect in part (c). In part (b), Lisa is indifferent between the two situations. Her income falls at the same time that the price of a movie falls and she substitutes movies for pop. The substitution effect always works in the same direction—the consumer slides along an indifference curve to buy more of the good whose relative price has fallen and less of the good whose relative price has risen. In part (c), prices are constant and Lisa's income returns to its original level. The direction of the income effect depends on whether the good is normal or inferior. By definition, normal goods are ones whose consumption increases as income increases. For Lisa, movies and pop are normal goods because the income effect increases their consumption. Both the income effect and the substitution effect increase Lisa's consumption of movies.

The arrows in parts (b) and (c) of Fig. 8.10

show the substitution and income effects of a price change. The move from point *c* to point *k* in part (b) is the substitution effect, and the move from point *k* to point *j* in part (c) is the income effect. For movies, the income effect reinforces the substitution effect with the result that Lisa increases her consumption of movies. For pop, the substitution effect and the income effect work in opposite directions with the result that Lisa decreases her consumption of pop.

Back to the Real World

We started this chapter by noting how consumer spending has changed over the years. We also noted that the way we spend our time has also changed. We can explain all of these patterns with the indifference curve model.

Consumer spending is determined by the choices that people make to make the best possible use of their limited income. Changes in prices and incomes lead to changes in the best affordable choices and change the pattern of consumer spending. As the prices of home videos and microwave popcorn have fallen, so the quantities bought have increased. As incomes have grown, the demand for some goods such as housing, transportation, and recreation have grown rapidly because they have a large income effect.

We can even explain how we allocate our time using these same ideas. Leisure time is a consumption good. Its opportunity cost is the goods and services we can buy with an hour of work—the *real* wage rate. As the real wage rate has increased the "price" of leisure has increased, so we have substituted work for leisure. But a higher real wage brings a higher income. And leisure is a normal good, so the higher income brings an increase in the demand for leisure. The income effect has been stronger than the substitution effect so over the years, the workweek has become shorter and the amount of leisure consumed has increased.

◆ You've now completed your study of household choices. *Reading Between the Lines* on pp. 182–183 uses the tools you've learned about to explain such everyday activities as going to the movies and enjoying a weekend of leisure. In the chapters that follow, we switch our attention from households' consumption choices to the decisions that firms make to produce goods and services.

Substitution and Income Effects

Essence of THE STORY

- The costs of almost all the items in the table in the news article have increased more quickly than the increase in disposable income.

- A University of Calgary finance professor says that "real wages" have fallen and taxes have increased during recent years.

- As a result, fewer family dollars are available to spend on fewer family outings.

CALGARY HERALD, January 14, 1996

Rising prices squeezing families

BY CHRIS DAWSON

It costs more to ski, more to camp, more to eat under the watchful eye of Ronald McDonald.

More to drive into Banff National Park—more to walk the streets at Heritage Park.

"It seems like everything is twice as much," says Calgary parent Gayle Peters. "Except our salaries."

Ay, there's the rub. While the cost of family outings has risen steadily over the years, the amount of disposable income hasn't kept pace.

There's no question "real wages" have declined throughout the 1990s, says University of Calgary finance Prof. Michael Robinson. "People are much more heavily taxed than they were ten years ago."...

Meanwhile, direct and hidden taxes continue to climb—as do user fees, admission charges and utility costs, Robinson says.

The result? Fewer family dollars to spend on fewer family outings.

Rising cost of family fun

The cost of various activities for a family of four (two adults and two school-age children) in 1996 and 1986 (unless otherwise noted).

Activities	1996 prices	1986 prices
■ A day pass to Heritage Park	Adults $10, child $6 **Total: $32***	Adults $5, child $2 **Total: $14**
■ A day of skiing at Canada Olympic Park (since 1988)	Adults $17, child[1] $9 **Total: $52***	Adults $12, child[2] $10 **Total: $44**
■ A day trip to Banff with a soak in the upper hot springs	Park pass $8; pool Adults $5, child $3 **Total: $24***	Park pass $3; pool Adults $2.75, child $1.75 **Total: $12**
■ A meal at McDonald's (assume each family member has one of each item)	Big Mac $2.55, m. pop $1.15, fries $0.95 **Total: $18.60**	Big Mac $1.79, m. pop $0.75, fries $0.59 **Total: $12.52**
■ Family day pass to the Southland Leisure Centre	$16.30*	$14
■ A day at the Glenbow Museum	Adults $5, student $3.50 **Total: $17***	Adults $2, student $1 **Total: $6**
■ Watching a Famous Players movie (assumes each family member has one of each item)	Adults $8, child $4.25, pop $2.34, popcorn $2.81, candy bar $0.93 **Total: $48.82***	Adults $6.50, child $2.75, pop $1.75, popcorn $2.50, candy bar $0.75 **Total: $38.50**
■ A night camping at a serviced provincial site in Kananaskis Country	$15 (firewood $4) **Total: $19***	$5 (firewood included)
■ A day at the zoo	Adults $8, child $4 **Total: $24***	Adults $4.50, child $2.25 **Total: $13.50**

[1] Age five to 12, [2] Age five to 17   *GST included

© 1996, *Calgary Herald*, Reprinted by permission.

Economic

A N A L Y S I S

■ The median Canadian family income after tax was about $34,000 in 1986 and about $44,000 in 1996. So over this decade, incomes increased by about 22 percent.

■ Over this same decade, the prices of "family fun" items listed in the table increased by amounts that range from a low of 16 percent (Southland Leisure Centre) to a high of 280 percent (camping in Kananaskis Country).

■ *Real incomes* have fallen but *relative prices* have changed. To see the change in relative prices most clearly, consider two family activities: (1) a meal at McDonald's and a night at the movies and (2) a fun weekend, camping and visiting a major outdoor site.

■ In 1986, each of these activities cost about $50. In 1996, a McDonald's and movie night cost $70 and a fun weekend cost $140.

■ Figure 1 shows how a family might have allocated its budget in 1986. Here, the family spends $2,600 on movie nights and fun weekends. At $50 each, it can buy just one of these items a week. The budget line shows these possibili-ties. One fun weekend costs one movie night.

■ The indifference curves illustrate the family's pref-erences. This family makes its best affordable choice by going to the movies 32 times and having 20 fun weekends.

■ Figure 2 shows the sit-uation in 1996. If the fami-ly spends the same per-centage of its income on these two goods as it did in 1986 (an assumption), it can now consume less of both goods.

■ If it spends all its fun money on movies, it can have 48 movie nights in the year. If it spends it all on weekend outings, it can have 24 a year. One fun weekend now costs *two* movie nights.

■ This family's best affordable choice is to have 38 movie nights and only 5 fun weekends. Because a movie night now costs less relative to a fun weekend, the family has substituted movie nights for fun weekends.

■ This outcome is consis-tent with the broad facts. Despite lower family incomes, families are going on fewer family outings than they did in 1986.

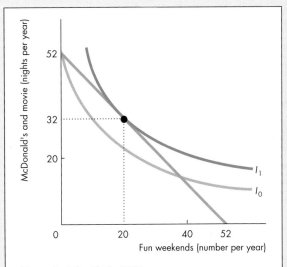

Figure 1 A family in 1986

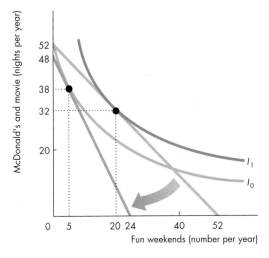

Figure 2 A family in 1996

S U M M A R Y

Key Points

Consumption Possibilities   The budget line is the boundary between what the household can and cannot afford. The point at which the budget line intersects the *y*-axis is the household's real income in terms of the good measured on that axis. The magnitude of the slope of the budget line is the relative price of the good measured on the *x*-axis in terms of the good measured on the *y*-axis. A change in price changes the slope of the budget line. A change in income shifts the budget line (rightward for an increase and leftward for a decrease) but does not change its slope. (pp. 169–172)

Preferences and Indifference Curves   A consumer's preferences can be represented by indifference curves. An indifference curve joins the combinations of goods among which the consumer is indifferent. The magnitude of the slope of an indifference curve is called the marginal rate of substitution. A key assumption is that the marginal rate of substitution diminishes as consumption of the good measured on the *y*-axis decreases and consumption of the good measured on the *x*-axis increases. (pp. 172–176)

The Household's Consumption Choice   A household consumes at its best affordable point. Such a point is on the budget line and on the highest attainable indifference curve. At that point, the indifference curve and the budget line have the same slope—the marginal rate of substitution equals the relative price. (pp. 176–177)

Predicting Consumer Behaviour   Other things remaining the same, when the price of a good falls, a household buys more of that good. Also, other things remaining the same, when income increases, a household buys more of all (normal) goods. A fall in the price of a good makes that good relatively less costly and increases real income. The fall in the relative price increases consumption of the good—the substitution effect—and the increase in real income increases consumption if the good is a normal good and decreases consumption if the good is an inferior good—the income effect. (pp. 177–181)

Key Figures

Key Terms

R E V I E W   Q U E S T I O N S

1. What determines the limits to a household's consumption choices?
2. What is the budget line?
3. What determines the intercept of the budget line on the *y*-axis?
4. What determines the slope of the budget line?
5. What do all the points on an indifference curve have in common?
6. What is the connection between the degree of substitutability and the shape of an indifference curve?
7. What is the marginal rate of substitution?
8. What two conditions are satisfied when a con-

sumer makes the best affordable consumption choice?
9. What is the effect of a change in income on consumption of a normal good?
10. What is the effect of a change in income on consumption of an inferior good?
11. What is the effect of a change in price on consumption of a normal good?
12. What is the price effect?
13. What is the substitution effect?
14. How do we isolate the substitution effect?
15. What is the direction of the substitution effect?

C R I T I C A L   T H I N K I N G

1. Study *Reading Between the Lines* on pp.182–183 and then answer the following questions:
   a. What happened to real incomes between 1986 and 1996?
   b. What were the changes in relative prices reported in the news article between 1986 and 1996?
   c. Use a figure similar to those on p. 183 to show how consumption patterns would have been different in 1996 if:
      (i) Real incomes were the same as in 1986 but relative prices were the same as in 1996.
      (ii) Real incomes were the same as in 1996 but relative prices were the same as in 1986.
   d. If the government put a tax on movies and fast food but no tax on other leisure goods and services, how would consumption patterns change? Answer by using a figure similar to those on p. 183.
2. The Liberal government of Jean Chrétien was elected on the promise that the Goods and Services Tax (GST) would be eliminated. If the GST, which is a tax on almost all goods and services, was replaced by a tax on only goods,

what effect would such a policy have on the quantities of goods and services that the average consumer buys?
3. Once in power, the government of Jean Chrétien adopted a policy of a uniform GST that merges the original GST and the provincial sales tax (PST). Currently, PST is a tax on goods but not services. If the uniform GST does get adopted, what effect would it have on the quantities of goods and services that the average consumer buys?
4. Jim, a Generation-Xer, spends his income on apartment rent, food, clothing, and vacations. He gets a pay raise from $2,000 a month to $3,000 a month. At the same time, air fares and other vacation related costs increase by 50 percent. Other prices don't change.
   a. How do you think Jim will change his spending pattern as a result of the changes in his income and prices?
   b. Can we say whether Jim is better off, worse off, or just as well off as before?
   c. How will Jim be affected by the merged PST and GST described in the previous question?

P R O B L E M S

1. Sara has an income of $12 a week. Popcorn costs $3 a bag and cola costs $3 a can.
   a. What is Sara's real income in terms of cola?
   b. What is her real income in terms of popcorn?
   c. What is the relative price of cola in terms of popcorn?
   d. What is the opportunity cost of a can of cola?
   e. Calculate the equation for Sara's budget line (placing bags of popcorn on the left side).
   f. Draw a graph of Sara's budget line with cola on the x-axis.
   g. In part (f), what is the slope of Sara's budget line? What is it equal to?

2. Sara's income and the prices she faces are the same as in problem 1. Her preferences are shown by her indifference curves in the figure.

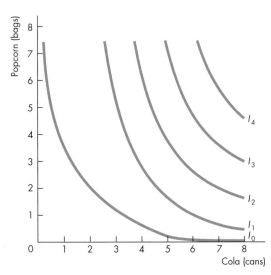

   a. What are the quantities of popcorn and cola that Sara buys?
   b. What is Sara's marginal rate of substitution of popcorn for cola at the point at which she consumes?

3. Now suppose that in the situation described in problem 2, the price of cola falls to $1.50 per can and the price of popcorn and Sara's income remain constant.
   a. Find the new quantities of cola and popcorn that Sara buys.
   b. Find two points on Sara's demand curve for cola.
   c. Find the substitution effect of the price change.
   d. Find the income effect of the price change.
   e. Is cola a normal good or an inferior good for Sara?
   f. Is popcorn a normal good or an inferior good for Sara?

4. Jerry buys cookies that cost $1 each and comic books that cost $2 each. Each month, Jerry buys 20 cookies and 10 comic books. He spends all of his income. Next month, the price of a cookie will fall to 50¢, but the price of a comic book will rise to $3.
   a. Will Jerry be able to buy 20 cookies and 10 comic books next month?
   b. Will he want to?
   c. If he changes his consumption, which good will he buy more of and which less of?
   d. Which situation does Jerry prefer: cookies at $1 and comic books at $2 or cookies at 50¢ and comic books at $3?
   e. When the prices change next month, will there be an income effect and a substitution effect at work or just one of them? If there is only one effect at work, which one will it be?

5. Now suppose that in the situation described in problem 4, the prices of cookies and comic books next month remain at $1 and $2 respectively. Jerry gets a pay raise of $10 a month. He now buys 16 comic books and 18 cookies. For Jerry, are cookies and comic books normal goods or inferior goods?

Organizing Production

After studying this chapter, you will be able to:

- Explain what a firm is, and describe the economic problems that *all* firms face

- Define and explain the principal–agent problem

- Describe and distinguish between different forms of business organization

- Explain how firms raise the funds to finance their operations

- Calculate a firm's opportunity cost and economic profit

- Explain why firms coordinate some economic activities and markets coordinate others

Realizing Dreams

In the summer of 1971, Greig Clark, a student at the University of Western Ontario, realized that he was going to need $3,000 to pay his bills for the coming year at school. He hit on the idea of hiring other students as workers to paint houses in his home town of Thunder Bay. So was born College Pro Painters, a tiny firm that today has grown into a profitable enterprise that hires thousands of students. By 1987, College Pro had more than 500 outlets across North America and sales of $35 million. College Pro was the target of a takeover in 1989 and today is part of First Service, one of some 2 million firms that operate in Canada today. They range from multinational giants to small family restaurants and corner stores. Three-quarters of all firms are operated by their owners, but corporations (like IBM) account for 90 percent of all business sales. What are the different forms a firm can take? Why do some remain small while others become giants? Why are most firms owner operated? ◆ Firms spend billions of dollars on buildings and production lines and on developing and marketing new products. How does a firm get the funds needed to pay for all these activities? What do investors expect in return when they put funds into a firm? And how do we measure a firm's economic health? ◆ Most of the components of an IBM personal computer are made by other firms. Another firm, Microsoft, created the operating system for the PC. Microsoft has now outgrown IBM, and its products such as DOS and Windows have become household names. Why doesn't IBM make its own computer components? Why didn't it create its own operating system? Why did it leave these activities to other firms? How do firms decide what to make themselves and what to buy in the marketplace from other firms?

◆ In this chapter, we are going to learn about firms and the choices they make to cope with scarcity. We begin by studying the economic problems and choices that all firms face.

The Firm and Its Economic Problem

THERE ARE 2 MILLION FIRMS IN CANADA, AND they differ enormously in size and in the scope of what they do. What do they have in common? What are the distinguishing characteristics of a firm? What are the different ways in which firms are organized? Why are there different forms of organization? These are the questions we'll tackle first.

What Is a Firm?

A **firm** is an institution that hires factors of production and that organizes those factors to produce and sell goods and services. Firms exist because of scarcity. They help us to cope with the fundamental economic problem of scarcity and they enable us to use our scarce resources efficiently. But each firm faces its own economic problem. That is, each firm must strive to get the most it can out of the scarce resources under its control. To do so, a firm must decide on the following:

- Which goods and services to produce and in what quantities

- Which of its inputs to produce itself and which to buy from other firms

- Which techniques of production to use

- Which factors of production to employ and in what quantities

- How to organize its management

- How to compensate its factors of production and suppliers

For the majority of firms, these decisions are made so that the firm makes the maximum possible profit. And for every firm, whether it is motivated by profit or some other goal, these decisions are made so that the firm produces its output at the lowest possible cost.

In the rest of this chapter and in Chapters 10 through 13, we are going to study the actions a firm must take to be efficient. We are going to see how we can predict a firm's behaviour by working out its efficient response to a change in its circumstances. But we are going to begin by looking a bit more closely at the fundamental problem the firm faces.

The fundamental problem for a firm is *organization*—the firm organizes the production of goods and services by combining and coordinating the factors of production it hires. Firms organize production by using a mixture of two systems:

- Command systems

- Incentive systems

Command Systems

A command system is a method of coordinating the factors of production that a firm hires that is based on a managerial hierarchy. A chief executive is at the top of the managerial ladder and directs the senior managers. The senior managers direct the middle managers, who in turn direct operations managers. This lowest level of management controls the workers who produce the goods and services. Commands pass downward through the managerial hierarchy and information passes upward. Managers spend most of their time collecting and processing information about the performance of the people under their control and making decisions about commands to issue and how best to get those commands implemented.

The number of layers of management depends on the complexity of the business and on the technology available for managing information. In the smallest and simplest organizations, perhaps one or two layers of managers are all that are needed. But in large organizations that undertake complex tasks, several layers of management are found. The computer and information revolution of the 1980s and 1990s has decreased the number of layers needed and has brought a big shake-out of middle managers.

Despite the enormous efforts they make to be well-informed, managers always have incomplete information about what is happening in the divisions of the firm under their control. It is for this reason that firms use incentive systems as well as command systems to organize production.

Incentive Systems

Incentive systems are market-like mechanisms that firms create inside their organizations. Such systems operate at all levels, from the chief executive down to the factory floor and the sales force. They arise because a firm's owners and managers cannot know everything that is relevant to the efficient operation of their business. What did Greig Clark contribute to the success of College Pro Painters? What role did Bill Gates play in the fortunes of Microsoft Corporation? These questions cannot be answered with certainty even long after the event. Yet College Pro Painters and Microsoft must put chief executive officers (CEOs) like these in charge of operations and give them *incentives* to succeed, even when the contribution they make cannot be measured directly.

At the bottom of the management ladder, some workers are more diligent than others and it is often difficult for managers to know who is working and who is shirking. Did sales fall last month because the sales force slacked off or because of some other unknown factor? Again, firms must devise incentives to ensure that the sales force works effectively.

Because of incomplete information, firms do not simply demand factors of production and pay them as if they were buying toothpaste at the drugstore. Instead, they enter into contracts and devise compensation packages that strengthen incentives and raise productivity. These contracts and compensation packages are called agency relationships and they are an attempt to solve what is called the principal–agent problem.

The Principal–Agent Problem

The **principal–agent problem** is to devise compensation rules that induce an *agent* to act in the best interest of a *principal*. For example, the relationship between the stockholders of the Royal Bank and the bank's managers is an agency relationship. The stockholders (the principals) want the managers (agents) to act in the stockholders' best interest. Another example of an agency relationship is that between Microsoft Corporation (a principal) and its programmers working on a new version of Windows (agents). Microsoft wants the programmers to work in the best interest of the firm.

Coping with the Principal–Agent Problem

Agents, whether they are managers or workers, pursue their own goals and often impose costs on a principal. For example, the goal of a stockholder of the Royal Bank (a principal) is to maximize the bank's profit. But the bank's profit depends on the actions of its managers (agents) who have their own goals.

Perhaps a manager takes a customer to a ball game on the pretence that she is building customer loyalty, when in fact she is simply taking on-the-job leisure. This same manager is also a principal and her tellers are agents. The manager wants the tellers to work hard and attract new customers so she can meet her operating targets. But the tellers enjoy conversations with each other and keep customers waiting in line. Nonetheless, the bank constantly strives to find ways of improving performance and increasing profits.

The principal–agent problem cannot be solved just by giving orders and having workers obey them. In most firms, it isn't possible for the shareholders to monitor the managers or even for the managers to monitor the workers. To achieve their goal, the firm's owners (principals) must induce its managers (agents) to pursue the maximum possible profit. And the managers (principals) must induce the workers and other firms (agents) to work efficiently. Each principal attempts to do this by creating incentives that induce each agent to work in the interests of the principal. The three main ways of coping with the principal–agent problem are

- Ownership

- Incentive pay

- Long-term contracts

Ownership By assigning a manager or worker ownership (or part-ownership) of a business, it is sometimes possible to induce a job performance that increases a firm's profits. Part-ownership schemes for senior managers are quite common, but they are less common for workers. This solution worked when in 1995 Canadian Pacific Ltd. sold off CP Express and Transport, Canada's third largest coast-to-coast trucking company, to its 3,500 employees.

Incentive Pay Incentive pay schemes—pay related to performance—are very common. They are based on a wide variety of performance criteria. For example, managers often share in a firm's profits for meeting profit targets, and workers get bonuses for meeting production or sales targets.

Long-Term Contracts Long-term contracts are a way of coping with the principal–agent problem because they tie the long-term fortunes of managers and workers (agents) to the success of the principal(s)—the owner(s) of the firm.

The principal–agent problem arises from incomplete information about the present. In addition, all firms must cope with uncertainty about the future.

Uncertainty About the Future

A firm's decisions are based on expectations of the consequences of their actions. But expectations often turn out to be wrong. The main reason is that almost every firm must commit to a project and spend huge amounts on it *before* it knows whether it will be able to sell its output in sufficient quantities and at a sufficiently high price to cover its outlays. For example, 30 years ago, French and British airplane makers spent several years and millions of dollars building a supersonic transatlantic passenger plane—the Concorde. They expected to be able to sell enough of these technologically sophisticated airplanes to recover their cost. But it turns out that too few people value the Concorde's extra speed for it to generate sales revenues equal to its cost. On a smaller scale, millions of people try their luck at opening coffee shops and other small businesses. They spend several thousand dollars setting up a business before they know how much revenue their business will earn. And many of them turn out to be too optimistic. The revenue falls short of the cost and the business fails.

The facts of incomplete information and uncertainty about the future give rise to different forms of business organization. Let's look at these different forms.

The Forms of Business Organization

The three main forms of business organization are

- Sole proprietorship
- Partnership
- Corporation

Which form a firm takes influences its management structure, how it compensates factors of production, how much tax its owners pay, and who receives its profits and is liable for its debts if it goes out of business.

Sole Proprietorship A *sole proprietorship* is a firm with a single owner—a proprietor—who has unlimit-

ed liability. *Unlimited liability* is the legal responsibility for all the debts of a firm up to an amount equal to the entire wealth of the owner. If a proprietorship cannot pay its debts, the personal property of the owner can be claimed by those to whom the firm owes money. Corner stores, computer programmers, and artists are all examples of sole proprietorships.

The proprietor makes the management decisions and is the firm's sole residual claimant. A firm's *residual claimant* is the person who receives the firm's profits and is responsible for its losses. The profits of a sole proprietorship are part of the income of the proprietor. They are added to the proprietor's other income and taxed as personal income.

Partnership A *partnership* is a firm with two or more owners who have unlimited liability. Partners must agree on an appropriate management structure and on how to divide the firm's profits among themselves. As in a sole proprietorship, the profits of a partnership are taxed as the personal income of the owners. But each partner is legally liable for all the debts of the partnership (only limited by the wealth of an individual partner). Liability for the full debts of the partnership is called *joint unlimited liability*. Most law firms and accounting firms are partnerships.

Corporation A *corporation* is a firm owned by one or more limited liability stockholders. *Limited liability* means the owners have legal liability only for the value of their initial investment. This limitation of liability means that if the corporation becomes bankrupt, the owners of the corporation, unlike the owners of a sole proprietorship or partnership, cannot be forced to use their personal wealth to pay the corporation's debts.

The stock of a corporation is divided into shares. A *share* is a fraction of the stock of a corporation. Shares in many corporations can be bought and sold on stock markets such as the Toronto Stock Exchange.

Some corporations, no bigger than a sole proprietorship, have just one effective owner and are managed in the same way as a sole proprietorship. Large corporations have elaborate management structures headed by a CEO and senior vice-presidents responsible for such areas as production, finance, marketing, and research. These senior executives are in turn served by a series of specialists. Each layer in the management structure knows enough about what happens in the layer below it to exercise control, but the entire management consists of specialists who concentrate on a narrow aspect of the corporation's activities.

The corporation receives its financial resources from its owners—the stockholders—and by borrowing. Corporations sometimes borrow from banks, but they can also borrow directly from households by issuing bonds—loans on which they pay a fixed number of dollars of interest.

If a corporation makes a profit, the residual claimants to that profit are the stockholders, who receive dividends. If a corporation incurs a loss on such a scale that it becomes bankrupt, the residual loss is absorbed by the banks and other corporations to whom the troubled corporation is in debt. The stockholders themselves, by virtue of their limited liability, are responsible for the debt of the corporation only up to the value of their initial investment.

The profits of a corporation are taxed independently of the incomes of its stockholders so corporate profits are, in effect, taxed twice. After a corporation has paid tax on its profits, the stockholders themselves pay taxes on the income they receive as dividends on stocks. They also pay tax on capital gains when they sell a stock. A **capital gain** is the income received by selling a stock (or a bond) for a higher price than the price paid for it. Corporate stocks generate capital gains when a corporation retains some of its profit and reinvests it in profitable activities instead of paying dividends. So even retained earnings are effectively taxed twice because the capital gains they generate are taxed.

The Pros and Cons of the Different Types of Firms

Because each of the three main types of firms exists, each type obviously has advantages in particular situations. Each type also has its disadvantages, a fact that explains why each type has not driven out the other two. These pros and cons of each type of firm are summarized in Table 9.1.

TABLE 9.1

The Pros and Cons of Different Types of Firms

Type of firm	Pros	Cons
Sole Proprietorship	■ Easy to set up ■ Simple decision making ■ Profits taxed only once as owner's income	■ Bad decisions not checked by need for consensus ■ Owner's entire wealth at risk ■ Firm dies with owner ■ Capital is expensive ■ Labour is expensive
Partnership	■ Easy to set up ■ Diversified decision making ■ Can survive withdrawal of partner ■ Profits taxed only once as owners' incomes	■ Achieving consensus may be slow and expensive ■ Owners' entire wealth at risk ■ Withdrawal of partner may create capital shortage ■ Capital is expensive
Corporation	■ Owners have limited liability ■ Large-scale, low-cost capital available ■ Professional management not restricted by ability of owners ■ Perpetual life ■ Long-term labour contracts cut labour costs	■ Complex management structure can make decisions slow and expensive ■ Profits taxed twice as company profit and as stockholders' income

- A firm is an institution that hires factors of production and organizes the production and sale of goods and services.
- Firms strive to be efficient and most firms aim to maximize profit but they face uncertainty and have incomplete information. To cope with these problems, firms enter into relationships—principal–agent relationships—with owners, managers, workers, and other firms and devise efficient legal structures and compensation schemes.
- Each main type of firm—sole proprietorship, partnership, and corporation—has its advantages, and each type plays a role in every sector of the economy.

Business Finance

EVERY YEAR FIRMS RAISE BILLIONS OF DOLLARS to enable them to buy capital equipment and to finance their inventory holdings. For example, an airline might raise hundreds of millions of dollars to buy a bigger fleet of jets. A steel manufacturer might raise hundreds of millions of dollars to build a new plant. A software producer might raise millions of dollars to pay programmers to develop a new computer game. Let's see how firms raise funds.

How Firms Raise Funds

All firms get some of their funds from their owners. The owner's stake in a business is called **equity**. Firms also borrow some of the funds they need from banks. Sole proprietorships and partnerships raise additional funds by borrowing from friends. The more permanent structure of corporations gives them two ways of raising large amounts of money that are not generally available to households and unincorporated businesses. They are

- Selling stock
- Selling bonds

Selling Stock

One major way in which a corporation can raise funds is by selling stock. Funds raised in this way are the corporation's *equity* because the stockholders of a corporation are its owners. They have bought shares of the corporation's stock.

Corporations sell shares of their stock, and these shares regularly trade on stock exchanges. A *stock exchange* is an organized market for trading in stock. Stock exchanges in Canada are located in Toronto, Montreal, and Vancouver.

Figure 9.1 shows an example of a firm raising funds by selling stock. In February 1994, Reebok International Ltd. sold 3 million shares of stock for $33.125 a share, thereby raising $99,375,000. There is no obligation for a firm that raises funds by selling stock to make dividend payments to its stockholders. But stockholders expect a dividend or a capital gain—otherwise no one will buy the shares.

FIGURE 9.1

Selling Stock

This announcement is neither an offer to sell nor a solicitation of offers to buy any of these securities. The offering is made only by the Prospectus.

February 25, 1994

3,000,000 Shares

Reebok International Ltd.

Common Stock
($0.1 par value)

Price $33.125 Per Share

Copies of the Prospectus may be obtained in any State in which this announcement is circulated only from such of the undersigned as may legally offer these securities in such State.

CS First Boston

Kidder, Peabody & Co.
Incorporated

Montgomery Securities

A share of the stock in a company entitles its holder to receive a dividend (if the directors vote to pay one). Reebok sold 3,000,000 shares of stock at $33.125 a share, thereby raising $99,375,000 of additional funds.

Selling Bonds

A **bond** is a legally enforceable debt obligation to pay specified amounts of money at specified future dates. Usually, a bond specifies that a certain amount of money called the *redemption value* of the bond will be paid at a certain future date called the *maturity date*. In addition, another amount will be paid each year between the date of sale of the bond and the maturity date. The amount of money paid each year is called the *coupon payment*.

Figure 9.2 gives an example of bond financing. On July 12, 1994, Kinpo Electronics Inc., a company based in Taiwan that plans to take on Apple Computers, Motorola, and Texas Instruments in a bid for the world market in personal digital assistants, raised $44 million by selling bonds. On that day, Kinpo obligated itself to making a coupon payment of $1.32 million (the equivalent of an interest rate of 3 percent a year) on July 12 each year through 2001 and to repaying the $44 million on July 12, 2001. So the total amount that Kinpo obligated itself to pay is $53.24 million, the $44 million borrowed plus $1.32 million a year for seven years.

When it makes a financing decision, a firm tries to minimize its cost of funds. If it can raise funds by selling bonds at a lower cost than from any other source, the firm will choose that method of financing. But how does it decide how much to borrow? To answer this question, we need to understand a key principle of business and personal finance.

Discounting and Present Value

When a firm raises funds, it receives money in the current period and takes on an obligation to make a series of payments in *future* periods. For example, Kinpo received $44 million in 1994 and took on an obligation to pay out $53.24 million through 2001. But also when a firm raises funds, it does so because it plans to use them to generate a future net inflow of cash from its business operations. For example, Kinpo borrowed $44 million because it planned to use it to manufacture and sell computer components and products that would bring in some future revenue.

To decide whether to borrow and how much to borrow, a firm must somehow compare money today with money in the future. If you are given a choice between a dollar today and a dollar a year from today, you will choose a dollar today. A dollar today

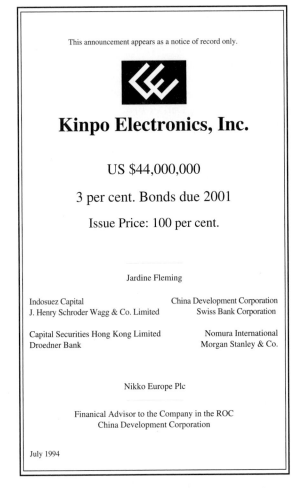

A bond is an obligation to make coupon payments and a redemption payment. Kinpo, a producer of computer components and personal digital assistants, sold bonds to raise $44 million in 1994. The company promised to pay $3 per $100 borrowed each year as a coupon payment and to redeem the bonds in 2001.

is worth more to you than a dollar in the future because you can invest today's dollar to earn interest. The same is true for a firm. To compare an amount of money in the future with an amount of money in the present, we calculate the present value of the future amount of money. The **present value** of a future amount of money is the amount which, if invested today, will grow to be as large as that future amount, when the interest that it will earn is taken into account. Let's express this idea with an equation:

Future amount = Present value + Interest income.

The interest income is equal to the present value multiplied by the interest rate, r, so

Future amount = Present value + ($r \times$ Present value)

or,

Future amount = Present value × (1 + r).

If you have $100 today and the interest rate is 10 percent a year ($r = 0.1$), one year from today you will have $110, the original $100 plus $10 interest. Check that the above formula delivers that answer: $100 × 1.1 = $110.

The formula that we have just used calculates a future amount one year from today from the present value and an interest rate. To calculate the present value, we just work backward. Instead of multiplying the present value by (1 + r), we divide the future amount by (1 + r). That is,

$$\text{Present value} = \frac{\text{Future amount}}{(1 + r)}.$$

You can use this formula to calculate present value. Calculating present value is called discounting. **Discounting** is the conversion of a future amount of money to its present value. Let's check that we can use the present value formula by calculating the present value of $110 one year from now when the interest rate is 10 percent a year. You'll be able to guess that the answer is $100 because we just calculated that $100 invested today at 10 percent a year becomes $110 in one year. Thus it follows immediately that the present value of $110 in one year's time is $100. But let's use the formula. Putting the numbers into the above formula we have

$$\text{Present value} = \frac{\$110}{(1 + 0.1)}$$

$$= \frac{\$110}{(1.1)}$$

$$= \$100.$$

Calculating the present value of an amount of money one year from now is the easiest case. But we can also calculate the present value of an amount any number of years in the future. As an example, let's see how we calculate the present value of an amount of money available two years from now.

Suppose that you invest $100 today for two years at an interest rate of 10 percent a year. The money will earn $10 in the first year, which means that by the end of the first year you will have $110. If the interest of $10 is invested, then the interest earned in the second year will be a further $10 on the original $100 plus $1 on the $10 interest. Thus the total interest earned in the second year will be $11. The total interest earned overall will be $21 ($10 in the first year and $11 in the second year). After two years, you will have $121. From the definition of present value, you can see that the present value of $121 two years hence is $100. That is, $100 is the present amount which, if invested at 10 percent interest, will grow to $121 two years from now.

To calculate the present value of an amount of money two years in the future we use the formula

$$\text{Present value} = \frac{\begin{array}{c}\text{Amount of money}\\ \text{two years in future}\end{array}}{(1 + r)^2}.$$

Let's check that the formula works by calculating the present value of $121 two years in the future when the interest rate is 10 percent a year. Putting these numbers into the formula gives

$$\text{Present value} = \frac{\$121}{(1 + 0.1)^2}$$

$$= \frac{\$121}{(1.1)^2}$$

$$= \frac{\$121}{1.21}$$

$$= \$100.$$

We can calculate the present value of an amount of money any number of years in the future by using a formula based on the two that we've already used. The general formula is

$$\text{Present value} = \frac{\begin{array}{c}\text{Amount of money}\\ n \text{ years in future}\end{array}}{(1 + r)^n}.$$

For example, if the interest rate is 10 percent a year, $100 to be received 10 years from now has a present value of $38.55. That is, if $38.55 is invested today at an interest rate of 10 percent, it will accumulate to $100 in 10 years. (You might check that calculation on your pocket calculator.)

Present Value and Marginal Analysis

Firms use the concept of present value to make their financing decisions. But they use it together with another fundamental principle, marginal analysis. In making any decision, only the additional benefit—*marginal benefit*—and additional cost—*marginal cost*—resulting from that decision are relevant. By evaluating the marginal benefit and marginal cost of borrowing, a firm is able to maximize its profit. Marginal benefit minus marginal cost is net benefit and the present value of net benefit is called *net* present value.

The firm decides how much to borrow by calculating the net present value of borrowing one additional dollar—the marginal dollar borrowed. If the present value of the marginal dollar borrowed is positive, then the firm increases its profit by increasing the amount it borrows. If present value of the marginal dollar borrowed is negative, then the firm increases its profit by *decreasing* its borrowing. When the present value of the marginal dollar borrowed is zero, then the firm is maximizing its profit.

R E V I E W

■ Firms finance capital equipment purchases by selling bonds—promises of a fixed income independent of the firm's profit—and selling stock—opportunities to share in the firm's profit.

■ Firms borrow if doing so increases the net present value of their cash flow.

■ The net present value of an amount of money n years in the future when the interest rate is r a year is equal to the amount of money divided by $(1 + r)^n$.

We've seen how firms pursue maximum profits by establishing appropriate types of business organization and by raising funds in the most profitable way. But how do firms measure their performance? How do they calculate their costs and profits? These are the questions we now study.

Opportunity Cost and Economic Profit

A FIRM'S OPPORTUNITY COST OF PRODUCING A good is the best alternative action that the firm forgoes to produce it. Equivalently, it is the firm's best alternative use for the factors of production it employs to produce a good. Opportunity cost is a real alternative forgone. But so that we can compare the opportunity cost of one action with that of another action, we often express opportunity cost in units of money. Even though we sometimes express opportunity cost in money units, it is the real alternative forgone and not the money value of that alternative.

A firm's opportunity cost of production has two components:

1. Explicit costs
2. Implicit costs

Explicit costs are paid directly in money—*money costs*. Implicit costs (measured in units of money) are opportunities forgone but not paid for directly in money. It is easy to measure explicit costs but harder to measure implicit costs.

A firm incurs explicit costs when it pays for a factor of production at the same time as it uses it. The money cost is the amount paid for the factor of production, but this same amount could have been spent on something else, so it is also the opportunity cost (expressed in dollars) of using this factor of production. For example, if a pizza restaurant hires a waiter, the wages paid are both the money cost and opportunity cost of hiring the waiter—the firm pays the waiter at the same time as it uses the services of the waiter. Labour is the factor of production whose money cost typically equals its opportunity cost.

A firm incurs implicit costs when it uses the following factors of production:

■ Capital
■ Inventories
■ Owner's resources

Cost of Capital

The cost of using capital equipment is an implicit cost because a firm usually buys its equipment—lays out some money—and then uses the equipment over a future period. For example, GM buys an assembly line, pays for it this year, and uses it for several years. What is the opportunity cost of using capital equipment bought several years earlier? This opportunity cost has two components:

- Depreciation
- Interest

Depreciation   **Economic depreciation i**s the change in the market price of a capital asset over a given period. It is calculated as the market price of the capital at the beginning of the period minus its market price at the end of the period. For example, suppose that Air Canada has a Boeing 747 jumbo jet that it could have sold on December 31, 1995, for $5 million. Suppose also that it could sell the same airplane on December 31, 1996, for $4 million. The $1 million fall in the market value is an implicit cost of using the airplane during 1996. Notice that the original cost of the airplane is not directly relevant to this calculation.

Economic depreciation occurs for a variety of reasons. The most common is that an older piece of equipment has a shorter future life. Also, it is often more costly to maintain in good working order. But economic depreciation also occurs simply because a piece of equipment has become obsolete. It still works fine and might do so for many years, but there is something new that works even better. For example, suppose Kinko bought some new copiers on January 1, 1996, that it expected to operate for three years. Then, during 1996, a faster copier became available and the market price of the slower copiers fell by 90 percent. This 90 percent price fall is the opportunity cost of using the copiers in 1996. Even though the copiers are new and still work fine, their economic depreciation—and opportunity cost—during 1996 is large.

Interest   The funds used to buy a capital asset could have been used for some other purpose. And in their next best alternative use, they would have yielded a return—an interest income. This forgone interest is part of the opportunity cost of using the capital asset. It is an opportunity cost regardless of whether a firm borrows the funds it uses to buy its capital. To see why, think about two cases: the firm borrows or uses its previous earnings.

If a firm borrows the money, then it makes an explicit interest payment, so the interest cost is an explicit cost. If the firm uses its own funds, then the

opportunity cost is the amount that could have been earned by allocating those funds to their best alternative use. Suppose the best alternative is for the firm to put the money in a bank deposit. The bank deposit interest forgone is the opportunity cost of using the capital.

Implicit Rental Rate   To measure the opportunity cost of using capital (buildings, plant, and equipment), we calculate the sum of economic depreciation and interest costs. This opportunity cost is the income that the firm forgoes by using the capital itself and not renting the capital to another firm instead. The firm actually rents the capital to itself. When a firm rents capital to itself, it pays an **implicit rental rate** for its use.

People commonly rent houses, apartments, cars, movies, VCRs, and videotapes. And firms commonly rent photocopiers, earthmoving equipment, satellite launching services, and so on. If a piece of equipment is rented, a dollar payment called an *explicit* rental rate is made. If a piece of equipment is bought and used by its owner rather than rented to someone else, an *implicit rental rate* is paid. The owner–user of a piece of equipment could have rented the equipment to someone else instead. And the income forgone is the opportunity cost of using the equipment. That opportunity cost is the *implicit* rental rate.

Market forces bring about an equality of the explicit rental rate and implicit rental rate. If renting had a lower opportunity cost than buying, everyone would want to rent and no one would want to buy. So renters would not be able to find anyone to rent from, and the (explicit) rental rate would rise. If renting had a higher opportunity cost than buying, everyone would want to buy and no one would want to rent. So owners would not be able to find anyone to rent to, and the (explicit) rental rate would fall. Only when the opportunity cost of renting and buying are equal—when the explicit rental rate and the implicit rental rate are equal—is there no incentive to switch between buying and renting.

Sunk Cost   The *past economic depreciation* of the firm's capital (building, plant, or equipment) is **sunk cost**. When the capital was purchased, an opportunity was forgone. But that past forgone opportunity is a bygone. The opportunity cannot be retrieved. Sunk cost is not an *opportunity cost*. In the Kinko copier example, Kinko incurred a high opportunity cost during 1996 when the market price of its slow copiers fell. But as Kinko looks forward to 1997, the fall in the value of its copiers in 1996 is a sunk cost. The opportunity cost of using the copiers during 1997 does *not* include that fall in value.

Accounting Measures   Accountants measure depreciation, but they do not usually measure *economic depreciation*. Instead, they assess this fall in the value of a capital asset by applying a conventional depreciation rate to the original purchase price. The conventions used are based on Revenue Canada's rules. For buildings, a conventional depreciation period is 20 years. Thus if a firm buys a new office building for $100,000, its accounts show one-twentieth of that amount, $5,000, as a cost of production each year. At the end of the first year, the firm's accounts record the value of the building as $95,000 (the original cost minus the $5,000 depreciation). Different depreciation rates are used for different types of capital. For example, for cars and computers, the conventional depreciation period is 3 years.

These accounting measures of depreciation do not measure economic depreciation and are not a correct measure of the depreciation component of the opportunity cost of using capital.

Cost of Inventories

Inventories are stocks of raw materials, semifinished goods, and finished goods held by firms. The opportunity cost of using an item from inventory is its current market price. Firms hold inventories to make the production process efficient. So when an item is taken out of inventory, it will have to be replaced by a new item. The cost of that new item is the opportunity cost of using the item taken from inventory. Another line of reasoning leads to the same conclusion. An alternative to *using* an item from inventory is to sell it for its current market price. So the opportunity forgone is the current market price.

To measure the cost of using inventories, accountants frequently use a money cost method called FIFO, which stands for "First In, First Out." This method of calculating the cost of an item taken from inventory assumes that the first item placed into the inventory is the first one out. An alternative accountant's measure is called LIFO, which stands for "Last In, First Out." This money cost of an item taken from inventory is the cost of the last one placed into inventory. Some firms have small inventories or inventories that turn

over very quickly. In such cases, the money cost of using an item from inventory and its opportunity cost are the same. When a production process requires inventories to be held for a long time, the two costs might differ. If prices are constant over long periods of time, FIFO and LIFO measure opportunity cost. But if prices are changing, FIFO is not a measure of opportunity cost, although LIFO is a good approximation to it if the price most recently paid is similar to the price paid to replace the used item.

Cost of Owner's Resources

The owner of a firm often puts a great deal of time and effort into organizing the firm. But the owner could have worked at some other activity and earned a wage. The opportunity cost of the owner's time spent working for the firm is the wage income forgone by not working in the best alternative job.

In addition to supplying labour to the firm, its owner also supplies *entrepreneurial ability* —the factor of production that organizes the business, makes business decisions, innovates, and bears the risk of running the business. These activities would not be undertaken without the expectation of a return. This expected return for supplying entrepreneurial ability is called **normal profit**. Normal profit is part of a firm's opportunity cost because it is the cost of a forgone alternative. The forgone alternative is running another firm.

Usually, the owner of a firm withdraws cash from the business to meet living expenses. Accountants regard such withdrawals of cash as part of the owner's profit from the business, rather than as part of the opportunity cost of the owner's time and entrepreneurial ability. But to the extent that they compensate for wages forgone and risk, they are part of the firm's opportunity cost.

Economic Profit

What is the bottom line—the profit or loss of the firm? A firm's **economic profit** is equal to its total revenue minus its opportunity cost. Its opportunity cost is the explicit and implicit cost of the best alternative actions forgone, including *normal profit.*

Economic profit is not the same as what accountants call profit. For the accountant, a firm's profit is equal to its total revenue minus its money cost and its conventional depreciation.

Opportunity Cost and Economic Profit: An Example

To help you get a clearer picture of the concepts of a firm's opportunity cost, normal profit, and economic profit, we'll look at a concrete example. We'll contrast the economic concepts of opportunity cost and profit with the accounting concepts of cost and profit.

Rocky owns a shop that sells bikes. His revenue, cost, and profit appear in Table 9.2. The accountant's cost calculations are on the left side and the economist's opportunity cost calculations are on the right.

Rocky sold $300,000 worth of bikes during the year. This amount appears as his total revenue. The wholesale cost of bikes was $150,000, he bought $20,000 worth of utilities and other services, and paid out $50,000 in wages to his mechanic and sales clerk. Rocky also paid $12,000 in interest to the bank. All of the items just mentioned appear in both the accountant's and the economist's statements. The remaining items differ between the two statements

and some notes at the foot of the table explain the differences.

The accountant's depreciation calculation is based on conventional life assumptions for Rocky's capital. The economist calculates the cost of Rocky's time, funds invested in the firm, and risk-bearing and also calculates economic depreciation. The accountant says Rocky's costs are $254,000 and his profit is $46,000. In contrast, the economist says that Rocky's year in business had an opportunity cost of $299,500 and yielded an economic profit of $500.

The accountant's calculation of Rocky's profit does not tell Rocky his economic profit because it omits some components of opportunity cost and measures others incorrectly. The economist's measure of economic profit tells Rocky how his business is doing compared with what he can normally expect. Any positive economic profit is good news for Rocky because his normal profit—the normal return on his entrepreneurial ability—is part of the opportunity cost of running his business.

TABLE 9.2

Rocky's Mountain Bikes' Revenue, Cost, and Profit Statement

The accountant		The economist	
Item	**Amount**	**Item**	**Amount**
Total revenue	$300,000	Total revenue	$300,000
Costs:		Costs:	
Wholesale cost of bikes	150,000	Wholesale cost of bikes	150,000
Utilities and other services	20,000	Utilities and other services	20,000
Wages	50,000	Wages	50,000
Depreciation	22,000	Fall in market value of assets[a]	10,000
		Rocky's wages (implicit)[b]	40,000
Bank interest	12,000	Bank interest	12,000
		Interest on Rocky's money[c] invested	
		in firm (implicit)	11,500
		Normal profit (implicit)[d]	6,000
Total cost	$254,000	Opportunity cost	$299,500
Profit	$46,000	Economic profit	$500

[a]The fall in the market value of the assets of the firm gives the opportunity cost of not selling them one year ago. That is part of the opportunity cost of using them for the year.
[b]Rocky could have worked elsewhere for $40 an hour, but he worked 1,000 hours on the firm's business, which means that the opportunity cost of his time is $40,000.

[c]Rocky has invested $115,000 in the firm. If the current interest rate is 10% a year, the opportunity cost of those funds is $11,500.
[d]Rocky could avoid the risk of running his own business, and he would be unwilling to take on the risk for a return of less than $6,000. This is his *normal profit*. (The magnitude of normal profit is assumed.)

REVIEW

■ A firm's economic profit is equal to its total revenue minus its opportunity cost of production.

■ Opportunity cost differs from money cost. Money cost measures cost as the money spent to hire inputs. Opportunity cost measures cost as the value of the best alternative forgone.

■ The main differences between money cost and opportunity cost arise from the cost of capital and inventories and the cost of the resources supplied directly by the owner. But opportunity cost also includes normal profit—the expected return for bearing risk.

We are interested in measuring the opportunity cost of production, not for its own sake, but so that we can compare the efficiency of alternative methods of production. What do we mean by efficiency?

Economic Efficiency

How DOES A FIRM CHOOSE AMONG ALTERNATIVE methods of production? What is the most efficient way of producing? There are two concepts of efficiency: technological efficiency and economic efficiency. **Technological efficiency** occurs when it is not possible to increase output without increasing inputs. **Economic efficiency** occurs when the cost of producing a given output is as low as possible.

Technological efficiency is an engineering matter. Given what is technologically feasible, something can or cannot be done. Economic efficiency depends on the prices of the factors of production. Something that is technologically efficient might not be economically efficient. But something that is economically efficient is always technologically efficient. Let's study technological efficiency and economic efficiency by looking at an example.

Suppose that there are four methods of making TV sets:

a. *Robot production.* One person monitors the entire computer-driven process.

b. *Production line.* Workers specialize in a small part of the job as the emerging TV set passes them on a production line.

c. *Human production.* Workers specialize in a small part of the job but walk from bench to bench to perform their tasks.

d. *Hand-tool production.* A single worker uses a few hand tools to make a TV set.

Table 9.3 sets out the amount of labour and capital required to make 10 TV sets a day by each of these four methods. Are all of these alternative methods technologically efficient? By inspecting the numbers in the figure, you will be able to see that method *c* is not technologically efficient. It requires 100 workers and 10 units of capital to produce 10 TV sets. Those same 10 TV sets can be produced by method *b* with 10 workers and the same 10 units of capital. Therefore method *c* is not technologically efficient.

Are any of the other methods not technologically efficient? The answer is no: Each of the other three methods is technologically efficient. Method *a* uses less labour and more capital than method *b*, and method *d* uses more labour and less capital than method *b*.

What about economic efficiency? Are all three methods economically efficient? To answer that question, we need to know the labour and capital costs. Let's suppose that labour costs $75 per person-day and that capital costs $250 per machine-day. Recall that economic efficiency occurs with the least expensive production process. Table 9.4 calculates the costs of using the four different methods of production. As you can see, the least expensive method of producing a TV set is *b*. Method *a* uses less labour but more capital. It costs much more to make a TV set using method *a* than by using method *b*. Method *d*, the

---

TABLE 9.3

Four Ways of Making 10 TV Sets a Day

		Quantities of inputs	
	Method	Labour	Capital
a	Robot production	1	1,000
b	Production line	10	10
c	Human production	100	10
d	Hand-tool production	1,000	1

TABLE 9.4

The Costs of Four Ways of Making 10 TV Sets a Day

Method	Labour cost ($75 per day)		Capital cost ($250 per day)		Total cost	Cost per TV set
a	$75	+	$250,000	=	$250,075	$25,007.50
b	750	+	2,500	=	3,250	325.00
c	7,500	+	2,500	=	10,000	1,000.00
d	75,000	+	250	=	75,250	7,525.00

---

other technologically efficient method, uses much more labour and hardly any capital. Like method *a*, it winds up costing far more to make a TV set using method *d* than method *b*.

Method *c* is technologically inefficient. It uses the same amount of capital as method *b* but 10 times as much labour. It is interesting to notice that although method *c* is technologically inefficient, it costs less to produce a TV set by using method *c* than it does by using methods *a* and *d*. But method *b* dominates method *c*. Because method *c* is not technologically efficient, there is always a lower-cost method available. That is, a technologically inefficient method is never economically efficient.

Although method *b* is the economically efficient method in this example, methods *a* or *d* could be economically efficient in other circumstances. Let's see when.

First, suppose that labour costs $150 a person-day and capital only $1 a machine-day. Table 9.5 now shows the costs of making a TV set. In this case, method *a* is economically efficient. Capital is now sufficiently cheap relative to labour so that the method using the most capital is the economically efficient method.

Now, suppose that labour costs only $1 a day while capital costs $1,000 a day. Table 9.6 shows the costs in this case. As you can see, method *d*, which uses a lot of labour and little capital, is now the economically efficient method.

A firm that does not use the economically efficient method of production makes a smaller profit. Natural selection favours firms that choose the economically efficient method of production and goes against firms that do not. In extreme cases, an inefficient firm may go bankrupt or be taken over by another firm that can see the possibilities for lower cost and greater profit. Efficient firms will be stronger and better able to survive temporary adversity than inefficient ones.

Our final topic in this chapter goes back to the economic fundamentals from which we began. It examines the reasons why firms coordinate the production of some goods and services and why markets coordinate some others.

TABLE 9.5

The Costs of Three Ways of Making 10 TV Sets: High Labour Costs

Method	Labour cost ($150 per day)		Capital cost ($1 per day)		Total cost	Cost per TV set
a	$150	+	$1,000	=	$1,150	$115.00
b	1,500	+	10	=	1,510	151.00
d	150,000	+	1	=	150,001	15,000.10

TABLE   9.6

The Costs of Three Ways of Making 10 TV Sets: High Capital Costs

Method	Labour cost ($1 per day)		Capital cost ($1,000 per day)		Total cost	Cost per TV set
a	$1	+	$1,000,000	=	$1,000,001	$100,000.10
b	10	+	10,000	=	10,010	1,001.00
d	1,000	+	1,000	=	2,000	200.00

Firms and Markets

AT THE BEGINNING OF THIS CHAPTER, WE DEFINED a firm as an institution that hires factors of production and organizes them to produce and sell goods and services. To organize production, firms coordinate the economic decisions and activities of many individuals. But firms are not the only coordinators of economic decisions. As we learned in Chapter 4, markets also coordinate decisions. By adjusting prices, markets make the decisions of buyers and sellers consistent—make the quantities demanded equal to the quantities supplied of the many different goods and services.

An example of market coordination is the production of a rock concert. A promoter hires a stadium, some stage equipment, audio and video recording engineers and technicians, some rock groups, a superstar, a publicity agent, and a ticket agent—all market transactions—and sells tickets to thousands of rock fans, audio rights to a recording company, and video and broadcasting rights to a television network—another set of market transactions. If rock concerts were produced like corn flakes, the firm producing them would own all the capital used (stadiums, stage, sound and video equipment) and would employ all the labour needed (singers, engineers, sales persons, and so on).

What determines whether a firm or markets coordinate a particular set of activities? The answer is cost. Taking account of the opportunity cost of time as well as the costs of the other inputs, people use the method that costs the least. In other words, they use the economically efficient method.

Firms coordinate economic activity when they can perform a task more efficiently than markets. In such a situation, it is profitable to set up a firm. If markets can perform a task more efficiently than a firm, people will use markets, and any attempt to set up a firm to replace such market coordination will be doomed to failure.

Why Firms?

There are three key reasons why, in many instances, firms are more efficient than markets as coordinators of economic activity. Firms achieve

- Lower transactions costs
- Economies of scale
- Economies of team production

Transactions Costs   The idea that firms exist because there are activities in which they are more efficient than markets was first suggested by University of Chicago economist and Nobel Laureate, Ronald Coase. Coase focused on the firm's ability to reduce or eliminate transactions costs. **Transactions costs** are the costs arising from finding someone with whom to do business, of reaching an agreement about the price and other aspects of the exchange, and of ensuring that the terms of the agreement are fulfilled. *Market* transactions require buyers and sellers to get together and to negotiate the terms and conditions of their trading. Sometimes lawyers have to be hired to draw up contracts. A broken contract leads to still more expenses. A *firm* can lower such transactions costs by reducing the number of individual transactions undertaken.

Consider, for example, two ways of getting your creaking car fixed.

1. *Firm coordination:* You take the car to the garage. Parts and tools as well as the mechanic's time are coordinated by the garage owner, and your car gets fixed. You pay one bill for the entire job.

2. *Market coordination:* You hire a mechanic who diagnoses the problems and makes a list of the parts and tools needed to fix them. You buy the parts from the local wrecker's yard and rent the tools from ABC Rentals. You hire the mechanic again to fix the problems. You return the tools and pay your bills—wages to the mechanic, rental to ABC, and the cost of the parts used to the wrecker.

What determines the method that you use? The answer is cost. Taking account of the opportunity cost of your own time as well as the costs of the other inputs that you'd have to buy, you will use the method that costs least. In other words, you will use the economically efficient method.

The first method requires that you undertake only one transaction with one firm. It's true that the firm has to undertake several transactions—hiring the labour and buying the parts and tools required to do the job. But the firm doesn't have to undertake those transactions simply to fix your car. One set of such transactions enables the firm to fix hundreds of cars. Thus there is an enormous reduction in the number of individual transactions that take place if people get their cars fixed at the garage rather than going through an elaborate sequence of market transactions.

Economies of Scale When the cost of producing a unit of a good falls as its output rate increases, **economies of scale** exist. Many industries experience economies of scale; automobile manufacturing is an example. One firm can produce 4 million cars a year at a lower cost per car than 200 firms each producing 20,000 cars a year. Economies of scale that arise from specialization and the division of labour can be reaped more effectively by firm coordination rather than market coordination.

Team Production A production process in which a group of individuals each specializes in mutually supportive tasks is *team production*. Sport provides the best example of team activity. Some team members specialize in pitching and some in batting, some

in defence and some in offence. The production of goods and services offers many examples of team activity. For example, production lines in automobile and TV manufacturing plants work most efficiently when individual activity is organized in teams, each specializing in a small task. You can also think of an entire firm as being a team. The team has buyers of raw material and other inputs, production workers, and salespersons. There are even specialists within these various groups. Each individual member of the team specializes, but the value of the output of the team and the profit that it earns depend on the coordinated activities of all the team's members. The idea that firms arise as a consequence of the economies of team production was first suggested by Armen Alchian and Harold Demsetz of the University of California at Los Angeles.

Because firms can economize on transactions costs, reap economies of scale, and organize efficient team production, it is firms rather than markets that coordinate most of our economic activity. But there are limits to the economic efficiency of firms. If a firm becomes too big or too diversified in the things that it seeks to do, the cost of management and monitoring per unit of output begins to rise and, at some point, the market becomes more efficient at coordinating the use of resources. IBM is an example of a firm that became too big to be efficient. In an attempt to restore efficient operations, IBM split up its large organization into a number of "Baby Blues," each of which specializes in segments of the computer market.

Sometimes firms enter into long-term relationships with each other that effectively cut out ordinary market transactions and make it difficult to see where one firm ends and another begins. For example, GM has long-term relationships with suppliers of windows, tires, and other parts. Wal-Mart has long-term relationships with suppliers of the goods it sells in its stores. Such relationships make transactions costs lower than they would be if GM or Wal-Mart went shopping in the open market each time they wanted new supplies.

◆ *Reading Between the Lines*, on pp. 204–205, shows you a recent real-world event—the merger of Tim Hortons and Wendy's—that illustrates some of the lessons you've learned in this chapter. In the next chapter, we are going to study more choices of firms. We will study their production decision and how they minimize costs.

Organizing the Production of Doughnuts

FINANCIAL POST, AUGUST 10, 1996

Tim Hortons dips into U.S. market

BY SCOTT ANDERSON

When Ron Joyce took over the first Tim Hortons franchise in Hamilton, Ont., in 1965 he believed a realistic goal was to see the fledging chain grow to 10 stores.

The company's 1,000th doughnut shop opened last week.

In fact, Joyce and his senior management team have a new goal—"2,000 by 2,000." And from all estimates, the target will be reached long before the turn of the century.

"As sure as I'm sitting here, this goal is going to happen, and I'll be there in the background making sure it happens," Joyce said in an interview yesterday.

In the background is exactly where the former policeman turned entrepreneur prefers to be—unlike this week, when Joyce became the headline story because he had sold Tim Hortons to U.S. fast food giant Wendy's International Inc. in a deal worth US$425 million.

The agreement sees Wendy's issue Joyce, co-founder and sole owner of Tim Hortons through TDL Group Ltd., 16.2 million shares, valued at approximately US$300 million, and assume about US$125 million of debt in exchange for all TDL shares.

This deal makes Joyce the largest shareholder of the hamburger chain with 13.5% of the shares, Wendy's senior chairman, Dave Thomas, who founded the chain, will hold only 5.7%. ...

Joyce says the two companies will be able to "share and learn together" adding they share great synergies.

Though Joyce said there are many benefits realized from a joining of the two companies, the primary advantage for the doughnut chain is the exposure the deal will bring in the United States as it rides on the coattails of the hamburger chain. ...

Joyce has a target of 40-50 stores per year opening across North America, with a further 15-20 Wendy's/Tim Hortons combo outlets springing up. ...

Though much of the concentration will be south of the border, Joyce said the company has not forgotten its roots and will stay firmly entrenched in Canada where it now occupies top spot in the Canadian doughnut industry with a 35.9% share of the market.

Essence of THE STORY

■ A former policeman, Ron Joyce, opened the first Tim Hortons franchise in Hamilton, Ont., in 1965.

■ He believed he might see the chain grow to 10 stores but by 1996, the company had 1,000 stores and a 35.9% share of the Canadian doughnut market.

■ In 1996, Wendy's International Inc. bought Tim Hortons for $425 million (U.S.) in a deal that made Joyce the largest shareholder of Wendy's.

■ The main advantage for Tim Hortons is better access to the U.S. market.

■ The plan is to open 40–50 stores plus 15–20 Wendy's/Tim Hortons combo outlets a year across North America.

Economic

ANALYSIS

■ Until August 1995, Tim Hortons was a private company based in Hamilton, Ont., and owned by Ron Joyce.

■ The company had 1,000 doughnut stores and a revenue in 1994 of $603 million.

■ Wendy's is the third largest hamburger chain after McDonald's and Burger King. In 1994, the company had a profit of $92.7 (U.S.) and a total revenue of $1.4 billion (U.S.).

■ Wendy's has 1,283 restaurants and 3,220 franchised restaurants in 34 countries. It has 200 restaurants in Canada.

■ By merging their operations, both Tim Hortons and Wendy's can deliver their services at lower cost and become more profitable.

■ Some of the savings: Senior management can be spread over a larger organization.

■ Marketing expenses can be spread over a larger volume of business.

■ Some stores can sell both the traditional Wendy's range and the traditional Tim Hortons range of goods.

■ The stock market value of Wendy's provides an estimate of the extra profitability of the new combined company.

■ On August 8, 1996, Wendy's stock was selling for $17.50 per share. On Thursday, after the merger was announced, its price increased by almost 6 percent to $18.50. The price remained in this area for the balance of the week, which suggests that the market was comfortable with the idea that the combined assets were worth 6 percent more than the assets managed separately in the two companies.

■ The new expanded Wendy's will use two solutions to the principal–agent problem: direct management (Fig. 1) and franchise agreements (Fig. 2).

■ With direct management, the senior management sets the detailed operating targets and monitors performance.

■ With a franchise, Wendy's senior managers collect a payment from the operator of the franchise but do not set detailed operating targets.

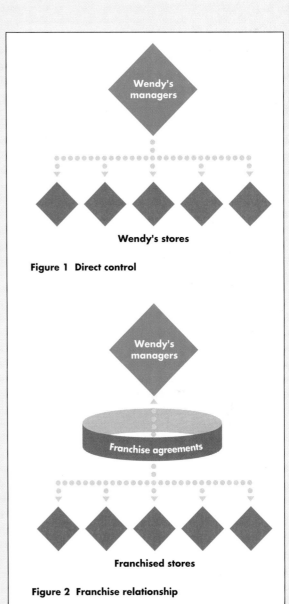

Figure 1 Direct control

Figure 2 Franchise relationship

S U M M A R Y

Key Points

The Firm and Its Economic Problem

Firms hire and organize factors of production to produce and sell goods and services. Firms strive to be efficient—to produce output at the lowest possible cost and to maximize profit. Uncertainty and incomplete information place limits on what a firm can attain. To operate efficiently, a firm's owners (principals) must induce its managers (agents) to pursue the maximum possible profit. The managers (principals) must induce the workers and other firms (agents) to work efficiently. But incentive schemes are imperfect and firms constantly strive to find ways of improving performance and increasing profits.

The main forms of business organization are sole proprietorships, partnerships, and corporations. (pp. 189–193)

Business Finance

Firms attempt to raise funds from the source that costs least. When a firm raises funds, it receives money in the current period and takes on an obligation to make a series of payments in future periods. The firm compares money received today with money paid out in the future by calculating the present value of the future payments. (pp. 193–196)

Opportunity Cost and Economic Profit

Economic profit is calculated as total revenue minus opportunity cost. The opportunity cost of producing a good is the best alternative action that was forgone to produce it. It has two components: explicit costs and implicit costs. Explicit costs are paid directly in money—money costs. Implicit costs (measured in units of money) are opportunities forgone but not paid for directly in money. A firm's implicit costs arise from its use of capital, inventories, and resources provided by its owner. Past economic depreciation of capital is not a current opportunity cost. It is a sunk cost—a bygone. The opportunity cost of the resources supplied by a firm's owner are the wages forgone by not working in the best alternative job and normal profit for supplying entrepreneurial ability. (pp. 196–200)

Economic Efficiency

A method of production is technologically efficient when it is not possible to increase output without using more inputs. A method of production is economically efficient when the cost of producing a given output is as low as possible. (pp. 200–202)

Firms and Markets

Firms coordinate economic activities when they can perform a task more efficiently—at lower cost—than markets. Firms can economize on transactions costs and achieve the benefits of economies of scale and of team production. (pp. 202–203)

Key Tables

Table 9.1   The Pros and Cons of Different Types of Firms, 192
Table 9.2   Rocky's Mountain Bikes' Revenue, Cost, and Profit Statement, 199
Table 9.3   Four Ways of Making 10 TV Sets a Day, 200

Key Terms

Bond, 194
Capital gain, 192
Discounting, 195
Economic depreciation, 197
Economic efficiency, 200
Economic profit, 198
Economies of scale, 203
Equity, 193
Firm, 189
Implicit rental rate, 197
Normal profit, 198
Present value, 194
Principal–agent problem, 190
Sunk cost, 197
Technological efficiency, 200
Transactions costs, 202

R E V I E W   Q U E S T I O N S

1. What is a firm and what are the economic problems that all firms face?
2. What are the two systems of organization that firms use?
3. Why do firms organize production by using both a command system and an incentive system?
4. What factors make it difficult for a firm to get the most out of its resources?
5. What is a principal–agent relationship and why does it arise?
6. In what ways can a principal cope with the principal–agent problem?
7. What are the main forms of business organization and the advantages and disadvantages of each?
8. What is the most common type of business and which type produces most of the economy's output?

9. What are the main ways in which firms can raise funds?
10. Describe and contrast a bond and a stock.
11. What do we mean by net present value?
12. What determines the value of a bond?
13. Explain how a firm uses marginal analysis when it makes a financing decision.
14. Distinguish between money cost and opportunity cost. What are the main items of opportunity cost that don't get counted as part of money cost?
15. Distinguish between implicit costs and explicit costs.
16. Distinguish between profit as defined by accountants, normal profit, and economic profit.
17. Distinguish between technological efficiency and economic efficiency.
18. Why do firms, rather than markets, coordinate such a large amount of economic activity?

C R I T I C A L   T H I N K I N G

1. Study *Reading Between the Lines* on pp. 204–205 and answer the following questions:
    a. What were the main sources of gain for Tim Hortons and Wendy's from the merger?
    b. How do we know that most likely there were some gains from the merger?
    c. What is a franchise?
    d. Why might a franchise be an efficient method of organizing a doughnut business?
2. Valentine's, a restaurant company, wants to expand across the country. In each location, it decides to sell a franchise. Why does it sell a franchise rather than open a restaurant and hire a manager?
3. All McDonald's outlets in Canada are owned and operated by one company, McDonald's Canada; whereas McDonald's outlets in the United States are franchises. Why aren't all McDonald's in North America either owned by one company or all franchises?

4. Some companies, such as Avon (a cosmetics company), sell their products by going door-to-door; others, such as Computerland, sell their products by mailing out catalogues; and others, such as Eaton's and the Bay, sell their products by opening a store. Why don't all companies operate like Eaton's and open a store?
5. Garry is thinking about setting up a gardening company in Prince Rupert. What information should he use to arrive at his decision? List the economic costs that Garry's company will incur in its first year of operation.
6. New technology based on the computer has been introduced in many industries and some jobs have almost disappeared. For example, ATMs have replaced many bank tellers; new telecommunication equipment has replaced many phone operators; and automated payment machines have replaced many parking attendants. Does new technology affect economic efficiency? Do we need to worry about machines replacing workers?

P R O B L E M S

1. Soap Bubbles, Inc. has a bank loan of $1 million on which it is paying an interest rate of 10 percent a year. The firm's financial advisor suggests paying off the loan by selling bonds. To sell bonds valued at $1 million, Soap Bubbles, Inc. must offer the following deal: One year from today, pay the bond holders $9 for each $100 of bonds; two years from today, redeem the bonds for $114 per $100 of bonds.
   a. Does it pay Soap Bubbles to sell the bonds to repay the bank loan?
   b. What is the present value of the profit or loss that would result from repaying the bank loan and selling the bonds?

2. One year ago, Jack and Jill set up a vinegar bottling firm (called JJVB). In that year
   a. Jack and Jill put $50,000 of their own money into the firm.
   b. They bought equipment for $30,000 and an inventory of bottles and vinegar for $15,000.
   c. They hired one employee to help them for an annual wage of $20,000.
   d. JJVB's sales for the year were $100,000.
   e. Jack gave up his previous job, at which he earned $30,000, and spent all his time working for JJVB.
   f. Jill kept her old job, which paid $30 an hour, but gave up 10 hours of leisure each week (for 50 weeks) to work for JJVB.
   g. The cash expenses of JJVB were $10,000 for the year.

   h. The inventory at the end of the year was worth $20,000.
   i. The market value of the equipment at the end of the year was $28,000.
   j. JJVB's accountant depreciated the equipment over 5 years.
   k. The interest rate at the bank is 5 percent a year.
      (i) Construct JJVB's profit and loss account as recorded by their accountant.
      (ii) Construct JJVB's profit and loss account based on opportunity cost.
      (iii) What is JJVB's economic profit?

3. There are three methods that you can use for doing your tax return: a personal computer, a pocket calculator, or a pencil and paper. With a PC, you complete the job in an hour; with a pocket calculator, it takes 12 hours; and with a pencil and paper, it takes two days. The PC and its software cost $1,000, the pocket calculator costs $10, and the pencil and paper cost $1.
   a. Which, if any, of the above methods is technologically efficient?
   b. Suppose that your wage rate is $5 an hour. Which of the above methods is economically efficient?
   c. Suppose that your wage rate is $50 an hour. Which of the above methods is economically efficient?
   d. Suppose your wage rate is $500 an hour. Which of the above methods is economically efficient?

Output and Costs

After studying this chapter, you will be able to:

- Explain what limits the profit a firm can make

- Explain the relationship between a firm's output and its costs

- Derive a firm's short-run cost curves

- Explain how cost changes when a firm's plant size changes

- Derive a firm's long-run average cost curve

Size does not guarantee survival in business. True, the Hudson's Bay Company has been around a long time and has grown pretty large. But most of the giants of fifty years ago don't even exist today. Remaining small does not guarantee survival either. Every year, millions of small businesses close down. Call a random selection of restaurants and fashion boutiques from *last* year's yellow pages and see how many have vanished.

Survival of the Fittest

What does a firm have to do to be one of the survivors? ◆ Firms differ in lots of ways—from Mom-and-Pop convenience stores to multinational giants producing hi-tech goods. But regardless of their size or what they produce, all firms must decide how much to produce and how to produce it. How do firms make these decisions? ◆ Most car makers in North America can produce far more cars than they can sell. Why do car makers have expensive equipment lying around that isn't fully used? Many electric utilities in North America don't have enough production equipment on hand to meet demand on the coldest and hottest days and have to buy power from other producers. Why don't such firms have a bigger production plant so that they can supply the market themselves?

◈ We are going to answer these questions in this chapter. To do so, we are going to study the economic decisions of a small, imaginary firm—Swanky, Inc., a producer of knitted sweaters. The firm is owned and operated by Sidney. By studying Swanky's economic problems and the way Sidney solves them, we will be able to get a clear view of the problems that face all firms—small ones like Swanky as well as the giants.

The Firm's Objective and Constraints

To UNDERSTAND AND PREDICT THE BEHAVIOUR of firms, we will start by describing a firm's objective—what it is trying to achieve.

The Objective: Profit Maximization

Individual firms and the entrepreneurs that run them have many different objectives. If you ask a group of entrepreneurs what their objectives were, you'd get lots of different answers. Some would talk about making a quality product, others about business growth, others about market share, and others about work force satisfaction. All of these objectives might be pursued, but they are not the fundamental objective. They are a means to a deeper objective, which is achieving the largest possible profit—*profit maximization.*

The firm that we will study has this single objective of profit maximization. A firm that seeks the largest possible profit is one that tries to use its scarce resources efficiently. And a firm that maximizes profit has the best chance of surviving in a competitive environment and of avoiding being taken over by another firm.

Two types of constraints limit the profit a firm can make. They are

- Market constraints
- Technology constraints

Market Constraints

A firm's market constraints are the conditions under which it can buy its inputs and sell its output. On the output side, people have a limited demand for each good or service and will buy additional quantities only at lower prices. On the input side, people have a limited supply of the factors of production that they own and will supply additional quantities only at higher prices.

We'll study these market constraints on firms in Chapters 11 through 16. Swanky, the firm that we'll study in this chapter, is small and cannot influence the prices at which it sells its output or buys its inputs. For such a firm, the market constraints are a set of given prices.

Technology Constraints

A firm's technology constraints are the limits to the quantity of output that can be produced by using given quantities of inputs—factors of production. To maximize profit, a firm chooses a *technologically efficient* method of production. It does not use more inputs than necessary to produce a given output. Equivalently, it does not waste resources. But a firm must also choose the *economically efficient* technique—the technique that produces a given output at the lowest possible cost. (See Chapter 9, pp. 200–202.)

The possibilities open to a firm depend on the length of the planning period over which it is making its decisions. A firm that wants to change its output rate overnight has fewer options than one that plans to change its output rate several months in the future. In studying the way a firm's technology constrains its actions, we distinguish between two planning horizons—the short run and the long run.

The Short Run and the Long Run

The **short run** is a period of time in which the quantity of at least one input is fixed and the quantities of the other inputs can be varied. The **long run** is a period of time in which the quantities of all inputs can be varied. Inputs whose quantity can be varied in the short run are called *variable inputs.* Inputs whose quantity cannot be varied in the short run are called *fixed inputs.*

There is no specific time that can be marked on the calendar to separate the short run from the long run. In some cases—for example, a laundromat or a copying service—the short run is a month or two. New premises can be rented and new machines installed quickly. In other cases—for example, an electric power company or a railroad company—the short run is several years. Bigger power generators and additional track and rolling stock take a few years to build.

In the short run, Swanky has a fixed amount of capital—knitting machines—so to vary its output in the short run it must vary the quantity of labour employed. For Swanky, the knitting equipment is the fixed input and labour is the variable input. In the long run, Swanky can vary the quantity of both inputs—knitting machines and labour employed.

Let's look more closely at the short-run technology constraint.

Short-Run Technology Constraint

TO INCREASE OUTPUT IN THE SHORT RUN, A FIRM must increase the quantity of a variable input. The effect of a change in the quantity of variable input can be described using three related concepts:

- Total product
- Marginal product
- Average product

Total Product

The total output produced with a given quantity of a fixed input is called **total product**. The *total product curve* shows the maximum output attainable with a given amount of capital as the amount of labour employed is varied. Equivalently, the relationship between total product and the amount of labour employed can be described by a schedule that lists the amounts of labour required with the given amount of capital to produce given amounts of output.

Figure 10.1 shows Swanky's total product schedule and curve. As you can see, when employment is zero, no sweaters are knitted. As employment increases, so does the number of sweaters knitted. Swanky's total product curve, *TP*, is based on the schedule in the figure. Points *a* through *f* on the curve correspond to the same rows in the table.

The total product curve is similar to the *production possibility frontier* (explained in Chapter 3). It separates the attainable output levels from those that are unattainable. All the points that lie above the curve are unattainable. Points that lie below the curve, in the orange area, are attainable. But they are inefficient—they use more labour than is necessary to produce a given output. Only the points *on* the total product curve are technologically efficient.

Marginal Product

The **marginal product** of an input is the increase in total product divided by the increase in the quantity of the input employed, holding the quantity of all other inputs constant. For example, the marginal product of labour is the increase in total product divided by the increase in the quantity of labour

FIGURE 10.1

Total Product

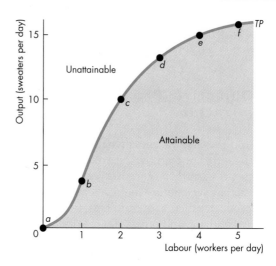

The table shows how many sweaters Swanky can produce when it uses 1 knitting machine and different amounts of labour. For example, using 1 knitting machine, 2 workers can produce 10 sweaters a day (row *c*). The total product curve, *TP*, is based on these data. Points *a* through *f* on the curve correspond to the rows of the table. The total product curve separates the attainable output from the unattainable.

	Labour (workers per day)	Output (sweaters per day)
a	0	0
b	1	4
c	2	10
d	3	13
e	4	15
f	5	16

employed, holding the quantity of capital constant. Equivalently, it is the change in total product resulting from a one-unit increase in the quantity of labour employed.

Table 10.1 shows the calculation of Swanky's marginal product of labour. For example, when the quantity of labour increases from 2 to 3 workers, total product increases from 10 to 13 sweaters. The change in total product—3 sweaters—is the marginal product of going from 2 to 3 workers.

Figure 10.2 illustrates Swanky's marginal product of labour. Part (a) reproduces the total product curve that you met in Fig. 10.1. Part (b) shows the marginal product curve, *MP*. In part (a), the orange bars illustrate the marginal product of labour. The height of each bar measures marginal product. Marginal product is also measured by the slope of the total product curve. Recall that the slope of a curve is the change in the value of the variable measured on the *y*-axis—output—divided by the change in the variable measured on the *x*-axis—labour input—as we move along the curve. A one-unit increase in labour input, from 2 to 3 workers, increases output from 10 to 13 sweaters, so the slope from point *c* to point *d* is 3, the same as the marginal product that we've just calculated.

TABLE 10.1

Calculating Marginal Product and Average Product

Labour (workers per day)	Output (sweaters per day)	Marginal product (sweaters per worker)	Average product (sweaters per worker)
a	0	0		
		·········· 4	
b	1	4	4.00
		·········· 6	
c	2	10	5.00
		·········· 3	
d	3	13	4.33
		·········· 2	
e	4	15	3.75
		·········· 1	
f	5	16	3.20

Marginal product of an input is the change in total product resulting from a one-unit increase in an input. For example, when labour increases from 2 to 3 workers a day (row *c* to row *d*), total product increases from 10 to 13 sweaters a day. The marginal product of increasing the number of workers from 2 to 3 is 3 sweaters.

Average product of an input is total product divided by the quantity of an input employed. For example, 3 workers produce 13 sweaters a day, so the average product of 3 workers is 4.33 sweaters per worker.

FIGURE 10.2

Marginal Product

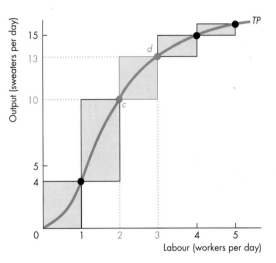

(a) Total product

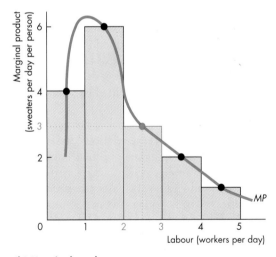

(b) Marginal product

Marginal product is illustrated by the orange bars. For example, when labour increases from 2 to 3, marginal product is the orange bar whose height is 3 sweaters. (Marginal product is shown midway between the labour inputs to emphasize that it is the result of *changing* inputs—moving from one level to the next.) The steeper the slope of the total product curve (*TP*) in part (a), the larger is marginal product (*MP*) in part (b). Marginal product increases to a maximum (when 1 worker is employed in this example) and then declines—diminishing marginal product.

We've calculated the marginal product of labour for a series of unit increases in the amount of labour. But labour is divisible into smaller units than one person. It is divisible into hours and even minutes. By varying the amount of labour in the smallest imaginable units, we can draw the marginal product curve shown in Fig. 10.2(b). The *height* of this curve measures the *slope* of the total product curve at a point. Part (a) shows that an increase in employment from 2 to 3 workers increases output from 10 to 13 sweaters (an increase of 3). The increase in output of 3 sweaters appears on the vertical axis of part (b) as the marginal product of going from 2 to 3 workers. We plot that marginal product at the midpoint between 2 and 3 workers. Notice that marginal product shown in Fig. 10.2(b) reaches a peak at 1 unit of labour and at that point marginal product is more than 6. The peak occurs at 1 unit of labour because the total product curve is steepest at 1 unit of labour.

Average Product

The **average product** of an input is equal to total product divided by the quantity of the input employed. Average product tells us how productive, on the average, a factor of production is. Table 10.1 shows Swanky's average product of labour. For example, 3 workers can knit 13 sweaters a day, so the average product of labour is 13 divided by 3, which is 4.33 sweaters per worker.

Figure 10.3 illustrates Swanky's average product of labour, *AP*, and shows the relationship between average product and marginal product. Points *b* through *f* on the average product curve correspond to those same rows in Table 10.1. Average product increases from 1 to 2 workers (its maximum value at point *c*) but then decreases as yet more workers are employed. Notice also that average product is largest when average product and marginal product are equal. That is, the marginal product curve cuts the average product curve at the point of maximum average product. For employment levels at which marginal product exceeds average product, average product is increasing. For employment levels at which marginal product is less than average product, average product is decreasing.

These relationships between the average and marginal product curves that you've just seen are a general feature of the relationship between the average and marginal values of any variable. Let's look at a familiar example.

FIGURE 10.3
Average Product

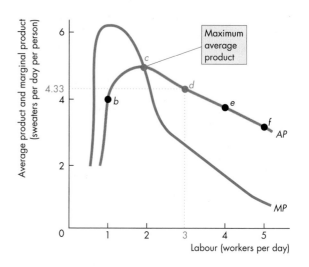

The figure shows the average product of labour and the connection between the average product and marginal product. With 1 worker per day, marginal product exceeds average product, so average product is increasing. With 2 workers per day, marginal product equals average product, so average product is at its maximum. With more than 2 workers per day, marginal product is less than average product, so average product is decreasing.

Marginal Grade and Grade Point Average

Figure 10.4 shows the performance over five semesters of Sidney, a part-time student who takes one course each semester. First, he takes a calculus course and, on a scale of 1 to 4, his grade is a 2. This grade is his marginal grade. It is also his grade point average (GPA). In the next semester, Sidney takes French and gets a 3. French is Sidney's marginal course and his marginal grade is 3. His GPA rises to 2.5. Because his marginal grade is greater than his average grade, it pulls his average up. In the third semester, Sidney takes economics, and gets a 4—his new marginal grade. Because his marginal grade is higher than his GPA, it again pulls his average up. In the fourth semester, Sidney takes history, and gets a 3. Because his marginal grade equals his average, his GPA does not change. In the fifth semester, Sidney takes

English and gets a 2. Because his marginal grade, a 2, is below his GPA of 3, his GPA falls.

This everyday relationship between marginal and average values agrees with the relationship between marginal and average product. Sidney's GPA increases when his marginal grade exceeds his GPA. His GPA falls when his marginal grade is below his GPA. And his GPA is constant when his marginal grade equals his GPA.

The Shapes of the Product Curves

Now let's get back to studying production. The total, marginal, and average product curves are different for different firms and different types of goods. Ford Motor Company's product curves are different from those of Jim's Burger Stand, which in turn are different from those of Sidney's sweater factory. But the shapes of the product curves are similar, because almost every production process incorporates two features:

■ Increasing marginal returns initially
■ Diminishing marginal returns eventually

Increasing Marginal Returns **Increasing marginal returns** occur when the marginal product of an additional worker exceeds the marginal product of the previous worker. If Sidney employs just one worker at Swanky, that person has to learn all the aspects of sweater production: running the knitting machines, fixing breakdowns, packaging and mailing sweaters, buying and checking the type and colour of the wool. All of these tasks have to be done by that one person. If Sidney hires a second person, the two workers can specialize in different parts of the production process. As a result, two workers produce more than twice as much as one. The marginal product of the second worker is greater than the marginal product of the first worker. Marginal returns are increasing.

Diminishing Marginal Returns *Increasing* marginal returns do not always occur, but all production processes eventually reach a point of *diminishing* marginal returns. **Diminishing marginal returns** occur when the marginal product of an additional worker is less than the marginal product of the previous worker. If Sidney hires a third worker, output increases but not by as much as it did when he added the second worker. In this case, after two workers are hired, all the gains from specialization and the division of labour have been exhausted. By hiring a third worker,

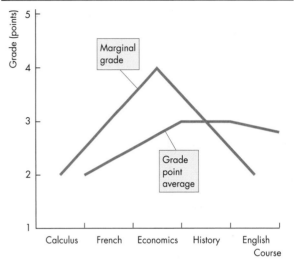

FIGURE 10.4

Marginal Grade and Grade Point Average

Sidney's first course is calculus, for which he gets a 2. His marginal grade is 2 and his GPA is 2. He then gets a 3 for French, which pulls his GPA up to 2.5. Next he gets a 4 for economics, which pulls his GPA up again to 3. On his next course, history, he gets a 3, which maintains his GPA. Then he gets a 2 for English. This marginal grade is below his GPA, and it pulls his average down.

the factory produces more sweaters, but the equipment is being operated closer to its limits. There are even times when the third worker has nothing to do because the plant is running without the need for further attention. Adding yet more and more workers continues to increase output but by successively smaller amounts. Marginal returns are diminishing. This phenomenon is such a pervasive one that it is called "the law of diminishing returns." The **law of diminishing returns** states that

As a firm uses more of a variable input, with a given quantity of fixed inputs, the marginal product of the variable input eventually diminishes.

Because marginal product eventually diminishes, so does average product. Recall that average product decreases when marginal product is less than average product. If marginal product is diminishing it must eventually become less than average product and, when it does so, average product begins to decline.

■ When marginal product exceeds average product, average product increases; when marginal product is less than average product, average product decreases; and when marginal product and average product are equal, average product is at its maximum.

■ Initially, as the labour input increases, marginal product and average product might increase.

■ But as the labour input increases further, marginal product eventually declines—the law of diminishing returns.

Why does Swanky care about total product, marginal product, and average product and whether marginal product and average product are increasing or decreasing? Swanky cares because the product curves influence its costs and the way costs change with the quantity of sweaters produced.

Short-Run Cost

TO PRODUCE MORE OUTPUT IN THE SHORT RUN, a firm must employ more labour. But if the firm employs more labour, its costs increase. Thus to produce more output, a firm must increase its costs. Let's study Swanky's costs to see how a firm's costs change with the level of production.

Swanky is a small firm, and we'll assume that it cannot influence the prices it pays for its inputs. Given the prices of its inputs, Swanky's lowest attainable cost of production for each output level is determined by its technology constraint. Let's see how.

Total Cost

A firm's **total cost** is the sum of the costs of all the inputs it uses in production. It includes the cost of renting land, buildings, and equipment, the wages paid to the firm's work force, and normal profit. Total cost is divided into two categories: fixed cost and variable cost.

A **fixed cost** is the cost of a fixed input. Because the quantity of a fixed input does not change as output changes, a fixed cost is a cost that is independent of the output level. For example, GM can change its output of cars without changing the amount it spends on advertising. The cost of advertising is a fixed cost.

A **variable cost** is a cost of a variable input. Because to change its output a firm must change the quantity of variable inputs, a variable cost is a cost that varies with the output level. For example, to produce more cars, GM must run its assembly lines for longer hours and hire more labour. The cost of this labour is a variable cost.

Total fixed cost is the total cost of the fixed inputs. **Total variable cost** is the total cost of the variable inputs. We call total cost TC, total fixed cost TFC, and total variable cost TVC. The total cost of production is the sum of total fixed cost and total variable cost. That is,

$$TC = TFC + TVC.$$

Table 10.2 shows Swanky's total cost and its division into total fixed cost and total variable cost. Swanky has one knitting machine and this is its fixed input. To produce more sweaters, Sidney must hire more labour; the first two columns of the table show how many sweaters can be produced at each level of employment. This is Swanky's technology constraint.

Swanky rents its knitting machine for $25 a day. This amount is its total fixed cost. It hires workers at a wage rate of $25 a day and its total variable cost is equal to the total wage bill. For example, if Swanky employs 3 workers, its total variable cost is ($3 \times $25), which equals $75. Total cost is the sum of total fixed cost and total variable cost. For example, when Swanky employs 3 workers, its total cost is $100— total fixed cost of $25 plus total variable cost of $75.

Marginal Cost

A firm's **marginal cost** is the increase in its total cost divided by the increase in its output. Equivalently, it is the change in total cost that results from a unit increase in output. For example, when output increases from 10 to 13 sweaters, total cost increases from $75 to $100. The change in output is 3 sweaters and the change in total cost is $25. The marginal cost of one of those 3 sweaters is ($25 ÷ 3), which equals $8.33.

Notice that when Swanky hires a second worker, marginal cost decreases, but when a third, fourth, and fifth worker are employed, marginal cost succes

TABLE 10.2

Calculating a Firm's Costs

Labour (workers per day)	Output (sweaters per day)	Total fixed cost (TFC)	Total variable cost (TVC)	Total cost (TC)	Marginal cost (MC)	Average fixed cost (AFC)	Average variable cost (AVC)	Average total cost (ATC)
		(dollars per day)			(dollars per sweater)			
0	0	25	0	25		—	—	—
					6.25			
1	4	25	25	50		6.25	6.25	12.50
					4.17			
2	10	25	50	75		2.50	5.00	7.50
					8.33			
3	13	25	75	100		1.92	5.77	7.69
					12.50			
4	15	25	100	125		1.67	6.67	8.33
					25.00			
5	16	25	125	150		1.56	7.81	9.38

sively increases. Marginal cost eventually increases because each additional worker produces a successively smaller addition to output—*the law of diminishing returns.* The law of diminishing returns means that each additional worker produces a successively smaller addition to output. So to get an additional unit of output, ever more workers are required. Because more workers are required to produce one additional unit of output, the cost of the additional output—marginal cost—must eventually increase.

Average Cost

Average cost is the cost per unit of output. There are three average costs:

1. Average fixed cost
2. Average variable cost
3. Average total cost

Average fixed cost (*AFC*) is total fixed cost per unit of output. **Average variable cost** (*AVC*) is total variable cost per unit of output. **Average total cost** (*ATC*) is total cost per unit of output. The average cost concepts are calculated from the total cost concepts as follows:

$$TC = TFC + TVC.$$

Divide each total cost term by the quantity produced, Q, to give

$$\frac{TC}{Q} = \frac{TFC}{Q} + \frac{TVC}{Q}$$

or,

$$ATC = AFC + AVC.$$

Average total cost equals average fixed cost plus average variable cost. Table 10.2 shows the calculation of average total cost. For example, when output is 10 sweaters, average fixed cost is ($25 ÷ 10), which equals $2.50, average variable cost is ($50 ÷ 10), which equals $5.00, and average total cost is ($75 ÷ 10), which equals $7.50. Equivalently, average total cost is equal to average fixed cost ($2.50) plus average variable cost ($5.00).

Short-Run Cost Curves

Figure 10.5(a) illustrates Swanky's short-run costs as the total cost curves. Total fixed cost is a constant $25. It appears in the figure as the horizontal green curve *TFC*. Total variable cost and total cost both increase with output. They are graphed as the purple total variable cost curve (*TVC*) and the blue total cost curve (*TC*). The vertical distance between those two curves

FIGURE 10.5
Short-Run Costs

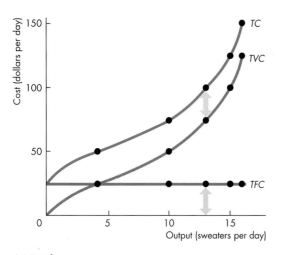

(a) Total costs

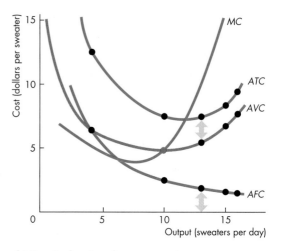

(b) Marginal cost and average costs

The short-run costs calculated in Table 10.2 are illustrated in the graphs. Part (a) shows the total cost curves. Total cost (*TC*) increases as output increases. Total fixed cost (*TFC*) is constant—it graphs as a horizontal line—and total variable cost (*TVC*) increases in a similar way to total cost. The vertical distance between the total cost curve and the total variable cost curve is total fixed cost, as illustrated by the two arrows.

Part (b) shows the average and marginal cost curves. Average fixed cost (*AFC*) decreases as output increases. The average total cost curve (*ATC*) and average variable cost curve (*AVC*) are U-shaped. The vertical distance between these two curves is equal to average fixed cost, as illustrated by the two arrows. The marginal cost curve (*MC*) is also U-shaped. It intersects the average variable cost curve and the average total cost curve at their minimum points.

is equal to total fixed cost—as shown by the two arrows. Because total fixed cost is a constant $25, the distance between the purple total variable cost curve and the blue total cost curve is a constant $25. Use your ruler to check that the distance is a constant $25.

Figure 10.5(b) shows the average cost curves. The green average fixed cost curve (*AFC*) slopes downward. As output increases, the same constant fixed cost is spread over a larger output. When Swanky produces 4 sweaters, average fixed cost is $6.25; when total product increases to 16 sweaters, average fixed cost decreases to $1.56.

The blue average total cost curve (*ATC*) and the purple average variable cost curve (*AVC*) are U-shaped. The vertical distance between the average total cost and average variable cost curves is equal to average fixed cost—as shown by the two arrows. That distance shrinks as output increases because average fixed cost declines with increasing output.

Figure 10.5(b) also illustrates the marginal cost curve. It is the red curve *MC*. This curve is also U-shaped. The marginal cost curve intersects the average variable cost curve and the average total cost curve at their minimum points. That is, when marginal cost is less than average cost, average cost is decreasing, and when marginal cost exceeds average cost, average cost is increasing. This relationship holds for both the *ATC* and the *AVC* curves and is just another example of the relationship you saw in Fig. 10.4 for Sidney's course grades.

Why the Average Total Cost Curve Is U-Shaped

Average total cost, *ATC*, is the sum of average fixed cost, *AFC*, and average variable cost, *AVC*. So the shape of the *ATC* curve combines the shapes of the

AFC and *AVC* curves. The U-shape of the average total cost curve arises from the influence of two opposing forces:

■ Spreading fixed cost over a larger output
■ Eventually diminishing returns

When output increases, the firm spreads its fixed costs over a larger output and its average fixed cost decreases—its average fixed cost curve slopes downward.

When output increases, diminishing returns eventually set in. That is, to produce an additional unit of output, ever larger amounts of labour are required. So average variable cost eventually increases and the firm's *AVC* curve eventually slopes upward.

The shape of the average total cost curve combines these two effects. Initially, as output increases, both average fixed cost and average variable cost decrease, so average total cost decreases and the *ATC* curve slopes downward. But as output increases further and diminishing returns set in, average variable cost begins to increase. Eventually, average variable cost increases more quickly than average fixed cost decreases, so average total cost increases and the *ATC* curve slopes upward. At the output level at which declining average fixed cost offsets increasing average variable cost, average total cost is constant and at its minimum.

Cost Curves and Product Curves

A firm's cost curves are determined by its technology and its product curves. Figure 10.6 shows the links between the product curves and the cost curves. The upper part of the figure shows the average product curve and the marginal product curve—just like Fig. 10.3. The lower part of the figure shows the average variable cost curve and the marginal cost curve—like those in Fig. 10.5(b).

Notice that over the output range in which marginal product and average product are rising, marginal cost and average variable cost are falling. Then, at the point of maximum marginal product, marginal cost is a minimum. At output levels above this point, marginal product diminishes and marginal cost increases. But there is an intermediate range of output over which average product is still rising and average variable cost is falling. Then an output is reached at which average product is a maximum and average variable cost is a minimum. At outputs above this level, average product diminishes and average variable cost increases.

FIGURE 10.6

Product Curves and Cost Curves

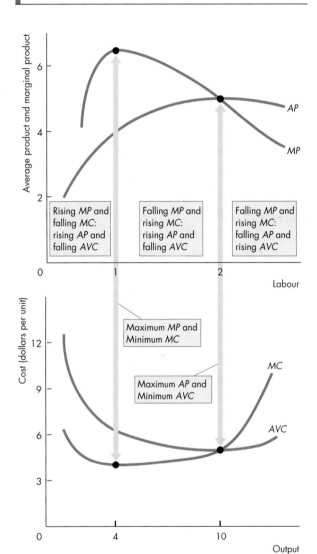

A firm's cost curves are linked to its product curves. Over the range of rising marginal product, marginal cost is falling. When marginal product is a maximum, marginal cost is a minimum. Over the range of rising average product, average *variable* cost is falling. When average product is a maximum, average variable cost is a minimum. Over the range of diminishing marginal product, marginal cost is rising. And over the range of diminishing average product, average *variable* cost is rising.

TABLE 10.3

A Compact Glossary of Costs

Term	Symbol	Definition	Equation
Fixed cost		Cost that is independent of the output level; cost of a fixed input	
Variable cost		Cost that varies with the output level; cost of a variable input	
Total fixed cost	TFC	Cost of the fixed inputs	
Total variable cost	TVC	Cost of the variable inputs	
Total cost	TC	Cost of all inputs	$TC = TFC + TVC$
Output (total product)	TP	Output produced	
Marginal cost	MC	Change in total cost resulting from a one-unit increase in total product	$MC = \Delta TC \div \Delta TP$
Average fixed cost	AFC	Total fixed cost per unit of output	$AFC = TFC \div TP$
Average variable cost	AVC	Total variable cost per unit of output	$AVC = TVC \div TP$
Average total cost	ATC	Total cost per unit of output	$ATC = AFC + AVC$

Shifts in the Cost Curves

The position of a firm's short-run cost curves depend on technology, described by its product curves, and by the prices it pays for its factors of production. If technology changes or if factor prices change, the firm's costs change and its cost curves shift.

A technological change that increases productivity shifts the product curves upward and shifts the cost curves downward. For example, advances in robotic production techniques have increased productivity in the automobile industry. As a result, the product curves of Chrysler, Ford, and GM have shifted upward and their cost curves have shifted downward. But the relationships between their product curves and cost curves have not changed. The curves are still linked in the way shown in Fig. 10.6.

An increase in factor prices increases costs and shifts the cost curves. But the way the curves shift depends on which factor prices change. A change in rent or some other component of *fixed* cost shifts the fixed cost curves (*TFC* and *AFC*) upward and shifts the total cost curve (*TC*) upward but leaves the variable cost curves (*AVC* and *TVC*) and the marginal cost (*MC*) unchanged. A change in wages or some

other component of *variable* cost shifts the variable curves (*TVC* and *AVC*) upward and shifts the total cost curve (*TC*) and the marginal cost curve (*MC*) upward but leaves the fixed cost curves (*AFC* and *TFC*) unchanged.

You've now completed your study of short-run costs. All the concepts that you have met are summarized in Table 10.3.

R E V I E W

■ A firm's short-run cost curves show the relationships between short-run cost and output.

■ Marginal cost eventually increases because of *diminishing returns*—each additional worker produces a successively smaller addition to output.

■ Average fixed cost decreases because as output increases, fixed costs are spread over a larger output.

■ The average total cost curve is U-shaped because as output increases, it combines the influences of falling average fixed cost and eventually diminishing returns.

Plant Size and Cost

W̶E HAVE STUDIED HOW THE COST OF production varies for a given sweater plant when different quantities of labour are used. We are now going to see how the cost of production varies when both plant size and the quantity of labour are varied. That is, we are going to study a firm's long-run costs. **Long-run cost** is the cost of production when a firm uses the economically efficient quantity of labour and plant size.

The behaviour of long-run cost depends on the firm's production function. A **production function** is the relationship between the maximum output attainable and the quantities of *all* inputs used.

The Production Function

Figure 10.7 shows Swanky's production function. The table lists the total product for four different plant sizes and five different quantities of labour. The numbers for Plant 1 are for the sweater factory whose short-run product and cost curves we've just studied. The other three plants have 2, 3, and 4 machines. If Sidney doubles the plant size to 2 knitting machines, the various amounts of labour can produce the outputs shown in the second column of the table. The other two columns show the outputs of yet larger plants.

The numbers in the table are graphed as the four total product curves in Fig. 10.7. Each total product curve has the same basic shape, but the larger the number of knitting machines, the larger is the number of sweaters knitted each day by a given number of workers.

Diminishing Returns

Diminishing returns occur in all four plants as the labour input increases. You can check that fact by doing similar calculations for the larger plants to those you've already done for a plant with 1 machine. Regardless of the plant size, as the labour input increases, its marginal product (eventually) decreases.

Diminishing Marginal Product of Capital Just as we can calculate the marginal product of labour for each plant size, we can also calculate the marginal product of capital for each quantity of labour. The *marginal product of capital* is the change in total product divided by the change in capital employed when the amount of labour employed is constant.

FIGURE 10.7

The Production Function

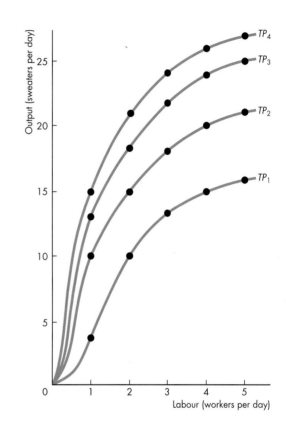

Labour	Output (sweaters per day)			
(workers per day)	Plant 1	Plant 2	Plant 3	Plant 4
1	4	10	13	15
2	10	15	18	21
3	13	18	22	24
4	15	20	24	26
5	16	21	25	27
Knitting machines (number)	1	2	3	4

The table shows the total product data for four plant sizes. These numbers are graphed as the total product curves, TP_1, TP_2, TP_3, and TP_4. The bigger the plant, the larger is the total product for any given amount of labour employed. But each total product curve displays diminishing marginal product.

Equivalently, it is the change in output resulting from a one-unit increase in the quantity of capital employed. For example, if Swanky has 3 workers and increases the number of machines from 1 to 2, output increases from 13 to 18 sweaters a day. The marginal product of capital is 5 sweaters per day. The marginal product of capital diminishes, just like the marginal product of labour. For example, if with 3 workers, Swanky increases the number of machines from 2 to 3, output increases from 18 to 22 sweaters per day. The marginal product of the third machine is 4 sweaters per day, down from 5 sweaters per day for the second machine.

The law of diminishing returns tells us what happens to output when a firm changes one input, either labour or capital, and holds the other input constant. But what happens to a firm's output if it changes *both* labour and capital?

Returns to Scale

A change in scale occurs when there is an equal percentage change in the use of all the firm's inputs. For example, if Swanky has been employing 1 worker and has 1 knitting machine and then doubles its use of both inputs (to use 2 workers and 2 knitting machines), the scale of the firm will double. **Returns to scale** are the increases in output that result from increasing all inputs by the same percentage. There are three possible cases:

■ Constant returns to scale
■ Increasing returns to scale
■ Decreasing returns to scale

Constant Returns to Scale **Constant returns to scale** occur when the percentage increase in a firm's output is equal to the percentage increase in its inputs. If constant returns to scale are present and a firm doubles all its inputs, its output exactly doubles. Constant returns to scale occur if an increase in output is achieved by replicating the original production process. For example, General Motors can double its production of Cavaliers by doubling its production facility for those cars. It can build an identical production line and hire an identical number of workers. With the two identical production lines, GM produces exactly twice as many cars.

Increasing Returns to Scale **Increasing returns to scale** occur when the percentage increase in out-

put exceeds the percentage increase in inputs. If increasing returns to scale are present and a firm doubles all its inputs, its output more than doubles. Increasing returns to scale occur in production processes where increased output enables a firm to increase the division of labour and to use more specialized labour and capital. For example, if GM produces only 100 cars a week, each worker and each machine must be capable of performing many different tasks. But if it produces 10,000 cars a week, each worker and each piece of equipment can be highly specialized. Workers specialize in a small number of tasks at which they become highly proficient. General Motors might use 100 times more capital and labour, but the number of cars produced increases by more than a hundredfold. General Motors experiences increasing returns to scale.

Decreasing Returns to Scale **Decreasing returns to scale** occur when the percentage increase in output is less than the percentage increase in inputs. If decreasing returns to scale are present and a firm doubles all its inputs, its output less than doubles. Decreasing returns to scale occur in all production processes at some output rate, but in some production processes perhaps only at a very large output rate. The most common source of decreasing returns to scale is the increasingly complex management and organizational structure required to control a large firm. The larger the organization, the greater is the number of layers in the management pyramid and the greater are the costs of monitoring and maintaining control of the production and marketing process.

Returns to Scale at Swanky Swanky's production possibilities, set out in Fig. 10.7, display both increasing returns to scale and decreasing returns to scale. If Sidney has 1 knitting machine and employs 1 worker, his factory will produce 4 sweaters a day. If he doubles the firm's inputs to 2 knitting machines and 2 workers, the factory's output increases almost fourfold to 15 sweaters a day. If he increases the firm's inputs by another 50 percent to 3 knitting machines and 3 workers, output increases to 22 sweaters a day—an increase of less than 50 percent. Doubling Swanky's scale from 1 to 2 units of each input gives rise to increasing returns to scale, but the further increase from 2 to 3 units of each input gives rise to decreasing returns to scale.

Whether a firm experiences increasing, constant, or decreasing returns to scale affects its long-run costs. Let's see how.

Short-Run Cost and Long-Run Cost

The cost curves in Fig. 10.5 apply to a plant with 1 knitting machine. There is a set of short-run cost curves like those shown in Fig. 10.5 for each different plant size. Let's look at the short-run costs for the four plants set out in Fig. 10.7 and see how plant size affects the cost curves.

We've already studied the costs of a plant with 1 knitting machine. We'll call the average total cost curve for that plant ATC_1 in Fig. 10.8. The average total cost curve for larger plants (with 2, 3, and 4 knitting machines respectively) are also shown in Fig. 10.8 as ATC_2 (for 2 machines), ATC_3 (for 3 machines), and ATC_4 (for 4 machines). The average total cost curve for each plant size has the same basic U-shape. And because larger plants produce larger outputs with the same amount of labour, the ATC curves for successively larger plants lie farther to the right. Which of these cost curves Swanky operates on depends on its plant size. For example, if Swanky has 1 machine, then its average total cost curve is ATC_1 and it costs $7.69 per sweater to knit 13 sweaters a day. But Swanky can produce 13 sweaters a day with any of these four plant sizes. If it uses 2 machines, the average total cost curve is ATC_2 and the average total cost of a sweater is $6.80. If it uses 3 machines, the average total cost curve is ATC_3 and the average total cost of a sweater is $7.69. And if it uses 4 machines, the average total cost curve is ATC_4, and the average total cost of a sweater is $9.50. If Swanky wants to produce 13 sweaters a day, the economically efficient plant size is 2 machines—the plant size with the lowest average total cost of production.

FIGURE 10.8

Short-Run Average Cost Curves

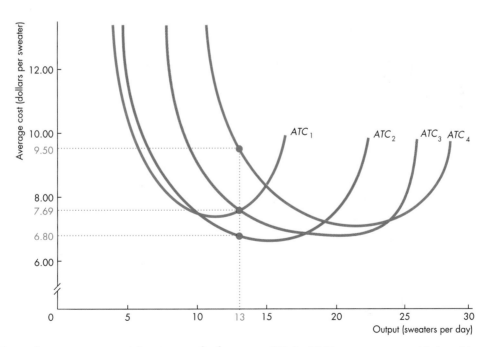

The figure shows short-run average total cost curves for four different plants. Swanky can produce 13 sweaters a day with 1 knitting machine on ATC_1 or with 3 knitting machines on ATC_3 for an average cost of $7.69 per sweater. It can produce the same number of sweaters by using 2 knitting machines on ATC_2 for $6.80 per sweater or with 4 machines on ATC_4 for $9.50 per sweater. If Swanky produces 13 sweaters a day, the least-cost method of production—the long-run method—is with 2 machines on ATC_2.

The Long-Run Average Cost Curve

The *long-run average cost curve* traces the relationship between the lowest attainable average total cost and output when both capital and labour inputs can be varied. This curve is illustrated in Fig. 10.9 as *LRAC*.

The long-run average cost curve is derived directly from the short-run average total cost curves that we have just reviewed in Fig. 10.8. As you can see, ATC_1 has the lowest average total cost for all output rates up to 10 sweaters a day. ATC_2 has the lowest average total cost for output rates between 10 and 18 sweaters a day. ATC_3 has the lowest average total cost for output rates between 18 and 24 sweaters a day. And ATC_4 has the lowest average total cost for output

rates in excess of 24 sweaters a day.

The segment of each of the four average total cost curves for which that plant has the lowest average total cost is highlighted in dark blue in Fig. 10.9. The scallop-shaped curve made up of these four segments is the long-run average cost curve.

Swanky will be on its long-run average cost curve if it does the following: To produce up to 10 sweaters a day it uses 1 machine; to produce between 10 and 18 sweaters a day it uses 2 machines; to produce between 18 and 24 sweaters a day it uses 3 machines; and, finally, to produce more than 24 sweaters a day it uses 4 machines. Within these ranges, Swanky varies its output by varying only the amount of labour employed.

FIGURE 10.9

Long-Run Average Cost Curve

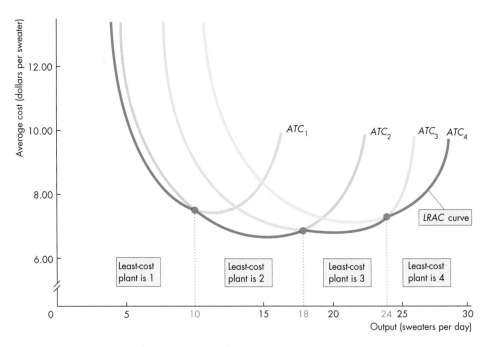

In the long run, Swanky can vary both capital and labour. The long-run average cost curve traces the lowest attainable average cost of production. Swanky produces on its long-run average cost curve if it uses 1 machine to produce up to 10 sweaters a day, 2 machines to produce between 10 and 18

sweaters a day, 3 machines to produce between 18 and 24 sweaters a day, and 4 machines to produce more than 24 sweaters a day. Within these ranges, Swanky varies its output by varying its labour input.

Economies and Diseconomies of Scale

Economies of scale are present when, as output increases, long-run average cost decreases. When economies of scale are present, the *LRAC* curve slopes downward. Swanky experiences economies of scale for outputs up to 15 sweaters a day. **Diseconomies of scale** are present when, as output increases, long-run average cost increases. When diseconomies of scale are present, the *LRAC* curve slopes upward. At outputs greater than 15 sweaters a day, Swanky experiences diseconomies of scale.

In general, plant size can be changed in small increments so there is an infinite number of plant sizes and an infinite number of short-run average total cost curves, one for each plant size.

Figure 10.10 illustrates the general case. With an infinite number of plant sizes, the long-run average cost curve is smooth, not scalloped like Swanky's. For outputs up to Q_1, there are economies of scale. For outputs that exceed Q_2, there are diseconomies of scale. For outputs between Q_1 and Q_2, there are neither economies nor diseconomies of scale.

Each plant size produces a single output at a lower cost than any other plant can produce it. For example, the quantity Q_0 can be produced at least cost by using the plant with the short-run average total cost curve, $SRAC_a$. This least cost is ATC_0. At the output Q_0, the short-run average total cost curve $SRAC_a$ just touches the long-run average cost curve at a single point. So too does $SRAC_b$. That is, each point on the long-run average cost curve is a single point on a short-run average total cost curve.

You've now studied the principles of long-run cost. Let's use what you've learned to answer some questions about real businesses.

Producing Cars and Generating Electric Power

At the beginning of this chapter, we noted that most car makers can produce far more cars than they can sell. We posed the question: Why do car makers have expensive equipment lying around that isn't fully used? You can see the answer in Fig. 10.10. Car producers experience economies of scale. The minimum cost of production occurs on a short-run average total cost curve that looks like $SRAC_a$.

We also noted that many electric utilities don't have enough production equipment on hand to meet demand on the coldest and hottest days and have to buy power from other producers. You can now see

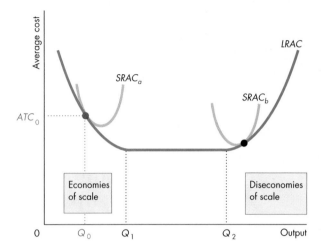

FIGURE 10.10

Economies of Scale

If capital can be varied in small units, the number of plant sizes is infinitely large, and there is an infinitely large number of short-run average total cost curves. Each short-run average total cost curve touches the long-run average cost curve at a single point. For example, the short-run average total cost curve ($SRAC_a$) touches the long-run average cost curve ($LRAC$) at the output rate Q_0 and average total cost ATC_0. For outputs up to Q_1, there are economies of scale; for outputs between Q_1 and Q_2, there are constant costs; and for outputs greater than Q_2, there are diseconomies of scale.

why this happens and why they don't build a bigger plant. Power producers experience diseconomies of scale. They have short-run average total cost curves like $SRAC_b$. If they had larger plants, their average total costs of producing their normal output would increase.

◆ *Reading Between the Lines* on pp. 226–227 shows you how you can use the cost curves that you've studied in this chapter to make sense of a recent innovation in some Winnipeg hospitals. There, you can see how some real-world cost curves are influenced by adopting a more capital-intensive technology.

Our next task is to study the interactions of firms and households in markets for goods and services and to see how prices, output, and profits are determined.

Changing a Hospital's Cost Curves

WINNIPEG FREE PRESS, JANUARY 20, 1996

Drug-dispensing robot frees nurses to give TLC

BY BUD ROBERTSON

A unique robotic arm developed in Winnipeg could help hospitals around the world cut costs while improving safety for staff.

The idea is not to eliminate jobs but to free up time for busy nurses and pharmacists and protect them from dangerous medicines.

"There's none like it in the world," said Harry Schulz, director of business operations with the St. Boniface General Hospital Research Centre.

Known as the Automated Pharmacy Admixture System, the $2-million project developed by Technology 2000 Inc.—a business subsidiary of the research centre—will completely automate the preparation of intravenous doses for hospitals. That job is currently done by hand by nurses or pharmacy staff.

If all goes as planned, the robot will serve Winnipeg's seven hospitals by the end of the year, said Schulz.

The arm is also to be installed next year in nine U.S. centres that contract out the job of filling IVs, including hospitals in Chicago, Los Angeles and Boston.

And while a final decision has yet to be made on where the arm will be made, Schulz said a new manufacturing plant could be established in Winnipeg. Most of the components are already manufactured in Manitoba. ...

While the robot requires only two or three staff members to process the 500,000 IV doses Winnipeg's hospitals use each year, Schulz said the intent is not to eliminate hospital jobs.

Rather, he said, it is to free up staff so that they can spend more time on other tasks, such as caring for patients.

It will also create jobs in the health industry, as orders for the new arm start to come in, Schulz predicted. ...

The arm also improves safety in handling certain hazardous products, such as those used in chemotherapy treatment for cancer, Schulz said.

The technology is the brainchild of scientists at the research centre, who were searching for a more efficient way to fill intravenous doses.

Essence of THE STORY

■ A $2-million robotic arm developed in Winnipeg will completely automate the preparation of intravenous doses for hospitals.

■ The job is currently done by hand by nurses or pharmacy staff.

■ The robot requires only two or three staff members to process the 500,000 IV doses Winnipeg's hospitals use each year.

■ Robots can also be used to handle other hazardous products.

Economic

A N A L Y S I S

■ When a hospital replaces labour with capital, its cost curves change.

■ Assuming the hospital can only lease robots on a long-term lease, but can hire nurses by the week, capital is a *fixed* input while labour is a *variable* input.

■ So if robots replace nurses, a hospital's fixed costs increase and its variable costs decrease. But what happens to its total cost and its average total cost? The answer depends on the scale of production.

■ The table shows some (hypothetical) data for a hospital. Column (1) lists the number of nurses employed and column (2) shows the maximum number of patients they can deal with if they have no robots. Column (3) shows how many patients the nurses can handle if they have 10 robots.

■ Figure 1 shows two total product curves that are based on these numbers. With no robots, total product is TP_0. With 10 robots, total product is TP_1. When the hospital leases some robots, total product increases.

■ Columns (4) and (5) of the table show the hospital's total cost of nurses and robots (ignoring its

other costs). It is based on $12 an hour (wages and benefits) to hire a nurse and $4 an hour to lease a robot.

■ Columns (6) and (7) of the table show the hospital's average total cost, which is total cost divided by total product.

■ Figure 2 shows the hospital's average total cost curves. With no robots, average total cost is ATC_0. With 10 robots, average total cost is ATC_1.

■ You can see that when the hospital leases 10 robots, its average total cost *increases* if it has fewer than 20 patients and decreases only when it has more than 20 patients.

■ So whether leasing robots cuts costs depends on the level of production.

■ This example is similar to the sweater factory case described in the chapter.

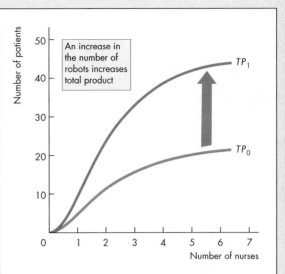

Figure 1 Total product

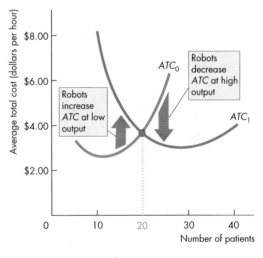

Figure 2 Average total cost

Number of nurses	Total product (TP)		Total cost (TC)		Average total cost (ATC)	
	(number of patients)		(dollars per hour)		(dollars per patient)	
(1)	(no robots) (2)	(10 robots) (3)	(no robots) (4)	(10 robots) (5)	(no robots) (6)	(10 robots) (7)
0	0	0	0.00	40.00		
1	4	8	12.00	52.00	3.00	6.50
2	10	20	24.00	64.00	2.40	3.20
3	14	28	36.00	76.00	2.57	2.71
4	17	34	48.00	88.00	2.82	2.59
5	19	38	60.00	100.00	3.16	2.63
6	20	40	72.00	112.00	3.60	2.80

Source: Winnipeg Free Press, January 20, 1996

S U M M A R Y

Key Points

The Firm's Objective and Constraints   Firms aim to maximize profit subject to constraints imposed by the market and by technology. (p. 211)

Short-Run Technology Constraint   A firm's total product curve separates attainable output levels from unattainable output levels. The slope of the total product curve is the marginal product of labour. Initially, marginal product increases as the quantity of labour increases, but eventually it diminishes. Average product also increases initially and eventually diminishes. Average product increases when marginal product exceeds average product and decreases when marginal product is less than average product. (pp. 212–216)

Short-Run Cost   Total cost is divided into total fixed cost and total variable cost. As output increases, total cost increases, because total variable cost increases. Average cost and marginal cost depend on how much a firm produces. Average fixed cost decreases as output increases. Average variable cost, average total cost, and marginal cost are U-shaped. Average cost decreases when marginal cost is less than average cost and increases when marginal cost exceeds average cost. Marginal cost equals average variable cost when it is a minimum, and marginal cost equals average total cost when it is a minimum. Average cost is linked to average product and marginal cost is linked to marginal product. (pp. 216–220)

Plant Size and Cost   Long-run cost is the cost of production when all inputs—labour and capital—have been adjusted to their economically efficient levels. When a firm increases all its inputs in equal proportions, it experiences returns to scale. Returns to scale can be constant, increasing, or decreasing. There is a set of short-run cost curves for each different plant size and one least-cost plant for each output. The larger the output, the larger is the plant that has the lowest average total cost. The long-run average cost curve traces the relationship between the lowest attainable average total cost and output when both capital and labour inputs are varied. With economies of scale, the long-run average cost curve slopes downward. With diseconomies of scale, the long-run average cost curve slopes upward. (pp. 221–225)

Key Figures and Tables

Key Terms

R E V I E W   Q U E S T I O N S

1. Why do firms try to maximize profit?
2. What are the constraints on a firm's ability to maximize profit?
3. Distinguish between the short run and the long run.
4. What does a firm's total product curve show?
5. What does a firm's marginal product curve show?
6. What does a firm's average product curve show?
7. Explain the relationship between a firm's total product curve and its marginal product curve.
8. Explain the relationship between a firm's average product curve and its marginal product curve.
9. What is the law of diminishing returns? What does this law imply about the shapes of the total, marginal, and average product curves?
10. Why does a firm's marginal product at first increase and eventually diminish?
11. Define total cost, total fixed cost, and total variable cost. What is the relationship among the three concepts of total cost?

12. Explain how the three total cost measures change as total product increases.
13. Define marginal cost. Why does marginal cost eventually increase as total product increases?
14. Define average total cost, average variable cost, and average fixed cost. What is the relationship among the three average cost concepts?
15. Explain how the three average cost concepts change as total product changes.
16. What is the relationship between average variable cost and marginal cost and between average total cost and marginal cost?
17. What is the relationship between the average product curve and the average variable cost curve and between the marginal product curve and the marginal cost curve?
18. What is the relationship between the long-run average cost curve and the short-run average total cost curves?
19. What effects do economies of scale and diseconomies of scale have on the shape of the long-run average cost curve?

C R I T I C A L   T H I N K I N G

1. Study *Reading Between the Lines* on pp. 226–227 and then explain
   a. How a hospital's cost curves change if it replaces nurses with robots.
   b. Why, at low production levels, using nurses rather than robots lowers average total cost.
   c. Why, at high production levels, using robots rather than nurses lowers average total cost.
2. If 1 person can paint a house in 26 days, can 26 people paint the same house in 1 day? Explain why or why not. What do you think the product curves—the average product curve and the marginal product curve—look like for house painting using the two different house-painting technologies? What do you think the cost curves—the average cost curves (*AFC, AVC, and ATC*) and the marginal cost curve (*MC*)—

for house painting look like using the two different technologies?
3. In recent years, phone companies have replaced most operators with computers. How has this change in technology changed a phone company's fixed cost, variable cost, and average total cost of a phone call? Sketch the average cost curves (*AFC, AVC,* and *ATC*) and the marginal cost curve (*MC*). Compare and contrast the average cost curves and the marginal cost curve before and after the change in technology.
4. China has been producing illegal copies of music and software CDs. Compare the fixed costs, variable costs, and average total costs of producing a rock group's CD in China and in North America.

P R O B L E M S

1. The total product schedule of Rubber Duckies, Inc., a firm making rubber boats, is described by the following:

Labour (workers per week)	Output (rubber boats per week)
1	1
2	3
3	6
4	10
5	15
6	21
7	26
8	30
9	33
10	35

a. Draw the total product curve.
b. Calculate the average product of labour and draw the average product curve.
c. Calculate the marginal product of labour and draw the marginal product curve.
d. What is the relationship between average product and marginal product when Rubber Duckies produces less than 30 boats a week? Why?
e. What is the relationship between average and marginal product when Rubber Duckies produces more than 30 boats a week? Why?

2. Suppose that the price of labour is $400 a week, the total fixed cost is $1,000 a week, and the total product schedule is the same as in problem 1.

a. Calculate total cost, total variable cost, and total fixed costs for each level of output.
b. Draw the total cost, total variable cost, and total fixed cost curves.
c. Calculate average total cost, average fixed cost, average variable cost, and marginal cost at each level of output.
d. Draw the following cost curves: average total cost, average variable cost, average fixed cost, and marginal cost.

3. Suppose that total fixed cost increases to $1,100 a week. What will happen to the firm's short-run cost curves in problem 2?

4. Suppose that total fixed cost remains at $1,000 a week, but that the price of labour increases to $450 a week. Using these new costs, rework problem 2.

5. Rubber Duckies, Inc. can buy an additional factory. If it does so and operates two factories, its total product schedule is

Labour (workers per week)	Output (rubber boats per week)
1	1
2	6
3	12
4	20
5	30
6	42
7	52
8	60
9	66
10	70

The total fixed cost of operating its current factory is $1,000 a week and the total fixed cost of operating the additional factory is also $1,000 a week. The wage rate is $400 a week.

a. Calculate the total cost for each of the outputs given for the new factory.
b. Calculate Rubber Duckies' average total cost of each output given.
c. Draw Rubber Duckies' long-run average cost curve.
d. Over what output range would it be efficient for Rubber Duckies to operate one factory?
e. Over what output range would it be efficient for Rubber Duckies to operate two factories?

6. In 1950, Air Canada transported passengers between Toronto and Vancouver in aircraft that travelled at 500 kilometres per hour, required refuelling stops, and carried around 100 passengers. In 1996, the airline used Boeing 747 (jumbo) airplanes that travel at 1,000 kilometres per hour, do the journey nonstop, and carry more than 400 passengers.

Assume the following costs (all expressed in 1996 dollars):

	1950	1996
Aircraft rental rate	$2,000	$10,000
Crew and other labour cost	$20,000	$10,000
Fuel cost	$78,000	$180,000
Total cost	$100,000	$200,000

a. Sketch average cost curves (*AFC*, *AVC*, and *ATC*) and the marginal cost curve (*MC*) per passenager carried from Toronto to Vancouver in 1950 and 1996.

b. Compare and contrast the average cost curves and the marginal cost curve in the two years.

7. The figure shows Swanky's short-run costs of producing sweaters.

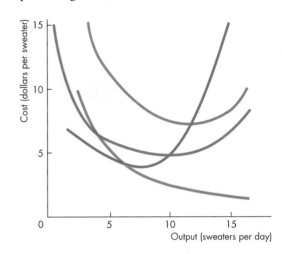

Over what output range is

a. The marginal cost of a sweater greater than the average total cost of a sweater?

b. The marginal cost of a sweater less than the average total cost of a sweater?

c. The marginal cost of a sweater greater than the average variable cost of a sweater?

d. The marginal cost of a sweater less than the average cost of a sweater?

e. The marginal product of Swanky's labour increasing?

f. The marginal product of Swanky's labour decreasing?

g. The average product of Swanky's labour increasing?

h. The average product of Swanky's labour decreasing?

Competition

After studying this chapter, you will be able to:

- Define perfect competition

- Explain how price and output are determined in a competitive industry

- Explain why firms sometimes shut down temporarily and lay off workers

- Explain why firms enter and leave an industry

- Predict the effects of a change in demand and of a technological advance

- Explain why perfect competition is efficient

Collision Course in Car Repairs

It is morning rush hour and a six-vehicle pile-up snarls the traffic on Toronto's busiest section of Highway 401. Human injuries are light, but the toll in dented car bodies, buckled wheels and damaged tires, and crushed mufflers is considerable. Competition to clean up the mess begins. Fifty towing companies compete for the initial clean-up. Several hundreds of body shops and repair shops battle for a place in a crowded market. How does competition affect prices and profits?

◆ Whether you want your car fixed, a new lock installed, your TV repaired, your furniture removed, a prescription filled, or a pizza delivered, you have lots of choice about the firm to call. Just look in the Yellow Pages if you're not convinced! In this fiercely competitive environment, new firms are entering and trying their luck while other firms are being squeezed out of the business. ◆ In June 1996, almost 1.5 million people were unemployed. Of these, 660,000 were unemployed because they had lost their jobs or were laid off by firms seeking to trim their costs and avoid bankruptcy. Retailers, ice cream producers, computer manufacturers, and firms in almost every sector of the economy laid off workers even though the economy was expanding and the total number of jobs was growing. Why do firms lay off workers? When will a firm temporarily shut down, laying off its workers?

◆ Over the past few years, there has been a dramatic fall in the prices of personal computers. For example, a slow computer cost almost $4,000 a few years ago, and a fast one costs only $2,000 today. What goes on in an industry when the price of its output falls sharply? What happens to the profits of the firms producing such goods?

◇ Ice cream, computers, and most other goods are produced by more than one firm, and these firms compete with each other for sales. To study competitive markets, we are going to build a model of a market in which competition is as fierce and extreme as possible—more extreme than in the examples we've just considered. We call this situation "perfect competition."

Perfect Competition

PERFECT COMPETITION IS AN EXTREME FORM OF competition. **Perfect competition** arises when

- There are many firms, each selling an identical product.
- There are many buyers.
- There are no restrictions on entry into the industry.
- Firms in the industry have no advantage over potential new entrants.
- Firms and buyers are completely informed about the prices of the products of each firm in the industry.

An industry can have a large number of firms only if the demand for its product is large relative to the output level at which average total cost is a minimum. For example, the worldwide demand for corn, rice, and other basic grains is many thousands of times larger than the output that can be produced by a single farm at minimum average total cost.

The conditions that define perfect competition imply that no individual firm can influence the price at which it sells its output. Firms in perfect competition are said to be price takers. A **price taker** is a firm that cannot influence the price of a good or service.

The key reasons why a perfectly competitive firm is a price taker are that it produces a tiny fraction of the total output of a particular good and buyers are well informed about the prices of other firms.

Imagine for a moment that you are a wheat farmer in Saskatchewan. You have 500 hectares under cultivation—which sounds like a lot. But then you go on a drive, first heading west. The flat lands turn into rolling hills as you head towards the Rocky Mountains, but everywhere you look you see hundreds and hundreds of hectares of wheat. The sun goes down in the west behind millions of hectares of golden plants. The next morning, it rises in the east above the same scene. Driving east to Manitoba or south to the Dakotas reveals similar vistas. You also find unbroken stretches of wheat in the United States, Argentina, Australia, and Ukraine. Your 500 hectares is a drop in the ocean.

Nothing makes your wheat any better than any other farmer's, and all the buyers of wheat know the price at which they can do business. If everybody else sells their wheat for $300 a tonne, and you want $310, why would people buy from you? They can simply go to the next farmer, and the one after that and buy all they need for $300 a tonne. You are a price taker. A price taker faces a perfectly elastic demand.

The market demand for wheat is not perfectly elastic. The market demand curve is downward sloping, and its elasticity depends on the substitutability of wheat for other grains such as barley, rye, corn, and rice. The demand for wheat from farm *A* is perfectly elastic because wheat from farm *A* is a *perfect substitute* for wheat from farm *B*.

Perfect competition does not occur frequently in the real world. But competition in many industries is so fierce that the model of perfect competition is of enormous help in predicting the behaviour of the firms in these industries. Wreck towing, panel beating and fixing, muffler fixing, farming, fishing, wood pulping and paper milling, manufacturing paper cups and plastic shopping bags, grocery retailing, photo finishing, lawn service, plumbing, painting, dry cleaning and the provision of laundry services are all examples of industries that are highly competitive.

Profit and Revenue

The goal of a firm is to maximize profit, which is the sum of normal profit and economic profit. **Normal profit** is the return that a firm's owner could obtain in the best alternative business. So it is a forgone alternative or *opportunity cost* and part of the firm's total cost. **Economic profit** is equal to total revenue minus total cost.

Total revenue is the value of a firm's sales. It equals the price of the firm's output multiplied by the number of units of output sold (price × quantity). **Average revenue** is total revenue divided by the total quantity sold—revenue per unit sold. Because total revenue equals price multiplied by quantity sold, average revenue (total revenue divided by quantity sold) equals price. **Marginal revenue** is the change in total revenue divided by the change in quantity. That is, marginal revenue is the change in total revenue resulting from a one-unit increase in the quantity sold. In perfect competition, the price remains constant when the quantity sold changes. So the change in total revenue resulting from a one-unit increase in the quantity sold equals price. Therefore, in perfect competition, marginal revenue equals price.

Figure 11.1 sets out an example of these revenue concepts for Swanky, Inc. The table shows three different quantities of sweaters sold. For a price taker, as the quantity sold varies, the price stays constant—in this example at $25. Total revenue is equal to price multiplied by quantity. For example, if Swanky sells 9 sweaters, total revenue is 9 times $25, which equals $225. Average revenue is total revenue divided by quantity. Again, if Swanky sells 9 sweaters, average revenue is total revenue ($225) divided by quantity (9), which equals $25. Marginal revenue is the change in total revenue resulting from a one-unit change in quantity. For example, when the quantity sold increases from 8 to 9, total revenue increases from $200 to $225, so marginal revenue is $25. (Notice that in the table, marginal revenue appears *between* the lines for the quantities sold. This arrangement presents a visual reminder that marginal revenue results from the *change* in the quantity sold.)

Suppose that Swanky is one of a thousand similar small producers of sweaters. Figure 11.1(a) shows the demand and supply curves for the entire sweater industry. Demand curve *D* intersects supply curve *S* at a price of $25 and a quantity of 9,000 sweaters. Figure 11.1(b) shows Swanky's demand curve. Because the firm is a price taker, it faces a perfectly elastic demand—the horizontal line at $25. The figure also illustrates Swanky's average and marginal revenues. Because average revenue and marginal revenue equal price, the firm's demand curve is also its average revenue curve (*AR*) and its marginal revenue curve (*MR*). Swanky's total revenue curve, *TR* (part c), shows the total revenue for each quantity sold. For example, when Swanky sells 9 sweaters, total revenue is $225 (point *a*). Because each additional sweater sold brings in a constant amount—$25—the total revenue curve is an upward-sloping straight line.

FIGURE 11.1

Demand, Price, and Revenue in Perfect Competition

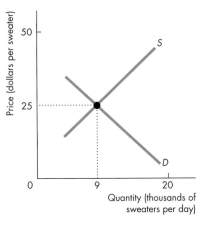

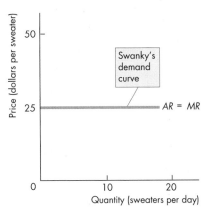

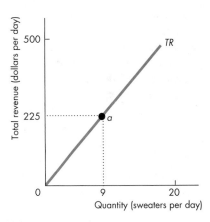

(a) Sweater industry

(b) Swanky's demand, average revenue, and marginal revenue

(c) Swanky's total revenue

Quantity sold (Q) (sweaters per day)	Price (P) (dollars per sweater)	Total revenue (TR = P × Q) (dollars)	Average revenue (AR = TR/Q) (dollars per sweater)	Marginal revenue (MR = ΔTR/ΔQ) (dollars per sweater)
8	25	200	25	
				25
9	25	225	25	
				25
10	25	250	25	

The industry demand and supply curves determine the market price. In part (a), the price is $25 a sweater and 9,000 sweaters are bought and sold. Swanky faces a perfectly elastic demand curve at the market price of $25 a sweater, part (b). The table calculates Swanky's total revenue, average revenue, and marginal revenue. Part (b) shows that Swanky's demand curve is also its average revenue curve (*AR*) and marginal revenue curve (*MR*). Part (c) shows Swanky's total revenue curve (*TR*). Point *a* corresponds to the second row of the table.

The Firm's Decisions in Perfect Competition

Firms in a perfectly competitive industry face a given market price and have the revenue curves that you've just studied. These revenue curves summarize the market constraint faced by a perfectly competitive firm.

Firms also have a technology constraint, which is described by the product curves (total product, average product, and marginal product) that you studied in Chapter 10. The technology available to the firm determines its costs, which are described by the cost curves (total cost, average cost, and marginal cost) that you also studied in Chapter 10.

The task of the competitive firm is to make the maximum profit possible, given the constraints it faces. To achieve this objective, a firm must make four key decisions: two in the short run and two in the long run.

Short-Run Decisions   The short run is a time frame in which each firm has a given plant and the number of firms in the industry is fixed. But many things can change in the short run and the firm must react to these changes. For example, the price for which the firm can sell its output might have a seasonal fluctuation or it might fluctuate with general business fluctuations.

The firm must react to such short-run price fluctuations and decide

1. Whether to produce or to shut down
2. If the decision is to produce, what quantity to produce

Long-Run Decisions   The long run is a time frame in which each firm can change the size of its plant and decide whether to leave the industry. Other firms can decide whether to enter the industry. So in the long run, both the plant size of each firm and the number of firms in the industry can change. Also in the long run, the constraints facing firms can change. For example, the demand for a good can permanently decrease. Or a technological advance can change an industry's costs.

The firm must react to such long-run changes and decide

1. Whether to increase or decrease its plant size
2. Whether to stay in the industry or leave it

The Firm and the Industry in the Short Run and the Long Run   To study a competitive industry, we begin by looking at an individual firm's short-run decisions. We then see how the short-run decisions of all the firms in a competitive industry combine to determine the industry price, output, and economic profit. Then we turn to the long run and study the effects of long-run decisions on the industry price, output, and economic profit. All decisions we study are driven by a single objective: to maximize profit.

Profit-Maximizing Output

A perfectly competitive firm maximizes profit in the short run by choosing its output level. One way of finding the profit-maximizing output is to study a firm's total revenue and total cost curves and to find the output level at which total revenue exceeds total cost by the largest amount. Figure 11.2 shows you how to do this for Swanky, Inc. The table lists Swanky's total revenue and total cost at different outputs and part (a) of the figure shows Swanky's total revenue and total cost curves. These curves are graphs of the numbers shown in the first three columns of the table. The total revenue curve (*TR*) is the same as that in Fig. 11.1(c). The total cost curve (*TC*) is similar to the one that you met in Chapter 10. As output increases, so does total cost.

Economic profit equals total revenue minus total cost. The fourth column of the table in Fig. 11.2 shows Swanky's economic profit, and part (b) of the figure illustrates Swanky's profit curve. This curve shows that Swanky makes an economic profit at outputs greater than 4 and less than 12 sweaters a day. At outputs less than 4 sweaters a day, Swanky incurs a loss. It also incurs a loss if output exceeds 12 sweaters a day. At outputs of 4 sweaters and 12 sweaters a day, total cost equals total revenue and Swanky's economic profit is zero. An output at which total cost equals total revenue is called a *break-even point*. The firm's economic profit is zero but because normal profit is part of total cost, a firm makes normal profit at a break-even point. That is, at the break-even point, the owner of the firm makes profit equal to the best alternative return forgone.

Notice the relationship between the total revenue, total cost, and profit curves. Economic profit is measured by the vertical distance between the total revenue and total cost curves. When the total revenue curve in part (a) is above the total cost curve,

FIGURE 11.2

Total Revenue, Total Cost, and Economic Profit

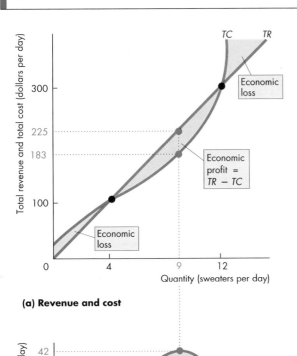

(a) Revenue and cost

(b) Economic profit and loss

Quantity (Q) (sweaters per day)	Total revenue (TR) (dollars)	Total cost (TC) (dollars)	Economic profit (TR – TC) (dollars)
0	0	22	–22
1	25	45	–20
2	50	66	–16
3	75	85	–10
4	100	100	0
5	125	114	11
6	150	126	24
7	175	141	34
8	200	160	40
9	225	183	42
10	250	210	40
11	275	245	30
12	300	300	0
13	325	360	–35

The table lists Swanky's total revenue, total cost, and economic profit. Part (a) graphs the total revenue and total cost curves. Economic profit, in part (a), is the height of the blue area between the total cost and total revenue curves. Swanky makes maximum economic profit, $42 a day ($225 – $183), when it produces 9 sweaters—the output at which the vertical distance between the total revenue and total cost curves is

at its largest. At outputs of 4 sweaters a day and 12 sweaters a day, Swanky makes zero economic profit—these are break-even points. At outputs less than 4 and greater than 12 sweaters a day, Swanky incurs an economic loss. Part (b) of the figure shows Swanky's profit curve. The profit curve is at its highest when profit is at a maximum and cuts the horizontal axis at the break-even points.

between 4 and 12 sweaters, the firm is making an economic profit and the profit curve in part (b) is above the horizontal axis. At the break-even point, where the total cost and total revenue curves intersect, the profit curve intersects the horizontal axis.

The profit curve is at its highest when the distance between TR and TC is greatest. In this example, profit maximization occurs at an output of 9 sweaters a day. At this output, Swanky's economic profit is $42 a day.

Marginal Analysis

Another way of finding the profit-maximizing output is to use *marginal analysis*. To use marginal analysis, a firm compares its marginal cost, *MC*, with its marginal revenue, *MR*. As output increases, marginal revenue is constant and marginal cost eventually increases. If marginal revenue exceeds marginal cost (if *MR* > *MC*), then the extra revenue from selling one more unit exceeds the extra cost incurred to produce it, so profit increases if output increases. If marginal revenue is less than marginal cost (if *MR* < *MC*), then the extra revenue from selling one more unit is less than the extra cost incurred to produce it, so profit increases if output *decreases*. If marginal revenue equals marginal cost (if *MR* = *MC*), profit is maximized. The rule *MR* = *MC* is a prime example of marginal analysis. Let's check that this rule works to find the profit-maximizing output by returning to Swanky's sweater factory.

Look at Fig. 11.3. The table records Swanky's marginal revenue and marginal cost. Focus on the highlighted rows of the table. If Swanky increases output from 8 sweaters to 9 sweaters, marginal revenue is $25 and marginal cost is $23. Because marginal revenue exceeds marginal cost, economic profit increases. The last column of the table shows that profit increases from $40 to $42, an increase of $2. This profit from the ninth sweater is shown as the blue area in the figure.

If output increases from 9 sweaters to 10 sweaters, marginal revenue is still $25, but marginal cost is $27. Because marginal revenue is less than marginal cost, economic profit decreases. The last column of the table shows that profit decreases from $42 to $40. This loss from the tenth sweater is shown as the red area in the figure.

Swanky maximizes profit by producing 9 sweaters a day, the quantity at which marginal revenue equals marginal cost.

Economic Profit in the Short Run

In the short run, when a firm has set its marginal cost equal to its marginal revenue and maximized profit, it might make an economic profit, break even (making normal profit), or incur an economic loss. To determine which of these three possible outcomes occurs, we need to compare the firm's total revenue and total cost. Alternatively, we can compare price with average total cost. If price exceeds average total

FIGURE 11.3
Profit-Maximizing Output

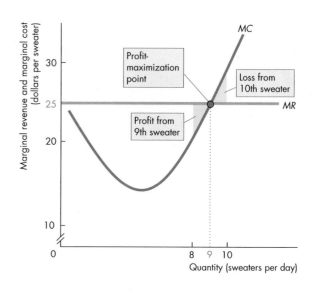

Quantity (Q) (sweaters per day)	Total revenue (TR) (dollars)	Marginal revenue (MR) (dollars per sweater)	Total cost (TC) (dollars)	Marginal cost (MC) (dollars per sweater)	Economic profit (TR – TC) (dollars)
7	175		141		34
		25		19	
8	200		160		40
		25		23	
9	225		183		42
		25		27	
10	250		210		40
		25		35	
11	275		245		30

Another way of finding the profit-maximizing output is to determine the output at which marginal revenue equals marginal cost. The table shows that if output increases from 8 to 9 sweaters, marginal cost is $23, which is less than the marginal revenue of $25. If output increases from 9 to 10 sweaters, marginal cost is $27, which exceeds the marginal revenue of $25. The figure shows that marginal cost and marginal revenue are equal when Swanky produces 9 sweaters a day. If marginal revenue exceeds marginal cost, an increase in output increases economic profit. If marginal revenue is less than marginal cost, an increase in output decreases economic profit. If marginal revenue equals marginal cost, economic profit is maximized.

cost, a firm makes an economic profit. If price equals average total cost, a firm makes a normal profit. If price is less than average total cost, a firm incurs an economic loss. But the economic loss incurred is the minimum possible loss. Profit maximization implies loss minimization. Let's look more closely at these three possible outcomes.

Three Possible Profit Outcomes Figure 11.4 shows the three possible profit outcomes in the short run. In part (a), price exceeds average total cost (*ATC*) and Swanky makes an economic profit. Price and marginal revenue (*MR*) are $25 a sweater, and the profit-maximizing output is 9 sweaters a day. Swanky's total revenue is $225 a day (9 × $25). Average total cost is $20.33 a sweater, and total cost is $183 a day (9 × $20.33). Swanky's economic profit is $42 a day. Economic profit equals total revenue minus total cost, which is $225 – $183 or $42 a day. Economic profit also equals economic profit per sweater, which is $4.67 ($25.00 – $20.33), multiplied by the number of sweaters ($4.67 × 9 = $42). The blue rectangle shows this economic profit. The height of that rectangle is profit per sweater, $4.67, and the length is the quantity

of sweaters produced, 9 a day, so the area of the rectangle measures Swanky's economic profit of $42 a day.

In part (b), price equals average total cost and Swanky breaks even—makes normal profit and zero economic profit. Price and marginal revenue are $20 a sweater, and the profit-maximizing output is 8 sweaters a day. At this output, average total cost is at its minimum.

In part (c), price is less than average total cost and Swanky incurs an economic loss. Price and marginal revenue are $17 a sweater and the profit-maximizing (loss-minimizing) output is 7 sweaters a day. Swanky's total revenue is $119 a day (7 × $17). Average total cost is $20.14 a sweater, and total cost is $141 a day (7 × $20.14). Swanky's economic loss is $22 a day, total revenue of $119 minus total cost of $141. Economic loss also equals economic loss per sweater, which is $3.14 ($20.14 – $17.00), multiplied by the number of sweaters ($3.14 × 7 = $22). The red rectangle shows this economic loss. The height of that rectangle is economic loss per sweater, $3.14, and the length is the quantity of sweaters produced, 7 a day, so the area of the rectangle measures Swanky's economic loss of $22 a day.

FIGURE 11.4
Three Possible Profit Outcomes in the Short Run

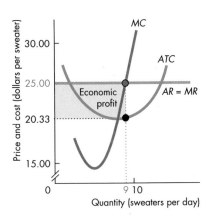

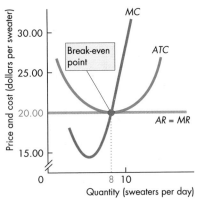

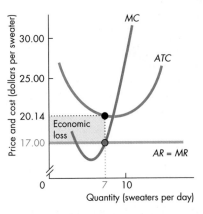

(a) Economic profit   **(b) Normal profit**   **(c) Economic loss**

In the short run, firms might make an economic profit, break even (making a normal profit), or incur an economic loss. If the market price exceeds the average total cost of producing the profit-maximizing output, the firm makes an economic profit (the blue rectangle in part a). If price equals minimum average total cost, the firm breaks even and makes a normal profit (part b). If the price is below minimum average total cost, the firm incurs an economic loss (the red rectangle in part c).

The Firm's Short-Run Supply Curve

A perfectly competitive firm's supply curve shows how the firm's profit-maximizing output varies as the market price varies, other things remaining constant. Figure 11.5 shows you how to derive Swanky's entire supply curve. Part (a) shows Swanky's marginal cost and average variable cost curves, and part (b) shows its supply curve. There is a direct link between the marginal cost and average variable cost curves and the supply curve. Let's see what that link is.

Temporary Plant Shutdown   In the short run, a firm cannot avoid incurring its fixed costs but it *can* avoid variable costs. If a firm produces no output, it incurs a loss equal to its total fixed cost. This loss is the largest the firm will incur. If the price falls below average variable cost, the firm's profit-maximizing action is to shut down temporarily, lay off its workers, and produce nothing. A firm's **shutdown point** is the output and price where the firm's total revenue is just enough to cover its total *variable* cost. At the shutdown point, the firm incurs an economic loss equal to its total fixed cost. If a firm did produce and sell its output for less than its average variable cost, its loss would exceed its fixed cost. Such a firm would not be maximizing profit (minimizing loss). Figure 11.5(a) shows the shutdown point. When the price is $17, the marginal revenue curve is MR_0 and the firm produces 7 sweaters a day at the shutdown point *s*. As the price falls below $17, the firm shuts down.

Short-Run Supply Curve   If the price is above minimum average variable cost, Swanky maximizes profit by producing the output at which marginal cost equals price. We can determine the quantity produced at each price from the marginal cost curve. At a price of $25, the marginal revenue curve is MR_1 and Swanky maximizes profit by producing 9 sweaters. At a price of $31, the marginal revenue curve is MR_2 and Swanky produces 10 sweaters.

The supply curve, shown in Fig. 11.5(b), has two separate parts: First, in the range of prices that exceed minimum average variable cost, the supply curve is the same as the marginal cost curve above the shutdown point (*s*). Second, at prices below minimum average variable cost, Swanky shuts down and produces nothing. Its supply curve runs along the vertical axis. At a price of $17, Swanky is indifferent between shutting down and producing 7 sweaters a day. Either way, it incurs a loss of $25 a day.

FIGURE 11.5

Swanky's Supply Curve

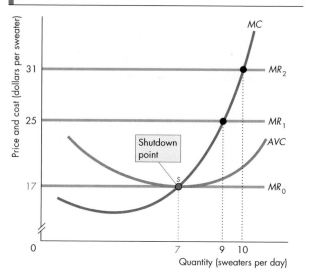

(a) Marginal cost and average variable cost

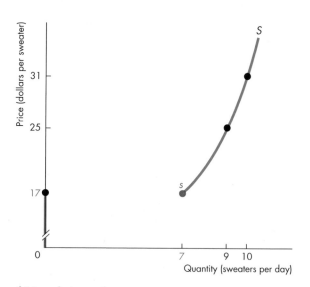

(b) Swanky's supply curve

Part (a) shows Swanky's profit-maximizing output at various prices. At $25 a sweater, Swanky produces 9 sweaters. At $17 a sweater, Swanky produces 7 sweaters. At any price below $17 a sweater, Swanky produces nothing. Swanky's shutdown point is *s*. Part (b) shows Swanky's supply curve—the number of sweaters Swanky will produce at each price. It is made up of its marginal cost curve (part a) at all points above the average variable cost curve and the vertical axis at all prices below minimum average variable cost.

Short-Run Industry Supply Curve

The **short-run industry supply curve** shows how the quantity supplied by the industry varies as the market price varies when the plant size of each firm and the number of firms in the industry remain the same. The quantity supplied by the industry at a given price is the sum of the quantities supplied by all firms in the industry at that price. To construct the industry supply curve, we sum horizontally the supply curves of the individual firms.

Suppose that the competitive sweater industry consists of 1,000 firms exactly like Swanky. Figure 11.6 illustrates the industry supply curve. Each of the 1,000 firms in the industry has a supply schedule like Swanky's. The table lists the quantities supplied by a firm and the industry at each price. At a price below $17, each firm in the industry will shut down; the industry will supply nothing. At $17, each firm is indifferent between shutting down and producing 7 sweaters. Because each firm is indifferent, some firms will produce and others will shut down. Industry supply can be anything between 0 (all firms shut down) and 7,000 (all firms producing 7 sweaters a day each). Thus at $17, the industry supply curve is horizontal. As the price rises above $17, each firm increases its quantity supplied and the quantity supplied by the industry increases by 1,000 times that of each firm.

The supply schedules set out in the table form the basis of the supply curve that is graphed in Fig. 11.6. The quantity supplied by the industry is 1,000 times the quantity supplied by a single firm. At a price of $17 a sweater, the firm supplies either nothing or 7 sweaters a day, so the industry supplies any quantity between zero and 7,000 sweaters. Over that range, the industry supply curve is perfectly elastic.

REVIEW

- In perfect competition, a firm is a price taker and its marginal revenue equals the market price.
- If price exceeds average variable cost, a firm maximizes profit by producing the output at which marginal cost equals marginal revenue (equals price). The lowest price at which a firm produces is equal to its minimum average variable cost.
- In the short run, a firm can make an economic profit, break even (make zero economic profit and earn normal profit), or incur an economic loss.

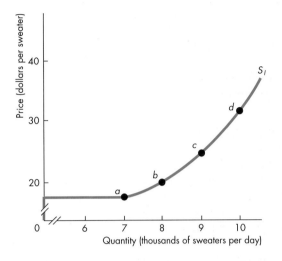

FIGURE 11.6
Industry Supply Curve

Price (dollars) per sweater)	Quantity supplied by Swanky, Inc. (sweaters per day)	Quantity supplied by industry (sweaters per day)
a	17	0 or 7	0 to 7,000
b	20	8	8,000
c	25	9	9,000
d	31	10	10,000

The industry supply schedule is the sum of the supply schedules of all individual firms. An industry that consists of 1,000 identical firms has a supply schedule similar to that of the individual firm, but the quantity supplied by the industry is 1,000 times as large as that of the individual firm (see table). The industry supply curve is S_I. Points a, b, c, and d correspond to the rows of the table. At the shutdown price of $17, each firm produces either 0 or 7 sweaters per day. The industry supply curve is perfectly elastic at the shutdown price.

The maximum economic loss that a firm incurs is equal to its total fixed cost.

So far, we have studied a single firm in isolation. We have seen that the firm's profit-maximizing actions depend on the market price, which the firm takes as given. But how is the market price determined? Let's find out.

Output, Price, and Profit in the Short Run

To DETERMINE THE MARKET PRICE AND THE quantity bought and sold in a perfectly competitive market, we need to study the market as a whole. That is, we need to study how market demand and market supply interact. We begin this process by studying a perfectly competitive market in the short run.

Short-Run Competitive Equilibrium

Market price and industry output are determined by industry demand and supply. Figure 11.7(a) shows three different possible short-run competitive equilibrium positions. The supply curve S is the same as S_I in Fig. 11.6. If the demand curve is D_1, the equilibrium price is $25 and industry output is 9,000 sweaters a day. If the

demand curve is D_2, the price is $20 and industry output is 8,000 sweaters a day. If the demand curve is D_3, the price is $17 and industry output is 7,000 sweaters a day.

Figure 11.7(b) shows the situation facing each individual firm. With demand curve D_1, the price is $25 a sweater, each firm produces 9 sweaters a day and makes an economic profit (the blue rectangle); if the demand curve is D_2, the price is $20 a sweater, each firm produces 8 sweaters a day and makes a zero economic profit (normal profit); and if the demand curve is D_3, the price is $17 a sweater, each firm produces 7 sweaters a day and incurs an economic loss (the red rectangle).

If the demand curve shifts farther leftward than D_3, the price remains constant at $17 because the industry supply curve is horizontal at that price. Some firms continue to produce 7 sweaters a day, and others shut down. Firms are indifferent between these two activities and, whichever they choose, they incur a loss equal to total fixed cost. The number of firms continuing to produce is just enough to satisfy the market demand at a price of $17.

FIGURE 11.7
Short-Run Equilibrium

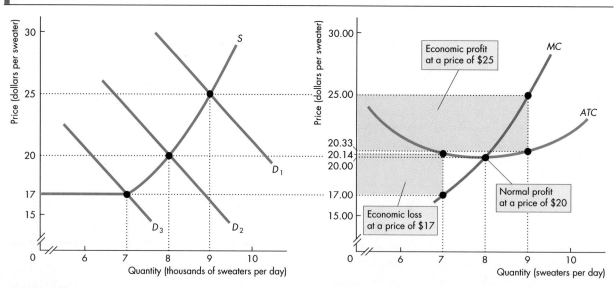

(a) Industry

(b) Firm

In part (a), the competitive sweater industry's supply curve is S. If demand is D_1, the price is $25 and the industry produces 9,000 sweaters. If demand is D_2, the price is $20, and industry output is 8,000 sweaters. If demand is D_3, the price is $17, and

industry output is 7,000 sweaters. In part (b), when the price is $25, an individual firm makes an economic profit; when the price is $20, it breaks even (making normal profit); and when the price is $17, it incurs an economic loss.

In the short run, the number of firms and plant size of each firm is fixed. In the long run, these features of an industry can change. Also, there are forces at work that will disturb some of the short-run situations we've just examined. Let's now look at the forces that operate in the long run.

Output, Price, and Profit in the Long Run

IN SHORT-RUN EQUILIBRIUM, A FIRM MIGHT MAKE an economic profit, incur an economic loss, or break even (make normal profit). Although each of these three situations is a short-run equilibrium, only one of them is a long-run equilibrium. To see why, we need to examine the forces at work in a competitive industry in the long run.

In the long run, an industry adjusts in two ways: The number of firms in the industry changes, and firms change the scale of their plants. Let's study the effects of these two forces in a competitive industry.

The number of firms in an industry changes as a result of entry and exit. *Entry* is the act of setting up a new firm in an industry. *Exit* is the act of a firm leaving an industry. Entry and exit are triggered by economic profit and economic loss, and entry and exit change economic profit and loss. Let's first see how economic profit and loss trigger entry and exit.

Economic Profit and Economic Loss as Signals

An industry in which firms are making an economic profit attracts new entrants; one in which firms are incurring an economic loss induces exits; and an industry in which firms are making normal profit (zero economic profit) induces neither entry nor exit. Thus economic profit and economic loss are the signals to which firms respond in making entry and exit decisions.

Temporary economic profits and temporary losses that are random, like the winnings and losings at a casino, do not trigger entry or exit. But the prospect of persistent economic profit or loss does.

Entry and exit influence market price, the quantity produced, and economic profit. The immediate effect of entry and exit is to shift the industry supply curve. If more firms enter an industry, the industry supply curve shifts rightward: Supply increases. If firms exit an industry, the industry supply curve shifts leftward: Supply decreases. Let's see what happens when new firms enter an industry.

The Effects of Entry

Figure 11.8 shows the effects of entry. Suppose that the demand curve for sweaters is D and the industry supply curve is S_A, so sweaters sell for $23 and 7,000 sweaters are being produced. Firms in the industry are making an economic profit. Some new firms enter the industry. As they do so, the industry supply curve shifts rightward to S_0. With the greater supply and unchanged demand, the market price falls from $23 to $20 a sweater and the quantity produced

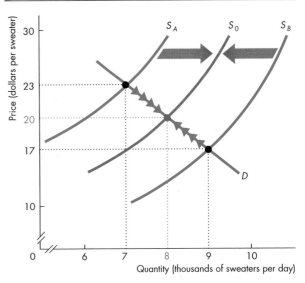

FIGURE 11.8

Entry and Exit

When new firms enter the sweater industry, the industry supply curve shifts rightward, from S_A to S_0. The equilibrium price falls from $23 to $20, and the quantity produced increases from 7,000 to 8,000 sweaters. When firms exit the sweater industry, the industry supply curve shifts leftward, from S_B to S_0. The equilibrium price rises from $17 to $20, and the quantity produced decreases from 9,000 to 8,000 sweaters.

increases from 7,000 to 8,000 sweaters a day. As the price falls, Swanky, like each other firm in the industry, moves down along its supply curve and decreases output. That is, for each existing firm in the industry, the profit-maximizing output decreases. Because the price falls and each firm sells less, economic profit decreases. When the price falls to $20, economic profit disappears and each firm makes a normal profit.

You have just discovered a key proposition:

As new firms enter an industry, the price falls and the economic profit of each existing firm decreases.

A good example of this process has occurred in the last few years in the personal computer industry. When IBM introduced its first personal computer in the early 1980s, there was little competition and the price of PCs gave IBM a big profit. But very quickly, new firms such as Compaq, NEC, Dell, and a host of others entered the industry with machines technologically identical to IBM's. In fact, they were so similar that they came to be called "clones." The massive wave of entry into the personal computer industry shifted the supply curve rightward and lowered the price and the economic profit for all firms.

Let's now see what happens when firms leave an industry.

The Effects of Exit

Figure 11.8 shows the effects of exit. Suppose that the demand curve is D and the supply curve is S_B, so the market price is $17 and 9,000 sweaters are being produced. Firms in the industry are incurring an economic loss. As firms leave the industry, the supply curve shifts leftward to S_0. With the decrease in supply, industry output decreases from 9,000 to 8,000 sweaters and the price rises from $17 to $20.

As the price rises, Swanky, like each other firm in the industry, moves up along its supply curve and increases output. That is, for each existing firm in the industry, the profit-maximizing output increases. Because the price rises and each firm sells more, economic loss decreases. When the price rises to $20, economic loss disappears and each firm makes a normal profit.

You have just discovered a second key proposition:

As firms leave an industry, the price rises and so do the economic profits of the remaining firms.

An example of a firm leaving an industry is Massey-Ferguson, a farm equipment manufacturer whose main centre of operation was in Brantford, Ontario. Another farm equipment manufacturer that exited the business was International Harvester. For decades, people associated the names of these two firms with tractors, combines, and other farm machines. But the industry became intensely competitive and several firms, including these two, began losing money. After years of losses and shrinking revenues, they got out of the farm equipment business, leaving it to John Deere and a host of smaller firms such as Agrimetal, Butler, Houle, as well as Japanese and European companies.

The exits of Massey-Ferguson and International Harvester decreased the industry supply of farm machinery and made it possible for the remaining firms in the industry to break even.

Long-Run Equilibrium

Long-run equilibrium occurs in a competitive industry when firms are earning normal profit and economic profit is zero.

If the firms in a competitive industry make an economic profit, new firms enter the industry and the supply curve shifts rightward. As a result, the market price falls and so does economic profit. Firms continue to enter and economic profit continues to decrease as long as firms in the industry are earning positive economic profits. Only when the economic profit has been eliminated and normal profit is being made do firms stop entering.

If the firms in a competitive industry incur an economic loss, some of the firms exit the industry and the supply curve shifts leftward. As a result, the market price rises and the economic loss incurred by the firms remaining in the industry shrinks. Firms continue to leave and economic loss continues to shrink as long as the industry is incurring an economic loss. Only when the economic loss has been eliminated and normal profit is being made, do firms stop exiting.

So in long-run equilibrium in a competitive industry, firms neither enter nor exit the industry. Each firm in the industry earns a normal profit.

Let's now examine the second way in which the competitive industry adjusts in the long run—by existing firms changing their plant size.

Changes in Plant Size

A firm changes its plant size if, by doing so, its profit increases. Figure 11.9 shows a situation in which Swanky can increase its profit by increasing its plant size. With its current plant, Swanky's marginal cost curve is MC_0 and its short-run average total cost curve is $SRAC_0$. The market price is $25 a sweater, so Swanky's marginal revenue curve is MR_0 and Swanky maximizes profit by producing 6 sweaters a day.

Swanky's long-run average cost curve is $LRAC$. By increasing its plant size—installing more knitting machines—Swanky can move along its long-run average cost curve. As Swanky increases its plant size, its short-run marginal cost curve shifts rightward.

FIGURE 11.9

Plant Size and Long-Run Equilibrium

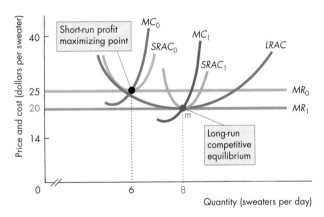

Initially, Swanky's plant has marginal cost curve MC_0 and short-run average total cost curve $SRAC_0$. The market price is $25 a sweater and Swanky's marginal revenue is MR_0. The short-run profit-maximizing quantity is 6 sweaters a day. Swanky can increase its profit by increasing its plant size. If all firms in the sweater industry increase their plant sizes, the short-run industry supply increases and the market price falls. In long-run equilibrium, a firm operates with the plant size that minimizes its average cost. Here, Swanky operates the plant with marginal cost MC_1 and short-run average cost $SRAC_1$. Swanky is also on its long-run average cost curve $LRAC$ and produces at point m. Its output is 8 sweaters a day, and its average total cost equals the price of a sweater—$20.

Recall that a firm's short-run supply curve is linked to its marginal cost curve. As Swanky's marginal cost curve shifts rightward, so does its supply curve. If Swanky and the other firms in the industry increase their plants, the short-run industry supply curve shifts rightward and the market price falls. The fall in the market price limits the extent to which Swanky can profit from increasing its plant size.

Figure 11.9 also shows Swanky in a long-run competitive equilibrium. This situation arises when the market price has fallen to $20 a sweater. Marginal revenue is MR_1, and Swanky maximizes profit by producing 8 sweaters a day. In this situation, Swanky cannot increase its profit by changing its plant size. It is producing at minimum long-run average cost (point m on $LRAC$).

Because Swanky is producing at minimum long-run average cost, it has no incentive to change its plant size. Either a bigger plant or a smaller plant has a higher long-run average cost. If Fig. 11.9 describes the situation of all firms in the sweater industry, the industry is in long-run equilibrium. No firm has an incentive to change its plant size. Also, because each firm is making zero economic profit (normal profit), no firm has an incentive to enter the industry or to leave it.

R E V I E W

Long-run competitive equilibrium is described by three conditions:

- Firms maximize profit by producing the quantity that makes marginal cost equal to marginal revenue and price.

- Economic profits are zero, so no firm has an incentive to enter or to leave the industry.

- Long-run average cost is at a minimum, so no firm has an incentive to change its plant size.

We've seen how economic loss triggers exit, which eventually eliminates the loss. We've also seen how economic profit triggers entry, which eventually eliminates the profit. In the long run, normal profit is earned. But a competitive industry is rarely in a long-run equilibrium. It is restlessly evolving towards such an equilibrium and the conditions the industry faces are constantly changing. The two most persistent sources of change are in tastes and technology. Let's see how a competitive industry reacts to such changes.

Changing Tastes and Advancing Technology

INCREASED AWARENESS OF THE HEALTH HAZARD of smoking has caused a decrease in the demand for tobacco and cigarettes. The development of inexpensive car and air transportation has caused a huge decrease in the demand for long-distance trains and buses. Solid-state electronics have caused a large decrease in the demand for TV and radio repair. The development of good-quality inexpensive clothing has decreased the demand for sewing machines. What happens in a competitive industry when there is a permanent decrease in the demand for its products?

The development of the microwave oven has produced an enormous increase in demand for paper, glass, and plastic cooking utensils and for plastic wrap. The demand for almost all products is steadily increasing as a result of increasing population and increasing incomes. What happens in a competitive industry when the demand for its product increases?

Advances in technology are constantly lowering the costs of production. New biotechnologies have dramatically lowered the costs of many food and pharmaceutical products. New electronic technologies have lowered the cost of producing just about every good and service. What happens in a competitive industry when technological change lowers its production costs?

Let's use the theory of perfect competition to answer these questions.

A Permanent Change in Demand

Figure 11.10(a) shows an industry that initially is in long-run competitive equilibrium. The demand curve is D_0, the supply curve is S_0, the market price is P_0, and industry output is Q_0. Figure 11.10(b) shows a single firm in this initial long-run equilibrium. The firm produces q_0 and makes a normal profit and zero economic profit.

Now suppose that demand decreases and the demand curve shifts leftward to D_1, as shown in part (a). The price falls to P_1 and the quantity supplied by the industry decreases from Q_0 to Q_1 as the industry slides down its short-run supply curve S_0. Part (b) shows the situation facing a firm. Price is now below minimum average total cost so the firm incurs an

economic loss. But to keep its loss to a minimum, the firm adjusts its output to keep price equal to marginal cost. At a price of P_1, each firm produces an output of q_1.

The industry is now in short-run equilibrium but not long-run equilibrium. It is in short-run equilibrium because each firm is maximizing profit. But it is not in long-run equilibrium because each firm is incurring an economic loss—its average total cost exceeds the price.

The economic loss is a signal for some firms to leave the industry. As they do so, short-run industry supply decreases and the supply curve shifts leftward. As supply decreases, the price rises. At each higher price, a firm's profit-maximizing output is greater, so the firms remaining in the industry increase their output as the price rises. Each firm slides up its marginal cost or supply curve (part b). That is, as firms exit the industry, industry output decreases but the output of the firms that remain in the industry increases. Eventually, enough firms leave the industry for the supply curve to have shifted to S_1 (part a). At this time, the price has returned to its original level, P_0. At this price, the firms remaining in the industry produce q_0, the same quantity as they produced before the decrease in demand. Because firms are now making normal profits and zero economic profit, no firm wants to enter or exit the industry. The industry supply curve remains at S_1 and industry output is Q_2. The industry is again in long-run equilibrium.

The difference between the initial long-run equilibrium and the final long-run equilibrium is the number of firms in the industry. A permanent decrease in demand has decreased the number of firms. Each remaining firm produces the same output in the new long-run equilibrium as it did initially and earns a normal profit. In the process of moving from the initial equilibrium to the new one, firms that remain in the industry incur losses.

We've just worked out how a competitive industry responds to a permanent *decrease* in demand. A permanent increase in demand triggers a similar response, except in the opposite direction. The increase in demand brings a higher price, profit, and entry. Entry increases industry supply and eventually lowers the price to its original level.

In the example that we have just studied, the price returns to its original level. This outcome does not always occur. The price can rise, fall, or remain unchanged, as we will now see.

FIGURE 11.10

A Decrease in Demand

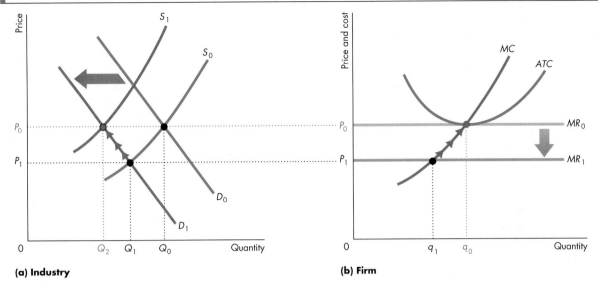

(a) Industry

(b) Firm

An industry starts out in long-run competitive equilibrium. Part (a) shows the industry demand curve D_0, the industry supply curve S_0, the equilibrium quantity Q_0, and the market price P_0. Each firm sells at price P_0, so its marginal revenue curve is MR_0 in part (b). Each firm produces q_0 and makes a normal profit. Demand decreases permanently from D_0 to D_1 (part a). The equilibrium price falls to P_1, each firm decreases its output to q_1 (part b), and industry output decreases to Q_1 (part a).

In this new situation, firms incur economic losses and some firms leave the industry. As they do so, the industry supply curve gradually shifts leftward, from S_0 to S_1. This shift gradually raises the market price from P_1 back to P_0. While the price is below P_0, firms incur economic losses and some firms leave the industry. Once the price has returned to P_0, each firm makes a normal profit. Firms have no further incentive to leave the industry. Each firm produces q_0, and industry output is Q_2.

External Economies and Diseconomies

The change in long-run equilibrium price depends on external economies and external diseconomies. **External economies** are factors beyond the control of an individual firm that lower its costs as *industry* output increases. **External diseconomies** are factors outside the control of a firm that raise its costs as *industry* output increases. With no external economies or external diseconomies, a firm's costs remain constant as industry output changes.

Figure 11.11 illustrates these three cases and introduces a new supply concept: the long-run industry supply curve. A **long-run industry supply curve** shows how the quantity supplied by an industry varies as the market price varies after all the possible adjustments have been made, including changes in plant size and changes in the number of firms in the industry.

Part (a) shows the case we have just studied—no external economies or diseconomies. The long-run industry supply curve (LS_A) is perfectly elastic. In this case, a permanent increase in demand from D_0 to D_1 has no effect on the price in the long run. The increase in demand brings a temporary increase in price to P_S and a short-run quantity increase from Q_0 to Q_S. Entry increases short-run supply from S_0 to S_1, which lowers the price to its original level, P_0, and increases the quantity to Q_1.

Part (b) shows the case of external diseconomies. In this case, the long-run supply industry curve (LS_B) slopes upward. A permanent increase in demand from D_0 to D_1 increases the price in both the short run and the long run. As in the previous case, the increase in demand brings a temporary increase in price to P_S and a short-run quantity increase from Q_0 to Q_S. Entry increases short-run supply from S_0 to S_2, which lowers the price to P_2 and increases the quantity to Q_2.

FIGURE 11.11

Long-Run Changes in Price and Quantity

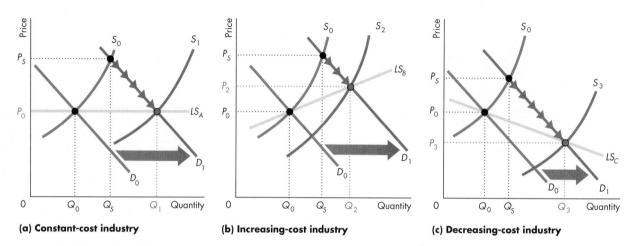

(a) Constant-cost industry   **(b) Increasing-cost industry**   **(c) Decreasing-cost industry**

Three possible changes in price and quantity occur in the long run. When demand increases from D_0 to D_1, entry occurs and the industry supply curve shifts rightward. In part (a), the long-run supply curve LS_A is horizontal. The quantity increases from Q_0 to Q_1 and the price remains constant at P_0. In part (b), the

long-run supply curve is LS_B; the price rises to P_2 and the quantity increases to Q_2. This case occurs in an industry with external diseconomies. In part (c), the long-run supply curve is LS_C; the price falls to P_3 and the quantity increases to Q_3. This case occurs in an industry with external economies.

Part (c) shows the case of external economies. In this case, the long-run industry supply curve (LS_C) slopes downward. A permanent increase in demand from D_0 to D_1 increases the price in the short run and lowers it in the long run. Again, the increase in demand brings a temporary increase in price to P_S and a short-run quantity increase from Q_0 to Q_S. Entry increases short-run supply from S_0 to S_3, which lowers the price to P_3 and increases the quantity to Q_3.

One of the best examples of external economies is the growth of specialist support services for an industry as it expands. As farm output increased in the nineteenth and early twentieth centuries, the services available to farmers expanded and average farm costs fell. For example, new firms specialized in the development and marketing of farm machinery and fertilizers. As a result, average farm costs decreased. Farms enjoyed the benefits of external economies. As a consequence, as the demand for farm products increased, the quantity produced increased but the price fell.

Over the long term, the prices of many goods and services have fallen, not because of external economies but because of technological change. Let's now study this influence on a competitive market.

Technological Change

Industries are constantly discovering lower-cost techniques of production. Most cost-saving production techniques cannot be implemented, however, without investing in new plant and equipment. As a consequence, it takes time for a technological advance to spread through an industry. Some firms whose plants are on the verge of being replaced will be quick to adopt the new technology, while other firms whose plants have recently been replaced will continue to operate with an old technology until they can no longer cover their average variable cost. Once average variable cost cannot be covered, a firm will scrap even a relatively new plant (embodying an old technology) in favour of a plant with a new technology.

New technology allows firms to produce at a lower cost. As a result, as firms adopt a new technology, their cost curves shift downward. With lower costs, firms are willing to supply a larger quantity at a given price. Supply increases and the supply curve shifts rightward. With a given demand, the quantity produced increases and the price falls.

Two forces are at work in an industry undergoing technological change. Firms that adopt the new technology make an economic profit. So there is entry by new-technology firms. Firms that stick with the old technology incur economic losses. They either exit the industry or switch to the new technology.

As old-technology firms disappear and new-technology firms enter, the price falls and the quantity produced increases. Eventually, the industry arrives at a long-run equilibrium in which all the firms use the new technology, produce at minimum long-run average cost, and make a zero economic profit (a normal profit). Because in the long run competition eliminates economic profit, technological change brings only temporary gains to producers. But the lower prices and better products that technological advances bring are permanent gains for consumers.

The process that we've just described is one in which some firms experience economic profits and others experience economic losses. It is a period of dynamic change for an industry. Some firms do well, and others do badly. Often, the process has a geographical dimension—the expanding new-technology firms bring prosperity to what was once the boondocks, and traditional industrial regions decline. Sometimes, the new-technology firms are in a foreign country, while the old-technology firms are in the domestic economy.

R E V I E W

- A decrease in demand in a competitive industry brings a fall in price, economic loss, and exit. Exit decreases industry supply, which brings a rise in price. In the long run, enough firms exit for those remaining to make a normal profit.
- An increase in demand in a competitive industry brings a rise in price, economic profit, and entry. Entry increases industry supply, which brings a fall in price. In the long run, enough firms enter for economic profit to decrease to zero and leave firms making a normal profit.
- A new technology lowers costs, increases industry supply, and lowers price. New-technology firms make an economic profit and enter. Old-technology firms incur an economic loss and exit. In the long run, all firms adopt the new technology and make normal profit.

Competition and Efficiency

DOES A PERFECTLY COMPETITIVE INDUSTRY produce the right quantities of goods and services at the right prices? Is perfect competition efficient?

Allocative Efficiency

If no one can be made better off without someone else being made worse off, **allocative efficiency** has been achieved. If someone can be made better off without anyone else being made worse off, the allocation is not efficient. For example, suppose a school has a computer that no one uses and that no one will ever use. Suppose also that the students in another school are clamouring for an extra computer. If the computer is reallocated from the first school to the second, some people are better off and no one is worse off.

Three conditions are met when the allocation of resources is efficient:

1. Consumer efficiency
2. Producer efficiency
3. Exchange efficiency

Consumer Efficiency When consumers cannot make themselves better off—cannot increase utility—by reallocating their budgets, they have achieved **consumer efficiency**. You've seen that along a household's demand curve, utility is maximized. So, when a household is on its demand curve, it has achieved consumer efficiency.

If there are no *external benefits*, an entire market achieves consumer efficiency at any point on the *market* demand curve. **External benefits** are benefits that accrue to people other than the buyer of a good. For example, you might get pleasure (utility) from your neighbour's expenditure on her garden. Your neighbour buys the quantities of garden plants that maximize her utility, not yours.

In the absence of external benefits, the market demand curve measures the value that consumers place on the various quantities and along the market demand curve, consumers cannot increase utility by reallocating their budgets.

Producer Efficiency When firms cannot lower the cost of producing a given output by changing the factors of production used, they have achieved **producer efficiency**. A firm achieves producer efficiency at any point on its marginal cost curve, or equivalently, on its supply curve.

If there are no *external costs*, an entire market achieves producer efficiency at any point on the *market* (or *industry*) supply curve. **External costs** are costs not borne by the producer of a good or service but costs borne by someone else. For example, a firm might lower its own costs by polluting the atmosphere. The cost of pollution is an external cost. Firms produce the output level that maximizes their own profit and they do not count the cost of pollution as a charge against their profit.

In the absence of externalities, the market supply curve measures the opportunity cost that firms incur to produce the various quantities of a good or service and along the market supply curve, firms cannot increase profit. (Two separate conditions are met when producer efficiency is achieved: *technological efficiency*—maximum possible output from factors of production—and *economic efficiency*—factor combination that minimizes cost. See Chapter 9, pp. 200–202.)

Exchange Efficiency   When all the gains from trade have been realized, **exchange efficiency** is achieved. The gains from trade for consumers are measured by **consumer surplus**, which is the value that consumers place on a good minus the price paid for it. Consumer surplus is measured by the area between the demand curve and the price paid. (See Chapter 7, pp. 160–161 for a more detailed explanation of consumer surplus.)

The gains from trade for producers are measured by **producer surplus**, which is the total revenue that producers receive for a good minus the opportunity cost of producing it. Opportunity cost equals marginal cost, and the competitive firm's marginal cost curve is its supply curve. Because producer surplus is revenue minus opportunity cost, it is measured by the area between the price received and the supply curve.

The total gains from trade are the sum of consumer surplus and producer surplus.

An Efficient Allocation   Figure 11.12 shows an efficient allocation. Consumer efficiency is achieved at all points on the demand curve, *D*. Producer efficiency is achieved at all points on the supply curve, *S*. Exchange efficiency is achieved at the quantity Q^* and price P^*. In this situation, the sum of producer sur-

FIGURE   11.12

Allocative Efficiency

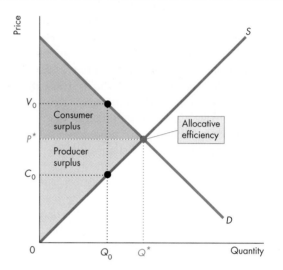

Allocative efficiency requires *producer efficiency*, which occurs when firms are on their supply curves; *consumer efficiency*, which occurs when consumers are on their demand curves; and *exchange efficiency*, which occurs when all the gains from trade are realized. Allocative efficiency occurs at the quantity Q^* and price P^*. The sum of consumer surplus (green area) and producer surplus (blue area) is maximized. If the output is Q_0, all the gains from trade are not realized. The cost of producing another unit, C_0, is less than the value consumers place on that unit, V_0. At the output Q_0, the sum of consumer surplus and producer surplus is not maximized.

plus (blue area) and consumer surplus (green area) is maximized.

To see that the gains from trade cannot be increased, imagine that output is restricted to Q_0. The cost of producing one more unit is C_0 and the value placed on one more unit by consumers is V_0. Producers could supply more of the good for a price lower than V_0. Consumers are willing to buy more of the good for a price higher than C_0. Everyone would like to trade more and get more consumer surplus and producer surplus. If output exceeded Q^*, the cost of producing one more unit would exceed the value placed on it. Only at Q^* does the value the consumer places on the last unit bought equal its cost of production and are the gains from trade maximized.

Efficiency of Perfect Competition

Perfect competition delivers allocative efficiency if there are no external benefits and costs. In such a case, all the benefits accrue to the buyers of a good and the costs are borne by its producer. The price and quantity are determined at the point of intersection of the demand and supply curves so, in Fig. 11.12, a perfectly competitive market produces an output of Q^* at a price P^* and allocative efficiency is achieved.

Adam Smith believed that competitive markets were efficient because each participant in the market was "led by an invisible hand to promote an end (an

efficient allocation of resources) which was no part of his intention." You can see the invisible hand at work in the cartoon. When there is no demand for ice cream but there is a demand for shade, the ice cream vendor temporarily exits the ice cream market and enters the sunshade market. A transaction occurs that makes two people better off.

There are two main obstacles to allocative efficiency:

1. External costs and external benefits
2. Monopoly

External Costs and External Benefits   Goods such as national defence, the enforcement of law and order, the provision of clean drinking water, and the disposal of sewage and garbage are examples of goods and services in which there are enormous external benefits. Left to competitive markets, too small a quantity of them would be produced. The production of steel and chemicals can generate air and water pollution and perfect competition might produce too large a quantity of these goods. Government institutions and policies (which we study in Chapters 19 and 21) arise, in part, because of external costs and benefits.

Monopoly   Monopoly (in Chapter 12) restricts output below its competitive level to raise price and increase profit. Government policies (in Chapter 20) arise to limit such use of monopoly power.

◆   We have now completed our study of perfect competition. The competitive model that you have studied in this chapter can be used to interpret many developments in today's world, and *Reading Between the Lines* on pp. 252–253 gives an interesting example of competition in the shopping malls.

Although many markets approximate the model of perfect competition, many do not. Our next task, in Chapters 12 and 13, is to study markets that depart from perfect competition. When we have completed this study, we'll have a toolkit of alternative models of markets that will enable us to study all the possible situations that arise in the real world. We begin, in the next chapter, by going to the opposite extreme of perfect competition—monopoly. Then, in Chapter 13, we'll study the markets between perfect competition and pure monopoly—monopolistic competition and oligopoly.

Drawing by M. Twohy; © 1985 The New Yorker Magazine, Inc.

Competition Among Shopping Malls

CALGARY HERALD, JUNE 1, 1996

Mall wars

BY CAROL HOWES

Calgarians have become extremely fickle in their love affair with shopping centres, says a retail design specialist.

Calgary is not overbuilt with shopping centres, but it has too many copycats, says Marcel Proskow, principal of Maxam Design International Inc. Many malls will have to reposition themselves over the next few years to avoid extinction.

"The problem is we have too many shopping centres that are the same," he says. "In repositioning, (malls) have to take a look at creating a niche that isn't there."

Proskow, who has just returned from Las Vegas where he spoke at an annual convention of the International Council of Shopping Centres, says because of overbuilding in the 1980s malls across Canada are struggling and dying at an alarming rate.

But by repositioning—not simply renovating—and targeting a specific market for a specific purpose, there is hope for them.

"The mantra of the shopping development community for the 1990s is the three Rs—renovate, remerchandise and reposition," says Mike Kehoe, a retail and real estate specialist with Fairfield Commercial.

Kehoe says despite what appears to be an over-abundance of shopping centres in Calgary, the city "is well within acceptable limits." Calgary has 18.6 square feet per capita of shopping area, compared to the national average of 12.2 square feet. But that does not take into account the large number of people who drive in from outside Calgary to shop.

Proskow, whose fledgling company is doing work on old or tired shopping centres across Canada and the U.S., says mall owners and developers are finally catching on to the fact that "just because you build it doesn't mean they're coming." ...

Proskow says most retail concepts only have a shelf life of about seven years.

He says a mix of value retail stores, destination stores and an entertainment component is the current trend for shopping malls. The idea behind the format is to keep shoppers in the centres longer. ...

Kehoe says the current crop of new projects under construction are likely to be the last for some time to come.

"There won't be any new malls built in Canada for the rest of the decade and likely into the next," he says. "We're at our limit."

Essence of THE STORY

■ Calgary has several almost identical competing shopping malls.

■ At 18.6 square feet per person, Calgary has more mall space than the Canadian average of 12.2 square feet. But a large number of people drive into Calgary to shop, so the city does not have too much space.

■ It is predicted that no new malls will be built in Canada for more than 10 years and because of over-building during the 1980s some malls are closing down.

■ Malls can increase their profitability by targeting specific markets but not simply by renovating.

Economic

A N A L Y S I S

■ Renting retail space in shopping malls is a very competitive business.

■ Owners of malls are price takers. If they try to rent space for more than the market price, retail stores will go to another mall.

■ Figure 1 shows the market for mall floor space during the 1980s and 1990s.

■ The demand for space is shown by the demand curve D. In the mid-1980s, the supply curve was S_0. The price of a square foot of space was P_0 and the quantity was Q_0.

■ Because mall owners anticipated an increase in demand during the 1990s, they built more retail space. The supply of mall space increased and the supply curve shifted rightward to S_1. The price to rent space fell to P_1 and the quantity of space available increased to Q_1.

■ Figure 2 shows what happened at a typical local mall. The mall owner's average total cost curve is ATC and marginal cost curve is MC.

■ When, during the 1980s, the price of a square foot of space was P_0, the quantity of space used was q_0. The mall was operating at capacity.

■ But when the price fell to P_1, the mall owner cut back the amount of space used to q_1. The reason is that the marginal cost of renovating and maintaining space in good condition exceeded the rental price.

■ But the mall in Fig. 2 is incurring a loss. So eventually, it will go out of business.

■ As malls incurring losses exit, the supply of space decreases, the supply curve shifts leftward back towards S_0 in Fig. 1, and the price rises back to P_0. When that has happened, malls will again be fully utilized as they were during the mid-1980s.

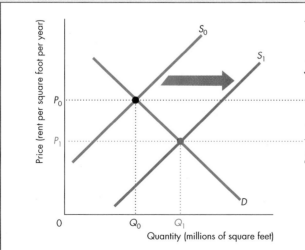

Figure 1 The market

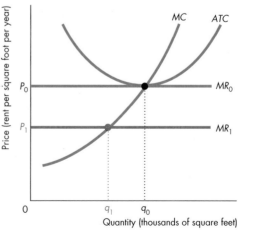

Figure 2 The individual mall owner

SUMMARY

Key Points

Perfect Competition   A perfectly competitive firm is a price taker. It maximizes profit by producing the quantity at which price equals marginal cost. The firm maximizes profit by temporarily shutting down when price is less than or equal to minimum average variable cost. The firm's supply curve is the upward-sloping part of its marginal cost curve above minimum average variable cost. (pp. 234–241)

Output, Price, and Profit in the Short Run Industry supply and demand determine the market price. Each firm takes the market price as given and chooses the output that maximizes profit. In short-run equilibrium, each firm can make an economic profit, incur an economic loss, or break even. (pp. 242–243)

Output, Price, and Profit in the Long Run   If firms make economic profits, new firms enter the industry and existing firms might increase their plant size. If firms incur economic losses, some will leave the industry and the remaining firms might decrease their plant size. Entry and exit and changes in plant size shift the short-run industry supply curve. Entry increases short-run supply, lowers price, and decreases economic profit. Exit decreases short-run supply, raises price, and increases economic profit (decreases economic loss). In long-run equilibrium, economic profit is zero. Each firm makes normal profit. In long-run competitive equilibrium, price equals marginal cost; economic profit is zero, there is no entry or exit, and each firm produces at the point of minimum long-run average cost. (pp. 243–245)

Changing Tastes and Advancing Technology   In a perfectly competitive market, a permanent decrease in demand leads to a smaller industry output and a smaller number of firms in the industry. A permanent increase in demand leads to an increase in industry output and an increase in the number of firms in the industry. As demand changes, the price can rise (external diseconomies), fall (external economies), or remain constant (no external economies or diseconomies) in the long run.

New technology increases the industry supply, and in the long run the market price falls and the quantity sold increases. (pp. 246–249)

Competition and Efficiency   Allocative efficiency occurs when no one can be made better off without making someone else worse off. Perfect competition is efficient when there are no external costs and external benefits. (pp. 249–251)

Key Figures

Key Terms

REVIEW QUESTIONS

1. What are the main features of a perfectly competitive industry?
2. Why can't a perfectly competitive firm influence the industry price?
3. List the four key decisions that a firm in a perfectly competitive industry has to make to maximize profit.
4. Why is marginal revenue equal to price in a perfectly competitive industry?
5. When will a perfectly competitive firm temporarily stop producing?
6. In a perfectly competitive industry, what is the connection between the supply curve and the marginal cost curve?
7. In a perfectly competitive industry, what is the relationship between a firm's supply curve and the short-run industry supply curve?
8. When will firms enter an industry and when will they leave it?
9. What happens to the short-run industry supply curve when firms enter a competitive industry?
10. What is the effect of entry on the price and quantity produced?
11. What is the effect of entry on economic profit?
12. Trace the effects of a permanent increase in demand on price, quantity sold, number of firms, and economic profit.
13. Trace the effects of a permanent decrease in demand on price, quantity sold, number of firms, and economic profit.
14. What are external economies and external diseconomies?
15. Under what circumstances will a perfectly competitive industry have
    a. A perfectly elastic long-run supply curve?
    b. An upward-sloping long-run supply curve?
    c. A downward-sloping long-run supply curve?
16. What is allocative efficiency and under what circumstances does it arise?
17. What are external costs and external benefits?
18. What is economic efficiency?
19. What is consumer efficiency?
20. Under what conditions is perfect competition not allocatively efficient?

CRITICAL THINKING

1. After you have studied *Reading Between the Lines* on pp. 252–253, answer the following questions:
    a. How would you characterize the shopping mall industry of 1996: in long-run equilibrium, making economic profit, incurring economic loss? What evidence enables you to reach your conclusion?
    b. Why are the shopping malls in the condition described in the news article?
    c. What do you predict will happen to the shopping mall industry during the next few years? Be specific about the quantity of malls, rents, and economic profits.
2. In commercial shopping areas close to universities across Canada, a new industry has sprung up in recent years: the copy centre. Explain why businesses such as Kinko's are flourishing. What has generated a sustained increase in the quantity of copying done? Has the price increased or decreased? (Be careful to use relative price—see Chapter 4, p. 68.) In answering this question, think about both demand-side and supply-side factors and draw careful figures to illustrate your answer.
3. Inline skates have become fashionable and roller skates have become unfashionable. At the same time, new technologies have vastly improved the quality of inline skates. What do you predict has happened in the inline skate industry and the roller skate industry to
    a. The number of producers?
    b. Prices?
    c. Quantities produced?
    d. Economic profit?
Draw four diagrams, one for each industry and one for a typical firm in each industry, to show the trends in these four variables over recent years.

P R O B L E M S

1. Quick Copy is one of the many copy shops near the campus. The figure shows Quick Copy's cost curves.
   a. If the market price of copying is 10¢ a page, what is Quick Copy's profit-maximizing output?
   b. Calculate Quick Copy's profit.
   c. With no change in demand or technology, how will the price and profit change in the long run?

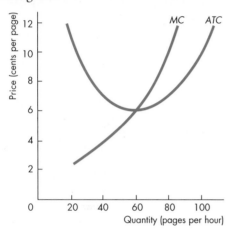

2. Pat's Pizza Kitchen is a price taker. It has the following hourly costs:

Output (pizzas per hour)	Total cost (dollars per hour)
0	10
1	21
2	30
3	41
4	54
5	79
6	96

   a. If pizzas sell for $14, what is Pat's profit-maximizing output per hour? How much economic profit does Pat make?
   b. What is Pat's shutdown point?
   c. Derive Pat's supply curve.
   d. What range of prices will cause Pat to leave the pizza industry?
   e. What range of prices will cause other firms with costs identical to Pat's to enter the industry?

   f. What is the long-run equilibrium price of a pizza?

3. The table sets out the market demand schedule for cassettes.

Price (dollars per cassette)	Quantity demanded (cassettes per week)
3.65	500,000
4.40	475,000
5.20	450,000
6.00	425,000
6.80	400,000
7.60	375,000
8.40	350,000
9.20	325,000
10.00	300,000
10.80	275,000
11.60	250,000
12.40	225,000
13.20	200,000
14.00	175,000
14.80	150,000

The market is perfectly competitive and each firm has the following cost structure:

Output (cassettes per week)	Marginal cost	Average variable cost	Average total cost
		(dollars per cassette)	
150	6.00	8.80	15.47
200	6.40	7.80	12.80
250	7.00	7.00	11.00
300	7.65	7.10	10.43
350	8.40	7.20	10.06
400	10.00	7.50	10.00
450	12.40	8.00	10.22
500	12.70	9.00	11.00

There are 1,000 firms in the industry.
   a. What is the market price?
   b. What is the industry's output?
   c. What is the output of each firm?
   d. What is the economic profit of each firm?
   e. What is the shutdown point?
   f. What is the long-run equilibrium price?
   g. What is the number of firms in the long run?

4. The same demand conditions as those in problem 3 prevail and there are still 1,000 firms in the industry, but fixed costs increase by $980.
   a. What is the short-run profit-maximizing output for each firm?
   b. Do firms enter or exit the industry in the long run?
   c. What is the new long-run equilibrium price?
   d. What is the new long-run equilibrium number of firms in the industry?

5. The same cost conditions as those in problem 3 prevail and there are 1,000 firms in the industry, but a fall in the price of compact discs decreases the demand for cassettes and the demand schedule becomes as follows:

Price (dollars per cassette)	Quantity demanded (cassettes per week)
2.95	500,000
3.54	475,000
4.13	450,000
4.71	425,000
5.30	400,000
5.89	375,000
6.48	350,000
7.06	325,000
7.65	300,000
8.24	275,000
8.83	250,000
9.41	225,000
10.00	200,000
10.59	175,000
11.18	150,000

   a. What is the short-run profit-maximizing output for each firm?
   b. Do firms enter or exit the industry in the long run?
   c. What is the new long-run equilibrium price?

   d. What is the new long-run equilibrium number of firms in the industry?
6. Why have the prices of pocket calculators and VCRs fallen?
7. What has been the effect of an increase in world population on the wheat market and the individual wheat farmer?
8. How has the diaper service industry been affected by the decrease in the Canadian birth rate and the development of disposable diapers?
9. The graph illustrates the copy market. There are no external costs and benefits from making copies.

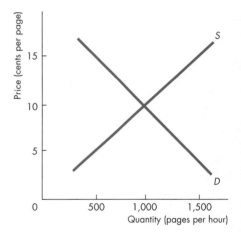

   a. What is the allocatively efficient number of copies per hour?
   b. If an industry produced 500 copies an hour, are the copy shops economically efficient?
   c. If the copy price were 15¢ a page and students made 500 copies an hour, is this outcome consumer efficient?
   d. If the copy industry created external costs of 1¢ a page, would the allocatively efficient output be larger or smaller than that when the industry created no external costs?

Monopoly

After studying this chapter, you will be able to:

- Define monopoly and explain the conditions under which it arises

- Distinguish between legal monopoly and natural monopoly

- Explain how a monopoly determines its price and output

- Define price discrimination and explain why it leads to a bigger profit

- Compare the performance of a competitive and monopolistic industry

- Define rent seeking and explain why it arises

- Explain the conditions under which monopoly is more efficient than competition

You have been reading a lot in this book about firms that want to maximize profit. But perhaps you've been looking around at some of the places where you do business and wondering if they are really so intent on profit. After all, don't you get a student's discount when you get a haircut? Don't museums and movie theatres give discounts to students, too? And what about the airline that gives a discount for buying a ticket in advance? Are your barber and movie theatre owner, as well as the museum and airline operators, simply generous folks to whom the model of profit-maximizing firms does not apply? Aren't they simply throwing away profit by cutting ticket prices and offering discounts? ◆ When you buy electric power, you don't shop around. You buy from your electric power utility, which is your only available supplier. If you live in the north of London, Ontario, and want cable TV service, you only have one option: Buy from Rogers Cablesystems. These are examples of a single producer of a good or service controlling its supply. Such firms are obviously not like firms in perfectly competitive industries. They don't face a market-determined price. They can choose their own price. How do such firms behave? How do they choose the quantity to produce and the price at which to sell it? How does their behaviour compare with firms in perfectly competitive industries? Do such firms charge prices that are too high and that damage the interests of consumers? Do such firms bring any benefits?

The Profits of Generosity

◇ In this chapter, we study markets in which an individual firm can influence the quantity of goods supplied and exert an influence on price. We also compare the performance of a firm in such markets with that of a competitive market and examine whether monopoly is as efficient as competition.

How Monopoly Arises

THE SUPPLIERS OF LOCAL PHONE SERVICES, GAS, electricity, and water are monopolies. A **monopoly** is an industry that produces a good or service for which no close substitute exists and in which there is one supplier that is protected from competition by a barrier preventing the entry of new firms. The suppliers of local phone services, gas, electricity, and water are examples of local monopolies—monopolies restricted to a given location. Microsoft Corp., the software developer that created DOS, the operating system used by most PCs, is an example of a global monopoly.

No Close Substitutes

The first key feature of a monopoly is that it has no close substitutes. If a good does have a close substitute, even though only one firm produces it, that firm effectively faces competition from the producers of substitutes.

Water supplied by a local public utility is an example of a good that does not have close substitutes. While it does have a close substitute for drinking—bottled mineral water—it has no effective substitutes for showering or washing a car.

Innovation and technological change create new products. Some of these are substitutes for existing products and so weaken existing monopolies. For example, with the arrival of national couriers such as FedEx and UPS and the development of the fax machine, the first-class letter monopoly of Canada Post has been greatly weakened. Similarly, the arrival of satellite dishes has greatly weakened the monopoly of local cable television companies. Advances in telecommunication technology have ended the telephone monopoly. Competition among long-distance carriers came first, and later, cellular telephones began to undermine the monopoly in local calls.

Other new products have poor substitutes and so create new monopolies. An example is Microsoft's monopoly in Windows. Similarly, research in the pharmaceutical industry is constantly creating new monopolies in drugs.

Barriers to Entry

The second key feature of a monopoly is the existence of barriers preventing the entry of new firms.

Barriers to entry are legal or natural impediments protecting a firm from competition from potential new entrants.

Legal Barriers to Entry Legal barriers to entry create legal monopoly. A **legal monopoly** is a market in which competition and entry are restricted by the granting of a public franchise, licence, patent or copyright, or in which a firm has acquired ownership of a significant portion of a key resource.

A *public franchise* is an exclusive right granted to a firm to supply a good or service. An example of a public franchise is Canada Post, which has the exclusive right to carry first-class mail. Another common form of public franchise occurs on highways where particular firms are given exclusive rights to sell gasoline and food services.

A *government licence* controls entry into particular occupations, professions, and industries. Government licensing in the professions is the most common example of this type of barrier to entry. For example, a licence is required to practise medicine, law, dentistry, school teaching, architecture, and a variety of other professional services. Licensing does not create monopoly, but it does restrict competition.

A *patent* is an exclusive right granted to the inventor of a product or service. A *copyright* is an exclusive right granted to the author or composer of a literary, musical, dramatic, or artistic work. Patents and copyrights are valid for a limited time period that varies from country to country. In Canada, a patent is valid for 20 years. Patents protect inventors by creating a property right and thereby encourage invention by preventing others from copying an invention until sufficient time has elapsed for the inventor to have reaped some benefits. They also stimulate *innovation*—the use of new inventions—by increasing the incentives for inventors to publicize their discoveries and offer them for use under licence.

In some industries, the government does not grant a legal monopoly, but a single firm acquires ownership of a significant proportion of a key resource. A past example of this type of monopoly is Alcoa, an aluminum producer that controlled a large proportion of the sources of supply of aluminum during the 1930s. A modern example is DeBeers, a South African firm that controls some 95 percent of the world's supply of natural diamonds.

Natural Barriers to Entry Natural barriers to entry give rise to natural monopoly. **Natural monopoly**

occurs when one firm can supply the entire market at a lower average total cost than two or more firms can. This situation arises when demand limits sales to a quantity at which economies of scale exist. Figure 12.1 shows such a situation. Here, the demand curve for electric power is *D* and the average total cost curve is *ATC*. Because average total cost decreases as output increases, economies of scale prevail over the entire length of the *ATC* curve. One firm can produce 4 million kilowatt-hours at 5¢ a kilowatt-hour. At this price, the quantity demanded is 4 million kilowatt-hours. So if the price was 5¢ a kilowatt-hour, one firm could supply the entire market. If two firms shared the market, it would cost each of them 10¢ a kilowatt-hour to produce a total of 4 million kilowatt-hours. If four firms shared the market, it would cost each of them 15¢ a kilowatt-hour to pro-

duce a total of 4 million kilowatt-hours. So, in conditions like those shown in Fig. 12.1, one firm can supply the entire market at a lower cost than two or more firms can. Electric power utilities are an example of natural monopoly. Another example is natural gas distribution.

Most monopolies in the real world, whether legal or natural, are regulated in some way by government or by government agencies. We will study such regulation in Chapter 20. Here we will study unregulated monopoly for two reasons. First, we can better understand why governments regulate monopolies and the effects of regulation if we also know how an unregulated monopoly behaves. Second, even in industries with more than one producer, firms often have a degree of monopoly power, arising from locational advantages or from differences in product quality protected by patents. The theory of monopoly sheds light on the behaviour of such firms and industries.

We begin by studying the behaviour of a single-price monopoly. A *single-price monopoly* is a monopoly that charges the same price for each and every unit of its output. How does a single-price monopoly determine the quantity to produce and the price to charge for its output?

FIGURE 12.1
Natural Monopoly

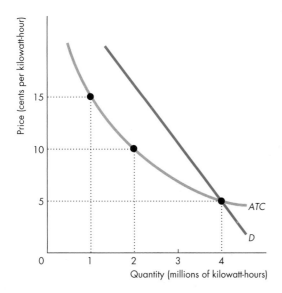

The demand curve for electric power is *D* and the average total cost curve is *ATC*. Economies of scale exist over the entire *ATC* curve. One firm can produce a total output of 4 million kilowatt-hours at a cost of 5¢ a kilowatt-hour. This same total output costs 10¢ a kilowatt-hour with two firms and 15¢ a kilowatt-hour with four firms. So one firm can meet the market demand at a lower cost than two or more firms can, and the market is a natural monopoly.

Single-Price Monopoly

THE STARTING POINT FOR UNDERSTANDING HOW a single-price monopoly chooses its price and output is to work out the relationship between the demand for the good produced by the monopoly and the monopoly's revenue.

Demand and Revenue

Because in a monopoly there is only one firm, the demand curve facing that firm is the industry demand curve. Let's look at an example: Bobbie's Barbershop, the sole supplier of haircuts in Trout River, Newfoundland. The demand schedule that Bobbie faces is set out in Table 12.1. At a price of $20, Bobbie sells no haircuts. The lower the price, the more haircuts per hour Bobbie is able to sell. For example, at a price of $12, consumers demand 4 haircuts per hour (row *e*) and at a price of $4, they demand 8 haircuts per hour (row *i*).

TABLE 12.1

Single-Price Monopoly's Revenue

	Price (P) (dollars per haircut)	Quantity demanded (Q) (haircuts per hour)	Total revenue (TR = P × Q) (dollars)	Marginal revenue (MR = ΔTR/ΔQ) (dollars per haircut)
a	20	0	0	
				18
b	18	1	18	
				14
c	16	2	32	
				10
d	14	3	42	
				6
e	12	4	48	
				2
f	10	5	50	
				−2
g	8	6	48	
				−6
h	6	7	42	
				−10
i	4	8	32	
				−14
j	2	9	18	
				−18
k	0	10	0	

The table shows Bobbie's demand schedule—the number of haircuts demanded per hour at each price. Total revenue (*TR*) is price multiplied by quantity sold. For example, row *c* shows that when the price is $16 a haircut, two haircuts are sold for a total revenue of $32. Marginal revenue (*MR*) is the change in total revenue resulting from a one-unit increase in the quantity sold. For example, when the price falls from $16 to $14 a haircut, the quantity sold increases from 2 to 3 haircuts and total revenue increases by $10. Marginal revenue is $10. Total revenue increases through row *f*, where 5 haircuts are sold for $10, and it decreases thereafter. Over the output range in which total revenue is increasing, marginal revenue is positive; over the output range in which total revenue is decreasing, marginal revenue is negative.

Total revenue (*TR*) is the price (*P*) multiplied by the quantity sold (*Q*). For example, in row *d*, Bobbie sells 3 haircuts at $14 each, so total revenue is $42. *Marginal revenue* (*MR*) is the change in total revenue (Δ*TR*) resulting from a one-unit increase in the quantity sold. For example, if the price falls from $18 (row *b*) to $16 (row *c*), the quantity sold increases

from 1 to 2 haircuts. Total revenue rises from $18 to $32, so the change in total revenue is $14. Because the quantity sold increases by 1 haircut, marginal revenue equals the change in total revenue and is $14. Marginal revenue is placed between the two rows to emphasize that marginal revenue relates to the *change* in the quantity sold.

Figure 12.2 shows Bobbie's demand curve (*D*). Each row of Table 12.1 corresponds to a point on the demand curve. For example, row *d* in the table and point *d* on the demand curve tell us that at a price of

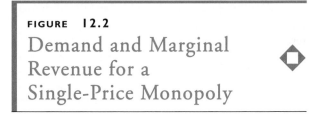

FIGURE 12.2

Demand and Marginal Revenue for a Single-Price Monopoly

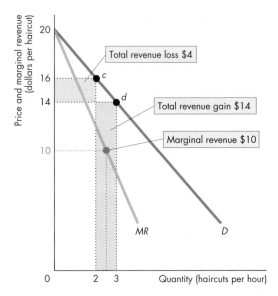

The monopoly demand curve (*D*) is based on the numbers in Table 12.1. At a price of $16 a haircut, Bobbie sells 2 haircuts an hour. If she lowers the price to $14, she sells 3 haircuts an hour. The sale of the third haircut brings a revenue gain of $14 (the price charged for the third haircut). But there is a revenue loss of $4 ($2 per haircut) on the initial 2 haircuts that she could have sold for $16 each. The marginal revenue (extra total revenue) from the third haircut is the revenue gain minus the revenue loss, which is $10. The marginal revenue curve (*MR*) shows the marginal revenue at each level of sales. Marginal revenue is lower than price.

$14, Bobbie sells 3 haircuts. The figure also shows Bobbie's marginal revenue curve (*MR*). Notice that the marginal revenue curve is below the demand curve. That is, at each level of output, marginal revenue is less than price. Why is marginal revenue less than price? It is because when the price is lowered to sell one more unit, there are two opposing effects on total revenue. The lower price results in a revenue loss, and the increased quantity sold results in a revenue gain. For example, at a price of $16, Bobbie sells 2 haircuts (point *c*). If she reduces the price to $14, she sells 3 haircuts and has a revenue gain of $14 on the third haircut. But she charges the same price for all haircuts, so she receives only $14 on each of the first two as well—$2 less than before. As a result, she loses $4 of revenue on the first 2 haircuts. She must deduct this amount from the revenue gain of $14. Marginal revenue—the difference between the revenue gain and the revenue loss—is $10.

Figure 12.3 shows Bobbie's demand curve, marginal revenue curve (*MR*), and total revenue curve (*TR*), and illustrates the connections among them. Again, each row in Table 12.1 corresponds to a point on the curves. For example, row *d* in the table and point *d* on the graphs tell us that when 3 haircuts are sold for $14 each (part a) total revenue is $42 (part b). Notice that as the quantity sold increases, total revenue rises to a peak of $50 (point *f*) and then declines. To understand the behaviour of total revenue, notice what happens to marginal revenue as the quantity sold increases. Over the range 0 to 5 haircuts, marginal revenue is positive. When more than 5 haircuts are sold, marginal revenue becomes negative. The output range over which marginal revenue is positive is the same as that over which total revenue increases. The output range over which marginal revenue is negative is the same as that over which total revenue decreases. When marginal revenue is 0, total revenue is at a maximum.

Revenue and Elasticity

The elasticity of demand is the absolute value of the percentage change in the quantity demanded divided by the percentage change in price. The demand for a good or service can be

1. Elastic
2. Inelastic
3. Unit elastic

Demand is *elastic* if a 1 percent decrease in price results in a greater than 1 percent increase in the quantity demanded. When demand is elastic, the elasticity of demand is greater than 1. Demand is *inelastic* if a 1 percent decrease in price results in a less than 1 percent increase in the quantity demanded. When demand is inelastic, the elasticity of demand is less than 1. Demand is *unit elastic* if a 1 percent decrease in price results in a 1 percent increase in the quantity demanded. When demand is *unit elastic*, the elasticity of demand is 1.

The elasticity of demand influences the change in total revenue resulting from a change in price. A fall in the price increases the quantity demanded along the firm's demand curve. But what happens to total revenue? If demand is elastic, total revenue increases—the increase in revenue from the increase in the quantity sold outweighs the decrease in revenue from the lower price. If demand is inelastic, total revenue decreases—the increase in revenue from the increase in the quantity sold is outweighed by the decrease in revenue from the lower price. If demand is unit elastic, total revenue does not change—the increase in revenue from the increase in the quantity sold offsets the decrease in revenue from the lower price. (Chapter 5, pp. 105–106, explains the relationship between total revenue and elasticity more fully.)

Figure 12.3 illustrates the relationship among marginal revenue, total revenue, and elasticity. As the price of a haircut gradually falls from $20 to $10, the quantity of haircuts demanded increases from 0 to 5 an hour. Over this output range, marginal revenue is positive (part a) and total revenue increases (part b). The demand for haircuts is elastic. As the price of a haircut gradually falls from $10 to $0, the quantity of haircuts demanded increases from 5 to 10 an hour. Over this output range, marginal revenue is negative (part a) and total revenue decreases (part b). The demand for haircuts is inelastic. When the price of a haircut is $10, marginal revenue is zero and total revenue is maximum. The demand for haircuts is unit elastic.

Monopoly Demand Always Elastic The relationship that you have just discovered implies that a profit-maximizing monopoly never produces an output in the inelastic range of its demand curve. If it did so, marginal revenue would be negative—each additional unit sold would lower total revenue. In such a situation, if the firm charges a higher price and produces a smaller quantity its profit increases because its total revenue rises and its total cost falls. But what price and quantity does a profit-maximizing monopoly choose?

FIGURE 12.3

A Single-Price Monopoly's Revenue Curves

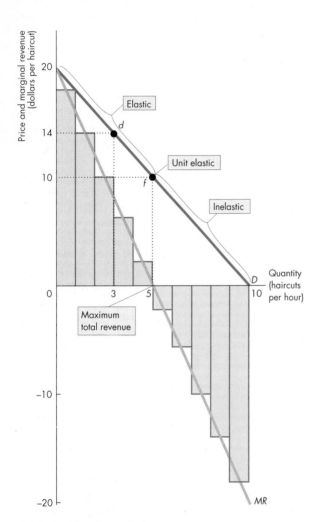

(a) Demand and marginal revenue curves

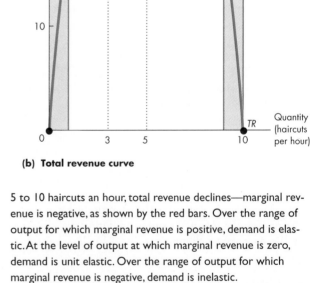

(b) Total revenue curve

Bobbie's demand curve (*D*) and marginal revenue curve (*MR*), shown in part (a), and total revenue curve (*TR*), shown in part (b), are based on the numbers in Table 12.1. For example, at a price of $14, Bobbie sells 3 haircuts an hour (point *d* in part a) for a total revenue of $42 (point *d* in part b). Over the range 0 to 5 haircuts an hour, total revenue is increasing and marginal revenue is positive, as shown by the blue bars. Over the range

5 to 10 haircuts an hour, total revenue declines—marginal revenue is negative, as shown by the red bars. Over the range of output for which marginal revenue is positive, demand is elastic. At the level of output at which marginal revenue is zero, demand is unit elastic. Over the range of output for which marginal revenue is negative, demand is inelastic.

Price and Output Decision

To determine the output level and price that maximize a monopoly's profit, we need to study the behaviour of both revenue and costs as output varies. A monopoly faces the same types of technology and cost constraints as a competitive firm. But it faces a different market constraint. The competitive firm is a price taker, whereas the monopoly's production decision influences the price it receives. Let's see how.

Bobbie's revenue that we studied in Table 12.1 is shown again in Table 12.2. The table also contains information on Bobbie's costs and economic profit. Total cost (*TC*) rises as output increases, and so does total revenue (*TR*). Economic profit equals total revenue minus total cost. As you can see in the table, the maximum profit ($12) occurs when Bobbie sells 3 haircuts for $14 each. If she sells 2 haircuts for $16 each or 4 haircuts for $12 each, her economic profit will be only $8.

You can see why 3 haircuts is the profit-maximizing output by looking at the marginal revenue and marginal cost columns. When Bobbie increases output from 2 to 3 haircuts, her marginal revenue is $10 and her marginal cost is $6. Profit increases by the difference—$4 an hour. If Bobbie increases output even further, from 3 to 4 haircuts, her marginal revenue is $6

and her marginal cost is $10. In this case, marginal cost exceeds marginal revenue by $4, so profit decreases by $4 an hour. When marginal revenue exceeds marginal cost, profit increases if output increases. And when marginal cost exceeds marginal revenue, profit increases if output decreases. When marginal cost and marginal revenue are equal, profit is maximized.

The information set out in Table 12.2 is shown graphically in Fig. 12.4. Part (a) shows Bobbie's total revenue curve (*TR*) and total cost curve (*TC*). Economic profit is the vertical distance between *TR* and *TC*. Bobbie maximizes her profit at 3 haircuts an hour—economic profit is $42 minus $30, or $12. Part (b) shows Bobbie's economic profit when she sells 3 haircuts.

A monopoly, like a competitive firm, maximizes profit by producing the output at which marginal revenue equals marginal cost. Figure 12.4(b) shows Bobbie's demand curve (*D*) and the marginal revenue curve (*MR*) along with the marginal cost curve (*MC*) and average total cost curve (*ATC*). Bobbie maximizes profit by doing 3 haircuts an hour. But what price does she charge for a haircut? To set the price, the monopoly uses the demand curve and finds the highest price at which the profit-maximizing output can be sold. In Bobbie's case, the price at which she can sell 3 haircuts an hour is $14.

TABLE 12.2

A Monopoly's Output and Price Decision

Price (P) (dollars per haircut)	Quantity demanded (Q) (haircuts per hour)	Total revenue (TR = P × Q) (dollars)	Marginal revenue (MR =ΔTR/ΔQ) (dollars per haircut)	Total cost (TC) (dollars)	Marginal cost (MC = ΔTC/ΔQ) (dollars per haircut)	Economic profit (TR – TC) (dollars)
20	0	0		20		−20
			 18		 1	
18	1	18		21		−3
			 14		 3	
16	2	32		24		+8
			 10		 6	
14	3	42		30		+12
			 6		 10	
12	4	48		40		+8
			 2		 15	
10	5	50		55		−5

The table gives the information needed to find the profit-maximizing output and price. Total revenue (*TR*) equals price multiplied by the quantity sold. Profit equals total revenue minus total cost (*TC*). Profit is maximized when the price is $14 and 3 haircuts are sold. Total revenue is $42, total cost is $30, and economic profit is $12 ($42 − $30).

FIGURE 12.4

A Monopoly's Output and Price

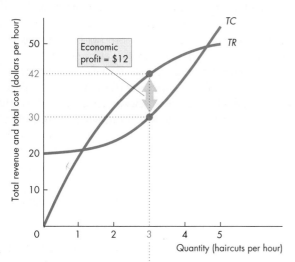

(a) Total revenue and total cost curves

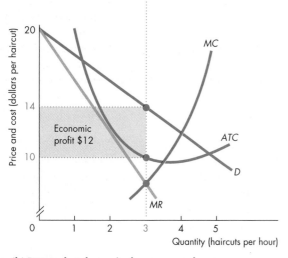

(b) Demand and marginal revenue and cost curves

This figure graphs the numbers in Table 12.2. In part (a), economic profit is the vertical distance between total revenue (*TR*) and total cost (*TC*), and is maximized at 3 haircuts an hour. In Part (b), economic profit is maximized when marginal cost (*MC*) equals marginal revenue (*MR*). The price is determined by the demand curve (*D*) and is $14 a haircut. Economic profit, the blue rectangle, is $12—the profit per haircut ($4) multiplied by 3 haircuts.

All firms maximize profit by producing the output at which marginal revenue equals marginal cost. For a competitive firm, price equals marginal revenue, so price equals marginal cost. For a monopoly, price exceeds marginal revenue, so price also exceeds marginal cost.

A monopoly charges a price that exceeds marginal cost, but does it always make an economic profit? In Bobbie's case, when she produces 3 haircuts an hour, her average total cost is $10 (read from the *ATC* curve) and her price is $14 (read from the *D* curve). Her profit per haircut is $4 ($14 minus $10). Bobbie's economic profit is shown by the blue rectangle, which equals the profit per haircut ($4) multiplied by the number of haircuts (3), for a total of $12.

Bobbie makes a positive economic profit. But suppose that the owner of the shop that Bobbie rents increases the amount she charges Bobbie. If Bobbie pays an additional $12 an hour, her fixed cost increases by $12 an hour. Her marginal cost and marginal revenue don't change, so her profit-maximizing output remains at 3 haircuts an hour. Her economic profit decreases by $12 an hour to zero. If Bobbie pays more than an additional $12 an hour for her shop rent, she incurs an economic loss. If this situation were permanent, Bobbie would go out of business. But entrepreneurs are a hardy lot, and Bobbie might find another shop where the rent is lower.

If firms in a perfectly competitive industry are making a positive economic profit, new firms enter. That does not happen in a monopolistic industry. Barriers to entry prevent new firms from entering. So a monopoly can make a positive economic profit and continue to do so indefinitely. Sometimes that profit is large, as in the international diamond business.

REVIEW

- A monopoly maximizes profit by producing an output at which marginal cost equals marginal revenue.
- At the profit-maximizing output, the monopoly charges the price that consumers are willing to pay, which is determined by the demand curve.
- Because in a monopoly price exceeds marginal revenue, price also exceeds marginal cost.
- A monopoly can make a positive economic profit even in the long run because barriers prevent the entry of new firms.

Price Discrimination

MOVIE THEATRES OFTEN CHARGE STUDENTS AND senior citizens a lower price than other adults to see a movie. Movie theatres practise price discrimination. **Price discrimination** is the practice of charging some customers a lower price than others for an identical good, or of charging an individual customer a lower price on a large purchase than on a small one, even though the cost of servicing all customers is the same. Another example of price discrimination is the common practice of barbers and hairdressers giving discounts to senior citizens and students. Price discrimination can be practised in varying degrees. *Perfect price discrimination* occurs when a firm charges a different price for each unit sold and charges each consumer the maximum price that he or she is willing to pay for the unit. Though firms in the real world do not practise perfect price discrimination, it shows the limit to which price discrimination can be taken.

Not all price *differences* imply price *discrimination*. In many situations, goods that are similar but not identical have different costs and sell for different prices *because* they have different costs. For example, the marginal cost of producing electricity depends on the time of day. If an electric power company charges a higher price for consumption between 7:00 and 9:00 in the morning and between 4:00 and 7:00 in the evening than it does at other times of the day, this practice is not called price discrimination. Price discrimination charges varying prices to consumers, not because of differences in the cost of producing the good, but because of differences in consumers' elasticities of demand for the good.

At first sight, it appears that price discrimination contradicts the assumption of profit maximization. Why would a movie operator allow children to see movies at half price? Why would a hairdresser or barber charge students and senior citizens less? Aren't these producers losing profit by being nice?

Deeper investigation shows that far from losing profit, price discriminators actually make a bigger profit than they would otherwise. Thus a monopoly has an incentive to try to find ways of discriminating among groups of consumers and charging each group the highest possible price. Some people might pay less with price discrimination, but others pay more. How does price discrimination bring in more total revenue?

Price Discrimination and Consumer Surplus

Demand curves slope down because the value that an individual places on a good falls as the quantity consumed of that good increases. When all the units consumed can be bought for a single price, consumers benefit. The benefit is the value the consumers get from each unit of the good minus the price actually paid for it. We call this benefit *consumer surplus*. (If you need to refresh your understanding of consumer surplus, flip back to Chapter 7, pp. 160–161.) Price discrimination can be seen as an attempt by a monopoly to capture the consumer surplus (or as much of the surplus as possible) for itself.

Discriminating Among Units of a Good

One form of price discrimination charges each single buyer a different price on each unit of a good bought. An example of this type of discrimination is a discount for bulk buying. The larger the order, the larger is the discount—and the lower is the price. This type of price discrimination works because each individual's demand curve slopes downward. Some discounts for bulk arise from lower costs of production for greater bulk. In these cases, such discounts are not price discrimination.

To extract every dollar of consumer surplus from every buyer, a monopoly would have to offer each individual customer a separate price schedule based on that customer's own demand curve. Clearly such price discrimination cannot be carried out in practice because a firm does not have enough information about each consumer's demand curve.

Discriminating Among Individuals

Even when it is not possible to charge each individual a different price for each unit bought, it might still be possible to discriminate among individuals. This possibility arises from the fact that some people place a higher value on consuming one more unit of a good than do other individuals. By charging such an individual a higher price, the producer can obtain some of the consumer surplus that would otherwise accrue to its customers.

Discriminating Between Two Groups

Price discrimination often takes the form of discriminating between different groups of consumers on the basis of age, employment status, or some other easily distinguished characteristic. This type of price discrimination works only if each group has a different price elasticity of demand for the product. But this situation is a common one. For example, the elasticity of demand for haircuts is lower for business people than for students, and the elasticity of demand for air travel is lower for business travellers than for vacation travellers. Let's see how an airline exploits the differences in demand by business and vacation travellers and increases its profit by price discriminating.

Global Air has a monopoly on an exotic route. Figure 12.5(a) shows the demand curve (*D*) and the marginal revenue curve (*MR*) for travel on this route. It also shows Global Air's marginal cost curve (*MC*). Marginal cost is constant, and fixed cost is zero. Global Air is a single-price monopoly and maximizes its profit by producing the output at which marginal revenue equals marginal cost. This output is 10,000 trips a year. The price at which Global can sell 10,000 trips is $1,500 per trip. Global Air's total revenue is $15 million a year. Its total cost is $10 million a year, so its economic profit is $5 million a year, as

shown by the blue rectangle in part (a).

Global is struck by the fact that most of its customers are business travellers. Global knows that its exotic route is ideal for vacationers, but it also knows that to attract more of these travellers, it must offer a lower fare than $1,500. At the same time, Global knows that if it cuts the fare, it will lose revenue on its business travellers. So Global decides to price discriminate between the two groups.

Global's first step is to determine the demand curve of business travellers and the demand curve of vacation travellers. The market demand curve (in Fig. 12.5a) is the horizontal sum of the demand curves for these two types of traveller. (See Chapter 7, p.158.) Global determines that the demand curve for business travel is *D_B* in Fig. 12.5(b) and the demand curve for vacation travel is *D_V* in Fig. 12.5(c). At the single fare of $1,500, the 10,000 trips that Global sells is made up of 6,000 to business travellers and 4,000 to vacation travellers. At $1,500 a trip, business travellers buy more trips than vacation travellers—6,000 business trips and 4,000 vacation trips—but at this price, the demand for business travel is much less elastic than vacation travel. As the price decreases below $1,500, the demand for business travel becomes perfectly inelastic while the demand for vacation travel is more elastic.

FIGURE 12.5

A Single Price of Air Travel

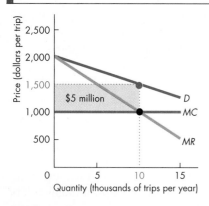

(a) All travellers

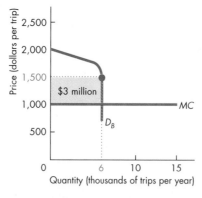

(b) Business travellers

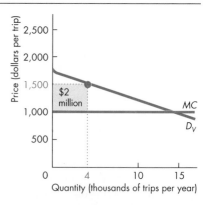

(c) Vacation travellers

Part (a) shows the demand curve (*D*), marginal revenue curve (*MR*), and marginal cost curve (*MC*) for a route on which Global Airlines has a monopoly. As a single-price monopoly, Global maximizes profit by selling 10,000 trips a year at $1,500 a trip. Its profit is $5 million, which is shown by the blue rectangle in

part (a). The demand curve in part (a) is the horizontal sum of the demand curve for business travel (*D_B*) in part (b) and the demand curve for vacation travel (*D_V*) in part (c). Global sells 6,000 trips to business travellers for a profit of $3 million and 4,000 trips to vacation travellers for a profit of $2 million.

Profiting by Price Discriminating

Global uses the profit-maximization rule: Produce the quantity at which marginal revenue equals marginal cost and set the price at the level the consumer is willing to pay. But now that Global has separated its market into two parts, it has two marginal revenue curves. Global's marginal revenue curve for business travel is MR_B as shown in Fig. 12.6(a) and its marginal revenue curve for vacation travel is MR_V as shown in Fig. 12.6(b).

In Fig. 12.6(a), marginal revenue from business travel equals marginal cost of $1,000 at 5,000 trips a year. The price that business travellers are willing to pay for this quantity of trips is $1,700 a trip, up $200 on the current price. In Fig. 12.6(b), marginal revenue from vacation travel equals marginal cost of $1,000 at 7,000 trips a year. The price that vacation travellers are willing to pay for this quantity of trips is $1,350 a trip, *down* $150 on the current price.

If Global can charge its business travellers a fare of $1,700 and its vacation travellers a fare of $1,350, it can increase its sales from 10,000 to 12,000 trips a

year and can increase its economic profit from $5 million a year to $5.95 million. On business travellers, it can make $3.5 million a year, which is $700 per trip on 5,000 trips. This economic profit is shown by the blue rectangle in Fig. 12.6(a). On vacation travellers, Global can make $2.45 million a year, which is $350 per trip on 7,000 trips. The blue rectangle in Fig. 12.6(b) illustrates this economic profit.

How can Global get its business travellers to pay $1,700? If it offers fares to vacation travellers for $1,350, won't business travellers claim to be vacationers? Not with the deal that Global comes up with.

Global has noticed that its business travellers never make reservations more than three weeks in advance. It conducts a survey, which reveals that these travellers never know more than a month in advance when they will need to travel. Its survey also reveals that vacation travellers always know at least a month in advance of their travel plans. So Global offers a deal to all travellers: The basic fare is $1,700, but if a traveller buys a nonrefundable ticket one month in advance of the date of travel, the fare is discounted by $350 to

---

FIGURE 12.6

Price Discrimination

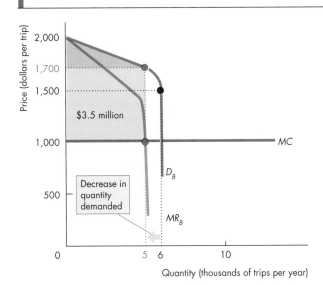

(a) Business travellers

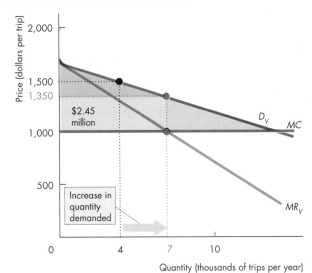

(b) Vacation travellers

The marginal revenue curve for business travel is (MR_B) in part (a) and for vacation travel is (MR_V) in part (b). Global maximizes profit by making marginal revenue equal to marginal cost for each type of travel. By increasing the business fare to $1,700 and by cutting the vacation fare to $1,350, Global increases its

economic profit. It now sells 5,000 business trips for a profit of $3.5 million (the blue rectangle in part a) and 7,000 vacation trips for a profit of $2.45 million (the blue rectangle in part b), so its total profit increases from $5 million with no price discrimination to $5.95 million with discrimination.

$1,350. By price discriminating between business and vacation travellers, Global increases the quantity of trips sold from 10,000 to 12,000 and increases its profit by $0.95 million a year.

More Perfect Price Discrimination

Global can do even better. Some of the business travellers are willing to pay more than $1,700 a trip. They make the consumer surplus shown by the green triangle in Fig. 12.6(a). Also, most of the vacation travellers who are paying $1,350 a trip are willing to pay more. They make the consumer surplus shown by the green triangle in Fig. 12.6(b). Further, some potential vacation travellers are not willing to pay $1,350 but are willing to pay at least $1,000. With a price of $1,000 a trip, potential vacation travellers make the consumer surplus as shown by the orange triangle in Fig. 12.6(b).

Global gets creative. It comes up with a host of special deals. For higher prices, it offers priority reservations and frills to business travellers. (These deals don't change Global's marginal cost.) It refines the list

of restrictions on its discount fares and creates many different fare categories, the lowest of which has lots of restrictions but is $1,000 a trip.

The quantity of seats sold increases until Global is selling 20,000 trips a year, 6,000 to business travellers at various prices between $1,500 and almost $2,000, and 14,000 to vacationers at prices ranging between $1,000 and $1,700 a trip. Global is now almost a perfect price discriminator.

Figure 12.7 shows that if Global is able to perfectly price discriminate, it captures the entire consumer surplus.

Price Discrimination in Practice

You can now see why price discrimination is profitable. Global's special offer—"Normal fare: $1,700, 30-day advance purchase special: $1,350"—is no generous gesture. It is profit-maximizing behaviour. The model of price discrimination that you have just studied explains a wide variety of familiar pricing practices, even by firms that are not pure monopolies.

FIGURE 12.7

Perfect Price Discrimination

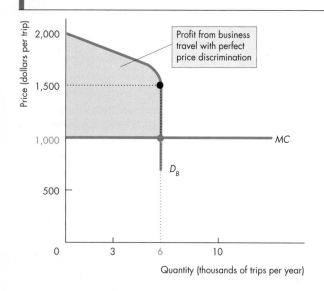

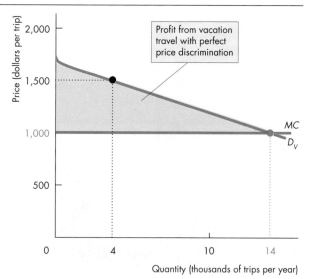

(a) Business travellers

(b) Vacation travellers

By offering a wide array of special fares, restrictions, and deals, Global tries to perfectly price discriminate. If it succeeds, it sells 6,000 trips to business travellers and 14,000 trips to

vacation travellers. It captures the entire consumer surplus. Its economic profit increases to the magnitude shown by the blue areas under the two demand curves.

For example, real airlines, not just the imaginary Global, offer lower fares for advance-purchase tickets than for last-minute travel. Last-minute travellers usually have a lower elasticity of demand than vacation travellers who can plan ahead. Retail stores of all kinds hold seasonal "sales" when they reduce their prices, often by substantial amounts. These "sales" are a form of price discrimination. Each season, the newest fashions carry a high price tag, but retailers do not expect to sell all their stock at such high prices. At the end of the season, they sell off what is left at a discount. Thus such stores discriminate between buyers who have an inelastic demand (for example, those who want to be instantly fashionable) and buyers who have a more elastic demand (for example, those who pay less attention to up-to-the-minute fashion and more attention to price).

Limits to Price Discrimination

If price discrimination is profitable, why don't more firms do it? What are the limits to price discrimination?

Profitable price discrimination can take place only under certain conditions. First, it is possible to price discriminate only if the good cannot be resold. If a good can be resold, then customers who get the good for the low price can resell it to someone willing to pay a higher price. Price discrimination breaks down. It is for this reason that price discrimination usually occurs in markets for services rather than in markets for storable goods. One major exception, price discrimination in the sale of fashion clothes, works because at the end of the season when the clothes go on sale, the fashion plates are looking for next season's fashions. People buying on sale have no one to whom they can resell the clothes at a higher price.

Second, a price-discriminating monopoly must be able to identify groups with different elasticities of demand. The characteristics used for discrimination must also be within the law. These requirements usually limit price discrimination to cases based on age, employment status, or the timing of the purchase.

Despite these limitations, there are some ingenious criteria used for discriminating. For example, Air Canada discriminates between four different passenger groups on many of its international flights. The economy class alternatives between Toronto and London in the summer of 1996 were

- $1,645—no restrictions
- $1,008—7-day advance purchase
- $958—14-day advance purchase
- $898—21-day advance purchase

These different prices discriminate between different groups of customers with different elasticities of demand. The $1,645 fare is probably paid by last-minute business travellers who have a lower elasticity of demand, whereas the $898 fare is probably paid by vacationers who have a higher elasticity of demand.

Would it bother you to hear how little I paid for this flight?

From William Hamilton, "Voodoo Economics," ©1992 by The Chronicle Publishing Company, p.3. Reprinted with permission of Chronicle Books.

REVIEW

- Price discrimination can increase a monopoly's profit.
- By charging the highest price for each unit of the good that each person is willing to pay, a monopoly perfectly price discriminates and captures all of the consumer surplus.
- Most price discrimination takes the form of discriminating among different groups of customers with different elasticities of demand.
- People with a lower elasticity of demand pay a higher price, and people with a higher elasticity of demand pay a lower price.
- A price-discriminating monopoly produces a larger output than a single-price monopoly.

Comparing Monopoly and Competition

WE HAVE NOW STUDIED A VARIETY OF WAYS IN which firms and households interact in markets for goods and services. In Chapter 11, we saw how perfectly competitive firms behave and discovered the price and output at which they operate. In this chapter, we have studied the price and output of a single-price monopoly and a monopoly that price discriminates. How do the quantities produced, prices, and profits of these different types of firms compare with each other?

To answer this question, let's imagine an industry made up of a large number of identical competitive firms. We will work out what the price charged and quantity produced will be in that industry. Then we will imagine that a single firm buys out all the individual firms and creates a monopoly. We will then work out the price charged and quantity produced by the monopoly, first when it charges a single price and second when it price discriminates.

Price and Output

We will conduct the analysis by using Fig. 12.8. The industry demand curve is *D,* and the industry supply curve is *S*. In perfect competition, the market equilibrium occurs where the supply curve and the demand curve intersect.

In Perfect Competition   The quantity produced by the industry is Q_C and the price is P_C. Each firm takes the price P_C and maximizes its profit by producing the output at which its own marginal cost equals the price. Because each firm is a small part of the total industry, there is no incentive for any firm to try to manipulate the price by varying its output.

With a Single-Price Monopoly   Now suppose that this industry is taken over by a single firm. No changes in production techniques occur, so the new combined firm has identical costs to the original separate firms. The new single firm recognizes that by varying output it can influence price. It also recognizes that its marginal revenue curve is *MR*. To maximize profit, the firm chooses an output at which marginal revenue equals marginal cost.

FIGURE 12.8
Monopoly and Competition Compared

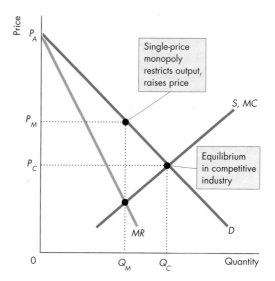

A competitive industry has a demand curve *D* and a supply curve *S*. Equilibrium occurs where the quantity demanded equals the quantity supplied at quantity Q_C and price P_C. If all firms in the industry are taken over by a single producer that sells the profit-maximizing output for a single price, marginal revenue is *MR* and the competitive industry supply curve, *S*, becomes the monopoly's marginal cost curve, *MC*. The monopoly produces the output at which marginal revenue equals marginal cost. A single-price monopoly produces Q_M and sells that output for the price P_M. A perfectly price-discriminating monopoly produces Q_C and charges a different price for each unit sold. The prices charged range from P_A to P_C.

Monopoly restricts output and raises the price. But the more perfectly a monopoly can price discriminate, the closer its output gets to the competitive output.

But what is the monopoly's marginal cost curve? To answer this question, you need to recall the relationship between the marginal cost curve and the supply curve of a competitive firm. The supply curve of an individual competitive firm is its marginal cost curve above minimum average variable cost. The industry supply curve is the industry's marginal cost curve. (The supply curve has also been labelled *MC* to remind you of this fact.) Therefore, when the industry is taken over by a single firm, that firm's marginal cost curve is the same as what used to be the competitive industry's supply curve.

We have seen that a competitive industry always operates at the point of intersection of its supply and demand curves. In Fig. 12.8, this is the point at which price is P_C and the industry produces the quantity Q_C. In contrast, the single-price monopoly maximizes profit by restricting output to Q_M, where marginal revenue equals marginal cost. Because the marginal revenue curve is below the demand curve, output Q_M will always be smaller than output Q_C. The monopoly charges the price for which output Q_M can be sold, and that price, which is determined by the demand curve, is P_M. We have just established a key proposition:

Compared to a perfectly competitive industry, a single-price monopoly restricts its output and charges a higher price.

With Perfect Price Discrimination   If a monopoly can perfectly price discriminate, it will charge a different price on each unit sold and increase output to Q_C. The highest price charged is P_A, and the lowest price charged is P_C, the price in a competitive market. The price P_A is the highest that is charged because at yet higher prices nothing can be sold. The price P_C is the lowest charged because when a monopoly perfectly price discriminates, its demand curve is also its marginal revenue curve and at prices below P_C, marginal cost exceeds marginal revenue. We have just established a second key proposition:

The more perfectly the monopoly can price discriminate, the closer its output gets to the competitive output.

We've seen how the output and price of a monopoly compare with those in a competitive industry. Let's now compare the efficiency of the two types of market.

Allocative Efficiency

Whether monopoly is less efficient than competition depends on how successfully the monopoly can price discriminate. A single-price monopoly is inefficient and a perfect price discriminating monopoly is efficient. Let's look at these two cases.

Inefficiency of a Single-Price Monopoly   Figure 12.9 compares perfect competition and a single-price monopoly. Under perfect competition (part a), consumers pay P_C for each unit bought. The maximum price that consumers are willing to pay for each unit is shown by the demand curve (D). This price measures the *value* of the good to the consumer. The value of a good minus its price is **consumer surplus.** (See Chapter 7, pp. 160–161, for a more detailed explanation of consumer surplus.)

In Fig. 12.9(a), consumer surplus is represented by the green triangle. A single-price monopoly (part b) restricts output to Q_M and sells that output for P_M. Consumer surplus is decreased to the smaller green triangle. Consumers lose partly by having to pay more for what is available and partly by getting less of the good. But is the consumers' loss equal to the monopoly's gain? Is there simply a redistribution of the gains from trade? A closer look at Fig. 12.9(b) will convince you that there is a reduction in the gains from trade. Some of the loss in consumer surplus accrues to the monopoly—the monopoly gets the difference between the higher price (P_M) and P_C on the quantity sold (Q_M). So the monopoly takes the part of the consumer surplus shown by the blue rectangle. This portion of the loss of consumer surplus is not a loss to society. It is a redistribution from consumers to the monopoly.

What, though, has become of the rest of the consumer surplus? The answer is that because output has been restricted, it is lost. But more than that has been lost. The total loss resulting from the lower monopoly output (Q_M) is the grey triangle in Fig. 12.9(b). The part of the grey triangle above P_C is the loss of consumer surplus, and the part of the triangle below P_C is a loss to the producer—a loss of producer surplus. **Producer surplus** is the difference between a producer's revenue and the opportunity cost of production. It is calculated as the sum of the differences between price and the marginal cost of producing each unit of output. Under competitive conditions, the producer sells the output between Q_M and Q_C for a price of P_C. The marginal cost of producing each extra unit of output through that range is shown by the marginal cost (supply) curve. Thus the vertical distance between the marginal cost curve and price represents a producer surplus. Part of the producer surplus is lost when a monopoly restricts output to less than its competitive level.

The grey triangle, which measures the total loss of both consumer and producer surplus, is called the deadweight loss. **Deadweight loss** measures allocative

FIGURE 12.9

Allocative Inefficiency of Monopoly

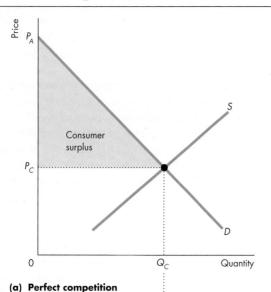

(a) Perfect competition

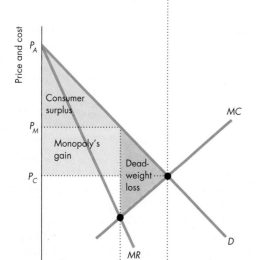

(b) Monopoly

In perfect competition (part a), demand curve D intersects supply curve S at quantity Q_C and price P_C. Consumer surplus is represented by the green triangle. In long-run equilibrium, firms' economic profits are zero and consumer surplus is maximized. Under a single-price monopoly (part b), output is restricted to Q_M and the price increases to P_M. Consumer surplus is reduced to the smaller green triangle. The monopoly takes the blue rectangle for itself and creates a deadweight loss (the grey triangle).

inefficiency as the reduction in consumer and producer surplus resulting from a restriction of output below its efficient level. The reduced output and higher price result in the monopoly capturing some of the consumer surplus. It also results in the elimination of the producer surplus and the consumer surplus on the output that a competitive industry would have produced but which the monopoly does not.

Usually a monopoly produces an output well below that at which average total cost is a minimum. It has far more capacity than it uses. But even if a monopoly produces the quantity at which average total cost is a minimum, which it might, the consumer does not have the opportunity of buying the good at that price. The price paid by the consumer always exceeds marginal cost.

Efficiency of Perfect Price Discrimination The deadweight loss if the monopoly practises perfect price discrimination is zero. A perfect price discriminator produces the same output as the competitive industry would. The price of the last item sold is P_C, the same as its marginal cost. The consumer surplus is zero but the deadweight loss is also zero. So perfect price discrimination achieves allocative efficiency. But what about the distribution of the gains from trade?

Redistribution

Under perfect competition, the consumer surplus is the green triangle in Fig. 12.9(a). Because of free entry, the long-run equilibrium economic profit of each perfectly competitive firm is zero. We've just seen that the creation of monopoly reduces consumer surplus. Further, in the case of a single-price monopoly, a deadweight loss arises. But what happens to the distribution of surpluses between producers and consumers? The answer is that the monopoly always wins. In the case of a single-price monopoly (Fig. 12.9b), the monopoly gains the blue rectangle at the expense of the consumer, but it loses part of its producer surplus—its share of the deadweight loss. This loss reduces its gain. But there is always a net gain for the monopoly and a net loss for the consumer. We also know that because there is a deadweight loss, the consumer loses more than the monopoly gains.

In the case of a perfect price-discriminating monopoly, there is no deadweight loss but there is an even larger redistribution of the gains from trade away from consumers to the monopoly. In this case, the monopoly captures the entire consumer surplus, the green triangle in Fig. 12.9(a).

It is because it creates a deadweight loss that monopoly is inefficient. It imposes a cost on society. This cost might be avoided by the break-up of a monopoly, and a considerable amount of law and regulation, which is described and explained in Chapter 20, is directed at this problem.

R E V I E W

- The creation of a monopoly results in a redistribution of economic gains away from consumers and to the monopoly producer.
- If a monopoly can perfectly price discriminate, it produces the same output as a competitive industry and achieves allocative efficiency but it captures the entire consumer surplus.
- If a monopoly cannot perfectly price discriminate, it restricts output below what a competitive industry would produce and creates a deadweight loss. The monopoly is allocative inefficient—the consumers' loss exceeds the monopoly's gain.

Rent Seeking

The activity of creating a monopoly from which an economic profit can be made is called **rent seeking**. The term "rent seeking" is used because "rent" (or "economic rent") is another name for consumer surplus, producer surplus, and economic profit. We've seen that a monopoly makes its economic profit by diverting part of the consumer surplus to itself. Thus the pursuit of an economic profit by a monopoly is rent seeking. It is the attempt to capture some consumer surplus.

Rent seeking is a profitable activity and one that is widely pursued. It is profitable because a monopoly can make an economic profit in the long run, while a firm in a competitive industry can hope to make an economic profit only in the short run. In a competitive industry, freedom of entry brings new firms and results in economic profit being competed away. In a monopoly, barriers to entry prevent this process. Because a monopoly can make an economic profit in the long run, there is an incentive to acquire a monopoly—to rent seek.

What do rent seekers do? One form of rent seeking is the searching out of existing monopoly rights

that can be bought for a lower price than the monopoly's economic profit—that is, seeking to acquire existing monopoly rights. An example of this type of rent-seeking activity is the purchase of taxicab licences. In most cities, taxicabs are regulated. The city restricts both the fares and the number of taxis that can operate. Operating a taxi results in economic profit or rent. A person who wants to operate a taxi must buy the right to do so from someone who already has one.

But buying an existing monopoly does not assure an economic profit. The reason is that there is freedom of entry into the activity of rent seeking. Rent seeking is like perfect competition. If an economic profit is available, a new entrant will try to get some of it. Competition among rent seekers pushes the price that must be paid for a monopoly right up to the point at which only a normal profit can be made by operating the monopoly. The economic profit—the rent—goes to the person who created the monopoly in the first place. For example, competition for the right to operate a taxi in Toronto leads to a price of more than $80,000, which is sufficiently high to eliminate long-run economic profit for the taxi operator. But the person who acquired the right in the first place collects the economic rent. This type of rent seeking transfers wealth from the buyer to the seller of the monopoly.

Although a great deal of rent-seeking activity involves searching out existing monopoly rights that can be profitably bought, much of it is devoted to the creation of monopoly. This type of rent-seeking activity takes the form of lobbying and seeking to influence the political process. Such influence is sometimes sought by making campaign contributions in exchange for legislative support or by indirectly seeking to influence political outcomes through publicity in the media or more direct contacts with politicians and bureaucrats. An example of a monopoly right created in this way is the government-imposed restrictions on the quantities of beef that may be imported into Canada. These are regulations that restrict output and increase price.

This type of rent seeking is a costly activity that uses up scarce resources. In aggregate, firms spend billions of dollars lobbying federal and provincial politicians and municipal officials in the pursuit of licences and laws that create barriers to entry and establish a monopoly right. Everyone has an incentive to rent seek, and because there are no barriers to entry into the rent-seeking activity, there is a great deal of competition for new monopoly rights.

What determines the value of the resources that a person will use to obtain a monopoly right? The answer is the monopoly's economic profit. If the value of resources spent trying to create a monopoly exceeds the monopoly's economic profit, the net result is an economic loss. But as long as the value of the resources used to create a monopoly falls short of the monopoly's economic profit, there is an economic profit to be earned. With no barrier to entry into rent seeking, the value of the resources used up in rent seeking equals the monopoly's economic profit.

Because of rent seeking, monopoly imposes a social cost that exceeds the deadweight loss that we calculated earlier. That social cost equals the value of the deadweight loss plus the value of resources used in rent seeking—the monopoly's entire economic profit because that is the value of the resources that it pays to use in rent seeking. Thus the social cost of monopoly is the deadweight loss plus the monopoly's economic profit.

Gains from Monopoly

So far, compared to perfect competition, monopoly has come out in a pretty bad light. If monopoly is so bad, why do we put up with it? Why don't we have laws that crack down on monopoly so hard that it never rears its head? We do indeed have laws that limit monopoly power (explained in Chapter 20). We also have laws that regulate the monopolies that exist. But monopoly is not all bad. Let's look at its potential advantages and some of the reasons for its existence.

The main reasons why monopoly might have some advantages are

- Economies of scale and economies of scope
- Incentives to innovate

Economies of Scale and Scope A firm experiences *economies of scale* when an increase in its production of a good or service brings a decrease in the average total cost of producing it—see Chapter 10, p. 225. **Economies of scope** arise when an increase in the *range of goods produced* brings a decrease in average total cost. Economies of scope occur when highly specialized (and usually expensive) technical inputs can be shared by different goods. For example, McDonald's can produce both hamburgers and french fries at an average total cost that is lower than what it would cost two separate firms to produce the same goods because at McDonald's hamburgers and french fries share the use of specialized food storage and preparation facilities. Firms producing a wide range of products can hire specialist computer programmers, designers, and marketing experts whose skills can be used across the product range, thereby spreading their costs and lowering the average total cost of production of each of the goods.

Large-scale firms that have control over supply and can influence price—and that therefore behave like the monopoly firm that we've been studying in this chapter—can reap these economies of scale and scope. Small, competitive firms cannot. As a consequence, there are situations in which the comparison of monopoly and competition that we made earlier in this chapter is not a valid one. Recall that we imagined the takeover of a large number of competitive firms by a single monopoly firm. But we also assumed that the monopoly would use exactly the same technology as the small firms and have the same costs. But if one large firm can reap economies of scale and scope, its marginal cost curve will lie below the supply curve of a competitive industry made up of thousands of small firms. It is possible for such economies of scale and scope to be so large as to result in a higher output and lower price under monopoly than a competitive industry would achieve.

Figure 12.10 illustrates such a situation. Here, the demand curve (D) is the same regardless of whether the industry is a competitive one or a monopoly. With a competitive industry, the supply curve is S, the quantity produced is Q_C, and the price is P_C. The marginal revenue curve for a monopoly is MR. With a monopoly that can exploit economies of scale and scope, the marginal cost curve is MC_M. The monopoly maximizes profit by producing the output (Q_M) at which marginal revenue equals marginal cost. The price that maximizes profit is P_M. By exploiting a superior technology that is not available to each small firm, the monopoly is able to achieve a larger output and lower price than the competitive industry.

There are many examples of industries in which economies of scale are so significant that they lead to an outcome similar to that shown in Fig. 12.10. Public utilities such as gas, electric power, water, local telephone service, and garbage collection are all such cases. There are also many examples where a combination of economies of scale and economies of scope arise, such as the brewing of beer, the manufacture of refrigerators and other household appliances, pharmaceuticals, and the refining of petroleum.

FIGURE 12.10

When Economies of Scale and Scope Make Monopoly More Efficient

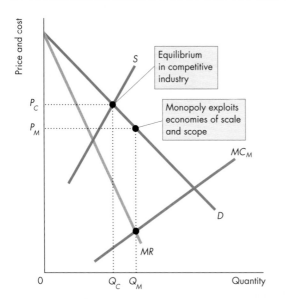

In some industries, economies of scale and economies of scope result in the monopoly's marginal cost curve (MC_M) lying below the competitive industry supply curve (S). In such a case, it is possible that the single-price monopoly output (Q_M) exceeds the competitive output (Q_C) and that the monopoly price (P_M) is below the competitive price (P_C).

Incentives to Innovate

Innovation is the first-time application of new knowledge in the production process. Innovation may take the form of developing a new product or a lower-cost way of making an existing product. Controversy has raged whether large firms with monopoly power or small competitive firms lacking such monopoly power are the most innovative. It is clear that some temporary monopoly power arises from innovation. A firm that develops a new product or process and patents it obtains exclusive right to that product or process for the term of the patent.

But does the granting of a monopoly, even a temporary one, to an innovator increase the pace of innovation? One line of reasoning suggests that it

does. With no protection, an innovator is not able to enjoy the profits from innovation for very long. Thus the incentive to innovate is weakened. A contrary argument is that monopolies can afford to be lazy while competitive firms cannot. Competitive firms must strive to innovate and cut costs even though they know that they cannot hang on to the benefits of their innovation for long. But that knowledge spurs them on to greater and faster innovation.

A matter such as this one cannot be resolved by listing arguments and counterarguments. It requires a careful empirical investigation. Many such investigations have been conducted. But the evidence is mixed. It shows that large firms do much more research and development than do small firms. It also shows that large firms are significantly more prominent at the development end of the research and development process. But measuring research and development is measuring the volume of inputs into the process of innovation. What matters is not input but output. Two measures of the output of research and development are the number of patents and the rate of productivity growth. On these measures, there is no clear evidence that big is best. But there is a clear pattern in the process of diffusion of technological knowledge. After innovation, a new process or product spreads gradually through the industry with large firms jumping on the bandwagon more quickly than the remaining small firms. Thus large firms speed the process of diffusion of technological advances.

In determining public policy towards monopoly (discussed in Chapter 20), laws and regulations are designed that balance the gains from monopoly (economies of scale and scope and innovation) against the deadweight loss and redistribution that it generates.

◆ We've now studied two models of market structure: perfect competition and monopoly. We've discovered the conditions under which perfect competition achieves allocative efficiency and we've compared the efficiency of competition with that of monopoly. *Reading Between the Lines* on pp. 278–279 looks at the situation developing in a monopoly that is being eroded by technological change, cable television.

Competition and monopoly are just two extreme market types. In the next chapter, we're going to study the middle ground between monopoly and competition. We're going to discover that many of the lessons that we learned from these two extreme models are still relevant and useful in understanding behaviour in real-world markets.

Falling Barriers to Entry

FINANCIAL POST, SEPTEMBER 12, 1996

Cable TV without the cable set for launch

BY BRENDA DALGLISH

Brandon, Man.-based SkyCable Inc. said yesterday it is just days away from launching the world's first "wireless cable" service.

SkyCable was awarded a licence for the first multichannel multipoint distribution system (MMDS) in Canada in December by the Canadian Radio-television and Telecommunications Commission.

With the launch of direct-to-home satellite TV in Canada delayed, SkyCable will probably provide the first legal direct competition for cable television.

"We're in the testing stage now," said Stuart Craig, president of SkyCable owner Craig Broadcasting Systems Inc.

"The first transmitter has been up and running for more than a month. The system is working perfectly."

In all, SkyCable intends to erect eight more transmitters to provide its service across most of Manitoba's populated areas.

Its commercial launch date will be announced within days, Craig said.

Broadband Networks Inc., a Winnipeg wireless communications company, has developed the technology, equipment and network design that SkyCable's system is based upon, Craig said.

SkyCable has the first installed digital MMDS system in the world, said David Graves, BNI's chairman and chief executive.

MMDS can do everything cable has the potential to do including transmitting high-quality video and audio signals and providing two-way interactive services that allow high-speed computer access to the Internet, Graves said.

The wireless MMDS technology relies on microwave transmissions beamed to individual home receivers from towers located about 100 kilometres apart.

Because the technology does not require high-cost infrastructure, proponents say it will be effective competition.

Essence of THE STORY

■ The Canadian Radio-television and Telecommunications Commission (CRTC) has licensed SkyCable Inc. of Brandon, Manitoba, to operate a multichannel-multipoint television distribution system (MMDS).

■ MMDS can do everything cable can do. It can transmit high-quality video and audio signals and provide two-way interactive services that allow high-speed computer access to the Internet.

■ The wireless MMDS technology uses microwave transmissions beamed to individual home receivers from towers located about 100 kilometres apart.

■ Because the technology does not require high-cost infrastructure, proponents say it will be effective competition for cable television.

Economic

A N A L Y S I S

■ Local cable television distributors have had a monopoly in providing home television signals.

■ Figure 1 shows a typical local cable monopoly. The demand curve is *D*, the marginal revenue curve is *MR*, the average total cost curve is *ATC*, and the marginal cost curve is *MC*.

■ With a monopoly, they have been able to make large profits.

■ The *ATC* curve slopes downward even where it intersects the demand curve because of economies of scale.

■ Using cable technology, the industry is a *natural monopoly*.

■ A cable company maximizes profit by connecting 100,000 homes and charging a monthly fee of $30. The blue rectangle shows the economic profit.

■ With the new MMDS technology, fixed costs are much lower than with cable. Figure 2 shows how the market operates with competition among MMDS suppliers. Part (a) is the market. The demand curve is the same as in Fig. 1.

■ Figure 2(b) shows the cost curves of SkyCable. Because fixed costs are lower, *ATC* is a minimum at a smaller number of homes connected (40,000 in this example).

■ At a monthly fee of $30, firms like SkyCable enter the industry and supply increases. Supply is *S* when entry stops (Fig. 2a). The price is $18 a month, and there are four firms, each supplying 40,000 homes.

■ With cable technology a company will break even at $20 a month. So at $18 a month all companies will use MMDS technology.

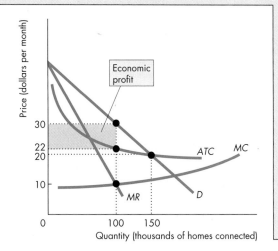

Figure 1 Cable monopoly

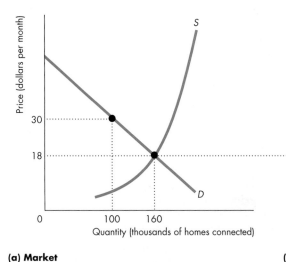

(a) Market

(b) SkyCable

Figure 2 Competition in television

SUMMARY

Key Points

How Monopoly Arises   A monopoly is the sole supplier of a good or service for which no close substitute exists. Monopoly arises because of legal or natural barriers to entry. Natural barriers can arise from economies of scale. (pp. 260–261)

Single-Price Monopoly   A monopoly's demand curve is the market demand curve. A single-price monopoly charges the same price for each unit of output. For a single-price monopoly, marginal revenue is less than price. A monopoly's technology and costs behave like those of any other type of firm. The monopoly maximizes profit by producing the output that makes marginal revenue equal to marginal cost and by charging the maximum price that consumers are willing to pay for that output. The price charged always exceeds marginal cost. (pp. 261–266)

Price Discrimination   Price discrimination is the practice of charging some consumers a higher price than others for an identical item or of charging an individual customer a higher price on a small purchase than on a large one. Price discrimination is an attempt by the monopoly to convert consumer surplus into economic profit. Perfect price discrimination extracts all the consumer surplus by charging a different price for each unit sold and obtaining the maximum price that each consumer is willing to pay. With perfect price discrimination, the monopoly produces the same output as would a perfectly competitive industry. A monopoly can discriminate between different groups of customers on the basis of age, employment status, or other distinguishable characteristics. Such price discrimination increases the monopoly's economic profit if each group has a different elasticity of demand for the product. Price discrimination can be practised only when it is impossible for a buyer to resell the good and when consumers with different elasticities can be identified. (pp. 267–271)

Comparing Monopoly and Competition   A single-price monopoly charges a higher price and produces a smaller quantity than would prevail in a perfectly competitive industry. A perfectly price-

discriminating monopoly produces the competitive quantity and sells the last unit for the competitive price. A single-price monopoly captures consumer surplus by restricting output and creating a deadweight loss. The more a monopoly price discriminates, the smaller is the deadweight loss, the smaller is the consumer surplus, but the larger is the monopoly's economic profit. Monopoly imposes costs that equal deadweight loss plus the cost of the resources devoted to rent seeking. The cost of rent seeking might be equal economic profit. So the maximum cost of monopoly equals deadweight loss plus economic profit. In industries with large economies of scale and scope, a monopoly's output is larger and its price lower than a competitive industry could achieve. Monopoly might be more innovative than competition. (pp. 272–277)

Key Figures and Table

Key Terms

R E V I E W   Q U E S T I O N S

1. Give examples of monopoly in your province.
2. How does monopoly arise?
3. What are barriers to entry? Give some examples of the various barriers to entry.
4. Distinguish between a legal monopoly and a natural monopoly. Give examples of each type.
5. Explain why a monopoly has to lower its price to be able to sell a larger quantity.
6. Explain why a monopoly's marginal revenue decreases as it sells a larger output.
7. Explain why marginal revenue of a single-price monopoly is always less than the price.
8. Does a single-price monopoly operate on the inelastic part of its demand curve? Explain why.
9. Explain how a single-price monopoly chooses its output and price.
10. Compare the monopoly's price and marginal revenue at its profit-maximizing output.
11. Does a monopoly always make a positive economic profit in the short run? Explain why or why not.
12. Does a monopoly make zero economic profit in the long run? Explain why or why not.
13. What is price discrimination? Under what conditions can a monopoly price discriminate?
14. Explain the effect of price discrimination on the quantity the monopoly sells and the monopoly's profit.
15. Explain why a single-price monopoly produces a smaller output than an equivalent competitive industry.
16. Is a single-price monopoly as efficient as competition?
17. What are consumer surplus, producer surplus, and deadweight loss?
18. As far as allocative efficiency is concerned, is a single-price monopoly better or worse than perfect price discrimination? Why?
19. Why do people engage in rent seeking?
20. What are economies of scale and economies of scope? What effects, if any, do they have on allocative efficiency of monopoly?

C R I T I C A L   T H I N K I N G

1. Study *Reading Between the Lines* on pp. 278–279 and then answer the following questions:
   a. What are the main technological changes taking place in telecommunications that are removing barriers to entry and ending a natural monopoly?
   b. What is happening to cable television prices and offerings in the area in which you live? Is it similar to or different from the developments reported in the news article? What do you predict will happen to television in your area during the next few years? Draw a figure similar to that on p. 279 to illustrate your predictions about prices, quantities, and economic profits.
   c. Suppose a new technology is invented that can be used in the home to receive and decode every television signal currently being transmitted for $100. What will happen to the cable television companies' demand, prices, and economic profits?

2. Do the owners of movie theatres throw away profit when they offer students discounts?
3. Until a few years ago, the government of Canada licensed one long-distance telephone company to operate in each province. Today, there is competition among a small number of long-distance carriers. What has happened to the price of a long-distance call, the number of calls made, the efficiency of the industry?
4. Your local cable company has a monopoly in supplying you with cable television. Your local telephone company has a monopoly in supplying you with local phone service. As new technology becomes available, the suppliers of cable and telephone services will converge. What will happen to the prices of these services?
5. If a good has only poor substitutes, the demand for it is inelastic. Is this good likely to be supplied by a monopoly or many competitive firms? [Hint: Check Chapter 5 to see the types of goods that have inelastic demands.]

PROBLEMS

1. The figure illustrates the situation facing the publisher of the only newspaper containing local news in an isolated community. Use the figure to answer the following questions.

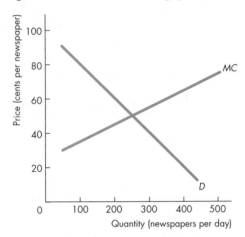

a. In the figure, draw the marginal revenue curve.
b. What quantity will maximize the publisher's profit?
c. What price will the publisher charge for a daily newspaper?
d. Compare the marginal revenue of the publisher with the price charged for a newspaper.
e. What is the publisher's daily total revenue?
f. At the price charged for a newspaper, is the demand for newspapers elastic or inelastic? Why?

2. Refer to the newspaper industry in problem 1. If this industry were allocatively efficient,
a. How many newspapers would be printed?
b. What would be the price of a newspaper?
c. Shade in the area on the graph that measures the consumer surplus. What is the value of the consumer surplus?
d. Shade in the area on the graph that measures the producer surplus.

3. Refer to the newspaper industry in problem 1.
a. What is the consumer surplus?
b. Shade in the area on the graph that measures the deadweight loss. What is the value of the deadweight loss created by the single-price monopoly?

4. Minnie's Mineral Springs, a single-price monopoly, faces the following demand schedule for bottled mineral water:

Price (dollars per bottle)	Quantity demanded (bottles)
10	0
8	1
6	2
4	3
2	4
0	5

a. Calculate Minnie's total revenue schedule.
b. Calculate its marginal revenue schedule.
c. At what price is the elasticity of demand equal to 1?

5. Minnie's Mineral Springs in problem 4 has the following total cost:

Quantity produced (bottles)	Total cost (dollars)
0	1
1	3
2	7
3	13
4	21
5	31

If Minnie's maximizes its profit,
a. What output does it produce?
b. What price does it charge?
c. What is its marginal cost?
d. What is its marginal revenue?
e. What is its economic profit?
f. Is Minnie's allocatively efficient? Explain your answer.

6. Suppose that Minnie's in problem 5 can perfectly price discriminate. Calculate its profit-maximizing
a. Output
b. Total revenue
c. Economic profit

7. What is the maximum price that someone would be willing to pay Minnie's for a licence to operate its mineral spring?

8. Two demand schedules for round-trip flights between Toronto and Mexico City are set out below. The schedule for weekday travellers is for those making round-trips on weekdays and returning within the same week. The schedule for weekend travellers is for those who stay through the weekend. (The former tend to be business travellers and the latter vacation and pleasure travellers.)

Weekday travellers		Weekend travellers	
Price (dollars per round-trip)	Quantity demanded (thousands of round-trips)	Price (dollars per round-trip)	Quantity demanded (thousands of round-trips)
1,500	0		
1,250	5		
1,000	10	750	0
750	15	500	5
500	15	200	10
250	15	0	15

The marginal cost of a round-trip is $500. If a single-price monopoly airline controls the Toronto–Mexico City route, use a graph to find out the following:

a. What price is charged?
b. How many passengers travel?
c. What is the consumer surplus for weekday travellers?
d. What is the consumer surplus for weekend travellers?
e. Is the market allocatively efficient? Explain your answer.

9. If the airline in problem 8 discriminates between round-trips during the week and round-trips through the weekend,
a. What is the price for the round-trip during the week?

b. What is the price of the airline ticket with a weekend stay?
c. What is the consumer surplus for weekday travellers?
d. What is the consumer surplus for weekend travellers?
e. Is the market allocatively efficient? Explain your answer.

10. If the airline in problem 8 could practise perfect price discrimination,
a. Calculate the travellers' consumer surplus.
b. Calculate the deadweight loss created by the airline.

11. Barbara runs a truck stop on the prairies, miles from anywhere. She has a monopoly and faces the following demand schedule for meals:

Price (dollars per meal)	Quantity demanded (meals per week)
5.00	0
4.50	20
4.00	40
3.50	60
3.00	80
2.50	100
2.00	120
1.50	140
1.00	160

Barbara's marginal cost and average total cost are a constant $2 per meal.
a. If Barbara charges all customers the same price for a meal, what price is it?
b. What is the consumer surplus of all the customers who buy a meal from Barbara?
c. What is the producer surplus?
d. What is the deadweight loss?

Monopolistic Competition and Oligopoly

After studying
this chapter,
you will be
able to:

■ Define monopolistic competition and
oligopoly

■ Explain how price and output are
determined in a monopolistically
competitive industry

■ Explain why the price might be sticky in
an oligopoly industry

■ Explain how price and output are
determined when an industry has one
dominant firm and several small firms

■ Use game theory to make predictions
about price wars and competition among
a small number of firms

Flyers and War Games

Every week, we receive a newspaper stuffed with supermarket flyers describing this week's "specials," providing coupons and other enticements, all designed to grab our attention and persuade us that A & P, Zehrs, Safeway, Loblaws, and Miracle Mart have the best deals in town. One claims the lowest price, another the best brands, yet another the best value for money even if its prices are not the lowest. How do firms locked in fierce competition with other firms set their prices, pick their products, and choose the quantities to produce? How are the profits of such firms affected by the actions of other firms? ◆ Until recently, only one firm made the chips that drive IBM and compatible PCs: Intel Corporation. During 1994, the prices of powerful personal computers based on Intel's fast 486 and Pentium chips collapsed. The reason: Intel suddenly faced competition from new chip producers such as Advanced Micro Devices Inc. and Cyrix Corp. The price of Intel's Pentium processor, set at more than $1,000 when it was launched in 1993, fell to less than $350 by spring 1995, and the price of a Pentium-based computer fell to less than $2,000. How did competition among a small number of chip makers bring such a rapid fall in the price of chips and computers?

◆ The theories of monopoly and perfect competition do not predict the kind of behaviour that we've just described. There are no flyers and coupons, best brands, or price wars in perfect competition because each firm produces an identical product and is a price taker. And there are none in monopoly because each monopoly firm has the entire market to itself. To understand coupons, flyers, and price wars, we need the richer models explained in this chapter.

Varieties of Market Structure

WE HAVE STUDIED TWO TYPES OF MARKET structure—perfect competition and monopoly. In perfect competition, a large number of firms produce identical goods and there are no barriers to the entry of new firms into the industry. In this situation, each firm is a price taker, and in the long run, there is no economic profit. The opposite extreme, monopoly, is an industry in which there is one firm. That firm is protected by barriers preventing the entry of new firms. The firm sets its price to maximize profit and might enjoy economic profit even in the long run.

Many real-world industries are not well described by the models of perfect competition and monopoly. They lie somewhere between these two cases. Two other market models have been developed to study the industries that lie between perfect competition and monopoly. They are

1. Monopolistic competition
2. Oligopoly

Monopolistic competition is a market structure in which a large number of firms compete with each other by making similar but slightly different products. Making a product slightly different from the product of a competing firm is called **product differentiation**. Because of product differentiation, a monopolistically competitive firm has an element of monopoly power. The firm is the sole producer of the particular version of the good in question. For example, in the market for microwave popcorn, only Nabisco makes Planters Premium Select. Only General Mills makes Pop Secret. And only American Popcorn makes Jolly Time. Each of these firms has a monopoly on a particular brand of microwave popcorn. Differentiated products are not necessarily different in an objective sense. For example, the different brands of aspirin are chemically identical and only differ in their packaging. What matters is that consumers perceive products to be differentiated.

Oligopoly is a market structure in which a small number of producers compete with each other. There are hundreds of examples of oligopolistic industries. Computer software, airplane manufacture, and international air transportation are but a few. In some oligopolistic industries, each firm produces an almost identical product, while in others, products are differ-

entiated. For example, oil and gasoline are essentially the same whether they are made by Petro-Canada or Exxon. But Chrysler's Cirrus is a differentiated commodity from Chevrolet's Lumina and Ford's Taurus.

Many features must be taken into account to determine which market structure describes a particular real-world market. But one of these factors is the extent to which the market is dominated by a small number of firms. To help measure this feature of markets, economists have developed indexes called measures of concentration. Let's look at these measures.

Measures of Concentration

To tell how close to the competitive or monopolistic extreme an industry comes or where in between these extremes it lies, economists have developed two measures of industrial concentration. They are

- Four-firm concentration ratio
- Herfindahl–Hirschman Index

Four-Firm Concentration Ratio   The **four-firm concentration ratio** is the percentage of the value of sales accounted for by the four largest firms in an industry. The range of the concentration ratio is from almost zero for perfect competition to 100 for monopoly. This ratio is the main measure used to assess market structure.

Table 13.1 sets out two hypothetical concentration ratio calculations, one for tires and one for printing. In this example, there are 14 firms in the tire industry. The biggest four have 80 percent of the sales of the industry, so the four-firm concentration ratio for that industry is 80. In the printing industry, with 1,004 firms, the top four firms account for only 0.5 percent of total industry sales. In that case, the four-firm concentration ratio is 0.5.

The idea behind calculating four-firm concentration ratios is to get information about the degree of competitiveness of a market: A low concentration ratio indicates a high degree of competition, and a high concentration ratio indicates an absence of competition. In the extreme case of monopoly, the concentration ratio is 100—the largest (and only) firm makes the entire industry sales. The four-firm concentration ratio is regarded as a useful indicator of the likelihood of collusion among firms in an oligopoly. If the ratio exceeds 60 percent, it is likely that firms will collude and behave like a monopoly. If the ratio is less than 40 percent, it is likely that the firms will compete effectively.

TABLE 13.1

Concentration Ratio Calculations

Tiremakers		Printers	
Firm	**Sales** (millions of dollars)	**Firm**	**Sales** (millions of dollars)
Top, Inc.	200	Fran's	2.5
ABC, Inc.	250	Ned's	2.0
Big, Inc.	150	Tom's	1.8
XYZ, Inc.	100	Jill's	1.7
Top 4 sales	700	Top 4 sales	8.0
Other 10 firms	175	Other 1,000 firms	1,592.0
Industry sales	875	Industry sales	1,600.0

Four-firm concentration ratios:

Tiremakers: $\dfrac{700}{875} \times 100 = 80\%$ Printers: $\dfrac{8}{1,600} \times 100 = 0.5\%$

The Herfindahl–Hirschman Index   The **Herfindahl–Hirschman Index**—also called the HHI—is calculated as the square of market share (percentage) of each firm summed over the largest 50 firms (or summed over all the firms if there are fewer than 50) in a market. For example, suppose there are four firms in a market. The market shares of the firms are 50 percent, 25 percent, 15 percent, and 10 percent. The Herfindahl–Hirschman Index is calculated as

$$HHI = 50^2 + 25^2 + 15^2 + 10^2 = 3{,}450.$$

If each of the largest 50 firms has a market share of 0.1 percent, the HHI is equal to $0.1^2 \times 50 = 0.5$. Such a market would be perfectly competitive. If a market has only one firm that has a 100 percent market share, the HHI is $100^2 = 10{,}000$. Such a market is a monopoly.

The HHI is an indicator of monopoly power. If the HHI is less than 1,800, a market is regarded as being competitive. (An HHI less than 1,000 is highly competitive and between 1,000 and 1,800 is moderately competitive.) But if the HHI exceeds 1,800, a market is regarded as being highly concentrated.

Although the HHI is a measure of concentration, it has not displaced the four-firm concentration ratio. Most users of the two measures find the concentra-

tion ratio more intuitive than the HHI and point out that the formula for the HHI is not derived from any theory or observations and is arbitrary.

Table 13.2 summarizes the characteristics of perfect competition, monopolistic competition, oligopoly, and monopoly and their concentration ratios.

Limitations of Concentration Measures

Although concentration ratios and HHIs are useful, they have some limitations and must be supplemented by other information to determine a market's structure. There are three key problems, which are

- The geographical scope of the market

- Barriers to entry and firm turnover

- The correspondence between a market and an industry

Geographical Scope of Market   Concentration ratio data are based on a national view of the market. Many goods are sold on a national market but some are sold on a regional market and some on a global one. The newspaper industry is a good example of one for which the local market is more relevant than the national market. Thus although the concentration ratio for newspapers is not high, there is a high degree of concentration in the newspaper industry in most cities. The car industry is an example of one for which there is a global market. Thus although the biggest four Canadian car producers account for almost 90 percent of all cars sold by Canadian producers, they account for a smaller percentage of the total Canadian car market (including imports) and an even smaller percentage of the global market for cars.

Barriers to Entry and Turnover   Measures of concentration do not tell us how severe are the barriers to entry in an industry. Some industries, for example, are highly concentrated but have virtually free entry and experience an enormous amount of turnover of firms. An example is the market in local restaurants. Many small towns have few restaurants. But there are no restrictions on entering the restaurant industry, and indeed firms do enter and exit with great regularity.

Even if there is not much entry and exit, an industry might be competitive because of potential entry—because the few firms in the market face potential competition from many firms that can easily enter the market.

Market and Industry   The classifications used to calculate concentration ratios allocate every firm in the Canadian economy to a particular industry. But markets for particular goods do not usually correspond to industries.

The main problem is that markets are usually much narrower than industries. For example, the pharmaceutical industry, which has a low concentration ratio, operates in many separate markets for individual products (drugs and treatments), each one of which has almost no substitute. So this industry, which looks competitive, operates in many somewhat monopolistic markets.

Another problem arises from the fact that firms make many products. For example, Labatt produces beer and milk, among many other products. So this one firm operates in many quite separate markets. But Labatt is classified by Statistics Canada as being in the brewing industry.

A further problem arises from the fact that firms switch from market to market depending on the profit opportunities that exist. Many firms have built their initial organization on one product but then diversified into a wide variety of others. For example, Canadian Pacific Ltd., which today provides hotels, forest products, coal, and petroleum products as well as rail services, has diversified from being just a railroad company; and publishers of newspapers, maga-

---

TABLE   13.2

Market Structure

Characteristics	Perfect competition	Monopolistic competition	Oligopoly	Monopoly
Number of firms in industry	Many	Many	Few	One
Product	Identical	Differentiated	Either identical or differentiated	No close substitutes
Barriers to entry	None	None	Scale and scope economies	Scale and scope economies or legal barriers
Firm's control over price	None	Some	Considerable	Considerable or regulated
Concentration ratio	0	Low	High	100
Examples	Wheat, corn	Food, clothing	Automobiles, cereals	Local phone service, electric and gas utilities

zines, and textbooks are today rapidly diversifying into multimedia products; and banks are diversifying into insurance, investment, and travel services.

Despite their limitations, combined with information about the geographical scope of the market, barriers to entry, and the extent to which large, multi-product firms straddle a variety of markets, concentration ratios provide a basis for determining the degree of concentration in an industry.

Concentration Measures in Canada

Statistics Canada uses data on individual firm's sales to calculate concentration ratios for a large number of industry groups. Figure 13.1 shows a selection of their calculations. As you can see, some industries—from pharmaceuticals to sawmills and planing mills and women's clothing—have low concentration ratios.

FIGURE 13.1

Some Concentration Measures in Canada

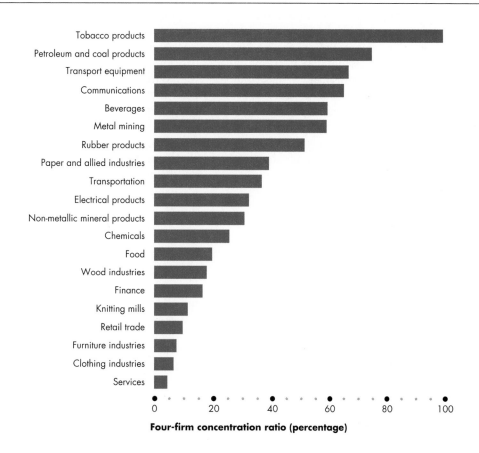

Four-firm concentration ratio (percentage)

Measured by the four-firm concentration ratio, industries producing tobacco products, petroleum and coal products, and transport equipment are highly concentrated, while the finance industry, knitting mills, retail trade, furniture and clothing industries, and services are highly competitive. Industries producing rubber products, transportation, and paper and allied industries have an intermediate degree of concentration.

Source: Statistics Canada.

These industries are highly competitive. At the other extreme are industries with a high concentration ratio such as brewing, motor vehicles, iron and steel, and aircraft manufacture. These are industries in which there is competition but among a small number of firms, each of which has considerable control over its price. Medium concentration ratios are found for such products as fish products and motor vehicle parts.

Market Structures in the Canadian Economy

Three-quarters of the value of goods and services bought and sold in Canada are traded in markets that are essentially competitive—markets that have almost perfect competition or monopolistic competition. Monopoly is rare—accounting for less than 3 percent of the value of goods and services in Canada—and is found mainly in public utilities and public transportation. A similarly small number of markets—accounting for less than 3 percent of the value of sales—are dominated by one or two firms, but are not monopolies. These, too, are in the public utilities and transportation sectors. Oligopoly, found mainly in manufacturing, accounts for about 18 percent of sales.

Monopolistic Competition

MONOPOLISTIC COMPETITION ARISES IN AN industry in which

- A large number of firms compete with each other.
- Each firm produces a differentiated product, which is a close but not a perfect substitute for the products of the other firms.
- Firms are free to enter and exit.

Makers of running shoes, pizza producers, auto-service stations, family restaurants, and realtors are all examples of firms that operate in monopolistic competition. In monopolistic competition, as in perfect competition, the industry consists of a large number of firms and each firm supplies a small part of the total industry output. Because each firm is small, no one firm can effectively influence what other firms do. If one firm changes its price, this action has no effect on the actions of the other firms.

Unlike perfect competition and like monopoly, a firm in monopolistic competition faces a downward-

sloping demand curve. The reason is that the firm's product is differentiated from the products of its competitors. Some people will pay more for one variety of the product, so when its price rises, the quantity demanded decreases but it does not (necessarily) decrease to zero. For example, Adidas, Asics, Diadora, Etonic, Fila, New Balance, Nike, Puma, and Reebok all make differentiated running shoes. Other things remaining the same, if the price of Adidas running shoes rises and the prices of the other shoes remain constant, Adidas sells fewer shoes and the other producers sell more. But Adidas shoes don't disappear unless the price rises by a large amount. Because a firm in monopolistic competition faces a downward-sloping demand curve, it maximizes profit by choosing both its price and its output.

Like competition and unlike monopoly, in monopolistic competition there is free entry and free exit. As a consequence, a firm in monopolistic competition cannot make an economic profit in the long run. When economic profit is being made, new firms enter the industry. This entry lowers prices and eventually eliminates economic profit. When economic losses are incurred, some firms leave the industry. This exit increases prices and profits and eventually eliminates the economic loss. In long-run equilibrium, firms neither enter nor leave the industry, and the firms in the industry make zero economic profit.

Price and Output in Monopolistic Competition

Figure 13.2 shows how price and output are determined by a firm in a monopolistically competitive industry. Part (a) deals with the short run and part (b) the long run. Let's concentrate initially on the short run (part a). The demand curve D shows the demand for the firm's own variety of the product. For example, it is the demand for Bayer aspirin rather than for painkillers in general or for McDonald's hamburgers rather than for hamburgers in general. The curve labelled MR is the marginal revenue curve associated with the demand curve. The figure also shows the firm's average total cost (ATC) and marginal cost (MC). The firm maximizes profit in the short run by producing output Q_S, where marginal revenue equals marginal cost, and charging the price P_S. The firm's average total cost is C_S and the firm makes a short-run economic profit, as measured by the blue rectangle.

FIGURE 13.2

Monopolistic Competition

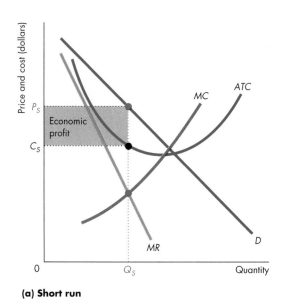

(a) Short run

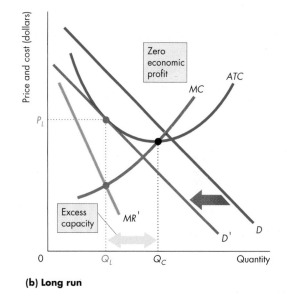

(b) Long run

Profit is maximized where marginal revenue equals marginal cost. Part (a) shows the short-run outcome. Profit is maximized by producing the quantity Q_S and selling it for the price P_S. Average total cost is C_S, and the firm makes an economic profit (the blue rectangle). Economic profit encourages new entrants in the long run.

Part (b) shows the long-run outcome. The entry of new

firms decreases each firm's demand, and the demand curve and marginal revenue curve shift leftward. When the demand curve has shifted from D to D', the marginal revenue curve is MR' and the firm is in a long-run equilibrium. The output that maximizes profit is Q_L, the price is P_L, and economic profit is zero. Because each firm produces less output than its capacity Q_C, it has excess capacity.

So far, the monopolistically competitive firm looks just like a monopoly. It produces the quantity at which marginal revenue equals marginal cost and then charges the price that buyers are willing to pay for that quantity, determined by the demand curve. The key difference between monopoly and monopolistic competition lies in what happens next.

There is no restriction on entry in monopolistic competition, so positive economic profit attracts new entrants. As new firms enter the industry, they introduce new varieties of the good. As a result, the demand for each particular variety decreases. The firm's demand curve and marginal revenue curve start to shift leftward. At each point in time, the firm maximizes its short-run profit by producing the quantity at which marginal revenue equals marginal

cost and by charging the price that buyers are willing to pay for this quantity. But as the demand curve shifts leftward, the profit-maximizing quantity and price fall.

Figure 13.2(b) shows the long-run equilibrium. The firm produces Q_L and sells it at a price of P_L. In this situation, the firm is making zero economic profit. There is no incentive for firms to enter or exit.

Excess Capacity   A firm's *capacity* output is the output produced at which average total cost is a minimum—the output at the bottom of the U-shaped *ATC* curve (Q_C in Fig. 13.2b). In monopolistic competition, in the long run, firms always have *excess capacity*. In Fig. 13.2(b), the firm produces Q_L and has excess capacity of $Q_C - Q_L$. That is, firms produce less output than that which minimizes average total cost. As a consequence, the consumer pays a price that exceeds minimum average total cost. This result arises from the fact that the firm faces a downward-sloping demand curve. The demand curve slopes down because of product differentiation—because one firm's product is not a perfect substitute for another firm's product. Thus it is product differentiation that produces excess capacity.

You can see the excess capacity in monopolistic competition all around you. Family restaurants (except for the truly outstanding ones) almost always have a few empty tables. You can always get a pizza delivered in less than 30 minutes. It is rare that every pump at a gas station is in use with customers waiting in line. There is always an abundance of realtors ready to help find or sell a home.

Efficiency of Monopolistic Competition

When we studied a perfectly competitive industry, we discovered that in some circumstances, such an industry achieves allocative efficiency. A key feature of allocative efficiency is that price equals marginal cost. Recall that price measures the value placed on the last unit bought by the consumer and marginal cost measures the firm's opportunity cost of producing the last unit. We also discovered that monopoly is allocatively inefficient because it restricts output below the level at which price equals marginal cost. As we have just discovered, monopolistic competition shares this feature with monopoly. Even though there is zero economic profit in long-run equilibrium, the monopolistically competitive industry produces an output at which price equals average total cost but exceeds marginal cost.

Because in monopolistic competition, price exceeds marginal cost, this market structure, like monopoly, is allocatively inefficient. The marginal cost of producing one more unit of output is less than the marginal benefit to the consumer, determined by the price the consumer is willing to pay. But the inefficiency of monopolistic competition arises from product differentiation—from product variety. Variety is valued by consumers, but it is achievable only if firms make differentiated products. So the loss in allocative efficiency that occurs in monopolistic competition must be weighed against the gain of greater product variety.

Product Innovation

Another source of gain from monopolistically competitive industries is product innovation. Monopolistically competitive firms are constantly seeking out new products that will provide them with a competitive edge, even if only temporarily. A firm that manages to introduce a new and differentiated variety will temporarily face a steeper demand curve than before and will be able to temporarily increase its price. It will make an economic profit. New firms that make close substitutes for the new product will enter and compete away the economic profit arising from this initial advantage.

Selling Costs

A large and increasing proportion of the prices we pay goes to cover the cost of selling the good, not the cost of making it. When you visit a major shopping mall, you see store designs, indoor gardens, and waterfalls that might be movie sets. The costs of these items are just a part of selling costs. Others are the costs of glossy catalogues and brochures, magazine and television advertising, and the salaries, airfares, and hotel bills of salespeople.

All these costs are incurred because monopolistically competitive firms strive to differentiate their products from those of other firms. Some product differentiation is achieved by designing and introducing products that are actually different from those of the other firms in the industry. But firms also attempt to differentiate the consumer's perception of the product. Marketing and advertising are the principal means whereby firms seek to achieve this end. Nike and Reebok make similar athletic shoes; Molson and Labatt make similar beers. But these companies spend millions of dollars building images and defining niches in crowded markets. Their goal is not to inform consumers about the small differences from their competitors in their athletic shoes and beer. It is to encourage consumers to believe that products with very similar physical characteristics will satisfy other wants as well and will enable the buyers of their products to live more exciting lives.

Selling costs increase a monopolistically competitive firm's costs above those of a competitive firm or a monopoly because it does not incur such selling costs. To the extent that selling costs provide consumers with services that are valued and with information about the precise nature of the differentiation of products, they serve a valuable purpose to the consumer and enable a better product choice to be made. But the opportunity cost of the additional services and information must be weighed against the gain to the consumer.

The bottom line on the question of allocative efficiency of monopolistic competition is ambiguous. In some cases, the gains from extra product variety unquestionably offset the selling and marketing costs and the extra cost arising from excess capacity. The tremendous varieties of books and magazines, of clothing, food, and drink are examples of such gains. It is less easy to see the gains from being able to buy brand-name drugs that have a chemical composition identical to a generic alternative. But some people see the brand name as a signal of qualtity and willingly pay more for the brand-name alternative.

R E V I E W

■ In monopolistic competition, a large number of firms compete with each other but, because each firm produces a differentiated product, it faces a downward-sloping demand curve.

■ In short-run equilibrium, firms can make economic profit.

■ Economic profit stimulates entry. In the long run, firms make zero economic profit—normal profit.

■ In long-run equilibrium, price equals average total cost but exceeds marginal cost and the quantity produced is less than that which minimizes average total cost.

■ The cost of monopolistic competition is excess capacity and high advertising expenditure; the gain is a wide product variety and valuable information to the consumer.

You've seen that monopolistic competition is a blend of monopoly and competition. As in monopoly, each firm faces a downward-sloping demand curve and sets its price. But as in perfect competition, economic profit triggers entry, so in long-run equilibrium, economic profits are competed away and firms make normal profit.

Oligopoly, which we now study, is fundamentally different from the other market types because each firm must take account of its actions on other firms.

Oligopoly

IN OLIGOPOLY, A SMALL NUMBER OF PRODUCERS compete with each other. The quantity sold by any one producer depends on that producer's price *and* the prices and quantities sold by the other producers. Each firm must take into account the effects of its own actions on the actions of other firms.

To see the interplay between prices and sales, suppose you run one of the three gas stations in a small town. If you lower your price and your two competitors don't lower theirs, your sales increase, but the sales of the other two firms decrease. In such a situation, the other firms will, most likely, lower their prices too. If they do cut their prices, your sales and profits will take a tumble. So, before deciding to cut your price, you try to predict how the other firms will react and you attempt to calculate the effects of those reactions on your own profit.

A variety of models has been developed to explain the determination of price and quantity in oligopoly markets, and no one theory has been found that can explain all the different types of behaviour that we observe in such markets. The models fall into two broad groups: traditional models and game theory models. We'll look at examples of both types, starting with two traditional models.

The Kinked Demand Curve Model

The kinked demand curve model is a model of oligopoly based on assumptions about the beliefs of each firm concerning the reactions of another firm (or firms) to its own actions. These beliefs are

■ If I increase my price, I will be on my own—others will not follow me.

■ If I decrease my price, so will everyone else.

Figure 13.3 shows a demand curve, D, that reflects these beliefs. The demand curve has a kink occurring at the current price, which is P. At prices above P, the demand curve is relatively elastic. It reflects the belief that if the firm raises its price above P, its price will be higher than the price of the other firms. So the quantity demanded will fall by a relatively large amount. At prices below P, the demand curve is less elastic. It reflects the belief that if the firm lowers its price, the other firms will lower their prices too. So the quantity demanded will increase by a relatively small amount.

FIGURE   13.3

The Kinked Demand Curve Model

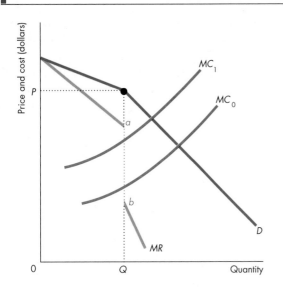

The price in an oligopoly market is P. Each firm believes it faces the demand curve D. At prices above P, demand is highly elastic because the firm believes that its price increases will not be matched by other firms. At prices below P, demand is less elastic because the firm believes its price cuts will be matched. Because the demand curve is kinked, the marginal revenue curve, MR, has a break ab. Profit is maximized by producing Q. The marginal cost curve passes through the break in the marginal revenue curve. Marginal cost changes inside the range ab leave the price and quantity unchanged.

The kink in demand curve D creates a break in the marginal revenue curve (MR). To maximize profit, the firm produces the quantity that makes marginal cost and marginal revenue equal. But that output, Q, is where the marginal cost curve passes through the discontinuity in the marginal revenue curve—the gap ab. If marginal cost fluctuates between a and b, as is shown in the figure with the marginal cost curves, MC_0 and MC_1, the firm will change neither its price nor its quantity of output. Only if marginal cost fluctuates outside the range ab will the firm change its price and quantity produced.

Thus the kinked demand curve model predicts that price and quantity will be insensitive to small

cost changes but will respond if cost changes are large enough. That is, the price will be sticky. But there are two problems with the kinked demand curve model:

1. It does not tell us how the price, P, is determined.
2. It does not tell us what happens if firms discover that their belief about the demand curve is incorrect.

Suppose, for example, that marginal cost increases by enough to cause the firm to increase its price and that all firms experience the same increase in marginal cost so they all increase their prices together. Each firm bases its action on the belief that other firms will not match its price increase, but that belief is incorrect. The firm's beliefs are inconsistent with reality, and the demand and marginal revenue curves that summarize those beliefs (such as those in Fig. 13.3) are not the correct ones for the purpose of calculating the new profit-maximizing price and output. A firm that bases its actions on beliefs that are wrong does not maximize profit and might well end up incurring an economic loss, leading to its eventual exit from the industry.

The kinked demand curve model is an attempt to understand price and output determination in an oligopoly in which the firms are of similar size. Another traditional model deals with the case in which firms differ in size and one firm dominates the industry.

Dominant Firm Oligopoly

A dominant firm oligopoly arises when one firm—the dominant firm—has a substantial cost advantage over the other firms and produces a large part of the industry output. The dominant firm sets the market price and the other firms are price takers. An example of a dominant firm oligopoly is a large gasoline retailer or a big video rental company that dominates its market in a particular city.

To see how a dominant firm oligopoly works, suppose that 11 firms operate gas stations in a city. Big-G is the dominant firm. It sells 50 percent of the city's gas. The other firms are small, and each sells 5 percent of the city's gas.

Figure 13.4 shows the market for gas in this city. In part (a), the demand curve D tells us how the total quantity of gas demanded in the city is influenced by its price. The supply curve S_{10} is the supply curve of the 10 small suppliers. These firms are price takers.

FIGURE   13.4

A Dominant Firm Oligopoly

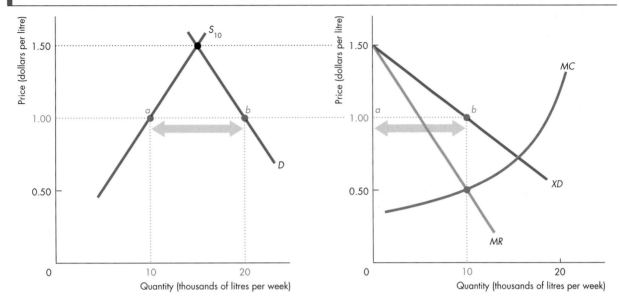

(a) Ten small firms and market demand

(b) Big-G's price and output decision

The demand curve for gas in a city is *D* in part (a). There are 10 small competitive firms that together have a supply curve of S_{10}. In addition, there is one large firm, Big-G, shown in part (b). Big-G faces the demand curve *XD*, determined as market demand *D* minus the supply of the other 10 firms S_{10}—the demand that is not satisfied by the small firms. Big-G's margin-

al revenue is *MR*, and marginal cost is *MC*. Big-G sets its output to maximize profit by equating marginal cost, *MC*, and marginal revenue, *MR*. This output is 10,000 litres. The price at which Big-G can sell this quantity is $1 a litre. The other 10 firms take this price and together they sell 10,000 litres a week. Each small firm sells 1,000 litres per week.

Part (b) shows the situation facing Big-G, the dominant firm. Big-G's marginal cost curve is *MC*. The demand curve for gasoline facing Big-G is *XD*. This curve is found by working out the amount of excess demand arising from the rest of the market. It graphs the difference between the quantity demanded and the quantity supplied in the rest of the market at each price. Thus, for example, at a price of $1 a litre, the distance *ab* in part (a) measures the excess quantity demand in the rest of the market. That same distance *ab* at the price $1 a litre in part (b) provides us with one point, point *b*, on Big-G's demand curve, *XD*.

If Big-G sold gasoline in a perfectly competitive city gas market, it would be willing to supply it at the prices indicated by its marginal cost curve. The city market would operate at the point of intersection of Big-G's marginal cost curve and its demand curve. But Big-G can do better for itself than that. Because it controls 50 percent of the city's gas market, it can

restrict its sales, decreasing the amount of gas available and increasing its price.

To maximize its profit, Big-G operates like a monopoly. Big-G's demand is the excess demand curve *XD*. To operate like a monopoly, Big-G must calculate its marginal revenue and find its marginal revenue curve. The curve is *MR* in Fig. 13.4(b). This curve tells us the extra revenue Big-G gets from selling one more litre of gas. To maximize profit, Big-G sells the quantity that makes its marginal revenue equal to its marginal cost. Thus it sells 10,000 litres of gas for $1 a litre. This price and quantity of sales gives Big-G the biggest possible profit. The 10 small firms are price takers, so they take the price of $1 a litre and behave competitively. The quantity of gas demanded in the entire city at $1 a litre is 20,000 litres, as shown in part (a). Of this amount, 10,000 litres are sold by Big-G and 10,000 litres are sold by the 10 small firms who sell 1,000 litres each.

<table>
<tr><td>

R E V I E W

- If a firm believes that a price cut will be matched by other firms but a price rise will not, the firm faces a demand curve with a kink at the current price and quantity and a marginal revenue curve with a break in it.
- If a firm faces a kinked demand curve, its price will be sticky.
- If one firm dominates the market because its costs are lower than the other firms' costs, the dominant firm acts like a monopoly and sets its price.
- When the dominant firm sets the price, other firms take this price and act like competitive firms.

The dominant firm model of oligopoly works for markets in which there is a producer that has a cost advantage over all the other firms. But the model doesn't explain why the dominant firm has a cost advantage or what happens if some of the smaller firms acquire the same technology and costs as the dominant firm. Also it does not predict prices and quantities in markets in which firms are of similar size. The kinked demand curve model attempts to deal with this alternative case. But, as we've seen, that model has some weaknesses.

The weaknesses of traditional theories of oligopoly and a widespread dissatisfaction with them is one of the main forces leading to the development of new oligopoly models based on game theory.

Game Theory

THE TOOL THAT ECONOMISTS USE TO ANALYSE *strategic behaviour*—behaviour that takes into account the expected behaviour of others and the mutual recognition of interdependence—is called **game theory**. Game theory was invented by John von Neumann in 1937 and extended by von Neumann and Oskar Morgenstern in 1944. Today, it is a major research field in economics.

Game theory seeks to understand oligopoly as well as political and social rivalries by using a method of analysis specifically designed to understand games of all types, including the familiar games of everyday life. We will begin our study of game theory, and its application to the behaviour of firms, by considering those familiar games.

</td><td>

Familiar Games: What They Have in Common

What is a game? At first thought, the question seems silly. After all, there are many different games. There are ball games and parlour games, games of chance and games of skill. What do games of such diversity and variety have in common? In answering this question, we will focus on those features of games that are relevant for game theory and for analysing oligopoly as a game. All games have three things in common:

- Rules
- Strategies
- Payoffs

Let's see how these common features of games apply to a game called "the prisoners' dilemma." This game, it turns out, captures some of the essential features of oligopoly and it gives a good illustration of how game theory works and how it leads to predictions about the behaviour of the players.

The Prisoners' Dilemma

Art and Bob have been caught red-handed stealing a car. Facing airtight cases, they will receive a sentence of two years each for their crime. During his interviews with the two prisoners, the Crown attorney begins to suspect that he has stumbled on the two people who were responsible for a multimillion-dollar bank robbery some months earlier. But he also knows that this is just a suspicion. The Crown attorney has no evidence on which he can convict them of the greater crime unless he can get each of them to confess. The Crown attorney decides to make the prisoners play a game with the following rules.

Rules   Each prisoner (player) is placed in a separate room, and there is no communication between them. Each is told that he is suspected of having carried out the bank robbery and that

- If both he and his accomplice confess to the larger crime, each will receive a 3-year sentence.
- If he alone confesses and his accomplice does not, he will receive an even shorter sentence of 1 year while his accomplice will receive a 10-year sentence.

Strategies   In game theory as in ordinary games, **strategies** are all the possible actions of each player.

</td></tr>
</table>

The strategies in the prisoners' dilemma game are simple. Each prisoner can do only one of two things:

1. Confess to the bank robbery.
2. Deny having committed the bank robbery.

Payoffs   Because there are two players, each with two strategies, there are four possible outcomes:

1. Neither player confesses.
2. Both players confess.
3. Art confesses but Bob does not.
4. Bob confesses but Art does not.

Each prisoner can work out exactly what will happen to him—his *payoff*—in each of these four situations. We can tabulate the four possible payoffs for each of the prisoners in what is called a payoff matrix for the game. A **payoff matrix** is a table that shows the payoffs for every possible action by each player for every possible action by the other player.

Table 13.3 shows a payoff matrix for Art and Bob. The squares show the payoffs for each prisoner—the red triangle in each square shows Art's and the blue triangle Bob's. If both prisoners confess (top left), they each get a prison term of 3 years. If Bob confesses but Art denies (top right), Art gets a 10-year sentence and Bob gets a 1-year sentence. If Art confesses and Bob denies (bottom left), Art gets a 1-year sentence and Bob gets a 10-year sentence. Finally, if both of them deny (bottom right), neither can be convicted of the bank robbery charge but both are sentenced for the car theft—a 2-year sentence.

Equilibrium

The equilibrium of the game occurs when player *A* takes the best possible action given the action of player *B*, and player *B* takes the best possible action given the action of player *A*. In the case of the prisoners' dilemma, the equilibrium occurs when Art makes his best choice given Bob's choice, and when Bob makes his best choice given Art's choice. Let's find the equilibrium of the prisoners' dilemma game.

Look at the situation from Art's point of view. Art realizes that his outcome depends on the action Bob takes. If Bob confesses, it pays Art to confess also, for in that case he will be sentenced to 3 years rather than 10 years. But if Bob does not confess, it still pays Art to confess, for in that case he will receive 1 year rather than 2 years. Art reasons that regardless

TABLE 13.3

Prisoners' Dilemma Payoff Matrix

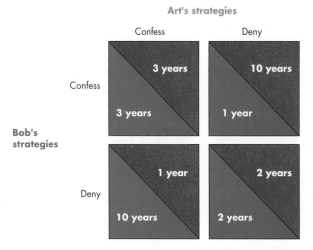

Each square shows the payoffs for the two players, Art and Bob, for each possible pair of actions. In each square, the red triangle shows Art's payoff and the blue triangle shows Bob's. For example, if both confess, the payoffs are in the top left square. The equilibrium of the game is for both players to confess and each gets a 3-year sentence.

of Bob's action, his own best action is to confess.

The problem from Bob's point of view is identical to Art's. Bob knows that if Art confesses, he will receive 10 years if he does not confess or 3 years if he does. Therefore if Art confesses, it pays Bob to confess. Similarly, if Art does not confess, Bob will receive 2 years for not confessing and 1 year if he confesses. Again, it pays Bob to confess. Bob's best action, regardless of Art's action, is to confess.

Each prisoner sees that regardless of what the other prisoner does, his own best action is to confess. Because each player's best action is to confess, each will confess, each will get a 3-year prison term, and the Crown attorney has solved the bank robbery. This is the equilibrium of the game.

Nash Equilibrium   The equilibrium—when player *A* takes the best possible action given the action of player *B*, and player *B* takes the best possible action given the action of player *A*—is called **Nash equilibrium**; it is so named because it was first proposed by

John Nash of Princeton University, who received the Nobel Prize for Economic Science in 1994.

The prisoners' dilemma has a special kind of Nash equilibrium called a dominant strategy equilibrium. A *dominant strategy* is a strategy that is the same regardless of the action taken by the other player. In other words, there is a unique best action regardless of what the other player does. A **dominant strategy equilibrium** occurs when there is a dominant strategy for each player. In the prisoners' dilemma, no matter what Bob does, Art's best strategy is to confess; and no matter what Art does, Bob's best strategy is to confess.

The Dilemma   Now that you have found the solution to the prisoners' dilemma, you can better appreciate the nature of the dilemma. The dilemma arises for each prisoner as he contemplates the consequences of confessing and not confessing. Each prisoner knows that if he and his accomplice remain silent about the bank robbery, they will only be sentenced to 2 years for stealing the car. But neither prisoner has any way of knowing that his accomplice will remain silent and refuse to confess. Each knows that if the other confesses and he denies, the other will receive only a 1-year sentence while he himself will receive a 10-year sentence. Each poses the following questions: Should I deny and rely on my accomplice to deny so that we might both get only 2 years? Or should I confess in the hope of getting just 1 year (providing my accomplice denies), but knowing that if my accomplice does confess we will both get 3 years in prison? Resolving the dilemma involves finding the equilibrium for the game.

A Bad Outcome   For the prisoners, the equilibrium of the game, with each confessing, is not the best outcome. If neither of them confesses, each will get only 2 years for the lesser crime. Isn't there some way in which this better outcome can be achieved? It seems that there is not, because the players cannot communicate with each other. Each player can put himself in the other player's place, and so each player can figure out that there is a dominant strategy for each of them. The prisoners are indeed in a dilemma. Each knows that he can serve 2 years only if he can trust the other not to confess. But each prisoner also knows that it is not in the best interest of the other to not confess. Thus each prisoner knows that he has to confess, thereby delivering a bad outcome for both.

Let's now see how we can use these ideas to understand the behaviour of firms in oligopoly.

Oligopoly Game

To UNDERSTAND HOW AN OLIGOPOLY GAME works, it is revealing to study a special case of oligopoly called duopoly. **Duopoly** is a market structure in which there are two producers of a commodity competing with each other. There are few cases of duopoly on a national and international scale but many cases of local duopolies. For example, in some communities, there are two suppliers of milk, two local newspapers, two taxi companies, or two car rental firms. But the main reason for studying duopoly is not its "realism." It is the fact that it captures all the essential features of oligopoly and yet is more manageable to analyse and understand.

To study a duopoly game, we're going to build a model of a duopoly industry.[1] Suppose that only two firms, Trick and Gear, make a particular kind of electric switchgear. Our goal is to make predictions about the prices charged and the outputs produced by each of the two firms. We are going to pursue that goal by constructing a duopoly game that the two firms will play. To set out the game, we need to specify the strategies of the players and the payoff matrix.

We will suppose that the two firms enter into a collusive agreement. A **collusive agreement** is an agreement between two (or more) producers to restrict output in order to raise prices and profits. Such an agreement is illegal in Canada and is undertaken in secret. A group of firms that has entered into a collusive agreement to restrict output and increase prices and profits is called a **cartel**. The strategies that firms in a cartel can pursue are to

■ Comply
■ Cheat

Complying simply means sticking to the agreement. Cheating means breaking the agreement in a manner designed to benefit the cheating firm.

Because each firm has two strategies, there are four possible combinations of actions for the two firms:

1. Both firms comply.
2. Both firms cheat.
3. Trick complies and Gear cheats.
4. Gear complies and Trick cheats.

---

[1]The model is inspired by a real-world case known as "the incredible electrical conspiracy." But don't lose sight of the fact that what follows is a *model*. It is not a description of a real historical episode.

We need to work out the payoffs to each firm from each of these four possible sets of actions. To do that we need to explore the costs and demand conditions in the industry.

Cost and Demand Conditions

The cost of producing switchgears is the same for both Trick and Gear. The average total cost curve (*ATC*) and the marginal cost curve (*MC*) for each firm are shown in Fig. 13.5(a). The market demand curve for switchgears (*D*) is shown in Fig. 13.5(b). Each firm produces an identical switchgear product, so one firm's switchgear is a perfect substitute for the other's. The market price of each firm's product, therefore, is identical. The quantity demanded depends on that price—the higher the price, the smaller is the quantity demanded.

Notice that in this industry, there is room for only two firms. For each firm, the *minimum efficient scale* of production is 3,000 switchgears a week. When the price equals the average total cost of production at the minimum efficient scale, total industry demand is 6,000 switchgears a week. There is no room for three firms in this industry. If there were three firms, at least one of them would incur an economic loss and exit. Thus the number of firms that an industry can sustain depends on the relationship between cost and the industry's demand conditions.

In the model industry that we're studying here, the particular cost and demand conditions assumed are designed to generate an industry in which two firms can survive in the long run. In real-world oligopoly and duopoly, barriers to entry might arise from economies of scale of the type featured in our model industry but there are other possible barriers as well (as discussed in Chapter 12, pp. 260–261).

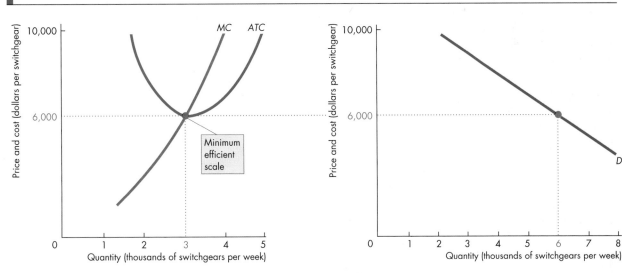

FIGURE 13.5

Costs and Demand

(a) Individual firm

(b) Industry

Part (a) shows the costs facing Trick and Gear, two duopolists that make switchgears. Each firm faces identical costs. The average total cost curve for each firm is *ATC*, and the marginal cost curve is *MC*. For each firm, the minimum efficient scale of production is 3,000 switchgears per week and the average total cost of producing that output is $6,000 a unit. Each firm makes zero economic profit (that is, normal profit).

Part (b) shows the industry demand curve. At a price of $6,000, the quantity demanded is 6,000 switchgears per week. With only two firms in the industry, each firm will make normal profit. But with more than two firms in the industry, they will incur economic losses. Sooner or later one firm will exit the industry. There is room for only two firms in this industry.

Colluding to Maximize Profits

Let's begin by working out the payoffs to the two firms if they collude to make the maximum industry profit by acting like a monopoly. The calculations that the two firms will perform are exactly the same calculations that a monopoly performs. (You studied these calculations in Chapter 12, pp. 265–266.) The only additional thing that the duopolists have to do is to agree on how much of the total output each of them will produce.

The price and quantity that maximizes industry profit for the duopolists is shown in Fig. 13.6. Part (a) shows the situation for each firm, and part (b) for the industry as a whole. The curve labelled MR is the industry marginal revenue curve. The curve labelled MC_I is the industry marginal cost curve if each firm produces the same level of output. That curve is constructed by adding together the outputs of the two firms at each level of marginal cost. That is, at each level of marginal cost, industry output is twice as much as the output of each individual firm. Thus the curve MC_I in part (b) is twice as far to the right as the curve MC in part (a).

To maximize industry profit, the duopolists agree to restrict output to the rate that makes the industry marginal cost and marginal revenue equal. That output rate, as shown in part (b), is 4,000 switchgears a week. The highest price for which the 4,000 switchgears can be sold is $9,000 each. Let's suppose that Trick and Gear agree to split the market equally so that each firm produces 2,000 switchgears a week. The average total cost (ATC) of producing 2,000 switchgears a week is $8,000, so the profit per unit is $1,000 and economic profit is $2 million (2,000 switchgears × $1,000 per unit). The economic profit of each firm is represented by the blue rectangle in Fig. 13.6(a).

FIGURE   13.6

Colluding to Make Monopoly Profits

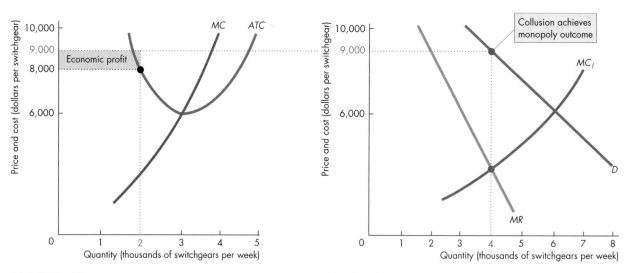

(a) Individual firm

(b) Industry

If Trick and Gear come to a collusive agreement, they can act as a single monopolist and maximize profit. First, the firms calculate the industry marginal cost curve, MC_I (part b), which is the horizontal sum of the two firms' marginal cost curves, MC (part a). Next they calculate the industry marginal revenue, MR. They then choose the output rate that makes marginal revenue equal to marginal cost (4,000 switchgears per week). They agree to sell that output for a price of $9,000, the price at which 4,000 switchgears are demanded.

Each firm has the same costs, so each produces half the total output—2,000 switchgears per week. Average total cost is $8,000 per unit, so each firm makes an economic profit of $2 million (the blue rectangle)—2,000 switchgears multiplied by $1,000 profit per unit.

We have just described one possible outcome for the duopoly game: The two firms collude to produce the monopoly profit-maximizing output and divide that output equally between themselves. From the industry point of view, this solution is identical to a monopoly. A duopoly that operates in this way is indistinguishable from a monopoly. The economic profit that is made by a monopoly is the maximum total profit that can be made by colluding duopolists.

Cheating on a Collusive Agreement

Each firm has an incentive to cheat on the collusive agreement because the price, $9,000 per switchgear, exceeds marginal cost, $8,000. So if one of the firms sold just one additional unit, its profit will increase. Because each firm has an incentive to cheat, there are two possible cheating situations: one in which one firm cheats and one in which both firms cheat.

One Firm Cheats What is the effect of one firm cheating on a collusive agreement? How much extra profit does the cheating firm make? What happens to

the profit of the firm that sticks to the agreement in the face of cheating by the other firm? Let's work out the answers to these questions.

There are many different ways for a firm to cheat. We will work out just one possibility. Suppose that Trick convinces Gear that the industry demand has decreased and that it cannot sell its share of the output at the agreed price. It tells Gear that it plans to cut its price in order to sell the agreed 2,000 switchgears each week. Because the two firms produce a virtually identical product, Gear has no alternative but to match Trick's price cut.

In fact, there has been no decrease in demand and the lower price has been calculated by Trick to be exactly the price needed to sell the additional output that it plans to produce. Gear, though lowering its price in line with that of Trick, restricts its output to the previously agreed level.

Figure 13.7 illustrates the consequences of Trick cheating in this way. Part (a) shows what happens to Gear (the complier); part (b) shows what happens to Trick (the cheat); and part (c) shows what is happening in the industry as a whole.

FIGURE 13.7
Cheating on a Collusive Agreement

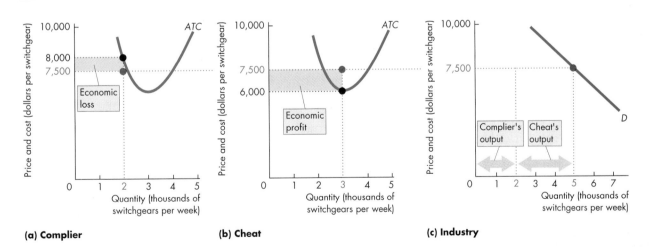

(a) Complier

(b) Cheat

(c) Industry

One firm, shown in part (a), complies with the agreement and produces 2,000 switchgears. The other firm, shown in part (b), cheats on the agreement and increases production to 3,000 switchgears. Given the market demand curve, shown in part (c), and with a total production of 5,000 switchgears a week,

the market price falls to $7,500.

At this price, the complier in part (a) incurs an economic loss of $1 million ($500 × 2,000 units), shown as the red rectangle. In part (b), the cheat makes an economic profit of $4.5 million ($1,500 × 3,000 units), shown as the blue rectangle.

Suppose that Trick decides to increase output from 2,000 to 3,000 switchgears a week—the output at which average total cost is minimized. It recognizes that if Gear sticks to the agreement to produce only 2,000 switchgears a week, total output will be 5,000 a week, and given demand in part (c), the price will have to be cut to $7,500 a unit.

Gear continues to produce 2,000 switchgears a week at a cost of $8,000 a unit and incurs a loss of $500 a unit or $1 million a week. This loss is represented by the red rectangle in part (a). Trick produces 3,000 switchgears a week at an average total cost of $6,000 each. With a price of $7,500, Trick makes a profit of $1,500 a unit and therefore an economic profit of $4.5 million. This economic profit is the blue rectangle in part (b).

We have now described a second possible outcome for the duopoly game—one of the firms cheats on the collusive agreement. In this case, the industry output is larger than the monopoly output and the industry price is lower than the monopoly price. The total economic profit made by the industry is also smaller than the monopoly's economic profit. Trick (the cheat) makes an economic profit of $4.5 million and Gear (the complier) incurs a loss of $1 million. The industry makes an economic profit of $3.5 million. Thus the industry profit is $0.5 million less than the economic profit a monopoly would make. But that profit is distributed unevenly. Trick makes a bigger economic profit than it would under the collusive agreement, while Gear incurs an economic loss.

We have just worked out what happens if Trick cheats and Gear complies with the collusive agreement. A similar outcome would arise if Gear cheated and Trick complied with the agreement. The industry profit and price would be the same, but in this case Gear (the cheat) would make an economic profit of $4.5 million and Trick (the complier) would incur an economic loss of $1 million.

There is yet another possible outcome: Both firms cheat on the agreement.

Both Firms Cheat   Suppose that instead of just one firm cheating on the collusive agreement, both firms cheat. In particular, suppose that each firm behaves in exactly the same way as the cheating firm that we have just analysed. Each tells the other that it is unable to sell its output at the going price and that it plans to cut its price. But because both firms cheat, each will propose a successively lower price. So long as price exceeds marginal cost, each firm has an incentive

to increase its production—to cheat. Only when price equals marginal cost is there no further incentive to cheat. This situation arises when the price has reached $6,000. At this price, marginal cost equals price. Also, price equals minimum average total cost. At a price of less than $6,000, each firm incurs an economic loss. At a price of $6,000, each firm covers all its costs and makes zero economic profit (makes normal profit). Also, at a price of $6,000, each firm wants to produce 3,000 switchgears a week, so the industry output is 6,000 switchgears a week. Given the demand conditions, 6,000 switchgears can be sold at a price of $6,000 each.

Figure 13.8 illustrates the situation just described. Each firm, shown in part (a) of the figure, is producing 3,000 switchgears a week, and at this output average total cost is a minimum ($6,000 per unit). The market as a whole, shown in part (b), operates at the point at which the demand curve (D) intersects the industry marginal cost curve. This marginal cost curve is constructed as the horizontal sum of the marginal cost curves of the two firms. Each firm has lowered its price and increased its output in order to try to gain an advantage over the other firm. Each has pushed this process as far as it can without incurring economic losses.

We have now described a third possible outcome of this duopoly game: Both firms cheat. If both firms cheat on the collusive agreement, the output of each firm is 3,000 switchgears a week and the price is $6,000. Each firm makes zero economic profit.

The Payoff Matrix

Now that we have described the strategies and payoffs in the duopoly game, let's summarize the strategies and the payoffs in the form of the game's payoff matrix and then calculate the equilibrium.

Table 13.4 sets out the payoff matrix for this game. It is constructed in exactly the same way as the payoff matrix for the prisoners' dilemma in Table 13.3. The squares show the payoffs for the two firms—Gear and Trick. In this case, the payoffs are profits. (In the case of the prisoners' dilemma, the payoffs were losses.)

The table shows that if both firms cheat (top left), they achieve the perfectly competitive outcome—each firm makes zero economic profit. If both firms comply (bottom right), the industry makes the monopoly profit and each firm earns an

FIGURE   13.8

Both Firms Cheat

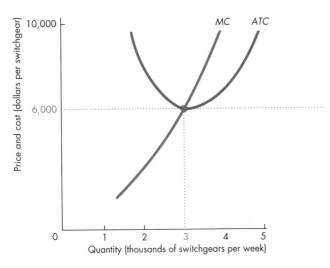

(a) Individual firm

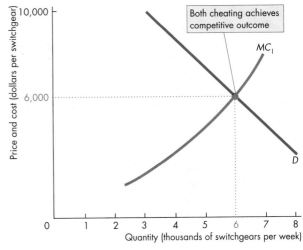

(b) Industry

If both firms cheat by increasing their output and lowering the price, the collusive agreement completely breaks down. The limit to the breakdown of the agreement is the competitive equilibrium. Neither firm will want to cut the price below $6,000 (minimum average total cost), for to do so will result in losses. Part (a) shows the situation facing each firm. At a price of $6,000, the firm's profit-maximizing output is 3,000 switchgears per week. At that output rate, price equals mar-

ginal cost, and it also equals average total cost. Economic profit is zero. Part (b) describes the situation in the industry as a whole. The industry marginal cost curve (MC_I)—the horizontal sum of the individual firms' marginal cost curves (MC)—intersects the demand curve at 6,000 switchgears per week and at a price of $6,000. This output and price is the one that would prevail in a competitive industry.

economic profit of $2 million. The top right and bottom left squares show what happens if one firm cheats while the other complies. The firm that cheats collects an economic profit of $4.5 million and the one that complies incurs a loss of $1 million.

This duopoly game is, in fact, the same as the prisoners' dilemma that we examined earlier in this chapter; it is a duopolist's dilemma.

The Duopolists' Dilemma

You can see why the duopolists have a dilemma by thinking about the situation that each faces. Under a collusive agreement, the colluding firms restrict output to make their joint marginal revenue equal to their joint marginal cost. They set the highest price for which the quantity produced can be sold—a price that is higher than marginal cost. In such a situation,

each firm recognizes that if it cheats on the agreement and increases its output, even though the price will fall below that agreed to, more will be added to its revenue than to its cost, so its profit will increase. Because each firm recognizes this fact, there is a temptation for each firm to cheat. The dilemma is just like that of the prisoners. If each firm could rely on the other one not to cheat, their joint profit would be maximized. But because it is in the individual best interest of each firm to cheat, each firm is led to that action. Let's confirm that this is the outcome of the duopolists' dilemma by finding its equilibrium.

Equilibrium of the Duopolists' Dilemma

To find the equilibrium, let's look at things from the point of view of Gear. Gear reasons as follows:

TABLE 13.4
Duopoly Payoff Matrix

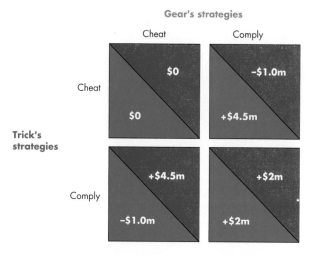

Each square shows the payoffs from a pair of actions. For example, if both firms comply with the collusive agreement, the payoffs are recorded in the bottom right square. The red triangle shows Gear's payoff and the blue triangle shows Trick's. The equilibrium is a Nash equilibrium in which both firms cheat.

Suppose that Trick cheats. If we comply with the agreement, we incur a loss of $1 million. If we also cheat, we make a zero economic profit. Zero economic profit is better than a $1 million loss, so it will pay us to cheat. But suppose Trick complies with the agreement. If we cheat, we will make a profit of $4.5 million, and if we comply, we will make a profit of $2 million. A $4.5 million profit is better than a $2 million profit, so it would again pay us to cheat. Thus regardless of whether Trick cheats or complies, it pays us to cheat. Gear's dominant strategy is to cheat.

Trick comes to the same conclusion as Gear. Therefore both firms will cheat. The equilibrium of this game then is that both firms cheat on the agreement. Although there are only two firms in the industry, the price and quantity are the same as in a competitive industry. Each firm makes zero economic profit.

Although we have done this analysis for only two firms, it would not make any difference (other than to increase the amount of arithmetic) if we were to play the game with three, four, or more firms. In other

words, though we have analysed duopoly, the game theory approach can also be used to analyse oligopoly. The analysis of oligopoly is much harder, but the essential ideas that we have learned also apply to oligopoly.

Repeated Games

The first game that we studied, the prisoners' dilemma, was played just once. The prisoners did not have an opportunity to observe the outcome of the game and then play it again. The duopolist game just described was also played only once. In contrast, most real-world duopolists do get opportunities to play repeatedly against each other. This fact suggests that real-world duopolists might find some way of learning to cooperate so that their efforts to collude are more effective.

If a game is played repeatedly, one player always has the opportunity to penalize the other player for previous "bad" behaviour. If Trick refuses to cooperate this week, then Gear can refuse to cooperate next week (and vice versa). If Gear cheats this week, perhaps Trick will cheat next week. Before Gear cheats this week, shouldn't it take account of the possibility of Trick cheating next week?

What is the equilibrium of this more complicated prisoners' dilemma game when it is repeated indefinitely? Actually there is more than one possibility. One is the Nash equilibrium that we have just analysed. Both players cheat with each making zero economic profit forever. In such a situation, it will never pay one of the players to start complying unilaterally, for to do so would result in a loss for that player and a profit for the other. The price and quantity will remain at the competitive levels forever.

But another equilibrium is possible—one in which the players make and share the monopoly profit. How might this equilibrium come about? Why wouldn't it always pay each firm to try to get away with cheating? The key to answering this question is the fact that when a prisoners' dilemma game is played repeatedly, the players have an increased array of strategies. Each player can punish the other player for previous actions.

There are two extremes of punishment. The smallest penalty that one player can impose on the other is what is called "tit-for-tat." A *tit-for-tat strategy* is one in which a player cooperates in the current period if the other player cooperated in the previous period, but cheats in the current period if the other player cheated in the previous period. The most severe form of punishment that one player can impose on the other arises in what is called a trigger strategy. A *trigger strategy* is one in which a player cooperates if the other player cooperates, but plays the Nash equilibrium strategy forever thereafter if the other player cheats. Because a tit-for-tat strategy and a trigger strategy are the extremes of punishment—the most mild and most severe—there are evidently other intermediate degrees of punishment. For example, if one player cheats on the agreement, the other player could punish by refusing to cooperate for a certain number of periods. In the duopoly game between Gear and Trick, a tit-for-tat strategy keeps both players cooperating and earning monopoly profits. Let's see why.

If both firms stick to the collusive agreement in period 1, they make an economic profit of $2 million each. Suppose that Trick contemplates cheating in period 2. The cheating produces a quick $4.5 million profit and inflicts a $1 million loss on Gear. Adding up the profits over two periods of play, Trick comes out ahead by cheating ($6.5 million compared with $4 million if it did not cheat). The next period Gear will hit Trick with its tit-for-tat response and cheat. With both firms cheating, each firm will make zero economic profit in period 3. If Trick reverts to cooperating, to induce Gear to cooperate in period 4, Gear now makes a profit of $4.5 million and Trick incurs a loss of $1 million. Adding up the profits over four periods of play, Trick would have made more profit by cooperating. In that case, its profit would have been $8 million compared with $5.5 million from cheating and generating Gear's tit-for-tat response.

What is true for Trick is also true for Gear. Because each firm makes a larger profit by sticking with the collusive agreement, both firms do so and the monopoly price, quantity, and profit prevail in the industry. This equilibrium is called a **cooperative equilibrium**—an equilibrium resulting from each player responding rationally to the credible threat of the other player to inflict heavy damage if the agreement is broken. But in order for this strategy to work, the threat must be credible: that is, each player must recognize that it is in the interest of the other player to respond with a "tit-for-tat." The tit-for-tat strategy is credible because if one player cheats, it clearly does not pay the other player to continue complying. So the threat of cheating next period is credible and sufficient to support the monopoly equilibrium outcome.

In reality, whether a cartel works like a one-play game or a repeated game depends primarily on the number of players and the ease of detecting and punishing cheating. The market for cellular telephone calls is restricted by regulation to two players in each area, and the high price of cellular telephone calls can be understood as the outcome of a repeated game between two players. The larger the number of players, the harder it is to achieve a monopoly outcome.

REVIEW

- A collusive agreement to restrict output and raise price creates a game like the prisoners' dilemma.
- Because price exceeds marginal cost, each firm can increase its profit at the expense of the other firm by cheating on the agreement and increasing production.
- If the game is played once, the agreement breaks down because the equilibrium strategy for each firm is to cheat.
- If the game is played repeatedly, punishment strategies such as tit-for-tat can be used that enable the agreement to persist.

Games and Price Wars

The theory of price and output determination under duopoly can help us understand real-world behaviour and, in particular, price wars. Some price wars can be interpreted as the implementation of a tit-for-tat strategy. We've seen that with a tit-for-tat strategy in place, firms have an incentive to stick to the monopoly price. But fluctuations in demand lead to fluctuations in the monopoly price, and sometimes, when the price changes, it might seem to one of the firms that the price has fallen because the other has cheated. In this case, a price war will break out. The price war will end only when each firm has satisfied itself that the other is ready to cooperate again. There will be cycles of price wars and the restoration of collusive agreements. Fluctuations in the world price of oil can be interpreted in this way.

Some price wars arise from the entry of a small number of firms into an industry that had been a monopoly. Although the industry has a small number of firms, the firms are in a prisoners' dilemma and they cannot impose effective penalties for price cutting. The behaviour of prices and outputs in the computer-chip industry during 1994 and 1995 can be explained in this way. Until 1994, the market for PC chips was dominated by one firm, Intel Corporation, which was able to make maximum economic profit by producing the quantity of chips at which marginal cost equalled marginal revenue. The price of Intel's chips was set to ensure that the quantity demanded equalled the quantity produced. Then, in 1994 and 1995, with the entry of a small number of new firms, the industry became an oligopoly. If the firms had maintained Intel's price and shared the market, together they could have made economic profits equal to Intel's profit. But the firms were in a prisoners' dilemma. So prices tumbled to competitive levels.

The Incredible Electrical Conspiracy

Price-fixing arrangements such as those we've just studied are illegal in Canada and the United States. This means that any conspiracies by firms to fix prices have to be undertaken in secrecy. As a result, we get to know about such agreements only after they have been cracked by the legal system.

One famous price-fixing arrangement, involving almost 30 firms in the United States, has been called "the incredible electrical conspiracy."[2] For most of the 1950s, 30 producers of electrical equipment, including such giants as General Electric and Westinghouse, fixed prices "on items ranging from $2 insulators to huge turbine generators costing several million dollars."[3]

Although the electrical equipment pricing conspiracy operated throughout the entire decade of the 1950s, the individual firms conspiring often changed. In particular, General Electric sometimes participated in the price-fixing agreement and sometimes dropped out, undercutting the agreed price and dragging down the industry price and profit in much the same way as the model that we've studied predicts.

Preserving Secrecy   Because collusion is illegal, one special problem that colluding firms face is hiding the fact of their collusion and preserving secrecy. "The incredible electrical conspiracy" provides a fascinating view of one way in which this problem has been solved. The particular device used in this conspiracy was called the "phases of the moon" pricing formula.

> [These pricing formulas were listed on] sheets of paper, each containing a half dozen columns of figures. . . . One group of columns established the bidding order of the seven switchgear manufacturers—a different company, each with its own code number, phasing into the priority position every two weeks (hence "phases of the moon"). A second group of columns, keyed into the company code numbers, established how much each company was to knock off the agreed-upon book price. For example, if it were No 1's (G.E.'s) turn to be low bidder at a certain number of dollars off book, then all Westinghouse (No 2), or Allis-Chalmers (No 3) had to do was look for their code number in the second group of columns to find how many dollars they were to bid above No 1. These bids would then be fuzzed up by having a little added to them or taken away by companies 2, 3, etc. Thus, there was not even a hint that the winning bid had been collusively arrived at.[4]

Before stumbling on the "phases of the moon" papers, the U.S. Justice Department was having a very hard time proving conspiracy but, with the formula in hand, they were able to put the conspiracy under the spotlight and end it.

Other Strategic Variables

We have focused here on firms that play a simple game and consider only two possible strategies—complying and cheating—concerning two variables—price and quantity produced. But the approach that we have used can be extended to deal with a much wider range of choices facing firms. For example, a firm has to decide whether to mount an expensive advertising campaign; whether to modify its product; how reliable to make its product (the more reliable a product, usually, the more expensive

[2]Richard A. Smith, "The Incredible Electrical Conspiracy," Part I and Part II, *Fortune* (April 1961): 132 and (May 1961): 161.
[3]James V. Koch, *Industrial Organization and Prices*, 2nd ed. (Englewood Cliffs, NJ: Prentice-Hall, 1980), 423.

[4]Richard A. Smith, "The Incredible Electrical Conspiracy," Part II, *Fortune* (May 1961): 210.

it is to produce); whether to price discriminate and, if so, among which groups of customers and to what degree; whether to undertake a large research and development (R&D) effort aimed at lowering production costs, or whether to enter or leave an industry. All of these choices can be analysed by using game theory. The basic method of analysis that you have studied can be applied to these problems by working out the payoff for each of the alternative strategies and then finding the equilibrium of the game.

We'll look at two examples. The first is an R&D game and the second is an entry-deterrence game—a game in which a firm tries to prevent other firms from entering an industry.

An R&D Game

Disposable diapers were first marketed in 1966. The two market leaders from the start of this industry have been Procter & Gamble (makers of Pampers) and Kimberly-Clark (makers of Huggies). Procter & Gamble has 60 to 70 percent of the total market while Kimberly-Clark has 25 percent. The disposable diaper industry is fiercely competitive. When the product was first introduced in 1966, it had to be cost-effective in competition against reusable, laundered diapers. A costly research and development effort resulted in the development of machines that could make disposable diapers at a low enough cost to achieve that initial competitive edge. But, as the industry has matured, a large number of firms have tried to get into the business and take market share away from the two industry leaders and the industry leaders themselves have battled against each other to maintain or increase their own market share.

The disposable diaper industry is one in which technological advances that result in small decreases in the average total cost of production can provide an individual firm with an enormous competitive advantage. The current machines can produce disposable diapers at a rate of 3,000 an hour—a rate that represents a tenfold increase on the output rate of just a decade earlier. The firm that develops and uses the least-cost technology gains a competitive edge, undercutting the rest of the market, increasing its market share, and increasing its profit. But the research and development effort that has to be undertaken to achieve even small cost reductions is itself very costly. This cost of research and development has to be deducted from the profit resulting from the increased market share that lower costs achieve. If no

firm does R&D, every firm can be better off, but if one firm initiates the R&D activity, all must.

Each firm is in a research and development dilemma situation that is similar to the game played by Art and Bob. Although the two firms play an ongoing game against each other, it has more in common with the one-shot game than a repeated game. The reason is that research and development is a long-term process. Effort is repeated, but payoffs occur only infrequently and uncertainly.

Table 13.5 illustrates the dilemma (with hypothetical numbers) for the R&D game that Kimberly-Clark and Procter & Gamble are playing. Each firm has two strategies: to spend $25 million a year on R&D or to spend nothing on R&D. If neither firm spends on R&D, they make a joint profit of $100 million, $30 million for Kimberly-Clark and $70

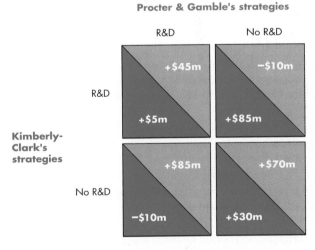

TABLE 13.5

Pampers Versus Huggies: An R&D Game

Procter & Gamble's strategies

	R&D	No R&D
R&D	+$45m / +$5m	−$10m / +$85m
No R&D	+$85m / −$10m	+$70m / +$30m

Kimberly-Clark's strategies (rows)

If both firms undertake R&D, their payoffs are those shown in the top left square. If neither firm undertakes R&D, their payoffs are in the bottom right square. When one firm undertakes R&D and the other one does not, their payoffs are in the top right and bottom left squares. The red triangle shows Procter & Gamble's payoff and the blue triangle shows Kimberly-Clark's. The dominant strategy equilibrium for this game is for both firms to undertake R&D. The structure of this game is the same as that of the prisoners' dilemma.

million for Procter & Gamble (bottom right square in payoff matrix). If each firm conducts R&D, market shares are maintained but each firm's profit is lower by the amount spent on R&D (top left square of payoff matrix). If Kimberly-Clark pays for R&D but Procter & Gamble does not, Kimberly-Clark gains a large part of Procter & Gamble's market. Kimberly-Clark profits and Procter & Gamble loses (top right square of payoff matrix). Finally, if Procter & Gamble invests in R&D, and Kimberly-Clark does not, Procter & Gamble gains market share from Kimberly-Clark, increasing its profit while Kimberly-Clark incurs a loss (bottom left square).

Confronted with the payoff matrix in Table 13.5, the two firms calculate their best strategies. Kimberly-Clark reasons as follows: If Procter & Gamble does not undertake R&D, we make $85 million if we do and $30 million if we do not; therefore it pays to conduct R&D. If Procter & Gamble conducts R&D, we lose $10 million if we don't and make $5 million if we do. Again, R&D pays off. Thus conducting R&D is a dominant strategy for Kimberly-Clark. Doing it pays regardless of Procter & Gamble's decision.

Procter & Gamble reasons similarly: If Kimberly-Clark does not undertake R&D, we make $70 million if we follow suit and $85 million if we conduct R&D. It therefore pays to conduct R&D. If Kimberly-Clark does undertake R&D, we make $45 million by doing the same and lose $10 million by not doing R&D. Again, it pays to conduct R&D. So, for Procter & Gamble, R&D is also a dominant strategy.

Because R&D is a dominant strategy for both players, it is the Nash equilibrium. The outcome of this game is that both firms conduct R&D. They make lower profits than they would if they could collude to achieve the cooperative outcome of no R&D.

The real-world situation has more players than Kimberly-Clark and Procter & Gamble. There are a large number of other firms sharing a small portion of the market, all of them ready to eat into the market share of Procter & Gamble and Kimberly-Clark. So, the R&D effort by these two firms not only serves the purpose of maintaining shares in their own battle, but also helps to keep barriers to entry high enough to preserve their joint market share.

Let's now study an entry-deterrence game in which a firm tries to prevent other firms from entering an industry. Such a game is played in a type of market called a contestable market.

Contestable Markets

A **contestable market** is a market in which one firm (or a small number of firms) operates but in which both entry and exit are free so that the firm (or firms) in the market faces perfect competition from *potential* entrants. Examples of contestable markets are routes served by airlines and by barge companies that operate on the major waterways. These markets are contestable because even though only one or a few firms actually operate on a particular air route or river, other firms could enter those markets if an opportunity for economic profit arose and could exit those markets if the opportunity for economic profit disappeared. The potential entrance prevents the single firm (or small number of firms) from making an economic profit.

If the four-firm concentration ratio is used to determine the degree of competition, a contestable market appears to be uncompetitive. It looks like an oligopoly or monopoly. But a contestable market behaves as if it were perfectly competitive. You can see why by thinking about a game that we'll call an entry-deterrence game.

Entry-Deterrence Game In the entry-deterrence game we'll study, there are two players. One player is Agile Air, the only firm operating on a particular route. The other player is Wanabe Inc., a potential entrant making a normal profit in its current business. The strategies for Agile Air are to set its price at the monopoly profit-maximizing level or at the competitive (zero economic profit) level. The strategies for Wanabe are to enter and set a price just below that of Agile or to not enter.

Table 13.6 shows the payoffs for the two firms. If Wanabe does not enter, Agile earns a normal profit by setting a competitive price and earns maximum monopoly profit (a positive economic profit) by setting the monopoly price. If Wanabe does enter and undercuts Agile's price, Agile incurs an economic loss regardless of whether it sets its price at the competitive or monopoly level. The reason is that Wanabe takes the market with the lower price, so Agile incurs a cost but has zero revenue. If Agile sets a competitive price, Wanabe earns a normal profit if it does not enter but incurs an economic loss if it enters and undercuts Agile by setting a price that is less than average total cost. If Agile sets the monopoly price, Wanabe earns a positive economic profit by entering and a normal profit by not entering.

TABLE 13.6

Agile Versus Wanabe: An Entry-Deterrence Game

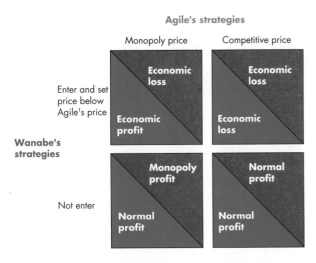

Agile's strategies

	Monopoly price	Competitive price
Enter and set price below Agile's price	Economic loss / Economic profit	Economic loss / Economic loss
Not enter	Monopoly profit / Normal profit	Normal profit / Normal profit

Wanabe's strategies

Agile is the only firm in a contestable market. If Agile sets the monopoly price, Wanabe earns an economic profit by entering and undercutting Agile's price, or a normal profit by not entering. So if Agile sets the price at the monopoly level, Wanabe will enter. If Agile sets the competitive price, Wanabe earns a normal profit if it does not enter or incurs an economic loss if it does enter. So if Agile sets the price at the competitive level, Wanabe will not enter. With entry, Agile incurs an economic loss regardless of the price it sets. The Nash equilibrium of this game is for Agile to set the competitive price, for Wanabe to not enter, and for both firms to make normal profit.

The Nash equilibrium for this game is a competitive price at which Agile Air earns a normal profit and Wanabe does not enter. If Agile raised the price to the monopoly level, Wanabe would enter and by undercutting Agile's price would take all the business, leaving Agile with an economic loss equal to total cost. Agile avoids this outcome by sticking with the competitive price and deterring Wanabe from entering.

Limit Pricing **Limit pricing** is the practice of charging a price below the monopoly profit-maximizing price and producing a quantity greater than that at which marginal revenue equals marginal cost in order to deter entry. The game that we've just

studied is an example of limit pricing but the practice is more general. For example, a firm can use limit pricing to try to convince potential entrants that its own costs are so low that new entrants will incur an economic loss if they enter the industry. To see how this works, lets go back to Agile and Wanabe.

Wanabe knows the current market price but does not know Agile's costs and profit. It can infer those costs though. Suppose Wanabe believes that marginal revenue is 50 percent of price. If the price is $100, then Wanabe estimates that marginal revenue is $50. Wanabe might assume that Agile is maximizing profit by setting marginal revenue equal to marginal cost. Given this assumption, Wanabe estimates Agile's marginal cost to be $50. If Wanabe's marginal cost is greater than $50, it can't compete with Agile, so it will drop the idea of entering this industry. But if its marginal cost is less than $50, it might be able not only to enter the industry, but also to drive Agile out.

Recognizing that Wanabe (and other potential entrants) reason in this way, Agile might decide to use limit pricing to send a false but possibly believable signal to them. It might cut its price to (say) $80 to make Wanabe believe that its marginal cost is only $40 (50 percent of $80). The lower Wanabe believes Agile's marginal cost to be, the less likely is Wanabe to enter. The strategic use of limit pricing makes it possible, in some situations, for a firm (or group of firms) to maintain a monopoly or collusive oligopoly and limit entry.

◆ *Reading Between the Lines* on pp. 310–311 gives you one further look at the power of the game theory approach to oligopoly. Here, we see the theory in action in a gas price war in Atlantic Canada.

We have now studied the four main market structures—perfect competition, monopolistic competition, oligopoly, and monopoly—and discovered how prices and outputs, revenue, cost, and economic profit are determined in these industries. A key element in our analysis of the markets for goods and services is the behaviour of costs. Costs are determined partly by technology and partly by the prices of factors of production. We are now going to see how factor prices are determined.

The firms decide *how* to produce; the interactions of households and firms in the markets for goods and services decide *what* will be produced. But the factor prices determined in the markets for factors of production determine *who* gets the various goods and services produced.

Policy
WATCH

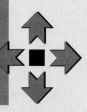

A Prisoners' Dilemma at the Gas Pump

Essence of THE STORY

FINANCIAL POST, JULY 29, 1996

Ultramar declares gasoline price war

BY GAVIN WILL

ST. JOHN'S—Residents of the Atlantic provinces, Quebec and Ontario's Ottawa Valley are basking in the warmth of a gasoline price war launched by Ultramar Canada Ltd. as part of its aggressive expansion campaign.

The opening salvo in what promises to be a happy summer of driving was fired just over a week ago when Ultramar declared a 1¢ per litre cut in prices for regular gas at each of its 1,400 service stations.

Since then, the company has slashed prices by as much as 12¢ a litre in Montreal, to 50¢. And Ultramar vows to meet and beat all competitors who dare to take them on.

"We want to be the lowest priced retailer, and as the competition tries to match us we'll respond by lowering prices below theirs," spokesman Louis Forget said. "We're losing money at some locations, but we're in this for the long term—this isn't a short-term strategy."

The company, which until a few years ago had been a minor gasoline retailer in Eastern Canada, has now become a sig-nificant regional player through a program of acquisitions and investment. ...

Ultramar is now the largest gasoline retailer in Quebec, Newfoundland and P.E.I., but is behind Irving Oil Co., Ltd. in Nova Scotia and New Brunswick.

It's the Irving factor that is sparking much of the speculation about Ultramar's motives in starting the price war. Florida-based industry analyst George Benson believes it was Irving's dominating presence that may have prompted Ultramar to start the campaign.

"Irving has always been a market leader in the Atlantic provinces, and Ultramar isn't going to accede to that," Benson said. "Ultramar is a growing company with new management, and this price war is a signal that they're not going to be pushed around by Irving any more." ...

As part of Ultramar's investment strategy, Forget said, 450 convenience stores will be upgraded and 50 stations built. It also plans to invest $80 million in acquiring more service stations, while expanding its home heating oil distribution networks.

■ Until recently, Irving Oil Co., Ltd. has been the major supplier of gasoline in the Atlantic provinces, and Ultramar Canada Ltd. has been a smaller player in this market.

■ Now, Ultramar is the largest gasoline retailer in Quebec, Newfoundland, and P.E.I., but it still lags Irving in Nova Scotia and New Brunswick.

■ Ultramar has expanded its sales in the Atlantic provinces, Quebec, and the Ottawa Valley by slashing prices.

■ Ultramar began with a 1 cent a litre price cut for regular gas at its 1,400 service stations, but the price eventually fell by up to 12 cents a litre in Montreal.

■ Ultramar says it will undercut any competitor's price.

■ At some service stations, Ultramar is incurring a loss, but the company regards its strategy as long term.

■ Ultramar plans to invest heavily in new outlets in Eastern Canada.

Economic

A N A L Y S I S

■ Two firms dominate the market for gasoline in Atlantic Canada, Quebec, and the Ottawa Valley.

■ So the market can be analysed by using a model of duopoly. (The other smaller firms in the market are price takers and behave like competitive firms.)

■ Figure 1 shows Ultramar's position before the price war. Its demand curve is D, marginal revenue curve is MR, marginal cost curve is MC, and average total cost curve is ATC.

■ Ultramar maximized its economic profit in the short run by selling Q_0 litres of gasoline a day (the quantity at which marginal revenue equals marginal cost) for a price of 62 cents a litre. The blue rectangle shows Ultramar's maximized economic profit.

■ Figure 2 shows what Ultramar hopes to accomplish from a price war with Irving Oil Co. By slashing its price to 50 cents a litre, Ultramar increases sales to Q_1 litres a day, but incurs a loss. The red rectangle shows the loss on this quantity at this price.

■ But Ultramar hopes to capture some of Irving's demand and increase its own. As competitors fail, Ultramar's demand will increase from D_0 to D_1, and Ultramar might eventually be able to raise its price and sell even more gasoline.

■ In the figure, Ultramar eventually raises its price back to 62 cents a litre and sells Q_2 litres a day. The blue rectangle shows its increased economic profit.

■ Figure 3 shows a possible payoff matrix for the game played by Ultramar and Irving. What is the equilibrium in this game?

You're

THE VOTER

■ Who benefits in the short run and in the long run from a price war like the one described in this news article?

■ Should the government step in and prevent such a price war?

■ Write a letter to your Member of Parliament setting out your views on these questions.

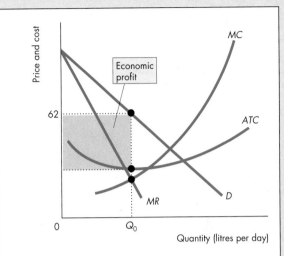

Figure 1 **Before the price war**

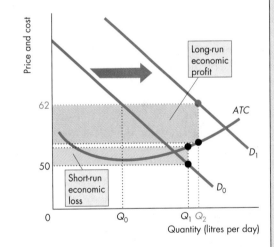

Figure 2 **After the price war**

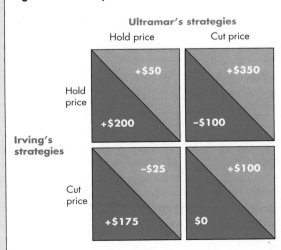

Figure 3 **Payoffs in price war game**

S U M M A R Y

Key Points

Varieties of Market Structure   Monopolistic competition occurs when a large number of firms compete with differentiated products. Oligopoly occurs when a small number of firms compete. A market with a small number of firms can be competitive if low barriers to entry bring competition from potential entrants. The four-firm concentration ratio and the Herfindahl–Hirschman Index are indicators of market power. In Canada, most industries are competitive, but there are some significant oligopoly and monopoly elements. (pp. 286–290)

Monopolistic Competition   In monopolistic competition, firms choose their price as well as their output. Free entry makes long-run economic profit zero. But firms operate with excess capacity. Monopolistic competition is inefficient because marginal cost is less than price, but the inefficiency must be weighed against product variety. (pp. 290–293)

Oligopoly   In oligopoly, firms take into account the effects of their own actions on the behaviour of other firms and the effects of the actions of other firms on their own profits.

  If competing firms match price cuts but not price increases, each firm faces a kinked demand curve and has a break in its marginal revenue curve. Fluctuations in marginal cost inside the range of the break in marginal revenue have no effects on either price or output.

  If one firm dominates an industry, it acts like a monopoly and sets a profit-maximizing price. The small firms take this price as given. (pp. 293–296)

Game Theory   Game theory is a method of analysing strategic behaviour. Players choose strategies and the combined strategies lead to the equilibrium of the game. In a classic game, the prisoners' dilemma, two prisoners, each acting in his own best interest, confess to a crime. (pp. 296–298)

Oligopoly Game   A duopoly can play a prisoners' dilemma game. The firms might collude to make

monopoly profits, or one might cheat on the collusive agreement and try to make a bigger profit at the expense of the other firm. If the game is played only once, both firms cheat. Output and price are the same as in perfect competition. If the game is repeated, a tit-for-tat punishment strategy can lead both firms to maintain a monopoly price.

  Most of the choices that face firms—whether to enter or leave an industry; how much to spend on advertising; whether to modify their products; whether to price discriminate; whether to undertake research and development—can be studied by using game theory. (pp. 298–309)

Key Figures and Tables

Key Terms

R E V I E W   Q U E S T I O N S

1. What are the main market structures and what are their main characteristics?
2. Explain how a firm can differentiate its product.
3. What is a four-firm concentration ratio? If the four-firm concentration ratio is 90 percent, what does that mean?
4. What is the Herfindahl–Hirschman Index and what does a large value of that index indicate?
5. Give some examples of Canadian industries that have a high concentration ratio and those that have a low concentration ratio.
6. What is the value of the four-firm concentration ratio for each market structure?
7. How do monopolistic competition and perfect competition differ?
8. Is monopolistic competition efficient? Explain your answer.
9. Why might the demand curve facing an oligopolist be kinked, and what happens to a firm's marginal revenue curve if its demand curve is kinked?

10. In what circumstances might the dominant firm model of oligopoly be relevant?
11. List the key features that all games have in common with each other.
12. What is the prisoners' dilemma?
13. What is a Nash equilibrium?
14. What is a dominant strategy equilibrium?
15. What are the features of duopoly that make it reasonable to treat duopoly as a game between two firms?
16. What is meant by a repeated game?
17. Explain what a tit-for-tat strategy is.
18. What is a price war? What is the effect of a price war on the profit of the firms in the industry and on the profitability of the industry?
19. What is a contestable market? Will the Herfindahl–Hirschman Index reveal such a market? How does a contestable market operate?
20. What is limit pricing? How might a firm try to use limit pricing to increase its economic profit?

C R I T I C A L   T H I N K I N G

1. After studying *Reading Between the Lines* on pp. 310–311, answer the following questions:
   a. Which market type best describes the retail gasoline market in Atlantic Canada, Quebec, and the Ottawa Valley?
   b. What strategies other than those discussed on pp. 310–311 might Ultramar and Irving Oil Co. have adopted? Explain how these additional strategies might change the nature of the game and the range of possible outcomes. [Hint: Think about the things that gas stations you buy from do to attract business.]
   c. Suppose a Mideast military crisis caused the world price of oil to increase by 100 percent. How would this event impact on the situation in Eastern Canada?
   d. Suppose PetroCan builds and operates a gas station in every community in Eastern Canada. How would that event impact on the market described in this news article? Would it be a wise action for PetroCan?

2. The next time you are watching television, pay close attention to the types of things advertised. Count the number of spots devoted to Nike and Reebok, Molson and Labatt beer, Kodak and other films, Coke and Pepsi, Apple and IBM computers, America Online and other Internet services.
   a. What type of industries do these firms operate in?
   b. Why do these firms spend so much on advertising?
   c. Use a game theory approach and set out a (hypothetical) payoff matrix for the game played by Nike and Reebok.
   d. Explain the equilibrium of the game.
   e. Do Nike and Reebok both gain, both lose, or does one gain and the other lose?
   f. Why do they play this game?

3. Give an example of a contestable market in your city or province. Explain why it is a contestable market. Use the analysis of this chapter to explain how the price, quantity, and economic profit are determined in this market.

P R O B L E M S

1. The figure shows the situation facing Lite and Kool Inc., a producer of running shoes.

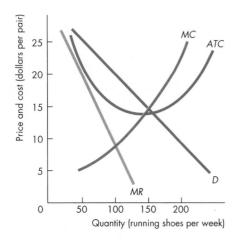

a. Classify this market for running shoes.
b. What quantity does Lite and Kool produce?
c. What price does it charge?
d. How much profit does Lite and Kool make?

2. A monopolistically competitive industry is in long-run equilibrium as illustrated in Fig. 13.2(b). Demand for the industry's product increases, increasing the demand for each firm's output. Using diagrams similar to those in Fig. 13.2, analyse the short-run and long-run effects on price, output, and economic profit of this increase in demand.

3. Another monopolistically competitive industry is in long-run equilibrium, as illustrated in Fig. 13.2(b), when it experiences a large increase in wages. Using diagrams similar to those in Fig. 13.2, analyse the short-run and long-run effects on price, output, and economic profit of this increase in wages.

4. A firm with a kinked demand curve experiences an increase in its variable cost. Explain the effects on the firm's price, output, and economic profit/loss.

5. An industry with one very large firm and 100 very small firms experiences an increase in the demand for its product. Use the dominant firm model to explain the effects on

a. The price, output, and economic profit of the large firm.
b. The price, output, and economic profit of a typical small firm.

6. Describe the game known as the prisoners' dilemma. In describing the game:
a. Make up a story that motivates the game.
b. Work out a payoff matrix.
c. Describe how the equilibrium of the game is arrived at.

7. Consider the following game. There are two players and they are each asked a question. They can answer the question honestly or they can lie. If they both answer honestly, they each receive a payoff of $100. If one answers honestly and the other lies, the liar gains at the expense of the honest player. In that event, the liar receives a profit of $500 and the honest player gets nothing. If they both lie then they each receive a payoff of $50.
a. Describe this game in terms of its players, strategies, and payoffs.
b. Construct the payoff matrix.
c. What is the equilibrium for this game?

8. Two firms, Soapy and Suddies Inc., are the only two producers of soap powder. They collude and agree to share the market equally. If neither firm cheats on the agreement, they can each make $1 million profit. If either firm cheats, the cheater can increase its profit to $1.5 million, while the firm that abides by the agreement incurs a loss of $0.5 million. Neither firm has any way of policing the actions of the other.
a. Describe the best strategy for each firm in a game that is played once.
b. What is the economic profit for each firm if they both cheat?
c. What is the payoff matrix of a game that is played just once?
d. What is the equilibrium if the game is played once?
e. If this duopolist game can be played many times, describe some of the strategies that each firm might adopt.

part 3

Markets for Factors of Production

Craig Riddell, who was born in Toronto in 1946, is a Professor of Economics and former Head of the Department of Economics at the University of British Columbia. He was an undergraduate at the Royal Military College of Canada and a graduate student at Queen's University, where he obtained his Ph.D. in 1977. He began teaching at the University of Alberta in 1975 and moved to the University of British Columbia in 1979. Professor Riddell has acted as economic advisor and consultant to numerous federal and provincial government departments as well as international agencies. He is Academic Co-Chair of the Canadian Employment Research Forum, an Associate of the Canadian Institute for Advanced Research, and Vice-President of the Canadian Economics Association.

Professor Riddell is a prolific researcher. In recent years he has examined a variety of issues in labour economics and labour relations. Robin Bade and Michael Parkin talked to Craig Riddell about his work and the Canadian labour market.

TALKING WITH Craig Riddell

How and why did you get into economics?

I started out in chemical engineering, but in the second year took an introductory course in economics. At the time I had little knowledge of what economics was—like many people, I confused the social science of economics with the professional program of business and commerce. Economics appealed to me for several reasons. Most of the subject matter was of immense social importance: What makes some countries rich and others poor? How should societies allocate their scarce resources in order to achieve the highest level of well-being for their citizens? What causes ups and downs of economics activity with the business cycle? and so on. I also liked the analytical rigour and the fact that the discipline seemed to have developed a set of tools that could be employed to address these "big questions"—as well as many smaller ones. Finally, the policy relevance of the subject was an attractive feature.

You have spent a lot of time in recent years studying unemployment. Why do you find this topic so absorbing?

One reason is the importance of the subject: unemployment may result in the underutilization of people's time and talents, reduce incomes and increase poverty. And persistent high unemployment raises questions in many observers' minds about the ability of the labour market to perform its key function of matching the demands of workers for jobs and of employers for workers. For these reasons, the unemployment rate is one of the most closely followed economic indicators.

Why in recent years has the Canadian unemployment rate remained so high compared with the U.S. unemployment rate?
At the outset, we need to recognize (or admit!) that we still don't fully understand the answer to this question, despite a fair amount of research. However, some important aspects are reasonably clear. First, it is important to distinguish between the 1980s and the 1990s. An unemployment rate gap of about 2 to 3 percentage points emerged beginning in the early 1980s, and this differential widened further in the 1990s. It is tempting to attribute the higher relative Canadian unemployment to weaker economic performance in Canada—that is, that the Canadian economy wasn't growing at a sufficiently rapid rate and wasn't creating enough jobs. This has been the case thus far in the 1990s—both output growth and employment growth have been much lower in Canada than in the United States. The widening of the unemployment gap in the 1990s can largely be attributed to this weaker economic growth in Canada, much of which in turn appears to be due to the much more aggressive anti-inflation policy pursued in Canada during the late 1980s and early 1990s. However, this same story does not apply to the 1980s. During that decade, the performance of the Canadian economy did not deteriorate relative to the United States. Indeed, both overall growth in the production of goods and services

Most of the unemployment gap during the 1980s can be attributed to the change in how Canadians spend their time when not employed relative to Americans, ...

and growth in employment were very similar in the two countries. Most of the unemployment gap during the 1980s can be attributed to the change in how Canadians spend their time when not employed relative to Americans, with Canadians becoming more likely to be engaged in job search, whereas Americans became more likely to drop out of the labour force when not employed. Understanding the causes of this change in behaviour is the key to understanding the emergence of the unemployment differential.

How does the Canadian labour market differ from that in the United States?
Relative to the differences that exist between most economies and societies, Canada and the United States are very similar. These similarities are evident in the labour market as well—for example, both countries have highly educated and skilled work forces, and similar industrial and occupational structures. But there are also a number of differences. Canadian labour market policies generally lie between the

extremes of the more *laissez-faire* American approach and the more highly regulated European approach. The principal Canadian income support programs for the working-age population—unemployment insurance and welfare—cover a large fraction of the population and provide higher levels than their U.S. counterparts.

One of the principal conclusions of recent comparative Canada–U.S. labour research is that these differences in labour market and income support policies do influence outcomes and behaviour in the two societies— they are "small differences that matter" (borrowing a phrase that summed up the conclusions of one set of studies).

Can you give an example from your own work that illustrates this "small differences that matter" idea?
The divergence in the importance of unions in the two countries during the past three decades is a good illustration. The extent of unionization in Canada and the United States was very similar as

recently as the mid-1960s, yet now union coverage in Canada is more than double that of the United States. A worker picked at random from either the public or the private sectors is more than twice as likely to be covered by a union contract in Canada than his or her counterpart in the United States.

A number of explanations have been offered for the decline of the unions in the United States and the emergence of a substantial Canada–U.S. unionization differential. These include: (i) changes in economic structure (decline of manufacturing employment, growth of service sector employment, growth of part-time work, growth of small firms, etc.); (ii) differences in social attitudes towards unions; (iii) greater demand for union coverage among Canadian workers; and (iv) differences between the two countries in labour laws relating to unionization and collective bargaining and in the administration and enforcement of these laws. My work on Canada–U.S. unionization finds very little support for the first three of these explanations, and points to the differences in the laws and their administration as the principal source of the differences in union coverage.

Another topic you have worked on is unemployment insurance. This has also been an area of considerable policy debate and reform in Canada. What role has the research played in this debate?
This case is a good illustration of progress in social science. In 1971, Canada made massive changes to its Unemployment Insurance program, including substantially increased coverage of the program, higher benefit levels, lower qualification requirements, and other major changes. At the time relatively little was known about the labour market

effects of Unemployment Insurance. Since then a substantial body of research on these effects—in Canada and elsewhere—has been built up. With hindsight, we now recognize that some of the 1971 changes were probably unwise. Recent reforms to the Unemployment Insurance program (now called "Employment Insurance") have had the advantage of a much greater base of information about the likely impacts of changes to the program. Indeed, the 1996 amendments to the Unemployment Insurance program had more research input than any previous package of reforms.

What type of labour market research do you foresee having the greatest payoff in the future?
International comparative research, an area that has seen some growth recently, seems likely to be able to pay dividends for some time. There are a wide variety of labour market policies and institutions across countries, and this great variation provides much scope for a richer understanding of the impacts of these institutions and policies.

I also believe that there is great potential to learn from social experiments—that is, situations in which there is random assignment into "treatment" and "control" groups. Economics will remain a largely nonexperimental science for a long time, and random assignment is not practical or even feasible in all circumstances. Nonetheless, there are many labour market interventions whose impacts on behaviour could be determined with greater confidence than now exists through the use of social experiments. Policy makers need to take a long-term view—that such experiments add to society's stock of knowledge about the probable effects of policy interventions, thus making it more

Economics requires a diverse set of skills ... it's a mistake to concentrate mainly on highly technical and analytical subjects. Having a good "tool kit" is necessary, but not sufficient.

likely that future policies will achieve their desired effects and making it clearer what the unintended consequences of these policies will be.

What subjects would you advise a student to pursue if he or she wants to become a professional economist today?
Economics requires a diverse set of skills, making it a challenging but also very interesting profession. On the one hand, it's important to have a solid grounding in mathematics and statistics. I would stress the value of good empirical skills—the manipulation and interpretation of data—because I expect economics to continue to become an increasingly empirical science. On the other hand, it's important to have a good knowledge of institutions and policy issues. Thus I believe it's a mistake to concentrate mainly on highly technical and analytical subjects. Having a good "tool kit" is necessary, but not sufficient. This argues for being exposed to a wide range of subjects rather than focusing narrowly.

Pricing and Allocating Factors of Production

After studying this chapter, you will be able to:

- Explain how firms choose the quantities of labour, capital, and land to demand

- Explain how households choose the quantities of labour, capital, land, and entrepreneurship to supply

- Explain how wages, interest, rent, and normal profit are determined in competitive factor markets

- Explain the concept of economic rent and distinguish between economic rent and transfer earnings

Many Happy Returns

It might not be your birthday, and even if it is, chances are you are spending most of it working. But at the end of the week or month (or, if you're devoting all your time to school, when you graduate), you will receive the *returns* from your labour. Those returns vary a lot. Ed Jones, who spends his chilly winter days in a small container suspended from the top of Toronto's First Canadian Place cleaning windows, makes a happy return of $12 an hour. Damon Stoudamire, who plays no more than 82 basketball games a year, makes a very happy return of $4.6 million over three years—including the gift of a Mercedes-Benz to his mother. Students working at what have been called McJobs—serving fast food or labouring in the fields of the Niagara Peninsula—earn just a few dollars an hour. Why aren't *all* jobs well paid? ◆ Most of us have little trouble spending our pay. But most of us do manage to save some of what we earn. What determines the amount of saving that people do and the returns they make on that saving? How do the returns on saving influence the allocation of savings across the many industries and activities that use our capital resources? ◆ Some people receive income from supplying land, but the amount earned varies enormously with the land's location and quality. For example, a hectare of farmland in Manitoba rents for about $1,000 a year, while a block in Toronto's Yorkville rents for several million dollars a year. What determines the rent that people are willing to pay for different blocks of land? Why are rents so enormously high in big cities and so relatively low in the great farming regions of the nation?

◆ In this chapter, we study the markets for factors of production—labour, capital, land, and entrepreneurship—and learn how their prices and people's incomes are determined.

Factor Prices and Incomes

GOODS AND SERVICES ARE PRODUCED BY USING the four factors of production—*labour, capital, land,* and *entrepreneurship.* (These factors of production are defined in Chapter 1, p. 19.) The owners of factors of production supply factor *services* and firms demand factor *services.* These factor services are *flows*—quantities *per unit of time.* Firms hire the *services* of factors of production and in return for the use of their factor services, factor owners receive incomes. These incomes are determined by the prices of the factor services—called *factor prices.* The factor prices are the *wage* rate for labour, the *interest* rate for capital, the *rental* rate for land, and the rate of *normal profit* for entrepreneurship.

In addition to the four factor incomes, a residual income, *economic profit* (or *economic loss*) is paid to (or borne by) firms' owners. A firm's owners might be the suppliers of any of the four factors of production. For a small firm, the owner is usually the entrepreneur. For a large corporation, the owners are the stockholders. In some cases, for example Algoma Steel Inc., a large part of the stock is owned by the firm's employees.

Factor Prices and Opportunity Costs

Factor prices, which generate incomes for the owners of factors of production, are *opportunity costs* for the firms that employ the factors. The wage rate is the opportunity cost of labour, the interest is the opportunity cost of capital, the land rental rate is the opportunity cost of land, and normal profit is the opportunity cost of entrepreneurship. This idea of factor prices as opportunity costs helps you to better understand the nature of the prices of the services of capital and land.

Why is the interest rate the factor price for capital? Why isn't the capital factor price the price of a piece of machinery—the price of a knitting machine for Swanky's sweater factory, the price of a computer for a tax consultant, or the price of an automobile assembly line for GM?

The answer is that these prices are not opportunity costs of *using* capital. They are prices at which capital can be bought *and sold*—the prices at which a piece of capital can change hands. But they are not the prices that must be paid for the use of capital.

The opportunity cost of *using* capital is the best alternative forgone. This alternative is using the funds tied up in the capital to earn some interest. So the interest rate paid on the funds tied up in the capital is the opportunity cost of using capital. These funds might be borrowed, in which case there is an explicit payment of interest to the lender. Or the funds might be owned by the firm, in which case there is an *implicit* interest cost—the interest that could have been earned by using those funds in some other way. Land is similar to capital. The opportunity cost of using land is its rental rate, not its purchase price.

An Overview of a Competitive Factor Market

We're going to learn how a competitive market for the services of a factor of production determines the price, the quantity used, and the income of the factor. But markets exist for only three of the factors of production—labour, capital, and land. The fourth factor, entrepreneurship, is special. It is demanded and supplied by each individual entrepreneur, who constantly seeks out economic profit opportunities. Entrepreneurs flow into industries that yield an economic profit, out of industries that incur an economic loss, and remain in industries that yield a normal profit. Entrepreneurs organize firms that create a demand for the other three factors of production. Let's look at a factor market.

We can study a factor market and the forces that determine the price and quantity in that market by using the model of demand and supply. The quantity of a factor of production demanded depends on the factor's price. That is, the quantity of labour demanded depends on the wage rate, the quantity of capital demanded depends on the interest rate, and the quantity of land demanded depends on the rental rate. The law of demand applies to factors of production just as it does to goods and services. The lower the price of a factor of production, other things remaining the same, the greater is the quantity demanded of the factor of production. Figure 14.1 shows the demand curve for a factor of production as the curve labelled *D.*

The quantity supplied of a factor of production also depends on its price. With a possible exception that we'll identify later in this chapter, the law of supply applies to factors of production. The higher the price of a factor of production, other things remaining the same, the greater is the quantity supplied of the factor. Figure 14.1 shows the supply curve of a factor of production as the curve labelled *S.*

FIGURE 14.1

Demand and Supply in a Factor Market

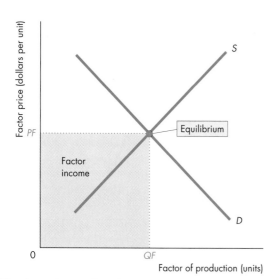

The demand curve for a factor of production (*D*) slopes downward and the supply curve (*S*) slopes upward. The intersection of the demand and supply curves determines the factor price (*PF*) and the quantity of a factor used (*QF*). The factor income is the product of the factor price and the quantity of the factor, as represented by the blue rectangle.

The point of intersection of the factor demand and factor supply curves determines the equilibrium factor price. Figure 14.1 shows such an equilibrium: *PF* is the factor price and *QF* is the quantity of the factor of production used.

The income earned by a factor of production is its price multiplied by the quantity used. In Fig. 14.1, the price is measured by the distance from the origin to *PF* and the quantity used is measured by the distance from the origin to *QF*. The factor income is the product of these two distances and equals the blue rectangle in the figure.

All influences on the quantity of a factor that a firm plans to employ other than its price result in a shift in the factor demand curve. We'll study what those influences are in the next section. For now, let's simply work out the effects of a change in the demand for a factor of production on its price, the quantity used of it, and the factor's income. An increase in

demand for a factor of production, as illustrated in Fig. 14.2(a), shifts the demand curve rightward, leading to an increase in its price and an increase in the quantity of the factor used. Thus when the demand curve shifts from D_0 to D_1, the price increases from PF_0 to PF_1 and the quantity used increases from QF_0 to QF_1. An increase in the demand for a factor of production increases that factor's income. The dark blue area in Fig. 14.2(a) illustrates the increase in income.

When the demand for a factor of production decreases, its demand curve shifts leftward. Figure 14.2(b) illustrates the effects of a decrease in demand. The demand curve shifts leftward from D_0 to D_2, the price decreases from PF_0 to PF_2 and the quantity used decreases from QF_0 to QF_2. When the demand for a factor of production decreases, the income of that factor also decreases. The light blue area in Fig. 14.2(b) illustrates the decrease in income.

The extent to which a change in the demand for a factor of production changes the factor price and the quantity used depends on the elasticity of supply. If the supply curve is very flat (supply is elastic), the change in the quantity used is large and the change in price is small. If the supply curve is very steep (supply is inelastic), the change in the price is large and the change in the quantity used is small.

A change in the supply of a factor of production changes the price and quantity used as well as the income earned by those supplying the factor. An increase in supply results in a decrease in the factor price and an increase in the quantity used. A decrease in supply results in an increase in the factor price and a decrease in the quantity used. But whether a change in supply increases or decreases the factor's income depends on the elasticity of demand for the factor.

Suppose that the quantity used of the factor of production illustrated in Fig. 14.3 decreases from 3 units to 2 units. Initially, the price is $10 a unit. If the demand for the factor is shown by the curve D_0, the decrease in supply results in an increase in the price of the factor but a decrease in the income of those supplying this factor of production. You can see that income decreases by multiplying the factor price by the quantity used. Initially, when the quantity is 3 units and the price is $10, the income earned by the suppliers of this factor of production is $30 ($20 light blue area plus $10 red area). When the quantity decreases to 2 units and the price increases to $14, income decreases by the $10 (red area) but increases by the $8 (dark blue area) for a net decrease of $2 to $28. Over the range of the price change that we've just considered, the demand for the factor is elastic.

FIGURE 14.2
Changes in Demand

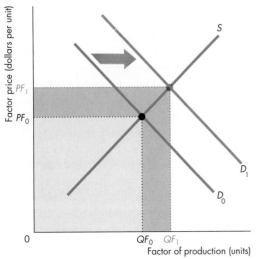

(a) An increase in demand

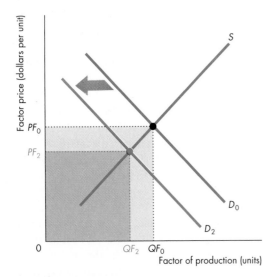

(b) A decrease in demand

An increase in the demand for a factor of production (part a) shifts its demand curve rightward—from D_0 to D_1. The quantity used increases from QF_0 to QF_1 and the price increases from PF_0 to PF_1. The factor income increases, and the dark blue area illustrates that increase in income. A decrease in the demand for a factor of production, from D_0 to D_2, results in a decrease in the quantity used, from QF_0 to QF_2, and a decrease in the factor price, from PF_0 to PF_2. The decrease in demand results in a decrease in the factor income, and the light blue area illustrates that decrease in income.

FIGURE 14.3
Factor Income and Demand Elasticity

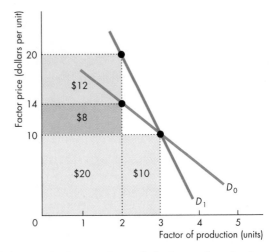

A decrease in the quantity used of a factor of production might result in a decrease or an increase in the factor's income. If the demand curve is D_0 (an elastic demand curve over the relevant range), a decrease in the quantity from 3 to 2 results in a decrease in the factor income from $30 to $28. If the demand curve is D_1 (an inelastic demand curve over the relevant range), a decrease in the quantity from 3 to 2 results in an increase in the factor's income from $30 to $40.

Conversely, suppose that the demand for the factor is shown by the curve D_1. In this case, when the quantity decreases to 2 units, the price increases to $20 a unit. Income increases to $40. The smaller quantity lowers income by $10 (red area), but the higher factor price increases income by $20 (dark blue plus green areas). Over the range of the price change that we've just considered, the demand for the factor is inelastic.

We've just seen how demand and supply in a factor market determine the price, quantity used, and income of a factor of production. We're going to spend the rest of this chapter exploring more closely the influences on the demand for and supply of factors of production. We're also going to study the influences of the elasticities of supply and demand for factors. These elasticities are important because of their effects on factor prices and the incomes earned. Let's begin by studying the demand for factors of production.

Demand for Factors

THE DEMAND FOR A FACTOR OF PRODUCTION IS A derived demand. A **derived demand** is a demand for an item not for its own sake but in order to use it in the production of goods and services. A firm's derived demand for factors depends on the constraints the firm faces—its technology constraint and its market constraint. It also depends on the firm's objective. We will study the behaviour of firms whose objective is to maximize profit.

Profit Maximization

In the short run, a firm's factors of production fall into two categories: variable and fixed. In most industries, the variable factor is labour and the fixed factors are capital (i.e., plant, machinery, and buildings) and land. A firm makes short-run changes in output by changing the quantity of labour it employs. It makes long-run changes in output by changing the quantities of labour, capital, and land it employs.

A profit-maximizing firm produces the output at which marginal cost equals marginal revenue. This principle holds whether the firm is a perfect competitor, in monopolistic competition, in oligopoly, or a monopoly. If one more unit of output adds less to total cost than it adds to total revenue, the firm can increase its profit by producing more. A firm maximizes profit by producing the output at which the additional cost of producing one more unit (marginal cost) equals the additional revenue from selling it (marginal revenue).

We can state the condition for maximum profit in terms of the quantity of each factor of production that the firm hires. To maximize profit, the firm hires the quantity of a factor of production that makes the marginal cost of the factor equal to the marginal revenue that the factor generates. Let's look at these two concepts.

Marginal Cost of a Factor The marginal cost of a factor of production is the addition to a firm's total cost that results from employing one more unit of a factor. For a firm that buys its factors of production in competitive factor markets, this marginal cost is the price of the factor. That is, in a competitive factor market, each firm is such a small user of the factor that it has no influence on the price it must pay for each unit employed. The firm simply has to pay the going factor price—market wage rate for labour, interest rate for capital, and rent for land.

Marginal Revenue Product To maximize profit, a firm must compare the marginal cost of a factor with the marginal revenue that the factor generates, which is called marginal revenue product. **Marginal revenue product** is the change in total revenue resulting from employing one more unit of a factor of production while the quantity of all other factors remains constant.

The concept of *marginal revenue product* sounds a bit like the concept of *marginal revenue* that you have met before. These concepts are indeed related but there is a crucial distinction between the two. Marginal revenue product is the extra revenue generated as a result of employing one extra unit of a factor; marginal revenue is the extra revenue generated as a result of selling one additional unit of output.

Quantity of Factor Demanded To maximize profit, a firm hires the quantity of a factor of production that makes the marginal revenue product equal to its price. If the marginal revenue product of a factor exceeds its price, the firm can increase its profit by increasing the quantity of the factor employed. If the marginal revenue product of a factor is less than its price, the firm can increase its profit by decreasing the quantity of the factor employed. But if the marginal revenue product of a factor is equal to its price, the firm can only decrease its profit by changing the quantity of the factor employed. At this point, the firm is maximizing profit.

As the price of a factor varies, the quantity demanded of it also varies. The lower the price of a factor, the larger is the quantity demanded of that factor. Let's illustrate this proposition by working through an example—that of labour.

The Firm's Demand for Labour

A *total product schedule* describes a firm's short-run technology constraint. The first two columns of Table 14.1 set out the total product schedule for a car wash operated by Max's Wash 'n' Wax. (This total product schedule is similar to the one we studied in Chapter 10, Fig. 10.1.) The numbers tell us how the maximum number of car washes each hour varies as the amount of labour employed varies. The third column of Table 14.1 shows the *marginal product of labour*—the change in output resulting from a one-unit increase in the quantity of labour employed.

Max's market constraint is the demand curve for his product. If, in the goods market, a firm is a monopoly or engaged in monopolistic competition or oligopoly, the demand curve for its product is downward sloping. If a firm is perfectly competitive, the demand curve for its product is perfectly elastic—the firm is a price taker. Assume that the car wash market is perfectly competitive. Max can sell as many washes as he chooses at $4 a wash. Given this information, we can calculate Max's total revenue (fourth column) by multiplying the number of cars washed per hour by $4. For example, if 9 cars are washed each hour (row c), total revenue is $36.

The fifth column shows the calculation of marginal revenue product of labour—the change in total revenue per unit change in labour. For example, if Max hires a second worker (row c), total revenue increases from $20 to $36, so marginal revenue product of labour is $16.

There is an alternative way of calculating the marginal revenue product of labour. The marginal product of labour tells us how many washes an additional worker produces. Marginal revenue tells the change in total revenue from selling one more wash. So an additional worker changes total revenue by an amount that equals marginal product multiplied by marginal revenue. That is, marginal revenue product equals marginal product multiplied by marginal revenue. For a perfectly competitive firm, marginal revenue equals price, so marginal revenue product equals marginal product multiplied by price.

To see that this method works, let's use the numbers in Table 14.1. Multiply the marginal product of hiring a second worker—4 cars an hour—by marginal revenue—$4 a car—and notice that the answer is $16, the same as we have already calculated.

Notice that as the quantity of labour increases, the marginal revenue product of labour declines. When Max hires the first worker, the marginal revenue product of labour is $20. If Max hires a second worker, the marginal revenue product of labour is $16. Marginal revenue product of labour continues to decline as Max hires more workers.

Marginal revenue product diminishes as Max hires more workers because of the principle of diminishing returns that we first studied in Chapter 10. With each additional worker hired, the marginal product of labour declines and so brings in a smaller marginal revenue product. Because Max's Wash 'n' Wax is a perfectly competitive firm, the price of each additional car wash is the same and brings in the same marginal revenue.

If Max had a monopoly in car washing, he would have to lower his price to sell more washes. In this case, the marginal revenue product of labour diminishes even more quickly than in perfectly competitive conditions. For a monopoly, marginal revenue product diminishes because of diminishing marginal product of labour and also because of diminishing marginal revenue.

TABLE 14.1

Marginal Revenue Product at Max's Wash 'n' Wax

	Quantity of labour (L) (workers)	Output (Q) (car washes per hour)	Marginal product (MP = ΔQ/ΔL) (washes per worker)	Total revenue (TR = P × Q) (dollars)	Marginal revenue product (MRP = ΔTR/ΔL) (dollars per worker)
a	0	0		0	
			5		20
b	1	5		20	
			4		16
c	2	9		36	
			3		12
d	3	12		48	
			2		8
e	4	14		56	
			1		4
f	5	15		60	

Max operates in a perfectly competitive car wash market and can sell any quantity of washes at $4 a wash. To calculate marginal revenue product, first work out total revenue. If Max hires 1 worker (row b), output is 5 washes an hour, and total revenue is $20. If he hires 2 workers (row c), output is 9 washes an hour, and total revenue is $36. By hiring the second worker, total revenue rises by $16—the marginal revenue product of labour is $16.

The Labour Demand Curve

Figure 14.4 shows how the labour demand curve is derived from the marginal revenue product curve. The *marginal revenue product curve* graphs the marginal revenue product of a factor at each quantity of the factor hired. Figure 14.4(a) illustrates the marginal revenue product curve for workers employed by Max. The horizontal axis measures the number of workers that Max hires and the vertical axis measures the marginal revenue product of labour. The blue bars show the marginal revenue product of labour as Max employs more workers. These bars correspond to the numbers in Table 14.1. The curve labelled *MRP* is Max's marginal revenue product curve.

The firm's demand for labour curve is based on its marginal revenue product curve. You can see Max's demand for labour curve (*D*) in Fig. 14.4(b). The horizontal axis measures the number of workers hired—the same as part (a). The vertical axis measures the wage rate in dollars per hour. The demand for labour curve is exactly the same as the firm's marginal revenue product curve. For example, when Max employs 3 workers an hour, his marginal revenue product is $10 an hour, as in Fig. 14.4(a); and at a wage rate of $10 an hour, Max hires 3 workers an hour, as in Fig. 14.4(b).

Why is the demand for labour curve identical to the marginal revenue product curve? Because the firm hires the profit-maximizing quantity of labour. If the cost of hiring one more worker—the wage rate—is less than the additional revenue that the worker brings in—the marginal revenue product of labour—then the firm can increase its profit by employing one more worker. Conversely, if the cost of hiring one more worker is greater than the additional revenue that the worker brings in—the wage rate exceeds the marginal revenue product—then the firm can increase its profit by employing one fewer worker. But if the cost of hiring one more worker is equal to the additional revenue that the worker brings in—the wage rate equals the marginal revenue product—then the firm cannot increase its profit by changing the number of workers it employs. The firm is making the maximum possible profit. This situation occurs when the wage rate equals the marginal revenue product of labour. Thus the quantity of labour demanded by the firm is such that the wage rate equals the marginal revenue product of labour.

Table 14.2 is a compact glossary of the factor market terms that you've just learned.

FIGURE 14.4

The Demand for Labour at Max's Wash 'n' Wax

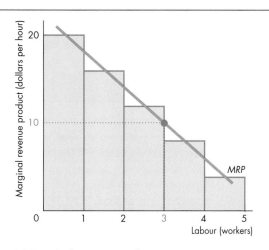

(a) Marginal revenue product

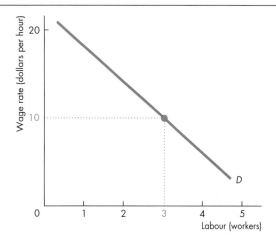

(b) Demand for labour

Max's Wash 'n' Wax operates in a perfectly competitive car wash market and can sell any quantity of washes at $4 a wash. The blue bars in part (a) represent the firm's marginal revenue product of labour. They are based on the numbers in Table 14.1. The orange line is the firm's marginal product of labour curve. Part (b) shows Max's demand for labour curve. This curve is identical to Max's marginal revenue product curve. Max demands the quantity of labour that makes the wage rate, which is the marginal cost of labour, equal to the marginal revenue product of labour.

TABLE 14.2

A Compact Glossary of Factor Market Terms

Factors of production	Labour, capital, land, and entrepreneurship
Factor prices	Wage—price of labour; interest—price of capital; rent—price of land; normal profit—price of entrepreneurship
Marginal product	The additional output produced by employing one additional unit of a factor; for example, the marginal product of labour is the additional output produced by employing one more person
Marginal revenue	The change in total revenue resulting from selling one additional unit of output
Marginal revenue product	The change in total revenue resulting from hiring one additional unit of a factor of production; for example, the marginal revenue product of labour is the additional total revenue resulting from selling the output produced by employing one more person

---

Two Conditions for Profit Maximization

When we studied firms' output decisions, we discovered that a condition for maximum profit is that marginal revenue equals marginal cost. We've now discovered another condition for maximum profit—marginal revenue product of a factor equals the factor's price. These two conditions are equivalent to each other as Table 14.3 shows. When a firm produces the output that maximizes profit, marginal revenue equals marginal cost and the firm's technological and market constraints imply that the firm is employing the amount of labour that makes the marginal revenue product of labour equal to the wage rate.

We have just derived the law of demand as it applies to the labour market. And we've discovered that the same principles that apply to the demand for goods and services apply here as well. The demand

---

TABLE 14.3

Two Conditions for Maximum Profit

SYMBOLS

Marginal product	**MP**
Marginal revenue	**MR**
Marginal cost	**MC**
Marginal revenue product	**MRP**
Factor price	**PF**

TWO CONDITIONS FOR MAXIMUM PROFIT

1.   **MR = MC**   2.   **MRP = PF**

EQUIVALENCE OF CONDITIONS

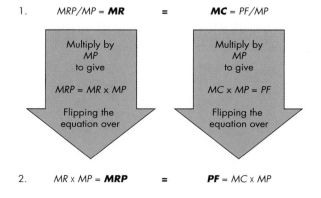

The two conditions for maximum profit are marginal revenue (MR) equals marginal cost (MC) and marginal revenue product (MRP) equals the price of the factor (PF). The two conditions for maximum profit are equivalent because marginal revenue product (MRP) equals marginal revenue (MR) multiplied by marginal product (MP), and the factor price (PF) equals marginal cost (MC) multiplied by marginal product (MP).

---

for labour curve slopes downward. Other things remaining the same, the lower the wage rate (the price of labour), the greater is the quantity of labour demanded. Let's now study the influences that change in the demand for labour and shift in the demand for labour curve.

Changes in the Demand for Labour

The position of a firm's demand for labour curve depends on three factors:

1. The price of the firm's output
2. The prices of other factors of production
3. Technology

The higher the price of a firm's output, the greater is the quantity of labour demanded by the firm, other things remaining the same. The price of output affects the demand for labour through its influence on marginal revenue product. A higher price for the firm's output increases marginal revenue which, in turn, increases the marginal revenue product of labour. A change in the price of a firm's output leads to a shift in the firm's demand for labour curve. If the output price increases, the demand for labour increases.

The other two influences on the demand for labour have their main effects not in the short run but in the long run. The *short-run demand for labour* is the relationship between the wage rate and the quantity of labour demanded when the firm's capital is fixed and labour is the only variable factor. The *long-run demand for labour* is the relationship between the wage rate and the quantity of labour demanded when all factors can be varied. A change in the relative price of factors of production—such as the relative price of labour and capital—leads to a substitution away from the factor whose relative price has increased and towards the factor whose relative price has decreased. Thus if the price of using capital decreases relative to that of using labour, the firm substitutes capital for labour, increasing the quantity of capital demanded and decreasing its demand for labour.

Finally, a new technology that influences the marginal product of labour also affects the demand for labour. For example, the development of electronic telephones with memories and a host of clever features decreased the marginal product of telephone operators and so decreased the demand for telephone operators. This same technological change increased the marginal product of telephone engineers and so increased the demand for telephone engineers. Again, these effects are felt in the long run when the firm adjusts all its factors and incorporates new technologies into its production process. Table 14.4 summarizes the influences on a firm's demand for labour.

We saw in Fig. 14.2 the effects of a change in the demand for a factor. We can now say why the demand for labour curve shifts. For example, an increase in the price of the firm's output, an increase

TABLE 14.4
A Firm's Demand for Labour

THE LAW OF DEMAND

The quantity of labour demanded by a firm

Decreases if:	*Increases if:*
■ The wage rate increases	■ The wage rate decreases

CHANGES IN DEMAND

A firm's demand for labour

Decreases if:	*Increases if:*
■ The firm's output price decreases	■ The firm's output price increases
■ The prices of other factors decrease	■ The prices of other factors increase
■ A new technology decreases the marginal product of labour	■ A new technology increases the marginal product of labour

in the price of capital, or a new technology that increases the marginal product of labour shifts the demand for labour curve from D_0 to D_1 in Fig. 14.2(a). Conversely, a decrease in the price of the firm's output, a decrease in the price of capital, or a new technology that lowers the marginal product of labour shifts the demand curve for labour from D_0 to D_2 in Fig. 14.2(b).

Market Demand

So far, we've studied only a firm's demand for labour. Let's now look at the market demand. The market demand for a factor is the total demand for that factor by all firms. Thus the market demand for labour curve is like the market demand curve for a good or service. The market demand curve for a good is obtained by adding together the quantities demanded of that good by all households at each price. The market demand curve for labour is obtained by adding together the quantities of labour demanded by all firms at each wage rate.

Elasticity of Demand for Labour

The elasticity of demand for labour measures the responsiveness of the quantity of labour demanded to the wage rate. We calculate this elasticity in the same way that we calculate a price elasticity: The elasticity of demand for labour equals the magnitude of the percentage change in the quantity of labour demanded divided by the percentage change in the wage rate.

The demand for labour is less elastic in the short run, when only labour can be varied, than in the long run, when labour and other factors can be varied. The elasticity of demand for labour depends on

- The labour intensity of the production process
- How rapidly the marginal product of labour diminishes
- The elasticity of demand for the product
- The substitutability of capital for labour

Labour Intensity   A labour-intensive production process is one that uses a lot of labour and little capital—a process that has a high ratio of labour to capital. Home building is an example. The larger the labour–capital ratio, the more elastic is the demand for labour, other things remaining the same. Let's see why.

If wages are 90 percent of total cost, a 10 percent increase in the wage rate increases total cost by 9 percent. Firms will be extremely sensitive to such a large change in total cost. If the wage rate increases, firms will decrease the quantity of labour demanded by a large amount. If wages are 10 percent of total cost, a 10 percent increase in the wage rate increases total cost by 1 percent. Firms will be less sensitive to this increase in cost. If wage rates increase in this case, firms will decrease the quantity of labour demanded by a small amount.

How Rapidly Marginal Product Diminishes   The more rapidly the marginal product of labour diminishes, the less elastic is the demand for labour, other things remaining the same. In some activities, marginal product diminishes quickly. For example, the marginal product of one bus driver is high, but the marginal product of a second driver on the same bus is close to zero. In other activities, marginal product diminishes slowly. For example, hiring a second window cleaner on a team almost doubles the amount of glass that can be cleaned in an hour—the marginal product of the second window cleaner is almost the same as the first.

The Elasticity of Demand for the Product   The greater the elasticity of demand for the good, the larger is the elasticity of demand for the factors of production used to produce it. To see why, think about what happens when the wage rate increases. An increase in the wage rate increases marginal cost and decreases the supply of the good. The decrease in the supply of the good increases the price of the good and decreases the quantity demanded of the good and the factors that produce it. The greater the elasticity of demand for the good, the larger is the decrease in the quantity demanded of the good and so the larger is the decrease in the quantities of the factors of production used to produce it.

The Substitutability of Capital for Labour   The substitutability of capital for labour influences the long-run elasticity of demand for labour but not the short-run elasticity. In the short run, capital is fixed. In the long run, capital can be varied, and the more easily capital can be substituted for labour in production, the more elastic is the long-run demand for labour. For example, it is fairly easy to substitute robots for assembly line workers in car factories and automatic picking machines for labour in vineyards and orchards. At the other extreme, it is difficult (though not impossible) to substitute robots for newspaper reporters, bank loan officers, and teachers. The more readily capital can be substituted for labour, the more elastic is the firm's demand for labour in the long run.

R E V I E W

- A firm chooses the quantity of labour to hire so that its profit is maximized.
- Profit is maximized when the marginal revenue product of labour equals the wage rate.
- The marginal revenue product of labour curve is the firm's demand for labour curve. The lower the wage rate, the greater is the quantity of labour demanded.
- The short-run elasticity of demand for labour depends on the labour intensity of production, how rapidly marginal product diminishes, and the elasticity of demand for the product.
- The long-run elasticity of demand for labour depends on these three conditions and on how easily capital can be substituted for labour.

Supply of Factors

THE SUPPLY OF FACTORS IS DETERMINED BY THE decisions of households. Households allocate the factors of production that they own to their most rewarding uses. The quantity supplied of any factor of production depends on its price. Usually, the higher the price of a factor of production, the larger is the quantity supplied. There is a possible exception to this general law of supply concerning the supply of labour. It arises from the fact that people have preferences about how they use their time.

Let's examine household factor supply decisions, beginning with the supply of labour.

Supply of Labour

A household chooses the number of hours per week of labour to supply as part of its time allocation decision. Time is allocated between two broad activities:

1. Market activity
2. Nonmarket activity

Market activity is the same thing as supplying labour. **Nonmarket activity** consists of everything else: leisure, nonmarket production activities including education and training, shopping, cooking, and other activities in the home. The household obtains a return from market activity in the form of a wage. Nonmarket activities generate a return in the form of goods and services produced in the home, a higher future income, or leisure, which is valued for its own sake and which is classified as a good.

In deciding how to allocate its time between market activity and nonmarket activity, a household weighs the returns that it can get from the different activities. We are interested in the effects of the wage rate on the household's allocation of its time and on how much labour it supplies.

Wages and Quantity of Labour Supplied To induce a household to supply labour, it must be offered a high enough wage rate. Nonmarket activities are valued by households either because the time is used in some productive activity or because of the value they attach to leisure. For it to be worthwhile to supply labour, a household has to be offered a wage rate that is at least equal to the value it places on the last hour it spends in nonmarket activities. This wage rate—the lowest one for which a household will supply labour to the market—is called its **reservation wage**. At wage rates below the reservation wage, the household supplies no labour. Once the wage rate reaches the reservation wage, the household begins to supply labour. As the wage rate rises above the reservation wage, the household varies the quantity of labour that it supplies. But a higher wage rate has two offsetting effects on the quantity of labour supplied—a *substitution effect* and an *income effect*.

Substitution Effect Other things remaining the same, the higher the wage rate, the more time people allocate to market activity and the less they allocate to nonmarket activities. Suppose, for example, that the market price of laundry services is $10 an hour. If the wage rate available to a household is less than $10 an hour, the household will provide its own laundry services—a nonmarket activity. If the household's wage rate rises above $10 an hour, it will be worthwhile for the household to work more hours and use part of its income to buy laundry services. The higher wage rate induces a switch of time from nonmarket activities to market activities.

Income Effect The higher the household's wage rate, the higher is its income. A higher income, other things remaining the same, induces a rise in demand for most goods. Leisure, a component of nonmarket activity, is one of those goods. Because an increase in income creates an increase in the demand for leisure, it also creates a decrease in the amount of time allocated to market activities and, therefore, to a fall in the quantity of labour supplied.

Backward-Bending Household Supply of Labour Curve The substitution effect and the income effect operate in opposite directions. The higher the wage rate, the higher is the quantity of labour supplied via the substitution effect but the lower is the quantity of labour supplied via the income effect. At low wage rates, the substitution effect is larger than the income effect. As the wage rate rises, the household supplies more labour. But as the wage rate continues to rise, there comes a point at which the substitution effect and the income effect just offset each other. At that point, a change in the wage rate has no effect on the quantity of labour supplied. If the wage rate continues to rise, the income effect begins to dominate the substitution effect and the quantity of labour supplied declines. The household's supply of labour curve does not slope upward throughout its entire length but begins to bend back on itself. It is called a *backward-bending supply curve.*

Figure 14.5(a) shows three individual household labour supply curves. Each household has a different reservation wage, and each household's labour supply curve is backward bending.

Market Supply   The quantity of labour supplied to the entire market is the total quantity supplied by all households. The market supply of labour curve is the sum of the supply curves of all the individual households. Figure 14.5(b) shows the market supply curve (S_M) derived from the supply curves of the three households (S_A, S_B, S_C) in Fig. 14.5(a). At wage rates of less than $1 an hour, the three households do only nonmarket activities such as laundry and cooking, and they do not supply any market labour. The household most eager to supply market labour has a reservation wage of $1 an hour. As the wage rate rises from $1 to $4 an hour, household A increases the quantity of labour that it supplies to the market. The reservation wage of household B is $4 an hour, so as the wage rate rises above $4 an hour, the quantity of labour supplied in the market is the sum of the labour supplied by households A and B. When the wage rate reaches $7 an hour, household C begins to supply some labour to the market. At wage rates above $7 an hour, the quantity supplied in the mar-

ket is equal to the sum of the quantities supplied by the three households.

Notice that the market supply curve S_M, like the individual household supply curves, eventually bends backward. But the market supply curve has a long upward-sloping section. The reason why the market supply curve slopes up for such a long stretch is that the reservation wage rates of individual households are not equal and at higher wage rates, additional households reach their reservation wage and so begin to supply labour.

Supply to Individual Firms   We've studied the labour supply decisions of individual households and seen how those decisions add up to the total market supply. But how is the supply of labour to each individual firm determined? The answer to this question depends on the degree of competitiveness in the labour market. In a perfectly competitive labour market (that we study here), each firm faces a perfectly elastic supply of labour. That is, the firm can hire any quantity of labour at the going market wage rate. This situation arises because the individual firm is such a small part of the total labour market that it has no influence on the wage rate.

FIGURE   14.5

The Supply of Labour

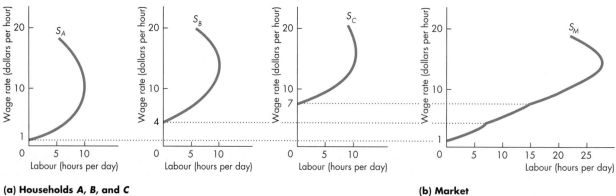

(a) Households A, B, and C

(b) Market

Part (a) shows the labour supply curves of three households (S_A, S_B, and S_C). Each household has a reservation wage below which it will supply no labour. As the wage rises, the quantity of labour supplied increases to a maximum. If the wage continues to rise, the quantity of labour supplied begins to decrease.

Each household's supply curve eventually bends backward. Part (b) shows how, by adding the quantities of labour supplied by the households at each wage rate, we derive the market supply curve of labour (S_M). The market supply curve has a long upward-sloping region before it bends backward.

REVIEW

- The labour supply curve is backward bending.
- The market supply of labour curve is the sum of the supply curves of individual households and is upward sloping.
- In a perfectly competitive labour market, each firm faces a perfectly elastic supply curve.

Supply of Capital

The supply of capital is more indirect than the supply of labour. It is determined by households' saving decisions. If households supplied capital in the same direct way that they supply labour, then all the buildings, machines, and other equipment would be owned by households and rented to firms. In fact, most capital is owned by firms, who in effect rent it to themselves. Households supply the funds, called *financial capital*, that firms use to buy capital. Households lend some of these funds to firms by buying their stocks and bonds and by making deposits in banks, which the banks lend to firms. Households also lend funds to firms in the form of retained earnings—profits that have not been paid out to the firms' owners, their stockholders.

The total amount of capital that firms can acquire and use depends on the total quantity of financial capital. This quantity is a *stock*—a quantity at a point in time. The stock of financial capital depends on the amounts that households have saved in previous years. Saving is a *flow*—a quantity per year—that adds to the stock of financial capital.

The most important factors determining a household's saving are

- Current income and expected future income
- The interest rate

Current Income and Expected Future Income
A household with a current income that is low compared with its expected future income saves little and might even have negative saving. A household with a current income that is high compared with its expected future income saves a great deal in the present in order to be able to consume more in the future. The stage in the household's life cycle is the main factor influencing whether current income is high or low compared with expected future income. Young house-

holds typically have a low current income compared with their expected future income, while older working households have a high current income relative to their expected future income. The consequence of this pattern in income over the life cycle is that young people have negative saving and older working people have positive saving. Thus the young incur debts (such as consumer credit) to acquire durable goods and to consume more than their income, while older working people save and accumulate assets (often in the form of pension and life insurance arrangements) to provide for their retirement years.

The Interest Rate   The interest rate is the opportunity cost of consuming in the current year rather than in the following year. If the interest rate is 10 percent a year, $100 consumed in the current year costs $110 of consumption in the following year. So by consuming $100 in the current year rather than in the following year, consumption falls by $10 or 10 percent of current consumption. Equivalently, $100 saved (not consumed) in the current year brings the possibility of increasing consumption by $110 in the following year—a net increase in consumption of $10 or 10 percent.

Other things remaining the same, the higher the interest rate, the greater is the amount of saving and the greater is the quantity of capital supplied. With a high interest rate, people have a strong incentive to cut consumption and increase their saving in order to take advantage of the high returns available. With a low interest rate, people have only a weak incentive to cut their consumption and save.

The Supply Curve of Capital

The quantity of capital supplied in the market is the sum of the quantities supplied by all the individual households. The market supply curve of capital shows how the quantity of capital supplied varies as the interest rate varies. In the short run, the supply of capital is inelastic and might even be perfectly inelastic. The vertical supply curve *SS* in Fig. 14.6 illustrates such a case. The reason is that households find it difficult to change their consumption plans quickly in response to changes in the interest rate. But given sufficient time to make the necessary substitutions, they do respond to a change in the interest rate. As a result, the long-run supply of capital is much more elastic. The supply curve *LS* in Fig. 14.6 illustrates such a case.

FIGURE   14.6

Short-Run and Long-Run Supply of Capital

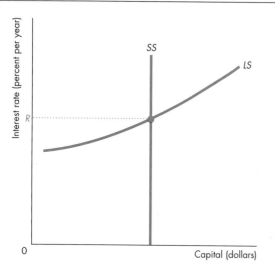

The long-run supply of capital (*LS*) is highly elastic. In the long run, if the interest rate is above *R*, households increase their saving and the quantity of capital supplied increases. Also, in the long run, if the interest rate is below *R*, households decrease their saving and the quantity of capital supplied decreases. The short-run supply of capital (*SS*) is inelastic (perfectly inelastic in the figure). In the short run, there is a fixed amount of capital and this quantity cannot be varied, no matter what the interest rate.

Supply to Individual Firms   In the short run, a firm can vary its labour but not its capital. Thus in the short run, the firm's supply of capital is fixed. It has a specific set of capital assets. For example, an auto producer has a production assembly line; a laundromat operator has a number of washing machines and dryers; the campus print shop has a number of photocopying and other printing machines. These pieces of capital cannot be quickly disposed of or added to.

In the long run, a firm can vary all its factors—capital as well as labour. A firm operating in a competitive capital market can obtain any amount of capital it chooses at the going market interest rate. Thus it faces a perfectly elastic supply of capital.

Let's complete our analysis of the supply of factors of production by examining the supply of land.

Supply of Land

Land is the stock of natural resources and its aggregate quantity supplied cannot be changed by any individual decisions. Individual households can vary the amount of land they own, but whatever land is acquired by one household is sold by another so that the aggregate quantity of land supplied of any particular type and in any particular location is fixed regardless of the decisions of any individual household. This fact means that the supply of each particular piece of land is perfectly inelastic. Figure 14.7 illustrates such a supply. Regardless of the rent available, the quantity of land supplied in Toronto's Yorkville is a fixed number of square metres.

Expensive land can be, and is, used more intensively than inexpensive land. For example, high-rise buildings enable land to be used more intensively. However, to use land more intensively, it has to be combined with another factor of production—capital. Increasing the amount of capital per block of land does not change the supply of land itself. But it does enable land to become more productive. A rising price of land strengthens the incentive to find ways of increasing its

FIGURE   14.7

The Supply of Land

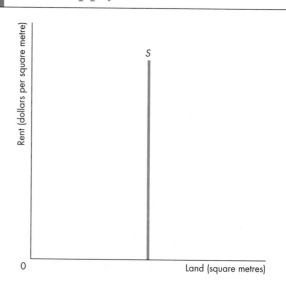

The supply of a given piece of land is perfectly inelastic. No matter what the rent, no more land than the quantity that exists can be supplied.

productivity. These issues are explored more fully in *Economics in History* on pp. 342–343.

Although the supply of each type of land is fixed and its supply is perfectly inelastic, each individual firm, operating in competitive land markets, faces an elastic supply of land. For example, Bloor Street in Toronto has a fixed amount of land, but Eddie Bauer, the leisure clothing store, could rent some space from The Bay, the department store. Each firm can rent the quantity of land that it demands at the going rent, which is determined in the marketplace. Thus provided land markets are highly competitive, firms are price takers in these markets, just as they are in the markets for other factors of production.

R E V I E W

■ The supply of capital is determined by households' saving decisions.

■ Other things remaining the same, the higher the interest rate, the greater is the amount of capital supplied. The supply of capital to individual firms is inelastic in the short run but perfectly elastic in the long run.

■ The supply of land is fixed—is perfectly inelastic. But the supply of land to individual firms is elastic.

We've now seen how demand and supply in factor markets determine incomes, and we've probed more deeply into the influences on the demand for and supply of factors of production. Let's now use what we've learned to see why some factors of production earn high incomes and others earn low ones. Let's also learn about economic rent and transfer earnings.

Incomes, Economic Rent, and Transfer Earnings

WE SAW AT THE BEGINNING OF THIS CHAPTER— in Figs. 14.1, 14.2, and 14.3—that the price of a factor of production and the quantity of it used are determined by the interaction of demand and supply. We've seen that demand is determined by marginal productivity and supply is determined by the resources available and by households' choices about their use. The interaction of demand and supply in factor markets determines who receives a large income and who receives a small income.

Large and Small Incomes

Why does an all-star basketball player earn a large income? It is because such a person has a very high marginal revenue product—reflected in the demand for his or her services—and the supply of people with the combination of talents needed for this kind of job is small—reflected in the supply. Equilibrium occurs at a high wage rate and a small quantity employed.

Why do McJobs pay low wages? It is because they have a low marginal revenue product—reflected in the demand—and there are many households able and willing to supply their labour for these jobs. Equilibrium occurs at a low wage rate and a large quantity employed.

If the demand for all-star basketball players increases, their incomes increase by a large amount and the number of all-star basketball players barely changes. If the demand for workers in McJobs increases, the number of people doing these jobs increases by a large amount and the wage rate barely changes.

The demand for a block of land is determined by its marginal revenue product. The marginal revenue product in turn depends on the uses to which the land can be put. In a central business district such as Vancouver, the marginal revenue product is high because a large number of people are concentrated in that area, making it a prime place for conducting business.

The rent charged for this piece of land depends entirely on its marginal revenue product—the demand curve. If the demand curve shifts rightward, the rent rises. If the demand curve shifts leftward, the rent falls. The quantity of land supplied remains constant.

Is coffee expensive in Vancouver because land rents are high or are land rents high because people in Vancouver are willing to pay a high price for coffee? If you asked McDonald's financial director this question, the answer you would get is that McDonald's charges a high price for coffee at its restaurant in the Vancouver business district because the rent they pay for the land is high. But this answer is not deep enough. The rent is high because McDonald's marginal revenue product of that land is high. That is, the rent of a Vancouver city block is determined by the demand for it and that demand, in turn, is determined by its marginal revenue product. Land has a high marginal revenue product because someone is willing to pay a high rent to use the land.

You can get a further insight into people's incomes by learning about the distinction between economic rent and transfer earnings.

Economic Rent and Transfer Earnings

The total income of a factor of production is made up of its economic rent and its transfer earnings. **Economic rent** is the income received by the owner of a factor over and above the amount required to induce that owner to offer the factor for use. Any factor of production can receive an economic rent. The income required to induce the supply of a factor of production is called transfer earnings. **Transfer earnings** are the opportunity cost of using a factor of production—the value of the factor in its next best use.

Figure 14.8 illustrates the concepts of economic rent and transfer earnings. The figure shows the market for a factor of production. It could be *any* factor of production—labour, capital, land, or entrepreneurship. The demand curve for the factor of production is *D*, and its supply curve is *S*. The factor price is *PF*, and the quantity of the factor used is *QF*. The income of the factor is the sum of the yellow and green areas. The yellow area below the supply curve measures transfer earnings, and the green area below the factor price but above the supply curve measures economic rent.

To see why the area below the supply curve measures transfer earnings, recall that a supply curve can be interpreted in two different ways. One interpretation is that a supply curve indicates the quantity supplied at a given price. But the alternative interpretation of a supply curve is that it shows the minimum price at which a given quantity is willingly supplied. If suppliers receive only the minimum amount required to induce them to supply each unit of the factor of production, they will be paid a different price for each unit. The prices will trace the supply curve, and the income received is entirely transfer earnings—the yellow area in Fig. 14.8.

The concept of economic rent is similar to the concept of consumer surplus that you met in Chapter 7, pp. 160–161. Recall that consumer surplus is the difference between the price the household pays for a good and the maximum price it would be willing to pay, as indicated by the demand curve. In a parallel sense, economic rent is the difference between the factor price a household actually receives and the minimum factor price at which it would be willing to supply a given amount of a factor of production.

Economic rent is not the same thing as *rent*. Rent is the price paid for the services of land. Economic rent is a component of the income received by any factor of production.

The portion of the income of a factor of production that consists of economic rent depends on the elasticity of the supply of the factor of production. When the supply of a factor of production is perfectly inelastic, its entire income is economic rent. Most of Garth Brooks' and Pearl Jam's income is economic rent. Also, a large part of the income of a major league baseball player is economic rent. When the supply of a factor of production is perfectly elastic, none of its income is economic rent. Most of the income of a babysitter is transfer earnings. In general, when the supply curve is neither perfectly elastic nor perfectly inelastic (like that illustrated in Fig. 14.8), some part of the factor income is economic rent and the other part transfer earnings.

Figure 14.9 illustrates the three possibilities. Part (a) of the figure shows the market for a particular parcel of land in Yorkville. The land is fixed in size at *L* square metres. Therefore the supply curve of the land is vertical—perfectly inelastic. No matter what

FIGURE 14.8
Economic Rent and Transfer Earnings

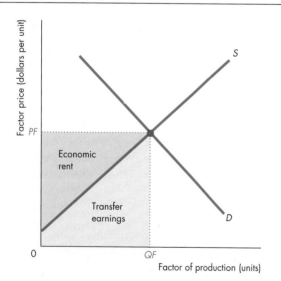

The total income of a factor of production is made up of its economic rent and its transfer earnings. Transfer earnings are measured by the yellow area under the supply curve, and economic rent is measured by the green area above the supply curve and below the factor price.

FIGURE 14.9

Economic Rent and Supply Elasticity

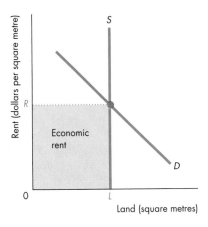

(a) All economic rent

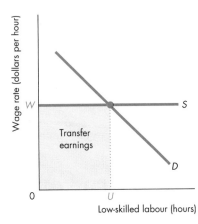

(b) All transfer earnings

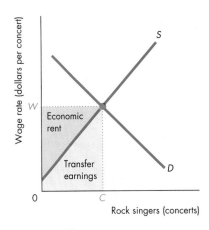

(c) Intermediate case

When the supply of a factor of production is perfectly inelastic (the supply curve is vertical), as in part (a), the entire factor income is economic rent. When the supply of the factor of production is perfectly elastic, as in part (b), the factor's entire income is transfer earnings. When a factor supply curve slopes upward, as in part (c), part of the factor income is economic rent and part is transfer earnings. Land is the example shown in part (a); low-skilled labour in poor countries such as India and China in part (b); and rock singers in part (c).

the rent on the land is, there is no way of increasing the quantity that can be supplied.

Suppose that the marginal revenue product of this block of land is shown by the demand curve in Fig. 14.9(a). Then it commands a rent of *R*. The entire income accruing to the owner of the land is the green area in the figure. This income is *economic rent*.

Figure 14.9(b) shows the market for a factor of production that is in perfectly elastic supply. An example of such a market might be that for low-skilled labour in a poor country such as India or China. In those countries, large amounts of labour flock to the cities and are available for work at the going wage rate (in this case, *W*). Thus in these situations the supply of labour is almost perfectly elastic. The entire income earned by this labour is transfer earnings. They receive no economic rent.

Figure 14.9(c) shows the market for rock singers. To induce rock singers to sing at a larger number of concerts, a higher income has to be offered—the supply curve of rock singers is upward sloping. The demand curve—measuring the marginal revenue product of the rock singer—is labelled *D* in the figure. Equilibrium occurs where rock singers receive a

wage of *W* and sing in *C* concerts. The green area above the rock singers' supply curve is economic rent, and the yellow area below the supply curve is the rock singers' transfer earnings. If rock singers are not offered at least the amount of the transfer earnings, then the singers will withdraw from the rock concert market and perform other alternative activities, such as recording CDs or teaching singing.

◆ We've seen how demand and supply determine factor prices and factor incomes. We've also seen how changes in demand and supply bring changes in factor prices and incomes. And we've seen the crucial role played by a factor's marginal revenue product. Finally, we've distinguished between economic rent and transfer earnings. Economic rent is a crucial element in the incomes of big earners such as movie stars and sports stars, as you can see in *Reading Between the Lines* on pp. 336–337.

In the next chapter, we're going to examine labour markets more closely and explain differences in wage rates among high- and low-skilled workers and between males and females.

Rents and Transfer Earnings on the Ice

GLOBE AND MAIL, SEPTEMBER 20, 1995

NHL pay raises still concern GMs

BY ALAN ADAMS

Two militants on the front line of last year's National Hockey League labour war say the 105-day lockout hasn't slowed troubling salary escalation.

Boston general manager Harry Sinden and his Edmonton counterpart, Glen Sather, say salaries are still rising too quickly and they doubt whether their peers will stop the increases.

"Obviously what happened last year didn't correct anything," Sather said. "I still think salaries are out of control."

Sinden fears other general managers won't use concessions won in the lockout in negotiating contracts.

"I think we will have the same amount of increase if not more (than last season)."

It was a year ago when owners insisted they needed a drag on salaries. In resolving the lockout, owners earned concessions to be used to hold salaries down, such as some players losing arbitration rights, restrictions on some free agents and a rookie salary cap.

"I have no reason to believe we know how to use them," Sinden said.

Last year's average salary was $730,000 and will be more than $800,000 this year, given some recent signings.

Before trading Sergei Zubov to Pittsburgh, the New York Rangers hiked his salary to $1.6-million (U.S.) from $275,000—a 482-per-cent increase.

St. Louis signed free agent Shayne Corson for $2.395-million— a 286-per-cent raise from the $850,000 (Canadian) Corson earned last year with Edmonton. Then the Blues gave Dale Hawerchuk $2.5-million (U.S.) for this season—89 per cent more than he made last year with Buffalo.

Even Sinden gave triple-digit increases to some Bruins—Ted Donato (200 per cent to $525,000), Kevin Stevens (123 per cent to $2.92-million) and Cam Neely (150 per cent to $2.5-million). ...

However, not everyone is cashing in. Marquee free agents like Trevor Linden, Curtis Joseph and Theo Fleury are still without jobs, as are veterans like Peter Zezel and Ron Tugnutt.

With just over three weeks to go before the season opens, money remains a hot topic at NHL rinks.

Reprinted with permission from *The Globe and Mail*.

Essence of THE STORY

■ The average NHL salary in 1994–1995 was $730,000. In 1995–1996, it was more than $800,000.

■ General managers Harry Sinden of Boston and Glen Sather of Edmonton say players' salaries are rising too quickly and the general managers can't stop the increases.

■ The New York Rangers hiked Sergei Zubov's salary to $1.6 million (U.S.) from $275,000—a 482 percent increase.

■ St. Louis pays Shayne Corson $2.395 million a year, up 286 percent from the $850,000 (Canadian) he earned the previous year with Edmonton.

■ The Blues pay Dale Hawerchuk $2.5 million (U.S.), 89 percent more than he made with Buffalo.

■ Sinden gave triple-digit increases to Ted Donato (200 percent to $525,000), Kevin Stevens (123 percent to $2.92 million), and Cam Neely (150 percent to $2.5 million).

Economic

A N A L Y S I S

■ The marginal revenue product of players of the quality of Shayne Corson, Dale Hawerchuk, and Cam Neely is enormous.

■ These players fill stadiums and generate huge revenues for their clubs.

■ The supply of top-performing hockey players is limited. At a wage rate below the minimum industrial wage, no one would be willing to work and train to perform at the standard of these players. The quantity supplied would be zero.

■ At a wage rate similar to the average industrial wage, a large number of people are willing to work and train to play competition quality hockey. But few have the talent to perform at the level of a Corson, Hawerchuk, or Neely.

■ No matter by how much the wage rate rises above the average industrial wage, the quantity of top performers does not increase. The supply is inelastic.

■ Figure I shows the supply of top-performing hockey players as the curve labelled S. The average industrial wage rate is a. As the wage rate for

hockey increases above this wage rate, the quantity of star players supplied increases, but up to a maximum of Q_0. This quantity is limited by the available talent pool.

■ The demand for top-performing players is determined by their marginal revenue product and is the curve D.

■ Equilibrium in the market for top-performing hockey players occurs when the wage rate is (an average of) $800,000 a year.

■ Most of this income is *economic rent*, which is shown as the green area. The rest, shown by the yellow area, is *transfer earnings*.

■ Figure 2 shows the situation facing an individual hockey club. The club faces a perfectly elastic supply of top-performing players shown by the curve S_i. The club's demand curve is D_i, and the club hired Q_i top-performing players.

■ If the clubs could collude, they might be able to keep players' wages down. But competition for the best players means that each club must pay the going market wage for its talent.

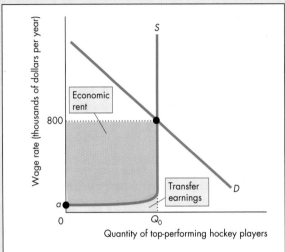

Figure 1 The market for hockey superstars

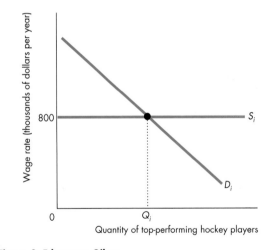

Figure 2 Edmonton Oilers

S U M M A R Y

Key Points

Factor Prices and Incomes   Factor prices are determined by the demand for and supply of factors of production. Incomes are determined by factor prices and the quantities of factors of production used. An increase in the demand for a factor of production increases its price and income. An increase in the supply of a factor of production decreases its price, increases the quantity used, and has an ambiguous effect on income. The effect depends on the elasticity of demand. (pp. 320–322)

Demand for Factors   A firm maximizes profit by hiring the quantity of a factor of production that makes the marginal revenue product of the factor equal to the factor's price. Firms can vary the amount of labour hired in both the short run and the long run, but they can vary the amount of capital used only in the long run. The short-run elasticity of demand for labour depends on the labour intensity of the production process, on how rapidly the marginal product of labour diminishes, and on the elasticity of demand for the firm's product. The long-run elasticity of demand for labour depends on these three conditions and on the ease with which capital can be substituted for labour. (pp. 323–328)

Supply of Factors   In choosing how much time to allocate to market activities, each household compares the wage rate that can be earned with the value of its time in nonmarket activities. At wage rates above the household's reservation wage, the quantity of labour supplied increases as long as the substitution effect of the higher wage rate is larger than the income effect. As the wage rate continues to rise, the income effect becomes larger than the substitution effect, and the quantity of labour supplied by the household decreases. Households supply capital by saving and firms use financial capital to buy physical capital. Saving and the quantity of capital supplied increase as the interest rate increases. The supply of capital to an individual firm is highly inelastic in the short run but highly elastic in the long run. The supply of land is fixed and independent of its rent. But the supply of land to individual firms is elastic. (pp. 329–333)

Incomes, Economic Rent, and Transfer Earnings   The price of a factor is high if the factor has a high marginal revenue product and a low supply. The price of a factor is low if the factor has a low marginal revenue product and a high supply. Economic rent is that part of the income received by a factor owner over and above the amount needed to induce the owner to supply the factor of production for use. The rest of a factor's income is transfer earnings. Transfer earnings are opportunity costs but economic rent is not. When the supply of a factor is perfectly inelastic, its entire income is made up of economic rent. Factors that have a perfectly elastic supply receive only transfer earnings. In general, the supply curve of a factor is upward sloping, and part of its income is transfer earnings (below the supply curve) and part is economic rent (above the supply curve but below the factor price). (pp. 333–335)

Key Figures and Tables

Key Terms

R E V I E W   Q U E S T I O N S

1. Explain what happens to the price of a factor of production and its income if the following occurs:
   a. The demand for the factor increases.
   b. The supply of the factor increases.
   c. The demand for the factor decreases.
   d. The supply of the factor decreases.
2. Explain why the effect of a change in supply of a factor on a factor's income depends on the elasticity of demand for the factor.
3. Define marginal revenue product and distinguish between marginal revenue product and marginal revenue.
4. Why does marginal revenue product decline as the quantity of a factor employed increases?
5. What is the relationship between the demand curve for a factor of production and its marginal revenue product curve? Why?
6. Show that the condition for maximum profit in the product market—marginal cost equals marginal revenue—is equivalent to the condition for maximum profit in the factor market—marginal revenue product equals marginal cost of factor (equals factor price in a competitive factor market).

7. Review the main influences on the demand for a factor of production—the influences that shift the demand curve for a factor.
8. What determines the short-run and the long-run elasticity of demand for labour?
9. What determines the supply of labour?
10. Why might the supply of labour curve bend backward at a high enough wage rate?
11. Explain why all-star basketball players receive such high salaries.
12. Explain why fast-food servers receive such low salaries.
13. What determines the supply of capital?
14. Explain why the supply of capital is more elastic in the long run than in the short run.
15. Explain why the rent on a block of land is determined by its marginal revenue product.
16. Define economic rent and transfer earnings and distinguish between these two components of income.
17. Suppose that a factor of production is in perfectly inelastic supply. If the marginal revenue product of the factor decreases, what happens to its price, quantity used, income, transfer earnings, and rent of the factor?

C R I T I C A L   T H I N K I N G

1. Study *Reading Between the Lines* on pp. 336–337 and answer the following questions:
   a. Why do the best hockey players have a high marginal revenue product?
   b. Why can't club owners pay players their transfer earnings?
   c. Suppose a special income tax was imposed on sports superstars. Aside from the outcry, what effect would the tax have on the wage rate paid by the clubs and the after-tax pay earned by the players?
2. Why do students who work at McJobs earn less than Damon Stoudamire?
3. Why does a square metre of land in Toronto's Yorkville cost so much more than a square metre of farmland in Manitoba?

4. Why do people protest when farmland on the edge of cities is used for suburban houses?
5. To win, the whole team has to play. So why aren't all members of a hockey team, a football team, or a baseball team paid the same salary?
6. What information do you need to be able to calculate the economic rent that Damon Stoudamire receives?
7. At the Olympic games held in Atlanta, Singapore paid each of its gold medallists almost $1 million, Australia paid only $25,000, and Canada paid nothing. What do you think determines the amount of money that governments around the world are willing to pay their gold medallists?

P R O B L E M S

1. The figure illustrates the market for blueberry pickers:

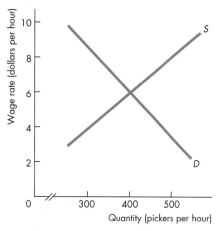

a. What is the wage rate paid to blueberry pickers?
b. How many blueberry pickers get hired?
c. What is the income received by blueberry pickers?
d. What is the marginal revenue product of blueberry pickers?
e. If the price of blueberries is $1 a carton, what is the marginal product of the last picker hired?

2. In problem 1, show on the figure the pickers'
a. Economic rent.
b. Transfer earnings.

3. In problem 1, if the demand for blueberry pickers increases by 100 a day,
a. What is the increase in the wage rate paid to the pickers?
b. How many additional pickers get hired?
c. What is the total income paid to pickers?
d. What now is the pickers' economic rent?
e. What now is the pickers' transfer earnings?

4. Wanda owns a fish shop. She employs students to sort and pack the fish. Students can pack the following amounts of fish in an hour:

Number of students	Quantity of fish (kilograms)
1	20
2	50
3	90
4	120
5	145
6	165
7	180
8	190

a. Draw the average and marginal product curves of these students.
b. If Wanda can sell her fish for 50¢ a kilogram, draw the average and marginal revenue product curves.
c. Draw Wanda's demand for labour curve.
d. If all fish shops in Wanda's area pay their packers $7.50 an hour, how many students will Wanda employ?

5. If , in problem 4, the price of fish falls to 33.33¢ a kilogram and fish packers' wages remain at $7.50 an hour, what happens to
a. Wanda's average and marginal product curves?
b. Wanda's average and marginal revenue product curves?
c. Wanda's demand for labour curve?
d. The number of students that Wanda employs?

6. If, in problem 4, fish packers' wages increase to $10 an hour but the price of fish remains at 50¢ a kilogram,
a. What happens to the average and marginal revenue product curves?
b. What happens to Wanda's demand curve?
c. How many pickers does Wanda hire?

7. Using the information provided in problem 4, calculate Wanda's marginal revenue and marginal cost, marginal revenue product, and marginal cost of labour. Show that when Wanda is making maximum profit, marginal cost equals marginal revenue and marginal revenue product equals the marginal cost of labour.

8. You are given the following information about the labour market in an isolated town in the Amazon rainforest: Everyone works for logging companies, but there are many logging companies in the town. The market for logging workers is perfectly competitive. The town's labour supply is given as follows:

Wage rate (cruzeiros per hour)	Quantity of labour supplied (hours)
200	120
300	160
400	200
500	240
600	280
700	320
800	360

The market demand for labour from all the logging firms in the town is as follows:

Wage rate (cruzeiros per hour)	Quantity of labour demanded (hours)
200	400
300	360
400	320
500	280
600	240
700	200
800	160

a. What is the competitive equilibrium wage rate and the quantity of labour employed?

b. What is total labour income?

c. How much of that labour income is economic rent and how much is transfer earnings? (You may find it easier to answer this question by drawing graphs of the demand and supply curves and then finding the economic rent and transfer earnings as areas on the graph in a manner similar to what was done in Fig. 14.8.)

"*Men, like all animals, naturally multiply in proportion to the means of their subsistence.*"

ADAM SMITH, *THE WEALTH OF NATIONS*

Running Out of Resources?

Is there a limit to economic growth, or can we expand production and population without effective limit? One of the most influential answers to these questions was given by Thomas Malthus in 1798. He believed that population, unchecked, would grow at a geometric rate—1, 2, 4, 8, 16, ..., while the food supply would grow at an arithmetic rate—1, 2, 3, 4, 5, ... To prevent the population from outstripping the available food supply, there would be periodic wars, famines, and plagues. In Malthus's view, only a change in the moral code by which people live could prevent such periodic disasters.

As industrialization proceeded through the nineteenth century, Malthus's idea came to be applied to all natural resources, especially those that are exhaustible. A modern-day Malthusian, ecologist Paul Ehrlich, believes that we are sitting on a "population bomb" and that the government must limit both population growth and the resources that may be used each year.

In 1931, Harold Hotelling developed a theory of natural resources with different predications from those of Malthus. The Hotelling Principle is that the relative price of an exhaustible natural resource will steadily rise, bringing a decline in the quantity used and an increase in the use of substitute resources.

Julian Simon, a contemporary economist, has challenged both the Malthusian gloom and the Hotelling Principle. He believes that *people* are the "ultimate resource," and predicts that a rising population *lessens* the pressure on natural resources. A bigger population provides a larger number of resourceful people who can work out more efficient ways of using scarce resources. As these solutions are found, the prices of exhaustible resources actually fall. To demonstrate his point, in 1980, Simon bet Ehrlich that the prices of five metals—copper, chrome, nickel, tin, and tungsten—would fall during the 1980s. Simon won the bet!

THEN . . .

NO MATTER whether it is agricultural land, an exhaustible natural resource, or Place Jacques-Cartier on market day and no matter whether it is 1997 or, as shown here, 1927, there is a limit to what is available, and we persistently push against that limit. Economists see urban congestion as a consequence of the value of doing business in the city centre relative to the cost. They see the price mechanism, bringing ever higher rents and prices of raw materials, as the means of allocating and rationing scarce natural resources. Malthusians, in contrast, explain congestion as the consequence of population pressure, and they see population control as the solution.

HUNT.

In Tokyo, the pressure on space is so great that in some residential neighbourhoods, a parking space costs $1,700 a month. To economize on this expensive space—and to lower the cost of car ownership and hence boost car sales—Honda, Nissan, and Toyota, three of Japan's big car producers, have developed a parking machine that enables two cars to occupy the space of one. The most basic of these machines costs a mere $10,000—less than 6 months' parking fees.

Thomas Robert Malthus

THE ECONOMISTS: THOMAS ROBERT MALTHUS AND HAROLD HOTELLING

Thomas Robert Malthus (1766–1834), an English parson and professor, was an extremely influential social scientist. In his best-selling *Essay on the Principle of Population*, published in 1798, he argued that population growth would outstrip food production. Modern-day Malthusians believe that his basic idea was right and that it applies to all natural resources.

The most profound work on the economics of natural resources is that of Harold Hotelling (1895–1973). Hotelling worked as a journalist, schoolteacher, and mathematical consultant before becoming an economics professor at Columbia University. He explained how the price mechanism allocates exhaustible resources, making them progressively more expensive. Their higher price encourages the development of new technologies, the discovery of new sources of supply, and the development of substitutes.

Harold Hotelling

After studying
this chapter,
you will be
able to:

- Explain why high-skilled workers earn
  more, on the average, than low-skilled
  workers

- Explain why university and college
  graduates earn more, on the average, than
  high school graduates

- Explain why union workers earn higher
  wages than nonunion workers

- Explain why, on the average, men earn
  more than women

- Predict the effects of pay equity legislation

As you well know, school is not just a party. Those exams and problem sets require a lot of time and effort. Are they worth the sweat that goes into them? What is the payoff? Is it sufficient to make up for the years of tuition, room and board, and lost wages? (You could, after all, be working now instead of slogging

The Sweat of Our Brows

through this economics course.) ◆ Many workers belong to labour unions. Usually, union workers earn a higher wage than nonunion workers in comparable jobs. Why? How are unions able to get higher wages for their members than the wages that nonunion workers are paid? ◆ Among the most visible and persistent differences in earnings are those between men and women. Men, on the average, earn incomes that are one-third higher than the incomes earned by women. Certainly a lot of individuals defy the averages. But why do women so consistently earn less than men? Is it because of discrimination and exploitation? Or is it because of economic factors? Or is it a combination of the two? ◆ Equal pay legislation has resulted in programs that try to ensure that jobs of equivalent value receive the same pay regardless of the pay set by the market. Can pay equity laws bring economic help to women?

◇ In this chapter, we answer questions such as these by continuing our study of labour markets. We begin by extending the competitive labour market model developed in Chapter 14 to analyse the effects of education and training on wages. We then study differences in union and nonunion wages and in pay between men and women. Finally, we analyse the effects of pay equity laws.

Skill Differentials

EVERYONE IS SKILLED BUT THE VALUE THE MARKET places on different types of skills varies a great deal so that differences in skills lead to large differences in earnings. For example, a clerk in a law firm earns less than a tenth of the earnings of the lawyer he assists. An operating room assistant earns less than a tenth of the earnings of the surgeon she works with. Differences in skills arise partly from differences in education and partly from differences in on-the-job training. Differences in earnings between workers with varying levels of education and training can be explained by using a model of competitive labour markets. In the real world, there are many different levels and varieties of education and training. To keep our analysis as clear as possible, we'll study a model economy in which there are just two different levels that result in two types of labour: high-skilled labour and low-skilled labour. We'll study the demand for and supply of these two types of labour and see why there is a difference in their wages and what determines that difference. Let's begin by looking at the demand for the two types of labour.

The Demand for High-Skilled and Low-Skilled Labour

High-skilled workers can perform a wide variety of tasks that low-skilled workers would perform badly or perhaps could not even perform at all. Imagine an untrained, inexperienced person performing surgery or piloting an airplane. High-skilled workers have a higher marginal revenue product than low-skilled workers. As we learned in Chapter 14, the demand for labour curve is derived from the marginal revenue product curve.

Figure 15.1(a) shows the demand curves for high-skilled and low-skilled labour. At any given level of employment, firms are willing to pay a higher wage to a high-skilled worker than to a low-skilled worker. The gap between the two wages is the difference between the marginal revenue products of a given number of high-skilled and low-skilled workers. This difference is the marginal revenue product of skill. For example, at an employment level of 2,000 hours, firms are willing to pay $12.50 for a high-skilled worker and only $5 for a low-skilled worker. The difference in the marginal revenue product of the two workers is $7.50 an hour. Thus the marginal revenue product of skill is $7.50 an hour.

The Supply of High-Skilled and Low-Skilled Labour

Skills are costly to acquire. Furthermore, a worker usually pays the cost of acquiring a skill before benefiting from a higher wage. For example, attending college or university usually leads to a higher income, but the higher income is not earned until after graduation. These facts imply that the acquisition of a skill is an investment. To emphasize the investment nature of acquiring a skill, we call that activity an investment in human capital. **Human capital** is the accumulated skill and knowledge of human beings.

The opportunity cost of acquiring a skill includes actual expenditures on such things as tuition and room and board, and also costs in the form of lost or reduced earnings while the skill is being acquired. When a person goes to school full time, that cost is the total earnings forgone. However, some people acquire skills on the job. Such skill acquisition is called on-the-job training. Usually a worker undergoing on-the-job training is paid a lower wage than one doing a comparable job but not undergoing training. In such a case, the cost of acquiring the skill is the difference between the wage paid to a person not being trained and that paid to a person being trained.

Supply Curves of High-Skilled and Low-Skilled Labour   The position of the supply curve of high-skilled workers reflects the cost of acquiring the skill. Figure 15.1(b) shows two supply curves, one for high-skilled workers and the other for low-skilled workers. The supply curve of high-skilled workers is S_H and of low-skilled workers S_L.

The high-skilled worker's supply curve lies above the low-skilled worker's supply curve. The vertical distance between the two supply curves is the compensation that high-skilled workers require for the cost of acquiring the skill. For example, suppose that the quantity of low-skilled labour supplied is 2,000 hours at a wage rate of $5 an hour. This wage rate compensates the low-skilled workers purely for their time on the job. Consider next the supply of high-skilled workers. To induce 2,000 hours of high-skilled labour to be supplied, firms must pay a wage rate of $8.50 an hour. This wage rate for high-skilled labour is higher than that for low-skilled labour because high-skilled labour must be compensated not only for the time on the job but also for the time and other costs of acquiring the skill.

FIGURE 15.1
Skill Differentials

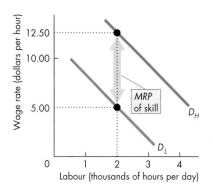

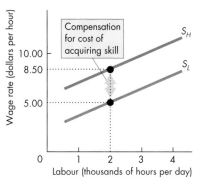

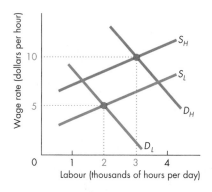

(a) Demand for high-skilled and low-skilled labour

(b) Supply of high-skilled and low-skilled labour

(c) Markets for high-skilled and low-skilled labour

Part (a) illustrates the marginal revenue product of skill. Low-skilled workers have a marginal revenue product that gives rise to the demand curve marked D_L. High-skilled workers have a higher marginal revenue product than low-skilled workers. Therefore the demand curve for high-skilled workers, D_H, lies to the right of D_L. The vertical distance between these two curves is the marginal revenue product of the skill.

Part (b) shows the effects of the cost of acquiring skills on the supply curves of labour. The supply curve for low-skilled workrs is S_L. The supply curve for high-skilled workers is S_H. The vertical distance between these two curves is the required compensation for the cost of acquiring a skill.

Part (c) shows the equilibrium employment and wage differential. Low-skilled workers earn a wage rate of $5 an hour and 2,000 hours of low-skilled workers are employed. High-skilled workers earn the wage rate $10 an hour and 3,000 hours of high-skilled workers are employed. The wage rate for high-skilled workers is always greater than that for low-skilled workers.

Wage Rates of High-Skilled and Low-Skilled Labour

To work out the wage rates of high-skilled and low-skilled labour, all we have to do is bring together the effects of skill on the demand for and supply of labour.

Figure 15.1(c) shows the demand curves and the supply curves for high-skilled and low-skilled labour. These curves are exactly the same as those plotted in parts (a) and (b). Equilibrium occurs in the market for low-skilled labour where the supply and demand curves for low-skilled labour intersect. The equilibrium wage rate is $5 an hour and the quantity of low-skilled labour employed is 2,000 hours. Equilibrium in the market for high-skilled workers occurs where the supply and demand curves for high-skilled workers intersect. The equilibrium wage rate is $10 an hour and the quantity of high-skilled labour employed is 3,000 hours.

As you can see in part (c), the equilibrium wage rate of high-skilled labour is higher than that of low-skilled labour. There are two reasons why this occurs: First, high-skilled labour has a higher marginal revenue product than low-skilled labour, so at a given wage rate the demand for high-skilled labour is greater than the demand for low-skilled labour. Second, skills are costly to acquire so that at a given wage rate the supply of high-skilled labour is less than the supply of low-skilled labour. The wage differential (in this case, $5 an hour) depends on both the marginal revenue product of the skill and the cost of acquiring it. The higher the marginal revenue product of the skill, the larger is the vertical distance between the demand curves for high-skilled and low-skilled labour. The more costly it is to acquire a skill, the larger is the vertical distance between the supplies of high-skilled and low-skilled labour. The larger the marginal revenue product of the skill and the more costly it is to acquire, the larger is the wage differential between high-skilled and low-skilled workers.

Do Education and Training Pay?

There are large and persistent differences in earnings based on the degree of education and training. An indication of those differences can be seen in Fig. 15.2. This figure highlights two important sources of earnings differences. The first is the degree of education itself. The higher the level of education, other things remaining the same, the higher are a person's earnings. The second source of earnings differences apparent in Fig. 15.2 is age. Age is strongly correlated with experience and the degree of on-the-job training a person has had. Thus as a person gets older, up to middle age, earnings increase.

We can see from Fig. 15.2 that going through high school, postsecondary, and university education leads to higher incomes. But do they pay in the sense of yielding a higher income that compensates for the cost of education and for the delay in the start of earnings? For most people, postsecondary education does indeed pay. Rates of return have been estimated to be in the range of 5 to 10 percent after allowing for inflation, which suggests that a postsecondary degree is a better investment than almost any other that a person can undertake.

Education is an important source of earnings differences. But there are others. One is the activities of labour unions. Let's see how unions affect wages and why, on the average, union wages exceed nonunion wages.

FIGURE 15.2

Education and Earnings

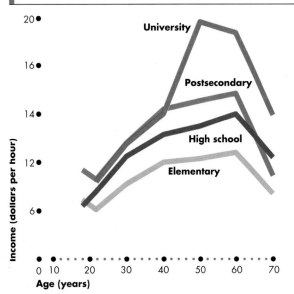

The figure shows average earnings of employees at various ages and with varying school levels. Earnings increase with length of education and also with age but only up to the mid-50s. Beyond that age, earnings decrease. These differences show the importance of experience and education in influencing skill differentials.

Source: Statistics Canada, *Survey of Consumer Finances,* 1993.*

*This analysis is based on Statistics Canada microdata tape. All computations on these microdata were prepared by Audra J. Bowlus, University of Western Ontario; the responsibility for the use and interpretation of these data is entirely that of the authors.

Union–Nonunion Wage Differentials

WAGE DIFFERENTIALS CAN ARISE FROM LABOUR market monopolies. The main source of these monopolies is the labour union. A **labour union** is an organized group of workers whose purpose it is to increase wages and influence other job conditions. A labour union acts in the labour market like a monopolist in the product market. The union seeks to restrict competition and, as a result, increases the price at which labour is traded.

There are two main types of union: craft unions and industrial unions. A **craft union** is a group of workers who have a similar range of skills but work for many different firms in many different industries and regions. An example is the carpenters' union. An **industrial union** is a group of workers who have a variety of skills and job types but work for the same firm or industry. The United Food and Commercial Workers (UFCW) is an example of an industrial union.

The most important national organization representing three-fifths of Canadian union members is the Canadian Labour Congress (CLC). The CLC was created in 1956 when two labour organizations combined: the Labour Council of Canada (TLC), which was founded in 1883 to organize craft unions, and the Canadian Congress of Labour (CCL), founded in 1940 to organize industrial unions. The CLC often acts as the national voice of organized labour in the media and in the political arena.

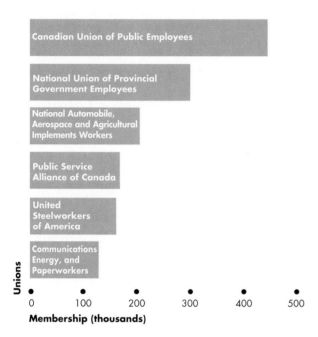

FIGURE 15.3
Unions with the Largest Membership

The labour unions with the largest membership in Canada are the two big public service unions. Together, they have almost 1 million members. The next 10 largest unions each have more than 50,000 members.

Source: Bureau of Labour Organization, *Directory of Labour Organizations.*

Unions vary enormously in size. Craft unions are the smallest and industrial unions are the biggest. Figure 15.3 shows the six largest unions in Canada—measured by number of members. Union strength peaked in 1983 when 40 percent of the work force belonged to unions. That percentage has fallen slightly since then. Changes in union membership, however, have been uneven in the past several decades. Some unions have declined dramatically while others, especially those in the government sector, have increased in strength.

In some firms or plants where a union operates, all workers are required to be members of the union. Such a situation is known as a closed shop. A *closed shop* is an arrangement in which only union members may be employed by a firm. There are other firms and plants in which the terms and conditions of employment are negotiated by a union but in which workers are not required to join the union. Nevertheless, in such situations, an arrangement called the Rand formula applies. The **Rand formula** is a rule (set out by Mr. Justice Ivan Rand in 1945) making it compulsory for all workers to contribute to the union whether or not they belong to the union.

Unions negotiate with employers or their representatives in a process called **collective bargaining**. The main weapons available to the union and the employer in collective bargaining are the strike and the lockout. A *strike* is a group decision to refuse to work under prevailing conditions. A *lockout* is a firm's refusal to operate its plant and pay its workers. Each party uses the threat of a strike or a lockout to try to get an agreement in its own favour. Sometimes when the two parties in the collective bargaining process cannot agree on the wage rate and other conditions of employment, they agree to submit their disagreement to binding arbitration. *Binding arbitration* is a process in which a third party—an arbitrator—determines wages and other employment conditions on behalf of the negotiating parties. A compact glossary of union terms can be found in Table 15.1.

Though not labour unions in a legal sense, professional associations act in many ways like labour unions. A *professional association* is an organized group of professional workers such as lawyers, dentists, or physicians (an example of which is the Ontario Medical Association—OMA). Professional associations control entry into the professions and license practitioners, ensuring the adherence to minimum standards of competence. But they also influence the compensation and other labour market conditions of their members.

Unions' Objectives and Constraints

A union has three broad objectives that it strives to achieve for its members:

1. To increase compensation
2. To improve working conditions
3. To expand job opportunities

Each of these objectives contains a series of more detailed goals. For example, in seeking to increase the compensation of its members, a union operates on a variety of fronts: wage rates, fringe benefits, retirement pay, and such things as vacation allowances. In seeking to improve working conditions, a union is concerned with occupational health and safety as well as the environmental quality of the workplace. In seeking to expand job opportunities, a union tries to obtain greater job security for existing union members and to find ways of creating additional jobs for them.

A union's ability to pursue its objectives is restricted by two sets of constraints—one on the supply side and the other on the demand side of the labour market. On the supply side, the union's activities are limited by how well it can restrict nonunion workers from offering their labour in the same market. The larger the fraction of the work force controlled by the union, the more effective the union can be. For example, unions in the construction industry can better pursue their goals because they can influence the number of people obtaining skills as electricians, plasterers, and carpenters. The professional associations of dentists and physicians are best able to restrict the supply of dentists and physicians. These groups control the number of qualified workers by controlling either the examinations that new entrants must pass or entrance into professional degree programs.

On the demand side of the labour market, the constraint facing a union is the fact that it cannot force firms to hire more labour than the quantity that maximizes their profits. Anything that increases the wage rate or other employment costs decreases the quantity of labour demanded.

Let's see how a union operates in a competitive labour market.

Unions in a Competitive Labour Market

When a union operates in an otherwise competitive labour market, it seeks to increase wages and other compensation and to limit employment reductions by increasing demand for the labour of its members.

Figure 15.4 illustrates a labour market. The demand curve is D_C and the supply curve is S_C. If the market is a competitive one with no union, the wage

---

TABLE 15.1

A Compact Glossary of Union Terms

Labour union	An organized group of workers that attempts to increase wages and improve other conditions of employment for its members
CLC	A federation of unions formed in 1956 by a merger of the Labour Council of Canada (TLC) and the Canadian Congress of Labour (CCL); acts as the voice of organized labour in media and political arenas
Craft union	A union in which workers have a similar range of skills but work for many firms and in many different industries
Industrial union	A union in which workers have a variety of skills and job types but work in the same industry
Closed shop	A place of work where only union members can be employed
Rand formula	A rule (set out by Mr. Justice Ivan Rand in 1945) making it compulsory for all workers in a unionized plant to contribute to the union whether or not they belong
Collective bargaining	Negotiations between representatives of employers and unions on wages and other employment conditions
Strike	A group decision to refuse to work under prevailing conditions
Lockout	A firm's refusal to allow its labour force to work
Binding arbitration	Determination of wages and other employment conditions by a third party (an arbitrator) acceptable to both parties

rate is $4 an hour and 100 hours of labour will be employed. Suppose that a union is formed to organize the workers in this market and that the union has sufficient control over the supply of labour to be able to artificially restrict that supply below its competitive level—to S_U. If that is all the union does, employment will fall to 85 hours of labour and the wage rate will rise to $5 an hour.

How Unions Try to Change the Demand for Labour

Unless the union can take actions that shift the

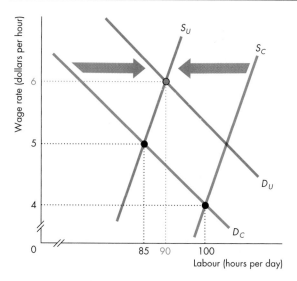

In a competitive labour market, the demand curve is D_C, the supply curve S_C, and equilibrium occurs at a wage rate of $4 an hour with 100 hours employed. By restricting employment below its competitive level, the union shifts the supply of labour to S_U. If the union can do no more than that, the wage rate will increase to $5 an hour, but employment will fall to 85 hours. If the union can increase the demand for labour (by increasing the demand for the good produced by the union members or by raising the price of substitute labour) and shift the demand curve to D_U, then it can increase the wage rate still higher to $6 an hour and achieve employment of 90 hours.

demand curve for the labour that it represents, it has to accept the fact that a higher wage rate can be obtained only at the price of lower employment. Recognizing the importance of the demand for labour curve, a union tries to make the demand for union labour inelastic and to increase the demand for it. If the union can make the demand for labour less elastic, it can increase the wage rate at a lower cost in terms of lost employment opportunities. And if it can increase the demand for labour, it might even be able to increase both the wage rate and the employment opportunities of its members. Some of the methods used by the unions to change the demand for the labour of its members are to

- Increase the marginal product of union members
- Encourage import restrictions
- Support minimum wage laws
- Support immigration restrictions
- Increase demand for the good produced

Unions try to increase the marginal product of their members, which in turn increases the demand for their labour, by organizing and sponsoring training schemes, by encouraging apprenticeship and other on-the-job training activities, and by professional certification.

One of the best examples of import restrictions is the support by the Canadian Autoworkers union for import restrictions on foreign cars. By reducing the quantity of foreign-produced cars, the demand for Canadian-produced cars will increase and so too will the demand for union labour.

Unions support minimum wage laws to increase the cost of employing low-skilled labour. An increase in the wage rate of low-skilled labour leads to a decrease in the quantity demanded of low-skilled labour and to an increase in demand for high-skilled union labour, a substitute for low-skilled labour.

Restrictive immigration laws decrease the supply and increase the wage rate of low-skilled workers. As a result, the demand for high-skilled union labour increases.

Because the demand for labour is a derived demand, an increase in the demand for the good produced increases the demand for union labour. The best examples of attempts by unions in this activity are in the textile and auto industries. The garment workers union urges us to buy union-made clothes and the CAW asks us to buy only cars made by union workers.

Figure 15.4 illustrates the effects of an increase in the demand for the labour of a union's members. If the union can also take steps that increase the demand for labour to D_U, it can achieve an even bigger increase in the wage rate with a smaller fall in employment. By maintaining the restricted labour supply at S_U, the union increases the wage rate to $6 an hour and achieves an employment level of 90 hours of labour.

Because a union restricts the supply of labour in the market in which it operates, its actions increase the supply of labour in nonunion markets. Workers who can't get union jobs must look elsewhere for work. This increase in supply in nonunion markets lowers the wage rate in those markets and further widens the union–nonunion differential. But low nonunion wages decrease the demand for union labour and limit the increase in wages that unions can achieve. For this reason, unions are strong supporters of minimum wage laws that keep nonunion wages high and limit the incentive to use nonunion labour.

Let's now turn our attention to the case in which employers have considerable influence in the labour market.

Monopsony

A **monopsony** is a market structure in which there is just a single buyer. With the growth of large-scale production over the last century, large manufacturing plants such as coal mines, steel and textile mills, and car manufacturers became the major employer of labour in some regions, and in some places a single firm employed almost all the labour. Such a firm has some monopsony power.

A monopsony can make a bigger profit than a group of firms that have to compete with each other for their labour. Figure 15.5 illustrates how a monopsony operates. The monopsony's marginal revenue product curve is *MRP*. This curve tells us the extra revenue from selling the output produced by the last hour of labour hired. The curve labelled *S* is the supply curve of labour. This curve tells us how many hours are supplied at each wage rate. It also tells us the minimum wage that is acceptable at each level of labour supplied.

In deciding how much labour to hire, the monopsony recognizes that to hire more labour it must pay a higher wage or, equivalently, by hiring less labour the monopsony can get away with paying a lower wage. The monopsony takes account of this fact when calculating its marginal cost of labour. The marginal cost of labour is shown by the curve *MCL*. The relationship between the marginal cost of labour curve and the supply curve is similar to the relationship between the marginal cost and average total cost curves that you studied in Chapter 10. The supply curve is like the average total cost of labour curve. For example, in Fig. 15.5 the firm can hire 50 hours of labour at $5 an hour, so its average total cost is $5 an hour. The total cost of labour is $5 an hour multiplied by 50 hours, which equals $250 an hour. But suppose that the firm hires slightly less than 50 hours of labour, say 49 hours. The wage rate at which 49 hours of labour can be hired is just below $4.90 an hour. The firm's total labour cost is $240. Hiring the fiftieth hour of labour increases the total cost of labour from $240 to $250, which is $10. The curve *MCL* shows the $10 marginal cost of hiring the fiftieth hour of labour.

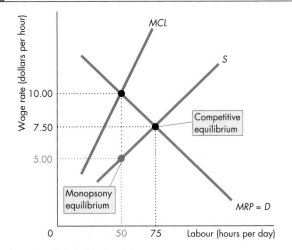

FIGURE 15.5

A Monopsony Labour Market

A monopsony is a market structure in which there is a single buyer. A monopsony in the labour market has marginal revenue product curve *MRP* and faces a labour curve *S*. The marginal cost of labour curve is *MCL*. Profit is maximized by making the marginal cost of labour equal to marginal revenue product. The monopsony hires 50 hours of labour and pays the lowest wage for which that labour will work, $5 an hour.

To calculate the profit-maximizing quantity of labour to hire, the firm sets the marginal cost of labour equal to the marginal revenue product of labour. That is, the firm wants the cost of the last worker hired to equal the extra revenue brought in. In Fig. 15.5, this outcome occurs when the monopsony employs 50 hours of labour. What is the wage rate that the monopsony pays? To hire 50 hours of labour, the firm must pay $5 an hour, as shown by the supply of labour curve. The marginal revenue product of labour, however, is $10 an hour, which means that the firm makes an economic profit of $5 on the last hour of labour that it hires. Each worker is paid $5 an hour.

Compare this outcome with that in a competitive labour market. If the labour market shown in Fig. 15.5 were competitive, equilibrium would occur at the point of intersection of the demand curve and the supply curve. The wage rate would be $7.50 an hour and 75 hours of labour a day would be employed. So, compared with a competitive labour market, a monopsony decreases both the wage rate and the level of employment.

The ability of a monopsony to lower the wage rate and employment level and make an economic profit depends on the elasticity of labour supply. The more elastic the supply of labour, the less opportunity a monopsony has to cut wages and employment and make an economic profit.

Monopsony Tendencies With today's low costs of transportation, it is unlikely that many pure monopsonies remain. Workers can easily commute long distances to a job, and so for most people there is not just one potential employer. But some firms do have a monopsony tendency. That is, while they are not pure monopsonies, they face an upward-sloping supply of labour curve and their marginal cost of labour exceeds the wage rate. Monopsony tendencies arise in isolated communities in which a single firm is the main employer. But in such situations, there is also, usually, a union and wage rates and employment are the result of interaction between the union and the firm. Let's see how unions and monopsonies interact.

Monopsony and Unions When we studied monopoly in Chapter 12, we discovered that a single seller in a market is able to determine the price in that market. We have just studied monopsony—a market with a single buyer—and discovered that in such a market the buyer is able to determine the price. Suppose that a union starts to operate in a monopsony labour market. A union is like a monopoly. It controls the supply of labour and acts like a single seller of labour. If the union (monopoly seller) faces a monopsony buyer, the situation is one of **bilateral monopoly**. In bilateral monopoly, the wage rate is determined by bargaining between the two sides. Let's study the bargaining process.

In Fig. 15.5, if the monopsony is free to determine the wage rate and the level of employment, it hires 50 hours of labour for a wage rate of $5 an hour. But suppose that a union represents the workers and can, if necessary, call a strike. Also suppose that the union agrees to maintain employment at 50 hours, but seeks the highest wage rate the employer can be forced to pay. That wage rate is $10 an hour. That is, the wage rate equals the marginal revenue product of labour. It is unlikely that the union will get the wage rate up to $10 an hour. But it is also unlikely that the firm will keep the wage rate down to $5 an hour. The monopsony firm and the union will bargain over the wage rate and the result will be an outcome between $10 an hour (the maximum that the union can achieve) and $5 an hour (the minimum that the firm can achieve).

The actual outcome of the bargaining depends on the costs that each party can inflict on the other as a result of a failure to agree on the wage rate. The firm can shut down the plant and lock out its workers, and the workers can shut down the plant by striking. Each party knows the strength of the other and knows what it will lose if it does not agree to the demands of the other. If the two parties are equally strong, and they realize it, they will split the difference and agree to a wage rate of $7.50 an hour. If one party is stronger than the other—and both parties know that—the agreed wage will favour the stronger party. The wage rate will be between $5.00 an hour and $7.50 an hour if the firm is the stronger party and between $7.50 an hour and $10 an hour if the union is stronger. Usually, an agreement is reached without a strike or a lockout. The threat—the knowledge that such an event can occur—is usually enough to bring the bargaining parties to an agreement. When strikes or lockouts do occur, it is usually because one party has misjudged the costs each party can inflict on the other.

Monopsony has an interesting implication for the effects of minimum wage laws. Let's now study these effects.

Monopsony and the Minimum Wage

A minimum wage that exceeds the equilibrium wage in a competitive labour market decreases employment — see Chapter 6, pp. 125–126. A minimum wage in a monopsony labour market can *increase* both the wage rate and employment. Let's see how.

Suppose that the labour market is that shown in Fig. 15.6 and that the wage rate is $5 an hour with 50 hours of labour employed. The government now passes a minimum wage law that prohibits anyone from hiring labour for less than $7.50 an hour. The monopsony now faces a perfectly elastic supply of labour at $7.50 an hour up to 75 hours. Above 75 hours, a higher wage than $7.50 an hour must be paid to hire additional hours of labour. Because the wage rate is a fixed $7.50 an hour up to 75 hours, the marginal cost of labour is also $7.50 up to 75 hours. Beyond 75 hours, the marginal cost of labour rises above $7.50 an hour. To maximize profit, the monopsony sets the marginal cost of labour equal to its marginal revenue product. That is, the monopsony hires 75 hours of labour at $7.50 an hour.

The minimum wage law has made the supply of labour perfectly elastic and made the marginal cost of labour the same as the wage rate up to 75 hours. The

law has not affected the supply of labour curve or the marginal cost of labour at employment levels above 75 hours. The minimum wage law has succeeded in raising the wage rate by $2.50 an hour and increasing the amount of labour employed by 25 hours.

The Scale of Union–Nonunion Wage Differentials

We have seen that unions can influence the wage rate by restricting the supply of labour and increasing the demand for labour. How much of a difference to wage rates do unions make in practice?

Union wage rates are, on the average, 30 percent higher than nonunion wage rates. In public administration, union and nonunion wage rates are similar. In manufacturing, transportation, communication and other utilities, and trade, finance, insurance, and real estate, the differential is between 5 and 21 percent. In primary industries, the differential is 30 percent. But in construction and community, business, and personal services, the differential is between 40 and 47 percent.

These union–nonunion differentials do not give a true measure of the effects of unions, however. In some industries, union wages are higher than non-union wages because union members do jobs that involve greater skill. Even without a union, those who perform such tasks receive a higher wage. To calculate the effects of unions, we have to examine the wages of unionized and nonunionized workers who do nearly identical work. The evidence suggests that after allowing for the effects of skill differentials, the union–nonunion wage differential lies between 10 percent and 35 percent.[1]

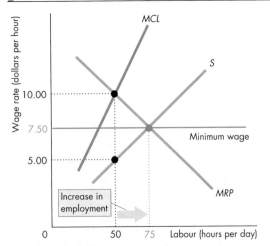

FIGURE 15.6
Minimum Wage in Monopsony

In a monopsony labour market, the wage rate is $5 an hour and 50 hours are hired. If a minimum wage law increases the wage rate to $7.50 an hour, employment increases to 75 hours.

R E V I E W

■ Differences in earnings based on skill or education level arise because high-skilled labour has a higher marginal revenue product than low-skilled labour and because skills are costly to acquire.

■ Union workers have higher wage rates than nonunion workers because a union is able to control the supply of labour and, indirectly, influence the marginal revenue product of its members.

---

[1] Chris Robinson, "The Joint Determination of Union Status and Union Wage Effects: Some Tests of Alternative Models," *Journal of Political Economy* 97, 3 (June 1989): 639–667.

Wage Differentials Between the Sexes

THE OBJECTIVE OF THIS SECTION IS TO SHOW you how to use economic analysis to address a controversial and emotionally charged issue: persistent earnings differentials between the sexes. Figure 15.7 gives a snapshot of these differences in 1991. For both part-time and full-time workers, Canadian women, on the average, earned 61.5 percent of Canadian men's earnings. For full-time workers, the earnings of women were 69.6 percent of men's earnings.

Why does this earnings differential exist? Does it arise because there is discrimination against women, or is there some other explanation? This controversial question generates an enormous amount of passion.

It is not our intention to make you angry, but that may happen as an unintended consequence of this discussion.

We are going to examine four possible explanations for this earnings difference:

- Job types
- Discrimination
- Differences in human capital
- Differences in degree of specialization

Job Types

Some of the difference in men's and women's wages arises from the fact that men and women do different jobs and, for the most part, men's jobs are better paid than women's jobs. But there are increasing numbers of women entering areas that were traditionally the preserve of men. This trend is particularly clear in professions such as architecture, medicine, economics, law, accounting, and pharmacology. The percentage of total enrolments in university courses in these subjects for women has increased from less than 20 percent in 1970 to approaching, and in some cases exceeding, 50 percent today. Women are also increasingly seen as bus drivers, police officers, and construction workers, all jobs that traditionally were done mainly by men.

But there are many situations in which women earn less than men, even when they do essentially the same job. One possible reason is that women are discriminated against. Let's see how discrimination might affect wage rates.

Discrimination

To see how discrimination can affect earnings, let's look at an example—the market for investment advisors. Suppose that there are two groups of investment advisors who are identical in their skills at picking good investments. One group consists of females and the other of males. Figure 15.8(a) shows the supply curve of females, S_F, and Fig. 15.8(b) shows the supply curve of males, S_M. These supply curves are identical. The marginal revenue product of investment advisors, whether they are female or male, is also identical, as shown by the two curves labelled MRP in parts (a) and (b). (Their revenues are the fees their customers pay for investment advice.)

FIGURE 15.7

Earnings Differentials

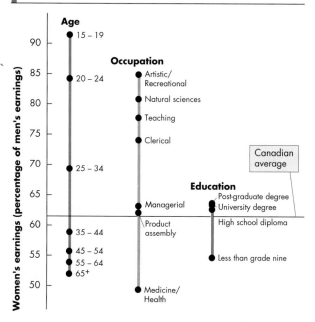

Women on the average earn about 61.5 percent of the amount earned by men. Much of this difference is accounted for by age—the incomes of younger women are much closer to those of men than are those of older women. The difference also arises from the fact that women predominate in lower-paid jobs. Education also plays a role.

Source: Statistics Canada, *Women in the Workplace,* 1993.

FIGURE 15.8
Discrimination

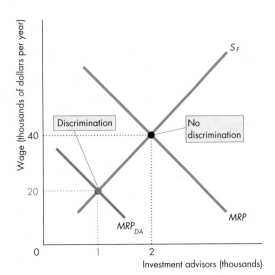

(a) Women

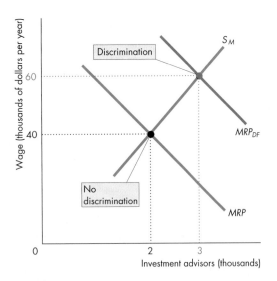

(b) Men

With no discrimination, the wage rate is $40,000 a year and 2,000 of each group are hired. With discrimination against women, the marginal revenue product curve in part (a) is MRP_{DA} and MRP_{DF} in part (b). The wage rate for women falls to $20,000 a year and only 1,000 are employed. The wage rate for males increases to $60,000 a year and 3,000 are employed.

Suppose that everyone in this society is free of prejudice about sex. The market for female investment advisors determines a wage rate of $40,000 a year and there are 2,000 female investment advisors. The male investment advisor market also determines a wage rate of $40,000 a year, and there are 2,000 male investment advisors.

In contrast to the situation just described, suppose that the customers of investment houses are prejudiced against women. The two types of investment advisors are equally able, as before, but the degree of prejudice is so strong that the customers are not willing to pay as much for investment advice given by a female as they will pay for advice from a male. Because of the differences in the amounts that people are willing to pay, based purely on their prejudices, the marginal revenue products of the two groups are different. The ability of the two groups is the same but the value that prejudiced consumers place on their outputs is not the same. Suppose that the marginal revenue product of the females, when discriminated against, is the line labelled MRP_{DA}—DA standing for "discriminated against." Suppose that the marginal revenue product for males, the group discriminated in favour of, is MRP_{DF}—DF standing for "discriminated in favour of." Given these marginal revenue product curves, the markets for the two groups of investment advisors will now determine very different wages and employment levels. Females will earn $20,000 a year and only 1,000 will work as investment advisors. Males will earn $60,000 a year and 3,000 of them will work as investment advisors. Thus, purely on the basis of the prejudice of the demanders of investment advice, women will earn one-third the wages of men, and three-quarters of all investment advisors will be men and only one-quarter will be women.

We've just examined a hypothetical example of how prejudice can produce differences in earnings. Economists disagree about whether prejudice actually causes wage differentials, and one line of reasoning suggests that it does not. In the example, the customers who buy from men pay a higher service charge for investment advice than the customers who buy from women. This price difference acts as an incentive to limit discrimination and encourages people who are prejudiced to buy from the people whom they are prejudiced against. This force could be so strong as to eliminate the effects of discrimination altogether. Suppose, as is true in manufacturing, that a firm's customers never meet its workers. If a manufacturing firm discriminated against women, it would not be able to compete with firms who hired women. So only those firms that do not discriminate are able to survive in a competitive industry. This line of reasoning suggests a test for discrimination. Customers who discriminate against women must pay a higher price for the services they buy from males than the prices paid by those willing to buy from women. And firms that discriminate must make lower profit rates than those that do not.

But while you can recognize prejudice when you see it, you cannot easily measure it objectively. The model we've studied shows that the sex differential might come from prejudice. But without a way of directly measuring prejudice, we cannot test that model in a completely convincing way to see whether it is true.

We need to make another point as well. Our model of prejudice, like all economic models, is in an equilibrium, albeit an unhappy one. But simply because a model is in equilibrium does not mean that such a real situation is either desirable or inevitable. Economic theory makes predictions about the way things will be, not moral statements about the way things ought to be. Policies designed to bring equal wages and employment prospects to women can be devised. But to be successful, such policies must be based on careful economic analysis. Good intentions are not enough to bring about equality.

A further source of wage rate differences lies in differences in human capital. Let's now examine the effects of human capital on wage rates.

Human Capital Differences

Wages are compensation in part for time spent on the job and in part for the cost incurred in acquiring skill—human capital. The more human capital a person possesses, the more that person earns, other things remaining the same. It is impossible to measure human capital precisely but there are some rough indicators. The three most useful indicators are

1. Years of schooling
2. Years of work experience
3. Number of job interruptions

In recent years, the median number of years in school for both sexes is almost equal at about 12 years.

Years of work experience and job interruptions

are interrelated. For people of a given age and given amount of schooling, a person who has had fewer job interruptions has usually had more years of work experience. But interruptions to a career disrupt and reduce the effectiveness of job experience, slow down the accumulation of human capital, and even sometimes result in the depreciation of human capital through its lack of use. Historically and today, job interruptions are more serious for women than for men. Traditionally, women's careers have been interrupted for bearing and rearing children. This factor is a possible source of lower wages, on the average, for women. But just as education differences are virtually disappearing, so career interruptions for women are becoming less common. Maternity leave and day-care facilities are providing an increasing number of women with uninterrupted employment that makes their human capital accumulation more similar to that of men.

Thus it seems that human capital differences possibly can account for earnings differentials between women and men in the past and for some of the differentials that still remain. The trends, however, suggest that wage differentials from this source will eventually disappear.

There is one final source of earnings differences that is likely to affect women's incomes adversely: the relative degree of specialization of women and men.

Degrees of Specialization

People undertake two kinds of production activities: They supply labour services to the market (market activities) and they undertake household production (nonmarket activities). *Household production* creates goods and services to be consumed within the household rather than to be supplied to the market. Such activities include cooking, cleaning, minor repair work, education, shopping, and various organizational services such as arranging vacations and leisure activities. Bearing and rearing children is another important nonmarket activity.

In Chapter 3, we discovered that people can gain from specializing in particular activities and trading their output with each other. Specialization and the gains from trade do not operate exclusively in the marketplace. They also operate within the household and among its members. It is not uncommon for each member of a household to specialize in a limited range of activities. For example, one does the shopping and cleaning while another does laundry and prepares meals. Specialization in bearing children is a biological necessity, although rearing them is not.

Consider, for example, a household that has two members—Bob and Sue. Bob and Sue have to decide how they will allocate their time between various nonmarket household production activities and market activity. One solution is for Bob to specialize in market activity and Sue to specialize in nonmarket activity. Another solution is to reverse the roles and have Sue specialize in market activity and Bob in nonmarket activity. Or for one or both of them to be diversified in market and nonmarket activities.

The allocation chosen by Bob and Sue will depend on their preferences and on the market earning potential of each of them. The choice of an increasing number of households is for each person to diversify between nonmarket and market activity. But most households, however, still choose an allocation that has Bob almost fully specialized in market activity and Sue diversified in market and nonmarket activities. It seems likely that with this allocation Bob will have higher earning potential in the marketplace than Sue. If Sue devotes time and effort to ensuring Bob's mental and physical well-being, the quality of Bob's market labour will be higher than if he were diversified. If the roles were reversed, Sue would be able to supply market labour capable of earning more than Bob.

Economists have attempted to test whether the degree of specialization can account for earnings differentials between the sexes by examining the wages of men and women where, as far as possible, the degree of specialization is held constant. For example, if the degree of specialization is an important factor influencing a person's wage, then men and women of identical ages and educational backgrounds in identical occupations will be paid different wages depending on whether they are single, married to a spouse who specializes in household production, or married to a spouse who has paid employment. Single men and women who live alone and who are equally specialized in household and market production and who have the same amounts of human capital and who do similar jobs will be paid the same wage. To make nonmarket factors as similar as possible, economists have studied two groups: "never married" men and "never married" women. The available evidence suggests that, on the average, when they have the same amount of human capital—measured by years of schooling, work experience, and career interrup-

tions—the wages of these two groups are not identical, but they are much closer than the difference between average wages for men and women. When allowance is made for degree of specialization and human capital, this wage differential comes down to between 5 and 10 percent, by some estimates. Some economists suspect the remaining discrepancy stems from discrimination against women, although the difficulty of measuring such discrimination makes this hypothesis hard to test.

Because labour markets do not seem to treat everyone in the same way, governments intervene in these markets to modify the wages and employment levels that they determine. One potentially far-reaching intervention is pay equity laws. Let's see how these laws work.

Pay Equity Laws

THE FEDERAL GOVERNMENT AND ALL PROVINCIAL governments have passed laws that require "equal pay for equal work without discrimination on the basis of sex."[2] Increasingly, attempts are being made to find ways of comparing jobs that are essentially different but require, on some criteria, similar degrees of skill. Such comparisons lead to a broader concept than "equal pay for equal work"; they call for equal pay for comparable work. Paying the same wage for different jobs that are judged to be comparable is called *pay equity*.

Advocates of pay equity laws argue that wages should be determined by analysing the characteristics of jobs and determining their worth on objective grounds. However, such a method of determining wage rates does not achieve the objectives sought by supporters of wage equality. Let's see why.

Figure 15.9 shows two markets: that for oil rig operators in part (a) and that for nurses in part (b). The marginal revenue product curves (MRP_R and MRP_N) and the supply curves (S_R and S_N) are shown for each type of labour. Competitive equilibrium generates a wage rate W_R for oil rig operators and W_N for nurses.

Suppose that the knowledge and skills required in those two occupations—the mental and physical demands, the responsibilities, and the working condi-

---

[2]N. Agarwal and Jain Harish, "Pay Discrimination Against Women in Canada," *International Labour Review* 117 (March–April 1978): 169–178.

FIGURE 15.9

The Problem with Pay Equity

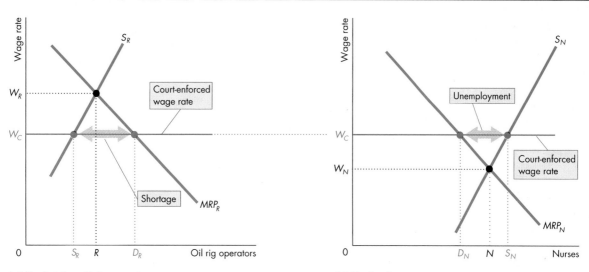

(a) Market for oil rig operators

(b) Market for nurses

Part (a) shows the demand for and supply of oil rig operators, MRP_R and S_R, and part (b) shows the demand for and supply of nurses, MRP_N and S_N. The competitive equilibrium wage rate for oil rig operators is W_R and that for nurses is W_N. If an evaluation of the two jobs finds that they have equal value and rules that the wage rate W_C be paid to both types of workers,

such a wage creates a shortage of oil rig operators and a surplus of nurses. Oil producers search for other labour-saving ways of producing oil (that are more expensive), and nurses search for other jobs (that are less desirable to them and probably are less well paid).

tions—result in a judgment that these two jobs are comparable. The wage rate that is judged to apply to each of them is W_C, and the courts enforce this wage rate. What happens? First, there is a shortage of oil rig operators. Oil rig companies are able to hire only S_R workers at the wage rate W_C. They cut back their production or build more expensive labour-saving oil rigs. Also the number of nurses employed decreases. But this decrease occurs because hospitals demand fewer nurses. At the higher wage W_C, hospitals demand only D_N nurses. The quantity of nurses supplied is S_N and the difference between S_N and D_N is the number of unemployed nurses looking for jobs. These nurses eventually accept non-nursing jobs (which they don't like as much as nursing jobs), and quite likely at a lower rate of pay than that of nurses.

Thus legislated equal pay for work of equal value might have serious and costly unintended consequences.

R E V I E W

■ Wage differences between the sexes might arise from differences in the types of jobs done, discrimination, differences in human capital, and differences in the degree of specialization of women and men.

■ The equalization of human capital and of the degree of specialization will lead to smaller differentials and possibly will eliminate them.

■ Pay equity laws cannot, themselves, eliminate wage differences.

◆ *Reading Between the Lines* on pp. 360–361 looks at one key lesson of this chapter—education pays. In the next chapter, we use the factor market model to deal with markets for capital and for natural resources.

Policy WATCH

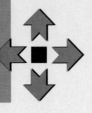

Investing in Human Capital

Essence of THE STORY

■ A private survey of wealthy Canadians (with average household incomes of $124,000 and average net worth of $441,000) has revealed the following facts.

■ Most of the wealthy Canadians were (1) born in the late 1940s—baby boomers—to poorer parents, (2) live in a two-income family, (3) have a university degree, (4) work hard, and (5) do not expect to inherit much.

■ Survey respondents ranked the sources of their high incomes as: (1) a willingness to work hard, (2) education, (3) intelligence, and (4) good luck.

TORONTO STAR, OCTOBER 12, 1995

Survey is proof university pays off

BY ART CHAMBERLAIN

The road to riches leads through university, wealthy Canadians say.

More than two-thirds of people with income in the top 10 per cent of all Canadians have a university degree, according to a survey done for Royal Trust.

Since only 18 per cent of Canadians have a degree, extra education clearly pays off, said Bruce Armstrong, director of marketing for retirement services.

The average household income of Royal Trust's survey was $124,000, with an average net worth of $441,000, including real estate.

In Ontario, the threshold to be considered wealthy was $100,000 in cities and $90,000 in rural areas. Retired people in Metro made the grade if their income was $80,000 or more.

"Despite their wealth, today's affluent are not basking in a life of luxury and leisure," Armstrong said yesterday. "This isn't Robin Leach. Instead, they are busy family managers balancing the responsibilities of career and families."

Most of the affluent families are Baby Boomers with two incomes and young children.

A willingness to work hard was the key ingredient in their success, said 83 per cent of the respondents to the survey done by Environics Research Group.

They ranked education next in importance, followed by intelligence and good luck.

Most of the affluent came from a lower economic background and few expect to inherit much of a nest egg.

Asked what advice they would give others, 27 per cent replied: Get as much education as possible. ...

Economic

A N A L Y S I S

■ Most people earn their income by working. And the income they earn depends on the demand for and supply of the skills they have to offer.

■ The figure illustrates the market for two types of labour: average-productivity labour and high-productivity labour.

■ The demand for labour with an average productivity is D_A and the supply of labour with an average productivity is S_A.

■ In equilibrium, average-productivity labour earns $25 an hour and works for 2,000 hours a year. Each person in this category earns $50,000 a year.

■ Some people earn more than the average and for two reasons: Their productivity is higher than average and the supply of such labour is limited.

■ A higher than average productivity means a greater demand. The demand for high-productivity labour is D_H in the figure.

■ The sources of high productivity are: (1) formal education, (2) on the job experience, and (3) motivation.

■ People with university degrees have had the most formal education.

■ People in mid-career (in the 1990s, they are the 45-year-old baby boomers) have had the most relevant job experience.

■ People with a low-income background often have a high degree of motivation.

■ The combination of these last three attributes, combined with some luck, create the highest productivity and the greatest demand.

■ But this same combination of schooling, experience, and motivation is relatively rare, so the supply of high-productivity labour is limited. In the figure, the supply curve is S_H.

■ In equilibrium, high-productivity labour earns $62 an hour and works the same 2,000 hours a year as the low-productivity labour. Each person in this category earns $124,000 a year.

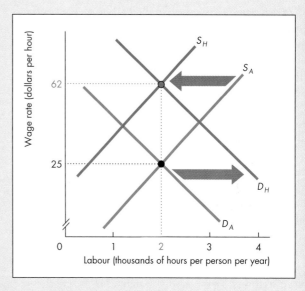

You're

THE VOTER

■ Does the big payoff from education mean that the government should spend more on education?

■ Or does it mean that because education pays higher incomes, the government should pay less for education and leave people to make their own choices based on the likely personal payoff?

■ Would you vote for more education dollars? Or would you vote for fewer education dollars and lower taxes through deductions for education expenses?

S U M M A R Y

Key Points

Skill Differentials   High-skilled labour has a higher marginal product than low-skilled labour, and skills are costly to acquire. So the demand for high-skilled labour is higher and the supply of high-skilled labour is lower than for low-skilled labour. As a result, the equilibrium wage rate for high-skilled labour exceeds that for low-skilled labour. The difference in wages reflects the higher marginal product of skill and the cost to acquire skill. (pp. 346–348)

Union–Nonunion Wage Differentials   Labour unions influence wages by controlling the supply of labour. In competitive labour markets, unions obtain higher wages only at the expense of lower employment. Unions in competitive industries also influence the marginal revenue product of their members by supporting import restrictions, minimum wages, and immigration restrictions; by increasing demand for the good they produce; and by increasing the marginal productivity of their members. In a monopsony—a market in which there is a single buyer—a union can increase the wage rate without sacrificing employment. Bilateral monopoly occurs when the union is a monopoly seller of labour, the firm is a monopsony buyer of labour, and the wage rate is determined by bargaining between the two parties. Also, in a monopsony, a minimum wage law can increase both the wage rate and the level of employment. In practice, union workers earn an estimated 10 to 35 percent more than comparable nonunion workers. (pp. 348–354)

Wage Differentials Between the Sexes   Earnings differentials between men and women arise from differences in types of jobs, discrimination, differences in human capital, and differences in degree of specialization. Well-paid jobs, such as those in the legal, medical, and other professions, and in higher ranks of management, are more likely to be held by men than by women. Women are more likely to be discriminated against than males, but discrimination is hard to measure objectively. Historically, males have had more human capital than women, but human capital differences arising from schooling differences have almost been eliminated. Differentials based on work experience have kept women's pay below that for men because women's careers have traditionally

been interrupted more frequently than those of men, resulting on the average in a smaller accumulation of human capital. This difference is less important today than in the past. Differentials arising from different degrees of specialization are probably important and might persist. Men have traditionally been more specialized in market activity, on the average, than women. Women have traditionally undertaken both nonmarket (household production) activities as well as market activities. Attempts to test for the importance of the degree of specialization suggest that it is an important source of the difference between the earnings of men and women. (pp. 355–358)

Pay Equity Laws   Pay equity laws determine wages by using objective characteristics rather than what the market will pay to assess the value of different types of jobs. Determining wages through pay equity will result in a cut in the number of people employed in those jobs on which the market places a lower value, and shortages of those workers that the market values more highly. Thus the attempt to achieve equal pay for work of equal value has costly, unintended consequences. (pp. 358–359)

Key Figures and Table

Key Terms

R E V I E W   Q U E S T I O N S

1. What is human capital? How is it acquired?
2. Explain why the demand curve for high-skilled labour lies to the right of the demand curve for low-skilled labour.
3. Explain why the supply curve for high-skilled labour lies to the left of the supply curve for low-skilled labour.
4. What is the influence of education and on-the-job training on earnings?
5. Explain why high-skilled workers are paid more than low-skilled workers.
6. What is a labour union? What are the main types of labour union?
7. What is collective bargaining? What are the main weapons in collective bargaining?
8. How does a union try to influence wages?
9. How might a union increase the demand for its members' labour?
10. Explain why the elasticity of supply of labour influences how much the union can raise the wage rate paid to union members.
11. What is monopsony? Where in Canada might a monopsony exist?
12. Explain why the supply of labour facing a monopsony is not the marginal cost of labour.
13. Explain why a monopsony maximizes its profit by paying labour a wage rate that is less than the marginal revenue product of labour.
14. Under what circumstances will the introduction of a minimum wage increase employment?
15. Why does discrimination against women influence the marginal revenue product of women?
16. What is the effect of discrimination on the basis of sex in a profession on the wage rate paid to women and the number of women hired?
17. What is a pay equity law?
18. How do pay equity laws work and what are their predicted effects?

C R I T I C A L   T H I N K I N G

1. Study *Reading Between the Lines* on pp. 360–361 and then answer the following questions:
   a. Why does a university graduate earn more than a nongraduate? Explain what a university education does to both the demand for and supply of high-skilled labour.
   b. If university graduates had to pay full tuition, which is currently about $20,000 a school year, what would happen to the demand for and supply of university graduates? What would happen to their wage rates?
   c. If the government paid people the average wage rate to go to university and also paid the tuition, what would happen to the demand for and supply of university graduates? What would happen to their wage rates?
2. In British Columbia and Saskatchewan, provincial governments have restricted the bidding on some government contracts to unionized firms. What do you think will be the effect of such a policy on the demand for union labour, the wage rate paid to union labour, and the cost to provincial taxpayers?
3. Advances in technology have led to a reduction in the demand for public sector workers. What methods have the public sector unions used to try to maintain the demand for union labour?
4. Union membership in Canada peaked in 1983. Why do you think workers are less inclined to join a union today than they were in 1983?
5. Sixty percent of teachers in Canada are women, but only 25 percent of school administrators are women. Why? Is this discrimination against women or the outcome of women's choices?
6. Only 7 percent of full professors are women and about 50 percent of lecturers and instructors are women. About half the students entering university are women. Do you expect the percentage of full professors who are women to change much over the next 20 years? Why or why not?

P R O B L E M S

1. The figure illustrates the demand for and supply of low-skilled workers.

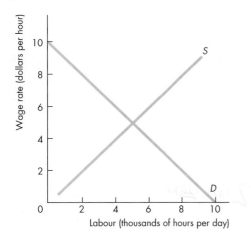

a. What is the wage rate of low-skilled labour?
b. What is the quantity of low-skilled labour employed?

2. The workers in problem 1 can be trained—can obtain a skill—and their marginal productivity doubles. (The marginal product at each employment level is twice the marginal product of a low-skilled worker.) But the compensation for the cost of acquiring skill adds $2 an hour to the wage that must be offered to attract high-skilled labour.
a. What is the wage rate of high-skilled labour?
b. What is the quantity of high-skilled labour employed?

3. Suppose that high-skilled workers become unionized and the union restricts entry into high-skilled work to 1,000 hours. What is the wage rate of high-skilled workers? How do low-skilled workers react to the new situation?

4. If in problem 1 the government introduces a minimum wage rate of $6 an hour for low-skilled workers,
a. What is the wage rate paid to low-skilled workers?
b. How many hours of low-skilled labour gets hired each day?

5. In an isolated part of the Amazon Basin a gold mining company faces the following labour market. The gold mine is a monopsony.

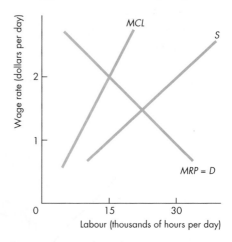

a. What wage rate does the company pay?
b. How many hours of labour does the gold mine hire?
c. What is the marginal revenue product of the last hour of labour?
d. How does the gold mine maximize its profit when it does not pay its workers their marginal revenue product?
e. If the world price of gold increases, what happens to the wage rate paid and the number of workers hired?

6. If in problem 5 the government imposes a minimum wage rate of $1.50 a day,
a. What wage rate does the gold mine pay?
b. Does the gold mine increase or decrease the number of hours of labour it hires?

Capital and Natural Resource Markets

After studying
this chapter,
you will be
able to:

- Describe the structure of capital markets in Canada today

- Explain how the demand for and supply of capital are determined

- Explain how interest rates and stock prices are determined and why stock prices fluctuate

- Explain how the prices of natural resources are determined

- Explain how markets regulate the pace at which we use exhaustible resources such as oil

Panic filled the Stock Exchanges of Toronto and Montreal on Monday, October 19, 1987. It had taken five years, from August 1982, for the average price of a common stock to climb 200 percent. But on that single day, stock prices fell an unheard-of 11.3 percent—knocking billions of dollars off the value of people's investments. Why does the stock market boom for several years and then crash suddenly and spectacularly?

Boom and Bust

◆ The Toronto Stock Exchange, large as it is, is only a part of the enormous worldwide capital market. Every year, trillions of dollars flow through the worldwide capital market. Saving flows through banks, insurance companies, and stock exchanges and ends up financing the purchases of machinery, factory and office buildings, cars, and homes. How does a dollar saved and placed on deposit in a bank enable Labatt to open a new beer-bottling plant? ◆ Many of our natural resources are exhaustible and yet we are using them up at a rapid rate. Every year we burn trillions of cubic metres of natural gas, billions of litres of petroleum, and millions of tonnes of coal. We extract bauxite to make aluminum and iron ore to make steel. Aren't we one day going to run out of these and other natural resources? How are their prices determined? Do their prices rise to encourage conservation, or does the market need help to ensure that we do not pillage nature's exhaustible endowments?

◆ In this chapter, we study capital and natural resource markets. We'll find out what determines the amount of saving and investment and how interest rates and stock prices are determined. We'll also see how market forces encourage the conservation and discovery of exhaustible natural resources.

The Structure of Capital Markets

CAPITAL MARKETS ARE THE CHANNELS THROUGH which households' saving flows into firms. Firms use the financial resources they obtain in capital markets to buy capital goods. Capital goods—goods such as buildings, machines, airplanes, and computers—are bought and sold, and they are rented. The markets in which capital goods are bought, sold, and rented are not capital markets. They are goods markets and factor rental markets. These markets coordinate the decisions of producers and buyers and of owners and renters of capital goods. In these markets, the forces of demand and supply, which you first met in Chapter 4, determine the prices and quantities of the various capital goods.

Capital markets coordinate the saving plans of households, which determine the supply of capital, and the investment plans of firms, which determine the demand for capital. The price of capital, which adjusts to make the quantity of capital supplied equal to the quantity demanded, is the interest rate.

The Flows of Funds

Figure 16.1 shows the main flows of saving through the capital markets. Households save part of their incomes and supply *financial capital*. Firms demand financial capital and use it to buy *physical capital*. Lying at the core of the financial markets are financial intermediaries. **Financial intermediaries** are the institutions that receive deposits, make loans, and facilitate transactions in the markets for stocks, bonds, and loans. The best-known financial intermediaries are chartered banks and trust companies, but others are money market funds, insurance companies, and retirement fund management companies. The green dotted lines in the figure illustrate the financial transactions. Households use their saving to buy stocks or bonds issued by firms and to make deposits with financial intermediaries. Financial intermediaries make loans to households and firms.

The three main types of capital market are

- Stock markets
- Bond markets
- Loan markets

FIGURE 16.1
Capital Market Flows

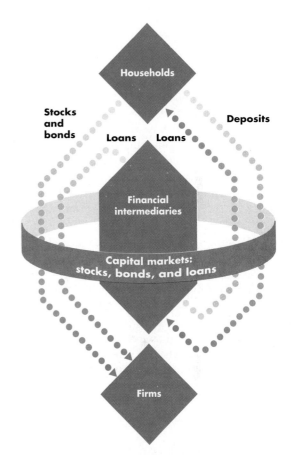

Households supply *financial* capital to firms, which use financial capital to buy *physical* capital. Households purchase stocks and bonds, and make deposits in financial intermediaries. Financial intermediaries lend to both households and firms. These flows are shown by the green dotted lines.

Stock Markets   A **stock market** is a market in which the stocks of corporations are traded. The most famous stock market, the *New York Stock Exchange* (*NYSE*) located on Wall Street, New York City, handles more than 2,000 of the most actively traded stocks, many of which are those of household names such as General Motors, Boeing Aircraft, and Exxon. Another stock exchange in New York City, NASDAQ, handles stocks that are not quite so heavily traded as those on the NYSE. Canada has four stock exchanges—Toronto, Montreal, Alberta, and

Vancouver. On a typical day, more than 20 million individual stocks are traded on the Toronto Stock Exchange. Outside North America, London, Paris, Frankfurt, Tokyo, Hong Kong, and other large cities have long-established stock exchanges that specialize in trading the stocks of tens of thousands of foreign companies. In recent years, stock markets have begun to operate in Shanghai, Taipei, Bangkok, Seoul, and other centres in the emerging market economies of East Asia.

If you want to buy or sell a stock on a stock exchange, you must give an instruction to a *broker* who in turn places a buy or sell order with a *specialist* who deals in the stock you want to trade. The specialist, who works on the *floor* of the stock exchange, continuously monitors demand and supply and tries to keep the price of the stock at the level at which the quantity demanded equals the quantity supplied.

Bond Markets   A **bond market** is a market in which the bonds of corporations and governments are traded. The distinction between a stock and a bond, described in Chapter 9, pp. 193–194, is that a stockholder receives a periodic dividend that depends on a firm's economic profit, while a bondholder receives a periodic fixed amount, called a coupon payment. Bond markets, like stock markets, are located in all the major financial centres. And bonds are issued in all the world's major currencies. For example, a business in Indonesia might borrow by issuing bonds denominated in Japanese yen or in U.S. dollars or in British pounds.

Also as in stock markets, if you want to buy or sell a bond, you must give an instruction to a broker who, working with specialist traders, maintains a balance between the quantities of bonds demanded and supplied.

Loan Markets   A **loan market** is a market in which households, firms, and financial intermediaries make and receive loans. Financial intermediaries make loan markets function and are the major players in these markets. When you make a deposit in a bank, you make a loan to the bank and the bank uses the funds it receives from depositors to make loans to businesses and households. Loans to businesses are used to finance investment in capital equipment and inventories. Loans to households are used to finance the purchase of homes and consumer durable goods.

Let's begin to learn how capital markets work by studying the demand for capital.

The Demand for Capital

A FIRM'S DEMAND FOR *financial* CAPITAL STEMS from its demand for *physical* capital and the amount that a firm plans to *borrow* in a given time period is determined by its planned *investment*.

Capital and Investment

Capital is a *stock*—the quantity of previously manufactured goods in existence at a given time that are used to produce other goods and services. Gross investment is a *flow*—the purchase of new capital during a given period. This amount is added to the capital stock. Capital is like the water in Lake Ontario at a given point in time and gross investment is like the water flowing over the Niagara Falls into the lake during a given period. The inflow adds to the water in the lake. Depreciation is another flow. **Depreciation** is the amount of existing capital that wears out in a given period. Depreciation is like the water flowing out of Lake Ontario into the St. Lawrence River. This outflow decreases the water in the lake. The change in the capital stock during a given period is called **net investment** and equals gross investment minus depreciation. Similarly, the change in the amount of water in Lake Ontario equals the inflow minus the outflow.

Investment Decisions

To decide how much to invest and borrow, a firm decides on the size of its capital stock. This decision, like a firm's decision about the amount of other factors of production to employ, is driven by its attempt to maximize profit.

As a firm increases the quantity of capital employed, other things remaining the same, the marginal revenue product of capital eventually diminishes. To maximize profit, a firm uses the rule: Employ the quantity of capital that makes the marginal revenue product of capital equal the price of using capital. The price of using capital is the interest rate. So a firm increases the quantity of capital employed until the additional revenue generated by using one extra unit of capital equals the interest rate.

The easiest way to see that the interest rate is the price of using capital is to think about capital that is actually rented. If a firm rents a computer from Computerland, it pays an annual rental rate. This rental rate gives Computerland a rate of return equal to the interest rate. If Computerland made a return less than the interest rate, it would sell some computers and buy some stocks and bonds that yield an interest rate higher than that on computers. If Computerland made a return greater than the interest rate, it would buy more computers and sell some stock or bonds that have an interest rate lower than that on computers.

But most capital is not rented. Firms *buy* buildings, plant, and equipment and operate them for several years. To decide how much capital equipment to buy, the firm compares the price to be paid here and now for the equipment with the returns—the future stream of marginal revenue products—that the equipment will generate over its life. The interest rate is still the price of using capital, even when it is bought rather than rented. The reason is that to decide how much capital to buy, the firm must convert a stream of *future* marginal revenue product into a *present value* so that it can be directly compared with the price of a new piece of capital equipment. Chapter 9 (pp. 194–196) explains the concept of present value.

The Net Present Value of a Computer   Let's see how a firm decides how much capital to buy by calculating the present value of a new computer. Table 16.1 summarizes the data. Tina runs Taxfile, Inc., a firm that sells advice to taxpayers. Tina is considering buying a new computer that costs $10,000. The computer has a life of two years, after which it will be worthless. If Tina buys the computer, she will pay out $10,000 now and she expects to generate business that will bring in an additional $5,900 at the end of each of the next two years.

To calculate the present value, *PV*, of the marginal revenue product of a new computer, Tina uses the formula

$$PV = \frac{MRP_1}{(1+r)} + \frac{MRP_2}{(1+r)^2}.$$

Here, MRP_1 is the marginal revenue product received by Tina at the end of the first year. It is converted to a present value by dividing it by $(1 + r)$. The term MRP_2 is the marginal revenue product received at the end of the second year. It is converted to a present value by dividing it by $(1 + r)^2$.

Table 16.1(b) puts Tina's numbers into the present value formula and calculates the present value of the

---

TABLE 16.1

Net Present Value of an Investment—Taxfile, Inc.

(a) Data

Price of computer	$10,000
Life of computer	2 years
Marginal revenue product	$5,900 a year
Interest rate	4% a year

(b) Present value of the flow of marginal revenue product

$$PV = \frac{MRP_1}{1+r} + \frac{MRP_2}{(1+r)^2}$$

$$= \frac{\$5,900}{1.04} + \frac{\$5,900}{(1.04)^2}$$

$$= \$5,673 + \$5,455$$

$$= \$11,128$$

(c) Net present value of investment

$$NPV = PV \text{ of Marginal revenue product} - \text{Cost of computer}$$

$$= \$11,128 - \$10,000$$

$$= \$1,128$$

---

marginal revenue product of a computer. Tina can borrow or lend at an interest rate of 4 percent a year. The present value (*PV*) of $5,900 one year in the future is $5,900 divided by 1.04 (4 percent as a proportion is 0.04). The present value of $5,900 two years in the future is $5,900 divided by $(1.04)^2$. Working out those two present values and then adding them gives Tina the present value of the future stream of marginal revenue products, which is $11,128.

Tina's Decision to Buy   Tina decides whether to buy the computer by comparing the present value of its future flow of marginal revenue product with its purchase price. She makes this comparison by calculating the net present value (*NPV*) of the computer. **Net present value** is the present value of the future flow of marginal revenue product generated by the capital minus the cost of the capital. If the net present value is positive, the firm buys additional capital. If the net present value is negative, the firm does not buy additional capital. Table 16.1(c) shows the calculation of Tina's net present value of a computer. The net present value is $1,128—greater than zero—so Tina buys the computer.

Tina can buy any number of computers that cost $10,000 and have a life of two years. But like all other factors of production, capital is subject to diminishing marginal returns. The greater the amount of capital employed, the smaller is its marginal revenue product. So if Tina buys a second computer or a third one, she gets successively smaller marginal revenue products from the additional machines.

Table 16.2(a) sets out Tina's marginal revenue products for one, two, and three computers. The marginal revenue product of one computer (the case just reviewed) is $5,900 a year. The marginal revenue product of a second computer is $5,600 a year, and the marginal revenue product of a third computer is $5,300 a year. Table 16.2(b) shows the calculations of the present values of the marginal revenue products of the first, the second, and the third computers.

You've seen that with an interest rate of 4 percent a year, the net present value of one computer is positive. At an interest rate of 4 percent a year, the present value of the marginal revenue product of a second computer is $10,562, which exceeds its price by $562. So Tina buys a second computer. But at an interest rate of 4 percent a year, the present value of the marginal revenue product of a third computer is $9,996, which is $4 less than the price of the computer. So Tina does not buy a third computer.

A Change in the Interest Rate   We've seen that at an interest rate of 4 percent a year, Tina buys two computers but not three. Suppose that the interest rate is 8 percent a year. In this case, the present value of the first computer is $10,521 (see Table 16.2b), so Tina still buys one machine because it has a positive net present value. At an interest rate of 8 percent a year, the net present value of the second computer is $9,986, which is less than $10,000, the price of the computer. So, at an interest rate of 8 percent a year, Tina buys only one computer.

Suppose that the interest rate is even higher at 12 percent a year. In this case, the present value of the marginal revenue product of one computer is $9,971 (see Table 16.2b). At this interest rate, Tina buys no computers.

TABLE 16.2

Taxfile's Investment Decision

(a) Data

Price of computer	$10,000
Life of computer	2 years
Marginal revenue product:	
Using 1 computer	$5,900 a year
Using 2 computers	$5,600 a year
Using 3 computers	$5,300 a year

(b) Present value of the flow of marginal revenue product

If interest rate is 0.04 (4% a year):

Using 1 computer: $PV = \dfrac{\$5,900}{1.04} + \dfrac{\$5,900}{(1.04)^2} = \$11,128$

Using 2 computers: $PV = \dfrac{\$5,600}{1.04} + \dfrac{\$5,600}{(1.04)^2} = \$10,562$

Using 3 computers: $PV = \dfrac{\$5,300}{1.04} + \dfrac{\$5,300}{(1.04)^2} = \$9,996$

If interest rate is 0.08 (8% a year):

Using 1 computer: $PV = \dfrac{\$5,900}{1.08} + \dfrac{\$5,900}{(1.08)^2} = \$10,521$

Using 2 computers: $PV = \dfrac{\$5,600}{1.08} + \dfrac{\$5,600}{(1.08)^2} = \$9,986$

If interest rate is 0.12 (12% a year):

Using 1 computer: $PV = \dfrac{\$5,900}{1.12} + \dfrac{\$5,900}{(1.12)^2} = \$9,971$

These calculations trace Taxfile's demand schedule for capital, which shows the value of computers demanded by Taxfile at each interest rate. Other things remaining the same, as the interest rate rises, the quantity of capital demanded decreases. The higher the interest rate, the smaller is the quantity of *physical* capital demanded. But to finance the purchase of *physical* capital, firms demand *financial* capital. So, the higher the interest rate, the smaller is the quantity of *financial* capital demanded.

Demand Curve for Capital

The quantity of capital demanded by a firm depends on the marginal revenue product of capital and the interest rate. A firm's demand curve for capital shows the relationship between the quantity of capital demanded and the interest rate, other things remaining the same. Figure 16.2 illustrates Taxfile's demand for computers (D_F). Points *a*, *b*, and *c* correspond to the example that we have just worked through. At an interest rate of 12 percent a year, Tina buys no computers—point *a*. At an interest rate of 8 percent, she buys 1 computer worth $10,000—point *b*. At an interest rate of 4 percent, she buys 2 computers worth $20,000—point *c*.

We've considered only one type of computer— one that costs $10,000. But Tina can buy different types of computers, the power of which can be expressed as a multiple or fraction of a $10,000 computer. For example, there may be a $5,000 computer that has half the power of a $10,000 machine. Or a $12,500 machine that has one and a quarter the power of a $10,000 machine. If we consider all the different computers that Tina can buy, we generate not just the three points, *a*, *b*, and *c*, but Taxfile's entire demand curve—the blue curve in Fig. 16.2.

The Market Demand for Capital

The market demand curve for capital is the horizontal sum of all the individual firm's demand curves. Figure 16.3 shows the market demand curve, which like the firm's demand curve slopes downward. When the interest rate rises, other things remaining the same, the quantity of capital demanded decreases along the demand curve. Figure 16.3 shows such a change by the movement along demand curve D_0.

FIGURE 16.2
A Firm's Demand for Capital

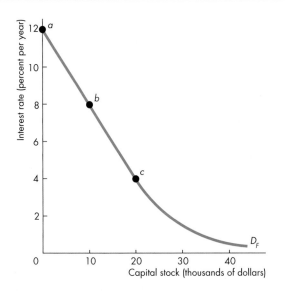

The lower the interest rate, the larger is the capital stock demanded. At an interest rate of 12 percent a year, Taxfile demands no computers (point *a*). At 8 percent a year, the firm demands 1 computer worth $10,000 (point *b*). At 4 percent a year, the firm demands 2 computers worth $20,000 (point *c*). If Taxfile can buy computers of different types (fractions of a $10,000 computer), the curve passing through points *a*, *b*, and *c* illustrates its demand.

FIGURE 16.3
The Demand for Capital

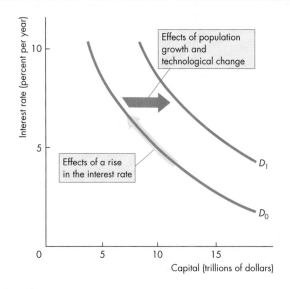

Other things remaining the same, the quantity of capital demanded decreases as the interest rate rises and there is a movement along the demand curve for capital. An increase in population and advances in technology increase the demand for capital and shift the demand curve rightward.

Changes in the Demand for Capital

The demand for capital changes when firms revise their expectations about the future marginal revenue product of capital. For example, Taxfile and other businesses might revise their expectations about marginal revenue product upward. If they do, the quantity of capital that has a positive present value increases at each interest rate. As a result, the demand for capital increases. The two main factors that change the marginal revenue product of capital and bring changes in the demand for capital are

1. Population growth
2. Technological change

Population growth brings a steady increase in the demand for capital. Technological change brings fluctuations in the demand for capital. Technological change increases the demand for some types of capital and decreases the demand for other types. For example, the development of diesel engines for railroad transportation decreased the demand for steam engines and increased the demand for diesel engines. In this case, the railroad industry's overall demand for capital did not change much. In contrast, the development of desktop computers increased the demand for office computing equipment, decreased the demand for electric typewriters, and increased the overall demand for capital in the office. Figure 16.3 shows such fluctuations in demand by a shift in the demand curve from D_0 to D_1.

R E V I E W

■ Firms' profit-maximization decisions determine the demand for capital—both *physical* and *financial*.

■ The quantity of capital demanded depends on the marginal revenue product of capital and the interest rate.

■ The higher the interest rate, the smaller is the present value of the future flow of marginal revenue products and the smaller is the quantity of capital demanded.

■ The demand for capital grows as population grows and fluctuates as technology changes.

The Supply of Capital

THE QUANTITY OF CAPITAL SUPPLIED RESULTS FROM people's saving decisions. Saving is a *flow*, which equals income minus consumption. The current market value of a household's past saving, together with any inheritances it has received, is the household's **wealth**, which is a *stock*. Households hold their wealth as financial capital such as stocks, bonds, and bank deposits, and as physical capital such as houses, cars, and other consumer durable goods. The wealth that households hold as financial capital is used by firms to finance the purchase of physical capital. So for the economy, wealth equals the value of physical capital—the total value of the physical capital of both households and firms.

Portfolio Choices   A household's decision about how to hold wealth is called a *portfolio choice*. In everyday language, we often refer to the purchase of stocks and bonds as investment. That everyday use of the word "investment" can cause confusion in economic analysis. It is to avoid this confusion that we use the term "portfolio choice" to refer to the choices that households make in allocating their wealth across the various assets available to them. *Investment* is the purchase of new physical capital.

The Saving Decision

The main factors that determine saving are

■ Income
■ Expected future income
■ Interest rate

Income   Saving is the act of converting *current* income into *future* consumption. Usually, the higher a household's income, the more it plans to consume both in the present and in the future. But to increase *future* consumption, the household must save. So, other things remaining the same, the higher a household's income, the more it saves.

Expected Future Income   Because a major reason for saving is to increase future consumption, the amount that a household saves depends not only on its current income but also on its *expected future income*. If a household's current income is high and its expected future income is low, it will have a high level of saving. But if its current income is low and its expected future income is high, it will have a low (perhaps even negative) level of saving.

Young people (especially students) usually have low current incomes compared with their expected future income. To smooth out their lifetime consumption, they consume more than they earn and incur debts. Such people have a negative amount of saving. In middle age, most people's incomes reach their peak. At this stage in life, saving is at its maximum. After retirement, people spend part of the wealth they have accumulated during their working lives.

Interest Rate　A dollar saved today grows into a dollar plus interest tomorrow. The higher the interest rate, the greater the amount that a dollar saved today becomes in the future. Thus the higher the interest rate, the greater is the opportunity cost of current consumption. Interest rates have two influences on saving. They are

1. Substitution effect
2. Income effect

1. *Substitution Effect.* Because a higher interest rate increases the future return from today's saving and increases the opportunity cost of current consumption, it stimulates saving. It encourages people to economize on current consumption and take advantage of the higher interest rate. That is, the substitution effect of interest rates on saving is positive. Other things remaining the same, the higher the interest rate, the greater is the quantity of saving.
2. *Income Effect.* A change in the interest rate changes a household's *future* income. Other things remaining the same, as a household's income increases, so too does its consumption. But the effect of a change in the interest rate on a household's income depends on whether the household is a net lender or a net borrower. For a net lender, an increase in interest rates increases future income, so it increases both current and future consumption and it decreases saving. The income effect opposes the substitution effect, and saving might increase or decrease depending on the relative strengths of the two effects. For a net borrower, an increase in interest rates decreases future income and decreases both current and future consumption. So saving increases. In this case, the income effect of a higher interest rate reinforces the substitution effect.

For individual households that are net lenders, the effect of a change in the interest rate on saving is ambiguous, but for households that are net borrowers, and for the economy as a whole, there is no ambiguity: Other things remaining the same, the higher the interest rate, the greater is the flow of saving in a given period and the greater is the stock of financial capital supplied.

Supply Curve of Capital

The quantity of capital supplied is the total value of accumulated saving—wealth. Figure 16.4 shows the supply curve of capital—the relationship between the quantity of capital supplied and the interest rate, other things remaining the same. An increase in the interest rate brings an increase in the quantity of capital supplied and a movement along the supply curve, as shown along the supply curve S_0. The supply curve is inelastic in the short run, but probably quite elastic in the long run. The reason is that in any given year, the

FIGURE　16.4

The Supply of Capital

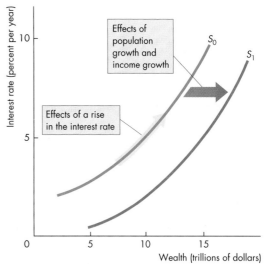

Other things remaining the same, the quantity of capital supplied increases as the interest rate rises and there is a movement along the supply curve for capital. An increase in population and rising incomes increase the supply of capital and shift the supply curve rightward.

total amount of saving is small relative to the stock of wealth. So even a large change in the saving rate brings only a small change in the supply of capital.

Changes in the Supply of Capital   A change in any influence on saving plans other than the interest rate changes the amount of saving and shifts the supply of capital curve. The main influences on the supply of capital are income and its distribution and the size and age distribution of the population.

Other things remaining the same, an increase in income or an increase in the population brings an increase in the supply of capital. Also, other things remaining the same, the more unequally income is distributed, the greater is the saving rate. The reason is that low-income and middle-income families have low saving rates, while families with high incomes have high saving rates. So the larger the proportion of total income earned by the highest income families, the greater is the amount of saving. Finally, and again other things remaining the same, the larger the proportion of middle-aged people, the higher is the saving rate. The reason is that middle-aged people do most of the saving as they build up a pension fund to provide an income in their retirement.

Any of the factors that increase the supply of capital shifts the supply curve of capital rightward, as shown in Fig. 16.4, where the supply of capital shifts from S_0 to S_1.

R E V I E W

■ The quantity of capital supplied is determined by saving decisions.

■ Other things remaining the same, the higher the interest rate, the larger the quantity of capital supplied.

■ The supply of capital changes as a result of changes in income and its distribution and in the population and its age composition. Income growth and population growth bring a steady increase in the supply of capital.

We have studied the demand for and supply of capital. We now bring these two sides of the capital market together and study the determination of interest rates and asset prices. We'll then be able to answer some of the questions posed at the beginning of this chapter about the stock market and understand the forces that produce stock market booms and crashes.

Interest Rates and Stock Prices

SAVING PLANS AND INVESTMENT PLANS ARE coordinated through capital markets. Interest rates, stock prices, and bond prices adjust to make these plans compatible. We are now going to study the way in which these market forces work. We are also going to discover what determines the stock market value of a firm.

Two Sides of the Same Coin

Interest rates and stock (and bond) prices can be viewed as two sides of the same coin. We'll look first at interest rates, then at stock (and bond) prices, and finally at the connection between them. The interest rate on a stock is called a *stock yield* and is the dividend on the stock, expressed as a percentage of the price of the stock. The interest rate on a bond is called a *bond yield* and is the coupon payment of the bond, expressed as a percentage of the price of the bond. So, to calculate a stock (or bond) yield, we divide the earnings of the stock (or bond) by its price. For example, if Taxfile, Inc. pays a dividend of $5 a share and if the price of a share is $50, then the stock yield is 10 percent ($5 divided by $50, expressed as a percentage). If Taxfile's dividend is $5 and the stock price is $100, then the stock yield is 5 percent.

These calculations show that for a given amount dividend, the higher the price of a stock, the lower its yield. This connection between the price of a stock and its yield or interest rate means that we can study the market forces in capital markets as simultaneously determining interest rates (yields) and stock and bond prices. We will first look at capital market equilibrium in terms of interest rate (or yield) determination and then in terms of the stock market value of a firm.

Equilibrium Interest Rate

Figure 16.5 shows the capital market. The horizontal axis measures the total quantity of capital. Notice that the axis is labelled "Capital stock and wealth." This label emphasizes the fact that the value of the capital stock and wealth are equivalent. The vertical axis measures the interest rate. The demand curve is D, and the supply curve is S. Equilibrium in the capital

FIGURE 16.5

Capital Market Equilibrium ◆

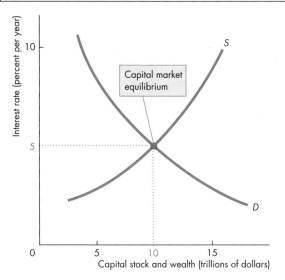

Capital market equilibrium occurs when the interest rate is such that the quantity of capital demanded equals the quantity of capital supplied. The demand curve is D and the supply curve is S. These curves intersect at an interest rate of 5 percent a year and a capital stock of $10 trillion.

market occurs where the quantity of capital supplied equals the quantity of capital demanded. In Fig. 16.5, this equilibrium is at an interest rate of 5 percent a year and $10 trillion of capital is supplied and demanded.

The market forces that bring about this equilibrium are the same as those that we studied in the markets for goods and services. If the interest rate exceeds 5 percent a year, the quantity of financial capital demanded is less than the quantity supplied. There is a surplus of funds in the capital market. In such a situation, as lenders compete to make loans, interest rates fall. The quantity of financial capital demanded increases as firms increase their borrowing and buy more capital goods. The interest rate continues to fall until lenders are able to lend all the funds they wish at that interest rate.

Conversely, if the interest rate is below 5 percent a year, the quantity of financial capital supplied is less than the quantity demanded. There is a shortage of funds in the capital market. Borrowers are unable to borrow all the funds they wish so they offer a higher interest rate. Interest rates increase until there are no unsatisfied borrowers. In either case, the interest rate converges on 5 percent a year, the equilibrium interest rate.

The institutions that specialize in trading in financial capital markets—banks, insurance companies, and specialized dealers—handle millions of dollars of business every day and maintain a near continuous equality between the quantity of capital demanded and the quantity supplied. These same competitive forces ensure that the interest rate is the same in all parts of the capital market, both across the regions of the nation and around the world.

The interest rate determined in Fig. 16.5 is the *average* interest rate. Interest rates on individual assets will be distributed around this average, based on the relative degree of riskiness of individual assets. An asset with a high degree of risk will earn an interest rate that exceeds the average, and a very safe asset will earn an interest rate that is below the average. The riskier asset earns a higher interest rate to compensate for the higher risk. For example, if the average interest rate is 5 percent a year as shown in Fig. 16.5, the interest rate on a bank deposit (a safer asset) might be 3 percent a year and that on the stock of a corporation (a riskier asset) might be 8 percent a year.

We've now seen how interest rates (yields) are determined. Let's look at the other side of the coin—stock (and bond) prices. To do so, we'll look at the stock market value of a firm.

Stock Market Value of a Firm

What determines the price of a firm's stock? The price of a firm's stock depends on the dividends the firm is expected to pay and on the investor's opportunity cost, which is the interest rate forgone. To see why, suppose that Pronto, a printing firm, is expected to pay a dividend of $10 per share in each future year and that the interest rate is 10 percent a year. The price of Pronto's stock will be $100 a share. At this price, Pronto's stock has an expected yield of 10 percent a year, which equals the opportunity cost of holding the stock—the interest rate. If the price of Pronto's stock was less than $100 a share, its expected yield would exceed 10 percent. In this case, people would buy Pronto's stock and its price would rise. If the price of Pronto's stock was more than $100 a share, its expected yield would be less than 10 percent a year. In this case, people would sell Pronto's stock and its price would fall. Only when the price of Pronto's stock is $100 a share and its expected yield is 10 percent a year—the same as the current interest rate—do people neither buy nor sell the stock. So only when its price is $100 does it remain constant. So if a firm is expected to pay a dividend of $10 a share and if the interest rate is 10 percent a year, the price of the firm's stock will be $100 a share. The stock market value of the firm equals the price of a share multiplied by the number of shares.

The price of a firm's stock increases if the expected dividend increases or if the interest rate falls. For example, if Pronto becomes more profitable and is expected to pay a dividend of $20 a share in each future year and the interest rate remains at 10 percent a year, the price of Pronto's stock will rise to $200 a share. And if Pronto is expected to pay a dividend of $10 a share each future year but the interest rate falls to 5 percent a year, the price of Pronto's stock will also rise to $200 a share.

Price-Earnings Ratio

A commonly used measure to describe the performance of a firm's stock is its price-earnings ratio. A *price-earnings ratio* is the current price of a share in a firm's stock divided by the most recent year's profit per share. In March 1982, the average price-earnings ratio of the stocks that formed the TSE 300 was 7.6. (The TSE 300 is an index of 300 stocks that are traded on the Toronto Stock Exchange.) By July 1987, the price-earnings ratio had risen to 21.6, but that was a peak year. The ratio then declined, and in January 1996, stood at 14.84.

What determines a price-earnings ratio? Why, in January 1996, was the Bank of Montreal's price-earnings ratio only 9.2 while the *Toronto Sun's* was 29.7? The higher a firm's *expected future* dividend, the higher is the *current* price of its stock. Expected future dividends depend on the firm's expected future profit. So the bigger the future profit is expected to be, the bigger is the future dividend people expected the firm to pay and the higher is the current price of its stock. Because the firm's price-earnings ratio is the ratio of its current price to its *current* profit, its price-earnings ratio depends on its expected future profit relative to its current profit. When expected future profit is high relative to current profit, the price-earnings ratio is high. Fluctuations in the price-earnings ratio arise from fluctuations in expected future profit relative to current profit.

Stock Market Volume and Prices

Sometimes stock prices rise or fall with little trading taking place. At other times, they rise or fall with an enormous volume of trading. What determines the volume of stock traded?

We've seen that stock prices rise and fall because of changes in expectations of future dividends and changes in interest rates. Suppose expected future dividends increase and suppose the source of this expectation is so obvious that everyone can see it. Everyone agrees that a firm's earnings are going to be higher in the future. In this situation, the price of the firm's shares rises but no one buys or sells shares. Shareholders are happy with the shares they already hold, and the price rises to make the expected yield (new expected dividend divided by the new price) equal to the interest rate on other assets. If the price rises further so that the expected yield is less than the interest rate, people will sell the stock and buy other assets. Their actions will lower the price until the expected yield equals the interest rate.

Conversely, suppose that an event occurs that will change this firm's future profit, but it is difficult to forecast how it will change. Some people believe that dividends will increase, and others believe that they will decrease. Call the first group optimists and the second group pessimists. The optimists will buy this firm's stock, and the pessimists will sell it. The price will not necessarily change, but a large volume of shares will be traded. What increases the volume traded is the disagreement, not the event that triggered the change in expected profitability. A large volume of shares traded on the stock market implies a large amount of disagreement.

Large changes in stock prices with small volumes of shares traded imply a great deal of agreement that something fundamental has changed. Large volumes traded with hardly any price change mean that the underlying changes are difficult to interpret: Some people predict that profitability will increase while others predict it will decrease.

Takeovers and Mergers

The theory of capital markets that you've now studied can be used to explain why takeovers and mergers occur. A **takeover** is the purchase of the stock of one firm by another firm. A takeover occurs when the stock market value of a firm is less than the present value of the expected future profits from operating the firm. For example, suppose that Taxfile, Inc. has a stock market value of $120,000. If the present value of its expected future profit is $150,000, someone will have an incentive to take over the firm. Takeover activity affects the price of a firm, and often the threat of a takeover drives the price to the point at which the takeover is no longer profitable.

But a takeover does occur if the profitability of the firm taken over is expected to be larger after the takeover than it was before. One recent example that illustrates this possibility is the takeover of Big V Pharmacies by Imasco. Imasco is a large company that owns the Shoppers Drug Mart and Pharmaprix chains. Imasco believed it could operate Big V stores more profitably than Big V could operate on its own. So Imasco was willing to offer a higher price for Big V's stock than the current market value.

A **merger** is the combining of the assets of two firms to form a single, new firm. Mergers take place when two firms perceive that, by combining their assets, they can increase their combined stock market values. For example, Tim Hortons and Wendy's (see Chapter 9, pp. 204–205) will be able to share and learn together and increase their profits as they expand the combo chain across North America.

R E V I E W

- An interest rate (or yield) is the dividend on a stock (or coupon payment on a bond) expressed as a percentage of the price of the stock (or bond).
- For a given dividend (or coupon payment), as the price of a stock (or bond) increases, its interest rate decreases.
- The average interest rate (and stock or bond price) makes the quantity of capital supplied equal to the quantity demanded.
- The stock market value of a firm fluctuates because its expected dividend fluctuates. The price-earnings ratio fluctuates because current profit relative to expected future profit changes.
- Takeovers and mergers occur when the current stock market value of the firm is less than the present value of the expected future profits that another firm believes it can generate.

The lessons that we've just learned about capital markets have wider application than explaining fluctuations in the stock market. They also help us to understand how natural resource markets work.

Natural Resource Markets

THE NONPRODUCED FACTORS OF PRODUCTION are **natural resources**. Natural resources fall into two categories: exhaustible and nonexhaustible. **Exhaustible natural resources** are natural resources that can be used only once and that cannot be replaced once used. Examples of exhaustible natural resources are coal, natural gas, and oil—the so-called hydrocarbon fuels. **Nonexhaustible natural resources** are natural resources that can be used repeatedly without depleting what is available for future use. Examples of nonexhaustible natural resources are land, seas, rivers and lakes, rain, air, and sunshine. Plants and animals are also examples of nonexhaustible natural resources. By careful cultivation and husbandry, more of these natural resources can be produced to replace those used up in production and consumption activities.

Natural resources have two important economic dimensions: a stock and a flow. Stocks are determined by nature and by the previous rate of use of the resource and flows—the rates of use—are determined by human choices. We first consider the stock dimension.

Supply and Demand in a Natural Resource Market

The stock of a natural resource supplied is the amount of the resource in existence. For example, the stock of oil supplied is the total volume of oil lying beneath the earth's surface. This amount is fixed independently of the price of the resource. Its supply is perfectly inelastic.

The actual stock supplied is not the same as the known (or proven) quantity. The known quantity of a natural resource is smaller than the actual quantity supplied, and the known quantity can actually increase even if the resource is being used. The known quantity of a natural resource increases for two reasons. First, advances in technology enable ever less accessible resources to be discovered. Second, as the price of a natural resource rises, other things remaining the same, the incentive to widen the search for additional reserves is strengthened. Both of these factors operated to double the known reserves of oil between 1970 and 1996. During this same period, the quantity of oil consumed exceeded the 1970 known reserves.

Demand for a Stock The stock of a natural resource demanded is determined by the *expected* rate of return or expected interest rate from holding the stock. The reason is that firms buy stocks of natural resources as an alternative to buying stocks, bonds, or physical capital, and they do so in the expectation of making a return.

What determines the expected interest rate on the stock of a natural resource? The answer is the rate of economic profit available from extracting and selling the stock, plus the rate at which the price of the resource is expected to rise. If the market for the extracted resource is competitive, firms will make only a normal profit on their extraction activity, so the return from holding a natural resource comes from increases in the price of the resource. The faster the price of a natural resource increases, the higher is the return from owning that natural resource. Because firms don't know the future, they must forecast this interest rate and the forecasted or *expected* interest rate is equal to the *expected* percentage increase in the price of the resource.

Stock Equilibrium Equilibrium occurs in the market for the stock of a natural resource when the price of the resource is *expected* to rise at a rate equal to the interest rate on similarly risky stocks and bonds. This proposition is called the **Hotelling Principle**.[1]

Why is the price of a natural resource expected to grow at a rate equal to the interest rate on similarly risky assets? It is to make the expected interest rate on the natural resource equal to the interest rate on other comparably risky stocks and bonds. Firms look for the highest returns they can find, holding risk constant. So if the expected interest rate on a stock of a natural resource exceeds that on stocks or bonds with similar risk, firms buy natural resources and sell stocks and bonds. Conversely, if the expected interest rate on a natural resource is less than that on stocks or bonds with similar risk, firms buy stocks and bonds and sell natural resources.

Equilibrium occurs in the market for the stock of a natural resource when prices and expectations about future prices have adjusted to make the *expected* interest rate earned on the natural resource equal to the interest rate on similarly risky stocks and bonds.

---

[1]The Hotelling Principle, discovered by Harold Hotelling, first appeared in "Economics of Exhaustible Resources," *Journal of Political Economy* 39 (April 1931): 137–175.

Supply and demand in the market for the stock of a natural resource determine the interest rate from owning that stock, which means that they determine the future *expected rate of change* of the price. But what determines the *current price* of the resource? To determine the *current* price of a natural resource, we must consider not only the supply of and demand for the stock of the resource but also the demand for its use.

Price of a Natural Resource

To determine the price of a natural resource, we must consider the influences on the demand for the use of the natural resource. Then we will study the equilibrium that emerges from the interaction of the demand for the use of the resource—the demand for a *flow*—with the demand to own the natural resource—the demand for a *stock*.

Demand for the Use of a Natural Resources

Figure 16.6(a) shows the demand curve, *D*, for the flow of a natural resource for use in production. This demand curve is determined in a similar way to that for the services of any other factor of production. A firm in a perfectly competitive market maximizes profit by using the quantity of a natural resource that makes the marginal revenue product of the resource equal to its price. Marginal revenue product diminishes as the quantity of the resource used increases so the lower the price of a resource, the greater is the quantity demanded for use in production.

For any resource, there is a price that is so high that no one uses it. The price at which no one uses a natural resource is called the **choke price**. It is the price at which the demand curve touches the price axis. In Fig. 16.6(a), the choke price is $144 a tonne. Everything has substitutes and at a high enough price—the choke price—only a substitute will be used. For example, we do not have to put soft drinks in aluminum cans; we can use plastic bottles instead. We do not have to power cars with gasoline; we can use alcohol, electricity, or natural gas instead. We do not have to generate electric power with coal, oil, or uranium; we can use solar or tidal energy instead. The natural resources that we *do* use are the least expensive resources available at the time they are used. They cost us less than the next best alternative would. For example, if the price of plastic makes the price of plastic bottles more expensive than aluminum cans, soft drink producers will use aluminum

FIGURE 16.6

The Market for an Exhaustible Natural Resource

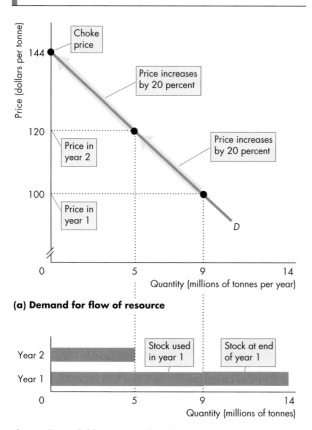

(a) Demand for flow of resource

(b) Stock available at start of each year

In part (a) at a price below $144—the *choke price*—the quantity demanded is positive and the lower the price, the larger is the quantity demanded. In part (b) the initial stock of the resource is 14 million tonnes. The interest rate is 20 percent a year. The current price is $100, which is determined by working backwards from the choke price. Starting from $100, the price rises by 20 percent a year to reach the choke price in two years. The demand curve (*D*) tells us that the quantity demanded (used) in the first year is 9 million tonnes and the quantity used in the second year is 5 million tonnes. Part (b) shows that the initial stock of 14 million tonnes is exhausted after two years.

Equilibrium Stock and Flow

The price of a natural resource and its rate of use depend on three things:

1. The interest rate
2. The demand for the flow of the resource
3. The stock of the resource

Figure 16.6 shows how these three factors combine to determine the price and rate of use of a natural resource. We start at the time the resource becomes depleted and work backwards. When the resource is depleted the quantity supplied is zero, so the quantity demanded must also be zero. The price that makes the quantity demanded zero is the choke price. So, at the end of the life of a resource, its price equals the choke price. In Fig. 16.6, this price is $144 a tonne.

With a given stock of the resource, its price must be expected to rise at a rate equal to the interest rate. Given this fact, the price in the year before the resource is depleted must be less than the choke price by a percentage amount determined by the interest rate. In Fig. 16.6(a), the interest rate is 20 percent a year, so the price in the year before depletion is $120 a tonne. A 20 percent price rise takes the price to the choke price of $144 a tonne the following year. We now repeat this type of calculation. The price two years before depletion is yet lower and in the example is $100 a tonne. A 20 percent increase takes the price to $120 tonne in the following year and to $144 a tonne in two years.

We repeat this calculation for as many years as necessary until the accumulated amount of the resource used up, which is determined by the demand curve and the sequence of prices we've calculated, just exhausts the current stock of the resource. In Fig. 16.6, the stock is exhausted in only two years. (This short life lets you see the principles more clearly.) To see that the stock depletes after two years, notice in part (b) of the figure that the stock at the start of year 1 is 14 million tonnes. In year 1, the price is $100 a tonne, and part (a) shows that the quantity used is 9 million tonnes. The blue bar in part (b) shows the stock used in year 1. In year 2, the price rises to $120 a tonne and the quantity used is 5 million tonnes, the red bar in part (b). The total quantity used, 9 million tonnes plus 5 million tonnes, exhausts the 14 million tonnes available at the start of year 1. The price of this natural resource starts at $100 a tonne in year 1 and rises by 20 percent a year for two years until it reaches its choke

cans. But as the price of aluminum increases, soft drink producers will substitute plastic bottles for aluminum cans.

price of $144 a tonne, at which time the natural resource is depleted. That is, the current price of the natural resource and the rate at which it is used is determined by the interest rate, the demand for the flow of the resource, and the current stock available.

The higher the interest rate, the lower is the current price of a natural resource. You can see this fact by recalling that the price must end up at the choke price. At a higher interest rate, the price must rise more quickly and end up at the same price (as determined by the demand for the flow), so its current price must be lower. But a lower price means that the resource is used up at a faster rate.

The greater the marginal revenue product of the natural resource—the larger the demand for the flow of the natural resource—the higher is the current price of the resource. A greater marginal revenue product means that the demand curve for the resource lies farther to the right and that the choke price is higher. A higher current price decreases the quantity of the resource demanded used to ensure that the current stock equals the quantities demanded over the remaining years of the life of the resource.

The larger the initial stock of the natural resource, the lower is the current price. The larger the known stock, the bigger is the quantity that must be used up before the choke price is reached. To induce an increase in the quantity used, the price of the resource must be lower.

Expected Prices and Actual Prices

Equilibrium in the market for a natural resource determines the current price of the resource and the *expected* rate of change of its future price. But the actual price rarely follows its expected path. For example, the price of oil between 1970 and 1994 did not follow the path predicted by the Hotelling Principle. Also, the prices of metals have tended to fall, as Fig. 16.7 shows. This fact was the basis of a famous wager between a conservationist and an economist—see *Economics in History* on pp. 342–343. Why do natural resource prices fluctuate and sometimes even fall rather than follow their expected path and increase over time?

The price of a natural resource depends on expectations about future events. In particular, it depends on expectations about the interest rate, the future demand for the use of the resource, and the size of the known stock, which in turn depends on

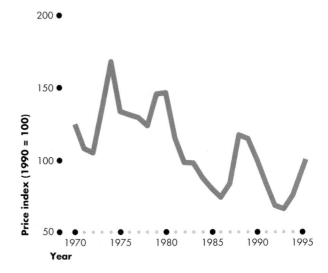

FIGURE   16.7

Falling Resource Prices

The prices of metals (here an average of the prices of aluminum, copper, iron ore, lead, manganese, nickel, silver, tin, and zinc) have tended to fall over time, not rise as expected by the Hotelling Principle. The reason is that advances in technology have decreased the cost of extracting resources and greatly increased the exploitable known reserves.

Source: International Monetary Fund, *International Financial Statistics,* Washington, DC (various issues).

the technologies and costs of extracting it. Natural resource markets are constantly being bombarded by new information that leads to new expectations. For example, new information about the stock of a resource or the technologies available for its use or extraction can lead to sudden and perhaps quite large changes in the price of a natural resource.

All of these forces have been at work in many of the markets for exhaustible natural resources in recent years. The market for oil illustrates these effects very well. The discovery of new sources of supply and of new extraction technologies has resulted in previously unforeseen increases in the known stock of oil. The development of energy-efficient automobile and airplane engines has slowed the growth in the quantity of oil used for transportation to below what was expected in the early 1970s. The combination of these factors has led to a fall in the price of oil. And changes in interest rates—up and down—have brought fluctuations in the price of oil.

An additional force leading to price changes in natural resource markets in general and in the oil market in particular is the degree of competitiveness in the markets. The model market that we have been studying is a perfectly competitive one. But the real-world market for oil has been dominated by the OPEC cartel, an oligopoly similar to that analysed in Chapter 13. The declining power of the OPEC cartel contributed significantly to the decline in the price of oil during the 1980s.

Conservation and Doomsday

The theory of the price of a natural resource and its expected change over time has important implications for the popular debate about the use of natural resources. Many people fear that we are using the earth's exhaustible natural resources at such a rapid pace that we will eventually (and perhaps in the not very distant future) run out of sources of energy and other crucial raw materials. Such people urge a slowing down in the rate at which we use exhaustible natural resources so that the limited stocks available today will last longer.

This topic is an emotional one and generates passionate debate. It is also a matter that involves economic issues that can be understood using the economic model of a depletable natural resource that you have just studied.

The economic analysis of an exhaustible natural resource market predicts that doomsday—the using up of the entire stock of a natural resource—will eventually arise if our use of natural resources is organized in competitive markets. The economic model also implies that a competitive market will provide an automatic conservation program arising from the steadily rising price. As the stock of a natural resource gets closer and closer to depletion, its price gets closer to the choke price—the price at which no one wants to use the resource any more. Each year, as the price rises, the quantity demanded of the flow declines.

But what if the resource gets completely used up? Don't we have a real problem then? We have the problem of scarcity but in no more acute a form than we had it before. Everything has substitutes. The resource that is no longer available was used because it was more efficient to use it than some alternative. For

example, it is more efficient to generate electricity today by using coal and oil rather than solar power. It is efficient to stop using an exhaustible resource only when a lower-cost alternative is available. This substitution might occur before the resource is depleted or at the same time as it becomes depleted. So, the market economy handles the depleting stocks of natural resources by persistently forcing up their prices. Higher prices cause us to ration our use and eventually drive the quantity demanded of the flow to zero. This happens when the supply of the stock disappears.

But will a competitive market lead us to use our scarce exhaustible natural resources at an efficient rate? Perfectly competitive markets for goods and services achieve allocative efficiency if there are no external costs and benefits. (See Chapter 11, pp. 249–251.) The same proposition applies to markets for natural resources. If there are no external costs or benefits arising from the use of a natural resource, then the rate of its use determined in a perfectly competitive exhaustible natural resource market is the efficient rate of use. But if external costs arise from the use of a natural resource, efficiency requires a slower rate of use of the resource than that in the competitive market. For example, if burning hydrocarbon fuels increases the carbon dioxide in the atmosphere and a warming of the earth's atmosphere results—the so-called greenhouse effect—the costs associated with this atmospheric change have to be added to the costs of using oil and coal as fuels. When these costs are taken into account, the allocatively efficient rate of use of these fuels is slower than that resulting from a perfectly competitive market. *Reading Between the Lines* on pp. 382–383 looks further at the issue of exhaustible fuel resources.

◆ We have now studied the way in which factor markets allocate scarce productive resources—labour, capital, and land—and the determination of factor prices and factor incomes. The prices and quantities determined in factor markets in turn determine the distribution of income among individuals and families. And that income distribution determines *for whom* goods and services are produced. But that outcome is uncertain. People decide what type of work to do, how much to save, and what to do with their savings with no sure knowledge of the incomes they'll receive from their decisions. In the next chapter, we study uncertainty and its consequences in a more systematic way and we discover some of the ways in which we cope with uncertainty.

Policy WATCH

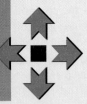

An Exhausting Natural Resource

Essence of THE STORY

■ World oil consumption was almost 65 million barrels per day (bpd) in 1994–1995 and is predicted to be 86 million bpd in 2010 and more than 100 million bpd in 2020.

■ Efforts to encourage alternative energy sources and high gasoline taxes have had little effect on consumption.

■ Up to 2050, there will be no shortage of crude oil and natural gas and no viable alternative to oil as the preferred fuel for transport.

■ Alberta's Athabasca oil sands and heavy oil deposits are large enough to serve Canada and maintain exports well into the next century.

■ Production from the Canadian West and from fields in the Middle East, Siberia, and South America should allow the world to avoid an oil shortage.

CALGARY HERALD, MAY 13, 1996

We're hooked on oil: we can't kick the habit

REUTER

The world's costly addiction to oil shows no signs of easing and is likely to continue right to the middle of the next century, energy experts, including a Calgarian, said Sunday.

Despite the efforts of environmental lobbies to encourage alternative energy sources and punitive government taxes imposed on gasoline, motorists and industrial users have not been weaned from the black liquid gold nor, on current predictions, are they likely to be.

"Politicians get very excited about alternative fuels. But there will be no alternative to oil and gas for many years to come. ...For the next 30 to 50 years oil will remain the foundation of energy," Hisham Khatib, a vice-chairman at the World Energy Council, told industry executives Sunday in Dubai, the United Arab Emirates.

"For the next few decades, probably up to 2050, there will be no shortage of global resources of crude oil and nat-ural gas...no viable alternative to oil as the preferred fuel for transport," Khatib added.

While the demand is growing, Alberta has abundant oil to meet that demand, Grant Billing, president of Norcen Energy Resources Ltd., and past chairman of the Canadian Association of Petroleum Producers, said Sunday.

He noted the Athabasca oil sands and heavy oil deposits in the Canadian West have more than enough supply to serve Canada and maintain exports well into the next century.

Those sources, and production from fields in the Middle East, Siberia and South America should allow the world [to] continue to defy earlier predictions of an oil shortage, said Khatib.

...

Led by the growing economies of the Pacific Rim and China, global demand of nearly 65 million barrels per day (bpd) in 1994-1995 is set to reach 86 million bpd in 2010 and more than 100 million bpd in 2020, according to Khati.

Economic

ANALYSIS

■ As the world economy expands, so does world oil consumption.

■ With this rapid economic growth, the world consumption of oil will continue to increase into the twenty-first century.

■ Because oil is a depletable natural resource, its price is predicted to rise steadily.

■ Figure I shows the price of oil from 1965 to 1995. The trend increase over this period is 1.75 percent per year.

■ But huge fluctuations above this trend occurred in 1973–1974 and 1979 when the Organization of Petroleum Exporting Countries (OPEC) created a cartel that charged the monopoly price.

■ With very high prices, new oil sources of supply were discovered and the OPEC cartel broke in the 1980s. As it did, the price of oil returned to the path predicted by the theory of natural resource pricing.

■ We don't know if events like the OPEC cartel will occur in the future or know how much undiscovered oil will be found. Both of these factors will influence the future price of oil.

■ The table shows some future prices of oil on two assumptions: One, the current trend, assumes the price continues to rise at 1.75 percent per year; the other assumes the rise is 2.5 percent a year. This number is closer to the long-term average real interest rate.

■ The news article predicts that world oil consumption will rise to 86 million barrels per day in 2010, to more than 100 million barrels per day in 2020, and that there will be no shortage, even in 2050.

■ We do not know what assumptions lie behind these predictions. But if the price follows the path predicted by the theory of natural resource prices, oil will likely remain a major fuel through 2050 and then start to be replaced by alternatives.

■ At a price of between $45 and $80 a barrel, oil will be at a similar price to that reached during the late 1970s and early 1980s. There is a big incentive to find alternatives, but there is not a big range of cost effective alternatives available.

■ At a price of between $105 and $280 a barrel, the range in the table for 2100, lots of cost effective alternatives to oil exist: for example, electric power generated by solar and tidal technologies.

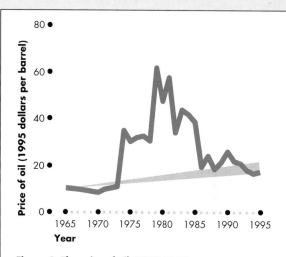

Figure 1 The price of oil: 1965–1995

The Future Price of Oil

Year	Current trend	2.5%-a-year trend
	(1995 dollars per barrel)	
2000	18.71	24.23
2010	22.25	31.01
2020	26.45	39.70
2050	44.47	83.27
2100	105.68	286.21

You're

THE VOTER

■ What should the government do today to deal with the fact that one day we will run out of oil?

■ Should the government leave the problem to market forces or should it intervene in some way to cut current consumption?

■ How would you vote on this issue? Give your reasons.

S U M M A R Y

Key Points

The Structure of Capital Markets   Capital markets determine interest rates, which coordinate the saving plans of households and the investment plans of firms. The stocks of corporations are traded in stock markets such as the Toronto Stock Exchange. The bonds of corporations and governments are traded in bond markets. Loans are made in loan markets in which financial intermediaries play the main role. (pp. 367–368)

The Demand for Capital   The demand for capital is determined by firms' profit-maximization decisions. The quantity of capital demanded by a firm is such that the marginal revenue product of capital equals its opportunity cost—the interest rate. Other things remaining the same, the lower the interest rate, the greater is the present value of the future flow of marginal revenue products and the greater is the quantity of capital equipment a firm buys. The demand curve for capital is downward sloping. The demand for capital changes when firms revise their expectations of the marginal revenue product of capital. The main influences on firms' expectations are population growth and technological change. The demand curve for capital shifts steadily rightward as a result of population growth, but technological change creates variability in the pace at which the demand for capital increases. (pp. 368–372)

The Supply of Capital   The supply of capital results from the saving decisions of households, which depend on current income, expected future income, and the interest rate. Other things remaining the same, as interest rates rise, the quantity of capital supplied increases—the supply curve of capital is upward sloping. Changes in the size and the age composition of the population and changes in income and its distribution change the supply of capital and shift the supply curve of capital over time. (pp. 372–374)

Interest Rates and Stock Prices   Interest rates and stock (or bond) prices can be viewed as two sides of the same coin. Interest rates and stock (or bond) prices adjust to achieve equality between the quantity of capital demanded and the quantity supplied.

Interest rates on particular assets are distributed around the average rate according to the degree of riskiness of different types of assets. The price of a firm's stock relative to its current profit is indicated by the price-earnings ratio and might be high or low. (pp. 374–377)

Natural Resource Markets   The price of a natural resource is determined by the interest rate, the marginal revenue product of the natural resource, and the stock of the natural resource. The price is such that its future price is expected to rise at a rate equal to the interest rate and to reach the choke price when the resource is exhausted. The actual price constantly changes with new information. Even though the future price is expected to rise, the actual price often falls because new information increases the estimated remaining stock or decreases the future demand. (pp. 377–381)

Key Figures

Figure 16.1   Capital Market Flows, 367
Figure 16.3   The Demand for Capital, 371
Figure 16.4   The Supply of Capital, 373
Figure 16.5   Capital Market Equilibrium, 375

Key Terms

Bond market, 368
Choke price, 378
Depreciation, 368
Exhaustible natural resources, 377
Financial intermediary, 367
Hotelling Principle, 378
Loan market, 368
Merger, 377
Natural resources, 377
Net investment, 368
Net present value, 369
Nonexhaustible natural resources, 377
Stock market, 367
Takeover, 376
Wealth, 372

REVIEW QUESTIONS

1. Describe the structure of the capital markets.
2. Distinguish between financial capital and physical capital.
3. Describe the main flows of funds in the capital markets.
4. Distinguish among the stock market, bond market, and loan market.
5. What is the net present value of an investment?
6. What are the main influences on the demand for capital?
7. Why does the quantity of capital demanded by a firm increase as the interest rate decreases?
8. What are the main factors that change the demand for capital and how do they change it?
9. What are the influences of the interest rate on the amount of saving and the supply of capital?
10. How does the age structure of the population influence the supply of capital?
11. What is the relationship between the interest rate and the price of a stock or bond?
12. How is the interest rate determined?
13. How are stock prices and bond prices determined?
14. Distinguish between a takeover and a merger. Explain why takeovers and mergers occur.
15. What is an exhaustible resource? Give some examples.
16. Distinguish between the stock and the flow of an exhaustible natural resource.
17. Explain what determines the demand for and supply of a stock of an exhaustible natural resource.
18. Explain what determines the demand for a flow of an exhaustible natural resource.
19. Explain why the price of an exhaustible natural resource is expected to rise at a rate equal to the interest rate.
20. What determines the price of a natural resource?

CRITICAL THINKING

1. Study *Reading Between the Lines* on pp. 382–383 and then answer the following questions:
   a. What will have happened to the price of oil if, by the mid-21st century, there have been no further discoveries of oil reserves and no further advances in the technology of extracting and refining oil?
   b. How would a big increase in the rate of economic growth in Asia affect the world market for oil in the first half of the 21st century?
   c. Suppose that in 2025, a breakthrough in fusion technology makes it possible to produce cheap and safe electric power from uranium. What will happen to the price of uranium and the prices of oil and coal as a result of the arrival of this new technology?
2. Use the theory of the price of an exhaustible natural resource to predict the effects on the price of oil of
   a. A rise in the real interest rate.
   b. The discovery of a huge new oil reserve.
   c. A breakthrough in electric car technology.
3. You've been hired by Greenpeace to make the economic case for conserving the world's stock of copper. Set out your best case and anticipate the arguments that an economist opposing you would make.
4. Geologists are always searching for new deposits of minerals. Recently, they found the world's largest known deposit of nickel in Newfoundland and the world's largest known deposit of zinc in Australia.
   a. What effect will these discoveries have on the prices of nickel and zinc?
   b. What effect will these discoveries have on the rates at which nickel and zinc are used?
5. Environmentalists are opposed to the use of carbon-based fuels—oil and coal. Suppose they persuade all countries to introduce a very large carbon fuel tax. What do you predict will happen to the world prices of oil and coal and to the stock prices of oil and coal companies?

P R O B L E M S

1. At the end of 1995, a firm had a plant worth $1,000,000. The plant depreciated during 1996 by 10 percent. During the same year, the firm also bought new capital for $250,000. What is the value of the firm's stock of capital at the end of 1996? What was the firm's gross investment and net investment during 1996?

2. After paying your taxes, you earn $20,000 a year for three years and you spend $16,000 a year. How much do you save each year? If the interest rate is 5 percent a year, what happens to your wealth during this three-year period?

3. A firm is considering buying a new machine. The marginal revenue product of the machine will be $10,000 a year for five years. The machine will have no scrap value at the end of five years. The interest rate is 10 percent a year.
   a. What is the maximum price that the firm will pay for the machine?
   b. If the machine costs $40,000, would the firm buy it at an interest rate of 10 percent? What is the highest interest rate at which the firm would buy the machine?

4. Suppose that exploration in China reveals a vast stock of natural gas that was previously undreamed of and that exceeds all the currently known stocks in China. What do you predict will happen to
   a. The world price of natural gas
      (i) At the moment the news of the discovery breaks?
      (ii) Over the following ten years?
   b. The rate of use of natural gas?

5. If the government increases the tax on oil and makes it more costly for people to use oil, what do you predict will happen to

a. The price of oil at the moment the tax is imposed and over the following ten years?
b. The rate of use of oil?

6. Doomsday is close for zapton, an exhaustible natural resource, the remaining stock of which is 6 million tonnes. The marginal revenue product schedule for zapton is

Quantity used (millions of tonnes)	Marginal revenue product (dollars per tonne)
0	16.11
1	14.64
2	13.31
3	12.10
4	11.00
5	10.00

The interest rate is 10 percent a year.
   a. What is the choke price of zapton?
   b. What is the current price of zapton?
   c. If there is no change in the marginal revenue product schedule for zapton, after how many years is its stock exhausted?

7. In problem 6, a new use is discovered for zapton that increases its marginal revenue product.
   a. Does the choke price of zapton rise, fall, or remain unchanged?
   b. Does the current price of zapton rise, fall, or remain unchanged?
   c. Does the number of years to zapton's exhaustion change?

8. The graphs show the prices of coal, iron ore, and lead (prices are in 1990 dollars to remove the effects of inflation). Explain the trends in these prices.

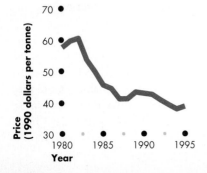

(a) Coal

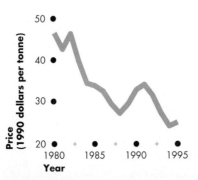

(b) Iron ore

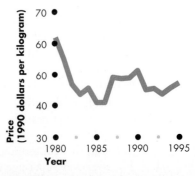

(c) Lead

Uncertainty and Information

After studying this chapter, you will be able to:

- Explain how people make decisions when they are uncertain about the consequences

- Explain why people buy insurance and how insurance companies make a profit

- Explain why buyers search and sellers advertise

- Explain how markets cope with private information

- Explain how performance-related compensation induces greater effort and higher profit

- Explain how people use financial markets to lower risk

Lotteries and Lemons

Life is like a lottery. You work hard in school, but what will the payoff be? Will you get an interesting, high-paying job or a miserable, low-paying one? You set up a small summer business and work hard at it. But will you make enough income to keep you in school next year or will you get wiped out? How do people make a decision when they don't know its consequences? ◆ As you drive across an intersection on a green light, you see a car on your left that's still moving. Will it stop or will it run the red light? You buy insurance against such a risk, and insurance companies gain from your business. Why are we willing to buy insurance at prices that leave insurance companies with a gain? ◆ Buying a new car—or a used car—is fun, but it's also scary. You could get stuck with a lemon. And cars are not unique. Just about every complicated product you buy could be defective. How do car dealers and retailers induce us to buy what may turn out to be a lemon? ◆ Not everyone is paid by the hour. For example, garment workers receive an income based on the number of shirts they make. Salespeople receive a percentage of the value of their sales. Tennis players and boxers are compensated by prize money. Why is there such variety in the ways people are compensated for their work? ◆ People keep some of their wealth in the bank, some in mutual funds, some in bonds, and some in stocks. Why don't people put all their wealth in the place that has the highest return? Why does it pay to diversify?

◇ In this chapter, we answer questions such as these. In doing so, we will extend and enrich the more abstract models of markets that we've studied in earlier chapters. We'll begin by explaining how people make decisions when they're uncertain about the consequences. We'll see how it pays to buy insurance, even if its price leaves the insurance company with a profit. We'll explain why we use scarce resources to generate and disseminate information. And we'll look at transactions in a wide variety of markets in which uncertainty and the cost of acquiring information play important roles.

Uncertainty and Risk

ALTHOUGH WE LIVE IN AN UNCERTAIN WORLD, we rarely ask what uncertainty is. Yet to explain how we make decisions and do business with each other in an uncertain world, we need to think more deeply about uncertainty. What exactly is uncertainty? We also live in a risky world. Is risk the same as uncertainty? Let's begin by defining uncertainty and risk and distinguishing between them.

Uncertainty is a situation in which more than one event might occur, but we don't know which one. For example, when farmers plant their crops, they are uncertain about the weather during the growing season.

In ordinary speech, risk is the probability of incurring a loss (or some other misfortune). In economics, **risk** is a situation in which more than one outcome may occur and the *probability* of each possible outcome can be estimated. A *probability* is a number between zero and one that measures the chance of some possible event occurring. A zero probability means the event will not happen. A probability of one means the event will occur for sure—with certainty. A probability of 0.5 means that the event is just as likely to occur as not. An example is the probability of a tossed coin falling heads. In a large number of tosses, about half of them will be heads and the other half tails.

Sometimes, probabilities can be measured. For example, the probability that a tossed coin will come down heads is based on the fact that, in a large number of tosses, half are heads and half are tails; the probability that an automobile in Montreal in 1997 will be involved in an accident can be estimated by using police and insurance records of previous accidents; the probability that you will win a lottery can be estimated by dividing the number of tickets you have bought by the total number of tickets bought.

Some situations cannot be described using probabilities based on past observed events. These situations may be unique events, such as the introduction of a new product. How much will sell and at what price? Because the product is new, there is no previous experience on which to base a probability. But the question can be answered by looking at past experience with *similar* new products, supported by some judgments. Such judgments are called *subjective probabilities*.

Regardless of whether the probability of some event occurring is based on actual data or judg-ments—or even guesses—we can use probability to study the way in which people make decisions in the face of uncertainty. The first step in doing this is to describe how people assess the cost of risk.

Measuring the Cost of Risk

Some people are more willing to bear risk than others, but everyone prefers less risk to more, other things remaining the same. We measure people's attitudes towards risk by using their utility of wealth schedules and curves. The **utility of wealth** is the amount of utility a person attaches to a given amount of wealth. The greater a person's wealth, other things remaining the same, the greater is the person's total utility. Not only does more wealth bring greater total utility, but as wealth increases, each additional unit of wealth increases total utility by a smaller amount. That is, the *marginal utility of wealth diminishes*.

Figure 17.1 sets out Tania's utility of wealth schedule and curve. Each point a through e on Tania's utility of wealth curve corresponds to the row of the table identified by the same letter. You can see that as her wealth increases, so does her total utility of wealth. You can also see that her marginal utility of wealth diminishes. When wealth increases from $3,000 to $6,000, total utility increases by 20 units, but when wealth increases by a further $3,000 to $9,000, total utility increases by only 10 units.

We can use Tania's utility of wealth curve to measure her cost of risk. Let's see how she evaluates two alternative summer jobs that involve different amounts of risk.

One job, working as a painter, pays enough for her to save $5,000 by the end of the summer. There is no uncertainty about the income from this job and hence no risk. If Tania takes this job, by the end of the summer her wealth will be $5,000. The other job, working as a telemarketer selling subscriptions to a magazine, is risky. If she takes this job, her wealth at the end of the summer depends entirely on her success at selling. She might be a good salesperson or a poor one. A good salesperson makes $9,000 in a summer and a poor one makes $3,000. Tania has never tried telemarketing before, so she doesn't know how successful she'll be. She assumes that there is an equal chance—a probability of 0.5—of making either $3,000 or $9,000. Which outcome does Tania prefer: $5,000 for sure from the painting job or a 50 percent chance of either $3,000 or $9,000 from the telemarketing job?

FIGURE 17.1
The Utility of Wealth

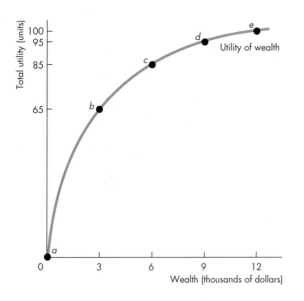

	Wealth (thousands of dollars)	Total utility (units)	Marginal utility (units)
a	0	0	
			65
b	3	65	
			20
c	6	85	
			10
d	9	95	
			5
e	12	100	

The table shows Tania's utility of wealth schedule, and the figure shows her utility of wealth curve. Utility increases as wealth increases, but the marginal utility of wealth diminishes.

When there is uncertainty, people do not know the *actual* utility they will get from taking a particular action. But it is possible to calculate the utility they *expect* to get. **Expected utility** is the average utility arising from all the possible outcomes. So, to choose her summer job, Tania calculates the expected utility arising from painting and telemarketing. Figure 17.2 shows how she does this.

If Tania takes the painting job, she has $5,000 of wealth and 80 units of utility. There is no uncertainty

FIGURE 17.2
Choice Under Uncertainty

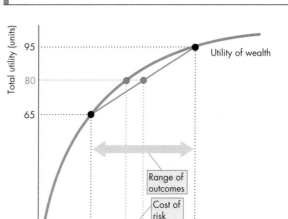

If Tania's wealth is $5,000 and she faces no risk, her utility is 80 units. If she faces an equal probability of having $9,000 with a utility of 95 or $3,000 with a utility of 65, her expected wealth is $6,000. But her expected utility is 80 units—the same as with $5,000 and no uncertainty. Tania is indifferent between these two alternatives. Tania's extra $1,000 of expected wealth is just enough to offset her extra risk.

in this case, so her expected utility equals her actual utility—80 units. But suppose she takes the telemarketing job. If she makes $9,000, her utility is 95 units, and if she makes $3,000, her utility is 65 units. Tania's *expected wealth* is the average of these two outcomes and is $6,000—calculated as ($9,000 × 0.5) + ($3,000 × 0.5). This average is called a *weighted average*, the weights being the probabilities of each outcome (both 0.5 in this case). Tania's *expected utility* is the average of these two possible total utilities and is 80 units—calculated as (95 × 0.5) + (65 × 0.5).

Tania chooses the job that maximizes her expected utility. In this case, the two alternatives give the same expected utility—80 units—so she is indifferent between them. She is equally likely to take either job. The difference between Tania's expected wealth of $6,000 from the risky job and $5,000 from the no-risk job—$1,000—is just large enough to offset the additional risk that Tania faces.

The calculations that we've just done enable us to measure Tania's cost of risk. The cost of risk is the amount by which expected wealth must be increased to give the same expected utility as a no-risk situation. In Tania's case, the cost of the risk arising from an uncertain income of $3,000 or $9,000 is $1,000.

If the amount Tania can make from painting remains at $5,000 and the expected wealth from telemarketing also remains constant while the range of uncertainty increases, Tania will take the painting job. To see this conclusion, suppose that good telemarketers make $12,000, and poor ones make nothing. The average income from telemarketing is unchanged at $6,000, but the range of uncertainty has increased. Looking at the table in Fig. 17.1 you can see that Tania gets 100 units of utility from a wealth of $12,000 and zero units of utility from a wealth of zero. Thus in this case, Tania's expected utility from telemarketing is 50 units—$(100 \times 0.5) + (0 \times 0.5)$. Because the expected utility from telemarketing is now less than that from painting, she chooses painting.

Risk Aversion and Risk Neutrality

There is an enormous difference between Scotty Bowman, coach of the Detroit Red Wings, who favours a cautious defensive game and Glen Sather, former coach of the Edmonton Oilers, who favours a risky offensive game. They have different attitudes towards risk. Scotty is much more risk averse than is Glen. Tania is also *risk averse*—other things remaining the same, she prefers situations with less risk. The shape of a person's utility of wealth curve tells us about the person's attitude towards risk—about the person's degree of *risk aversion*. The more rapidly a person's marginal utility of wealth diminishes, the more the person dislikes risk—the more risk averse that person is. You can see this fact best by considering the case of *risk neutrality*. A risk-neutral person is one for whom risk is costless. Such a person cares only about *expected wealth* and does not mind how much uncertainty there is.

Figure 17.3 shows the utility of wealth curve of a risk-neutral person. It is a straight line and the marginal utility of wealth is constant. If this person has an expected wealth of $6,000, expected utility is 50 units regardless of the range of uncertainty around that average. An equal probability of having $3,000 or $9,000 gives the same expected utility as an equal probability of having $0 or $12,000, which is also the expected

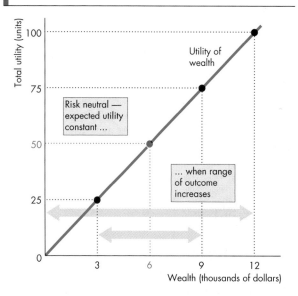

FIGURE 17.3
Risk Neutrality

People's dislike of risk implies a diminishing marginal utility of wealth. A (hypothetical) risk-neutral person has a linear utility of wealth curve and a constant marginal utility of wealth. For a risk-neutral person, expected utility does not depend on the range of uncertainty, and the cost of risk is zero.

utility of a certain $6,000. Real people are risk averse, and their utility of wealth curves look like Tania's. But the case of risk neutrality illustrates the importance and the consequences of the shape of the utility of wealth curve for a person's degree of risk aversion.

R E V I E W

- Faced with uncertain outcomes, people take the actions that maximize expected utility.
- The cost of risk can be measured as the amount by which expected wealth must be increased to give the same expected utility as in a no-risk situation.
- The cost of risk depends on the degree of *risk aversion*. The greater the degree of risk aversion, the greater is the cost of risk.
- For a *risk-neutral* person, risk is costless.

Most people are risk averse. Let's now see how insurance enables them to reduce the risk they face.

Insurance

ONE WAY OF REDUCING THE RISK WE FACE IS TO buy insurance. How does insurance reduce risk? Why do people buy insurance? How does insurance work?

How Insurance Works

Insurance works by pooling risks. It is possible and profitable because people are risk averse. The probability of any one person having a serious auto accident is small, but the cost of an accident to the person involved is enormous. For a large population, the probability of one person having an accident is the proportion of the population that does have an accident. Because this probability can be estimated, the total cost of accidents can be predicted. An insurance company can pool the risks of a large population and share the costs. It does so by collecting premiums from everyone and paying out benefits to those who suffer a loss. If the insurance company does its calculations correctly, it collects at least as much in premiums as it pays out in benefits and operating costs.

To see why people buy insurance and why it is profitable, let's consider an example. Dan has the utility of wealth curve shown in Fig. 17.4. He owns a car worth $10,000 and that is his only wealth. If there is no risk of his having an accident, his utility will be 100 units. But there is a 10 percent chance (a probability of 0.1) that he will have an accident within a year. Suppose Dan does not buy insurance. If he does have an accident his car is worthless, and with no insurance, he has no wealth and no utility. Because the probability of an accident is 0.1, the probability of *not* having an accident is 0.9. Dan's expected wealth, therefore, is $9,000 ($10,000 × 0.9 + $0 × 0.1), and his expected utility is 90 units (100 × 0.9 + 0 × 0.1).

Given his utility of wealth curve, Dan has 90 units of utility if his wealth is $7,000 and he faces no uncertainty. That is, Dan's utility of a guaranteed wealth of $7,000 is the same as his utility of a 90 percent chance of having wealth of $10,000 and a 10 percent chance of having nothing. If the cost of an insurance policy that pays out in the event of an accident is less than $3,000 ($10,000 − $7,000), Dan will buy the policy. Thus Dan has a demand for auto insurance at premiums less than $3,000.

Suppose there are lots of people like Dan, each with a $10,000 car and each with a 10 percent

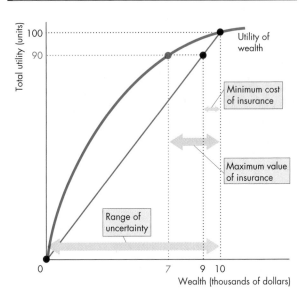

FIGURE   17.4

The Gains from Insurance

Dan has a car valued at $10,000 that gives him a utility of 100 units, but there is a 0.1 probability that he will have an accident making his car worthless (wealth and utility equal to zero). With no insurance, his expected utility is 90 units and he is willing to pay up to $3,000 for insurance. An insurance company (with no operating expenses) can offer insurance to Dan and other car owners for $1,000. There is a potential gain from insurance for both Dan and the insurance company.

chance of having an accident within the year. If an insurance company agrees to pay each person who has an accident $10,000, the company will pay out $10,000 to one-tenth of the population, or an average of $1,000 per person. This amount is the insurance company's minimum premium for such insurance. It is less than the value of insurance to Dan because Dan is risk averse. He is willing to pay something to reduce the risk he faces.

Now suppose that the insurance company's operating expenses are a further $1,000 and that it offers insurance for $2,000. The company now covers all its costs—the amounts paid out to policyholders for their losses plus the company's operating expenses. Dan—and all the other people like him—will maximize their utility by buying this insurance.

Information

WE SPEND A HUGE QUANTITY OF OUR SCARCE resources on economic information. **Economic information** includes data on the prices, quantities, and qualities of goods and services and factors of production.

In the models of perfect competition, monopoly, and monopolistic competition, information is free. Everyone has all the information he or she needs. Households are completely informed about the prices of the goods and services they buy and the factors of production they sell. Similarly, firms are completely informed.

In contrast, information is scarce in the real world. If it were not, we wouldn't need *The Financial Post* and CBC. And we wouldn't need to shop around for bargains or spend time looking for a job. The opportunity cost of economic information—the cost of acquiring information on prices, quantities, and qualities of goods and services and factors of production—is called **information cost**.

The fact that many economic models ignore information costs does not make these models useless. They give us insights into the forces generating trends in prices and quantities over periods long enough for information limits not to be important. But to understand how markets work hour by hour and day by day, we must take information problems into account. Let's look at some of the consequences of information cost.

Searching for Price Information

When many firms sell the same good or service, there is a range of prices and buyers want to find the lowest price. But searching takes time and is costly. So buyers must balance the expected gain from further search against the cost of further search. To perform this balancing act, buyers use a decision rule called the *optimal-search rule*—or *optimal-stopping rule*. The optimal-search rule is

■ Search for a lower price until the expected marginal benefit of search equals the marginal cost of search.

■ When the expected marginal benefit from additional search is less than or equal to the marginal cost, stop searching and buy.

To implement the optimal-search rule, each buyer chooses her or his own reservation price. The buyer's **reservation price** is the highest price that the buyer is willing to pay for a good. The buyer will continue to search for a lower price if the lowest price so far found exceeds the reservation price, but will stop searching and buy if the lowest price found is less than or equal to the reservation price. At the buyer's reservation price, the expected marginal benefit of search equals the marginal cost of search.

Figure 17.5 illustrates the optimal-search rule. Suppose you've decided to buy a used Mazda Miata. Your marginal cost of search is $\$C$ per dealer visited and is shown by the horizontal orange line in the figure. This cost includes the value of your time, which is the amount that you could have earned by working instead of cruising around used car lots, and the

---

FIGURE 17.5

Optimal-Search Rule

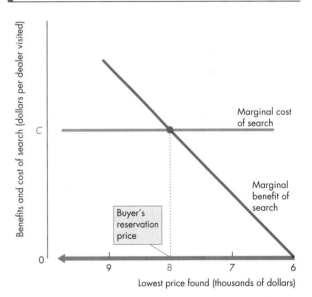

The marginal cost of search is constant at $\$C$. As the lowest price found (measured from right to left on the horizontal axis) declines, the expected marginal utility of further search diminishes. The lowest price found at which the marginal cost equals the expected marginal benefit is the reservation price. The optimal-search rule is to search until a price equal to (or lower than) the reservation price is found and then buy at that lowest found price.

amount spent on transportation and advice. Your expected marginal benefit of visiting one more dealer depends on the lowest price that you've found. The lower the price you've already found, the lower is your expected marginal benefit of visiting one more dealer, as shown by the blue curve in the figure.

The price at which expected marginal benefit equals marginal cost is your reservation price—$8,000 in the figure. If you find a price below your reservation price, you stop searching and buy. If you find a price that exceeds your reservation price, you continue to search for a lower price. Individual shoppers differ in their marginal cost of search and so have different reservation prices. As a result, identical items can be found selling for a range of prices.

A Real Car Shopping Trip   Real car shoppers are confronted with a much bigger problem than the one we've just studied. There are many more dimensions of the car they are looking for than its price. They could spend almost forever gathering information about the alternatives. But at some point in their search, they decide they've done enough looking and make a decision to buy. Your imaginary shopping trip to buy a used Mazda Miata rationalizes their decision. A real shopper thinks that the benefits expected from further search are insufficient to make it worth going on with the process. Real shoppers don't do the calculations we've just done—at least, not explicitly—but their actions can be explained by those calculations. But buyers are not alone in creating information. Sellers do a lot of it too—in the form of advertising. Let's see what the effects of advertising are.

Advertising

Advertising constantly surrounds us—on television, radio, and billboards and in newspapers and magazines—and costs billions of dollars. How do firms decide how much to spend on advertising? Does advertising create information, or does it just persuade us to buy things we don't really want? What does it do to prices?

Advertising for Profit Maximization   A firm's advertising decision is part of its overall profit-maximization strategy. Firms in perfect competition don't advertise because everyone has all the information there is. But firms selling differentiated products in monopolistic competition and firms locked in the struggle of survival in oligopoly advertise a lot.

The amount of advertising undertaken by firms in monopolistic competition is such that the marginal revenue product of advertising equals its marginal cost. The amount of advertising undertaken by firms in oligopoly is determined by the game they are playing. If that game is a *prisoners' dilemma*, they might spend amounts that lower their combined profits but they can't avoid advertising without being wiped out by other firms in the industry.

Persuasion or Information   Much advertising is designed to persuade us that the product being advertised is the best in its class. For example, the Pepsi advertisement tells us that Pepsi is really better than Coke. The Coca-Cola advertisement tells us that Coke is really better than Pepsi. But advertising also informs. It provides information about the quality and price of a good or service.

Does advertising mainly persuade or mainly inform? The answer varies for different goods and different types of markets. Goods whose quality can be assessed *before* they are bought are called *search goods*. Typically, the advertising of search goods mainly informs—gives information about price, quality, and location of suppliers. Examples of such goods are gasoline, basic foods, and household goods. Goods whose quality can only be assessed *after* they are bought are called *experience goods*. Typically, the advertising of experience goods mainly persuades—encourages the consumer to buy now and make a judgment later about quality, based on experience with the good. Examples of such goods are perfume, cosmetics, cigarettes, and alcoholic beverages.

Because most advertising involves experience goods, it is likely that advertising is more often persuasive rather than merely informative. But persuasive advertising doesn't necessarily harm the consumer. It might result in lower prices.

Advertising and Prices   Advertising is costly, but does it increase the price of the good advertised? It might, but two lines of reasoning tell us that advertising can lower prices. The first is that if advertising is informative, it *increases* competition. By informing potential buyers about alternative sources of supply, advertising forces firms to keep their prices low. There is evidence of such effects, especially in retailing. The second is that if advertising enables firms to increase their output and reap economies of scale, it is possible that the price of the good will be lower with advertising than without it, provided competition prevents monopoly pricing.

R E V I E W

- Data on the prices, quantities, and qualities of goods and services and factors of production—economic information—is scarce and people economize on its use.
- Buyers searching for price information stop when they find a price at or below their reservation price, the price that makes the expected marginal benefit of search equal the marginal cost of search.
- Sellers advertise to inform potential buyers of the good or to persuade them to buy it.
- Advertising can increase competition and may raise or lower the price of the advertised good.

Private Information

SO FAR WE HAVE LOOKED AT SITUATIONS IN which information is available to everyone and can be obtained with an expenditure of resources. But not all situations are like this. For example, someone might have private information. **Private information** is information that is available to one person but too costly for anyone else to obtain.

Private information affects many economic transactions. One is your knowledge about your driving. You know much more than your auto insurance company does about how carefully and defensively you drive. Another is your knowledge about your work effort. You know far more than your employer about how hard you work. Yet another is your knowledge about the quality of your car. You know whether it's a lemon. But the person to whom you are about to sell it does not and can't find out until after he has purchased it from you.

Private information creates two problems:

1. Moral hazard
2. Adverse selection

Moral hazard exists when one of the parties to an agreement has an incentive, *after the agreement is made*, to act in a manner that brings additional benefits to himself or herself at the expense of the other party. Moral hazard arises because it is too costly for the injured party to monitor the actions of the advantaged party. For example, Jackie hires Mitch as a salesperson and pays him a fixed wage regardless of his sales. Mitch faces a moral hazard. He has an incentive to put in the

least possible effort, benefiting himself and lowering Jackie's profits. For this reason, salespeople are usually paid by a formula that makes their income higher the greater is the volume (or value) of their sales.

Adverse selection is the tendency for people to enter into agreements in which they can use their private information to their own advantage and to the disadvantage of the less informed party. For example, if Jackie offers salespeople a fixed wage, she will attract lazy salespeople. Hardworking salespeople will prefer *not* to work for Jackie because they can earn more by working for someone who pays by results. The fixed-wage contract adversely selects those with private information (knowledge about their work habits) who can use that knowledge to their own advantage and to the disadvantage of the other party.

A variety of devices have evolved that enable markets to function in the face of moral hazard and adverse selection. We've just seen one, the use of incentive payments for salespeople. Let's look at some others and also see how moral hazard and adverse selection influence three real-world markets:

- The market for used cars
- The market for loans
- The market for insurance

The Market for Used Cars

When a person buys a car, it might turn out to be a lemon. If the car is a lemon, it is worth less to the person who bought it and to everyone else than if it has no defects. Does the used car market have two prices reflecting these two values—a low price for lemons and a higher price for cars without defects? It does not. To see why, let's look at a used car market, first with no dealer warranties and second with warranties.

Used Cars Without Warranties   To make the points as clearly as possible, we'll make some extreme assumptions. There are just two kinds of cars, lemons and those without defects. A lemon is worth $1,000 both to its current owner and to anyone who buys it. A car without defects is worth $5,000 to its current and potential future owners. Whether a car is a lemon is private information to the person who owns it and who has spent enough time driving it to discover its quality. Buyers of used cars can't tell whether they are buying a lemon until *after* they have bought the car and learned as much about it as its current owner knows. There are no dealer warranties.

Because buyers can't tell the difference between a lemon and a good car, they are willing to pay only one price for a used car. What is that price? Are they willing to pay $5,000, the value of a good car? They are not, because there is at least some probability that they are buying a lemon worth only $1,000. If buyers are not willing to pay $5,000 for a used car, are the owners of good cars willing to sell? They are not, because a good car is worth $5,000 to them, so they hang on to their cars. Only the owners of lemons are willing to sell—as long as the price is $1,000 or higher. But, reason the buyers, if only the owners of lemons are selling, all the used cars available are lemons so the maximum price worth paying is $1,000. Thus the market for used cars is a market for lemons and the price is $1,000.

Moral hazard exists in the car market because sellers have an incentive to claim that lemons are good cars. But, given the assumptions in the above description of the car market, no one believes such claims. Adverse selection exists, resulting in only lemons actually being traded. The market for used cars is not working well. Good used cars just don't get bought and sold, but people want to be able to exchange good used cars. How can they do so? The answer is by introducing warranties into the market.

Used Cars with Warranties　Buyers of used cars can't tell a lemon from a good car but car dealers can. For example, they might have regularly serviced the car. They know, therefore, whether they are buying a lemon or a good car and can offer $1,000 for lemons and $5,000 for good cars.[1] But how can they convince buyers that it is worth paying $5,000 for what might be a lemon? The answer is by giving a guarantee in the form of a warranty. The dealer *signals* which cars are good ones and which are lemons. A **signal** is an action taken outside a market that conveys information that can be used by that market. Students' grades are an example of a signal—a signal to the job market. In the case of the used cars, dealers take actions in the market for car repairs that can be used by the market for cars. For each good car sold, the dealer gives a warranty. The dealer agrees to pay the costs of repairing the car if it turns out to have a defect. Cars with a warranty are good; cars without a warranty are lemons.

Why do buyers believe the signal? It is because the cost of sending a false signal is high. A dealer who gives a warranty on a lemon ends up paying the high cost of repairs—and risks gaining a bad reputation. A dealer who gives a warranty only on good cars has no repair costs and a reputation that gets better and better. It pays to send an accurate signal. It is rational, therefore, for buyers to believe the signal. Warranties break the lemon problem and enable the used car market to function with two prices, one for lemons and one for good cars.

The Market for Loans

The market for bank loans is one in which private information plays a crucial role. Let's see how.

The quantity of loans demanded by borrowers depends on the interest rate. The lower the interest rate, the greater is the quantity of loans demanded—the demand curve for loans is downward sloping. The supply of loans by banks and other lenders depends on the cost of lending. This cost has two parts. One is interest and this interest cost is determined in the market for bank deposits—the market in which the banks borrow the funds that they lend. The other part of the cost of lending is the cost of bad loans—loans that are not repaid—called the default cost. The interest cost of a loan is the same for all borrowers. The default cost of a loan depends on the quality of the borrower.

Suppose that borrowers fall into two classes: low-risk and high-risk. Low-risk borrowers only default on their debts for reasons beyond their control. For example, a firm might borrow to finance a project that fails and be unable to repay the bank. High-risk borrowers take high risks with the money they borrow and frequently default on their loans. For example, a firm might borrow to speculate in high-risk mineral prospecting that has a very small chance of paying off.

If banks could separate borrowers into the two risk categories, they would supply loans to low-risk borrowers at one interest rate and to high-risk borrowers at another, higher interest rate.

But banks cannot separate their borrowers. They have no sure way of knowing whether they are lending to a low-risk or a high-risk borrower.

So the banks must charge a single interest rate to both low-risk and high-risk borrowers. If they offered loans to everyone at the low-risk interest rate, borrowers would face moral hazard and the banks would

---

[1]In this example, to keep the numbers simple, we'll ignore dealers' profit margins and other costs of doing business and suppose that dealers buy cars for the same price as they sell them. The principles are the same with dealers' profit margins.

attract a lot of high-risk borrowers—adverse selection. Most borrowers would default and the banks would incur economic losses. If the banks offered loans to everyone at the high-risk interest rate, most low-risk borrowers, with whom the banks would like to do profitable business, would be unwilling to borrow.

Faced with moral hazard and adverse selection, banks use *signals* to discriminate between borrowers and they *ration* or limit loans to amounts below the amounts demanded. To restrict the amounts they are willing to lend to borrowers, banks use signals such as length of time in a job, ownership of a home, marital status, age, and business record.

Figure 17.6 shows how the market for loans works in the face of moral hazard and adverse selection. The demand for loans is D, and the supply is S. The supply curve is horizontal—perfectly elastic supply—because it is assumed that banks have access to a large quantity of funds that have a constant marginal cost of r. With no loan limits, the interest rate is r and the quantity of loans is Q. Because of moral hazard and adverse selection, the banks set loan limits based on signals and restrict the total loans made to L. At the interest rate r, there is an excess demand for loans. A bank cannot increase its profit by making more loans because it can't identify the type of borrower taking the loans. And because the signals used mean that more high-risk borrowers are unsatisfied than low-risk borrowers, it is likely that any additional lending will be biased towards high-risk (and high-cost) borrowers.

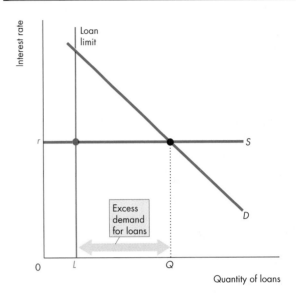

FIGURE 17.6
The Market for Loans

If a bank supplied loans on demand at the going interest rate r, the quantity of loans would be Q, but most of the loans would be taken by high-risk borrowers. Banks use signals to distinguish between low-risk and high-risk borrowers, and they ration loans. Banks have no incentive to increase interest rates and increase the quantity of loans because the additional loans would be to high-risk borrowers.

The Market for Insurance

People who buy insurance face a moral hazard problem, and insurance companies face an adverse selection problem. The moral hazard problem is that a person with insurance coverage for a loss has less incentive than an uninsured person to avoid such a loss. For example, a business with fire insurance has less incentive to take precautions against fire such as installing a fire alarm or sprinkler system than a business with no fire insurance. The adverse selection problem is that people who face greater risks are more likely to buy insurance. For example, a person with a family history of serious illness is more likely to buy accident and disability insurance than a person with a family history of good health.

Insurance companies have an incentive to find ways around the moral hazard and adverse selection problems. By doing so, they can lower premiums and

increase the amount of business they do. Real-world insurance markets have developed a variety of devices for overcoming or at least moderating these private information problems. Let's see how signals work in markets for insurance by looking at the example of auto insurance.

One of the clearest signals a person can give an auto insurance company is her or his driving record. Suppose that Dan is a good driver and rarely has an accident. If he can demonstrate to the insurance company that his driving record is impeccable over a long enough period, then the insurance company will recognize him as a good driver. Dan will work hard at establishing a reputation as a good driver because he will be able to get his insurance at a lower price.

If all drivers, good and bad alike, can establish good records, then simply having a good record will not convey any information. For the signal to be informative, it must be difficult for bad drivers to fake low risk by having a good record. The signals used in car insurance are the "no-claim" bonuses that drivers accumulate when they do not make an insurance claim.

Another device used by insurance companies is the deductible. A deductible is the amount of a loss that the insured agrees to bear. For example, most auto insurance policies have the insurer paying the first few hundred dollars worth of damage. The premium varies with the deductible and in a significant way. That is, the decrease in the premium is more than proportionate to the increase in the deductible. By offering insurance with full coverage—no deductible—on terms attractive only to the highest-risk people and then by offering coverage with a deductible on more favourable terms, insurance companies can do profitable business with everyone. High-risk people choose policies with low deductibles and high premiums, while low-risk people choose policies with high deductibles and low premiums.

R E V I E W

■ Private information creates moral hazard and adverse selection.
■ In markets for cars, loans, and insurance, methods such as warranties, loan limits, and no-claim bonuses and deductibles have been devised to limit the problems caused by private information.

Asymmetric Information in Labour Markets

IN MANY JOBS, THE VALUE OF A WORKER DEPENDS not on the number of hours worked but on the amount of effort exerted. For example, a salesperson who works hard to find new clients and who puts a lot of effort into discovering the right formula to persuade a client to buy her product is more valuable to a firm than a salesperson who mixes business with pleasure to the point at which almost no business gets done. A footballer who trains hard and gets pumped up is more valuable than one who skips training sessions and has a laid-back attitude. A chief executive who works hard to develop new products, inspire the sales force, and win new orders is more valuable than one who treats the office as a vacation place.

But in all these cases (and many others) it is difficult and perhaps impossible for an employer to monitor the efforts of the employee. The employee has more information than the employer about the effort being exerted. When there is asymmetric information about effort, it is necessary to use a compensation scheme that spurs the employee to take actions that, even though not monitored by the employer, bring maximum profit. But an efficient compensation scheme must not only maximize profit. It must also be acceptable to the employee.

We will examine three types of compensation schemes that are often used. They are

■ Sales commissions
■ Prize money
■ Profit shares

Let's see how these compensation schemes work.

Sales Commissions

Jenny has invented a revolutionary new vacuum cleaner—the Dustbeater—and she is going to hire some people to go on the road and sell her product. She knows that a salesperson can put in a great deal of effort or take a lot of on-the-job leisure. The salesperson who takes leisure on the job is not going to encounter many potential customers but might get lucky and find a few customers with filthy rugs and worn-out vacuum cleaners. The salesperson who works hard might have bad luck and do no better than the lazy salesperson. But Jenny does not have the time to follow the salespersons around checking on their sales efforts. How is she to tell the difference between a hard-working salesperson who has bad luck and a lazy one who has good luck?

She does so by offering the appropriate compensation scheme for salespersons. In figuring out the appropriate scheme, Jenny must first work out the effects of the salesperson's efforts on her profit.

Income, Effort, and Luck Suppose that the total income of Jenny and each salesperson depends on only two things, the salesperson's effort and luck. In a real selling situation, a salesperson's effort and luck can vary over a wide range and result in many different possible outcomes. To keep things simple and to enable us to focus on the principles involved rather than getting bogged down in detail, we'll suppose that there are only two levels of effort—"work" and "shirk"—and two levels of luck—"good" and "bad."

Commission Compensation ◆

TOTAL INCOMES, EFFORT, AND LUCK

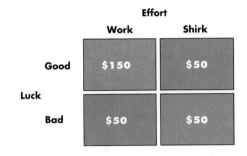

There is an equal (50 percent) chance of good luck or bad luck.

SALESPERSON'S PREFERENCES AND ALTERNATIVE EMPLOYMENT

Value of time spent working is $20 per day.
Income from alternative employment is $70 per day.
Value of work is $70 minus $20, which is $50 per day.

COMPENSATION SCHEMES AND OUTCOMES

Scheme 1: **Pays salesperson $50 a day.**

	Value to salesperson
If the salesperson works:	$50 − $20 = $30
If the salesperson shirks:	$50 − $0 = $50

Outcome: **Salesperson's choice is to shirk.**

Total income	=	profit	+	salesperson's income
$50	=	$0	+	$50

Scheme 2: **Pays salesperson $20 a day plus 51 percent of value of output.**

	Value to salesperson

If the salesperson works:

$$\$20 + 0.51 \left(\frac{\$150}{2} + \frac{\$50}{2} \right) - \$20 = \$51.00$$

If the salesperson shirks:

$$\$20 + 0.51\,(\$50) - \$0 = \$45.50$$

Outcome: **Salesperson's choice is to work.**

Total income	=	profit	+	salesperson's income
$100	=	$29	+	$71

With these possibilities for Jenny to consider, there are only four possible outcomes. The total income that Jenny and the salesperson can earn depends on the combination of effort and luck. The income arising in each of the four cases is set out in Table 17.1. If the salesperson shirks, total income is $50 regardless of whether there is good or bad luck. If the salesperson works, total income is $150 if there is good luck and $50 if there is bad luck. The probability of good luck is one-half (or 50 percent).

Jenny can figure out the four possible outcomes shown in Table 17.1, but she cannot observe the effort of the salespersons or tell whether they have good or bad luck. The salespersons know if they are shirking, but they have no incentive to tell Jenny, and Jenny has no reason to believe them.

Salesperson's Preferences and Alternatives   The salespersons have preferences that Jenny must take into account in designating the compensation package. Suppose that the value a salesperson places on shirking is $20 a day. That is, a salesperson prefers shirking to working, but a day of working for $20 and a day of shirking for a zero income are equally acceptable to a salesperson. The cost of working is $20 a day. Jenny must take this cost into account.

Salespersons also have alternative employment prospects. For example, selling encyclopedias and not shirking earns $70 a day. Jenny must also take the salesperson's alternative employment into account. To hire a salesperson on a deal that induces the person to work and not shirk, Jenny must offer a package that generates at least $70 a day. To hire someone who shirks, Jenny must offer at least $50 a day. In this case, the salesperson receives a further $20—the value placed on shirking.

Two Alternative Compensation Schemes   Jenny considers two compensation schemes for her salespersons. Scheme 1 pays a guaranteed wage of $50 a day. Contemplating this scheme, Jenny reasons as follows. If someone accepts my offer and works, a day is worth $30—an income of $50 minus the cost of working $20. If someone accepts my offer and shirks, a day is worth $50, since no compensation is needed for effort. But an encyclopedia salesperson who works earns $70 a day. So, to such a person, a day is worth $50—an income of $70 minus $20 cost of working. Since working for me is worth less than working for the encyclopedia company and shirking for me is worth the same as working for the encyclopedia company, anyone who accepts my offer will shirk.

Furthermore, Jenny continues to reason: I'll end up with nothing because a salesperson who shirks generates only $50 a day, the amount I would have paid the person.

Scheme 2 is a flat $20 a day plus a sales commission equal to 51 percent of total income. Jenny reasons in the following way: If the salesperson shirks, he generates a total income of $50 a day. He receives 51 percent of this amount—$25.50—plus the daily amount of $20. His income from shirking is $45.50. But selling encyclopedias generates $50 a day ($70 minus the $20 cost of working), so no one will accept my offer and shirk.

If the salesperson works, the income he generates depends on luck. If he is lucky, he generates a total income of $150 and if he is unlucky, he generates a total income of $50. The expected total income from accepting my offer and working is $100 a day (0.5 × $150 + 0.5 × $50). The salesperson will receive 51 percent of this amount—$51—plus the flat amount of $20, which is an *expected* daily income from working of $71. Since working for me is worth more than working for the encyclopedia company, anyone who accepts my offer will work. Furthermore, Jenny continues to reason: I'll end up with a profit of $29 a day from each salesperson—the $100 of income generated minus the $71 I pay out to each salesperson.

Since both Jenny and the salesperson earn more with Scheme 2, that's the one she offers. This example illustrates why most salespersons are compensated for their work by a commission rather than a fixed daily wage.

The compensation scheme we've just considered arises when the employer can observe the employee's output. In some situations it is not possible to observe the output of a worker, but it *is* possible to observe the worker's rank in some "game." In such a case, compensation can take the form of a prize based on rank. Let's see how such a scheme works.

Prize Money

Compensation based on rank delivers a payment related not to the *absolute* performance of a worker but based on the performance of one worker *relative* to another. This type of compensation is common in sports and, for that reason, it is called a rank-tournament compensation scheme. A **rank-tournament compensation scheme** is one in which the payment to a worker depends on the worker's rank in a tournament or game.

Let's see how a rank-tournament compensation scheme works by using the example set out in Table 17.2. There are 10 workers, each one of whom generates a value of output based on effort and luck in the same way as in Table 17.1. Each worker has the same preferences as before and an alternative employment opportunity that generates a net return of $50 a day for working. Scheme 1 is a flat daily wage rate of $50. Anyone accepting this deal will shirk because the alternative is to work for $70. In this case, total output is $500 and this entire amount is paid to the workers, leaving a zero profit.

Scheme 2 pays everyone a daily wage of $45 and in addition offers a prize of $260 to the worker who wins the tournament. The tournament in this case is producing output. The winner is the one who produces most. If two or more workers produce the highest output (tie), the prize is shared among them. To see how this scheme works, imagine that one worker works and the others shirk. The worker receives $305 ($45 plus the prize of $260) and the shirkers receive $45. There are 10 employees and each one works to be in the running for the $260 prize. But because they all work, they all win and they share the prize, receiving $26 each. The total daily income is $71 ($45 plus $26), a dollar more than the income received from a day working hard to sell encyclopedias. The total amount produced by the 10 workers is $1,000—with good luck (50 percent chance) each worker produces $150 and with bad luck each produces $50. So the expected total outcome is $1,000. The profit for the firm is $290, being equal to the total amount produced of $1,000 minus $710 (10 × $71) paid to the workers. Comparing the outcomes of the two schemes, both the firm and the workers gain by adopting Scheme 2.

In practice, rank tournaments usually involve one outright winner rather than a tie, but such schemes work for exactly the reason that this example works. When an employee is given an incentive to try for a prize, he or she finds it advantageous to work, thereby increasing the income of the firm as well as that of the worker.

Professional tennis illustrates this type of compensation scheme very well. If Steffi Graff and Monica Seles were paid by the hour, it would be in their interests to play a match in which the length of the game was such that the cost to each of them of the last hour played equalled the hourly wage rate. If the wage rate was high, the match would be long and boring. If the wage rate was low, the match would be

TABLE 17.2

Rank-Tournament Compensation

VALUE OF OUTPUT OF EACH EMPLOYEE

		Effort	
		Work	**Shirk**
Luck	**Good**	$150	$50
	Bad	$50	$50

There is an equal (50 percent) chance of good luck or bad luck. There are 10 employees and the output of each employee is observable.

COMPENSATION SCHEMES AND OUTCOMES

Scheme 1: Pays employee $50 a day.

Outcome: Each employee's choice is to shirk.

Total income	=	profit	+	employee's income
$500	=	$0	+	$500

Scheme 2: Pays each employee $45 and a prize of $260 to the employee with highest output. A tie results in sharing the prize.

Value to employee

If the employee works:	(1/10)($260) + ($45) − $20	= $51
If the employee shirks:	$45 − $0	= $45

Outcome: Each employee's choice is to work.

Total income	=	profit	+	employees' income
$1,000	=	$290	+	$710

short (and probably equally boring). Compensating such people with a prize for the winner induces each to try to win and produces a greater total output—a higher-quality and more exciting game of tennis that people are willing to pay more to watch.

Similar situations can be found in the executive suites and boardrooms of large corporations. Here, the tournament is climbing the corporate ladder. The one who climbs highest wins the prize. Having large differences in compensation between the chief executive officer and the people on the next rung below that level and so on down the executive ladder creates a competitive environment similar to that of a tennis tournament. The result is an average level of effort that, though not observed and monitored by anyone, is greater than it would be otherwise. Paying the chief executive twice as much as everyone else makes everyone work harder.

Profit Shares

The compensation schemes that we've considered so far require that the output of each worker be observable, or that their rank in some "game" be observable. But in many situations, the value of output depends on team effort and it is not possible to determine the direct contribution of any one member of the team. In such situations, compensation can be based only on total or team output. The most comprehensive team compensation scheme is profit sharing.

Since the objective of any firm is to maximize profit, it seems that profit sharing is a sensible compensation arrangement. Why aren't *all* employees compensated by an agreed share of the firm's profit? The answer is that for many workers, there is too weak a connection between effort and profit. Profit is the consequence of the joint output of all the firm's inputs.

But profit is a good indicator of the effectiveness of senior managers. It is their job to coordinate the efforts of others to achieve maximum profit. And that is why profit-sharing arrangements are usually part of the compensation of senior managers.

Many individuals are compensated by a combination of the schemes that we have just reviewed. For example, some senior executives are rewarded with a fixed annual salary, a prize for their rank in the corporate promotion ladder tournament, and a share in the firm's profits.

We have now seen how simple compensation schemes can spur employees to work hard for their firms even when much of their effort cannot be observed. If it is actually impossible to observe a worker's actions, a firm has no choice but to use such schemes. But in many other situations, where it *is* possible but costly to monitor the workers, monitoring costs can be avoided by using compensation schemes like the ones we've just examined.

R E V I E W

■ Compensation schemes based on output such as sales commissions, or on rank such as prize money for tournaments, or on profit sharing can induce an employee to work and enable a firm to maximize profit even though the efforts of the employees are not monitored.

■ The key is to structure the compensation scheme so that the interests of the employee are the same as those of the employer—to make employees better off only when they take the action that maximizes profit.

Your final task in this chapter is to study the role played by financial markets in helping people to cope with uncertainty.

Managing Risk in Financial Markets

RISK IS A DOMINANT FEATURE OF MARKETS FOR stocks and bonds—indeed for any asset whose price fluctuates. One thing people do to cope with risky asset prices is to diversify their asset holdings.

Diversification to Lower Risk

The idea that diversification lowers risk is very natural. It is just an application of not putting all one's eggs into the same basket. How exactly does diversification reduce risk? The best way to answer this question is to consider an example.

Suppose there are two risky projects that you can undertake. Each involves investing $100,000. The two projects are independent of each other, but they each promise the same degree of risk and return.

On each project, you will either make $50,000 or lose $25,000, and the chance that either of these things will happen is 50 percent. The expected return on each project is ($50,000 × 0.5) + (–$25,000 × 0.5), which is $12,500. But because the two projects are completely independent, the outcome of one project in no way influences or is related to the outcome of the other.

Undiversified   Suppose you put all your eggs in one basket, investing the $100,000 in either Project 1 or Project 2. You will either make $50,000 or lose $25,000, and the probability of each of these outcomes is 50 percent. Your expected return is the average of these two outcomes—an expected return of $12,500. But in this case in which only one project is chosen, there is no chance that you will actually make a return of $12,500.

Diversified   Suppose instead that you diversify by putting 50 percent of your money into Project 1 and 50 percent into Project 2. (Someone else is putting up the other money in these two projects.) Because the two projects are independent, you now have *four* possible returns:

1. Lose $12,500 on each project, and your return is –$25,000.
2. Make $25,000 on Project 1 and lose $12,500 on Project 2, and your return is $12,500.
3. Lose $12,500 on Project 1 and make $25,000 on Project 2, and your return is $12,500.
4. Make $25,000 on each project, and your return is $50,000.

Each of these four possible outcomes is equally probable—each has a 25 percent chance of occurring. You have lowered the chance that you will earn $50,000, but you have also lowered the chance that you will lose $25,000. And you have increased the chance that you will actually make your expected return of $12,500. By diversifying your portfolio of assets, you have reduced its riskiness while maintaining an expected return of $12,500.

If you are risk averse—that is, if your utility of wealth curve looks like Tania's, which you studied earlier in this chapter—you'll prefer the diversified portfolio to the one that is not diversified. That is, your *expected utility* with a diversified set of assets is greater.

A common way to diversify is to buy stocks in different corporations. Let's look at the market in which these stocks are traded.

The Stock Market

The prices of the stocks are determined by demand and supply. But demand and supply in the stock market is dominated by one thing: the expected future price. If the price of a stock today is higher than the expected price tomorrow, people will sell the stock today. If the price of a stock today is less than its expected price tomorrow, people will buy the stock today. As a result of such trading, today's price equals tomorrow's expected price, and so today's price embodies all the relevant information that is available about the stock. A market in which the actual price embodies all currently available relevant information is called an **efficient market**.

In an efficient market, it is impossible to forecast changes in price. Why? If your forecast is that the price is going to rise tomorrow you will buy now. Your action of buying today is an increase in demand today and increases *today's* price. It's true that your action—the action of a single trader—is not going to make much difference to a big market like the Toronto Stock Exchange. But if traders in general expect a higher price tomorrow and they all act today on the basis of that expectation, then today's price will rise. It will keep on rising until it reaches the expected future price, because only at that price do traders see no profit in buying more stock today.

There is an apparent paradox about efficient markets. Markets are efficient because people try to make a profit. They seek a profit by buying at a low price and selling at a high price. But the very act of buying and selling to make a profit means that the market price moves to equal its expected future value. Having done that, no one, not even those who are seeking to profit, can *predictably* make a profit. Every profit opportunity seen by traders leads to an action that produces a price change that removes the profit opportunity for others. Even the probability of an intergalactic attack is taken into account in determining stock market prices—see the cartoon.

Thus an efficient market has two features:

1. Its price equals the expected future price and embodies all the available information.
2. There are no forecastable profit opportunities available.

"Drat! I suppose the market has already discounted this, too."

Drawing by Lorenz; © 1986 The New Yorker Magazine, Inc.

The key thing to understand about an efficient market such as the stock market is that if something can be anticipated, it will be, and the anticipation will affect the current price of a stock.

Volatility in Stock Prices If the price of a stock is always equal to its expected future price, why is the stock market so volatile? The answer must be that expectations themselves are subject to fluctuation. Expectations depend on the information available. As new information becomes available, stock traders form new expectations about the future state of the economy and in turn new expectations of future stock prices. New information comes randomly so prices change randomly.

◆ We've studied the way people cope with uncertainty and how markets work when there are important information problems. One of the most pervasive consequences of the absence of complete information, the huge volume of advertising, is studied further in *Reading Between the Lines* on pp. 404–405. In the following chapters, we're going to study some problems that the market economy has difficulty coping with and that give rise to government economic activity. We'll learn how government actions and programs modify the outcome of a pure market economy and influence the distribution of income and wealth.

Policy
WATCH

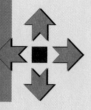

Advertising in Action

Essence of
THE STORY

Super Bowl ads are often better than the game

BY KEITH MARDER

There's a good chance that more people will be talking tomorrow morning about Deion Sanders's starring role in a Pepsi commercial with Wile E. Coyote than about anything he does for the Dallas Cowboys in today's Super Bowl XXX against the Pittsburgh Steelers.

That's because apart from the football, Super Bowl Sunday has become a battleground for a second clash of egos—among advertisers. Super Bowl party etiquette now dictates that breaks in the action are times to shush or be shushed because advertising agencies pull out all the stops for the most expensive commercials of the year.

Advertisers on today's game are spending up to $1.3 million for a half-minute of air time, or $43,333.33 a second. The average fee for today's 30-second commercial spot is $1.1 million. The average three decades ago: $40,000 for 30 seconds.

The price of advertising admission doesn't count the hundreds of thousands of dol-lars in production costs or the millions to sign a celebrity to endorse a product.

"It's two weeks of hype-o-mania that's not possible for any other event," said Michael Bernacchi of the University of Detroit Mercy, who tracks marketing trends, including the Super Bowl, in a newsletter. ...

The Super Bowl blowout is not always the best use of an advertising budget, however. According to Paul Schulman, a New York-based media buyer, a company can buy three commercials in the top-rated ER for the same price as one Super Bowl ad.

Another study showed that for less than the price of one Super Bowl ad, which cost an average of $900,000 in 1994, a company could buy a week of prime-time TV ads.

"Rather than be in the Super Bowl with one single sitting, you can buy one unit a night on highly rated shows," said Burton of the University of Oregon. "But you could be targeting the person watching the Super Bowl. That could be your target demographic."

- Advertising agencies produce expensive commercials for Super Bowl Sunday.

- The average fee for a 30-second TV commercial on Super Bowl Sunday is $1.1 million. This fee does not include production costs or celebrity endorsement fees.

- Advertisers can buy a whole week of prime-time TV ads for less than the price of one Super Bowl ad, so paying a big price for a Super Bowl ad might not be the best use of an advertising budget.

- But the Super Bowl lets advertisers reach a specific demographic group that might be exactly the right target.

Economic

A N A L Y S I S

■ Firms that advertise produce a product that is similar to that produced by other firms, a situation called *product differentiation*.

■ Product differentiation can occur in monopolistic competition (see Chapter 13, pp. 290–293) or oligopoly (see Chapter 13, pp. 293–295).

■ Most of the products advertised on television are differentiated products.

■ Firms advertise to increase their *economic profit*. And provided their profit is maximized, they might spend a huge sum on advertising.

■ Figures 1 and 2 show how advertising can increase a firm's economic profit in monopolistic competition, at least in the short run. (In the long run, entry competes economic profit away in monopolistic competition.)

■ In Fig. 1, the firm does not advertise. Its demand curve is D_0, its marginal revenue curve is MR_0, its average total cost curve is ATC_0, and its marginal cost curve is MC.

■ The firm maximizes profit by producing Q_0, the quantity at which marginal revenue equals marginal cost, and selling it for P_0. Economic profit is shown by the blue rectangle.

■ Advertising costs are fixed costs. When the firm buys television ads, its average total cost curve shifts upward to ATC_1 in Fig. 2.

■ Because advertising costs are fixed costs, marginal cost does not change. So in Fig. 2, the marginal cost curve remains at MC.

■ Well-targeted advertising increases the demand for a product, and the demand curve and marginal revenue curve shift rightward to D_1 and MR_1 in Fig. 2.

■ Again the firm maximizes profit by producing the quantity at which marginal revenue equals marginal cost. In Fig. 2, that quantity is Q_1. Price is P_1 and economic profit is shown by the enlarged blue rectangle.

■ In this example, advertising increases economic profit. But the consumer pays more and the good costs more.

■ Extremely large advertising expenses, like the ones described in the news article, can be justified by a profit calculation like the one you've just studied.

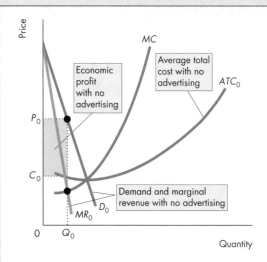

Figure 1 No advertising

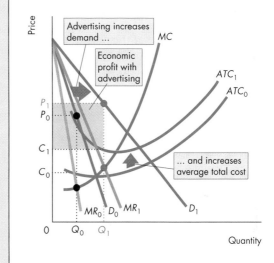

Figure 2 Advertising

You're

THE VOTER

■ In the example on this page, if the firm was not permitted to advertise, this good would be sold for a lower price and would cost less to produce and market.

■ Because of this possible outcome, some people want to limit advertising expenditures.

■ Suppose the government proposed a new law that limited or even outlawed expensive television advertising. Would you vote for such a proposal? Why or why not?

S U M M A R Y

Key Points

Uncertainty and Risk   To describe uncertainty and risk, we use the concept of probability (a number between zero and one), which measures the chance of an event occurring. Sometimes probabilities can be measured, and sometimes they are subjective. A person's attitude towards risk, called risk aversion, is described by the utility of wealth. Greater wealth brings greater utility, but as wealth increases, the marginal utility of wealth diminishes. Faced with uncertainty, people choose the action that maximizes expected utility. (pp. 389–391)

Insurance   Insurance is one of the most important ways we use to reduce risk. Insurance works by pooling risks, and it pays to insure because people are risk averse. By pooling risks, insurance companies can reduce risks at a lower cost than the value of the lower risk. (p. 392)

Information   Buyers search for price information—looking for the least-cost source of supply. They use the optimal-search rule: stop when the expected marginal benefit of search equals the marginal cost of search. Sellers advertise, sometimes to persuade and sometimes to provide information. A widely held idea is that advertising raises prices. But it can increase competition or bring economies of scale that lower prices. (pp. 393–395)

Private Information   Private information is one person's knowledge that is too costly for anyone else to discover. Private information creates the problems of moral hazard—the use of private information to the advantage of the informed and the disadvantage of the uninformed—and adverse selection—the tendency for the people who accept contracts to be those with private information that can be used to their own advantage and to the disadvantage of the less informed party. Devices that enable markets to function in the face of moral hazard and adverse selection are incentive payments, guarantees and warranties, and signals. (pp. 395–398)

Asymmetric Information in Labour Markets
When there is asymmetric information about effort, it is necessary to use compensation schemes that spur employees to take unmonitored actions that maximize profit. The three main compensation schemes used are sales commissions, prize money, and profit sharing. All such schemes work by confronting employees with alternatives that induce them to choose the actions that make both themselves and the firm better off. (pp. 398–402)

Managing Risk in Financial Markets   Risk can be reduced by diversifying asset holdings. A common way to diversify is to buy stocks in different corporations. Stock prices are determined by the expected future price of the stock. Expectations about future stock prices are based on all the information that is available and regarded as relevant. If the price is expected to rise, people buy and the actual price rises until it equals the expected price. If the price is expected to fall, people sell and the actual price falls until it equals the expected price. A market in which the price equals the expected price is an efficient market. (pp. 402–403)

Key Figures and Tables

Key Terms

R E V I E W   Q U E S T I O N S

1. Distinguish between uncertainty and risk.
2. How do we measure a person's attitude towards risk? How do these attitudes vary from one person to another?
3. What is a risk-neutral person and what does such a person's utility of wealth curve look like?
4. What is risk aversion and how could you tell which of two people is the more risk averse by looking at their utility of wealth curves?
5. Why do people buy insurance and why do insurance companies make a profit?
6. Why is information valuable?
7. What determines the amount of searching you do for a bargain?
8. Why do firms advertise?
9. Does advertising always increase prices? Why might it lower them?
10. What are moral hazard and adverse selection, and how do they influence the way markets for loans and insurance work?
11. What is a lemon and how does the lemon problem arise?
12. Explain how the used car market works.
13. Why do firms give warranties and guarantees?
14. Why do banks limit the amounts they are willing to lend?
15. How do deductibles make insurance more efficient and enable insurance companies to discriminate between high-risk and low-risk customers?
16. What are the main types of compensation schemes that arise to cope with asymmetric information in labour markets?
17. How does a sales commission work to induce greater effort from a salesperson?
18. How does a prize for the winner produce a more valuable game?
19. Why don't all employees get paid with a fixed share in the profits of their employer?
20. What is the most common way of diversifying assets?
21. How does diversification lower risk?
22. How is a stock price determined and what role does the expected future price play?
23. What is an efficient market? What types of markets are efficient?

C R I T I C A L   T H I N K I N G

1. Study *Reading Between the Lines* on pp. 404–405 and then answer the following questions:
   a. Why do firms spend huge sums on advertisments on Super Bowl Sunday?
   b. What information are firms using to target particular potential customers?
   c. Why don't we get lots of political advertisements on Super Bowl Sunday?
   d. How can firms be maximizing profits if they spend such huge amounts on advertising? Explain your answer by using the analysis presented on p. 405.

2. Why do you think it is not possible to buy insurance against having to put up with a low-paying and miserable job? Explain why such a market would not work.

3. Although you can't buy insurance against the risk of being sold a lemon, the market does give you some protection. How? What are the main ways in which markets overcome the lemon problem?

4. You and your friend have decided to set up a lawn service company. The plan is to hire six workers who will work with you and your friend in two teams: your team and your mate's team. What compensation scheme do you predict will most likely bring the company maximum profit?

5. Explain why the salary of the president of a company is much greater than the salary of the vice-president.

6. A new wonder drug is discovered by Merck that is expected to bring big profits. Describe in detail what happens in the stock market and how these actions influence the price of Merck's stock. Why would people diversify rather than put all their wealth into Merck's stock?

P R O B L E M S

1. The figure shows Lee's utility of wealth curve. Lee is offered a job as a salesperson in which there is a 50 percent chance she will make $4,000 a month and a 50 percent chance she will make nothing.

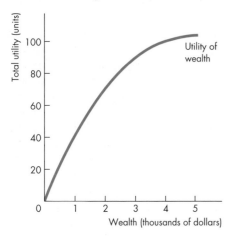

a. What is Lee's expected wealth from taking this job?
b. What is Lee's expected utility from taking this job?
c. How much (approximately) would another firm have to offer Lee with certainty to persuade her not to take the risky sales job?

2. The figure shows Colleen's utility of wealth curve. Colleen is offered the same kind of sales job as Lee in problem 1—a 50 percent chance of making $4,000 a month and a 50 percent chance of making nothing.

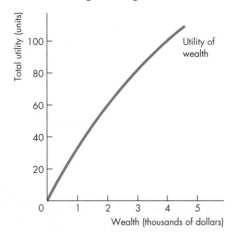

a. What is Colleen's expected wealth from taking this job?
b. What is Colleen's expected utility from taking this job?
c. Explain who is more likely to be willing to take this risky job, Lee or Colleen.

3. Jimmy and Zenda have the following utility of wealth schedules:

Wealth	Jimmy's utility	Zenda's utility
0	0	0
100	200	512
200	300	640
300	350	672
400	375	678
500	387	681
600	393	683
700	396	684

Who is more risk averse, Jimmy or Zenda?

4. Suppose that Jimmy and Zenda in problem 3 have $400 each and that each sees a business project that involves committing the entire $400 to the project. They reckon that the project could return $600 (a profit of $200) with a probability of 0.85 or $200 (a loss of $200) with a probability of 0.15. Who goes for the project and who hangs on to the initial $400?

5. In problem 3, who is more likely to buy insurance, Jimmy or Zenda, and why?

part 4 Markets and Government

Michael Walker is Executive Director of The Fraser Institute, an economic policy think tank located in Vancouver. In this position since 1974, he has become one of Canada's most articulate critics of government economic policy. He is a prolific writer of books and articles and a frequent contributor to current affairs programs on television and radio. Michael Walker prepared for his role of policy critic inside the policy machine at the Bank of Canada and the Department of Finance. Born in Corner Brook, Newfoundland, in 1945, he was an undergraduate at St. Francis Xavier University and a graduate student at the University of Western Ontario, where he completed the work for his Ph.D. in 1969. He has taught economics at the University of Western Ontario and statistics at Carleton University. Robin Bade and Michael Parkin talked with Michael Walker about his work and his views about the proper role for government in the Canadian economy.

TALKING WITH Michael Walker

What drew you to economics?
I was attracted to economics by the fact that it seemed to provide answers to many questions that had puzzled me as a student growing up in Newfoundland. Newfoundland is a province that has many natural attributes but has been perennially poor. During all of my life it has had the highest unemployment rates in Canada, notwithstanding what seemed to be the best efforts of government to redress this situation with industrial development programs and huge influxes of money from "the mainland."

But I think the central reason I took up the study of economics was because of the influence of one of my teachers. Actually, I had gone to St. Francis Xavier to study history and, although I find history a fascinating subject, I was even more fascinated when introduced to economics by Professor A.J. Wintermans who had had quite a colourful history as an economist in the "real world" before going to teach at university.

You began your professional career in the public sector. Why did you leave the security of such a job and pursue your current career?
I was recruited by the Bank of Canada because they were aware

of the research which I was doing at Western on econometric models.

Having worked at the Bank for four years, I was recruited by the Department of Finance to work with the policy branches to equip the department with a modelling capability similar to that at the Bank. During this period it began to dawn on me that many of the key decisions about the conduct of economic policy were not being taken for the purely technical reason that they could accomplish a well-defined economic objective. Rather, they were taken for ideological or purely political reasons and the economic impact was neither well understood nor involved in the decision-making process.

These emerging difficulties led eventually to my decision to leave Ottawa to join with some other people to form the Fraser Institute in 1974.

What is the Fraser Institute? How is it financed? Whose views does it push?
The Fraser Institute is a nonprofit research and educational organization that operates throughout North and South America and has some activities in Europe and Asia. It was established as a body that would provide an independent view about economic policy and to that end the editorial function of the Institute was devised to be independent from the funding and financial management function of the Institute. An Editorial Board was established comprised of leading economists—during its history the members of the Board have included H.G. Johnson, Friedrich Von Hayek, James Buchanan, George Stigler, Michael Parkin, Herbert Grubel, and Sir Alan Walters. It has been

supplemented from time to time with help from Milton Friedman and Gary Becker.

The Fraser Institute is a tax-exempt organization in Canada and the United States and is financed by contributions from nearly 3,000 individual corporate and foundation supporters. Roughly 39 percent of the contributions come from corporate and individual sponsors, with foundations, sales of publications, and interest on the Institute's endowment providing the rest of the financing.

The objective of the Fraser Institute is to constantly remind policy makers and the general public about the role that can be played by markets in the solution of economic problems. We regard this as similar to the function of physicists in reminding people about the role that gravity plays in the conduct of their everyday affairs. So the views that we "push" are really the methodology of positive economics as applied to real-world problems.

You have spent most of your professional life arguing that government is too big and that it causes more problems than it cures. What is the essence of your argument?
I think that the essence of the argument is that the government ignores the central function that markets provide to society. Friedrich Hayek encouraged us to think about markets as a way of processing the huge amounts of information that we had to deal with effectively if we were going to utilize society's resources in the best way to answer the questions, "what should be produced?," "how should it be produced?," "for whom should it be produced?," and "when should it be produced?" In Hayek's conception, relative prices are the key signalling devices that cause members of society to behave optimally, according to their best assessment

The objective of the Fraser Institute is to ... remind policy makers and the general public about the role that can be played by markets in the solution of economic problems.

of their abilities and interest, in such a way as to deal with the fundamental problem of scarcity.

Very often, government produces short circuits in this information transfer process so that good information is not passed to economic actors so they can modify their behaviour appropriately. Or, in the worst case, government actually sends the wrong message to people so that they do modify their behaviour, but in a way that is not helpful. Examples of the first kind are where government, for example, imposes some kind of price control, like rent control, or wage and price controls more generally, or imposes a quota on imports or in some other way tampers with the information flow that is being produced by the market itself.

An example of the second kind of intervention is where the government engages in tax and transfer policies of a kind that distort behaviour in a malevolent way. For example, unemployment insurance, I think, is increasingly recognized as a tax and transfer mechanism that induces people into behaviours which are not helpful either to society or the individual. Certainly the operation of unemployment insurance in Newfoundland has had an absolutely debilitating and, I think, unintended consequence of this kind—at least unanticipated by many of the well-meaning people who promoted unemployment insurance as a useful social policy.

What are the worst examples of misguided government intervention in our economy?
I would say that the worst examples are those policies that involve the double whammy of a tax which drives a wedge between the

effort that people undertake and the reward which they receive for that effort, on the one hand, and then transfers the proceeds of this tax to other individuals who are induced by the transfer not to engage in useful economic activity. Once again, the unemployment insurance program, as it has operated in the Maritime provinces, provides a particularly poignant illustration of this effect. A recent report on Newfoundland has noted that half of the 19-year-olds are on unemployment insurance and, of those, half have less than a grade 9 education. The reason is that during three generations the people of Newfoundland have been taught that one of the best routes to acquiring a reasonable standard of living is to become dependent on the unemployment insurance system. This dependency requires no particular education and indeed, if the unemployment insurance dependency route is the best that one can hope for, engaging in education is simply a waste of resources. We are now beginning to realize, I think, the devastating impact of this kind of policy.

How should decisions be made about the appropriate scale of provision of public goods?
There are clearly public goods, but the range we should regard as such is not a given but is technologically sensitive. Infectious disease control is a public good and likely to remain one. On the other hand, "public roads and bridges" are largely a vestige of the days when it was difficult to collect user fees from autos. The principle of charging for the use of roads was never really an issue since road-use taxes are universally added to gasoline in order to tax

... the essence of the argument is that the government ignores the central function that markets provide to society.

in proportion to use and, of course, users have always been charged for parking on the roadways. The fact that transducers can be used to assess user charges inexpensively will eventually revolutionize the road and bridge business and eliminate them from the list of public goods.

Policing, fire protection, and garbage removal have public good features, but that does not mean that they must be provided by the public sector. In some jurisdictions these services are paid for via taxation but the services are contracted out to private suppliers. That will increasingly be the case.

So we must be quite modest in our pretensions of knowledge about the services which are "public goods." The extent of public goods production, once there is a determination not to rely on the market, can only be done imperfectly.

Does the distribution of income bother you? Do you want to see any redistributive taxes?
Of course the distribution of income bothers me. Don't forget, I got into economics because of the failure of income levels in Newfoundland to catch up with

those elsewhere in the country. I would like to see everybody have the maximum level of income possible. The rub is that if we try to achieve that in the wrong way, not only will we not achieve our objective, the incomes of everybody will be lower than otherwise.

One of the methods of boosting incomes, which backfires, presumes that governments can permanently raise the incomes of one group in society significantly by reducing the incomes of others. The taxes required to accomplish this redistribution send out the message that the taxed activity—earning a high income—ought to be avoided. Moreover, it rewards those who have not earned a high income with the transfer, thus encouraging low-income earning as a trait to develop in society.

I think that the redistributive role of government ought to be limited to providing basic levels of income support to those who, due to misfortune, find that they are unable to provide for themselves. This group would include those who are physically or mentally incapable of supporting themselves and the victims of misfortune outside their control.

Can externalities always be handled by assigning private property rights?
In principle, yes. The practical problems are technological and related to the cost of enforcing the property right. As with the case of public goods, we are finding that allocation of property rights can solve many more externality problems than we would have dreamed possible only a few years ago. Such "problems" include sulfur dioxide emissions, elephant slaughter, crocodile survival, salmon protection, and codfish stock protection.

Take a look at *Economics and the Environment—A Reconciliation*, which is available on our Web site.

Are there any monopoly or anti-competition actions of firms that you believe the government should seek to regulate?
No. I don't believe that firms can sustain a monopoly without the contrivance of government, and all of the "monopoly" problems I can think of have in fact been the result of the government awarding an exclusive franchise to some firm to produce some good or service. Telephone, television, electricity, and other utilities are the sort of things I am talking about.

There was a time when we thought that there were "natural monopolies." Now we have found that there are substitutes for every imaginable service provided that the market incentives are permitted to operate. High long-distance telephone costs lead to the development of satellite competitors for land line systems which in turn convert to glass fibre to reduce the cost per call. Railways and pipelines find competition from trucking.

Even if markets are slow to adjust and produce abnormal profits for their owners, these send out signals to the market that eventually bring a competitive response. During the transition, it may seem that "monopoly regulation" might make sense. However, this presumes that the regulation will be done on behalf of the consumers. Considerable evidence accumulated in the past 50 years suggests that regulations bring their own problems and often higher costs.

The Fraser Institute publishes a Canadian tax reckoner each year.

What does this publication seek to achieve?
The purpose of the Tax Freedom Day calculation and the book *Tax Facts* upon which it is based, is to inform Canadians of the extent to which governments at all levels are removing from them the ability to dispose of their income according to their own private assessment of priorities. It is the tax equivalent of the Consumer Price Index since it compiles the total cost of government and makes this available to people. Tax Freedom Day is one of the few macroeconomic measures that Canadians are able to recall correctly—i.e., that they work nearly half a year to pay their total tax bill.

Many young people want to make an impact on the public policy debate. How can they be most effective in pursuing this goal?
I would tell them to get involved in our student program. We host regular public policy seminars and a student leader colloquium series. We hire summer interns. We publish the *Canadian Student Review* —articles by young people about public policy issues. We also publish the ideas of young people in *Fraser Forum*. Many of the "graduates" of our programs are now working in Ottawa and in provincial capitals where they make a direct contribution to the development of the government policies of tomorrow.

The route of writing to your Member of Parliament, legislative assembly representative, or mayor is also open, but to do that effectively a student needs the facts and a well-formed point of view. Our student programs and well-stocked Web site help young people to be more effective in expressing their point of view, whatever it may be.

Market Failure and Public Choice

After studying this chapter, you will be able to:

- Describe the structure and size of the government sector of the Canadian economy

- Explain how an economic role for government arises from market failure and inequity

- Distinguish between public goods and private goods and explain the free-rider problem

- Explain how the quantity of public goods is determined

- Explain why most of the government's revenue comes from income taxes and why some goods are taxed at a high rate

Government—The Solution or the Problem?

In 1995, the federal, provincial, and local governments in Canada employed 1.4 million people and spent 46¢ of every dollar earned by Canadians. Do we need this much government? Is government, as conservatives sometimes suggest, too big? Is government "the problem"? Or, despite its enormous size, is government too small to do all the things it must attend to? Is government, as liberals sometimes suggest, not contributing enough to economic life? ◆ Government touches many aspects of our lives. It is present at our birth, supporting the hospitals in which we are born and helping to train the doctors and nurses who deliver us. It is present throughout our education, supporting schools, colleges, and universities, and helping to train our teachers. It is present throughout our working lives, taxing our incomes, regulating our work environment, and paying us benefits when we are unemployed. It is present throughout our retirement, paying us a small income, and when we die, taxing our bequests. Government also provides services such as the enforcement of law and order and the provision of national defence. But the government does not make all our choices. We decide what work to do, how much to save, and what to spend our income on. Why does the government participate in some aspects of our lives but not others? ◆ Almost everyone, from the poor single mother to the wealthy taxpayer, grumbles about government services. Why is the bureaucracy so unpopular? And what determines the scale on which public services are provided?

◆ In this chapter and the next three, we study the interactions of governments and markets. We begin by describing the government sector and explaining how, in the absence of a government, the market economy fails to achieve an efficient allocation of resources. We also explain how the scale of government is determined.

The Government Sector

THE GOVERNMENT SECTOR OF THE CANADIAN economy consists of more than 40,000 separate organizations, some tiny like rural municipalities, and some enormous like the government of Canada and the governments of the larger provinces. The total outlays by the government sector equal 46 percent of total income in Canada, and 10.5 percent of the labour force is employed in the government sector.

There are three levels of government in Canada: federal, provincial, and local. Each level of government is organized into departments. Departments are the bureaucracies that run the day-to-day business of government. The largest federal government departments are National Defence, Employment and Immigration, National Revenue, Transport, and Justice.

The Scale and Growth of Government

The scale of government has changed over the years, as Fig. 18.1(a) shows. In 1970, government outlays were 34 percent of total income. Government outlays gradually increased to 50 percent of total income in 1992. In 1995, government outlays were 46 percent of total income. Government employment peaked at 13.3 percent of the labour force in 1975, as Fig. 18.1(b) shows. Since then, government employment has decreased. In 1995, it was 10.5 percent of the labour force.

The growth of government outlays and employment understates the growth of government influence on economic life. That influence stems not only from the government's share of expenditure and employment but also from the mushrooming of laws and regulations that affect the economic actions of households and firms. We look at this aspect of government in Chapter 20, where we study regulation and competition policy.

Why does the government sector become an ever larger part of the economy? And why has the government's share in employment declined? We'll discover the answers to these and other questions about government later in this chapter and in the following three chapters. But first let's look at the economic role the government plays.

FIGURE 18.1

The Size of Government

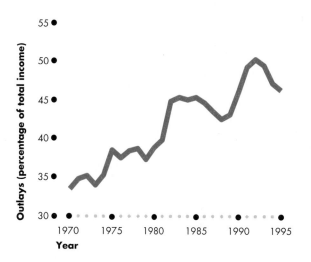

(a) Government outlays

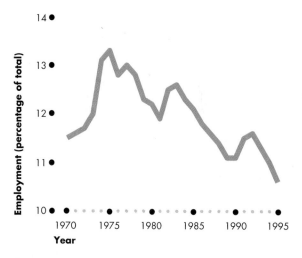

(b) Government employment

Government outlays in Canada have grown from 34 percent of the total income in 1970 to a peak of 50 percent in 1992. In 1995, they were 46 percent of total income. Government employment peaked at 13.3 percent of the labour force and since then has declined. In 1995, 10.5 percent of the labour force worked in the government.

Source: Statistics Canada, *StatCan: CANSIM Disc,* March 1996.

The Economic Theory of Government

WE ALL HAVE OPINIONS ON POLITICAL MATTERS, and some of those opinions are strongly held. As students of economics, our task is to understand, explain, and predict the economic choices that the government sector makes. Although we cannot suppress our political views, it is important, if we are to make progress in studying political behaviour, to continually remind ourselves of the important distinction between positive and normative analysis. We first reviewed that distinction in Chapter 1 (p. 12). But because the distinction is so important for the economic study of political behaviour, let's remind ourselves of what that distinction is.

Positive and Normative Analysis

An economic analysis of government choices may be either *positive* or *normative*. The positive analysis of government seeks to explain the reasons for and effects of government economic choices. A normative analysis seeks to evaluate the desirability of a government action and argues for or against some particular proposal. Positive analysis seeks to understand what *is*; normative analysis seeks to reach conclusions on what *ought* to be. The economic analysis used in both of these activities is similar. But the use to which the analysis is put differs.

Here we undertake a positive study of government action; that is, we seek to understand the reasons for and the effects of the actions that we see being undertaken by governments in Canada today. We do not seek to establish the desirability of any particular course of action or to argue for or against any particular policy.

Government economic activity arises, in part, because an unregulated market economy does not achieve an *efficient allocation of resources*, a situation called **market failure**. When market failure occurs, the market economy produces too many of some goods and services and too few of some others. In these cases, the marginal social cost of each good and service does not equal its marginal benefit. By reallocating resources, it is possible to make some people better off, while making no one worse off. So some government activity is an attempt to modify the market outcome to moderate the effects of market failure.

Government economic activity also arises because an unregulated market economy does not achieve what most people regard as an *equitable distribution of income*. So some government activity is an attempt to modify the market outcome to redistribute income and wealth, sometimes from the rich to the poor, sometimes among the rich and sometimes from the poor to the rich.

There are four broad problems that create market failure and inequity. They are

- Public goods
- Economic inequality
- Monopoly
- Externalities

Public Goods

A **public good** is a good or service that can be consumed simultaneously by everyone and from which no one can be excluded. The first feature of a public good is called nonrivalry. A good is a **nonrival good** if for a given level of production, the consumption of it by one person does not decrease the consumption of it by another person. An example of a nonrival good is a television show. The opposite of nonrival is rival. A good is a **rival good** if for a given level of production, the consumption of it by one person decreases the consumption of it by another person. An example of a rival good is a hot dog.

The second feature of a public good is that it is nonexcludable. A good is a **nonexcludable good** if it is impossible, or extremely costly, to prevent someone from benefiting from a good. An example of a nonexcludable good is national defence. It would be difficult to exclude someone from being defended. The opposite to nonexcludable is excludable. A good is an **excludable good** if it is possible to prevent a person from enjoying the benefits of a good. An example of an excludable good is cable television. Cable companies can ensure that only those people who have paid the fee receive programs.

Figure 18.2 classifies goods according to two criteria and gives some examples of goods in each category. Goods in the bottom right-hand corner are known as *pure* public goods. The classic example of a pure public good is a lighthouse. A modern example is national defence. One person's security that is provided by our national defence system does not decrease the amount of security available for someone else—defence is a nonrival good. And the military cannot select those

FIGURE 18.2
Public Goods and Private Goods

	Rival	Nonrival
Excludable	**Pure private goods** Food Car House	**Excludable and nonrival** Cable television Bridge Highway
Non-excludable	**Nonexcludable and rival** Fish in the ocean Air	**Pure public goods** Lighthouse National defence

A pure public good (bottom right) is one for which consumption is nonrival and from which it is impossible to exclude a consumer. Pure public goods pose a free-rider problem. A pure private good (top left) is one for which consumption is rival and from which consumers can be excluded. Some goods are nonexcludable but are rival (bottom left), and some goods are nonrival but are excludable (top right).

Source: Adapted from and inspired by E.S. Savas, *Privatizing the Public Sector* (Chatham, NJ: Chatham House Publishers, 1982), p. 34.

whom it will protect and those whom it will leave exposed to threats—defence is a nonexcludable good.

Many goods have a public element but are not pure public goods. An example is a highway. A highway is a nonrival good until it becomes congested. One more car on a highway with plenty of space does not reduce the transportation services available to anyone else. But once the highway becomes congested, one extra vehicle lowers the quality of the service available for everyone else—the highway becomes a rival good, like a private good. Also, users can be excluded from a highway by tollgates. Another good that has a public element is fish in the ocean. Ocean fish are rival goods because a fish taken by one person is not available for anyone else. Ocean fish are also nonexcludable goods because it is difficult (at least outside a country's territorial limits) to prevent anyone from taking them.

Public goods create a free-rider problem. A **free rider** is a person who consumes a good without paying for it. Public goods create a *free-rider problem* because the quantity of the good that the person is able to consume is not influenced by the amount the person pays for the good. So no one has an incentive to pay for a public good. We'll see how government can help to cope with the free-rider problem later in this chapter. But first let's look at the other sources of government economic activity.

Economic Inequality

The market economy produces unequal incomes. It does so because many people own few resources or own resources that command a low price. Also, the market economy does not provide insurance against an unlucky draw in the income distribution sweepstakes. Inequality creates two types of problems. First, it creates a situation that many people regard as unfair. Second, it creates social and political unrest that can increase the crime rate and, in extreme cases, produce political insurrection and revolution.

To lessen the degree of inequality, governments redistribute income. They tax some people and pay benefits to others. But not all government redistribution goes from the rich to the poor. The creation of monopoly and government protection of cartels often redistributes income from the poor (and the middle) to the rich. We study economic inequality and the way governments try to lessen it in Chapter 19.

Monopoly

Rent seeking and *monopoly* prevent the allocation of resources from being efficient. Every business tries to maximize profit and when monopoly power exists, it is usually possible to increase profit by restricting output and increasing price. Until a few years ago, for example, Bell Canada had a monopoly on long-distance telephone services and the quantity of long-distance services was much smaller and the price much higher than it is today.

Although some monopolies arise from *legal barriers to entry*—barriers to entry created by governments—a major activity of government is to regulate monopoly and to enforce laws that prevent cartels and other restrictions on competition. We study these regulations and laws in Chapter 20.

Externalities

An **externality** is a cost or a benefit arising from an economic transaction that falls on people who do not participate in that transaction. For example, when a chemical factory (legally) dumps its waste into a river and kills the fish, it imposes an externality—in this case, an external cost—on the fisherman who lives downstream. External costs and benefits are not usually taken into account by the people whose actions create them. For example, the chemical factory does not take its effects on the fish into account when deciding whether to dump waste into the river. When a homeowner fills her garden with spring bulbs, she generates an external benefit for all the joggers and walkers who pass by. In deciding how much to spend on this lavish display, she takes into account only the benefits accruing to herself. We study externalities and the way governments and markets cope with them in Chapter 21.

Before we begin to study each of these problems from which government activity arises, let's look at the arena in which governments operate, the "political marketplace."

Public Choice and the Political Marketplace

GOVERNMENT IS A COMPLEX ORGANIZATION made up of millions of individuals, each with their *own* economic objectives. Government policy choices are the outcome of the choices made by these individuals. To analyse these choices, economists have developed a theory of the political marketplace that parallels theories of markets for goods and services—*public choice theory*.

In public choice theory, the actors in the political marketplace are

- Voters
- Politicians
- Bureaucrats

The choices and interactions of these actors are illustrated in Fig. 18.3. Let's look at each in turn.

Voters

Voters are the consumers of the political process. In markets for goods and services, people express their demands by their willingness to pay. In the political marketplace, they express their demands by voting, by making campaign contributions, and by lobbying.

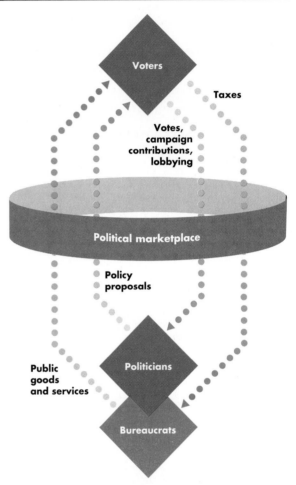

FIGURE 18.3

The Political Marketplace

Voters express their demands for policies by voting, making campaign contributions, and lobbying. Politicians propose policies to appeal to a majority of voters. Bureaucrats try to maximize the budgets of their bureaus. If voters are well informed, the political equilibrium is efficient. If voters are rationally ignorant, the provision of public goods exceeds the efficient level.

Economic models of public choice assume that people support policies that they believe will make them better off and oppose policies that they believe will make them worse off. They neither oppose nor support—they are indifferent among—policies that they believe have no effect on them. Voters' *perceptions* rather than reality are what guide their choices.

Politicians

Politicians are the elected administrators and legislators in federal, provincial, and local government—from the chief executives (the prime minister, premier, or mayor) to members of the legislatures and city councils.

Economic models of public choice assume that the objective of a politician is to get elected and to remain in office. Votes, to a politician, are like dollars to a firm. To get enough votes, politicians form coalitions—political parties—that develop policy proposals, which they expect will appeal to a majority of voters.

Bureaucrats

Bureaucrats are the hired officials who work in government departments, again at the federal, provincial, and local levels. The most senior bureaucrats are hired by politicians. Junior bureaucrats are hired by senior ones.

Economic models of public choice assume that bureaucrats aim to maximize their own utility. To achieve this objective, they try to maximize the budget of the agency in which they work. The bigger the budget of the agency, the greater is the prestige of the agency chief and the larger is the opportunity for promotion for people further down the bureaucratic ladder. Thus all the members of an agency have an interest in maximizing the agency's budget. To maximize their budgets, bureaucrats devise programs that they expect will appeal to politicians and they help politicians to sell programs to voters.

Political Equilibrium

Voters, politicians, and bureaucrats make their economic choices to best further their own objectives. But each group is constrained in two ways: by the preferences of the other groups and by what is technologically feasible. The outcome of the choices of voters, politicians, and bureaucrats is the political equilibrium. The **political equilibrium** is a situation in which the choices made by voters, politicians, and bureaucrats are all compatible and in which no group can improve its position by making a different choice.

A political equilibrium is similar to a market equilibrium. In a market equilibrium, buyers maximize utility and sellers maximize profits. But the equilibrium can be inefficient. That is, there can be *market failure*. A key reason for government action is to overcome market failure. But it is possible that in the attempt to overcome a market failure, the political process will create its own efficiencies and result in *government failure*. We're going to see how government actions might achieve an efficient outcome and how government failure might occur. We begin in the next section by looking at government actions to produce public goods.

Let's see how voters, politicians, and bureaucrats interact to determine the quantity of public goods.

Public Goods

WHY DOES THE GOVERNMENT PROVIDE GOODS and services such as national defence, environmental protection, public health services, a legal system, schools, and highways? Why don't we leave the provision of these goods and services to private firms that sell their output in markets? Why don't we buy our environmental protection from Arctic Ozone, Inc., a private firm that competes for our dollars in the marketplace in the same way that Tim Hortons and Coca-Cola do? The answer to these questions lies in the free-rider problem.

The Free-Rider Problem

Suppose that an effective method of controlling sulphur dioxide emissions has been developed, one that makes it possible to eliminate acid rain. Imagine also that specially designed acid-rain checks can monitor the level of acid rain. One acid-rain check can do part of the job required. But the larger the number of acid-rain checks deployed, the greater is the degree of security.

Acid-rain checks are expensive, and to build them, resources are diverted from other productive activities. The larger the number of acid-rain checks installed, the greater is their marginal cost.

Our task is to work out the number of acid-rain checks to install to achieve allocative efficiency. We'll then examine whether private provision can achieve allocative efficiency, and we'll discover that it cannot—that there is a free-rider problem.

Cost–Benefit Analysis

The benefit provided by an acid-rain check is based on the preferences and beliefs of the consumers of its services. It is the *value* of its services. The *value* to an individual of a *private* good is the maximum amount that the person is willing to pay for one more unit of the good. And the individual's demand curve tells us this value. Similarly, the value to an individual of a *public* good is the maximum amount that the person is willing to pay for one more unit of the good.

To calculate the value a person places on one more unit of a public good, we can use a total benefit schedule. *Total benefit* is the total dollar value that a person places on a given level of provision of a public good. The greater the quantity, the larger is a person's total benefit. **Marginal benefit** is the increase in total benefit resulting from a one-unit increase in the quantity of a public good.

Figure 18.4 shows an example of the marginal benefit that arises from acid-rain checks for a society with just two members, Lisa and Max. Lisa's and Max's marginal benefits are graphed as MB_L and MB_M, respectively, in parts (a) and (b) of the figure. The marginal benefit from a public good is similar to the marginal utility from a private good—its magnitude diminishes as the quantity of the good increases. For Lisa, the marginal benefit of the first acid-rain check is $80, and for the second it is $60. By the time 4 acid-rain checks are deployed, Lisa perceives no additional benefits. For Max, the marginal utility of the first acid-rain check is $50, and for the second it is $40. By the time 4 acid-rain checks are deployed, Max perceives only $10 worth of marginal benefit.

Part (c) of the figure shows the economy's marginal benefit curve, *MB* (where the economy has only two people, Lisa and Max). An individual's marginal benefit curve for a public good is similar to the individual's demand curve for a private good. But the economy's marginal benefit curve for a public good is different from the market demand curve for a private good. To obtain the market demand curve for a private good, we add up the quantities demanded by each individual at each price. In other words, we sum the individual demand curves horizontally. In contrast, to find the economy's marginal benefit curve of a public good, we add the marginal benefit of each individual at each quantity of provision. That is, we sum the individual marginal benefit curves vertically. The resulting marginal benefit for the economy made up of Lisa and Max is the economy's marginal benefit

Benefits of a Public Good

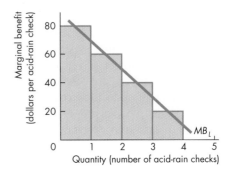

(a) Lisa's marginal benefit

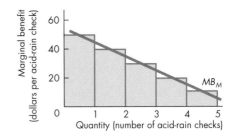

(b) Max's marginal benefit

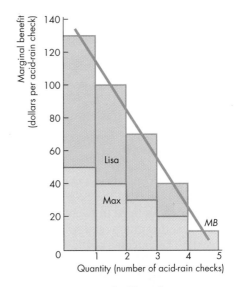

(c) Economy's marginal benefit

The marginal benefit to the economy at each quantity of the public good is the sum of the marginal benefits to each individual. The marginal benefit curves are MB_L for Lisa, MB_M for Max, and MB for the economy.

curve graphed in part (c)—the curve *MB*.

In reality, an economy with two people would not buy any acid-rain checks—the total benefit falls far short of the cost. But an economy with 25 million people might. To determine the efficient quantity, we need to take cost as well as benefit into account. The cost of an acid-rain check is based on technology and

the prices of the factors of production used to produce it. It is an opportunity cost and is derived in the same way as the cost of producing sweaters (explained in Chapter 10). The efficient quantity is the one that maximizes net benefit—total benefit minus total cost.

Figure 18.5 illustrates the efficient quantity of

FIGURE 18.5
The Efficient Quantity of a Public Good

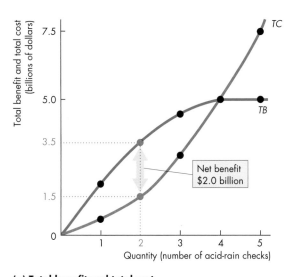

(a) Total benefit and total cost

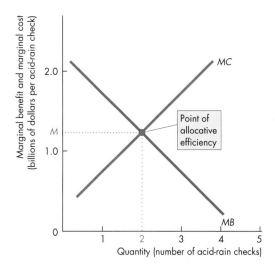

(b) Marginal benefit and marginal cost

Quantity (number of acid-rain checks)	Total benefit (billions of dollars)	Marginal benefit (billions of dollars per acid-rain check)	Total cost (billions of dollars)	Marginal cost (billions of dollars per acid-rain check)	Net benefit (billions of dollars)
0	0		0		0
		2.0		0.5	
1	2.0		0.5		1.5
		1.5		1.0	
2	3.5		1.5		2.0
		1.0		1.5	
3	4.5		3.0		1.5
		0.5		2.0	
4	5.0		5.0		0
		0		2.5	
5	5.0		7.5		−2.5

Total benefit and total cost are graphed in part (a) as the total benefit curve, *TB*, and the total cost curve, *TC*. Net benefit—the vertical distance between the two curves—is maximized when 2 acid-rain checks are installed.

Part (b) shows the marginal benefit curve, *MB*, and marginal cost curve, *MC*. When marginal cost equals marginal benefit, net benefit is maximized and allocative efficiency is achieved.

acid-rain checks. The second and third columns of the table show the total and marginal benefits to an economy. The next two columns show the total and marginal cost of producing acid-rain checks. The final column shows net benefit. Total benefit, *TB*, and total cost, *TC*, are graphed in part (a). Net benefit (total benefit minus total cost) is maximized when the vertical distance between the *TB* and *TC* curves is at its largest, a situation that occurs with 2 acid-rain checks. This is the efficient quantity.

The fundamental principles of marginal analysis that you have used to explain how consumers maximize utility and how firms maximize profit can also be used to calculate the efficient scale of provision of a public good. Figure 18.5(b) shows this alternative approach. The marginal benefit curve is *MB* and the marginal cost curve is *MC*. When marginal benefit exceeds marginal cost, net benefit increases if the quantity produced increases. When marginal cost exceeds marginal benefit, net benefit increases if the quantity produced decreases. Marginal benefit equals marginal cost with 2 acid-rain checks. So making marginal cost equal to marginal benefit maximizes net benefit and achieves allocative efficiency.

Private Provision

We have now worked out the quantity of acid-rain checks that maximizes net benefit. Would a private firm—Arctic Ozone, Inc.—deliver that quantity? It would not. To do so, it would have to collect $1.5 billion to cover its costs—or $60 from each of the 25 million people in the economy. But no one would have an incentive to buy his or her "share" of the acid-rain check system. Each person would reason as follows: The number of acid-rain checks provided by Arctic Ozone, Inc., is not affected by my $60. But my own private consumption is greater if I free-ride and do not pay my share of the cost of the acid-rain check system. If I do not pay, I enjoy the same level of security and can buy more private goods. Therefore I will spend my $60 on other goods and free-ride on the public good.

If everyone reasons the same way, Arctic Ozone, Inc. has zero revenue and so provides no acid-rain checks. Because 2 acid-rain checks is the efficient level, private provision is inefficient. Even if a few people made a contribution to Arctic Ozone so that the company could provide some level of service, this level would fall far short of the efficient.

Public Provision

Suppose there are two political parties, the Greens and the Smokes, that agree with each other on all issues except for acid-rain checks. The Greens would like to provide 4 acid-rain checks at a cost of $5.0 billion, with benefits of $5.0 billion and a net benefit of zero, as shown in Fig. 18.6. The Smokes would like to provide 1 acid-rain check at a cost of $0.5 billion, a benefit of $2.0 billion and a net benefit of $1.5 billion—see Fig. 18.6.

Before deciding on the platforms, the two political parties do a "what-if" analysis. Each party reasons as follows. If each party offers the acid-rain check program it wants—Greens 4 acid-rain checks and Smokes 1 acid-rain check—the voters will get a net

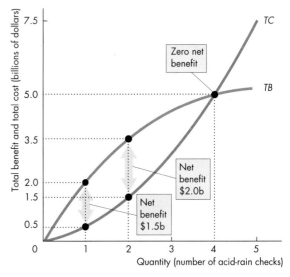

FIGURE 18.6

Provision of a Public Good in a Political System ◆

Net benefit is maximized if 2 acid-rain checks are installed, with a total benefit of $3.5 billion and a total cost of $1.5 billion. The Smokes would like 1 acid-rain check, and the Greens would like 4. But each party recognizes that its only hope of being elected is to provide 2 acid-rain checks—the quantity that maximizes net benefit and so leaves no room for the other party to improve on. If voters are well informed about the cost and benefit of a public good, competition between political parties for their votes achieves the efficient outcome.

benefit of $1.5 billion from the Smokes, zero net benefit from the Greens, and the Smokes will win the election.

Contemplating this outcome, the Greens realize that their party is too "green" to get elected. They figure that they must offer net benefits in excess of $1.5 billion if they are to beat the Smokes. So they scale back their proposal to 2 acid-rain checks. At this level of provision, total cost is $1.5 billion, total benefit is $3.5 billion, and net benefit is $2.0 billion. If the Smokes stick with 1 acid-rain check, the Greens will win the election.

But contemplating this outcome, the Smokes realize that the best they can do is to match the Greens. They too propose to provide 2 acid-rain checks on exactly the same terms as the Greens. If the two parties offer the same number of acid-rain checks, the voters are indifferent between the parties. They flip coins to decide their votes and each party receives around 50 percent of the vote.

The result of the politicians' "what-if" analysis is that each party offers 2 acid-rain checks, so regardless of who wins the election, this is the quantity of acid-rain checks installed. And this quantity is efficient. It maximizes the perceived net benefit of the voters. Thus in this example, competition in the political marketplace results in the efficient provision of a public good. But for this outcome to occur, voters must be well informed and evaluate the alternatives. We'll see below that they do not always have an incentive to do so.

In the example we've just studied, both parties propose identical policies. This tendency towards identical policies is called the principle of minimum differentiation.

The Principle of Minimum Differentiation The **principle of minimum differentiation** is the tendency for competitors to make themselves identical in order to appeal to the maximum number of clients or voters. You can see the principle of minimum differentiation in many familiar situations. Let's look at one.

Figure 18.7 shows a beach that is one kilometre long from *A* to *B*. Sunbathers lounge at equal intervals over the entire beach and buy their ice cream from the nearest vendor. Also, the farther they must walk, the fewer ice creams they buy. An ice cream vendor arrives at the beach and sets up a stand. Where will she locate? The answer is at position *C*— exactly halfway between *A* and *B*. By locating in this position, the farthest that anyone must walk to buy

FIGURE 18.7

The Principle of Minimum Differentiation

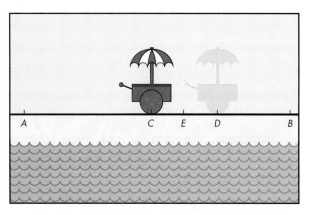

A beach stretches from *A* to *B*. Sunbathers are distributed at even intervals along the whole beach. An ice cream vendor sets up a stand at point *C*. The distance that people must walk for ice cream is the same no matter on which side of the ice cream stand they are located. If a second ice cream vendor sets up a stand, it will pay to place it exactly next to *C* in the middle of the beach. If the second stand is placed at *D*, only the customers on the beach between *E* and *B* will buy ice cream from *D*. Those between *A* and *E* will go to *C*. By moving as close to *C* as possible, the second ice cream vendor picks up half the ice cream customers.

an ice cream is a kilometre (half a kilometre to the ice cream stand and half a kilometre back to the beach towel), so she gets the maximum possible number of customers.

Now suppose a second ice cream vendor arrives on the beach. Where will he place his ice cream stand? The answer is right next to the original one at point *C*. To understand why, imagine that the second vendor locates his stand at point *D*—halfway between *C* and *B*. How many customers will he attract and how many will go to the stand at *C*? The stand at *D* will pick up all the customers on the beach between *B* and *D*, because this stand is closer for them. It will also pick up all the customers between *D* and *E* (the point halfway between *C* and *D*), because they too will have a shorter trip for an ice cream by going to *D* than by going to *C*. All the people between *A* and *C* and all those between *C* and *E* will go to stand *C.* So the ice cream stand located at *C* will pick up all the people on the beach between *A* and *E,* and the stand located at *D* will pick up all the people located between *E* and *B.*

Now suppose that the vendor with a stand at *D* moves to *C.* There are now two stands at *C.* Half the customers will go to the first vendor and the other half to the second vendor. Only by locating exactly in the centre of the beach can each pick up half the customers. If either of them moves slightly away from the centre, then that vendor picks up less than half the customers and the one remaining at the centre picks up a majority of the customers.

This example illustrates the principle of minimum differentiation. By having no differentiation in location, both ice cream vendors do as well as they can and share the market evenly.

The principle of minimum differentiation has been used to explain a wide variety of choices—how radio stations choose their playlists; how TV stations show programs that mimic those of their rival stations; and how political parties choose their platforms.

We have analysed the behaviour of politicians but not that of the bureaucrats who translate the choices of the politicians into programs. Let's now see how the economic choices of bureaucrats influence the political equilibrium.

The Role of Bureaucrats

We've seen, in Fig. 18.5 and Fig. 18.6, that 2 acid-rain checks at a cost of $1.5 billion maximize net benefit and that competition between two political parties delivers this outcome. But will the bureaucrats at Environment Canada cooperate?

The objective of bureaucrats at Environment Canada is to maximize their budget, as shown in Fig. 18.8. To achieve their objective, the bureaucrats will try to persuade the politicians that 2 acid-rain checks cost more than $1.5 billion. As Fig. 18.8 shows, if possible, Environment Canada would like to convince Parliament that the acid-rain checks cost $3.5 billion—the entire benefit. And pressing its position even more strongly, Environment Canada will argue for more acid-rain checks. It will press for 4 acid-rain checks and a budget of $5.0 billion. In this situation, total benefit and total cost are equal and net benefit is zero.

The bureaucrats at Environment Canada want to maximize their budget but won't the politicians prevent them from doing so to maximize votes?

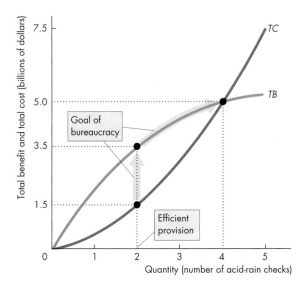

FIGURE 18.8

Bureaucratic Overprovision

The goal of a bureaucracy is to maximize its budget. A bureau that maximizes its budget will seek to increase its budget so that its total cost equals total benefit and then to use that budget to expand output and expenditure. Here, Environment Canada tries to get $3.5 billion to provide 2 acid-rain checks. It would like to increase the quantity of acid-rain checks to 4 with a budget of $5.0 billion.

Politicians will if voters are well informed and know what is best for them. But voters might be rationally ignorant. In this case, well-informed interest groups might enable the bureaucrats at Environment Canada to achieve their objective.

Voter Ignorance and Well-Informed Interest Groups   A principle of public choice theory is that it is rational for a voter to be ignorant about an issue unless that issue has a perceptible effect on the voter's income. **Rational ignorance** is the decision *not* to acquire information because the cost of doing so exceeds the expected benefit. For example, each voter knows that he or she can make virtually no difference to the government's clean air policy. Each voter also knows that it would take an enormous amount of time and effort to become even moderately well informed about alternative technologies for monitoring sulphur dioxide emissions. So voters remain relatively uninformed about the technicalities of clean air issues. (Though we are using clean air policy as an example, the same applies to all aspects of government economic activity.)

All voters are consumers of clean air. But not all voters are producers of equipment used to monitor sulphur dioxide emissions. Only a small number are in this latter category. Those voters who own or work for firms that produce such monitoring equipment have a direct personal interest in the quality of our air because it affects their incomes. These voters have an incentive to become well informed about monitoring issues and to operate a political lobby aimed at furthering their own interests. In collaboration with the bureaucracy at Environment Canada, these voters exert a larger influence than the relatively uninformed voters who only consume this public good.

When the rationality of the uninformed voter and special interest groups are taken into account, the political equilibrium provides public goods in excess of the efficient quantity. So, in the acid-rain check example, 3 or 4 acid-rain checks might be installed rather than the efficient quantity, which is 2 acid-rain checks.

Why Government Grows

We saw at the beginning of this chapter that government has grown over the years. Now that we know how the quantity of public goods is determined, we can explain part of the reason for the growth of government. Government grows, in part, because the demand for some public goods increases at a faster rate than the demand for private goods. There are two possible reasons for this growth:

- Voter preferences
- Inefficient overprovision

Voter Preferences   The growth of government can be explained by voter preferences in the following way. As voters' incomes increase (as they usually do in most years), the quantity of public goods demanded increases more quickly than income. (Technically, the *income elasticity of demand* for public goods is greater than 1—see Chapter 5, pp. 107–108.) Many (and the most expensive) public goods are in this category. They include communication systems such as highways, airports, and air-traffic control systems; public health; education; the environment; and defence. So this first reason for government growth seems convincing.

Inefficient Overprovision   Inefficient overprovision might explain the *size* of government, but not its *growth rate*. It (possibly) explains why government is *larger* than its efficient scale, but it does not explain why governments spend an increasing proportion of total income. In fact, while government outlays as a proportion of total income in the economy have steadily increased, government sector employment has shrunk relative to total employment since 1975—see Fig. 18.1.

Voters Strike Back

If government grows too large, relative to what voters are willing to accept, there might be a voter backlash against government programs and a large bureaucracy. The success of Mike Harris's Conservative Party in the 1995 Ontario election might be interpreted as such a backlash.

Another way that voters—and politicians—can try to counter the tendency of bureaucrats to expand their budgets is to privatize the *production* of public goods. Government *provision* of a public good does not automatically imply that a government-operated bureau must *produce* the good.

REVIEW

- Private provision of a public good creates a free-rider problem and provides less than the efficient quantity of the good.
- Competition between politicians for votes can achieve an efficient quantity of a public good, provided voters are well informed.
- If consumers of a public good are less well informed than producers of that good, bureaucrats supported by well-informed voters have a larger influence than uninformed voters and the quantity of public goods exceeds the efficient quantity.

We've now seen how voters, politicians, and bureaucrats interact to determine the quantity of a public good. We have recognized that voters must forgo some private consumption to give governments the resources used to provide public goods. But we have not explicitly studied the structure of taxes. How does the political marketplace determine the scale and variety of taxes that we pay?

Taxes

Taxes generate the financial resources that governments use to provide voters with public goods and other benefits. For the federal government in 1995, 59 percent of total revenue came from income taxes and 21 percent from indirect taxes (such as the Goods and Services Tax). For provincial governments, 30 percent of total revenue came from sales taxes, and 37 percent from income taxes. Why do income taxes provide such a large proportion of the government's revenue?

Income Taxes

Income taxes are such a prominent source of government revenue because of the way they distribute the costs and benefits of government. The amounts that people pay in income tax and receive in benefits from government programs depend on their income. Other things remaining the same, the higher a person's income, the greater is the amount of income tax paid and the smaller is the amount of benefit received. So as a rule, high-income people tend to vote for a political party that proposes low benefits and a low income tax rate, while low-income people tend to vote for a political party that proposes high benefits and a high income tax rate. The politicians' task is to find the income tax rate and benefits program that attract the votes of a majority of voters.

A model of the attempt of politicians to balance the interests of the high-income voters and low-income voters is based on the median voter theorem.

The Median Voter Theorem   The **median voter theorem** states that political parties will pursue policies that maximize the net benefit of the median voter. The median member of a population is the one in the middle—one-half of the population lies on one side and one-half on the other. Let's see how the median voter theorem applies to the questions of how large a benefits program to provide and how large an income tax to impose.

Imagine a list of all the possible levels of benefits from government programs and the associated income tax rates needed to finance them. The list begins with the highest possible level of benefits and income tax rate and ends with no benefits and a zero income tax rate. We can identify each entry in the list by the income tax rate associated with it.

Next imagine arranging all the voters along a line running from A to D, as shown in Fig. 18.9. The voter who favours the highest income tax rate (and the highest benefit level) is at A. The voter who favours a zero tax rate (and no benefits) is at D. All the other voters are arranged along the line based on the tax rate (and benefits) that they favour most. The curve in the figure shows the tax rate favoured most by each voter between A and D. The median voter in the example in Fig. 18.9 favours most a tax rate of 30 percent.

Suppose that there are two political parties and that they propose similar but not quite identical income tax rates. The high-tax party proposes a tax rate of 61 percent and the low-tax party proposes a tax rate of 59 percent. Given this choice, all the voters between A and B prefer the higher tax rate and will vote for the high-tax party. All the voters between B and D prefer the lower tax and will vote for the low-tax party. The low-tax party will win the election.

Alternatively, suppose that the high-tax party proposes a tax rate of 11 percent and the low-tax party proposes a tax rate of 9 percent. The voters between A and C will vote for the high-tax party and those between C and D will vote for the low-tax party. This time, the high-tax party will win the election.

In either of the two situations we've just examined, the party that wins the election is the one closer to the position preferred by the median voter. So each party can improve its election performance by moving closer to the median than the other party. But each party has the same incentive, so each moves towards the median. Once the two parties are offering the tax rate favoured most by the median voter, neither can increase its vote by changing its proposal. One party will get the votes between A and the median, and the other party will get the votes between the median and D.

All the voters except those at the median will be dissatisfied—for those between A and the median, the benefits and tax rate are too low, and for those between D and the median, the benefits and the tax rate are too high. But no political party can propose programs other than those that can be financed with a 30 percent tax rate and expect to win the election. If the two parties propose identical programs and a 30 percent tax rate, the voters are indifferent and either don't vote or flip a coin to decide which party to vote for.

The median voter theorem implies the principle of minimum differentiation that we've already studied. Both political parties locate at the same point on the political spectrum. But this implication does not

FIGURE 18.9

Voting for Income Taxes

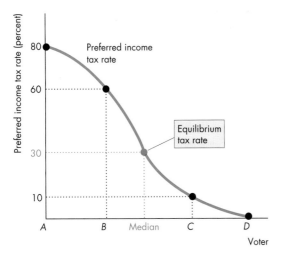

A political party can win an election by proposing policies that appeal to the median voter and to all the other voters on one side of the median. If the median voter favours a policy, that policy will be proposed. In the figure, voters have different preferences concerning the income tax rate (and benefit rate). They are ranked in descending order of their preferred tax. A's preferred tax rate is highest (80 percent) and D's is lowest (0 percent).

There are two political parties. If one proposes a 61 percent tax and the other a 59 percent tax, the low-tax party will win the election—voters between A and B will vote for the high tax and those between B and D for the low tax. If both parties propose low taxes—11 percent and 9 percent—the high-tax party will win. It will pick up the votes between A and C, leaving only the votes between C and D for the low-tax party. Each party has an incentive to move towards the tax rate preferred by the median voter. At that point, each party picks up half the votes and neither can improve its share.

mean that all political parties will be identical in all respects. One party might be ideologically aligned with the wealthy and another with the poor. The two parties will pursue similar policies but each will maintain a rhetoric designed to further the goals of their supporters. One party will talk about higher taxes and better programs and the other will talk about cutting taxes and programs, but neither will actually carry such policies to excess for fear of losing the support of the median voter.

Excise Taxes

An **excise tax** is a tax on the sale of a particular commodity. Let's study the effects of an excise tax by considering the tax on gasoline shown in Fig. 18.10. The demand curve for gasoline is *D,* and the supply curve is *S*. If there is no tax on gasoline, its price is 30¢ a litre and 400 million litres of gasoline a day are bought and sold.

Now suppose that a tax is imposed on gasoline at the rate of 30¢ a litre. If producers are willing to supply 400 million litres a day for 30¢ when there is no tax, then they are willing to supply that same quantity in the face of a 30¢ tax only if the price increases to 60¢ a litre. That is, they want to get the 30¢ a litre they received before, plus the additional 30¢ that they now have to hand over to the government in the form of a gasoline tax. As a result of the tax, the supply of gasoline decreases and the supply curve shifts leftward. The magnitude of the shift is such that the vertical distance between the original and the new supply curve is the amount of the tax. The new supply curve is the red curve *S + tax*. The new supply curve intersects the demand curve at 300 million litres a day and 55¢ a litre. This situation is the new equilibrium after the imposition of the tax.

Why Tax Rates Vary

Why do we tax gasoline, alcohol, and tobacco at high rates and some goods not at all? One reason is that taxes create *deadweight losses*. Deadweight loss is the reduction in consumer and producer surplus that results from the tax. (You first encountered the concept of deadweight loss when you studied monopoly in Chapter 12, pp. 273–274.) It is impossible to avoid deadweight losses from taxes, but by levying taxes at different rates on different commodities, the deadweight loss arising from raising a given amount of revenue can be minimized.

Minimizing the Deadweight Loss of Taxes   You can see that taxes create deadweight loss by looking again at Fig. 18.10. Without a tax, 400 million litres of gasoline a day are consumed at a price of 30¢ a litre. With a 30¢ tax, the price paid by the consumer rises to 55¢ a litre and the quantity consumed declines to 300 million litres a day. There is a loss of consumer surplus arising from this price increase and quantity decrease. The light grey triangle illustrates the loss of consumer surplus. On the 300 millionth

An Excise Tax

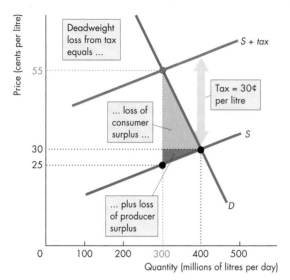

The demand curve for gasoline is *D*, and the supply curve is *S*. In the absence of any taxes, gasoline will sell for 30¢ a litre and 400 million litres a day will be bought and sold. When a tax of 30¢ a litre is imposed, the supply curve shifts leftward to become the curve *S + tax*. The new equilibrium price is 55¢ a litre and 300 million litres a day are bought and sold. The excise tax creates a deadweight loss represented by the sum of the two grey triangles. The tax revenue collected is 30¢ a litre on 300 million litres, which is $90 million a day. The deadweight loss from the tax is $15 million a day. That is, to raise tax revenue of $90 million a day, a deadweight loss of $15 million a day is incurred.

litre bought—the marginal unit bought—the consumer pays 55¢ compared with 30¢ in the absence of a tax. So 25¢ of consumer surplus is lost on this unit. On each successive unit up to the 400 millionth, there is a successively smaller loss of consumer surplus. The total loss of consumer surplus equals the area of the light grey triangle, which is $12.5 million a day.[1]

There is also a loss of producer surplus. The dark

grey triangle illustrates the loss of producer surplus. On the 300 millionth litre sold—the marginal unit sold—the producer receives 25¢ compared with 30¢ in the absence of a tax. So 5¢ of producer surplus is lost on this unit. On each successive unit up to the 400 millionth, there is a successively smaller loss of producer surplus. The total loss of producer surplus equals the area of the dark grey triangle, which is $2.5 million a day.[2]

The deadweight loss is the sum of the consumer surplus lost and the producer surplus lost, which is the sum of the two grey triangles in Fig. 18.10. The dollar value of that deadweight loss is $15 million a day. But how much revenue is raised by this tax? Since 300 million litres of gasoline are sold each day and since the tax is 30¢ a litre, total revenue from the gasoline tax is $90 million a day (300 million litres multiplied by 30¢ a litre). Thus to raise tax revenue of $90 million dollars a day using the gasoline tax, a deadweight loss of $15 million a day—one-sixth of the tax revenue—is incurred.

One of the main influences on the deadweight loss arising from a tax is the price elasticity of demand for the product. The demand for gasoline is fairly inelastic. As a consequence, when a tax is imposed the quantity demanded falls by a smaller percentage than the percentage rise in price. In the example that we've just studied, the quantity demanded falls by 25 percent but the price increases by 83.33 percent.

To see the importance of the elasticity of demand, let's consider a different commodity—orange juice. So that we can make a quick and direct comparison, let's assume that the orange juice market is exactly as big as the market for gasoline. Figure 18.11 illustrates this market. The demand curve for orange juice is *D*, and the supply curve is *S*. Orange juice is not taxed, and so the price of orange juice is 30¢ a litre—where the supply curve and the demand curve intersect—and the quantity of orange juice traded is 400 million litres a day.

Now suppose that the government contemplates abolishing the gasoline tax and taxing orange juice instead. The demand for orange juice is more elastic than the demand for gasoline. It has many more good substitutes in the form of other fruit juices. The

---

[1]You can calculate the area of that triangle by using the formula: (Base × height)/2. The base is 100 million litres per day, the decrease in quantity. The height is the price increase—25¢ per litre. Multiplying 100 million litres per day by 25¢ per litre and dividing by 2 gives $12.5 million a day.

[2]The base is 100 million litres per day, the decrease in quantity. The height is the price decrease for the producer—5¢ per litre. Multiplying 100 million litres per day by 5¢ per litre and dividing by 2 gives $2.5 million a day.

government wants to raise $90 million a day so that its total revenue is not affected by this tax change. The government's economists, armed with their statistical estimates of the demand and supply curves for orange juice that appear in Fig. 18.11, work out that a tax of 45¢ a litre will do the job. With such a tax, the supply curve shifts upward to the red curve labelled *S + tax*. This new supply curve intersects the demand curve at a price of 65¢ a litre and at a quantity of 200 million litres a day. The price at which suppliers are willing to produce 200 million litres a day is 20¢ a litre. The gov-

ernment collects a tax of 45¢ a litre on 200 million litres a day, so it collects a total revenue of $90 million a day—exactly the amount that it requires.

But what is the deadweight loss in this case? The answer can be seen by looking at the grey triangle in Fig. 18.11. The magnitude of that deadweight loss is $45 million.[3] Notice how much bigger the deadweight loss is from taxing orange juice than that from taxing gasoline. In the case of orange juice, the deadweight loss is one-half the revenue raised, while in the case of gasoline it is only one-sixth. What accounts for this difference? The supply curves are identical in each case and the examples were also set up to ensure that the initial no-tax prices and quantities were identical. The difference between the two cases is the elasticity of demand: In the case of gasoline, the quantity demanded falls by only 25 percent when the price almost doubles. In the case of orange juice, the quantity demanded falls by 50 percent when the price only slightly more than doubles.

You can see why taxing orange juice is not on the political agenda of any of the major parties. Vote-seeking politicians seek out taxes that benefit the median voter. Other things remaining the same, they try to minimize the deadweight loss of raising a given amount of revenue. Equivalently, they tax items with poor substitutes more heavily than items with close substitutes.

 We've seen that markets do not always achieve allocative efficiency and an equitable distribution of income—there is market failure. We've also seen how it is possible for public choices to overcome market failure in the provision of public goods. But we've also seen that bureaucrats can overprovide a public good—that there can also be government failure. *Reading Between the Lines* on pp. 430–431 looks at a current public good and free-rider issue—B.C. lighthouses. Finally, we've seen how public choices result in income taxes and high tax rates on items whose elasticity of demand is low. In the next three chapters, we are going to look more closely at the other sources of market failure—economic inequality, monopoly, and externalities—and the way public choices cope with them.

FIGURE 18.11

Why We Don't Tax Orange Juice

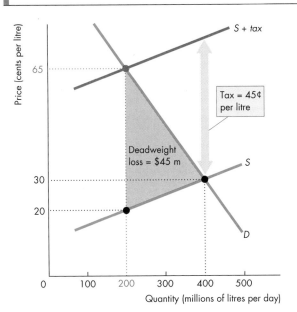

The demand curve for orange juice is *D*, and the supply curve is *S*. The equilibrium price is 30¢ a litre and 400 million litres of juice a day are traded. To raise $90 million of tax revenue, a tax of 45¢ a litre will have to be imposed. The introduction of this tax shifts the supply curve to *S + tax*. The price rises to 65¢ a litre and the quantity bought and sold falls to 200 million litres a day. The deadweight loss is represented by the grey triangle and equals $45 million a day. The deadweight loss from taxing orange juice is much larger than that from taxing gasoline (Fig. 18.10) because the demand for orange juice is more elastic than the demand for gasoline. Items that have a low elasticity of demand are taxed more heavily than items that have a high elasticity of demand.

---

[3]This deadweight loss is calculated in exactly the same way as our previous calculation of the deadweight loss from the gasoline tax. The loss of consumer surplus is 200 million litres per day multiplied by 35¢ per litre, divided by 2, which equals $35 million a day. The loss of producer surplus is 200 million litres per day multiplied by 10¢ per litre, divided by 2, which equals $10 million a day. The deadweight loss is the sum of the two losses, which equals $45 million a day.

Policy
WATCH

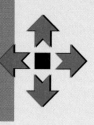

The End of a Free Ride?

VANCOUVER SUN, May 30, 1996

Fuel tax, recreation boat licences urged as way to keep lighthouses

BY STEWART BELL

The B.C. government is considering imposing new taxes on boaters and airplane pilots to help offset the cost of operating West Coast lighthouses, the Vancouver Sun has learned.

A marine and aviation fuel tax and a recreational boat licence fee are among "possible revenue sources" suggested in a study commissioned last fall by Premier Glen Clark.

"Both of these would be new fees on certain provincial taxpayers," said the 74-page report by the accounting firm KPMG.

The study explores alternatives to Ottawa's controversial plan to save money by removing the keepers from B.C. lighthouses. The so-called "destaffing" begins this weekend at the Point Atkinson lighthouse in West Vancouver.

The study found B.C. would have to pay about $7 million a year to run the province's 35 staffed lighthouses. But it said about $6 million of that could be recovered from the federal government, while the remainder could be generated through new taxes and user-fees.

A 0.1 cent-per-litre tax on marine and aviation gas would raise $855,000 annually, or a one-cent tax would bring in $8.55 mil-

lion, enough to run the lighthouses without federal help, the report said.

"If the provincial government were to change its policy on user fees or taxes, significant revenues could be collected from moderate taxes on marine diesel fuel, gasoline sold for marine purposes and aviation gas," said the report.

The province could also earn up to $2 million a year by collecting a $10 levy from recreational boaters, the report said. The report also says that a planned federal boat-licensing scheme should make it possible for the province to collect sales taxes on the sale of second-hand boats. ...

Although Clark promised tax relief to British Columbians during the election campaign, boaters have indicated they would be willing to pay a small fee to ensure lightkeepers will remain at their outposts along the rugged B.C. coast.

Many coastal mariners and pilots fear that if lightkeepers are replaced with machines, more lives will be lost along an already treacherous coastline. At public hearings held over the past few years, coastal residents were virtually unanimous in their opposition to lighthouse automation, arguing it will compromise safety for the sake of minor cost saving.

Essence of THE STORY

■ The federal government plans to stop paying for B.C. lighthouse keepers.

■ The B.C. government is considering imposing a tax on marine and aviation gas and a licence fee on each boat.

■ Boaters say they are willing to pay to ensure lighthouse keepers remain at their outposts along the rugged B.C. coast.

Economic

A N A L Y S I S

- A lighthouse is a public good. So the provision of lighthouse services creates a free-rider problem.

- To overcome this problem, the federal government had paid for lighthouses with funds collected in taxes.

- But now there is a proposal to stop funding the wages of lighthouse keepers.

- British Columbia, which has a rugged coast line, plans to maintain the original lighthouse services by paying for them with taxes paid by boaters (and aviators).

- Figure 1 shows the cost and benefits curves for a lighthouse system. Total cost, TC, increases with the number of lighthouses operated and at an increasing rate. That is, marginal cost rises.

- Total benefit, TB, also increases with the number of lighthouses operated, but at a decreasing rate. That is, marginal benefit diminishes.

- The B.C. government can provide the efficient amount of lighthouse services at Q^*, which brings a total benefit of B^*, by spending C^*.

- To raise the funds, the B.C. government proposes taxing boaters. Figure 2 shows the effects of these actions in the market for boating.

- With no taxes and with inferior lighthouse services, the supply of boating is S and the demand for boating is D. The quantity of boating is Q_0 and the price is P_0.

- With the efficient provision of lighthouse services, more people feel secure boating and the demand for boating increases to D_1. But with the tax on fuel and a licence fee added to other costs, the supply curve becomes $S + taxes$.

- Assuming that the increase in benefit exceeds the tax cost (as it does in Fig. 1) the price of boating rises to P_1 but the quantity increases to Q_1.

- Boaters say that they are willing to pay the tax, but lighthouses are public goods and the free-rider problem remains—boaters (and aviators) might buy their fuel outside British Columbia and avoid paying the tax. In this case, the B.C. government will raise insufficient funds to pay for the lighthouse services.

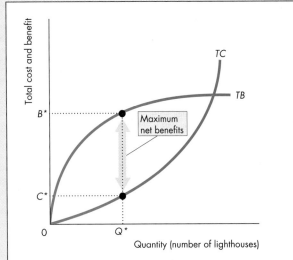

Figure 1 Cost and benefits of lighthouses

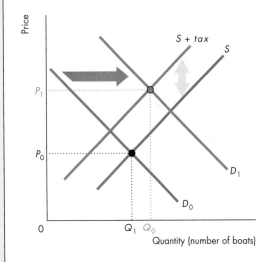

Figure 2 Market for boating

You're

THE VOTER

- Can you think of other public goods that benefit particular groups that might be taxed?

- Considering a tax on these public goods, which ones would you be willing to vote for and why?

S U M M A R Y

Key Points

The Government Sector   In 1995, the government sector of the Canadian economy spent 46 percent of total income and employed 10.5 percent of the labour force. Spending has increased and employment has decreased in recent years. (p. 415)

The Economic Theory of Government   Government economic activity arises in an attempt to cope with public goods, economic inequality, monopoly, and externalities. Public goods create a free-rider problem. Economic inequality is generally regarded as unfair. Monopoly and externalities result in an inefficient allocation of resources. (pp. 416–418)

Public Choice and the Political Marketplace
Public choice theory is based on the idea that government operates in a political marketplace in which voters, politicians, and bureaucrats interact. Voters are the consumers of the political process, and they express their demands through their votes, campaign contributions, and lobbying. Politicians propose policies, and their objective is to win elections. Bureaucrats implement policies, and their objective is to maximize their budgets. The outcome of the interaction of voters, politicians, and bureaucrats is a political equilibrium that might or might not be efficient. (pp. 418–419)

Public Goods   The efficient provision of a public good is the level at which total benefit minus total cost is at a maximum—at which marginal benefit equals marginal cost. Because of the free-rider problem too little is available from private provision. Government can finance a public good with tax revenue. Competition among political parties can lead to an efficient provision. Bureaucrats try to maximize their budgets, but they are constrained by what the voters will tolerate. If voters are well informed, provision of public goods is efficient. If voters are rationally ignorant, producer interest can result in an over-provision of public goods. (pp. 419–425)

Taxes   Government revenue comes from income taxes, expenditure taxes, sales taxes, and excise taxes on gasoline, alcoholic beverages, and tobacco products that are taxed at high rates. Income tax rates are

set to appeal to the median voter. Voters with a high income pay for more benefits than they receive and prefer a lower tax rate. Voters with a low income pay for fewer benefits than they receive and prefer a higher tax rate. Even political parties that represent the interests of the rich and the poor propose taxes and benefits that appeal to the median voter. To do otherwise would lose the election.

Taxes create deadweight losses, the size of which depends on the price elasticity of demand. By taxing goods that have inelastic demands, the deadweight loss of raising a given amount of tax revenue is lowered. (pp. 426–429)

Key Figures

Key Terms

R E V I E W   Q U E S T I O N S

1. Describe the growth of the government sector of the Canadian economy over the past 25 years.
2. Distinguish between a positive and a normative economic analysis of government choices.
3. What is market failure? Explain how it arises.
4. What are the features of a good that make it a public good? Give three examples of public goods.
5. What is the free-rider problem and how does government help overcome it?
6. What is economic inequity? What are the problems that economic inequity creates?
7. What is monopoly? How can it arise?
8. What is an externality? Give some examples of an external cost and an external benefit.
9. Describe the three actors in the political marketplace.
10. Describe how the marginal benefit from a public good is measured.
11. Explain why the private provision of a public good is inefficient.
12. Describe the economic functions of voters and explain how they make their economic choices.
13. Describe the economic functions of politicians and explain how they make their economic choices.
14. Describe the economic functions of bureaucrats and explain how they make their economic choices.
15. What is meant by political equilibrium?
16. What is the principle of minimum differentiation?
17. How does the principle of minimum differentiation explain political parties' policy platforms?
18. Explain why it is likely that the quantity of a public good provided will exceed its efficient scale.
19. Why is it rational for voters to be ignorant?
20. What is the median voter theorem?
21. What features of political choices does the median voter theorem explain?

C R I T I C A L   T H I N K I N G

1. Study *Reading Between the Lines* on pp. 430–431 and then answer the following questions:
   a. Do you agree that a lighthouse is a public good? Why or why not?
   b. Explain how a tax on boaters and aviators can enable the B.C. government to provide an efficient level of lighthouse services.
   c. Suppose lighthouses were paid for by the B.C. government out of the provincial income tax revenues. Would it still be possible to achieve an efficient amount of lighthouse services?
   d. Could a private market be set up to provide an efficient solution to the lighthouse problem?
2. Your local city council is contemplating upgrading its system for controlling traffic signals. It believes that by installing computers it can improve the speed of the traffic flow. The bigger the computer it buys, the better job it can do. The mayor and the other elected officials who are working on the proposal want to determine the scale of the system that will win them the most votes. The city bureaucrats want to maximize their budget. Suppose that you are an economist who is observing this public choice. Your job is to calculate the quantity of this public good that achieves allocative efficiency.
   a. What data would you need in order to reach your own conclusions?
   b. What does the public choice theory predict will be the quantity chosen?
   c. How could you, as an informed voter, attempt to influence the choice?
3. Some airports in Canada such as the airport in Vancouver are privately owned and others such as the one in Toronto are publicly owned. Why aren't all airports either privately owned or publicly owned? Under what circumstances might voters support a political party that proposes making
   (i) The airport in Vancouver publicly owned?
   (ii) The airport in Toronto privately owned?

P R O B L E M S

1. The figure illustrates the marginal benefit and marginal cost of sewage disposal systems of varying capacity. The city has 1 million inhabitants.

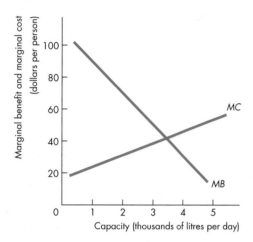

a. What is the capacity that achieves maximum net benefit?
b. How much will each person have to pay in taxes to pay for the efficient capacity level?
c. What is the political equilibrium if voters are well informed?
d. What is the political equilibrium if voters are rationally ignorant and bureaucrats achieve the highest attainable budget?

2. An economy with nine groups of people, *A* through *I*, has net benefits from different income tax rates:

A	B	C	D	E	F	G	H	I
90	80	70	60	50	0	0	0	0

If two political parties compete for office, what income tax rate would the parties propose?

3. In the market for cookies:

Price (dollars per kilogram)	Quantity demanded (kilograms per month)	Quantity supplied (kilograms per month)
10	0	36
8	3	30
6	6	24
4	9	18
2	12	12
0	15	0

a. What are the competitive equilibrium price and quantity bought and sold?
b. Suppose that a 10 percent tax is imposed on cookies.
   (i)   What is the new price of cookies?
   (ii)   What is the new quantity bought and sold?
   (iii) What is the total amount of tax revenue raised by the government?
   (iv)   What is the deadweight loss?

Chapter

19

Inequality and Redistribution

After studying this chapter, you will be able to:

- Describe the inequality in income and wealth in Canada

- Explain why wealth inequality is greater than income inequality

- Explain how economic inequality arises

- Explain the effects of taxes, social security, and welfare programs on economic inequality

Ken Thomson's family fortune, earned from the activities of the International Thomson Organization, is estimated as Canada's largest at $8.3 billion. Other billionaire Canadians are Charles Bronfman, owner of the Seagram Company, and Derek A. Price, owner of Starlaw Holdings, a massive Montreal firm that supplies investment and financial services. In stark con-

Riches and Rags

trast to these richest Canadians are the poorest, who can be seen any evening sleeping on park benches in our major cities and lined up at food banks. Here are men and women who have no visible wealth at all other than their meagre clothes and a few possessions. ◆ Most Canadians are not as poor as those who seek nourishment from food banks, but there is a large amount of relative poverty in our nation. One in ten households has an income that is so low that it spends close to half its income on rent. ◆ Why are some people exceedingly rich while others are very poor and own almost nothing? Are the rich getting richer and the poor getting poorer? Does the information we have about the inequality of income and wealth in Canada paint an accurate picture or a misleading one? How do taxes, social security, and welfare programs influence economic inequality?

◇ In this chapter, we study economic inequality—its extent, its sources, and its potential remedies. We also look at taxes and government programs that redistribute incomes and study their effects on economic inequality in Canada. Let's begin by looking at some facts about economic inequality.

Economic Inequality in Canada

WE CAN STUDY INEQUALITY EITHER BY LOOKING at the distribution of income or at the distribution of wealth. A family's income is the amount that it receives in a given period of time. A family's wealth is the value of the things it owns at a point in time. We can measure income inequality by looking at the percentage of total income received by a given percentage of families. And we can measure wealth inequality by looking at the percentage of total wealth owned by a given percentage of families.

In 1994, the average Canadian family income (excluding transfers) was $47,380. But there was considerable inequality around that average. The poorest 20 percent of families received 2.0 percent of total income. The next poorest 20 percent of families received 10.2 percent of total income. But the richest 20 percent of families received 44.1 percent of total income.

The wealth distribution shows even greater inequality. Wealth is measured as the value of holdings of real estate and financial assets. The most recent data available measure wealth in 1984. The median family wealth was a little more than $40,000. The variation around this value was enormous. The poorest 40 percent of families owned only 2 percent of total wealth. The richest 10 percent owned more than 50 percent of total wealth. And the richest 1 percent owned around 24 percent of total wealth.

Lorenz Curves

Figure 19.1 shows the distribution of income. The table divides families into five groups, called *quintiles*, ranging from the lowest income (row *a*) to highest income (row *e*), and shows the percentages of income of each of these groups. For example, row *a* tells us that the lowest quintile of families receives 2.0 percent of total income. The table also shows the *cumulative* percentages of families and income. For example, row *b* tells us that the lowest two quintiles (lowest 40 percent) of families receive 12.2 percent of total income (2.0 percent for the lowest quintile and 10.2 percent for the next lowest). The data on cumulative income shares are illustrated by a Lorenz curve. A **Lorenz curve** graphs the cumulative percentage of income against the cumulative percentage of families.

FIGURE 19.1

Lorenz Curves for Income and Wealth

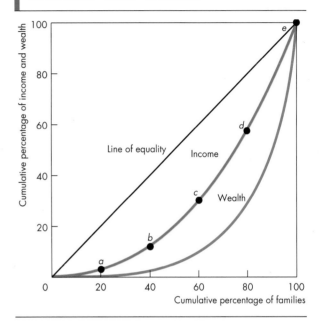

	Families		Income	
	Percentage	Cumulative percentage	Percentage	Cumulative percentage
a	Lowest 20	20	2.0	2.0
b	Second 20	40	10.2	12.2
c	Third 20	60	17.9	30.1
d	Fourth 20	80	25.9	56.0
e	Highest 20	100	44.1	100.0

The cumulative percentages of income and wealth are graphed against the cumulative percentage of families. If income and wealth were distributed equally, each 20 percent of families would have 20 percent of the income and wealth—the line of equality. Points *a* through *e* on the Lorenz curve for income correspond to the rows of the table. The Lorenz curve for wealth shows that wealth is more unequally distributed than income.

Sources: Income: Statistics Canada, *Income Distributions by Size in Canada*, 1994. Wealth: James B. Davies, "Distribution of Wealth in Canada," *Research in Economic Inequality: Studies in the Distribution of Household Wealth* (Greenwich, CT: JAI Press, 1993), and Lars Osberg, "Canada's Economic Performance: Inequality, Poverty, and Growth," in *False Promises, The Failure of Conservative Economics* (Vancouver: New Star Books, 1992).

If income was distributed equally to every family, the cumulative percentages of income received by the cumulative percentages of families would fall along the straight line labelled "Line of equality." The actual distribution of income is shown by the Lorenz curve labelled "Income."

The figure also shows a Lorenz curve for wealth. The curve is based on the distribution described above. Half the wealth is owned by richest 10 percent with the poorest 40 percent of families owning only 2 percent of total wealth.

The Lorenz curve illustrates the degree of inequality. The closer the Lorenz curve is to the line of equality, the more equal is the distribution. As you can see from the two Lorenz curves in Fig. 19.1, the Lorenz curve for wealth is much farther away from the line of equality than the Lorenz curve for income is, so the distribution of wealth is much more unequal than the distribution of income.

Inequality over Time

Figure 19.2 shows how the distribution of income has changed over the years. The first impression is that the distribution has been constant. But a closer look shows that from 1980 to 1994, the distribution became more equal—the poorest 40 percent gained slightly, the third fifth remained constant, the fourth fifth became poorer, and the richest fifth lost slightly. The lowest two-fifths are protected by a social safety net, paid for by taxes on the two highest income groups. The two highest income groups have gained because rapid technological change has increased the value of and return to education. The highest income group was able to pay its taxes and maintain its income level, but the second highest group was not.

Who Are the Rich and the Poor?

What are the characteristics of poor and rich families? The lowest-income person in Canada today is most likely to be a single-parent mother, less than 25 years old, who has no job and lives in Quebec. The highest-income family is a married couple, who both have jobs, are between 45 and 54 years old, and live in Ontario.

These snapshot profiles are the extremes in Fig. 19.3. That figure illustrates the importance of source

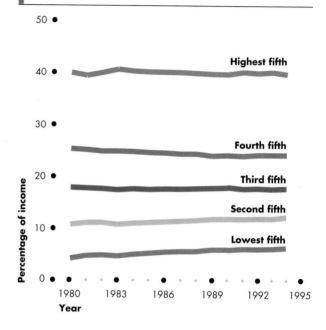

FIGURE   19.2
Trends in the Distribution of Income: 1980–1994

The distribution of income in Canada became slightly more equal in the 1980s and 1990s. The fifth with the highest income lost a little and the two-fifths with the lowest income gained. The third fifth remained constant and the fourth fifth lost.

Source: Statistics Canada, *Income Distributions by Size in Canada*, 1994.

of income, family type, sex of the household head, age of the household head, labour force status, number of children, education, and region of residence in influencing the size of a family's income.

Poverty

Families at the low end of the income distribution are so poor that they are considered to be living in poverty. **Poverty** is a state in which a family's income is too low to be able to buy the quantities of food, shelter, and clothing that are deemed necessary. Poverty is a relative concept. Millions of people living in Africa and Asia survive on incomes of less than $400 a year. In Canada, poverty is measured in terms of a low-income cutoff. The **low-income cutoff** is the income

FIGURE **19.3**

The Incidence of Low Income by Family Characteristics

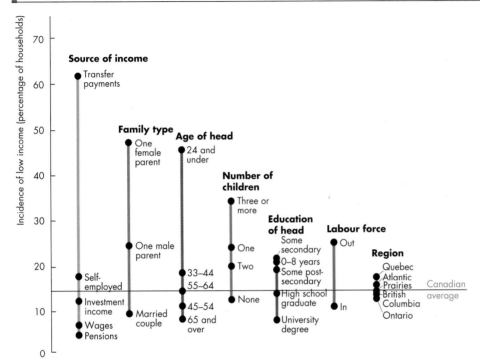

Source: Statistics Canada, *Income Distributions by Size in Canada*, 1994.

The vertical axis shows the incidence of low income—the percentage of households whose income falls below a low-income cutoff (the income level such that 54.7 percent of income is spent on food, shelter, and clothing). For Canada, on the average, 13.5 percent of families have incomes below the low-income cutoff. But that percentage varies depending on source of income, family type, sex and age of household head, number of children, education, and region of residence as indicated by the figure. Source of income, family type, sex and age of household head are by far the most important factors influencing incidence of low income.

level, determined separately for different types of families (for example, single persons, couples, one parent), that is selected such that families with incomes below that limit normally spend 54.7 percent or more of their income on food, shelter, and clothing. The low-income cutoffs currently used by Statistics Canada are based on family expenditure data for 1992. Statistics Canada measures the incidence of low income as the percentage of households whose income falls below a low-income cutoff.

Figure 19.3 shows how the incidence of low income is related to other family characteristics. Poverty is heavily influenced by source of income and family type. More than 60 percent of families receiving transfer payments from the government are below the poverty line. About 46 percent of families in which the household head is a female and no husband is present is below the poverty level, while fewer than 9 percent of families with a married couple present are. More than 44 percent of families with the head 24 years or under live in poverty, while only 17

percent of families with the head 35 to 44 years do. More than 16 percent of families in Quebec live in poverty, while less than 12 percent of families in Ontario do. Almost 20 percent of families in which the head has 8 or less years of education are below the poverty line, while only 7 percent of families in which the head is a university graduate are.

R E V I E W

- Income and wealth are distributed unequally, but wealth is more unequal than income.
- From 1980 to 1994, the distribution of income became slightly more equal.
- The main influences on a family's income, in decreasing order of importance, are source of income, family type, age of the household head, number of children, education of head, labour force status, and region of residence.

Comparing Like with Like

To determine the degree of inequality, we compare one person's economic situation with another person's. But what is the correct measure of a person's economic situation? Is it income or is it wealth? And is it *annual* income, the measure we've used so far in this chapter, or income over a longer time period—for example, over a family's lifetime?

Wealth Versus Income

Wealth is the stock of assets and income is the flow of earnings that results from the stock of wealth. Suppose that a person owns assets worth $1 million—has a wealth of $1 million. If the rate of return on assets is 5 percent a year, then this person receives an income of $50,000 a year in perpetuity from those assets. We can describe this person's economic condition by using either the wealth of $1 million or the income of $50,000. When the rate of return is 5 percent a year, $1 million of wealth *equals* $50,000 of income in perpetuity. Wealth and income are simply different ways of looking at the same thing.

But in Fig. 19.1, the distribution of wealth is much more unequal than the distribution of income. Why? It is because the wealth data measure tangible assets and exclude the value of human capital while the income data measure income from both tangible assets and human capital.

Table 19.1 illustrates the consequence of omitting human capital from the wealth data. Lee has twice the wealth and twice the income of Peter (they are the same age). But Lee's human capital is less than Peter's—$200,000 compared with $499,000. And Lee's income from human capital of $10,000 is less than Peter's income from human capital of $24,950. Lee's nonhuman capital is larger than Peter's—$800,000 compared with $1,000. And Lee's income from nonhuman capital of $40,000 is larger than Peter's income from nonhuman capital of $50.

The national wealth and income surveys record their incomes of $50,000 and $25,000 respectively, which indicates that Lee is twice as well off as Peter. And they record their tangible assets of $800,000 and $1,000 respectively, which indicates that Lee is 800 times as wealthy as Peter. Because the national survey of wealth excludes human capital, the income distribution is a more accurate measure of economic inequality than the wealth distribution.

TABLE 19.1
Capital, Wealth, and Income

	Lee		Peter	
	Wealth	**Income**	**Wealth**	**Income**
Human capital	200,000	10,000	499,000	24,950
Nonhuman capital	800,000	40,000	1,000	50
Total	$1,000,000	$50,000	$500,000	$25,000

When wealth is measured to include the value of human capital as well as nonhuman capital, the distribution of income and the distribution of wealth display the same degree of inequality.

Annual or Lifetime Income and Wealth?

A typical family's income changes over time. It starts out low, grows to a peak when the family's workers reach retirement age, and then falls after retirement. Also, like income, a typical family's wealth starts out low, grows to a peak at the point of retirement, and then falls. Suppose that three families have identical lifetime incomes. One family is young, one is middle aged, and one is retired. The middle-aged family has the highest income and wealth, the retired family has the lowest, and the young family falls in the middle. The distributions of annual income and wealth in a given year are unequal but the distributions of lifetime income and wealth are equal. So some of the measured inequality arises from the fact that families are at different stages in the life cycle and this overstates the degree of lifetime inequality.

R E V I E W

■ The distribution of income is a more accurate indicator of the degree of economic inequality than the distribution of wealth because wealth data exclude human capital.
■ The distribution of lifetime income is a more accurate indicator of the degree of economic inequality than the distribution of annual income because income varies over a family's life cycle.

Let's look at the sources of economic inequality.

Factor Prices, Endowments, and Choices

A FAMILY'S INCOME DEPENDS ON THE PRICES OF the factors of production supplied, the endowment of the factors owned by the family, and the choices the family members make. To what extent do differences in income arise from differences in factor prices and from differences in the quantities of factors that people supply?

Labour Market and Wages

We've seen that the biggest single source of income is labour. To what extent do variations in wage rates account for the unequal distribution of income? Table 19.2 helps answer this question. It sets out the average hourly earnings of private sector employees in nine occupations in 1994 along with the average hourly earnings in all industrial occupations. There is a large spread around the average of $14.34, ranging from $6.84 an hour for a barber in Newfoundland up to $31.02 for a skilled oil-rig worker in Alberta.

We can measure the spread between the highest- and lowest-paid workers in these employment categories by calculating the wage differential, which is the ratio of one wage to another. Taking the highest wage in Alberta ($31.02) and dividing it by the lowest wage in Alberta ($10.55) gives a wage differential of 2.9. That is, the highest-paid worker in Alberta earns 2.9 times the wage of the lowest-paid worker in Alberta. Similarly, in Ontario the highest paid worker ($24.07) earns 2.8 times the lowest paid worker ($8.55). But, in British Columbia the highest paid worker ($24.63) earns 3.4 times the lowest paid worker ($7.34).

The wage rate difference probably reflects, to some degree, differences in training and skill. For example, a skilled autoworker in Ontario has had much more training and has a great deal more work experience than an unskilled movie theatre worker. You can see other examples in the table.

Differences in wage rates are one source of income inequality. Differences in endowments of factors of production are another.

Distribution of Endowments

There is a large amount of variety in a family's endowments of abilities. Physical and mental differences (some inherited, some learned) are such an

TABLE 19.2

Average Hourly Earnings in 1994

Occupation/Location	Average wage rate (dollars per hour)
Barber in Newfoundland	6.84
Bar waiter in British Columbia	7.34
Movie theatre worker in Ontario	8.55
Furniture retail clerk in Alberta	10.55
Auto dealer in Manitoba	11.53
Truck driver in Ontario	17.39
Auto worker in Ontario	24.07
Pulp and paper worker in British Columbia	24.63
Oil rig worker in Alberta	31.02
Average, all Canada	**14.34**

Average hourly earnings show considerable inequality across occupations. But the range of inequality is much lower than the inequality of income. For example, the highest-paid worker in this list, a oil rig worker in Alberta, earns almost 5 times the income of the lowest-paid worker, a barber in Newfoundland, who earns **$6.84** an hour.

Source: Statistics Canada, *StatCan: CANSIM Disc,* March 1996.

obvious feature of human life that they hardly need mentioning. These differences across individuals have a normal, or bell-shaped distribution—like the distribution of heights or weights.

The distribution of ability across individuals is a major source of inequality in income and wealth. But it is not the only source. If it were, the distributions of income and wealth would look like the bell-shaped curve that describes the distribution of heights. In fact, these distributions are skewed towards high incomes and look like the curve in Fig. 19.4.

This figure shows income on the horizontal axis and the percentage of families receiving each income on the vertical axis. The median income—the income that separates the population into two groups of equal size—in 1994 was $48,091. The most common income is less than the median income. The average income is greater than the median income and in 1994 was $54,153. A skewed distribution like the one shown in Fig. 19.4 is one in which many more people have incomes below the average than above it, a large number of people have very low incomes, and a small number of people have very high incomes. The distribution of (nonhuman) wealth has a similar shape to the distribution of income, but is even more skewed.

The skewed shape of the distribution of income cannot be explained by the bell-shaped distribution of individual abilities. It results from the choices that people make.

Choices

The distribution of income and wealth depends partly on factor prices and partly on the quantities of factors that people choose to supply. In most cases, people can't influence the prices of the factors of production. People can't demand higher wages than the equilibrium wage for their babysitting, car washing, truck driving, or tutoring. An investment banker earns more than a parking lot attendant because of differences in human capital, but the market still determines the wages at which labour is traded.

In contrast, people choose how much of each of the factors of production that they own to supply. They also choose whether to babysit or look for a job in a bank, whether to put their savings in the bank or in stocks. We are going to discover that the choices people make exaggerate the differences among families. Their choices make the distribution of income more unequal than the distribution of abilities, and they make the distribution of income skewed.

Wages and the Supply of Labour   Other things remaining the same, the quantity of labour that a person supplies increases as that person's wage rate increases. A person who has a low wage rate chooses to work fewer hours than a person who has a high wage rate. Compare two people, one whose wage rate is $10 an hour and another whose wage rate is $20 an hour. If each person works the same number of hours, one has an income that is twice as much as the other. But a higher wage rate can induce a greater number of hours of work. So if the person whose wage is $20 an hour chooses to work more hours, she earns an income that exceeds twice the income of the other person.

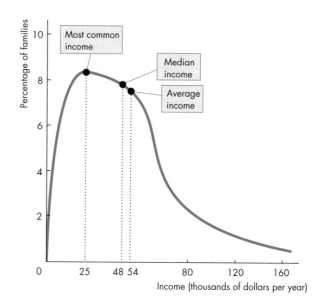

FIGURE   19.4

The Distribution of Income

The distribution of income in Canada in 1994 is unequal and is not symmetric around the average. There are many more people below the average than above it. Also, the distribution has a long thin upper tail representing a small number of people earning very large incomes.

Source: Statistics Canada, *Income Distributions by Size in Canada*, 1994.

Thus because the quantity of labour supplied increases as the wage rate increases, the distribution of income is more unequal than the distribution of hourly wages. It is also skewed like the distribution shown in Fig. 19.4. People whose wage rates are below the average tend to work fewer hours than the average, and their incomes bunch together below the average. People whose wage rates are above the average tend to work more hours than the average, and their incomes stretch out above the average.

Saving and Bequests   Another choice that results in unequal distributions in income and wealth is the decision to save and make bequests. A *bequest* is a gift from one generation to the next. The higher a family's income, the more that family tends to save and bequeath to later generations. By making a bequest, a family can spread consumption across the generations. One very common way in which people make bequests is to provide educational resources for their children and grandchildren.

Saving and bequests are not inevitably a source of increased inequality. If a family saves to redistribute an uneven income over the life cycle and enable consumption to be constant, the act of saving decreases the degree of inequality. If a lucky generation that has a high income saves a large amount and makes a bequest to a generation that is unlucky, this act of saving also decreases the degree of inequality. But there are two important features of bequests that do make intergenerational transfers of wealth a source of increased inequality:

■ Debts cannot be bequeathed
■ Mating is assortative

Debts Cannot Be Bequeathed   Although a person may die with debts that exceed assets—with negative wealth—debts cannot be forced onto other family members. Because a zero inheritance is the smallest inheritance that anyone can receive, bequests can only add to future generations' wealth and income potential.

The vast majority of people inherit nothing or a very small amount. A few people inherit enormous fortunes. As a result, bequests make the distribution of income and wealth not only more unequal than the distribution of ability and job skills but also more persistent. A family that is poor in one generation is more likely to be poor in the next. A family that is wealthy in one generation is likely to be wealthy in the next. But there is a tendency for income and wealth to converge, across generations, to the average. Although there can be long runs of good luck or bad luck, or good judgment or bad judgment, such long runs are uncommon across the generations. But one feature of human behaviour slows the convergence of wealth to the average and makes inequalities persist. That feature is assortative mating.

Assortative Mating   *Assortative mating* is the tendency for people to marry within their own socioeconomic class. In the vernacular, "like attracts like." Although there is a good deal of folklore that "opposites attract," perhaps such Cinderella tales appeal to us because they are so rare in reality. Marriage partners tend to have similar socioeconomic characteristics. Wealthy individuals seek wealthy partners. The consequence of assortative mating is that inherited wealth becomes more unequally distributed.

R E V I E W

■ Income inequality arises from unequal wage rates, unequal endowments, and choices.
■ Wage rates are unequal because of differences in skills or human capital.
■ Endowments are unequal and have a bell-shaped distribution.
■ The distribution of income is skewed because people with higher wage rates tend to work longer hours and so make a disproportionately larger income.
■ The distribution of wealth is skewed because people with higher incomes save more, bequeath more to the next generation, and marry people with similar wealth.

Income Redistribution

GOVERNMENTS IN CANADA REDISTRIBUTE income in three main ways:

■ Income taxes
■ Income maintenance programs
■ Provision of goods and services below opportunity cost

Income Taxes

The scale of redistribution of income achieved through income taxes depends on the form that the income taxes take. Income taxes may be progressive, regressive, or proportional. A **progressive income tax** is one that taxes income at a marginal rate that increases with the level of income. The term "marginal," applied to income tax rates, refers to the fraction of the last dollar earned that is paid in taxes. A **regressive income tax** is one that taxes income at a marginal rate that decreases with the level of income. A **proportional income tax** (also called a *flat-rate income tax*) is one that taxes income at a constant rate regardless of the level of income.

The income tax rates that apply in Canada are composed of two parts: federal and provincial taxes. There is variety in the detailed tax arrangements in the individual provinces but the tax system, at both the federal and provincial levels, is progressive. The poorest families pay no income tax. Most Canadians who earn between $10,000 and $30,000 a year, except for those living in Quebec, pay around 25 percent of their taxable income. In Quebec, for the same income range, the marginal tax rate ranges from 30 to almost 40 percent. Canadians with incomes between $30,000 and $60,000 a year pay between 40 and 45 percent and those with incomes above $60,000 pay a marginal tax rate of 45 to 50 percent.

Income Maintenance Programs

Three main types of programs redistribute income by making direct payments to people in the lower part of the income distribution. They are

- Social security programs
- Employment Insurance system
- Welfare programs

Social Security   Three programs, Old Age Security (OAS), Guaranteed Income Supplement (GIS), and Spouse Allowance (SPA), ensure a minimum level of income for the elderly. Monthly cash payments to retired or disabled workers or their surviving spouses are paid for by compulsory payroll taxes on both employers and employees. In 1996, the maximum GIS was $469.13 for a single person and $611.14 for a married couple, and the maximum SPA was $773.16.

Employment Insurance   To provide an income to unemployed workers, the federal government has established income benefits to unemployed workers. The Employment Insurance system is funded by employee and employer contributions, and after a qualifying period the worker is entitled to receive a benefit if the worker becomes unemployed. The maximum income benefit is 55 percent of average earnings over the previous 20 weeks.

Welfare Programs   Other federal welfare programs provide income maintenance for families and persons. They are

- Canada Assistance Plan, a plan shared equally by the federal and provincial governments that gives financial assistance to families and individuals who are in need, regardless of the cause; the assistance includes food, shelter, fuel, utilities, household supplies, items required to carry on a trade, certain welfare services, and specified health and social services

- Family Allowance and Child Tax Credit programs, designed to help families who have inadequate financial support
- Canada/Quebec Pension Plans, funded equally by employee and employer contributions, provide retirement benefits, survivor benefits, disability benefits, and death benefits
- Workers' Compensation, a provincial program funded by employers, designed to provide financial assistance as well as medical care and rehabilitation of workers injured at work

Provision of Goods and Services Below Cost

A great deal of redistribution takes place in Canada through the provision of goods and services by the government at prices far below the cost of production. The taxpayers who consume these goods and services receive a transfer in kind from the taxpayers who do not consume them. The two most important areas in which this form of redistribution takes place are education—both kindergarten through grade 12 and college and university—and health care.

In 1995, Canadian students enrolled in the universities in Ontario paid annual tuition fees of around $3,000. The cost of one year's education at one of these universities in 1995 was about $15,000. Thus families with a member enrolled in these institutions received a benefit from the government of about $12,000 a year. Those with several college or university students received proportionately higher benefits.

Government provision of health care to all residents has brought high-quality and high-cost health care to millions of people who earn too little to buy such services themselves. As a result, this program has contributed a great deal to reducing inequality.

Let's now bring all the different methods of income redistribution together and look at the overall scale of redistribution they achieve. And we will examine some income redistribution reform proposals.

The Scale of Income Redistribution

A family's income in the absence of government redistribution is called *market income*. One way of measuring the scale of income redistribution is to calculate the percentage of market income paid in taxes and the percentage received in benefits at each income level. Making such a calculation in a way that takes into account the value of the services provided by the government is almost impossible. The only calculations available ignore this aspect of redistribution and focus on taxes and cash benefits.

Figure 19.5 shows how much redistribution in aggregate takes place in Canada. The income distribution that takes account of government policies is called the *distribution after taxes and transfers*. Figure 19.5(a) illustrates the amount of redistribution that takes place among the five income groups is 18.7 percent of total income. The amount taken from the richest group is 5.7 percent, from the second-richest group, 3.2 percent, and from the middle group, 0.4 percent. The poorest group receives 7.3 percent, and the second-poorest group receives 2.1 percent. The effects of redistribution can also be seen by comparing the Lorenz curve for the market distribution and the distribution after taxes and transfers. Figure 19.5(b) shows these Lorenz curves. As you can see, there is considerable redistribution, especially to boost the incomes of the very poor, but a great deal of inequality remains after the redistribution.

The Big Tradeoff

The redistribution of income creates what has been called the **big tradeoff**, a tradeoff between inequality and efficiency[1]. The big tradeoff arises because redistribution uses scarce resources and weakens incentives.

A dollar collected from a rich person does not translate into a dollar received by a poor person. Some of it gets used up in the process of redistribution. Tax-collecting agencies such as Revenue Canada, welfare-administering agencies, tax accountants, and lawyers use skilled labour, computers, and other scarce resources to do their work. The bigger the scale of redistribution, the greater is the opportunity cost of administering it.

Redistribution weakens incentives. For example, taxing people's income from their work and saving lowers the after-tax income they receive. This lower income makes them work and save less. Less work and less saving result in smaller output and less consumption not only for the rich who pay the taxes but

---

[1]The term comes from the title of a book by Arthur Okun, chairman of the Council of Economic Advisors to President Lyndon Johnson, *Equality and Efficiency: The Big Tradeoff* (Washington, DC: Brookings Institution, 1975).

FIGURE 19.5

Income Redistribution

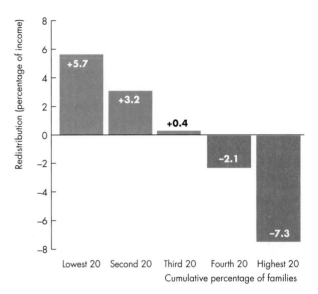

(a) Redistribution of income

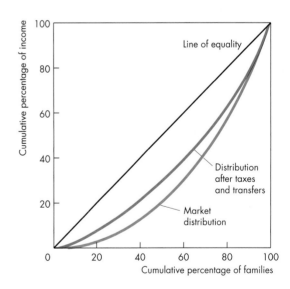

(b) Lorenz curve before and after redistribution

Taxes and transfers reduce the degree of inequality that the market generates. Part (a) shows the percentages of income taken from the richest groups and redistributed to the poorest groups. Part (b) shows the effects of this redistribution on the Lorenz curve for income. The Lorenz curve moves closer to the line of equality, which indicates a reduction in inequality.

also for the poor who receive the benefits. So the scale and methods of income redistribution involve striking a balance between greater equality and lower average consumption.

Some of the weakest incentives are those faced by families that benefit under programs such as Guaranteed Income Supplement. When a person in one of these families gets a job, benefits are withdrawn and the family in effect pays a tax of 100 percent on its earnings. This marginal tax rate is higher than that paid by the wealthiest Canadians, and it helps lock poor families in a welfare trap.

Reform Proposals

There are two broad ways in which the problem of the "big tradeoff" can be tackled. They are

- Piecemeal reforms
- Radical reforms

Piecemeal Reforms   For practical reasons, most reforms that actually get implemented are piecemeal. They are a response to the most pressing problems of the day. The critical aspect of welfare that is receiving attention is the removal of disincentives to work and the encouragement of people on welfare to find jobs. This process began with the new Employment Insurance Act. It set a limit on the income benefit and the length of time that an unemployed person can obtain income benefits.

Radical Reforms   A more radical reform proposal that is not on the current political agenda but is popular among economists is a negative income tax. A **negative income tax** gives every family a *guaranteed annual income* and decreases the family's benefit at a specified *benefit–loss rate* as its market income increases. For example, suppose the guaranteed annual income is $10,000 and the benefit–loss rate is 25 percent. A family with no earnings receives the $10,000 guaranteed income. A family with earnings of $8,000 loses 25 percent of that amount ($2,000) and receives a total income of $16,000 ($8,000 earnings plus $10,000 guaranteed income minus $2,000 benefit–loss). A family earning $40,000 receives an income of $40,000 ($40,000 earnings plus $10,000 guaranteed income minus $10,000 benefit–loss). Such a family is at the break-even income level. Families with earnings exceeding $40,000 pay more in taxes than they receive in benefits.

Figure 19.6 illustrates a negative income tax and compares it with our current arrangements. In both parts of the figure, the horizontal axis measures *market income*—that is income *before* taxes are paid and benefits received—and the vertical axis measures income *after* taxes are paid and benefits received. The 45° line shows the hypothetical case of "no redistribution."

Figure 19.6(a) shows the current redistribution arrangements—the blue curve. Benefits of *G* are paid to those with no income. As incomes increase from zero to *A*, benefits are withdrawn, *lowering* income after redistribution below *G*. This arrangement creates a *welfare trap*—it does not pay a person to work if the income he or she can earn is less than *A*. The welfare trap is shown as the grey triangle in the figure. Over the income range *A* to *C*, each additional dollar of market income increases income after redistribution by a dollar. At incomes greater than *C*, income taxes are paid and at successively higher rates, so income after redistribution is smaller than market income.

Figure 19.6(b) shows the negative income tax. The guaranteed annual income is *G,* and the break-even income is *B*. Families with market incomes below *B* receive a net benefit (blue area) and those with incomes above *B* pay taxes (red area). You can see why such a scheme is called a negative income tax. Every family receives a guaranteed minimum income and every family pays a tax on its market income—but families with incomes below the break-even income receive more than they pay and so, in total, they pay a negative amount of tax.

A negative income tax removes the welfare trap and gives greater encouragement to low-income families to seek additional employment, even at a low wage. It also overcomes many of the other problems arising from existing income maintenance programs. These conclusions about the effects of negative income tax schemes are supported by a good deal of evidence from negative income tax experiments. The latest of these experiments is the Canadian self-sufficiency project, which is being monitored by David Card and Philip Robins of Princeton University.

So why don't we have a negative income tax scheme? The main reason is cost. To implement a guaranteed annual income that puts every family above the official *low-income cutoff* level would impose a large tax increase on families with incomes above this level (as shown in Fig. 19.6b). Less generous negative income tax schemes are feasible, but most welfare experts believe that a better job can be done by a more piecemeal approach to reform.

FIGURE 19.6

Comparing Current Social Programs and a Negative Income Tax

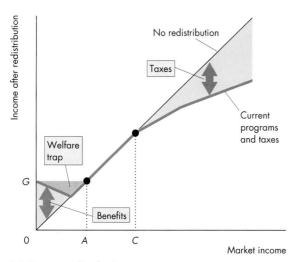

(a) Current redistribution arrangements

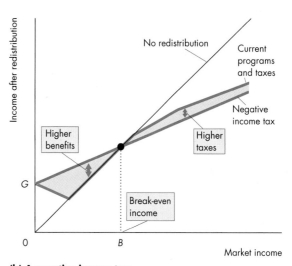

(b) A negative income tax

The 45° line shows the hypothetical case of no redistribution. Part (a) shows the current redistribution arrangements—the blue curve. Benefits of G are paid to those with no income. As incomes increase from zero to A, benefits are withdrawn, *lowering* income after redistribution below G and creating a welfare trap—the grey triangle. In the range A to C, there is no redistribution. As incomes increase above C, income taxes are paid at successively higher rates.

In part (b), a negative income tax gives a guaranteed annual income of G and decreases benefits at the same rate as the tax rate on incomes. The red line shows how market incomes translate into income after redistribution. Families with market incomes below B, the break-even income, receive net benefits. Those with market incomes above B pay net taxes.

R E V I E W

■ Governments redistribute income in Canada by using income taxes and income maintenance programs—social security, unemployment compensation, and welfare—and providing goods and services below cost.

■ Existing programs discourage work and are costly to administer.

■ Welfare reform seeks to strengthen the incentive to find a job. A more radical reform proposal is a negative income tax.

◆ We've now examined economic inequality in Canada. *Reading Between the Lines* on pp. 448–449 looks more closely at one aspect of this inequality, that between men and women. We've seen that there is a large amount of economic inequality across families and individuals. Some of that inequality arises from comparing families at different stages in the life cycle. But even taking a lifetime view, inequality remains. Some of that inequality arises from differences in wage rates. And economic choices accentuate those differences. We've seen that actions in the political marketplace redistribute income to alleviate the worst aspects of poverty.

Our next task is to look at the final area in which government actions modify the outcome of the market economy—the regulation of monopolies.

Policy WATCH

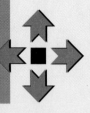

Income Distribution Between Men and Women

Essence of **THE STORY**

■ According to Statistics Canada, in 1994, full-time working women earned 70 cents for every dollar earned by men.

■ According to a study by Kathleen Lahey of Queen's University, Kingston, women receive 30 per cent of income earned from all sources before taxes and 25 per cent after taxes.

■ Lahey says the Statistics Canada data look only at full-time workers and are misleading.

■ More women than men rely entirely on government transfers. Also, says Lahey, women spend more caring for others, are hit harder by the GST, sales taxes, and are not helped by the flattening of income tax rates.

TORONTO STAR, MAY 7, 1996

Men's income much higher, study says

BY ELAINE CAREY

The income gap between men and women just got a whole lot wider.

A study at Queen's University in Kingston found that women are getting only 30 per cent of income earned in Canada from all sources.

And once taxes are applied, the gap gets even wider, leaving women with only 25 per cent, show the preliminary results of a study by tax expert Kathleen Lahey.

The findings fly in the face of Statistics Canada wage gap figures, she said, because the federal agency only looks at full-time workers.

StatsCan said that in 1994, full-time working women earned 70 cents for every dollar earned by men.

But when all income—including government transfers—is taken into account, women as a whole receive much less, Lahey said.

"The emphasis on a wage gap which just looks at the difference in pre-tax salaries obscures the larger picture," she said in an interview.

Far more women than men—particularly single parents—have no income at all and rely on government transfers, she said.

And that isn't accounted for in traditional wage gap figures.

Over-all, women start with lower incomes and they have greater responsibility for caring for others, she said.

They have to spend all their money on necessities, so they're hit harder by the goods and services tax and provincial taxes.

That combined with the "flattening" of income tax rates, means women are getting a far smaller share of the pie, she said. ...

Sue Genge, vice-president of the National Action Committee on the Status of Women, said her organization is aware of the factors affecting the income of women "but it's quite shocking." ...

Economic

A N A L Y S I S

■ Kathleen Lahey of Queen's University has increased our knowledge about the distribution of income between women and men.

■ She has measured the share of total income received by women on two definitions of income: (1) income from all sources before tax and (2) income from all sources after tax.

■ On Kathleen Lahey's findings, women received only 30 percent of total income before taxes and 25 percent of total income after taxes.

■ In 1994, the year to which the data apply, 51 percent of the adult population of Canada was female so 51 percent of the population received only 30 (25 after tax) percent of total income.

■ Women who have full-time jobs earn 70 percent of men's earnings on the average and this percentage has increased over the years.

■ If women earn 70 percent of the wages of men, how can they receive only 30 percent of total income?

■ The reason is that fewer women than men have full-time jobs. Figure 1 shows the differences in women's and men's employment in 1995. In that year, 37 percent of women and 59 percent of men had full-time jobs.

■ But the employment situation of women has improved. Figure 2 shows that in 1976 only 32 percent of women had full-time jobs while 69 percent of men did.

■ The news article suggests a further set of reasons why income data might not give a good measure of inequality. The economically relevant variable for judging inequality is consumption, not income. For many single-parent women, consumption is much less than income because they must support their child(ren).

■ But it must also be recognized that most men also support children and to make a valid comparison on a consumption basis, we would need data on family size and number of dependents as well as family income.

■ Also, to judge inequality, we must take into account lifetime rather than annual experiences, which go well beyond the scope of the survey reported in this news article.

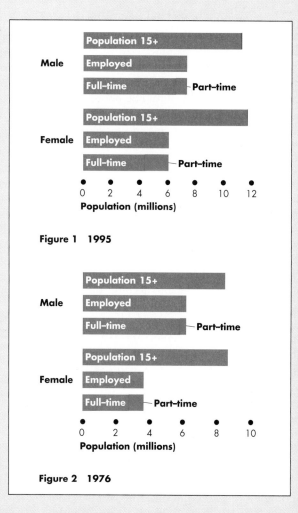

Figure 1 1995

Figure 2 1976

You're

THE VOTER

■ You have been hired by a political party that wants to enact new tax laws that give women a fair deal.

■ What are the main elements in your proposed tax reform that will achieve this desire?

■ What are the drawbacks to your proposal?

READING BETWEEN THE LINES

S U M M A R Y

Key Points

Economic Inequality in Canada   The richest 1 percent of Canadians own 24 percent of the total wealth in the country. Income is distributed less unevenly than wealth. The income distribution has changed only slightly over time but in the direction of a greater degree of equality. The poorest families in Canada are most likely to be those with a young, single, out-of-work mother living in Quebec. The richest families are most likely to live in Ontario and to be middle aged with husband and wife living together. (pp. 437–439)

Comparing Like with Like   The measured distribution of wealth exaggerates the degree of economic inequality because it fails to take human capital into account. The distributions of annual income and wealth exaggerate the degree of lifetime inequality because they do not take into account the family's stage in the life cycle. (p. 440)

Factor Prices, Endowments, and Choices
Differences in income and wealth arise partly from differences in individual endowments and partly from differences in factor prices. Wage rates vary considerably, depending on skill and other factors. But these differences, on their own, are not enough to account for differences in the distribution of income and wealth. Those differences get exaggerated by the economic choices that people make.

The economic choices that people make have an important influence on income and wealth. People who face a high wage rate generally work longer hours than those who face a low wage rate. As a result, the distribution of income becomes more unequal than the distribution of wage rates. The distribution also becomes skewed. A large proportion of the population earns less than the average income and a small proportion earns more than the average. Also, saving and bequests affect wealth across the generations. Bequests accentuate the inequality in the distribution of wealth because of assortative mating. (pp. 441–443)

Income Redistribution   Governments redistribute income in Canada today through income taxes, income maintenance programs, and the provision of goods and services below cost.

Income taxes are progressive. The poorest families pay no income tax. Most families that earn $10,000 to $30,000 pay a marginal tax rate of around 25 percent; those that earn $30,000 to $60,000 pay a marginal tax rate of between 40 and 45 percent; and those with taxable incomes above $60,000 pay 45 to 50 percent.

Income maintenance programs are social security programs, employment insurance system, and welfare programs. Social security programs include Old Age Security (OAS), Guaranteed Income Supplement (GIS), and Spousal Allowance (SPA). Welfare programs, such as Canada Assistance, provide income maintenance for families and persons who do not qualify for social security or unemployment compensation.

The poorest families receive more benefits than they pay in taxes—they receive net benefits—and the richest pay more in taxes than they receive in benefits—they pay net taxes. The main problem with income maintenance programs is that they create a welfare trap that discourages work. Reform of income maintenance programs includes tightening of the conditions for unemployment compensation. A more radical negative income tax would strengthen the incentives for those on welfare to find work. (pp. 443–447)

Key Figures

Key Terms

R E V I E W   Q U E S T I O N S

1. Which of the following statements describe the distributions of personal income and wealth in Canada today?
   a. The distributions of income and wealth are best represented by normal or bell-shaped curves.
   b. More than 50 percent of the population is wealthier than the average.
   c. More than 50 percent of the population is poorer than the average.

2. What is a Lorenz curve? How does a Lorenz curve illustrate inequality? Explain how the Lorenz curves for the distributions of income and wealth in Canada differ from each other.

3. Which is more unequally distributed, income or wealth? In answering this question, pay careful attention both to the way in which income and wealth are measured by official statistics and to the fundamental concepts of income and wealth.

4. How has the distribution of income in Canada changed since 1980? Which groups have gained and which have lost?

5. What is wrong with the way in which the official statistics measure the distribution of wealth?

6. Explain why the work/leisure choices made by individuals can result in a distribution of income that is more unequal than the distribution of ability. If ability is distributed normally (bell-shaped), will the resulting distribution of income also be bell-shaped?

7. Explain how the distribution of income and wealth is influenced by bequests and assortative mating.

8. What are the main ways in which governments redistribute income in Canada?

9. Explain the "big tradeoff."

10. What is a negative income tax? Explain how a negative income tax works and why we don't have one.

C R I T I C A L   T H I N K I N G

1. After studying *Reading Between the Lines* on pp. 448–449, answer the following questions:
   a. Describe how the percentage of women who work full-time and part-time has changed since 1976.
   b. Describe how the percentage of men who work full-time and part-time has changed since 1976.
   c. Explain how the GST and sales taxes hit women and men. Why are women hit harder than men?
   d. Consider the characteristics of those below the low-income cutoff in Fig. 19.3 along with the information that 4.2 percent of these families worked full-time, 22.7 percent worked part-time, and 28.3 percent did no work. Does this information help support the statement that "women are getting a far smaller share of the pie"?

2. From 1990 to 1995, 10 percent of all clerical jobs disappeared as computer technology— automatic teller machines and automatic phone answering machines, for example— wiped out many traditional office jobs that were open to people with little education and narrow skills. What effect do you predict that such new technology will have on the distribution of income?

3. From 1989 to 1996, the average before-tax income in Canada fell by 2.4 percent, but the average after-tax income fell by 5.1 percent. Can you explain these changes in average Canadian incomes?

4. The biggest source of income for Canadians is wages and salaries. Other major sources of income are transfers from the government, such as unemployment benefits, and interest and dividends on investments. Typically, poor people receive most transfers and rich people earn most interest and dividends. As the economy goes into a roll or into a slump, how might the distribution of income change?

P R O B L E M S

1. Imagine an economy in which there are five people who are identical in all respects. They each live for 70 years. For the first 14 of those years, they earn no income. For the next 35 years, they work and earn $30,000 a year from their work. For their remaining years, they are retired and have no income from labour. To make the arithmetic easy, let's suppose that the interest rate in this economy is zero; the individuals consume all their income during their lifetime and at a constant annual rate. What are the distributions of income and wealth in this economy if the individuals have the following ages:

   a.   All are 45

   b.   25, 35, 45, 55, 65

   Is case (a) one of greater inequality than case (b)?

2. You are given the following information about income and wealth shares:

	Income shares (percent)	Wealth shares (percent)
Lowest 20%	5	0
Second 20%	11	1
Third 20%	17	3
Fourth 20%	24	11
Highest 20%	43	85

   Draw the Lorenz curves for income and wealth for this economy. Explain which of the two variables—income or wealth—is more unequally distributed.

3. An economy consists of 10 people, each of whom has the following labour supply schedule:

Wage rate (dollars per hour)	Hours worked per day
1	0
2	1
3	2
4	3
5	4

   The people differ in ability and earn different wage rates. The distribution of *wage rates* is as follows:

Wage rate (dollars per hour)	Number of people
1	1
2	2
3	4
4	2
5	1

   a.   Calculate the average wage rate.

   b.   Calculate the ratio of the highest to the lowest wage rate.

   c.   Calculate the average daily income.

   d.   Calculate the ratio of the highest to the lowest daily income.

   e.   Sketch the distribution of hourly wage rates.

   f.   Sketch the distribution of daily incomes.

   g.   What important lesson is illustrated by this problem?

4. From Statistics Canada's page on social trends on the World Wide Web (http://www.statcan.ca/ Documents/English/SocTrends/social.html) collect data so that you can answer the following questions:

   a.   How has the percentage of the population receiving UI benefits changed over the past five years? Is this percentage related to the unemployment rate?

   b.   How has the percentage of the population receiving OAS, GIS, or Canada Assistance Plan benefits changed over the past five years? Is there a relationship between this percentage and the percentage of families with low incomes?

5. Use the Child and Family Canada's page on the distribution of income on the World Wide Web (http://cfc-efc.cymbiont.ca/docs/00000327.htm).

   a.   Draw the Lorenz curves to show the distributions of income in 1991 of families, unattached individuals, and all households. For which group is income distributed most unequally?

   b.   Draw the Lorenz curves of the distributions of income of unattached individuals in 1981, 1986, and 1991. How has the distribution of income of unattached individuals changed?

20

Competition Policy

After studying
this chapter,
you will be
able to:

- Define regulation, public ownership, and anti-combine law

- Distinguish between the public interest and capture theories of regulation

- Explain how regulation affects prices, outputs, profits, and the distribution of the gains from trade between consumers and producers

- Explain how public ownership affects prices, outputs, and allocative efficiency

- Explain how anti-combine law is used in Canada today

Public Interest or Special Interests?

When you consume water, electric power, natural gas, cable TV, or local telephone service, you buy from a regulated monopoly. Why do we regulate the industries that produce these goods and services? How do we regulate them? Does regulation work in the interests of consumers—the public interest—or does it serve the interests of producers—special interests? ◆ Regulation extends beyond monopoly to oligopoly. For example, until 1978 airline prices and routes were regulated. But in 1978, domestic air travel was deregulated and the airlines are free to choose their own routes and fares. Railways, interprovincial trucking, banking, and insurance were regulated in the past but in recent years they have been deregulated. Why do we regulate and then deregulate an industry? ◆ The government used its anti-combine laws to end Northern Telecom's monopoly on phone equipment and Bell Canada's monopoly on long-distance phone calls as well as the installation of phone lines. This action brought competition into all three markets. Now you can choose where to buy your phone equipment, which long-distance telephone service to use, and the company to install your phone line. What are the anti-combine laws? How have they evolved over the years? How are they used today? Do they serve the public interest of consumers or the special interests of producers?

◆ This chapter studies government actions to influence markets for goods and services. The chapter draws on your earlier study of how markets work and on your knowledge of consumer surplus and producer surplus. It shows how consumers and producers might redistribute those gains in the political marketplace, and it identifies who stands to gain and who stands to lose from various types of government intervention.

Market Intervention

THE GOVERNMENT INTERVENES IN MONOPOLISTIC and oligopolistic markets to influence *what*, *how*, and *for whom* various goods and services are produced in three main ways:

- Regulation
- Public ownership
- Anti-combine law

Regulation

Regulation consists of rules administered by a government agency to influence economic activity by determining prices, product standards and types, and the conditions under which new firms may enter an industry. To implement its regulations, the government establishes agencies to oversee the regulations and ensure their enforcement. The first such economic regulation in Canada was the Railway Act of 1888, which regulated railway rates. Since then and up to the late 1970s, regulation spread to banking and financial services, telecommunications, gas and electric utilities, railways, trucking, airlines and buses, and dozens of agricultural products. Since the early 1980s, there has been a tendency to deregulate the Canadian economy.

Deregulation is the process of removing restrictions on prices, product standards and types, and entry conditions. In recent years, deregulation has occurred in domestic air transportation, telephone service, interprovincial trucking, and banking and financial services.

Public Ownership

In Canada, publicly owned firms are called **Crown corporations**. The most important Crown corporations are Canada Post, the CBC, CN, VIA Rail, and Atomic Energy of Canada. There are many provincial Crown corporations, the most important of which are the provincial hydro companies. Just as there has been a tendency to deregulate the Canadian economy in recent years, there has also been a tendency to privatize it. **Privatization** is the process of selling a publicly owned corporation to private shareholders. Petro-Canada was privatized in 1991.

Anti-Combine Law

An **anti-combine law** is a law that regulates and prohibits certain kinds of market behaviour, such as monopoly and monopolistic practices. The main thrust of the anti-combine law is the prohibition of monopoly practices and of restricting output in order to achieve higher prices and profits. In Canada, unlike the United States, the anti-combine law was, until 1971, part of the Criminal Code. As a consequence, private lawsuits could not be filed. Also, the test of guilt is much more stringent under the Criminal Code than under civil law. As a result, Canada's anti-combine laws have been used less vigorously than the parallel laws (called "anti-trust laws") south of the border.

To understand why the government intervenes in the markets for goods and services and to work out the effects of its interventions, we need to identify the gains and losses that government actions can create. These gains and losses are the consumer surplus and producer surplus associated with different output levels and prices. Let's refresh our understanding of these concepts.

Surpluses and Their Distribution

Consumer surplus is the gain from trade accruing to consumers. It is calculated as the maximum price that consumers are willing to pay minus the price actually paid for each unit bought, summed over all the units bought (see Chapter 7, pp. 160–161). *Producer surplus* is the gain from trade accruing to producers. It is calculated as price minus marginal cost (opportunity cost) for each unit produced, summed over all the units produced (see Chapter 11, p. 250). *Total surplus* is the sum of consumer surplus and producer surplus.

Figure 20.1 shows these two surpluses. In Fig. 20.1(a) there is perfect competition. The market demand curve is D, and the market supply curve is S. The price is P_C and the quantity is Q_C. Because the demand curve shows the maximum price that consumers are willing to pay for each unit bought, consumer surplus is the amount shown by the green triangle. Because the supply curve shows marginal cost, producer surplus is the amount shown by the blue triangle. Total surplus is the amount shown by the combined green and blue triangles.

In Fig. 20.1(b), the industry is a (single-price) monopoly. The supply curve for a perfectly competi-

Consumer and Producer Surplus

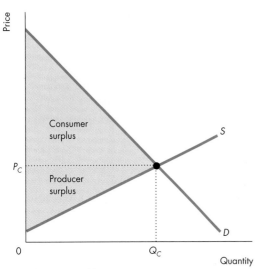

(a) Perfect competition

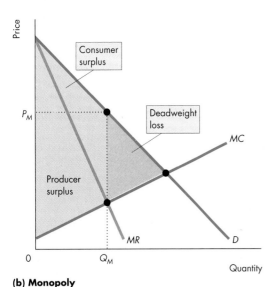

(b) Monopoly

With perfect competition (part a), consumer surplus is shown by the green triangle and producer surplus is shown by the blue triangle. Total surplus is the sum of consumer surplus and producer surplus. With monopoly (part b), the firm restricts output and consumer surplus decreases, producer surplus increases, and a deadweight loss, shown by the grey triangle, arises. Total surplus is maximized under perfect competition.

tive industry is the marginal cost curve for a monopoly. The firm's marginal revenue curve is *MR*. To maximize profit, the firm restricts output to Q_M, the quantity at which marginal revenue equals marginal cost, and sells the quantity Q_M at the price P_M. The smaller green triangle illustrates consumer surplus and the blue area illustrates producer surplus. Compared with perfect competition, consumer surplus is smaller and producer surplus is larger. Some of the consumer surplus becomes a producer surplus but some of it disappears. Also, some of the producer surplus is lost. The lost consumer surplus and producer surplus is *deadweight loss*. The grey triangle illustrates the deadweight loss. (See Chapter 12, pp. 273–274.)

Total surplus is maximized when deadweight loss is zero. When output is restricted to increase the price and increase producer surplus, total surplus decreases. Thus there is a tension between the consumer interest and producer interest. This tension is the key to understanding the economic theory of regulation. Let's examine that theory.

Economic Theory of Regulation

THE ECONOMIC THEORY OF REGULATION IS PART of the broader theory of public choice that is explained in Chapter 18. We're going to re-examine the main features of public choice theory but with an emphasis on the regulatory aspects of government behaviour. We'll examine the demand for government actions, the supply of those actions, and the political equilibrium—the balancing of demands and supplies.

Demand for Regulation

The demand for regulation is expressed through political activity—voting, lobbying, and making campaign contributions. But engaging in political activity is costly and people demand political action only if the benefit that they individually receive from such action exceeds their individual costs in obtaining the action. The four main factors that affect the demand for regulation are

1. Consumer surplus per buyer
2. Number of buyers

3. Producer surplus per firm

4. Number of firms

The larger the consumer surplus per buyer resulting from regulation, the greater is the demand for regulation by buyers. Also, as the number of buyers increases, so does the demand for regulation. But numbers alone do not necessarily translate into an effective political force. The larger the number of buyers, the greater is the cost of organizing them, so the demand for regulation does not increase proportionately with the number of buyers.

The larger the producer surplus per firm arising from a particular regulation, the larger is the demand for that regulation by firms. Also, as the number of firms that might benefit from some regulation increases, so does the demand for that regulation. But again, large numbers do not necessarily mean an effective political force. The larger the number of firms, the greater is the cost of organizing them.

For a given surplus, consumer or producer, the smaller the number of households or firms who share that surplus, the larger is the demand for the regulation that creates it.

Supply of Regulation

Regulation is supplied by politicians and bureaucrats. According to public choice theory, politicians choose policies that appeal to a majority of voters, thereby enabling themselves to achieve and maintain office. Bureaucrats support policies that maximize their budgets (see Chapter 18, p. 424). Given these objectives of politicians and bureaucrats, the supply of regulation depends on the following factors:

1. Consumer surplus per buyer

2. Producer surplus per firm

3. The number of persons affected

The larger the consumer surplus per buyer or producer surplus per firm generated and the larger the number of persons affected by a regulation, the greater is the tendency for politicians to supply that regulation. Politicians are likely to supply regulation that benefits a large number of people by a large amount per person. They are also likely to supply regulation that benefits a *small* number of people when the benefit per person is large and cost is spread widely and not easily identified. But they are unlikely to supply regulation that brings a small benefit per person.

Political Equilibrium

In a political equilibrium, no interest group plans to use resources to press for changes and no group of politicians plans to offer different regulations. Being in a political equilibrium is not the same thing as everyone being in agreement. Lobby groups will devote resources to trying to change regulations that are already in place. And others will devote resources to maintaining the existing regulations. But no one will feel it is worthwhile to *increase* the resources they are devoting to such activities. Also, political parties might not agree with each other. Some support the existing regulations, and others propose different regulations. In equilibrium, no one wants to change the proposals that they are making.

What will a political equilibrium look like? The answer depends on whether the regulation serves the public interest or the interest of the producer. Let's look at these two possibilities.

Public Interest Theory   The **public interest theory** is that regulations are supplied to satisfy the demand of consumers and producers to maximize total surplus—that is, to attain allocative efficiency. Public interest theory implies that the political process relentlessly seeks out deadweight loss and introduces regulations that eliminate it. For example, where monopoly practices exist, the political process will introduce price regulations to ensure that outputs increase and prices fall to their competitive levels.

Capture Theory   The **capture theory** is that the regulations are supplied to satisfy the demand of producers to maximize producer surplus—that is, to maximize economic profit. The key idea of capture theory is that the cost of regulation is high and only those regulations that increase the surplus of small, easily identified groups and that have low organization costs are supplied by the political process. Consumers bear the cost of such regulation but the costs are spread thinly and widely so they do not lose votes.

The predictions of the capture theory are less clear-cut than the predictions of the public interest theory. According to the capture theory, regulations benefit cohesive interest groups by large and visible amounts and impose small costs on everyone else. But those costs are so small, in per person terms, that no one feels it is worthwhile to incur the cost of organizing an interest group to avoid them. To make these predictions concrete enough to be useful, the capture theory needs a model of the costs of political organization.

Whichever theory of regulation is correct, according to public choice theory, the political system delivers amounts and types of regulations that best further the electoral success of politicians. Because producer-oriented and consumer-oriented regulation are in conflict with each other, the political process can't satisfy both groups in any particular industry. Only one group can win. This makes the regulatory actions of government a bit like a unique product—for example, a painting by Emily Carr. There is only one original and it will be sold to just one buyer. Normally, a unique commodity is sold through an auction; the highest bidder takes the prize. Equilibrium in the regulatory process can be thought of in much the same way: The suppliers of regulation will satisfy the demands of the higher bidder. If the producer demand offers a bigger return to the politicians, either directly through votes or indirectly through campaign contributions, then the regulation will serve the producers' interests. If the consumer demand translates into a larger number of votes, then the regulation will serve the consumers' interests.

R E V I E W

■ The demand for regulation is expressed by both consumers and producers who spend scarce resources voting, lobbying, and campaigning for regulations that best further their own interests.

■ Regulation is supplied by politicians and bureaucrats. Politicians choose actions that appeal to a majority of voters, and bureaucrats choose actions that maximize their budgets.

■ The regulation that exists is the political equilibrium that balances the opposing demand and supply forces. The political equilibrium achieves either efficiency—the public interest theory—or maximizes producer surplus—the capture theory.

We have now completed our study of the *theory* of regulation in the marketplace. Let's turn our attention to the regulations that exist in our economy today. Which theory of regulation best explains these real-world regulations? Which of these regulations are in the public interest and which are in the interest of producers?

Regulation and Deregulation

THE PAST DECADE OR SO HAS SEEN DRAMATIC changes in the way in which the government has regulated the Canadian economy. We're going to examine some of these changes. To begin we'll look at what the government regulates and also at the scope of regulation. Then we'll turn to the regulatory process itself and examine how regulators control prices and other aspects of market behaviour. Finally, we'll tackle the more difficult and controversial questions: Why does the government regulate some things but not others? Who benefits from the regulation that we have—consumers or producers?

The Scope of Regulation

Regulation touches a wide range of economic activity in Canada. Table 20.1 sets out the major federal regulatory agencies, together with a brief statement of their responsibilities. As you can see by inspecting that table, the predominant sectors subject to regulation are agriculture, energy, transport, and telecommunications.

Provincial and municipal governments also establish regulations covering a wide range of economic activity. Some of these—for example, municipal regulation of the taxicab industry—have important direct effects on the marketplace. Our analysis of the regulatory process and the effects of regulation applies with equal force to price, output, and profit regulation at these other governmental levels.

What exactly do regulatory agencies do? How do they regulate?

The Regulatory Process

Though regulatory agencies vary in size and scope and in the detailed aspects of economic life that they control, there are certain features common to all agencies.

First, the government appoints the senior bureaucrats who are the key decision makers in a regulatory agency. In addition, all agencies have a permanent bureaucracy made up of experts in the industry being regulated and often recruited from the regulated firms. Agencies have financial resources,

TABLE 20.1

Federal Regulatory Agencies

Agency	Responsiblility
Atomic Energy Control Board	Administers the Atomic Energy Control Act governing all uses of radioactive material.
Canadian Dairy Commission	Administers national dairy policy, which seeks to give producers an adequate return and keep the price to consumers low.
Canadian Radio-Television and Telecommunications Commission	Regulates all aspects of radio, television, and telecommunications.
Canadian Grain Commission	Regulates grain handling, establishes and maintains quality standards, audits grain stocks, and supervises future trading.
Canadian Wheat Board	Regulates exports of wheat and barley and domestic sales for human consumption.
National Energy Board	Regulates oil, gas, and electrical industries.
National Farm Products Marketing Council	Advises government on the establishment and operation of national agricultural marketing agencies and works with those agencies and provincial governments to promote marketing of farm products. Chicken, egg, and turkey agencies have been established under its aegis.
Canadian Transport Commission	Regulates transport under federal jurisdiction including rail, air, water, and pipeline and some interprovincial commercial motor transport.

Source: Statistics Canada, *Canada Year Book,* 1992.

voted by Parliament, to cover the costs of their operations.

Second, each agency adopts a set of practices or operating rules for controlling prices and other aspects of economic performance. These rules and practices are based on well-defined physical and financial accounting procedures that are relatively easy to administer and to monitor.

In a regulated industry, individual firms are usually free to determine the technology that they will use in production. But they are not free to determine the prices at which they will sell their output, the quantities that they will sell, or the markets that they will serve. The regulatory agency grants certification to a company to serve a particular market and with a particular line of products. The agency also determines the level and structure of prices that the company can charge. In some cases, the agency also determines the scale of output permitted.

To analyse the way in which regulation works, it is convenient to distinguish between the regulation of natural monopoly and the regulation of cartels. Let's begin with the regulation of natural monopoly.

Natural Monopoly

Natural monopoly was defined in Chapter 12 (pp. 260–261) as an industry in which one firm can supply the entire market at a lower price than two or more firms can. As a consequence, a natural monopoly experiences economies of scale, no matter how large an output rate it produces. Examples of natural monopolies include local distribution of cable television signals, electricity and gas, and urban rail services. It is much more expensive to have two or more competing sets of wires, pipes, and train lines serving every neighbourhood than it is to have a single set. (What is a natural monopoly changes over time as technology changes. With the introduction of fibre optic cables, both telephone companies and cable television companies will be able to compete with each other in both markets, so what is a natural monopoly will become a more competitive industry.)

Let's consider the example of cable TV, which is shown in Fig. 20.2. The demand curve for cable TV is *D*. The cable TV company's marginal cost curve is *MC*. That marginal cost curve is (assumed to be) hor-

FIGURE   20.2

Natural Monopoly: Marginal Cost Pricing

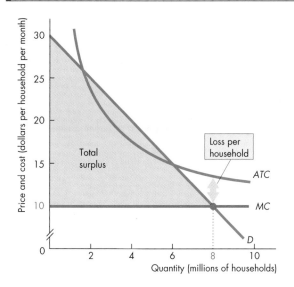

A natural monopoly is an industry in which average total cost is falling even when the entire market demand is satisfied. A cable TV operator faces a demand curve D. The firm's marginal cost is constant at $10 per household per month, as shown by the curve labelled MC. Fixed costs are large, and the average total cost curve, which includes average fixed cost, is shown as ATC. A marginal cost pricing rule that maximizes total surplus sets the price per household at $10 per month, with 8 million households being served. The resulting consumer surplus is shown as the green area. The firm incurs a loss on each household, indicated by the red arrow. To remain in business, the firm must price discriminate, use a two-part tariff, or receive a subsidy.

izontal at $10 per household per month—that is, the cost of providing each additional household with a month of cable programming is $10. The cable company has a heavy investment in satellite receiving dishes, cables, and control equipment and so has high fixed costs. These fixed costs are part of the company's average total cost curve, shown as ATC. The average total cost curve slopes downward because as the number of households served increases, the fixed cost is spread over a larger number of households. (If you need to refresh your memory on how the average total cost curve is calculated, take a quick look back at Chapter 10, pp. 217–219.)

Regulation in the Public Interest   How will cable TV be regulated according to the public interest theory? In the public interest theory, regulation maximizes total surplus, which occurs if marginal cost equals price. As you can see in Fig. 20.2, that outcome occurs if the price is regulated at $10 per household per month and if 8 million households are served. Such a regulation is called a **marginal cost pricing rule**. A marginal cost pricing rule sets price equal to marginal cost. It maximizes total surplus in the regulated industry.

A natural monopoly that is regulated to set price equal to marginal cost incurs an economic loss. Because its average total cost curve is falling, marginal cost is below average total cost. Because price equals marginal cost, price is below average total cost. Average total cost minus price is the loss per unit produced. It's pretty obvious that a cable TV company that is required to use a marginal cost pricing rule will not stay in business for long. How can a company cover its costs and, at the same time, obey a marginal cost pricing rule?

One possibility is price discrimination (see Chapter 12, pp. 267–271). Another possibility is to use a two-part price (called a two-part tariff). For example, local telephone companies can charge consumers a monthly fee for being connected to the telephone system and then charge a price equal to marginal cost for each local call. A cable TV operator can charge a one-time connection fee that covers its fixed cost and then charge a monthly fee equal to marginal cost.

But a natural monopoly cannot always cover its costs in these ways. If a natural monopoly cannot cover its total cost from its customers, and if the government wants it to follow a marginal cost pricing rule, the government must give the firm a subsidy. In such a case, the government raises the revenue for the subsidy by taxing some other activity. But as we saw in Chapter 18, taxes themselves generate deadweight loss. Thus the deadweight loss resulting from additional taxes must be subtracted from the allocative efficiency gained by forcing the natural monopoly to adopt a marginal cost pricing rule.

Deadweight loss might be minimized by making the natural monopoly cover its cost rather than by taxing another sector of the economy. When a monopoly covers its costs, it uses an average cost pricing rule. An **average cost pricing rule** sets price equal to average total cost. Figure 20.3 shows the average cost pricing solution. The cable TV operator charges $15 a month and serves 6 million households. A deadweight loss arises, which is shown by the grey triangle in the figure.

FIGURE 20.3
Natural Monopoly: Average Cost Pricing

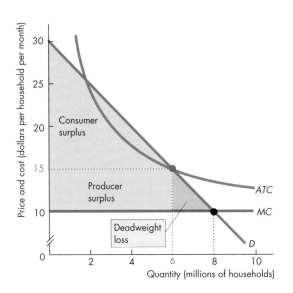

Average cost pricing sets price equal to average total cost. The cable TV operator charges $15 per month and serves 6 million households. In this situation, the firm breaks even—average total cost equals price. Deadweight loss, shown by the grey triangle, is generated. Consumer surplus is reduced to the green area.

FIGURE 20.4
Natural Monopoly: Profit Maximization

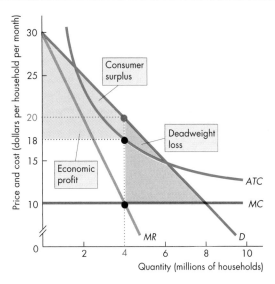

The cable TV operator would like to maximize profit. To do so, marginal revenue (MR) is made equal to marginal cost. At a price of $20 per month, 4 million households buy cable service. Consumer surplus is reduced to the green triangle. The deadweight loss increases to the grey triangle. The monopoly makes the profit shown by the blue rectangle. If the producer can capture the regulator, the outcome will be the situation shown here.

Capturing the Regulator   What does the capture theory predict about the regulation of this industry? According to the capture theory, regulation serves the interests of the producer, which means maximizing profit. To work out the price that achieves this goal, we need to look at the relationship between marginal revenue and marginal cost. A monopoly maximizes profit by producing the output at which marginal revenue equals marginal cost. The monopoly's marginal revenue curve in Fig. 20.4 is the curve labelled *MR*. Marginal revenue equals marginal cost when output is 4 million households and the price is $20 a month. Thus a regulation that best serves the interest of the producer will set the price at this level.

But how can a producer go about capturing the regulator and obtaining regulation that results in this monopoly profit-maximizing outcome? To answer

this question, we need to look at the way in which agencies determine a regulated price. A key method used is called rate of return regulation.

Rate of Return Regulation   Rate of return regulation determines a regulated price by setting the price at a level that enables the regulated firm to earn a specified target percent return on its capital. The target rate of return is determined with reference to what is normal in competitive industries. This rate of return is part of the opportunity cost of the natural monopolist and is included in the firm's average total cost. By examining the firm's total cost, including the normal rate of return on capital, the regulator attempts to determine the price at which average total cost is covered. Thus rate of return regulation is equivalent to average cost pricing.

In Fig. 20.3, average cost pricing results in a regulated price of $15 a month with 6 million households being served. Thus rate of return regulation, based on a correct assessment of the producer's average total cost curve, results in a price that favours the consumer and does not enable the producer to maximize monopoly profit. The special interest group will have failed to capture the regulator, and the outcome will be closer to that predicted by the public interest theory of regulation.

But there is a feature of many real-world situations that the above analysis does not take into account: the ability of the monopoly firm to mislead the regulator about its true costs.

Inflating Costs   The managers of a firm might be able to inflate the firm's costs by spending part of the firm's revenue on inputs that are not strictly required for the production of the good. By this device, the firm's apparent costs exceed the true costs. On-the-job luxury in the form of sumptuous office suites, limousines, free baseball tickets (disguised as public relations expenses), company jets, lavish international travel, and entertainment are all ways in which managers can inflate costs.

If the cable TV operator makes the regulator believe that its true cost is *ATC (inflated)* in Fig. 20.5, then the regulator will set the price at $20 a month. In this example, the price and quantity will be the same as those under unregulated monopoly. It might be impossible for firms to inflate their costs by as much as the amount shown in the figure. But to the extent that costs can be inflated, the apparent average total cost curve lies somewhere between the true average total cost curve and *ATC (inflated)*. The greater the ability of the firm to pad its costs in this way, the more closely its profit (measured in economic terms) approaches the maximum possible. The shareholders of this firm don't receive this economic profit because it is used up in baseball tickets, luxury offices, and the other actions taken by the firm's managers to inflate the company's costs.

Public Interest or Capture?

It is not clear whether actual regulation produces prices and quantities that more closely correspond with the predictions of capture theory or with public interest theory. One thing is clear, however. Price regulation does not require natural monopolies to use

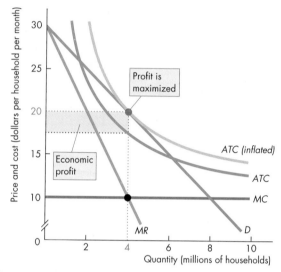

FIGURE   20.5

Natural Monopoly: Inflating Costs

If the cable TV operator is able to inflate its costs to *ATC (inflated)* and persuade the regulator that these are genuine minimum costs of production, rate of return regulation results in a price of $20 per month—the profit-maximizing price. To the extent that the producer can inflate costs above average total cost, the price rises, output falls, and deadweight loss increases. The profit is captured by the managers, not the shareholders (owners) of the firm.

the marginal cost pricing rule. If it did, most natural monopolies would make losses and receive hefty government subsidies to enable them to remain in business. But there are even exceptions to this conclusion. For example, many local telephone companies do appear to use marginal cost pricing for local telephone calls. They cover their total cost by charging a flat fee each month for being connected to their telephone system but then permitting each call to be made at its marginal cost—zero or something very close to it.

We can test whether natural monopoly regulation is in the public interest or producer interest by comparing the rates of return in regulated natural monopolies with average returns. If regulated natural monopolies have rates of return significantly higher than those in the rest of the economy, then, to some degree, the regulator may have been captured by the producer. There is plenty of empirical evidence that many natural monopolies in Canada do earn higher rates of return than the economy average.

One recent striking example is cable television service; telephone service is another. The rates of return in these two industries exceed 10 percent a year, approaching double the economy average. Perhaps the most dramatic piece of evidence that regulation benefits the regulated firm is the profits of Bell Canada Enterprises (BCE), prior to deregulation of long-distance phone services. BCE is a conglomerate that produced *regulated* long-distance telephone services and *unregulated* phone equipment (Northern Telecom) and financial services (Montreal Trustco). In 1992, BCE made a total profit of $1.4 billion on total assets of $12.3 billion, a profit rate of 11.4 percent. But this total was made up of a profit of $0.9 billion on assets of $7 billion—a return of 12.9 percent—for the regulated Bell Canada and a profit of $0.5 billion on assets of $5.3 billion—9.4 percent—for all BCE's *unregulated* operation.

Until the early 1990s, long-distance telephone service was a natural monopoly, but technological advances in telecommunications have changed the situation. Today, the industry is an oligopoly. But oligopoly is also regulated. Let's examine regulation in oligopolistic industries—the regulation of cartels.

Cartel Regulation

A *cartel* is a collusive agreement among a number of firms designed to restrict output and achieve a higher profit for the cartel's members. Cartels are illegal in Canada and in most other countries. But international cartels can sometimes operate legally, such as the international cartel of oil producers known as OPEC (the Organization of Petroleum Exporting Countries).

Illegal cartels can arise in oligopolistic industries. An oligopoly is a market structure in which a small number of firms compete with each other. We studied oligopoly (and duopoly—two firms competing for a market) in Chapter 13. There we saw that if firms manage to collude and behave like a monopoly, they can set the same price and sell the same total quantity as a monopoly firm would. But we also discovered that in such a situation, each firm will be tempted to cheat, increasing its own output and profit at the expense of the other firms. The result of such cheating on the collusive agreement is the unravelling

of the monopoly equilibrium and the emergence of a competitive outcome with zero economic profit for producers. Such an outcome benefits consumers at the expense of producers.

How is oligopoly regulated? Does regulation prevent monopoly practices or does it encourage those practices?

According to the public interest theory, oligopoly is regulated to ensure a competitive outcome. Consider, for example, the market for trucking tomatoes from the fields of southwestern Ontario to a ketchup factory at Leamington, illustrated in Fig. 20.6. The demand curve for trips is *D*. The industry marginal cost curve—and the competitive supply curve—is *MC*. Public interest regulation will regulate the price of a trip at $20 and there will be 300 trips a week.

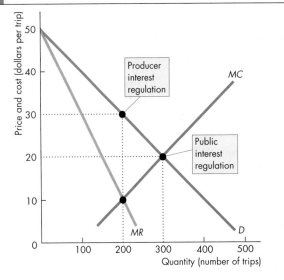

FIGURE 20.6

Collusive Oligopoly

Ten trucking firms transport tomatoes from southwestern Ontario to Leamington. The demand curve is *D*, and the industry marginal cost curve is *MC*. Under competition, the *MC* curve is the industry supply curve. If the industry is competitive, the price of a trip will be $20 and 300 trips will be made each week. Producers will demand regulation that restricts entry and limits output to 200 trips a week where the industry marginal revenue (*MR*) equals the industry marginal cost (*MC*). This regulation raises the price to $30 a trip and results in each producer making maximum profit—as if it is a monopoly.

How would this industry be regulated according to the capture theory? Regulation that is in the producer interest will maximize profit. To find the outcome in this case, we need to determine the price and quantity when marginal cost equals marginal revenue. The marginal revenue curve is *MR*. So, marginal revenue equals marginal cost at 200 trips a week. The price of a trip is $30.

One way of achieving this outcome is to place an output limit on each firm in the industry. If there are 10 trucking companies, an output limit of 20 trips per company ensures that the total number of trips in a week is 200. Penalties can be imposed to ensure that no single producer exceeds its output limit.

All the firms in the industry would support this type of regulation because it helps to prevent cheating and to maintain a monopoly outcome. Each firm knows that without effectively enforced production quotas, every firm has an incentive to increase output. (For each firm, price exceeds marginal cost, so a greater output brings a larger profit.) So each firm wants a method of preventing output from rising above the industry's profit-maximizing level, and the quotas enforced by regulation achieve this end. With this type of cartel regulation, the regulator enables a cartel to operate legally and in its own best interest.

What does cartel regulation do in practice? Although there is disagreement about the matter, the consensus view is that regulation tends to favour the producer. Trucking and airlines (when they were regulated by the Canadian Transport Commission) and taxicabs (regulated by cities) are specific examples in which profits of producers increased as a result of regulation. But the most dramatic examples of regulation favouring the producer are in agriculture. An Economic Council of Canada study, based on the situation prevailing in the early 1980s, estimated that regulation of the egg-producing and broiler chicken industries alone transferred more than $100 million a year to just 4,600 individual producers.[1]

Further evidence on cartel and oligopoly regulation can be obtained from the performance of prices and profit following deregulation. If, following deregulation, prices and profit fall, then, to some degree, the regulation must have been serving the interest of the producer. In contrast, if, following deregulation, prices and profits remain constant or increase, then

the regulation may be presumed to have been serving the public interest. Because there has been a substantial amount of deregulation in recent years, we may use this test of oligopoly regulation to see which of the two theories better fits the facts. The evidence is mixed, but in the cases of airlines, trucking, and long-distance phone calls, three oligopolies to be deregulated, prices fell and there was a large increase in the volume of business.

Making Predictions

Most industries have a few producers and many consumers. In these cases, public choice theory predicts that regulation will protect producer interests because a small number of people stand to gain a large amount and so they will be fairly easy to organize as a cohesive lobby. Under such circumstances, politicians will be rewarded with campaign contributions rather than votes. But there are situations in which the consumer interest is sufficiently strong and well organized and thus able to prevail. There are also cases in which the balance switches from producer to consumer, as seen in the deregulation process that began in the late 1970s.

Deregulation raises some hard questions for economists seeking to understand and make predictions about regulation. Why were the transportation and telecommunication sectors deregulated? If producers gained from regulation and if the producer lobby was strong enough to achieve regulation, what happened in the 1970s to change the equilibrium to one in which the consumer interest prevailed? We do not have a complete answer to this question at the present time. But regulation had become so costly to consumers, and the potential benefits to them from deregulation so great, that the cost of organizing the consumer voice became a price worth paying.

One factor that increased the cost of regulation borne by consumers and brought deregulation in the transportation sector was the large increase in energy prices in the 1970s. These price hikes made route regulation by the Canadian Transport Commission extremely costly and changed the balance in favour of consumers in the political equilibrium. Technological change was the main factor at work in the telecommunication sector. New satellite-based, computer-controlled long-distance technologies enabled smaller producers to offer low-cost services. These producers wanted a share of Bell Canada's business—and profit.

[1] J.D. Forbes, R.D. Hughes, and T.K. Warley, *Economic Intervention and Regulation in Canadian Agriculture* (Ottawa: Department of Supply and Services, 1982).

Furthermore, as communication technology improved, the cost of communication fell and the cost of organizing larger groups of consumers also fell. If this line of reasoning is correct, we can expect to see more consumer-oriented regulation in the future. In practice, more consumer-oriented regulation often means deregulation—removing the regulations that are already in place to serve the interests of producer groups.

R E V I E W

- Regulation of a natural monopoly in the public interest sets price equal to marginal cost or, to avoid a tax-financed subsidy, sets price equal to average total cost.
- In practice, natural monopolies face rate of return regulation. With rate of return regulation, firms have an incentive to inflate costs and move as closely as possible to the profit-maximizing output.
- Cartel regulation that establishes output levels for each firm can help perpetuate a cartel and work against the public interest.

Let's now turn to the second method of intervention in markets—public ownership.

Public Ownership

CROWN CORPPORATIONS HAVE A SIGNIFICANT AND historical presence in Canadian society. Before Confederation, Crown corporations were used for building canals and operating ports and harbours. The establishment of the Canadian nation involved a commitment to build an international railway to link New Brunswick and Nova Scotia to central Canada. Over the years, vast distances, a sparse population, the presence of a powerful neighbour, strong and distinct national interests, and the existence of two main cultural and linguistic groups nurtured the establishment of Crown corporations.

A Crown corporation is a corporation in which the government has 100 percent ownership. There

are federal and provincial Crown corporations, and they are involved in many sectors of the economy, including transporation; energy and resources; agricultural and fisheries; development and construction; government services; culture; financial intermediaries; telecommunications and broadcasting; provincial lotteries; housing; and alcoholic beverages. Examples of Crown corporations include the Business Development Bank of Canada, the Canadian Museum of Nature, and the Ontario Lottery Corporation.

Public ownership provides another way in which the government can influence the behaviour of natural monopoly. What are the effects of this method of natural monopoly control? How does a publicly owned corporation operate? Let's explore some alternative patterns of behaviour for such corporations.

Efficient Crown Corporation

One possibility is that a Crown corporation is operated in a manner that results in economic efficiency—maximization of total surplus. Let's consider the example of a railway. Figure 20.7(a) illustrates the demand for freight service and the railway's costs. The demand curve is *D*. The marginal cost curve is *MC*. Notice that the marginal cost curve is horizontal at $2 a tonne. The railway has a heavy investment in track, trains, and control equipment, so it has large fixed costs. These fixed costs feature in the company's average total cost curve *ATC*. The average total cost curve slopes downward because as the number of tonnes of freight carried increases, the fixed costs are spread over a larger number of tonnes. To be efficient, a Crown corporation obeys the rule:

Produce an output such that price equals marginal cost.

In this example, that output level is 8 billion tonnes a year at a price—and marginal cost—of $2 a tonne. To be able to operate in this manner, a publicly owned railway has to be subsidized; the subsidy on each unit of output must equal the difference between average total cost and marginal cost. And the subsidy has to be collected other than through the price of the good or service produced—in other words, by taxation. If the government taxes each household a fixed amount, the consumer surplus will shrink to the green triangle shown in Fig. 20.7(a), but consumer surplus will be at its maximum.

FIGURE 20.7
Public Enterprise

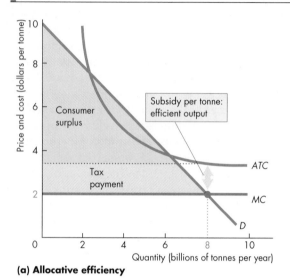

(a) Allocative efficiency

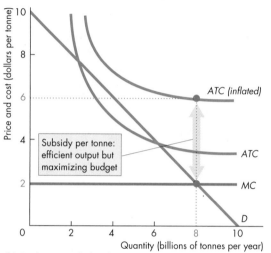

(b) Budget maximization

A railway operated by a Crown corporation that achieves allocative efficiency is shown in part (a). It produces the output at which price equals marginal cost. Its output is 8 billion tonnes a year and the price is $2 a tonne. The enterprise receives a subsidy that enables it to cover its average total cost and that cost is the minimum possible cost of providing the service.

If the managers of the enterprise pursue their own interest, maximizing their budget, costs are padded and the maximum possible cost rises to *ATC (inflated)* in part (b). If the corporation is constrained to keep price equal to marginal cost it continues to produce an output that achieves allocative efficiency, but the managers of the bureau divert the entire consumer surplus to themselves.

The situation depicted in Fig. 20.7(a) achieves allocative efficiency because consumer surplus is maximized. But it is not an outcome that is necessarily compatible with the interests of the managers of the Crown corporation. One model of the behaviour of managers is that suggested by the economic theory of bureaucracy. What does that alternative model predict about Crown corporation behaviour?

A Bureaucracy Model of Public Enterprise

The basic assumption of the economic theory of bureaucracy is that bureaucrats aim to maximize the budget of their bureau. The equivalent assumption for the managers of a Crown corporation is that they seek to maximize the budget of their corporation. To work out what the pursuit of this objective implies

for the behaviour of a Crown corporation, we need to know the constraints under which its managers are operating. We will consider two alternatives: (1) make price equal to marginal cost; and (2) make the service available at zero cost to the consumer.

Budget Maximization with Marginal Cost Pricing
If the bureau maximizes its budget but obeys the marginal cost pricing rule, it will remain allocatively efficient. It will produce 8 billion tonnes a year and it will sell its output for $2 a tonne, as Fig. 20.7(b) illustrates. But the corporation will not minimize its production cost. It will pad its costs and become inefficient. It will hire more workers than the number required to produce 8 billion tonnes a year, and its internal control mechanisms, which would ensure internal efficiency, as in a private profit-maximizing firm, will be weak. As a result, the average total cost of the corporation will rise to *ATC (inflated)*.

What determines the limit on the extent to which the corporation can pad its costs? The answer is the maximum amount that the users of the output can be made to pay through taxation. That maximum is the total consumer surplus. That maximum consumer surplus is the area beneath the demand curve and above the marginal cost curve. You can work out how big it is by using the usual formula for the area of the triangle. The height of this triangle is $8 and its base is 8 billion tonnes a year, so the consumer surplus is $32 billion. This will be the upper limit that any government—in a political democracy—can extract from the taxpayer-consumers of the product of this corporation. Spread over 8 billion tonnes, $32 billion gives a subsidy of $4 a tonne, the amount shown in the figure.

Budget Maximization at Zero Price   What happens if a government bureau provides its goods or services free? Of course, it is improbable that a publicly owned railway would be able to persuade politicians and taxpayers that its activities should be expanded to the point of providing its services free. But there are several examples of publicly provided goods that are indeed free. Primary and secondary education and health care are two outstanding examples. For the sake of comparison, we'll continue with our railway, improbable though it is.

If in Fig. 20.7(b) the bureau increases output to the point at which the price that consumers are willing to pay for the last unit produced is zero, output rises to 10 billion tonnes a year. A deadweight loss is created because the marginal cost of production, $2 a tonne, is higher than the marginal benefit or willingness to pay, $0 per tonne. The bureau will be inefficient in its internal operations and inflate its costs. The subsidy will increase to the highest that the public will be willing to pay. The maximum subsidy will equal the consumer surplus. If the subsidy were higher, people would vote to shut down the Crown corporation because the subsidy would exceed the consumer surplus.

Compromise Outcome   There will be a tendency for the corporation to overproduce and to inflate its budget, but not to the extent shown in Fig. 20.7(b). There will be a tendency for consumer interest to have some influence, but not to the degree shown in Fig. 20.7(a). The basic prediction about the behaviour of a Crown corporation, then, is that it will overproduce and be less efficient than a private firm.

Crown Corporations in Reality

How do actual Crown corporations behave? Several studies have been directed to answering this question. One of the most fruitful ways of approaching the question is to compare public and private enterprises in which, as far as possible, other things are equal. There are two well-known and well-studied cases for which other things do seem to be fairly equal. One such comparison is of Canada's public and private railways—Canadian National (CN) and Canadian Pacific (CP). The other is from Australia, which has two domestic airlines, one private and the other public, that fly almost identical routes at almost identical times every day. Economists have studied the costs of these similar enterprises and concluded that each of the publicly owned enterprises operates with a cost structure that is significantly higher than that of the corresponding private firm. In the case of CN and CP, the estimated difference was 14 percent.[2]

Privatization

Largely because of an increasing understanding of how bureaucracies work and of the inefficiency of publicly operated enterprises, there has been a move, in Canada and around the world, to sell off publicly owned corporations. Since the mid-1980s, the federal government has sold a dozen companies, including Air Canada. Companies that are too unprofitable to sell, such as CN, are being savagely cut back. As this process takes place, we are witnessing a gradual change in the political equilibrium—with the interest of the consumer having a larger weight placed on it and that of the producer a smaller weight.

Economists are divided on the question of whether privatization has gone too far to achieve allocative efficiency. Some believe that privatization is not necessary if a public corporation is operating in competition with private enterprises. Others believe that the tendency for bureaucracies to inflate costs is so strong that even more privatization is needed.

Let's now turn to anti-combine law.

---

[2] W.S.W. Caves and Lauritis Christensen, "The Relative Efficiency of Public *v.* Private Firms in a Competitive Environment: the Case of Canada's Railroads," *Journal of Political Economy* 88, 5 (September-October 1980), 958–76.

Anti-Combine Law

ANTI-COMBINE LAW GIVES POWERS TO THE COURTS and to government agencies to influence markets. Like regulation, anti-combine law can work in the public interest to maximize total surplus or in private interests to maximize the surpluses of particular special interest groups such as producers. We'll describe Canada's anti-combine law and then examine some recent cases.

Canada's Anti-Combine Law

Canada's anti-combine law dates from 1889. At that time, monopoly was a major political issue and people were concerned about the absence of competition in industries as diverse as sugar and groceries, biscuits and confectionery, coal, binder twine, agricultural implements, stoves, coffins, eggs, and fire insurance.

Canada's anti-combine law today is defined in the Competition Act of 1986, which is described in Table 20.3. The Competition Act distinguishes between actions that are

- Criminal
- Non-criminal

Criminal actions include conspiracy to fix prices, bid-rigging, other anti-competitive price-fixing actions, and false advertising. These actions are dealt with by the courts, where the alleged offence must be proven beyond a reasonable doubt. Non-criminal actions include mergers, abuse of a dominant market position, refusal to deal, and other actions designed to limit competition such as exclusive dealing. These actions are examined by a Competition Tribunal.

The Competition Act is administered by the Competition Bureau and decisions to send a case to the courts or the Competition Tribunal are made by the Director of the Competition Bureau.

Some Recent Anti-Combine Cases

Let's see how the Competition Act has been working by looking at some recent cases. The first case we'll examine is important because it confirms the Competition Tribunal's power to enforce its orders.

Chrysler   In 1986, Chrysler stopped supplying auto parts to Richard Brunet, a Montreal auto dealer.

Chrysler also discouraged other dealers from supplying Brunet. The Competition Tribunal claimed that Chrysler wanted Brunet's business for itself and ordered Chrysler to resume doing business with Brunet. Chrysler did not resume sending supplies and the Tribunal cited Chrysler for contempt. Appeals against this ruling eventually reached the Supreme Court of Canada, which confirmed the Tribunal's power over contempt for its ruling. But the Tribunal subsequently dropped its contempt charge.

The second case we'll look at concerns aspartame, the sweetener in many soft drinks.

NutraSweet   NutraSweet, the maker of aspartame, tried to gain a monopoly in aspartame. It did so by licensing the use of its "swirl" only on products for which it had an exclusive deal. The Competition Tribunal ruled that this action unduly limited competition and told NutraSweet that it may not enforce existing contracts, enter into new contracts in which it is the exclusive supplier, or give inducements to encourage the display of its "swirl." The result of this case is expected to be an increase in competition and a large fall in the price of aspartame in Canada.

The third case we'll examine concerns a publication you use almost every day: the Yellow Pages.

Bell Canada Enterprises   Two subsidiaries of Bell Canada Enterprises have a 90 percent share of the market for the publication of telephone directories in their territories. These companies tie the sale of *advertising services* to the sale of *advertising space* in the Yellow Pages. If you want to advertise in the Yellow Pages, you must buy the advertising services of one of these two companies. As a result, other advertising agencies cannot effectively compete for business in Yellow Pages advertising. The Director of the Competition Bureau applied for an order prohibiting the tied-sale practice of these two companies.

Other Recent Anti-Competitive Agreements
During 1995 and 1996, the Competition Bureau took action against several anti-competitive agreements. Among such cases were driving schools in Sherbrooke, ready-mix concrete in the Saguenay-Lac St-Jean region, real estate dealing in Calgary, the importing of Australian mandarin oranges, wire for baling pulp, and ambulance services in Alberta.

The Competition Bureau is extremely active in reviewing and, in some cases, blocking mergers. The next cases we examine fall into this category.

TABLE 20.2

Canada's Anti-Combine Law: The Competition Act, 1986

Abuse of Dominant Position

79 (1)   Where on application by the Director, the Tribunal finds that:

   (a)   one or more persons substantially or completely control, throughout Canada or any area thereof, a class or species of business,

   (b)   that person or those persons have engaged in or are engaging in a practice of anti-competitive acts, and

   (c)   the practice has had, is having or is likely to have the effect of preventing or lessening competition substantially in a market, the Tribunal may make an order prohibiting all or any of those persons from engaging in that practice.

Mergers

92(1)   Where on application by the Director, the Tribunal finds that a merger or proposed merger prevents or lessens, or is likely to prevent or lessen, competition substantially ... the Tribunal may ...[,] in the case of a completed merger, order any party to the merger

   (i)   to dissolve the merger...

   (ii)   to dispose of assets and shares...

   [or]

   in the case of a proposed merger, make an order directed against any party to the proposed merger

   (i)   ordering the person ... not to proceed with the merger

   (ii)   ordering the person not to proceed with part of the merger

---

Canada Packers and Labatt   Canada Packers Inc. and John Labatt Ltd. proposed a merger of their flour milling operations that would have made them the biggest miller in Canada and the fifth biggest in North America. The Competition Tribunal stopped this merger, saying that the Canadian flour milling business had been run too much like a cartel and that more, not less, competition was needed.

Not all mergers are prevented by the Competition Bureau and the next case is an example.

Smiths and Coles Book Stores   In 1994, FICG Inc., the company that operates SmithBooks, and Coles Book Stores Ltd. announced a merger of their two book-store chains. The new combined operation would account for half of all English-language book sales in Canada. The Director of the Competition Bureau decided that this case was not sufficiently serious to require a ruling from the Tribunal. The main reason for the Director's decision is an assessment that barriers to entry in book retailing are low. With low barriers to entry, a large market share does not translate into large market power. But this case will be monitored by the Bureau through 1997.

Public or Special Interest?

The intent of anti-combine law is to protect the public interest and restrain the profit-seeking and anti-competitive actions of producers. On the whole, the overall thrust of the law and its enforcement has been in line with its intent and has served the public interest. Further, if the recent cases we have examined are setting a trend, we can expect a continuation of pro-consumer decisions from the courts and the Competition Tribunal in future cases.

◆ In this chapter, we've seen how the government intervenes in markets to affect prices, quantities, the gains from trade, and the division of those gains between consumers and producers. We've seen that there is a conflict between the pursuit of the public interest—achieving allocative efficiency—and the pursuit of the special interests of producers—maximizing producer surplus or economic profit. The political and legal arenas are the places in which these conflicts are resolved. *Reading Between the Lines* on pp. 470–471 looks at a recent example that has a potentially wide-ranging effect on your life.

The Competition Tribunal in Action

Essence of THE STORY

■ Manufacturers of consumer products pay $70 million a year for data scanned from package bar codes at checkouts.

■ Nielsen Marketing Research became a monopoly in this market by entering into agreements with retailers that gave it exclusive access to the bar code data.

■ The Competition Tribunal has ruled that Nielsen may not enforce these contracts.

■ Chicago-based Information Resources Inc. is a potential competitor for Nielsen.

■ The introduction of competition is expected to lower the price of data and bring lower prices in grocery and drug stores.

CALGARY HERALD, AUGUST 31, 1995

Ruling could bring lower food, drug prices

BY ROB CARRICK

Canada's competition cops have struck a blow against a market research company that could bring lower prices to grocery and drug stores.

The federal Competition Tribunal ruled Wednesday that Nielsen Marketing Research can no longer enforce contracts that give it exclusive access to data from electronic price scanners.

The move breaks Nielsen's monopoly on the $70-million-a-year market for scanner data and paves the way for the entry of a new competitor, Chicago-based Information Resources Inc.

Scanner data is read from package bar codes at checkouts. The data is bought by companies such as Nielsen, analysed and sold to manufacturers of consumer products that want an idea of demand for their goods.

Introducing competition is expected to lower the price of data for these manufacturers and improve the quality.

"Hopefully, that would be reflected in lower costs to consumers," said George Addy, head of the Bureau of Competition Policy.

Addy launched a six-month investigation into Nielsen's practices after receiving a complaint in 1993.

The matter went to the tribunal last fall. The tribunal, an independent court-like body made up of Federal Court judges and lay people, ruled Nielsen controls the supply of scanner-based data through its exclusivity contracts.

Addy said the implications of the case go beyond scanner data to all kinds of electronic information, which is particularly important as the world moves into an information-based economy.

The Canadian Press.

Economic

A N A L Y S I S

■ If a manufacturer can get data on the prices and quantities sold of its own and its competitors' products, then the manufacturer can use the information to develop more profitable pricing strategies.

■ Data is an input and the demand for data is like the demand for a factor of production. The demand for data is determined by the marginal revenue product of the data.

■ Figure 1 shows the demand curve for data, D_0.

■ Nielsen Marketing Research has developed a technology for gathering such data by scanning bar codes at supermarket checkouts.

■ Figure 1 shows the (assumed) average total cost curve *ATC* and the marginal cost curve *MC* of gathering data.

■ By entering into agreements with stores that give it exclusive access to data, Nielsen gained a monopoly in this market. As a monopoly, Nielsen has a marginal revenue curve MR_0.

■ Neilsen maximizes profit by producing Q_0 bits of information and selling the information for P_0 per bit.

■ With Nielsen's monopoly broken, Information Resources Inc. and other firms enter the market. With differentiated data, the market for data becomes monopolistically competitive.

■ Figure 2 shows the result. Nielsen's demand curve shifts leftward and so does its marginal revenue curve.

■ In the long run, Nielsen sells Q_1 bits of information at a price of P_1 per bit. The firm's total revenue falls from its current $70 million a year to a smaller amount.

■ With a lower price for information, manufacturers' costs of producing goods decrease and so do the prices that consumers pay.

■ But the price fall is unlikely to be large. The total information market is $70 million a year, which is less than 0.5 percent of the value of food and drug sales.

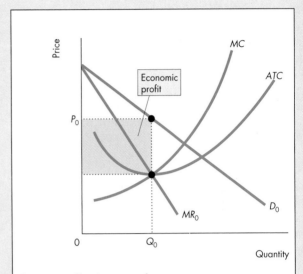

Figure 1 Neilsen's monopoly

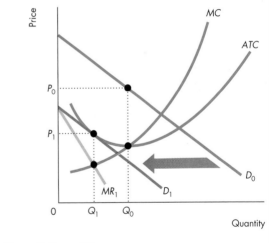

Figure 2 Competition

S U M M A R Y

Key Terms

Market Intervention   The government intervenes to regulate monopoly and oligopoly in three ways: regulation, public ownership, and anti-combine law. Government action can influence consumer surplus, producer surplus, and total surplus. Total surplus is maximized under competition. Under monopoly, producer surplus is increased and consumer surplus decreased, and a deadweight loss is created. (pp. 455–456)

Economic Theory of Regulation   Consumers and producers express their demand for the regulation that influences their surpluses by voting, lobbying, and making campaign contributions. The larger the surplus that can be generated by a particular regulation and the smaller the number of people adversely affected, the larger is the demand for the regulation. But the greater the number of people, the greater is the cost of organizing them into an effective political lobby. Regulation is supplied by politicians who pursue their own best interest. The larger the surplus per person generated and the larger the number of persons affected by it, the larger is the supply of regulation. In equilibrium, the regulation that exists is such that no interest group feels it is worthwhile to employ additional scarce resources to press for further changes. Public interest theory predicts that total surplus will be maximized. Capture theory predicts that producer surplus will be maximized. (pp. 456–458)

Regulation and Deregulation   Natural monopolies and cartels are regulated by agencies controlled by politically appointed bureaucrats and staffed by a permanent bureaucracy of experts. Regulated firms must comply with rules about price, product quality, and output levels. Regulation has not lowered the profit rates of regulated firms. This outcome is closer to the predictions of the capture theory of regulation than to the predictions of the public interest theory. (pp. 458–465)

Public Ownership   More than 100 federal and provincial Crown corporations in Canada produce such items as rail transport, hydroelectric power, and telecommunications. The economic model of public enterprise is based on the assumption that managers aim to maximize their budget. The political process constrains that aim. The outcome is a tendency for public enterprises to be inefficient: They overproduce and their costs are too high. In recent years, there has been a tendency for the consumer interest to be more assertive, and a process of privatization or cut-backs in the scale of public enterprises has occurred. (pp. 465–467)

Anti-Combine Law   Anti-combine law provides an alternative way for government to control monopoly and monopolistic practices. The original law was brief, and its interpretation tended to favour the consumer. The overall thrust of the law was directed towards serving the public interest. The Competition Act of 1986 radically reformed anti-combine law and placed responsibility for enforcement with the Competition Tribunal. (pp. 468–469)

Key Figures and Tables

Key Terms

R E V I E W   Q U E S T I O N S

1. What are the three main ways in which the government can intervene in the marketplace?
2. What is consumer surplus? How is it calculated and how is it represented in a diagram?
3. What is producer surplus? How is it calculated and how is it represented in a diagram?
4. What is total surplus? How is it calculated and how is it represented in a diagram?
5. Why do consumers demand regulation? In what kinds of industries would their demands for regulation be greatest?
6. Why do producers demand regulation? In what kinds of industries would their demands for regulation be greatest?
7. Explain the public interest and capture theories of the supply of regulation. What does each theory imply about the behaviour of politicians?

8. How is oligopoly regulated in Canada? In whose interest is it regulated?
9. Why do Crown corporations tend to be inefficient? Explain how a Crown corporation chooses the output to produce and the price of its service.
10. What was the original anti-combine law in Canada?
11. What is the anti-combine law in Canada today? How does it differ from the original law?
12. Describe the case against Chrysler.
13. Describe the case against NutraSweet. What was the outcome?
14. Describe the case against the merger of John Labatt Ltd. and Canada Packers Inc. What was the outcome?

C R I T I C A L   T H I N K I N G

1. After you have studied *Reading Between the Lines* on pp. 470–471, answer the following questions:
   a. What is the source of Nielsen's monopoly power? Was Nielsen a natural monopoly, a legal monopoly, or not a monopoly at all? (Refer to pp. 260–261 for a refresher on the distinction between natural monopoly and legal monopoly and the definition of monopoly.)
   b. Why did the Competition Tribunal rule against Nielsen?
   c. Would you expect retail margins to fall by a lot or a little as a result of the changes described in this news article? Explain.
2. The government of Canada regulates the production and sale of many goods and services. For example, the prices of local phone and cable TV services, the acreage that each wheat and cereal farmer can sow, the grain prices paid to these farmers, and to whom they can sell the grain. The suppliers of local phone and cable TV services are monopolies, but there are many grain farmers. Why are grain farmers regulated?

Is the regulation in the interest of grain farmers or consumers?
3. "Now that Canada has free trade with the United States, the government of Canada should not regulate monopolies in Canada because they are in direct competition with U.S. producers." Do you agree with this argument? If so, explain why. If not, explain why the argument is incorrect.
4. Study the *Interac* case on the Competition Tribunal's page on the World Wide Web (http://www.ct-tc.gc.ca/rcteng.htm).
   a. Explain the case against the owners of the *Interac*.
   b. What do you predict will be the effect of the consent order on the price the customer pays and the number of locations of *Interac* ATMs?
5. Check the World Wide Web page on Competition Law Review (http://ohh1.osler.com/Resources/maincomp.html). Look for cases of collusive agreement, abuse of dominant position, and mergers to restrict competition. In each case, describe the means cited as used to lessen competition.

P R O B L E M S

1. Elixir Springs, Inc., is an unregulated natural monopoly that bottles Elixir, a unique health product with no substitutes. The total fixed cost incurred by Elixir Springs is $160,000 and its marginal cost is 10¢ a bottle. The figure illustrates the demand for Elixir.

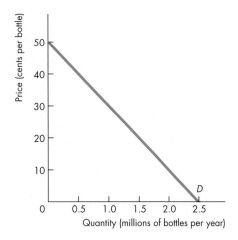

a. What is the price of a bottle of Elixir?
b. How many bottles does Elixir Springs sell?
c. Does Elixir Springs maximize total surplus or producer surplus?

2. The government regulates Elixir Springs in problem 1 by imposing a marginal cost pricing rule.
   a. What is the price of a bottle of Elixir?
   b. How many bottles does Elixir Springs sell?
   c. What is the producer surplus?
   d. What is the consumer surplus?
   e. Is the regulation in the public interest or in the private interest?

3. The government regulates Elixir Springs in problem 1 by imposing an average cost pricing rule.
   a. What is the price of a bottle of Elixir?
   b. How many bottles does Elixir Springs sell?
   c. What is the producer surplus?
   d. What is the consumer surplus?
   e. Is the regulation in the public interest or in the private interest?

4. The value of the capital invested in Elixir Springs in problem 1 is $2 million. The government introduces a rate of return regulation requiring the firm to sell its Elixir for a price that gives it a rate of return of 5 percent on its capital.
   a. What is the price of a bottle of Elixir?
   b. How many bottles does Elixir Springs sell?
   c. What is the producer surplus?
   d. What is the consumer surplus?
   e. Is the regulation in the public interest or in the private interest?

5. Faced with the rate of return regulation of problem 4, Elixir Springs pads its costs by paying a special bonus to its owner that it counts as a cost.
   a. Counting the bonus as part of the producer surplus, what is the size of the bonus that maximizes producer surplus and that makes the measured rate of return equal to 5 percent as required by the regulation?
   b. How many bottles does Elixir Springs sell?
   c. What is the producer surplus?
   d. What is the consumer surplus?
   e. Is the regulation in the public interest or in the private interest?

Externalities, the Environment, and Knowledge

After studying this chapter, you will be able to:

■ Explain how property rights can sometimes be used to overcome externalities

■ Explain how emission charges, marketable permits, and taxes may be used to achieve efficiency in the face of external costs

■ Explain how subsidies may be used to achieve efficiency in the face of external benefits

■ Explain how scholarships, below-cost tuition, and research grants make the quantity of education and invention more efficient

■ Explain how patents increase the efficiency of the process of developing new products and processes

Greener and Smarter

We hear a lot about our endangered planet. We burn huge quantities of fossil fuels—coal, natural gas, and oil—that cause acid rain and possibly global warming. The persistent and large-scale use of chlorofluorocarbons (CFCs) may have caused irreparable damage to the earth's ozone layer, thereby exposing us to additional ultraviolet rays, which increases the incidence of skin cancer. We dump toxic waste in rivers, lakes, and oceans. These environmental issues are simultaneously everybody's problem and nobody's problem. What, if anything, can government do to protect our environment? How can government action help us to take account of the damage that we cause others every time we turn on our heating or air conditioning systems? ◆ Almost every day, we hear about a new discovery—in medicine, engineering, chemistry, physics, or even economics. The advance of knowledge seems boundless. And more and more people are learning more and more of what is already known. Today, two in every five young Canadians receive an education beyond high school, and the proportion has been getting bigger every year. The stock of knowledge—what is known and how many people know it—is increasing apparently without bound. We are getting smarter. But is our stock of knowledge advancing fast enough? Are we spending enough on research and development? And do we spend enough on education? Do enough people remain in school for long enough? And do we work hard enough at school? Would we be better off if we spent more on research and education?

◇ In this chapter, we study the problems that arise because many of our actions affect other people, for ill or good, in ways that we do not take into account when we make our own economic choices. We study two big areas—the environment and the accumulation of knowledge—in which these problems are especially important. But first, we study the general problem of externalities.

Externalities

A COST OR BENEFIT OF A PRODUCTION OR CONsumption activity that spills over to affect people other than those who decide the scale of the activity is called an **externality**. An *external cost* is the cost of producing a good or service that is not borne by its consumers but by other people. An *external benefit* is the benefit of consuming a good or service that does not accrue to its consumers but to other people. Let's consider some examples.

External Costs

When a chemical factory dumps toxic waste products into a river and kills the fish, it imposes an external cost on the members of the fishing club located downstream. Because these costs are not borne by the chemical factory, the chemical company does not take these costs into account in deciding whether, and in what quantities, to dump waste into the river. When in the 1970s a person in Montreal drove a car fuelled by leaded gasoline, an external cost was imposed on everyone who tried to breathe the toxic air. Again, because most of these costs were not borne by the driver, they were not taken into account when deciding how often to drive.

Two particularly dramatic external costs have received a lot of attention in recent years. One arises from the use of chlorofluorocarbons (CFCs). These chemicals are used in a wide variety of products—from coolants in refrigerators and air conditioners, to plastic phones, to cleaning solvents for computer circuits. Although the precise chemistry of the process is not understood and is a subject of dispute, many atmospheric physicists believe that CFCs damage the atmosphere's protective ozone layer. Discoveries of depleted ozone over Antarctica in 1983 heightened fears of extended ozone depletion. Scientists have estimated that a 1 percent drop in ozone levels might cause a 2 percent rise in the incidence of skin cancer. Diminished ozone is also believed to be a possible cause of cataracts. When you switch on the air conditioner on a steamy August evening, you do not count the cost of an increase in the incidence of skin cancer as part of the price that has to be paid for a comfortable night's sleep. You count only the cost that *you* incur.

The other external cost arises from burning fossil fuels that add carbon dioxide and other gases to the atmosphere that prevent infrared radiation from escaping. These gases are collectively known as "greenhouse gases" because they maintain the earth's temperature. An increase in the concentration of these gases might be responsible for an increase in the earth's average temperature—an increase that could continue into the next century and beyond. If the greenhouse scenario is correct (which is by no means certain), much of the Prairies in Canada and the Midwest of the United States will become a dustbowl and many parts of North America's eastern seaboard, especially the Gulf Coast of the United States, will disappear under an expanded Atlantic Ocean. When you take a car trip—and burn gasoline—you do not count as part of the cost the effects of a warmer planet. You compare your private benefit with your own cost.

Not all externalities are negative—they are not always external costs. Let's look at some activities that bring external benefits.

External Benefits

When a homeowner renovates her house and landscapes her yard, she generates an external benefit for her neighbours—their property values increase. In deciding how much to spend on this lavish display, she pays more attention to the pleasure she receives herself than the pleasure she gives to others.

The biggest external benefits are in our schools, colleges, universities, and research laboratories. Welleducated people derive many benefits for themselves—such as higher incomes and the enjoyment of a wide range of artistic and cultural activities. But they also bring benefits to others through social interaction. People find more exciting partners and spouses, children get more imaginative parents, and we get to see more creative and entertaining movies and television shows. The list is almost endless. Despite all these external benefits, each one of us decides how much education to undertake by assessing our own costs and benefits, not those enjoyed by the wider community.

Health services also create external benefits. The pursuit of good health and personal hygiene reduces the risk that the people with whom we come into contact will be infected by transmitted diseases. Again, in making economic choices about the scale of resources to devote to health and hygiene, we mainly take account of the costs borne by ourselves and the benefits accruing to ourselves and not the greater benefit that our actions bring to others.

Market Failure and Public Choice

External costs and external benefits are the major sources of *market failure.* The market economy tends to overproduce goods and services that have external costs and to underproduce those that have external benefits. That is, externalities create inefficiency.

When market failure occurs, either we must live with the inefficiency it creates or try to achieve greater efficiency by making some *public choices* and using the instruments of government to intervene in the market economy. Governments can take several types of action to achieve a more efficient allocation of resources in the face of externalities—to decrease production where there are external costs and increase it where there are external benefits. This chapter explains these actions. It begins this task by studying external costs that affect the environment.

The Economics of the Environment

ENVIRONMENTAL PROBLEMS ARE NOT NEW AND they are not restricted to rich industrial countries. Pre-industrial towns and cities in Europe had severe sewage disposal problems that created cholera epidemics and scourges that killed tens of millions of people. Nor is the desire to find solutions to environmental problems new. The development in the fourteenth century of pure water supplies and of garbage and sewage disposal are spectacular examples of early contributions to improving the quality of the environment.

Popular discussions of the environment usually pay little attention to economics. They focus on physical aspects of the environment, not costs and benefits. A common assumption is that if people's actions cause *any* environmental degradation, those actions must cease. In contrast, an economic study of the environment emphasizes costs and benefits. An economist talks about the efficient amount of pollution or environmental damage. This emphasis on costs and benefits does not mean that economists, as citizens, do not share the same goals as others and value a healthy environment. Nor does it mean that economists have the right answers and everyone else has the wrong ones (or vice versa). Economics provides a set of tools and principles which clarify the issues. It does not provide an agreed list of solutions. The starting point for an economic analysis of the environment is the demand for a healthy environment.

The Demand for Environmental Quality

The demand for a clean and healthy environment has grown and is higher today than it has ever been. We join organizations that lobby governments for environmental regulations and policies. We vote for politicians who convince us they have the environmental polices that we want to see implemented. (All politicians at least pay lip-service to the environment today.) And we buy "green" products and avoid hazardous products, even if we pay a bit more to be green. Figure 21.1 gives one indicator of the growth in the demand for a better environment: the growth in the number of people who pay subscriptions to environmental organizations.

FIGURE   21.1

Membership of Environmental Groups

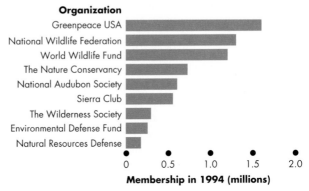

(a) Organizations

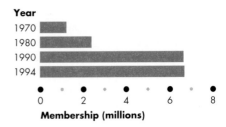

(b) Membership trend

In 1994, almost 7 million people were members of environmental groups. Membership doubled during the 1970s and almost tripled during the 1980s.

Sources: Outside, March 1994, and Francis Cairncross, *Costing the Earth* (The Economist Books Ltd.,) p. 13.

The demand for a better environment has grown for two reasons:

1. Increased incomes
2. Increased knowledge of the sources of environmental problems

As our incomes increase, we demand a larger range of goods and services and one of these "goods" is a high-quality environment. We value clean air, unspoiled natural scenery, and wildlife, and we are willing to pay to protect these valuable resources.

As our knowledge of the effects of our actions on the environment grows, so we are able to take measures that improve the environment. For example, now that we know how sulfur dioxide causes acid rain and how clearing rainforests destroys natural stores of carbon dioxide, we are able, in principle, to design measures that limit these problems.

Let's look at the range of environmental problems that have been identified and the actions that create those problems.

The Sources of Environmental Problems

Environmental problems arise from pollution of the air, water, and land and these individual sources of pollution interact through the *ecosystem*.

Air Pollution   Figure 21.2(a) shows the five economic activities that create most of our air pollution. It also shows the relative contributions of each activity. More than two-thirds of air pollution comes from road transportation and industrial processes. Only one-sixth arises from electric power generation.

A common belief is that air pollution is getting worse. On many fronts, as we will see later in this chapter, *global* air pollution *is* getting worse. But air pollution in North America is becoming less severe for most substances. Figure 21.2(b) shows the trends in the concentrations of six air pollutants. While lead has been almost eliminated from our air and sulfur dioxide and carbon monoxide have been reduced

---

FIGURE 21.2

Air Pollution

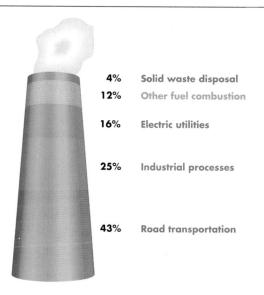

4%	Solid waste disposal
12%	Other fuel combustion
16%	Electric utilities
25%	Industrial processes
43%	Road transportation

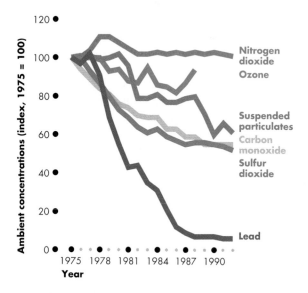

Part (a) shows that road transportation is the largest source of air pollution, followed by industrial processes and electric utilities. Part (b) shows that lead has almost been eliminated

from our air, and concentrations of carbon monoxide and sulfur dioxide have decreased. Ozone has decreased slightly but nitrogen dioxide has persisted at close to its 1975 level.

Source: U.S. Environmental Protection Agency, *National Air Quality and Emissions Trends Report, 1994*, February 1994.

substantially, other pollutants are more stable.

Although the facts about the sources and trends in air pollution are not in doubt, there is considerable disagreement in the scientific community about the *effects* of air pollution. The least controversial problem is *acid rain,* which is caused by sulfur dioxide and nitrogen oxide emissions from coal and oil-fired generators of electric utilities. Acid rain begins with air pollution, and then leads to water pollution and damages vegetation.

More controversial are airborne substances (suspended particulates) such as lead from leaded gasoline. Some scientists believe that in sufficiently large concentrations, these substances (currently 189 of which have been identified) cause cancer and other life-threatening conditions.

Even more controversial is *global warming*, which some scientists believe results from the carbon dioxide emissions of road transportation and electric utilities, methane created by cows and other livestock, nitrous oxide emissions of electric utilities and from fertilizers, and chlorofluorocarbons or CFCs from refrigeration equipment and (in the past) aerosols. The earth's average temperature has increased over the past 100 years, but most of the increase occurred *before* 1940. Determining what causes changes in the earth's temperature and separating out the effect of carbon dioxide and other factors is proving very difficult.

Equally controversial is the problem of *ozone layer depletion.* There is no doubt that a hole in the ozone layer exists over Antarctica, and that the ozone layer protects us from cancer-causing ultraviolet rays from the sun. But how our industrial activity influences the ozone layer is simply not understood at this time.

One air pollution problem has almost been eliminated: lead from gasoline. In part, this happened because the cost of living without leaded gasoline, it turns out, is not high. But sulfur dioxide and the so-called greenhouse gases are a much tougher problem to tackle. Their alternatives are costly or have environmental problems of their own. The major sources of these pollutants are road vehicles and electric utilities. Road vehicles can be made "greener" in a variety of ways. One is with new fuels, and some alternatives being investigated are alcohol, natural gas, propane and butane, and hydrogen. Another way of making cars and trucks "greener" is to change the chemistry of gasoline. Refiners are working on reformulations of gasoline that cut tailpipe emissions. Similarly, electric power can be generated in cleaner ways by harnessing solar power, tidal power, or geothermal pow-er. Technically possible, these methods are more costly than conventional carbon-fuelled generators. Another alternative is nuclear power. This method is good for air pollution but bad for land and water pollution because there is no known safe method of disposing of spent nuclear fuel.

Water Pollution The largest sources of water pollution are the dumping of industrial waste and treated sewage in lakes and rivers and the runoff from fertilizers. A more dramatic source is the accidental spilling of crude oil into the oceans, such as the *Exxon Valdez* spill in Alaska in 1989 and an even larger spill in the Russian Arctic in 1994. The most frightening is the dumping of nuclear waste in the ocean by the former Soviet Union.

There are two main alternatives to polluting the waterways and oceans. One is the chemical processing of waste to render it inert or biodegradable. The other, in wide use for nuclear waste, is to use land sites for storage in secure containers.

Land Pollution Land pollution arises from dumping toxic waste products. Ordinary household garbage does not pose a pollution problem unless dumped garbage seeps into the water supply. This possibility increases as less suitable landfill sites are used. It is estimated that 80 percent of existing landfills will be full by 2010. Some regions (New York and New Jersey) and some countries (Japan and the Netherlands) have run out of landfills already. The alternatives to landfill are recycling and incineration. Recycling is an apparently attractive alternative, but it requires an investment in new technologies to be effective. Incineration is a high-cost alternative to landfill, and it produces air pollution.

We've seen that the demand for a quality environment has grown, and we've described the range of environmental problems. Let's now look at the ways these problems can be handled. We'll begin by looking at property rights and how they relate to environmental externalities.

Property Rights and Environmental Externalities

Externalities arise because of an *absence* of property rights. **Property rights** are social arrangements that govern the ownership, use, and disposal of factors of production and goods and services. In modern societies, a property right is a legally established title that is enforceable in the courts.

By thinking about the examples we've already reviewed, you can see that property rights are absent when externalities arise. No one owns the air, the rivers, and the oceans. So it is no one's private business to ensure that these resources are used in an efficient way. In fact, there is an incentive to use them more than if there were property rights.

Figure 21.3 illustrates how an environmental externality arises in the absence of property rights. A chemical factory (part a) upstream from a fishing club must decide how to dispose of its waste.

The *MPB* curve in part (a) is the factory's marginal benefit curve. It tells us how much an additional tonne of waste dumped into the river is worth to the factory. The value to the firm of dumping a marginal tonne of waste in the river falls as the quantity increases. The *MPB* curve is the firm's demand curve for the use of the river, which is a factor of production. The demand for a factor of production slopes downward because of the law of diminishing returns (see Chapter 14, pp. 323–325).

The *MSC* curve in part (b) is the marginal social cost curve. It tells us the cost imposed by the chemical factory on the fishing club by one additional tonne of waste dumped into the river. The cost to the club of the firm dumping a marginal tonne of waste in the river rises as the quantity increases.

If no one owns the stream, the factory dumps the amount of waste that maximizes its total benefit. Because the marginal cost of waste disposal is zero, it dumps the quantity that makes its marginal benefit zero. The quantity dumped is 8 tonnes a week. The cost of this amount of waste, which is borne by the fishing club, is $200 a tonne. The marginal social cost of the waste is $200 a tonne and the marginal benefit is zero, so this outcome is inefficient. Stopping the dumping of waste is worth more to the fishing club than the benefit of dumping waste is worth to the factory.

Sometimes it is possible to correct an externality by establishing a property right where one does not currently exist. For example, suppose that the property right in the river was assigned to the chemical factory. Because the river is now the property of the factory, the fishing club must pay the factory for the right to fish in the river. But the price that the club is willing to pay depends on the number and quality of fish, which in turn depends on how much waste the factory dumps in the river. The greater the amount of

FIGURE 21.3

An Externality

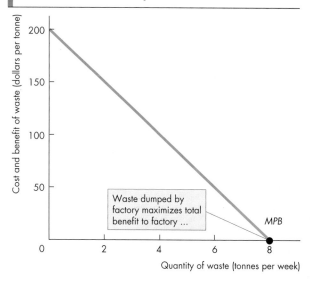

(a) Chemical factory

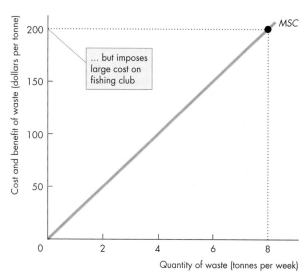

(b) Fishing club

A chemical factory's marginal benefit from dumping its waste into the river is *MPB* (part a) and a fishing club's marginal cost of having waste dumped is *MSC* (part b). With no property rights, the factory maximizes total benefit by dumping 8 tonnes a week, the quantity at which the marginal benefit of dumping equals the marginal cost (zero). With this quantity of waste, the fishing club bears a marginal cost of $200 per tonne. This outcome is inefficient because the marginal social cost exceeds the marginal benefit.

pollution, the smaller is the amount the fishing club is willing to pay for the right to fish. Similarly, the smaller the amount of pollution, the greater is the amount the fishing club is willing to pay for the right to fish. The chemical factory is now confronted with the cost of its pollution decision. It might still decide to pollute, but if it does, it faces the opportunity cost of its actions—forgone revenue from the fishing club.

Suppose that the fishing club, not the chemical factory, owns the river. In this case, the factory must pay a fee to the fishing club for the right to dump its waste. The more waste it dumps (equivalently, the more fish it kills), the more it must pay. Again, the factory faces an opportunity cost for the pollution it creates—the fee paid to the fishing club.

The Coase Theorem

We've considered two alternatives: assigning the property right to the polluter and to the victim of the pollution. Does it matter how property rights are assigned? At first thought, the assignment seems crucial. And until 1960, that is what everyone thought—including economists who had thought about the problem for longer than a few minutes. But in 1960, Ronald Coase had a remarkable insight, now known as the Coase theorem. The **Coase theorem** is the proposition that if property rights exist and transactions costs are low, private transactions are efficient. Equivalently, with property rights and low transactions costs, there are no externalities. All the costs and benefits are taken into account by the transacting parties. So the allocation of resources is the same regardless of how the property rights are assigned. How property rights are assigned affects the distribution of costs and benefits, but it does not affect the allocation of resources.

Figure 21.4 illustrates the Coase theorem. It brings together the chemical factory's marginal benefit curve and the fishing club's marginal cost curve that you saw in Fig. 21.3. With property rights in place, the *MPB* curve becomes the factory's demand curve for dumping waste. It tells us what the factory is willing to pay to dump. The *MSC* curve is the fishing club's supply curve of river use to the firm. It tells us what the club's members must be paid if they are to put up with inferior fishing and supply the firm with a permit to dump.

The efficient level of waste is 4 tonnes a week. At this level, the club bears a cost of $100 for the last

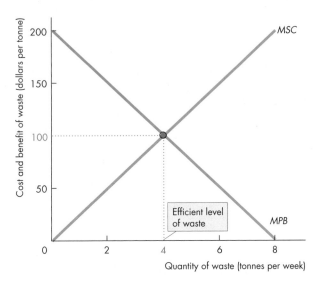

FIGURE   21.4

The Coase Theorem

Pollution of a river imposes a marginal social cost, *MSC*, on the victim and provides a marginal benefit, *MPB*, to the polluter. The efficient amount of pollution is the quantity that makes marginal benefit equal to marginal social cost—in this example, 4 tonnes per week. If the polluter owns the river, the victim will pay $400 a week ($100 a tonne × 4 tonnes a week) to the polluter for the assurance that pollution will not exceed 4 tonnes a week. If the victim owns the river, the polluter will pay $400 for pollution rights to dump 4 tonnes a week.

tonne dumped in the river, and the factory get a benefit of that amount. If waste disposal is restricted below 4 tonnes a week, an increase in waste disposal benefits the factory more than it costs the club. The factory can pay the club to put up with more waste disposal and both the club and the factory can gain. If waste disposal exceeds 4 tonnes a week, an increase in waste disposal costs the club more than it benefits the factory. The club can now pay the factory to cut its waste disposal, and again, both the club and the factory can gain. Only when the level of waste disposal is 4 tonnes a week can neither party do any better. This is the efficient level of waste disposal.

The amount of waste disposal is the same regardless of who owns the river. If the factory owns it, the club pays $400 for fishing rights and for an agreement that waste disposal will not exceed 4 tonnes a week. If the club owns the river, the factory pays $400 for the right to dump 4 tonnes of waste a week. In both cases, the amount of waste disposable is the efficient amount.

Property rights work in this example because the transactions costs are low. The factory and the fishing club can easily sit down and negotiate the deal that produces the efficient outcome.

But in many situations, transactions costs are high and property rights cannot be enforced. Imagine, for example, the transactions costs if the 50 million people who live in the northeastern of the United States and Canada tried to negotiate an agreement with the 20,000 factories that emit sulfur dioxide and cause acid rain! In a case such as this, governments resort to alternative methods of coping with externalities. In Canada, the federal government has established a department, Environment Canada, to coordinate and administer the nation's environment policies. The tools available to Environment Canada work indirectly through their influence on the decisions that businesses and individuals make and that are coordinated through markets. The three key tools are

- Emission charges
- Marketable permits
- Taxes

Let's look at these tools and see how they work.

Emission Charges

Emission charges are a method of using the market to achieve efficiency, even in the face of externalities. The government (or the regulatory agency established by government) sets the emission charges, which are, in effect, a price per unit of pollution. The more pollution a firm creates, the more it pays in emission charges. This method of dealing with environmental externalities has been used only modestly in North America, but it is common in Europe. For example, water polluters in France, Germany, and the Netherlands pay a waste disposal charge.

To work out the emission charge that achieves efficiency, the regulator must determine the marginal social cost and marginal social benefit of pollution. **Marginal social cost** is the marginal cost incurred by the producer of a good—marginal private cost—*plus* the marginal cost imposed on others—the external cost. **Marginal social benefit** is the marginal benefit received by the consumer of a good—marginal private benefit—*plus*

the marginal benefit to others—the external benefit. To achieve efficiency, the price per unit of pollution must be set to make the marginal social cost of the pollution equal to its marginal social benefit.

Figure 21.5 illustrates an efficient emission charge. The marginal benefit of pollution is *MPB* and accrues to the polluters—there is no *external* benefit. The marginal social cost of pollution is *MSC* and is entirely an external cost. The efficient level of sulfur dioxide emissions is 10 million tonnes a year, which is achieved with an emission charge of $10 per tonne. At this price, polluters do not find it worthwhile to buy the permission to pollute in excess of 10 million tonnes a year.

In practice, it is hard to determine the marginal benefit of pollution. And the people who are best informed about the marginal benefit, the polluters,

FIGURE 21.5

Emission Charges

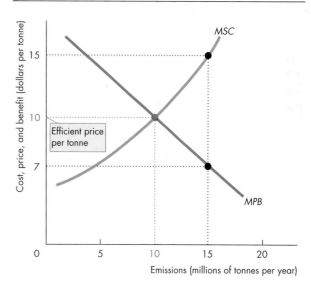

Electric utilities obtain marginal benefits from sulfur dioxide emissions of *MPB*, and everyone else bears a marginal social cost of *MSC*. The efficient level of pollution—10 million tonnes a year in this example—is achieved by imposing an emission charge on the utilities of $10 a tonne. If the emission charge is set too low, at $7 a tonne, the resulting amount of pollution is greater than the efficient amount—at 15 million tonnes a year in this example. In this case, the marginal social cost is $15 a tonne, and it exceeds the marginal benefit of $7 a tonne.

have an incentive to mislead the regulators about the benefit. As a result, if a pollution charge is used, the most likely outcome is for the price to be set too low. For example, in Fig. 21.5, the price might be set at $7 per tonne. At this price, polluters find it worthwhile to pay for 15 million tonnes a year. At this level of pollution, the marginal social cost is $15 a tonne and the amount of pollution exceeds the efficient level.

One way of overcoming excess pollution is to impose a quantitative limit. The most sophisticated way of doing this is with marketable permits. Let's look at this alternative.

Marketable Permits

Instead of imposing emission charges on polluters, each potential polluter might be given a pollution limit. To achieve efficiency, marginal benefit and marginal cost must be assessed just as in the case of emission charges. Provided that these benefit–cost calculations are correct, the same efficient outcome can be achieved with quantitative limits as with emission charges. But in the case of quantitative limits, a cap must be set for each polluter. To set these caps at their efficient levels, the marginal benefit of *each* producer must be assessed. If firm *H* has a higher marginal benefit than firm *L*, an efficiency gain can be achieved by decreasing the cap of firm *L* and increasing that for firm *H*. It is virtually impossible to determine the marginal benefits of each firm, so in practice, quantitative restrictions cannot be allocated to each producer in an efficient way.

Marketable permits are a clever way of overcoming the need for the regulator to know every firm's marginal benefit schedule. Each firm can be allocated a permit to emit a certain amount of pollution, and firms can buy and sell such permits.

Figure 21.6 shows how such a system works and can achieve efficiency. Some firms have low marginal benefits from sulfur emissions, shown as MPB_L in part (a). Others have a high marginal benefit, shown as MPB_H in part (b). For the economy as a whole, the marginal benefit is MPB_E in part (c). The marginal social cost of sulfur emissions is MSC, also shown in part (c). The efficient level of emissions is 10 million tonnes a year, the quantity at which marginal social cost equals marginal social benefit.

FIGURE   21.6

Marketable Pollution Permits

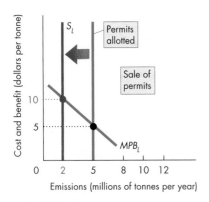

(a) Low-benefit firms

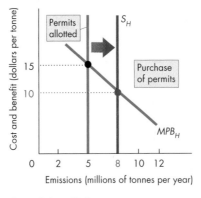

(b) High-benefit firms

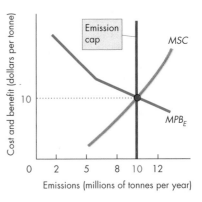

(c) Economy

Some firms obtain low marginal benefits from pollution, MPB_L in part (a), and some obtain high marginal benefits, MPB_H in part (b). Marginal benefit for the economy, MPB_E in part (c), is the horizontal sum of MPB_L and MPB_H. Marginal social cost is MSC in part (c). Permits for 10 million tonnes a year (the efficient level) are issued. Each type of firm gets 5 million tonnes a year. Initially, low-benefit firms value their permits at $5 a tonne and high-benefit firms value their permits at $15 a tonne. High-benefit firms buy permits for 3 million tonnes of pollution from low-benefit firms for a market price of $10 a tonne.

Suppose that Environment Canada allocates permits for a total of 10 million tonnes of sulfur emissions a year. And suppose the permits are allocated equally to the two groups of firms—5 million tonnes each. The firms in part (a) value their last tonne of pollution permitted at $5 a tonne. The firms in part (b) value their last tonne of pollution permitted at $15 a tonne. With a market in permits, the firms in part (a) sell some of their permits to those in part (b). Both types of firm gain from the trade.

If the market in permits is competitive, the price at which permits trade is $10 per tonne. At this price, low-benefit firms (part a) sell permits for 3 million tonnes of sulfur emissions to the high-benefit firms (part b). After these transactions, the low-benefit firms (part a) have S_L permits and the high-benefit firms (part b) have S_H permits and the allocation is efficient.

Real-World Market for Emissions   Environment Canada has not used marketable permits but the Environmental Protection Agency (EPA) in the United States has. The EPA issued marketable emission permits following the passage of the Clean Air Act in 1970. Trading in lead pollution permits was very common during the 1980s, and this marketable permit program has been rated a success. It enabled lead to be virtually eliminated from the atmosphere of the United States. But this success might not easily translate to other situations because lead pollution has some special features. First, most lead pollution came from a single source, leaded gasoline. Second, lead in gasoline is easily monitored. And third, the objective of the program was clear—eliminate lead in gasoline.

The EPA is currently considering using marketable permits to promote efficiency in the control of chlorofluorocarbons—the gases that are believed to damage the ozone layer.

Taxes and External Costs

Taxes can be used to provide incentives for producers or consumers to cut back on an activity that creates external costs. To see how taxes work, consider the market for transportation services. Figure 21.7 shows this market. The demand curve for transportation services, D, is also the marginal benefit curve, MPB. This curve tells us how much consumers value each different level of output of transportation services.

The curve MPC measures the marginal *private* cost of producing transportation services—the costs directly incurred by the producers of these services.

The costs borne by the producers of transportation services are not the only costs. External costs arise from the airborne particulates and greenhouse gases caused by vehicle emissions. Further, one person's decision to use a highway imposes congestion costs on others. These costs are also external costs. When all the external marginal costs are added to the marginal cost faced by the producer, we obtain the marginal *social* cost of transportation services, shown by MSC in the figure.

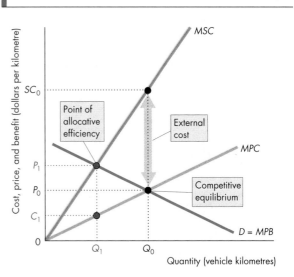

FIGURE   21.7

Taxes and Pollution

The demand curve for road transportation services is also the marginal benefit curve ($D = MPB$). The marginal private cost curve is MPC. If the market is competitive, output is Q_0 vehicle kilometres and the price is P_0 per kilometre. Marginal social cost is SC_0 per kilometre. Because of congestion and environmental pollution, the marginal cost of providing transportation services exceeds the marginal private cost. Marginal social cost is shown by curve MSC. If the government imposes a tax so that producers of transportation services are confronted with the marginal social cost, the MSC curve becomes the relevant marginal cost curve for suppliers' decisions. The price increases to P_1 per kilometre and the quantity decreases to Q_1 vehicle kilometres. Allocative efficiency is achieved.

If the transportation market is competitive and unregulated, road users will balance their own marginal cost, *MPC*, against their own marginal benefit, *MPB*, and travel Q_0 vehicle kilometres at a price (and cost) of P_0 per kilometre. At this scale of transportation services, the marginal social cost is SC_0. The marginal social cost minus the marginal private cost, $SC_0 - P_0$, is the marginal cost imposed on others—the marginal external cost.

Suppose the government taxes road transportation and that it sets the tax equal to the external marginal cost. By imposing such a tax, the government makes the suppliers of transportation services incur a marginal cost equal to the marginal social cost. That is, the marginal private cost plus the tax equals the marginal social cost. The market supply curve is now the same as the *MSC* curve. The price rises to P_1 a kilometre, and at this price, people travel Q_1 vehicle kilometres. The marginal private cost of the resources used in producing Q_1 vehicle kilometres is C_1, and the marginal external cost is P_1 minus C_1. That marginal external cost is paid by the consumer through the tax.

The situation at the price P_1 and the quantity Q_1 is efficient. At an output rate above Q_1, marginal social cost exceeds marginal benefit, so net benefit increases by decreasing the quantity of transport services. At a quantity less that Q_1, marginal benefit exceeds marginal social cost, so net benefit increases by increasing the quantity of transportation services.

Although taxes can be used to achieve an efficient outcome, it is difficult to ensure that they do not also change the distribution of costs and benefits. A tax on transportation is likely to impose most of the costs on producers of vehicles and truck drivers. A tax on forest depletion is likely to impose most of the costs on loggers. Finding politically acceptable ways of using taxes to achieve efficiency also involves complementary taxes and subsidies that preserve the original distribution of net benefit.

A Carbon-Fuel Tax?   A tax can be imposed on any activity that creates external costs. For example, we could tax *all* air-polluting activities. Because the carbon fuels that we use to power our vehicles and generate our electric power are a major source of pollution, why don't we have a broad-based tax on all activities that burn carbon fuel and set the tax rate high enough to give a large reduction in carbon emissions?

The question becomes even more pressing when we consider not only the current levels of greenhouse gases but also their projected future levels. In 1990, annual carbon emissions worldwide were a staggering 6 billion tonnes. By 2050, with current policies, that annual total is predicted to be 24 billion tonnes.

Uncertainty About Global Warming   Part of the reason we do not have a high, broad-based, carbon-fuel tax is that the scientific evidence that carbon emissions produce global warming is not accepted by everyone. Climatologists are uncertain about how carbon emissions translate into atmospheric concentrations—about how the *flow* of emissions translates into a *stock* of pollution. The main uncertainty arises because carbon drains from the atmosphere into the oceans and vegetation at a rate that is not well understood. Climatologists are also uncertain about the connection between carbon concentration and temperature. And economists are uncertain about how a temperature increase translates into economic costs and benefits. Some economists believe the costs and benefits are almost zero, while others believe that a temperature increase of 3° Celsius by 2090 will cut the total output of goods and services by 20 percent.

Present Cost and Future Benefit   Another factor weighing against a large change in fuel use is that the costs would be borne now, while the benefits, if any, would accrue many years in the future. To compare future benefits with current costs, we must use an interest rate. If the interest rate is 1 percent a year, $1.00 today becomes $7.30 in 200 years. If the interest rate is 5 percent a year, $1.00 today becomes more than $17,000 in 200 years. So, at an interest rate of 1 percent a year, it is worth spending $1 million in 1996 on pollution control to avoid $7.3 million in environmental damage in 2196. At an interest rate of 5 percent a year it is worth spending $1 million in 1996 only if this expenditure avoids $17 billion in environmental damage in 2196.

Because large uncertain future benefits are needed to justify small current costs, a general tax on carbon fuels is not a high priority on the political agenda.

International Factors   A final factor against a large change in fuel use is the international pattern of the use of carbon fuels. Right now, carbon pollution comes in even doses from the industrial countries and the developing countries. But by 2050, three-quarters of the carbon pollution will come from the developing countries (if the trends persist).

One reason for the high pollution rate in some

developing countries (notably Russia, China, and other Eastern European countries) is that those governments *subsidize* the use of coal or oil. These subsidies lower producers' marginal costs and encourage the use of these fuels. The result is that the quantity of carbon fuels consumed exceeds the efficient quantity—and by a large amount. It is estimated that by 2050, these subsidies will induce annual global carbon emissions of some 10 billion tonnes—about two-fifths of total emissions. If the subsidies were removed, global emissions in 2050 would be 10 billion tonnes a year less.

A Global Warming Dilemma

With the high output rate of greenhouse gases in the developing world, Canada, the United States, and the other industrial countries are faced with a global warming dilemma.[1] Decreasing pollution is costly and brings benefits. But the benefits depend on all countries taking action to limit pollution. If one country acts alone, it bears the cost of limiting pollution and gets almost no benefits. So it is only worthwhile taking steps to limit global pollution if all nations act together.

Table 21.1 shows the global warming dilemma faced by the industrial countries and the developing countries. The numbers are hypothetical. Each group of countries has two possible policies: to control carbon emissions or to pollute. If each group pollutes, it receives a zero net return (by assumption) shown in the top left square in the table. If each group controls carbon emissions, it bears the cost of using more expensive fuels and gets the benefit of less pollution. Its net return is $25 billion, as shown in the bottom right square of the table. If the industrial countries control carbon emissions but the developing countries do not, the industrial countries alone bear the cost of using alternative fuels, and both the industrial countries and the developing countries enjoy a lower level of pollution. In this example, the industrial countries pay $50 billion more than they benefit and the developing countries benefit by $50 billion more than they pay, as shown in the top right corner of the table. Finally, if the developing countries control

TABLE 21.1

A Global Warming Dilemma

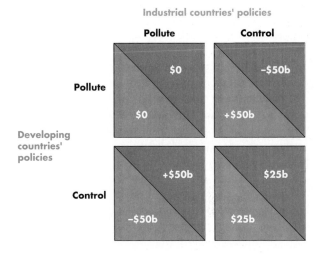

If the industrial countries and developing countries both pollute, their payoffs are those shown in the top left square. If neither pollutes, their payoffs are shown in the bottom right square. When one group of countries pollutes and the other one does not, their payoffs are shown in the top right and bottom left squares. The outcome of this game is for both groups to pollute. The structure of this game is the same as that of the prisoners' dilemma.

emissions and the industrial countries do not, the developing countries bear the cost and the industrial countries share the gains so the developing countries lose $50 billion and the industrial countries gain this amount, as shown in the bottom left corner of the table.

Confronted with these possible payoffs, the industrial countries and the developing countries decide their policies. The industrial countries reason as follows: If the developing countries do not control carbon emissions, we break even if we pollute and we lose $50 billion if we control our emissions. Conclusion: We are better off polluting. If the developing countries do control carbon emissions, we gain $50 billion if we pollute and $25 billion if we control emissions. Again, we are better off polluting. The developing countries reach the same conclusion. So no one controls emissions and pollution continues unabated.

---

[1]This dilemma is like the "prisoners' dilemma" that is explained in Chapter 13 on pp. 296–298.

Treaties and International Agreements

To break the dilemma, international agreements—treaties—might be negotiated. But such treaties must have incentives for countries to comply with their agreements. Otherwise, even with a treaty, the situation remains as we've just described and illustrated in Table 21.1.

One such international agreement is the *climate convention* that came into effect on March 21, 1994. This convention is an agreement among 60 countries to limit their output of greenhouse gases. But the convention does not have economic teeth. The poorer countries are merely asked to list their sources of greenhouse gases. The rich countries must show how, by 2000, they will return to their 1990 emission levels.

To return to the 1990 emission levels, the rich countries will need stiff increases in energy taxes, and such taxes will be costly. Energy taxes will induce a substitution towards more costly, but cleaner alternative fuels. Without energy taxes, only a large technological advance in solar, wind, tidal, or nuclear power that makes these sources less costly than coal can create the incentive needed to give up carbon fuels.

There are no simple solutions to the environment problem. But there are plenty of sensible solutions. And the insights that economics brings to the environment debate are central to finding those sensible solutions.

REVIEW

■ When externalities are present, the market allocation is not efficient.

■ If an externality can be eliminated by assigning property rights, an efficient allocation can be achieved.

■ If the government confronts firms with emission charges, imposes pollution limits, or imposes taxes equivalent to marginal external cost, it induces them to produce the efficient quantity of pollution, even in the face of externalities.

■ When an externality goes beyond the scope of one country, effective international cooperation is necessary to achieve an efficient outcome.

The Economics of Knowledge

KNOWLEDGE, THE THINGS PEOPLE KNOW AND understand, has a profound effect on the economy. The economics of knowledge is an attempt to understand that effect. It is also an attempt to understand the process of knowledge accumulation and the incentives people face to discover, to learn, and to pass on what they know to others. It is an economic analysis of the scientific and engineering processes that lead to the discovery and development of new technologies. And it is a study of the education process of teaching and learning.

You can think of knowledge as being both a consumer good and a factor of production. The demand for knowledge—the willingness to pay to acquire knowledge—depends on the marginal benefit it provides to its possessor. As a consumer good, knowledge provides utility, and this is one source of its marginal benefit. As a factor of production—part of the stock of capital—knowledge increases productivity, and this is another source of its marginal benefit.

Knowledge creates benefits not only for its possessor but also for others—external benefits. External benefits arise from education—passing on existing knowledge to others. When children learn the basics of reading, writing, and numbers in grade school, they are equipping themselves to be better neighbours for each other and better able to communicate and interact with each other. The process continues through high school and college or university. But when people make decisions about how much schooling to undertake, they undervalue the external benefits that it creates.

External benefits also arise from research and development activities that lead to the creation of new knowledge. Once someone has worked out how to do something, others can copy the basic idea. They do have to work to copy an idea, so they face an opportunity cost. But they do not usually have to pay the person who made the discovery to use it. When Isaac Newton worked out the formulas for calculating the rate of response of one variable to another—calculus—everyone was free to use his method. When a spreadsheet program called VisiCalc was invented, others were free to copy the basic idea and develop their own. Lotus Corporation developed its 1-2-3 and later Microsoft created Excel, and both became highly successful, but they did not pay for the key idea first used in VisiCalc. When the first shopping mall was built and found to be a successful way of arranging retailing, everyone was free to copy the idea and malls spread like mushrooms.

When people make decisions about the quantity of education to undertake or the amount of research and development to do, they balance the *private* marginal costs against the private marginal benefits. They undervalue the external benefits. As a result, if we were to leave education and research and development to unregulated market forces we would get too little of these activities. To deliver them in efficient quantities, we make public choices through governments to modify the market outcome.

Three devices that governments can use to achieve an efficient allocation of resources in the presence of the external benefits from education and research and development are

- Subsidies
- Below-cost provision
- Patents and copyrights

Subsidies

A **subsidy** is a payment made by the government to producers that depends on the level of output. By subsidizing private activities, government can in principle encourage private decisions to be taken in the public interest. A government subsidy program might alternatively enable private producers to capture resources for themselves. Although subsidies cannot be guaranteed to work successfully, we'll study an example in which they do achieve their desired goal.

Imagine that all the schools in Canada are private. We buy all our education from schools, colleges, and universities just like we now buy driving instruction from private driving schools. Suppose that the marginal cost of educating a student per year is $20,000. To cover their costs, the price of education in the competitive market is also $20,000 a year. At this price, you might guess that a large number of people would not go to school. The quantity of education would be far less than today. There would be a *market failure.*

Figure 21.8 shows the situation we've just described. It also shows how subsidizing education can achieve allocative efficiency. We've assumed that the marginal cost of a student-year of education is $20,000. We'll assume this to be both the private marginal cost, *MPC,* and the social marginal cost, *MSC.* That is, there are no external costs in produc-

ing education. This marginal cost is shown by the curve *MPC = MSC.*

The maximum price that students (or parents) are willing to pay for an additional year of education determines the marginal *private* benefit curve and the demand curve for education. That curve is *MPB = D.* In this example, a competitive market in private education results in 20,000 students a year being enrolled and tuition of $20,000 a year.

Suppose that the external benefit—the benefit derived by people other than those who receive the

---

FIGURE 21.8

The Efficient Quantity of Education

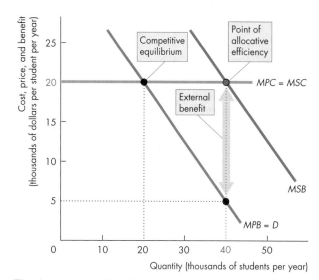

The demand curve for education measures the marginal private benefit to education (*MPB = D*). The curve *MSC* shows the marginal social cost of education—in this example, $20,000 per student per year. If education is provided in a competitive market, tuition is $20,000 a year and 20,000 students will enroll. Education produces an external benefit and adding the external benefit to the marginal private benefit gives marginal social benefit, *MSB.* Allocative efficiency is achieved if the government provides education services on a scale such that marginal social cost equals marginal social benefit. This scale of provision is 40,000 students a year, which is achieved if the government either subsidizes private schools or provides education below cost in public schools. In this example, people pay an annual tuition of $5,000 and the government pays a subsidy of $15,000.

education—when added to the marginal private benefit results in marginal social benefits described by the curve *MSB*. Allocative efficiency occurs when marginal social cost equals marginal social benefit. In the example in Fig. 21.8, this equality occurs when 40,000 students are enrolled. One way of getting 40,000 students to enroll is to subsidize private schools. In the example, a subsidy of $15,000 per student per year paid to the schools does the job. With a subsidy of $15,000 and marginal cost of $20,000, schools earn an economic profit if the annual tuition exceeds $5,000. Competition among the schools would drive the tuition down to $5,000, and at this price, 40,000 students will enroll. So a subsidy can achieve an efficient outcome.

The lessons in this example can be applied to stimulating the rate of increase in the stock of knowledge—research and development. By subsidizing these activities, the government can move the allocation of resources towards a more efficient outcome. The mechanism the government uses for this purpose is a research and development grant. In 1995, through agencies such as the National Sciences and Engineering Council and the Social Sciences and Humanities Research Council of Canada, the government made research and development grants of more than $600 million.

Another way to achieve an efficient amount of education and research and development is through public provision below cost.

Below-Cost Provision

Instead of subsidizing private schools, the government can establish its own schools (public schools) that provide education below cost. And instead of subsidizing research and development in industry and the universities, the government can establish its own research facilities and make discoveries available to others. Let's see how this approach works by returning to the example in Fig. 21.8.

By establishing public schools with places for 40,000 students, the government can supply the efficient quantity of education directly. To ensure that this number of places is taken up, the public schools would charge a tuition, in this example, of $5,000 per student per year. At this price, the number of people who choose to go to school makes the marginal social benefit of education equal to its marginal cost.

We've now looked at two examples of how government action can help market participants take

account of the external benefits deriving from education to achieve an outcome different from that of a private unregulated market. In Canada, governments run their own institutions and sell their services at below cost. But in the United States, governments use both methods of encouraging an efficient quantity of education. They subsidize private schools and universities and they run their own institutions and sell their services at below cost. But in education, the public sector is by far the larger. In research and development, subsidies to the private sector are far larger than the government direct provision.

Patents and Copyrights

Knowledge may well be the only factor of production that does not display *diminishing marginal productivity*. More knowledge (about the right things) makes people more productive. And there seems to be no tendency for the additional productivity from additional knowledge to diminish.

For example, in just 15 years, advances in knowledge about microprocessors have given us a sequence of processor chips that has made our personal computers increasingly powerful. Each advance in knowledge about how to design and manufacture a processor chip has brought apparently ever larger increments in performance and productivity. Similarly, each advance in knowledge about how to design and build an airplane has brought apparently ever larger increments in performance: Orville and Wilbur Wright's "Flyer 1" was a one-seat plane that could hop a farmer's field; the Lockheed Constellation was an airplane that could fly 120 passengers from New York to London, but with two refuelling stops in Newfoundland and Ireland; the latest version of the Boeing 747 can carry 400 people nonstop from Los Angeles to Sydney or New York to Tokyo (flights of 12,000 kilometres that take $13^1/_2$ hours). These examples can be repeated again and again in fields as diverse as agriculture, biogenetics, communications, engineering, entertainment, medicine, and publishing.

A key reason why the stock of knowledge increases without diminishing returns is the sheer number of different techniques that can in principle be tried. Paul Romer explains this fact with an amazing example. Suppose, says Romer,

that to make a finished good, 20 different parts have to be attached to a frame, one at a time. A worker could proceed in numerical order, attaching part one first, then part two....Or the worker could proceed in some other order, starting with part 10, then adding part seven....With 20 parts, a standard (but incredible) calculation shows that there are about 10^{18} different sequences one can use for assembling the final good. This number is larger than the total number of seconds that have elapsed since the big bang created the universe, so we can be confident that in all activities, only a very small fraction of the possible sequences have ever been tried.[2]

Think about all the processes and all the products and all the different bits and pieces that go into each, and you can see that we have only begun to scratch around the edges of what is possible.

Because knowledge is productive and creates external benefits, it is necessary to use public policies to ensure that those who develop new ideas face incentives that encourage an efficient level of effort. The main way of creating the right incentives is to provide the creators of knowledge with property rights in their discoveries—called **intellectual property rights**. The legal device for creating intellectual property rights is the patent or copyright. A **patent** or **copyright** is a government-sanctioned exclusive right granted to the inventor of a good, service, or productive process, to produce, use, and sell the invention for a given number of years. A patent enables the developer of a new idea to prevent, for a limited number of years, others from benefiting freely from an invention. But to obtain the protection of the law, an inventor must make knowledge of the invention public.

Although patents encourage invention and innovation, they do so at an economic cost. While a patent is in place, its holder is a monopoly. And monopoly is another type of market failure. To maximize profit, a monopoly (patent holder) produces the quantity at which marginal cost equals marginal revenue. The monopoly sets the price above marginal

cost and equal to the highest price at which the profit-maximizing quantity can be sold. In this situation, consumers value the good more highly (are willing to pay more for one more unit of it) than its marginal cost. So the quantity of the good available is less than the efficient quantity.

But without a patent, the effort to develop new goods, services, or processes is diminished and the flow of new inventions is slowed. So the efficient outcome is a compromise that balances the benefits of more inventions against the cost of temporary monopoly power in newly invented activities.

R E V I E W

- Knowledge is a good and a factor of production that creates external benefits.
- External benefits arise both from education—passing on existing knowledge to others—and from research and development—creating new knowledge.
- Three devices used by governments to achieve an efficient stock of knowledge are subsidies, below-cost provision, and patents and copyrights.
- Subsidies or below-cost provision can deliver an efficient amount of education.
- Knowledge does not seem to have diminishing returns, so incentives must exist to encourage the development of new ideas.
- Patents and copyrights can stimulate research but they create a temporary monopoly, so the gain from more knowledge must be balanced against the loss from monopoly.

◆ *Reading Between the Lines* on pp. 492–493 looks at one of the issues you've studied in this chapter, that of limiting the pollution of our urban air by automobiles and the pursuit of a clean alternative. Study this item as a current example of how we are trying to cope with an externality.

We've now completed our study of microeconomics. We've learned how all economic problems arise from scarcity. People choose what goods to buy and what factors of production to sell to maximize utility. Firms choose what goods to sell and what factors to buy to maximize profit. People and firms interact in markets. By providing public goods, redistributing income, curbing monopoly power, and coping with externalities, public choice modifies the market outcome.

---

[2] From "Ideas and Things," in *The Future Surveyed*, a supplement to *The Economist*, 11 September 1993, pp. 71–72. The "standard calculation" that Romer refers to is the number of ways of selecting and arranging in order 20 objects from 20 objects—also called the number of permutations of 20 objects 20 at a time. This number is *factorial* 20, or 20! = $20 \times 19 \times 18 \times ... \times 2 \times 1$ = $10^{18.4}$. A standard theory (challenged by observations made by the Hubble Space Telescope in 1994) is that a big bang started the universe 15 billion years, or $10^{17.7}$ seconds, ago. Although $10^{18.4}$ and $10^{17.7}$ look similar, $10^{18.4}$ is *five* times as large as $10^{17.7}$, so if you started trying alternative sequences at the moment of the big bang and took only one second per trial you would still have tried only one-fifth of the possibilities. Amazing?

Policy
WATCH

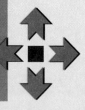

The Costs of Clean Air

Essence of
THE STORY

■ General Motors, Ford, and Chrysler are testing electric vehicles in the United States and all have plans to make electric vehicles for use in Canada.

■ But electric cars and battery packs still cost too much and electric cars only travel around 100 kilometres per battery charge. A recharge takes up to six hours.

■ Electric vehicles work least well in low temperatures and hilly terrains.

■ Mass production will first come in areas such as California and Arizona, where the weather is warm and terrain is flat.

THE DAILY GLEANER, JULY 24, 1996

Canadian drivers ready to test electric cars

BY TONY VAN ALPHEN

TORONTO—Non-polluting electric cars work, but they still need a push and researchers have found that's easier said than done.

In Canada, General Motors is about to roll out the first electric car for testing, but cost, convenience and climate factors have slowed production.

The car and its battery packs still cost too much and motorists can't travel far without a lengthy recharge. Cold weather and hills suck valuable energy.

"We're still some time away from offering an electric vehicle for retail customers," says Karen Holtschneider, a spokeswoman for Ford Motor Co. in Detroit. "Perhaps we can do it in less than five years."

GM is starting mass production of the two-seat EV1 car this fall, but only for four areas in the California and Arizona markets where the weather is warm and terrain is flat.

Ford will start producing the 1998 Ford Ranger EV in the fall of 1998. And Chrysler plans to make the Epic electric minivan in Windsor, Ont., within two years. ...

GM, Ford and Chrysler have started testing electric vehicles with fleet owners through the co-operation of utilities in about a dozen U.S. markets.

Twenty Vancouver drivers will take part in a GM test program until November, travelling up to 80 kilometres a day to work or school in Impact electric vehicles. The drivers' homes will be equipped with charging systems.

The GM program is a co-operative effort with the B.C. government and B.C. Hydro.

Cold weather means the cars need added energy, said Bryan Swift, GM Canada's manager of government relations. Low temperatures increase resistance and drag on the car's body shell.

"All this adds up to a substantial energy drain," he says. "The batteries don't have the capabilities to store a lot of energy. A critical element for acceptance of electric vehicles is the convenience of recharging."

Most electric vehicles now can't travel more than 100 kilometres without a recharge. A full recharge takes up to six hours and facilities exist in only a few areas.

Economic

A N A L Y S I S

■ As incomes have increased, the demand for vehicles has increased, as shown by the shift in the demand curve in Fig. 1 from D_0 to D_1.

■ During the same time that demand has increased, advances in technology have lowered the cost of producing vehicles and supply has increased, as shown by the shift in the supply curve in Fig. 1 from S_0 to S_1.

■ With an increase in both demand and supply, the quantity of vehicles has increased from Q_0 to Q_1 in Fig. 1.

■ This increase in quantity has been enormous. In Canada, the number of vehicles in 1996 was 18 million, compared with 7 million in 1966. In the United States, the number of vehicles in 1996 was 195 million, compared with 94 million in 1966.

■ Quality adjusted, the price of a vehicle has fallen from P_0 to P_1 in Fig. 1.

■ Road vehicles pollute. In 1966, 300 billion litres of gasoline were consumed in Canada and the United States. In 1996, that quantity was 560 billion litres.

■ But our air quality has improved. The reason is we have spent more on limiting emissions of pollutants.

■ Figure 2 shows the marginal social benefit and marginal social cost of clean air. Clean air is costly to produce, as shown by the marginal social cost curve *MSC* in Fig. 2.

■ As incomes have increased, the marginal benefit of clean air, as measured by people's willingness to pay for it, has increased. In Fig. 2, this increase is illustrated by the shift in the marginal social benefit curve from MSB_0 to MSB_1.

■ The quantity of clean air has increased from Q_0 to Q_1 and the marginal cost and benefit have increased from CB_0 to CB_1 in Fig. 2.

■ Electric cars are more costly to produce than conventional cars. So, if we produce more electric cars and fewer conventional cars, the supply curve of cars will shift leftward. The price of a car will rise and the quantity decreases.

■ But can electric vehicles help in the battle to get cleaner air? The answer depends on what happens to the marginal cost of clean air.

■ If the marginal social cost curve shifts downward, to MSC_1, electric cars help but if they shift the marginal social cost curve upward to MSC_2, they hinder the push for cleaner air.

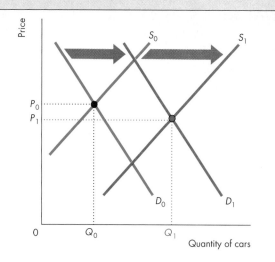

Figure 1 Market for cars

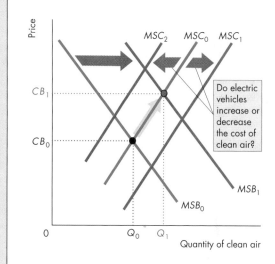

Do electric vehicles increase or decrease the cost of clean air?

Figure 2 Marginal benefit and marginal cost

■ It is not obvious that electric cars will lower the cost of clean air. They are expensive to produce, inconvenient to use, and their batteries must be recharged with electricity that is generated by power stations that themselves pollute.

You're

THE VOTER

■ Would you vote for or against a law that requires car producers to sell, after some specified future date, only cars that don't pollute? Explain in detail how you reach your decision.

S U M M A R Y

Key Points

Externalities   An external cost is the cost of producing a good or service that is not borne by its consumers but by other people. An external benefit is the benefit of consuming a good or service that does not accrue to its consumers but to other people.

The main external costs arise in connection with the environment and are the costs of air, land, and water pollution. The main external benefits arise in education and scientific research. The market economy overproduces goods and services that have external costs and underproduces goods and services that have external benefits. (pp. 477–478)

The Economics of the Environment   The demand for environmental policies has grown because incomes have grown and awareness of the connection between actions and the environment has increased. Air pollution arises from road transportation, electric utilities, and industrial processes. In North America, the trends in most types of air pollution are downward. Water pollution arises from dumping industrial waste, treated sewage, and fertilizers in lakes and rivers and spilling oil and dumping waste in the oceans. Land pollution arises from dumping garbage and toxic products.

Environmental externalities arise when property rights are absent. Sometimes it is possible to overcome an externality by assigning a property right. When property rights cannot be assigned, governments might overcome environmental externalities by using emission charges, marketable permits, or taxes. Marketable permits were used successfully to virtually eliminate lead from our air. Global externalities, such as greenhouse gases and substances that deplete the earth's ozone layer, can only be overcome by international action. Each country acting alone has insufficient incentive to act in the interest of the world as a whole. But there is a great deal of scientific uncertainty and disagreement about the effects of greenhouse gases and ozone depletion, and in the face of this uncertainty, international resolve to act is weak. Also, the world is locked in a type of "prisoners' dilemma" game, in which it is in every country's self-interest to let other countries carry the costs of environmental policies. (pp. 478–488)

The Economics of Knowledge   Knowledge is both a consumer good and a factor of production that creates external benefits. External benefits from education—passing on existing knowledge to others—arise because the basic reading, writing, and number skills equip people to interact and communicate more effectively. External benefits from research—creating new knowledge—arise because once someone has worked out how to do something, others can copy the basic idea. To enable the efficient amount of education and innovation to take place, we make public choices through governments to modify the market outcome. Three devices are available to governments: subsidies, below-cost provision, and patents and copyrights. Subsidies to private schools or the provision of public education below cost can achieve an efficient provision of education. Patents and copyrights create intellectual property rights and increase the incentive to innovate. But they do so by creating a temporary monopoly, the cost of which must be balanced against the benefit of more inventive activity. (pp. 488–491)

Key Figures

Key Terms

R E V I E W   Q U E S T I O N S

1. What are externalities? Give some examples of positive and negative externalities.
2. Why is an external cost a problem?
3. Why does the existence of external costs and external benefits lead to market failure?
4. How can an external benefit pose an economic problem?
5. Why has the demand for a better environment increased?
6. Describe the various types of pollution and identify their sources.
7. What are the main economic activities that cause air pollution?
8. What do property rights have to do with externalities?
9. State the Coase theorem. Under what conditions does the Coase theorem apply?
10. Explain why property rights assigned either to the polluter or the victim of pollution give an efficient amount of pollution if transactions costs are low.

11. What is an emission charge and how does it work?
12. What is a marketable pollution permit and how does it work?
13. How might a tax be used to overcome an external cost?
14. What are the pros and cons of a high, broad-based carbon tax and why don't we have such a tax?
15. Which countries have high pollution rates?
16. Why do some countries have high pollution rates?
17. Is the efficient rate of pollution zero? Explain your answer.
18. What is the global warming dilemma?
19. What are the externalities problems posed by knowledge?
20 Why do we have free primary and secondary education?
21. What is a patent and how does it work?

C R I T I C A L   T H I N K I N G

1. After you have studied *Reading Between the Lines* on pp. 492–493, answer the following questions:
   a. What will be the cost of switching to electric cars?
   b. Who will benefit from such a switch?
   c. Who will lose from such a switch?
   d. What policies could the government adopt to retain the current net benefit of drivers?
2. Good health has a positive externality. Explain why when the government supplies health care at below cost, the health care industry is more allocatively efficient than it would be if health care was supplied privately by the market.
3. Since its beginning 25 years ago, Greenpeace has fought for a cleaner and safer environment. What impact has Greenpeace had on the environment in your province? Has pollution been eliminated? If not, why not?
4. In recent years, many provincial governments increased university tuition fees. What effect will this increase have on the number of univer-

sity graduates in coming years and the allocative efficiency of university education?
5. To reduce the amount of overfishing in New Zealand waters, the New Zealand government introduced private property rights with an allocation of Individual Transferable Quotas (ITQs) in 1986. To check out the results to date of such a policy, go to the Fraser Institute's home page on the World Wide Web (http:\\www.fraserinstitute.ca) and read the article: "ITQs in New Zealand: Bureaucratic Management versus Private Property. The Score after Ten Years."
   a. Would the introduction of private property rights such as the tradeable quotas in New Zealand help replenish Canadian fish stocks? Explain your answer.
   b. Explain why tradeable quotas would be an incentive to stop overfishing.
   c. Who would oppose such a policy? Explain why.

P R O B L E M S

1. A trout farmer and a pesticide maker are located next to each other on the side of a lake. The pesticide maker can dispose of waste by dumping it in the lake or by trucking it to a safe land storage place. The marginal cost of trucking is a constant $100 a tonne. The trout farmer's profit depends on how much waste the pesticide maker dumps in the lake and is as follows:

Quantity of waste (tonnes per week)	Trout farmer's profit (dollars per week)
0	1,000
1	950
2	875
3	775
4	650
5	500
6	325
7	125

a. What is the efficient amount of waste to be dumped in the lake?
b. If the trout farmer owns the lake, how much waste will be dumped and how much will the pesticide maker pay to the farmer for each tonne dumped?
c. If the pesticide maker owns the lake, how much waste will be dumped and how much will the farmer pay to the factory to rent space on the lake?

2. Using the information given in problem 1, suppose that no one owns the lake, and that the government introduces a pollution tax.
a. What is the tax per tonne of waste dumped that will achieve an efficient outcome?
b. Explain the connection between the answer to this problem and the answer to problem 1.

3. Using the information given in problem 1, suppose that no one owns the lake, and that the government issues marketable pollution permits to both the farmer and the factory. They may each dump equal amounts of waste in the lake and the total that may be dumped is the efficient amount.
a. What is the quantity that may be dumped in the lake?

b. What is the market price of a permit? Who buys and who sells?
c. What is the connection between the answer to this problem and the answers to problems 1 and 2?

4. The figure illustrates the marginal private benefit to education. The marginal cost of educating a student is $5,000 a year and is constant.

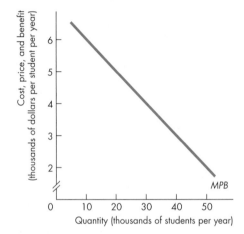

a. With no government involvement in education and if the schools are competitive, how many students are enrolled in school and what is the annual tuition?
b. Suppose the external benefit from education is $2,000 per student year and is constant. If the government provides the efficient amount of education, how many school places does it offer and what is the annual tuition?

5. Canada passed the Environment Act in 1988. To find out how our environment has changed, go to the Government of Canada's World Wide Web site (http://www.aia.gc.ca/ro/doc/launchgc.htm) and select Environment Canada.
a. Use Canada's National Environment Indicators to describe the change in air pollution in our cities and acid rain.
b. Compare the stratospheric ozone level in Canada with that in the world.
c. Has Canada's Environment Act improved our environment?
d. What information that is not on available on this web site do you need to be able to evaluate the economics of the Environment Act?

part 9

The Global Economy

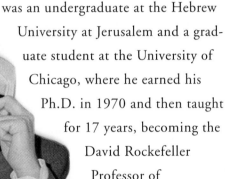

Jacob A. Frenkel, who is Governor of the Bank of Israel, was born in Tel Aviv, in 1943. He was an undergraduate at the Hebrew University at Jerusalem and a graduate student at the University of Chicago, where he earned his Ph.D. in 1970 and then taught for 17 years, becoming the David Rockefeller Professor of International Economics. He left Chicago to become the Economic Counsellor and Director of Research at the International Monetary Fund from 1987–1991.

TALKING WITH Jacob A. Frenkel

Dr. Frenkel is an influential international economist who has made many contributions to improving our understanding of the forces that influence exchange rates, interest rates, and the balance of international payments. Robin Bade and Michael Parkin talked with Jacob Frenkel about his work and about the challenges facing the world economy in the 1990s.

Dr. Frenkel, what drew you into economics?
The choice was rather accidental. When I started my undergraduate studies, I was working polishing diamonds and attended evening classes. I had only four courses to choose from: economics, political science, statistics, and sociology. I chose to study economics and political science and quickly became intrigued by economics, particularly by macroeconomics. As a graduate student at the University of Chicago I was fortunate to have courses in monetary economics and international economics from the giants of the time, including Milton Friedman, Lloyd Metzler, Harry Johnson, and Bob Mundell.

The International Monetary Fund (IMF), where you made an outstanding contribution to research on international economic questions, was established to help manage a world of fixed exchange rates. What was your role in the IMF?
My own entry into the IMF was in the context of participating in the G7 discussions on the interdependent world economy. My initial task was to provide a global perspective on the debate and design of economic policies. During this period, the research department developed a variety of analytical and empirical perspectives on these issues including economic indicators, the role of

the international reserves, and the evolving world.

We recognized that we were gravitating at that time toward a world in which there was no single reserve currency, greater unification within Europe, and with the emergence of a new economic centre in the Pacific. In this period, the exchange system was evolving. Small developing countries with no well-developed capital markets—and later transitional economies—had to make choices of the appropriate exchange rate regimes.

What is the IMF's role in today's world of floating exchange rates?
Today, the IMF has three major roles. The first is its traditional role: It assists developing countries to design stabilization policies, accompanied by structural measures, that enhance the flexibility of the economy. The IMF monitors their economic development and acts as a catalyst for financial assistance.

The second is to provide advice to countries even when they do not borrow from the IMF. This function will increase in importance because in the longer run, private capital markets will provide financial assistance.

The third ties these things together: The IMF interacts with countries within a multilateral setting where the global perspective is taken.

What does the Governor of the Bank of Israel do?
The Governor of the Bank of Israel wears two hats. First, he is in charge of monetary policy and the traditional tasks of the central bank including bank supervision. The central bank in Israel is highly independent. Monetary policy decisions that concern interest rates are made exclusively by the Bank of Israel without any involvement of the government. The Bank of Israel is also responsible for the day-to-day operation of the exchange market.

Second, the governor is the chief economic advisor to the government, which is unique to Israel. In this capacity, he participates in

cabinet meetings that involve economic matters and is involved in the broad range of economic issues that go beyond the narrow scope of monetary policy.

How does your involvement in the broader political arena influence the independence of the Bank?
It requires a very delicate balance between the economic advisor role that calls for proximity to government and the independence necessary for the conduct of monetary policy that calls for distance. I think that each governor finds his own balance. As far as I'm concerned, I have no doubt that monetary policy in Israel is conducted with complete independence and with a focus that is entirely set on proper professional economic consideration.

Israel has had extraordinary economic growth in the past year. To what do you attribute this economic success story?
In 1994, real GDP growth was $6\frac{1}{2}$ percent. This was healthy growth, with the business sector growing at $7\frac{1}{2}$ percent. Each year since 1990, growth has ranged around 6 percent.

A major impetus to economic performance during the first part of this decade has been the influx of immigrants, primarily from the former Soviet Union. They have proven to be a major engine of

> *[Governments] do not have the discipline of profit and loss and the guidance and discipline of shareholders.*

growth. As in all countries, absorbing new immigrants into society and into the work force is not an easy task. However, I think that we have been successful.

Our strategy relies heavily on the private sector to absorb immigrants. Since the beginning of the decade our population has increased by about one-fifth, yet our unemployment rate is now significantly lower than what it was before the start of the mass immigration. This means that our economy is capable of generating more new jobs than new entrants to the labour market. A large percentage of immigrants have gained employment.

I think that our rapid growth is the result of consistent economic policy, coupled with good immigration policies. Every year our exports have increased at a double-digit rate, which is much faster than the growth of GDP. This has happened despite our markets abroad being in recession at the beginning of the decade. In the last two years, we've penetrated into completely new markets, especially in Asia, China, and India.

Can you say more about the content of your economic policy?

First, budget deficit reduction. We have a budget-deficit reduction law, which requires continuous reduction in the budget deficit: Each year the budget deficit must be a smaller percentage of GDP than it was in the preceding year. We are now in the fourth year, and we are on track. I project the budget deficit in 1994 will be about 2 percent of GDP. At the beginning of the decade, it was more than 6 percent.

Second, trade liberalization. We have a free trade agreement with the United States and also a special agreement with the European Union. Vis-à-vis Third World countries, four years ago, we adopted a unilateral multi-year tariff-reduction scheme. Each year we cut our tariffs unilaterally. As we have opened up our economy to international competition, competition at home has increased significantly. The government has committed itself to a trajectory of multi-year tariff reductions. So far, so good.

Third, inflation target. Since the beginning of 1992, we have adopted an inflation target and it has served us very well. Also since 1992, we have adopted an exchange rate regime, which we call a "crawling band." We set the slope of the band to be consistent with our inflation target. At the beginning of the year, we set an inflation target. Then we subtract from it the average inflation rate in our trading partners, and this is the slope of the "crawling band." That is, we set the trajectory for the nominal magnitude of the economy. We are forward looking. We do not change the slope of our "crawling band" according to past inflation but rather according to targeted inflation. All the nominal magnitudes of the economy converge to be consistent with that target.

To summarize, our economic policy is cast in the medium term: multi-year budget deficit reduction, multi-year trade liberalization, and a forward-looking exchange rate regime that is consistent with our long-term inflation target.

If we think of the world economy as an economic laboratory in which experiments are being conducted, what, for you, are the clearest lessons for economic policy that come from the experiments currently being undertaken?

Lesson No. 1: To control inflation, a country must have an independent central bank. If you divide countries into those with low inflation and high inflation, or rising and falling inflation, I think that you can see the degree of the independence of the central banks. The degree of independence reflects the reality of the political system, which typically has a shorter time horizon than the economic system requires. Therefore, society must protect itelf from that reality by having an independent central bank.

Lesson No. 2: A country can't have sustainable growth without engaging in the world trading system. The interaction of trade policies, structural policies that ensure flexibility and nondistortion, and economic stability is becoming more important and apparent. If you look at the real cost of reform in Eastern Europe and transformation in Central Europe, you realize that a very large fraction of that cost comes from the collapse of their trading systems. Put the other way around, I think it is suggestive of the cure. For me, the GATT agreement is much more than just the dismantling of tariffs; rather it's an extraordinary victory of philosophy that in the new world, no country can afford to be a small island at the side of the larger economic world. A small country's only chance is to become an integral part of that world, and the only way to survive as an integral part of that world is to have a competitive, efficient economic system.

Lesson No. 3: The private sector stands no chance in competing against government. Governments are guided by different considerations. They do not have the discipline of profit and loss and the guidance and discipline of shareholders. Therefore, in the long term, large governments lose and in the short term, the private sector loses. It is in the best interest of the economy to get the size of the public sector as small as you can.

Lesson No. 4: The future is much closer to the present than many politicians think. Which means that if a country is running large budget deficits that are not sustainable, the marketplace will not be patient. The market extrapolates the consequences into the future and translates them immediately into the present.

Suppose a student wants to pursue a career in economics with an international policy orientation. What is the best combination of undergraduate courses to pursue?

Courses that build analytical skills are useful. In addition to economics, take a range of courses including philosophy, math, history, and political science. Seek out professors and peers who will challenge and inspire you to excel. It's also important to remain attentive to the economic and political changes in the world by reading, travelling, and exposing yourself to diverse cultures. Know who the policy makers are and what impact their decisions have on the world.

Chapter

37

Trading with the World

After studying
this chapter,
you will be
able to:

- Describe the trends and patterns in international trade

- Explain comparative advantage and why all countries can gain from international trade

- Explain how economies of scale and diversity of taste lead to gains from trade

- Explain why trade restrictions reduce the volume of imports and exports and reduce our consumption possibilities

- Explain the arguments used to justify trade restrictions and show how they are flawed

- Describe the Canada–United States Free Trade Agreement and explain its influence on the volume of trade

Silk Routes and Sucking Sounds

Since ancient times, people have striven to expand their trading as far as technology allowed. Marco Polo opened up the silk route between Europe and China in the thirteenth century. Today, container ships laden with cars and machines, and Boeing 747s stuffed with farm-fresh foods ply sea and air routes, carrying billions of dollars worth of goods. Why do people go to such great lengths to trade with those in other nations? ◆ Low-wage Mexico has entered into a free trade agreement with high-wage Canada and the United States—the North American Free Trade Agreement or NAFTA. According to Texas billionaire Ross Perot, this agreement will cause a "giant sucking sound" as jobs are transferred from Canada and the United States to Mexico. Is Ross Perot right? How can Canada compete with a country that pays its workers a fraction of our wages? Are there any industries in which we have an advantage? ◆ Tariffs —taxes on goods imported from other countries—have been a source of government revenue in Canada since before Confederation and were the centrepiece of Sir John A. Macdonald's national economic policy of the 1870s. After World War II, a process of trade liberalization brought about the creation of the General Agreement on Tariffs and Trade (GATT) and a gradual reduction of tariffs. What are the effects of tariffs on international trade? Why don't we have completely unrestricted international trade?

◈ In this chapter, we're going to learn about international trade. We'll discover how *all* nations can gain by specializing in producing the goods and services at which they have a comparative advantage and trading with other countries. We'll discover that all countries can compete, no matter how high their wages. We'll also explain why, despite the fact that international trade brings benefits to all, countries restrict trade.

Patterns and Trends in International Trade

THE GOODS AND SERVICES THAT WE BUY FROM people in other countries are called **imports**. The goods and services that we sell to people in other countries are called **exports**. What are the most important things that we import and export? Most people would probably guess that a resource-rich nation such as Canada imports manufactured goods and exports raw materials. While that is one feature of Canadian international trade, it is not its most important feature. The vast bulk of our exports *and* imports are manufactured goods. We sell foreigners automobiles, software, aircraft, chemicals, and electronic equipment, and we buy televisions, VCRs, blue jeans, and T-shirts from them. Also, we are a major exporter of raw materials and lumber products. We also import and export a huge volume of services. Let's look at Canada's international trade in a recent year.

Canada's International Trade

The **balance of trade** is the value of exports minus the value of imports. If the value of exports exceeds the value of imports, then the balance of trade is positive and Canada is a **net exporter**. If the value of imports exceeds the value of exports, then the balance of trade is negative and Canada is a **net importer**. Canada's balance of trade fluctuates but is usually positive.

Trade in Goods   Figure 37.1 highlights some of the major items of Canada's imports and exports of goods. By far the largest item in Canada's international trade is motor vehicles. Most of this trade crosses the border with the United States and is the result of an agreement, known as the Auto Pact, between the two countries. Automobiles and automobile parts are permitted to cross the border without any restriction and, in return for this freedom of movement, automobile manufacturers agree to undertake a sizeable amount of

---

FIGURE   37.1

Canadian Exports and Imports: 1995

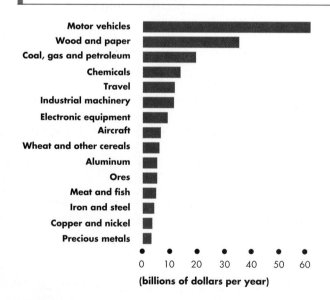

(a) Exports

Canada exports more motor vehicles than any other individual category of goods and services. Wood and paper, coal, gas and petroleum, chemicals, and travel are also major exports.

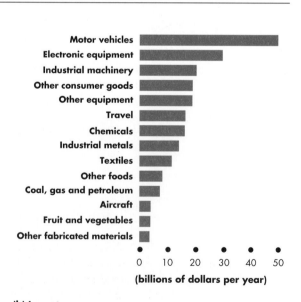

(b) Imports

Motor vehicles, electronic equipment, industrial machinery, other consumer goods and equipment, and travel are major imports.

Source: Statistics Canada, *StatCan: CANSIM Disc,* March 1996.

their manufacturing in Canada. Our second biggest export is wood and paper—the products of the forestry industry.

Motor vehicles are also our largest import. Other big import items are electronic equipment, industrial machinery, other consumer goods, and other equipment.

Trade in Services   One-fifth of Canada's international trade is not in goods but in services. You might be wondering how a country can "export" and "import" services. Let's look at some examples.

Suppose that you decided to vacation in France, travelling there on an Air France flight from Toronto. What you buy from Air France is not a good, but a transportation service. Although the concept might sound odd at first, in economic terms you are importing that service from France. The money you spend in France on hotel bills, restaurant meals, and other things are also classified as the import of services. Similarly, the vacation taken by a French student in Canada counts as an export of services to France. Canadians travel abroad a great deal and more so than foreigners travel to Canada. Travel is Canada's sixth largest import item.

When we import TV sets from South Korea, the owner of the ship that carries those TV sets might be Greek and the company that insures the cargo might be British. The payments that we make for the transportation and insurance to the Greek and British companies are also payments for the import of services. Similarly, when a Canadian shipping line transports newsprint to Tokyo, the transportation cost is an export of a service to Japan. Commercial services and transportation services are Canada's next largest imported services.

Geographical Patterns

Canada has trading links with almost every part of the world. Figure 37.2 shows the scale of these links and the way they have grown since 1975. In 1975, our trade was primarily with the United States. The United Kingdom, other countries in the European Union, Japan, and other OECD countries were smaller trading partners. By 1995, our trade with the United States more than doubled, trade with Europe remained steady, and trade with Japan increased. Our trade with the rest of the world also increased. Mexico is included in "Other OECD countries"

FIGURE   37.2

The Geographical Pattern of Canadian International Trade

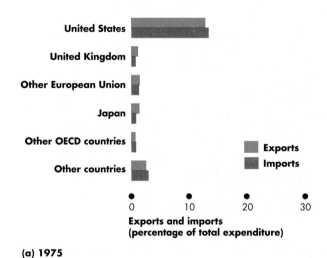

(a) 1975

(b) 1995

In 1975, Canada's largest trading partners were the United States, the United Kingdom, and the other countries of the European Union. By 1995, trade with the United States as a percentage of total expenditure had more than doubled. Trade with Japan and other countries as a percentage of total expenditure increased.

Source: Statistics Canada, *StatCan: CANSIM Disc,* March, 1996.

along with Australia and New Zealand. Asian countries such as China, Hong Kong, Singapore, South Korea, and Taiwan are included in "Other countries." In 1975, Canada had a small trade deficit with the United States but by 1995, Canada had a large trade surplus. This trade surplus is largely the result of the North American Free Trade Agreement (NAFTA) that came into effect in 1994.

Trends in Trade

International trade has become an increasingly important part of our economic life. In 1975, we exported 20 percent of total output and imported 20 percent of the goods and services that we consumed ourselves. Over the years since then, these percentages have steadily increased and today they are almost double their levels of 1975.

On the export side, all the major commodity categories have shared in the increased volume of international trade. Motor vehicles have become the largest component of exports, and forestry products (wood, paper, and pulp) are now the second largest component.

But there have been dramatic changes in the composition of imports. Food and raw material imports have declined steadily. Imports of fuel increased dramatically in the 1970s but declined in the 1980s. Imports of machinery of all kinds, after being a fairly stable percentage of total imports until the middle 1980s, now approach 50 percent of total imports.

Figure 37.3 shows Canada's overall *balance of trade* (of goods and services) since 1970. In the period 1970 to 1988, the balance was usually positive—Canada was a net exporter. But in the years immediately following the huge increase in world oil prices in the mid-1970s, the increased cost of imported oil temporarily threw our balance of trade into a deficit. From 1989 to 1993, Canada was a net importer and the excess of imports over exports (negative balance of trade) increased from 1989 to 1991 and then decreased. Canada became a net exporter again in 1994.

Balance of Trade and International Borrowing

When people buy more than they sell, they have to finance the difference by borrowing or by selling

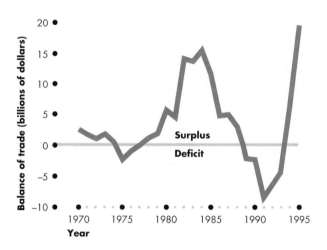

FIGURE 37.3
Canada's Balance of Trade

Canada's balance of trade in goods and services with the rest of the world fluctuates but is usually positive—we are a net exporter. We had a deficit in the mid-1970s and from 1989 to 1993, but in 1994 we returned to a surplus.

Source: Statistics Canada, *StatCan: CANSIM Disc,* March 1996.

assets. When they sell more than they buy, they can use the surplus to make loans to others or to buy assets. This simple principle that governs the income and expenditure and borrowing and lending of individuals and firms is also a feature of our balance of trade. If we import more than we export, we have to finance the difference by borrowing from foreigners or by selling our assets to them. When we export more than we import, we make loans to foreigners or buy their assets to enable them to buy goods in excess of the value of the goods they have sold to us.

This chapter does *not* cover the factors that determine the balance of trade and the scale of international borrowing and lending that finance that balance. It is concerned with understanding the volume, pattern, and directions of international trade rather than its balance. So that we can keep our focus on these topics, we'll build a model in which there is no international borrowing and lending—just international trade in goods and services. Because there is no international borrowing or lending, the trade balance must be zero. We'll find that we are able to understand what determines the volume, pattern, and direction of international trade and also establish its benefits and the costs of trade restrictions within this framework. This model can be expanded to include international borrowing and lending, but this extension does not change the conclusions that we'll reach here about the factors that determine the volume, pattern, directions, and benefits of international trade.

Let's now begin to study those factors.

Opportunity Cost and Comparative Advantage

LET'S APPLY THE LESSONS THAT WE LEARNED IN Chapter 3 about the gains from trade between Mark and Marjorie to the trade between nations. We'll begin by recalling how we can use the production possibility frontier to measure opportunity cost.

Opportunity Cost in Farmland

Farmland (a fictitious country) can produce grain and cars at any point inside or along the production possibility frontier shown in Fig. 37.4. (We're holding constant the output of all the other goods that Farmland produces.) The Farmers (the people of Farmland) are consuming all the grain and cars that they produce and they are operating at point *a* in the figure. That is, Farmland is producing and consuming 15 million tonnes of grain and 8 million cars each year. What is the opportunity cost of a car in Farmland?

We can answer that question by calculating the slope of the production possibility frontier at point *a*. The magnitude of the slope of the frontier measures the opportunity cost of one good in terms of the other. To measure the slope of the frontier at point *a*, place a straight line tangential to the frontier at point *a* and calculate the slope of that straight line. Recall that the formula for the slope of a line is the change in the value of the variable measured on the *y*-axis divided by the change in the value of the variable measured on the *x*-axis as we move along the line. Here, the variable measured on the *y*-axis is millions of tonnes of grain and the variable measured on the *x*-axis is millions of cars. So the slope is the change in

FIGURE 37.4

Opportunity Cost in Farmland

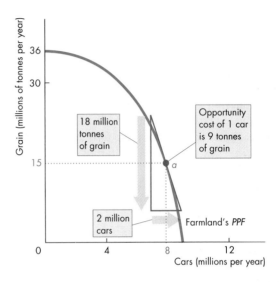

Farmland produces and consumes 15 million tonnes of grain and 8 million cars a year. That is, it produces and consumes at point *a* on its production possibility frontier. Opportunity cost is equal to the magnitude of the slope of the production possibility frontier. The red triangle tells us that at point *a*, 18 million tonnes of grain must be forgone to get 2 million cars. That is, at point *a*, 2 million cars cost 18 million tonnes of grain. Equivalently, 1 car costs 9 tonnes of grain or 9 tonnes of grain cost 1 car.

the number of tonnes of grain divided by the change in the number of cars.

As you can see from the red triangle at point *a* in the figure, if the number of cars produced increases by 2 million, grain production decreases by 18 million tonnes. Therefore the magnitude of the slope is 18 million divided by 2 million, which equals 9. To get one more car, the people of Farmland must give up 9 tonnes of grain. Thus the opportunity cost of 1 car is 9 tonnes of grain. Equivalently, 9 tonnes of grain cost 1 car. For the people of Farmland, these opportunity costs are the prices they face. The price of a car is 9 tonnes of grain, and the price of 9 tonnes of grain is 1 car.

Opportunity Cost in Mobilia

Now consider the production possibility frontier in Mobilia (another fictitious country and the only other country in our model world). Figure 37.5 illustrates its production possibility frontier. Like the Farmers, the Mobilians consume all the grain and cars that they produce. Mobilia consumes 18 million tonnes of grain a year and 4 million cars, at point a'.

Let's calculate the opportunity costs in Mobilia. At point a', the opportunity cost of a car is equal to the magnitude of the slope of the red line tangential to the production possibility frontier (*PPF*). You can see from the red triangle that the magnitude of the slope of Mobilia's production possibility frontier is 6 million tonnes of grain divided by 6 million cars, which equals 1 tonne of grain per car. To get one more car, the people of Mobilia must give up 1 tonne of grain. Thus the opportunity cost of 1 car is 1 tonne of grain, or, equivalently, the opportunity cost of 1 tonne of grain is 1 car. These are the prices faced in Mobilia.

Comparative Advantage

Cars are cheaper in Mobilia than in Farmland. One car costs 9 tonnes of grain in Farmland but only 1 tonne of grain in Mobilia. But grain is cheaper in Farmland than in Mobilia—9 tonnes of grain cost only 1 car in Farmland while that same amount of grain costs 9 cars in Mobilia.

Mobilia has a comparative advantage in car production. Farmland has a comparative advantage in grain production. A country has a **comparative advantage** in producing a good if it can produce that good at a lower opportunity cost than any other country. Let's see how opportunity cost differences and comparative advantage generate gains from international trade.

Opportunity Cost in Mobilia

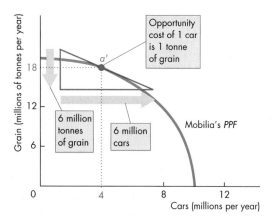

Mobilia produces and consumes 18 million tonnes of grain and 4 million cars a year. That is, it produces and consumes at point a' on its production possibility frontier. Opportunity cost is equal to the magnitude of the slope of the production possibility frontier. The red triangle tells us that at point a', 6 million tonnes of grain must be forgone to get 6 million cars. That is, at point a', 6 million cars cost 6 million tonnes of grain. Equivalently, 1 car costs 1 tonne of grain or 1 tonne of grain costs 1 car.

Gains from Trade

IF MOBILIA BOUGHT GRAIN FOR WHAT IT COSTS Farmland to produce it, then Mobilia could buy 9 tonnes of grain for 1 car. That cost is much lower than the cost of growing grain in Mobilia, where it costs 9 cars to produce 9 tonnes of grain. If the Mobilians can buy grain at the low Farmland price, they will reap some gains.

If the Farmers can buy cars for what it costs Mobilia to produce them, they will be able to obtain a car for 1 tonne of grain. Because it costs 9 tonnes of grain to produce a car in Farmland, the Farmers would gain from such an opportunity.

In this situation, it makes sense for Mobilians to buy their grain from Farmers and for Farmers to buy their cars from Mobilians. Let's see how such profitable international trade comes about.

Reaping the Gains from Trade

We've seen that the Farmers would like to buy their cars from the Mobilians and that the Mobilians would like to buy their grain from the Farmers. Let's see how the two groups do business with each other, concentrating attention on the international market for cars.

Figure 37.6 illustrates such a market. The quantity of cars *traded internationally* is measured on the *x*-axis. On the *y*-axis we measure the price of a car. This price is expressed as the number of tonnes of grain that a car costs—the opportunity cost of a car. If no international trade takes place, the price of a car in Farmland is 9 tonnes of grain, indicated by point *a* in the figure. Again, if no trade takes place, the price of a car in Mobilia is 1 tonne of grain, indicated by point *a'* in the figure. The no-trade points *a* and *a'* in

Fig. 37.6 correspond to the points identified by those same letters in Figs. 37.4 and 37.5. The lower the price of a car (in terms of grain), the greater is the quantity of cars that the Farmers are willing to import from the Mobilians. This fact is illustrated in the downward-sloping curve, which shows Farmland's import demand for cars.

The Mobilians respond in the opposite direction. The higher the price of cars (in terms of tonnes of grain), the greater is the quantity of cars that Mobilians are willing to export to Farmers. This fact is reflected in Mobilia's export supply of cars—the upward-sloping line in Fig. 37.6.

The international market in cars determines the equilibrium price and quantity traded. This equilibrium occurs where the import demand curve intersects the export supply curve. In this case, the equilibrium price of a car is 3 tonnes of grain. Four million cars a year are exported by Mobilia and imported by Farmland. Notice that the price at which cars are traded is lower than the initial price in Farmland but higher than the initial price in Mobilia.

FIGURE 37.6

International Trade in Cars

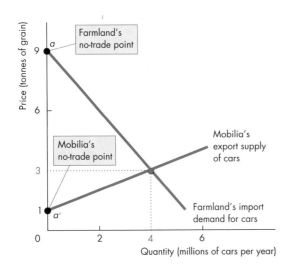

As the price of a car decreases, the quantity of imports demanded by Farmland increases—Farmland's import demand curve for cars is downward sloping. As the price of a car increases, the quantity of cars supplied by Mobilia for export increases—Mobilia's export supply curve of cars is upward sloping. With no international trade, the price of a car is 9 tonnes of grain in Farmland (point *a*) and 1 tonne of grain in Mobilia (point *a'*).

With free international trade, the price of a car is determined where the export supply curve intersects the import demand curve—at a price of 3 tonnes of grain. At that price, 4 million cars a year are imported by Farmland and exported by Mobilia. The value of grain exported by Farmland and imported by Mobilia is 12 million tonnes a year, the quantity required to pay for the cars imported.

Balanced Trade

Notice that the number of cars exported by Mobilia—4 million a year—is exactly equal to the number of cars imported by Farmland. How does Farmland pay for its cars? By exporting grain. How much grain does Farmland export? You can find the answer by noticing that Farmland has to pay 3 tonnes of grain for 1 car. So for 4 million cars, Farmland has to pay 12 million tonnes of grain. Thus Farmland's exports of grain are 12 million tonnes a year. Mobilia imports this same quantity of grain.

Mobilia is exchanging 4 million cars for 12 million tonnes of grain each year and Farmland is doing the opposite, exchanging 12 million tonnes of grain for 4 million cars. Trade is balanced between these two countries. The value received from exports equals the value paid for imports.

Changes in Production and Consumption

We've seen that international trade makes it possible for Farmers to buy cars at a lower price than they can produce them for themselves. Equivalently, Farmers can sell their grain for a higher price. International trade also enables Mobilians to sell their cars for a higher price. Equivalently, Mobilians can buy grain for a lower price. Thus everybody gains. How is it possible for *everyone* to gain? What are the changes in production and consumption that accompany these gains?

An economy that does not trade with other economies has identical production and consumption possibilities. Without trade, the economy can only consume what it produces. But with international trade, an economy can consume different quantities of goods from those that it produces. The production possibility frontier describes the limit of what a country can produce but it does not describe the limits to what it can consume. Figure 37.7 will help you to see the distinction between production possibilities and consumption possibilities when a country trades with other countries.

First of all, notice that the figure has two parts: part (a) for Farmland and part (b) for Mobilia. The production possibility frontiers that you saw in Figs. 37.4 and 37.5 are reproduced here. The slopes of the two black lines represent the opportunity costs in the two countries when there is no international trade. Farmland produces and consumes at point *a*, and Mobilia produces and consumes at *a'*. Cars cost 9 tonnes of grain in Farmland and 1 tonne of grain in Mobilia.

Consumption Possibilities The red line in each part of Fig. 37.7 shows the country's consumption possibilities with international trade. These two red lines have the same slope, and the magnitude of that slope is the opportunity cost of a car in terms of grain on the world market—3 tonnes per car. The *slope* of the consumption possibilities line is common to both countries because its magnitude equals the *world* price. But the position of a country's consumption possibilities line depends on the country's production possibilities. A country cannot produce outside its production possibility frontier so its consumption possibility line touches its production possibility frontier. Thus Farmland could choose to consume at point *b* with no international trade or at any point on its red consumption possibilities line with international trade.

Free Trade Equilibrium With international trade, the producers of cars in Mobilia can get a higher price for their output. As a result, they increase the quantity of car production. At the same time, grain

producers in Mobilia are getting a lower price for their grain and so they reduce production. Producers in Mobilia adjust their output by moving along their production possibility frontier until the opportunity cost in Mobilia equals world price (the opportunity cost in the world market). This situation arises when Mobilia is producing at point *b'* in Fig. 37.7(b).

But the Mobilians do not consume at point *b'*. That is, they do not increase their consumption of cars and decrease their consumption of grain. Instead, they sell some of their car production to Farmland in exchange for some of Farmland's grain. They trade internationally. But to see how that works out, we first need to check in with Farmland to see what's happening there.

In Farmland, producers of cars now get a lower price and producers of grain get a higher price. As a consequence, producers in Farmland decrease car production and increase grain production. They adjust their outputs by moving along the production possibility frontier until the opportunity cost of a car in terms of grain equals the world price (the opportunity cost on the world market). They move to point *b*, in part (a). But the Farmers do not consume at point *b*. Instead, they exchange some of their additional grain production for the now cheaper cars from Mobilia.

The figure shows us the quantities consumed in the two countries. We saw in Fig. 37.6 that Mobilia exports 4 million cars a year and Farmland imports those cars. We also saw that Farmland exports 12 million tonnes of grain a year and Mobilia imports that grain. Thus Farmland's consumption of grain is 12 million tonnes a year less than it produces and its consumption of cars is 4 million a year more than it produces. Farmland consumes at point *c* in Fig. 37.7(a).

Similarly, we know that Mobilia consumes 12 million tonnes of grain more than it produces and 4 million cars fewer than it produces. Thus Mobilia consumes at *c'* in Fig. 37.7(b).

Calculating the Gains from Trade You can now literally see the gains from trade for Farmland and Mobilia in Fig. 37.7. Without trade, Farmers produce and consume at *a* (part a)—a point on Farmland's production possibility frontier. With international trade, Farmers consume at point *c* in part (a)—a point *outside* the production possibility frontier. At point *c*, Farmers are consuming 3 million tonnes of grain a year and 1 million cars a year more

FIGURE **37.7**

Expanding Consumption Possibilities

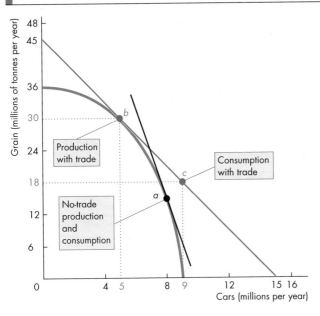

(a) Farmland

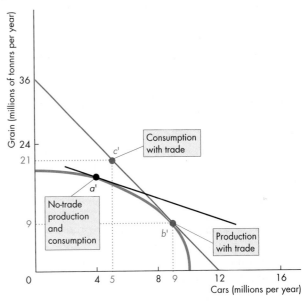

(b) Mobilia

With no international trade, the Farmers produce and consume at point *a* and the opportunity cost of a car is 9 tonnes of grain (the slope of the black line in part a). Also, with no international trade, the Mobilians produce and consume at point *a'* and the opportunity cost of 1 tonne of grain is 1 car (the slope of the black line in part b).

Goods can be traded internationally at a price of 3 tonnes of grain for 1 car along the red line in each part of the figure. In part (a), Farmland decreases its production of cars and increases its production of grain, moving from *a* to *b*. It

exports grain and imports cars, and it consumes at point *c*. The Farmers have more of both cars and grain than they would if they produced all their own consumption goods—at point *a*.

In part (b), Mobilia increases car production and decreases grain production, moving from *a'* to *b'*. Mobilia exports cars and imports grain, and it consumes at point *c'*. The Mobilians have more of both cars and grain than they would if they produced all their own consumption goods—at point *a'*.

than before. These increases in consumption of both cars and grain, beyond the limits of the production possibility frontier, are the gains from international trade for Farmland.

Mobilians also gain. Without trade, they consume at point *a'* in part (b)—a point on Mobilia's production possibility frontier. With international trade, they consume at point *c'*—a point outside the production possibility frontier. With international trade, Mobilia consumes 3 million tonnes of grain a year and 1 million cars a year more than without trade. These are the gains from international trade for Mobilia.

Gains for All

In popular discussions about international trade, we hear about the need for a "level playing field" and other measures to protect people from foreign competition. International trade seems like a type of contest in which there are winners and losers. But the trade between the Farmers and the Mobilians that you've just studied does not create winners and losers. Everyone wins. Sellers add the net demand of foreigners to their domestic demand, and so their market expands. Buyers are faced with domestic supply plus net foreign supply and so have a larger total supply available to them. As you know, the price rises when demand increases and falls when supply increases. So the increased demand (from foreigners) for exports increases their price and the increased supply (from foreigners) of imports decreases their price. Gains in one country do not bring losses in another. Everyone, in this example, gains from international trade.

Absolute Advantage

Suppose that in Mobilia, fewer workers are needed to produce any given output of either grain or cars than in Farmland—productivity is higher in Mobilia than in Farmland. In this situation, Mobilia has an absolute advantage over Farmland. A country has an **absolute advantage** in all goods if it has greater productivity than another country in the production of all goods. With an absolute advantage, can't Mobilia outsell Farmland in the markets for both cars and grain? Why, if Mobilia has greater productivity than Farmland, does it pay Mobilia to buy *anything* from Farmland?

The answer is that the cost of production in terms of the factors of production employed is irrelevant for determining the gains from trade. It does not matter how many resources are required to produce a tonne of grain or a car. What matters is how many cars must be given up to produce an additional tonne of grain or how much grain must be given up to produce an additional car. That is, what matters is the opportunity cost of one good in terms of the other good. (For a further explanation of why absolute advantage does not influence the gains from trade, see Chapter 3, pp. 55–56.)

Mobilia might have an absolute advantage in the production of all goods, but it cannot have a comparative advantage in the production of all goods. The statement that the opportunity cost of a car in Mobilia is less than that in Farmland is identical to the statement that the opportunity cost of grain is greater in Mobilia than in Farmland. Thus *whenever opportunity costs diverge, everyone has a comparative advantage in something.* All countries can potentially gain from international trade.

This lesson has powerful implications for the world economy today. It means that countries like Canada that have high productivity can gain from trade with countries that have low productivity, like Mexico.

The story of the discovery of the logic of the gains from international trade is presented in *Economics in History* on pp. 930–931.

REVIEW

■ When countries have divergent opportunity costs, they can gain from international trade.

■ Each country can buy some goods and services from another country at a lower opportunity cost than it can produce them for itself.

■ Gains arise when each country increases its production of those goods and services in which it has a comparative advantage (goods and services that it can produce at an opportunity cost that is lower than that of other countries) and trades some of its production for that of other countries.

■ All countries gain from international trade. Everyone has a comparative advantage at something.

Gains from Trade in Reality

THE GAINS FROM TRADE THAT WE HAVE JUST studied between Farmland and Mobilia in grain and cars occur in a model economy—in a world economy that we have imagined. But these same phenomena occur every day in the real global economy.

Comparative Advantage in the Global Economy

We buy cars made in Japan, and Canadian producers of grain and lumber sell large amounts of their output to Japanese households and firms. We buy airplanes and vegetables from the U.S. producers and sell natural gas and forest products to Americans in return. We buy shirts and fashion goods from the people of Hong Kong and sell them machinery in return. We buy TV sets and VCRs from South Korea and Taiwan and sell them financial and other services as well as manufactured goods in return. We make some kinds of manufactured goods and Europeans and the Japanese make other kinds, and we exchange one type of manufactured good for another.

These are all examples of international trade generated by comparative advantage, just like the international trade between Farmland and Mobilia in our model economy. All international trade arises from comparative advantage, even when it is trade in similar goods such as cars and machines. At first thought, it seems puzzling that countries exchange manufactured goods. Why doesn't each developed country produce all the manufactured goods its citizens want to buy? Let's look a bit more closely at this question.

Trade in Similar Goods

Why does it make sense for Canada to produce automobiles for export and at the same time to import large quantities of them from the United States, Japan, Korea, and Western Europe? Wouldn't it make more sense to produce all the cars that we buy here in Canada? After all, we have access to the best technology available for producing cars. Autoworkers in Canada are surely as productive as their fellow workers in the United States, Western Europe, and the Pacific countries. Capital equipment, production lines, robots, and the like used in the manufacture of cars are as available to Canadian car producers as they are to any others. This line of reasoning leaves a puzzle concerning the sources of international exchange of similar commodities produced by similar people using similar equipment. Why does it happen? Why does Canada have a comparative advantage in some types of cars and the United States, Japan, and Europe in others?

Diversity of Taste The first part of the answer to the puzzle is that people have a tremendous diversity of taste. Let's stick with the example of cars. Some people prefer a sports car, some prefer a limousine, some a regular, full-size car, and some prefer a mini-van. In addition to size and type of car, there are many other dimensions in which cars vary. Some have low fuel consumption, some have high performance, some are spacious and comfortable, some have a large trunk, some have four-wheel drive, some have front-wheel drive, some have manual transmission, some have automatic transmission, some are durable, some are flashy, some have a radiator grill that looks like a Greek temple, others look like a wedge. People's preferences across these many dimensions vary.

The tremendous diversity in tastes for cars means that people would be dissatisfied if they were forced to consume from a limited range of standardized cars. People value variety and are willing to pay for it in the marketplace.

Economies of Scale The second part of the answer to the puzzle is economies of scale. *Economies of scale* are the tendency, present in many production processes, for the average cost of production to be lower, the larger the scale of production. In such situations, larger and larger production runs lead to ever lower average production costs. Many manufactured goods, including cars, experience economies of scale. For example, if a car producer makes only a few hundred (or perhaps a few thousand) cars of a particular type and design, the producer must use production techniques that are much more labour-intensive and much less automated than those employed to make hundreds of thousands of cars in a particular model. With short production runs and labour-intensive production techniques, costs are high. With very large production runs and automated assembly lines, production costs are much lower. But to obtain lower costs, the automated assembly lines have to produce a large number of cars.

It is the combination of diversity of taste and economies of scale that produces comparative advantages and generates such a large amount of international trade in similar commodities. If every car bought in Canada today was made in Canada—no cars are imported—and if the present range of diversity and variety was available, production runs would be remarkably short. Car producers would not be able to reap economies of scale.

But with international trade, each manufacturer of cars has the whole world market to serve. Each producer can specialize in a limited range of products and then sell its output to the entire world market. This arrangement enables large production runs on the most popular cars and feasible production runs even on the most customized cars demanded by only a handful of people in each country.

The situation in the market for cars is also present in many other industries, especially those producing specialized equipment and parts. For example, Canada exports illustrator software but imports memory chips, exports mainframe computers but imports PCs, exports telecommunications equipment but imports VCRs. Thus international exchange of similar but slightly differentiated manufactured products is a highly profitable activity.

This type of trade can be understood with exactly the same model of international trade that we studied earlier. Although we normally think of cars as a single commodity, we have to think of sports cars and sedans and so on as different goods. Different countries, by specializing in a few of these "goods," are able to enjoy economies of scale and, therefore, a comparative advantage in their production.

You can see that comparative advantage and international trade bring gains regardless of the goods being traded. When the rich countries of the European Union, Japan, and the United States import raw materials from the Third World and from Australia and Canada, the rich importing countries gain and so do the exporting countries. When we buy cheap TV sets, VCRs, shirts, and other goods from low-wage countries, both we and the exporters gain from the trade. It's true that if we increase our imports of cars and produce fewer cars ourselves, jobs in our car industry disappear. But jobs in other industries, industries in which we have a comparative advantage, expand. After the adjustment is completed, people whose jobs have been lost find employment in the expanding industries and can buy goods produced in other countries at even lower prices than those at which they were available before. The gains from international trade are not necessarily gains for some at the expense of losses for others.

But changes in comparative advantage that lead to changes in international trade patterns can take a long time to adjust to. For example, the increase in automobile imports and the corresponding relative decline in domestic car production have not brought increased wealth for displaced autoworkers. Good new jobs take time to find and often people go through a period of prolonged search putting up with inferior jobs and lower wages than they had before. Thus only in the long run does everyone potentially gain from international specialization and trade. Short-run adjustment costs that can be large and relatively prolonged are borne by the people who have lost their comparative advantage. Some of the people who lose their jobs might be too old for it to be worth their while making the move to another region of the country or industry, and so they never share in the gains.

Partly because of the costs of adjustment to changing international trade patterns, but partly also for other reasons, governments intervene in international trade, restricting its volume. Let's examine what happens when governments restrict internation-

al trade. We'll see that free trade brings the greatest possible benefits. We'll also see why, in spite of the benefits of free trade, governments sometimes restrict trade.

Trade Restrictions

GOVERNMENTS RESTRICT INTERNATIONAL TRADE in order to protect domestic industries from foreign competition. The restriction of international trade is called **protectionism**. There are two main protectionist methods employed by governments:

1. Tariffs
2. Nontariff barriers

A **tariff** is a tax that is imposed by the importing country when an imported good crosses its international boundary. A **nontariff barrier** is any action other than a tariff that restricts international trade. Examples of nontariff barriers are quantitative restrictions and licensing regulations that limit imports. We'll consider nontariff barriers in more detail below. First, let's look at tariffs.

The History of Tariffs

The Canadian economy has always been protected by a tariff. Figure 37.8 illustrates the history of that tariff, from Confederation to 1995. The figure shows tariffs as a percentage of total imports—the average tariff rate. As you can see, the average tariff rate climbed from the early 1870s to exceed 20 percent by the 1890s. The rate fluctuated but then steadily declined through the 1930s. After World War II, there was a stronger trend decline in tariff rates.

The reduction in tariffs since World War II followed the establishment of the General Agreement on Tariffs and Trade (GATT). The **General Agreement on Tariffs and Trade** is an international agreement designed to limit government intervention to restrict international trade. It was negotiated immediately following World War II and was signed in October 1947. Its goal is to liberalize trading activity and to provide an organization to administer more liberal trading arrangements. GATT has a small bureaucracy located in Geneva, Switzerland.

Since the formation of GATT, several rounds of negotiations have taken place that have resulted in

FIGURE 37.8

Canadian Tariffs: 1860–1995

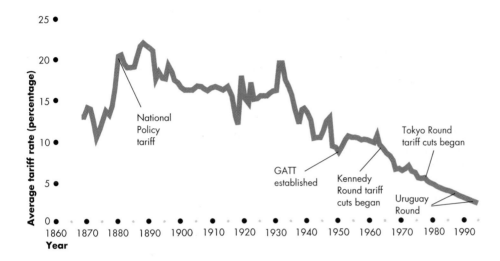

Canadian tariffs were in place before Confederation. Tariffs increased sharply in the 1870s and remained high until the 1930s. Since the establishment of GATT in 1947, tariffs have steadily declined in a series of negotiating rounds, the most significant of which are identified in the figure. Tariffs are now as low as they have ever been.

Sources: Statistics Canada, *Historical Statistics of Canada,* Series **G485,** and *StatCan: CANSIM Disc,* March 1996.

general tariff reductions. One of these, the Kennedy Round that began in the early 1960s, resulted in large tariff cuts starting in 1967. Another, the Tokyo Round, resulted in further tariff cuts in 1979.

The most recent, the Uruguay Round, which started in 1986 and was completed in 1994, was the most ambitious and comprehensive of the rounds. It was an agreement among 115 countries to lower tariffs and to prevent protection through subsidies or favourable treatment from government purchases. The agreement has been described as the biggest tax cut in the history of the world and the gains from greater specialization and trade are predicted to boost world output by 1 percent a year.

The most significant parts of the Uruguay Round agreement are the phasing out of many agricultural subsidies, the strengthening of intellectual property rights (copyrights and patents), and the creation of a new World Trade Organization (WTO). Membership in the WTO brings greater obligations on countries to observe the GATT rules and makes subsidies much harder to use as an alternative to tariffs and other forms of protection. Canada signed the Uruguay Round agreements in 1994.

In addition to the agreements under the GATT and the WTO, Canada is a party to the North American Free Trade Agreement (NAFTA), which became effective on January 1, 1994. Under this agreement, barriers to international trade among Canada, the United States, and Mexico will be virtually eliminated after a 15-year phasing-in period (10 years for Canada–U.S. trade under an earlier Canada–United States Free Trade Agreement that became effective on January 1, 1989). NAFTA appears to be boosting both exports and imports among the three members.

In other parts of the world, trade barriers have virtually been eliminated among the member countries of the European Union, which has created the largest unified tariff-free market in the world. In 1994, discussions among the Asia–Pacific Economic group (APEC) led to an agreement in principle to work towards a free trade area that embraces China, all the economies of East Asia and the South Pacific, together with Canada and the United States. These countries include the fastest-growing economies and hold the promise of heralding a global free trade area.

The effort to achieve freer trade underlines the

fact that trade in some goods is still subject to extremely high tariffs. The highest tariffs faced by Canadian buyers are those on textiles and footwear. A tariff of more than 10 percent (on the average) is imposed on almost all our imports of textiles and footwear. For example, when you buy a pair of blue jeans for $20, you pay a tariff of about $5. In other words, with free trade in textiles, a pair of jeans that today costs $20 would cost only $15. Other goods protected by tariffs are agricultural products, energy and chemicals, minerals and metals. The meat and cheese that you consume costs significantly more because of protection than it would with free international trade.

The temptation, on governments, to impose tariffs is a strong one. First, tariffs provide revenue to the government. Second, they enable the government to satisfy special interest groups in import-competing industries. But, as we'll see, free international trade brings enormous benefits that are reduced when tariffs are imposed. Let's see how.

How Tariffs Work

To analyse how tariffs work, let's return to the example of trade between Farmland and Mobilia. Figure 37.9 shows the international market for cars in which these two countries are the only traders.

The volume of trade and the price of a car are determined at the point of intersection of Mobilia's export supply curve of cars and Farmland's import demand curve for cars.

In Fig. 37.9, these two countries are trading cars and grain in exactly the same way that we analysed before in Fig. 37.6. Mobilia exports cars and Farmland exports grain. The volume of car imports into Farmland is 4 million a year, and the world market price of a car is 3 tonnes of grain. To make the example more concrete and real, Fig. 37.9 expresses prices in dollars rather than in units of grain and is based on a money price of grain of $1,000 a tonne. With grain costing $1,000 a tonne, the money price of a car is $3,000.

Now suppose that the government of Farmland, perhaps under pressure from car producers, decides to impose a tariff on imported cars. In particular, suppose that a tariff of $4,000 per car is imposed. (This is a huge tariff, but the car producers of Farmland are pretty fed up with competition from Mobilia.) What happens?

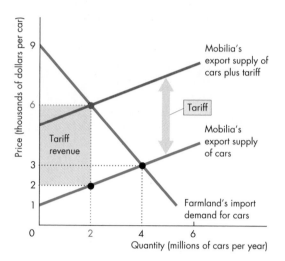

FIGURE 37.9
The Effects of a Tariff

Farmland imposes a tariff on car imports from Mobilia. The tariff increases the price that Farmers have to pay for cars. It shifts the supply curve of cars in Farmland leftward. The vertical distance between the original supply curve and the new one is the amount of the tariff, $4,000 per car. The price of cars in Farmland increases and the quantity of cars imported decreases. The government of Farmland collects a tariff revenue of $4,000 per car—a total of $8 billion on the 2 million cars imported. Farmland's exports of grain decrease because Mobilia now has a smaller income from its exports of cars.

The first part of the answer is obtained by studying the effects on the supply of cars in Farmland. Cars are no longer going to be available at the Mobilia export supply price. The tariff of $4,000 must be added to that price—the amount paid to the government of Farmland on each car imported. As a consequence, the supply curve in Farmland shifts upward by the amount of the tariff as shown in Fig. 37.9. The new supply curve becomes that labelled "Mobilia's export supply of cars plus tariff." The vertical distance between Mobilia's export supply curve and the new supply curve is the tariff imposed by the government of Farmland—$4,000 a car.

The next part of the answer is found by determining the new equilibrium. Imposing a tariff has no effect on the demand for cars in Farmland and so has no effect on Farmland's import demand for cars. Thus Farmland's import demand curve is unchanged. The new equilibrium occurs where the new supply curve intersects Farmland's import demand curve for cars. That equilibrium is at a price of $6,000 a car and with 2 million cars a year being imported. Imports decrease from 4 million to 2 million cars a year. At the higher price of $6,000 a car, domestic car producers increase their production. Domestic grain production decreases as resources are moved into the expanding car industry.

The total expenditure on imported cars by the Farmers is $6,000 a car multiplied by the 2 million cars imported ($12 billion). But not all of that money goes to the Mobilians. They receive $2,000 a car or $4 billion for the 2 million cars. The difference— $4,000 a car or a total of $8 billion for the 2 million cars—is collected by the government of Farmland as tariff revenue.

Obviously, the government of Farmland is happy with this situation. It is now collecting $8 billion that it didn't have before. But what about the Farmers? How do they view the new situation? The demand curve tells us the maximum price that a buyer is willing to pay for one more unit of a good. As you can see from Farmland's import demand curve for cars, if one more car could be imported, someone would be willing to pay almost $6,000 for it. Mobilia's export supply curve of cars tells us the minimum price at which additional cars are available. As you can see, one additional car would be supplied by Mobilia for a price only slightly more than $2,000. Thus because someone is willing to pay almost $6,000 for a car and someone else is willing to supply one for little more than $2,000, there is obviously a gain to be had from trading an extra car. In fact, there are gains to be had—willingness to pay exceeds the minimum supply price—all the way up to 4 million cars a year. Only when 4 million cars are being traded is the maximum price that a Farmer is willing to pay equal to the minimum price that is acceptable to a Mobilian. Thus a tariff on imports reduces the quantity of imports, raises the price of the good in the importing country and reduces the gains from trade.

It is easy to see that the tariff has lowered the total amount Farmland pays for imports. With free trade, Farmland was paying $3,000 a car and buying 4 million cars a year from Mobilia. Thus the total amount paid to Mobilia for imports was $12 billion a year. With a tariff, Farmland's imports have been cut to 2 million cars a year and the price paid to Mobilia

has also been cut to only $2,000 a car. Thus the total amount paid to Mobilia for imports has been cut to $4 billion a year. Doesn't this fact mean that Farmland is now importing less than it is exporting and has a balance of trade surplus?

To answer that question, we need to figure out what's happening in Mobilia. We've just seen that the price that Mobilia receives for cars has fallen from $3,000 to $2,000 a car. Thus the price of a car in Mobilia has fallen. But the price of grain remains at $1,000 a tonne. So the relative price of a car has fallen and the relative price of grain has increased. With free trade, the Mobilians could buy 3 tonnes of grain for one car. Now they can buy only 2 tonnes for a car. With a higher relative price of grain, the quantity demanded by the Mobilians decreases. As a result, Mobilia imports less grain. But because Mobilia imports less grain, Farmland exports less grain. In fact, Farmland's grain industry suffers from two sources. First, there is a decrease in the quantity of grain sold to Mobilia. Second, there is increased competition for inputs from the now expanded car industry. Thus the tariff leads to a contraction in the scale of the grain industry in Farmland.

It seems paradoxical at first that a country imposing a tariff on cars would hurt its own export industry, reducing its exports of grain. It might help to think of it this way: Mobilians buy grain with the money they make from exporting cars to Farmland. If they export fewer cars, they cannot afford to buy as much grain. In fact, in the absence of any international borrowing and lending, Mobilia has to cut its imports of grain by exactly the same amount as the loss in revenue from its export of cars. Grain imports into Mobilia will be cut back to a value of $4 billion, the amount that can be paid for by the new lower revenue from Mobilia's car exports. Thus trade is still balanced in this post-tariff situation. Although the tariff has cut imports, it has also cut exports, and the cut in the value of exports is exactly equal to the cut in the value of imports. The tariff, therefore, has no effect on the balance of trade—it reduces the volume of trade.

The result that we have just derived is perhaps one of the most misunderstood aspects of international economics. On countless occasions, politicians and others have called for tariffs in order to remove a balance of trade deficit or have argued that lowering tariffs would produce a balance of trade deficit. They reach this conclusion by failing to work out all the implications of a tariff. Because a tariff raises the price of imports and cuts imports, the easy conclusion is that the tariff reduces the balance of trade deficit. But there is a second round effect: The tariff changes the *volume* of exports as well. The equilibrium effects of a tariff are to reduce the volume of trade in both directions and the value of imports and exports by the same amount. The balance of trade itself is left unaffected.

Learning the Hard Way   Although the analysis that we have just worked through leads to the clear conclusion that tariffs cut both imports and exports and make both countries worse off, we have not found that conclusion easy to accept. Time and again in our history, we have imposed high tariff barriers on international trade (as Fig. 37.8 illustrates). Whenever tariff barriers are increased, trade collapses. The most vivid historical example of this interaction of tariffs and trade occurred during the Great Depression years of the early 1930s when the world's largest trading nation, the United States, increased its tariffs and set off a retaliatory round of tariff changes in many other countries. As a consequence of these high tariffs, world trade almost dried up.

Let's now turn our attention to the other range of protectionist weapons—nontariff barriers.

Nontariff Barriers

There are two important forms of nontariff barriers:

1. Quotas
2. Voluntary export restraints

A **quota** is a quantitative restriction on the import of a particular good. It specifies the maximum amount of the good that may be imported in a given period of time. Quotas are set for the import of many items, one of which is cheese. A **voluntary export restraint** is an agreement between two governments in which the government of the exporting country agrees to restrain the volume of its own exports. Voluntary export restraints are often called VERs. An example of a VER is a lumber agreement between British Columbia and the United States.

Nontariff barriers have become important features of international trading arrangements in the period since World War II, and there is general agreement that nontariff barriers are now a more severe impediment to international trade than tariffs.

Quotas are especially important in the textile industries, where there exists an international agreement called the Multifibre Arrangement, which establishes quotas on a wide range of textile products. Agricultural products are also subject to extensive quotas. Voluntary export restraints are particularly important in regulating the international trade in cars between Japan and North America.

It is difficult to quantify the effects of nontariff barriers in a way that makes them easy to compare with tariffs, but some studies have attempted to do just that. Such studies attempt to assess the tariff rate that would restrict trade by the same amount as the nontariff barriers do. With such calculations, nontariff barriers and tariffs can be added together to assess the total amount of protection. When we add nontariff barriers to tariffs for Canada, the overall amount of protection increases more than three-fold. Even so, Canada is one of the least protectionist countries in the world. Total protection in the European Union is higher, and higher still in other developed countries and Japan. The less developed countries and some of the newly industrializing countries have the highest protection rates of all.

How Quotas and VERs Work

To understand how nontariff barriers affect international trade, let's return to the example of trade between Farmland and Mobilia. Suppose that Farmland imposes a quota on car imports. Specifically, suppose that the quota restricts imports to no more than 2 million cars a year. What are the effects of this action?

The answer is found in Fig. 37.10. The quota is shown by the vertical red line at 2 million cars a year. Because it is illegal to import more than that number of cars, car importers buy only that quantity from Mobilia producers. They pay $2,000 a car to the Mobilia producer. But what do they sell their cars for? The answer is $6,000 each. Because the import supply of cars is restricted to 2 million cars a year, people with cars for sale will be able to get $6,000 each for them. The quantity of cars imported equals the quantity determined by the quota.

Importing cars is now obviously a profitable business. An importer gets $6,000 for an item that costs only $2,000. Thus there is severe competition among car importers for the available quotas. The pursuit of the profits from quotas is called "rent seeking."

FIGURE 37.10
The Effects of a Quota

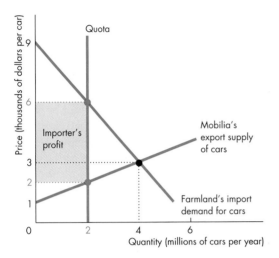

Farmland imposes a quota of 2 million cars a year on car imports from Mobilia. That quantity appears as the vertical line labelled "Quota." Because the quantity of cars supplied by Mobilia is restricted to 2 million, the price of a car in Farmland increases to $6,000. Importing cars is profitable because Mobilia is willing to supply cars at $2,000 each. There is competition for import quotas—rent seeking.

The value of imports—the amount paid to Mobilia—declines to $4 billion, exactly the same as in the case of the tariff. Thus with lower incomes from car exports and with a higher relative price of grain, Mobilians cut back on their imports of grain in exactly the same way they did under a tariff.

The key difference between a quota and a tariff lies in who gets the profit represented by the difference between the import supply price and the domestic selling price. In the case of a tariff, that difference goes to the government of the importing country. In the case of a quota, that difference goes to the person who has the right to import under the import-quota regulations.

A voluntary export restraint is like a quota arrangement where quotas are allocated to each exporting country. The effects of voluntary export restraints are similar to those of quotas but differ from them in that the gap between the domestic price and the export price is captured not by domestic importers but by the foreign exporter. The government of the exporting country has to establish procedures for allocating the restricted volume of exports among its producers.

"Invisible" Nontariff Barriers

In addition to quotas and VERs, there are thousands of nontariff barriers that are virtually impossible to detect—that are almost invisible. They arise from domestic laws that are not (necessarily) aimed at restricting foreign competition but they have that effect. For example, in a few countries (most notably the United Kingdom, Japan, Australia, and New Zealand), highway traffic drives on the left. This apparently harmless law effectively restricts competition from foreign car makers. Of course, a car produced in Canada can be fitted out with its steering wheel and controls on the right but only at an additional cost. And the cost depends on the volume of sales.

R E V I E W

- When a country opens itself up to international trade and trades freely at world market prices, it expands its consumption possibilities.
- When trade is restricted, some of the gains from trade are lost.
- A country might be better off with restricted trade than with no trade but not as well off as it could be if it engaged in free trade.
- A tariff reduces the volume of imports, but it also reduces the volume of exports.
- Under both free trade and restricted trade (and without international borrowing and lending), the value of imports equals the value of exports. With restricted trade, both the total value of exports and the total value of imports are lower than under free trade, but trade is still balanced.

We have now learned about the gains from international trade and we've studied the effects of different ways in which trade can be restricted. Let's now look at the arguments about restricting international trade.

The Case Against Protection

FOR AS LONG AS NATIONS AND INTERNATIONAL trade have existed, people have debated whether a country is better off with free international trade or with protection from foreign competition. The debate continues, but for most economists a verdict has been delivered and is the one you have just explored. Free trade is the arrangement most conducive to prosperity, and protection creates more problems than it solves. We've seen the most powerful case for free trade in the example of how Farmland and Mobilia both benefit from their comparative advantage. But there is a broader range of issues in the free trade versus protection debate. Let's review these issues.

A country might restrict international trade and impose tariffs or quotas in an attempt to achieve three goals. They are

■ Achieving national security
■ Stimulating the growth of new industries
■ Encouraging competition and restraining monopoly

Let's see how protection might be used to try to achieve these goals.

National Security

The national security argument for protection is that a country is better off if it protects its strategic industries—industries that produce defence equipment and armaments and the industries on which the defence industries rely for their raw materials and other intermediate inputs. This argument for protection runs into three overwhelming counterarguments.

First, it is an argument for the protection of *every* industry. In a time of war, there is no industry that does not contribute to national defence. Agriculture, ore and coal mining, oil and natural gas extraction, the manufacture of steel and other metals, vehicles, aircraft, ships, machinery of all kinds, and services such as banking and insurance are all vital to a nation's defence. To protect every industry would require a tariff or quota on the import of all goods and services that can be traded.

Second, the cost of lower output must be weighed against the benefit of greater national security. There is no clear and objective way of making this cost-benefit calculation. In practice, it is made in the political arena and once a national security argument is given respectability, it is exploited by anyone who can lay remote claim to it being relevant. Makers of paper clips and nail scissors will lobby as vigorously as weapons designers and shipbuilders.

Third, even if the case is made for maintaining or increasing the output of a strategic industry, there is always a more efficient way of doing so than by protecting the industry from international competition. A direct subsidy to the firms in a strategic industry that is financed out of taxes on all sectors of the economy keeps the industry operating at the scale judged appropriate, and the presence of unfettered international competition prevents the prices faced by consumers from rising.

New Industries

The second argument that is used to justify protection is the **infant-industry argument**—the proposition that protection is necessary to enable an infant industry to grow into a mature industry that can compete in world markets. The argument is based on the idea of *dynamic comparative advantage*, which can arise from *learning-by-doing* (see Chapter 3).

There is no doubt that learning-by-doing is a powerful engine of productivity growth and that comparative advantage evolves and changes because of on-the-job experience. But these facts do not justify protection.

First, the infant-industry argument is valid only if the benefits of learning-by-doing *not only* accrue to the owners and workers of the firms in the infant industry but also *spill over* to other industries and parts of the economy. For example, there are huge productivity gains from learning-by-doing in the manufacture of telecommunications equipment. But almost all of these gains benefit the stockholders and workers of companies like Northern Telecom. Because the people making the decisions, bearing the risk, and doing the work are the ones who benefit, they take the dynamic gains into account when they decide on the scale of their activities. In this case, almost no benefits spill over to other parts of the economy, so there is no need for government assistance to achieve an efficient outcome.

Second, even if the case is made for protecting an infant industry, it is more efficient to do so by a subsidy to the firms in the infant industry, with the subsidy financed out of taxes. Such a subsidy would keep the industry operating at the scale judged appropriate, and free international trade would keep the prices faced by consumers at their world market levels.

Restraining Monopoly

The third argument used to justify protection is the dumping argument. **Dumping** occurs when a foreign firm sells its exports at a price below its cost of production. Dumping might be used by a firm that wants to gain a global monopoly. In this case, the foreign firm sells its output at a price below its cost in order to drive domestic firms out of business. When the domestic firms have gone, the foreign firm takes advantage of its monopoly position and charges a higher price for its product. Under GATT, dumping is illegal and anti-dumping duties can be imposed on foreign producers if Canadian producers can show that they have been injured by dumping.

But there are powerful reasons to resist the dumping argument for protection. First, it is virtually impossible to detect dumping because it is hard to determine a firm's costs. As a result, the test for dumping is whether a firm's export price is below its domestic price. But this test is a weak one because it can be rational for a firm to charge a low price in markets in which the quantity demanded is highly sensitive to price and a higher price in markets in which demand is less price sensitive.

Second, there are virtually no goods that are natural global monopolies. So even if all the domestic firms were driven out of business in some industry, it would always be possible to find several and usually many alternative foreign sources of supply and to buy at prices determined in competitive markets.

Third, if a good or service was a truly global natural monopoly, the best way of dealing with it would be by regulation—just as in the case of domestic monopolies. Such regulation would require international cooperation.

Countervailing duties are tariffs that are imposed to enable domestic producers to compete with subsidized foreign producers. Often, foreign governments subsidize some of their domestic industries. Under the Special Import Measures Act, if Canada determines that a foreign government is unfairly subsidizing its exports to Canada, a countervailing duty may be imposed. Governments often subsidize some of their domestic industries, but defining what is a subsidy and what is a legitimate form of government aid (or simply a different government approach) can be a problem. The Canadian lumber industry offers an example. U.S. producers say it is subsidized, but Canadian governments, which own much of our timberland, say their method of renting it to producers simply differs from the U.S. method.

The three arguments for protection that we've just examined have an element of credibility. The counterarguments are in general stronger so these arguments do not make the case for protection. But they are not the only arguments that you might encounter. The many other arguments commonly heard are quite simply wrong. They are fatally flawed. The most common of them are that protection

- Saves jobs
- Allows us to compete with cheap foreign labour
- Brings diversity and stability
- Penalizes lax environmental standards
- Prevents rich countries from exploiting developing countries

Saves Jobs

The argument is: When we buy shoes from Brazil or shirts from Taiwan, Canadian workers lose their jobs. With no earnings and poor prospects, these workers become a drain on welfare and they spend less, causing a ripple effect of further job losses. The proposed solution to this problem is to ban imports of cheap foreign goods and protect Canadian jobs. The proposal is flawed for the following reasons.

First, free trade does cost some jobs, but it also creates other jobs. It brings about a global rationalization of labour and allocates labour resources to their highest value activities. As a result of international trade in textiles, thousands of workers in Canada have lost jobs because textile mills and other factories have closed. But thousands of workers in other countries have gotten jobs because textile mills have opened there. And thousands of Canadian workers have gotten better-paying jobs than textile workers because other industries have expanded and created more jobs than have been destroyed.

Second, imports create jobs. They create jobs for

retailers who sell imported goods and firms who service those goods. They also create jobs by creating incomes in the rest of the world, some of which are spent on Canadian-made goods and services.

Allows Us to Compete with Cheap Foreign Labour

With the removal of protective tariffs in Canada–U.S. trade with Mexico, Ross Perot said he could hear a "giant sucking sound" of jobs rushing to Mexico (one of which is shown in the cartoon). Let's see what's wrong with this view.

The labour cost of a unit of output equals the wage rate divided by labour productivity. For example, if a Canadian autoworker earns $30 an hour and produces 10 units of output an hour, the average labour cost of a unit of output is $3. If a Mexican autoworker earns $3 an hour and produces 1 unit of output an hour, the average labour cost of a unit of output is $3. Other things remaining the same, the higher a worker's productivity, the higher is the worker's wage rate. High-wage workers have high productivity. Low-wage workers have low productivity.

Although high-wage Canadian workers are more productive, on the average, than low-wage Mexican

"I don't know what the hell happened—one minute I'm at work in Flint, Michigan, then there's a giant sucking sound and suddenly here I am in Mexico."

Drawing by M. Stevens; © 1993
The New Yorker Magazine, Inc.

workers, there are differences across industries. Canadian labour is relatively more productive at some activities than others. For example, the productivity of Canadian workers in producing graphics software, financial services, and telecommunications equipment is relatively higher than in the production of furniture and some standardized machine parts. The activities in which Canadian workers are relatively more productive than their Mexican counterparts are those in which Canada has a *comparative advantage*. By engaging in free trade, increasing our production and exports of the goods at which we have a comparative advantage, and decreasing our production and increasing our imports of the goods at which our trading partners have a comparative advantage, we can make ourselves and the citizens of other countries better off.

Brings Diversity and Stability

A diversified investment portfolio is less risky than one that has all the eggs in one basket. The same is true for an economy's production. A diversified economy fluctuates less than an economy that produces only one or two goods.

But big, rich, diversified economies like Canada, the United States, Japan, and the European Union do not have this type of stability problem. And even a country like Saudi Arabia that produces almost only one good (oil) can benefit from specializing in the activity at which it has a comparative advantage and then investing in a wide range of other countries to bring greater stability to its income and consumption.

Penalizes Lax Environmental Standards

A new argument for protection that was used extensively in the Uruguay Round of GATT and in the NAFTA negotiations is that many poorer countries, such as Mexico, do not have the same environmental policies that we have and, because they are willing to pollute and we are not, we cannot compete with them without tariffs. So if they want free trade with the richer and "greener" countries, they must clean up their environments to our standards.

The environment argument for trade restrictions is weak. First, it is not true that all poorer countries have significantly lower environmental protection standards than Canada has. Many poor countries and the former communist countries of Eastern Europe do have bad records on the environment. Second, a poor country cannot afford to be as concerned about its environment as a rich country can. The best hope for a better environment in Mexico and in other developing countries is rapid income growth through free trade. As their incomes grow, developing countries such as Mexico will have the *means* to match their desires to improve their environments.

Prevents Rich Countries from Exploiting Developing Countries

Another new argument for protection is that international trade must be restricted to prevent the people of the rich industrial world from exploiting the poorer people of the developing countries, forcing them to work for slave wages.

Wage rates in some developing countries are indeed very low. But by trading with developing countries, we increase the demand for the goods that these countries produce, and, more significantly, we increase the demand for their labour. When the demand for labour in developing countries increases, the wage rate also increases. So, far from exploiting people in developing countries, trade improves their opportunities and increases their incomes.

We have reviewed the arguments commonly heard in favour of protection and the counterarguments against them. There is one counterargument to protection that is general and quite overwhelming: Protection invites retaliation and can trigger a trade war. The best example of such a trade war occurred during the Great Depression of the 1930s when the United States introduced the Smoot–Hawley Tariff. Country after country retaliated with its own tariff and in a short period, world trade had almost disappeared. The costs to all countries were large and led to a renewed international resolve to avoid such self-defeating moves in the future. They also led to the creation of GATT and are the impetus behind NAFTA, APEC, and the European Union.

Why Is Trade Restricted?

Why, despite all the arguments against protection, is international trade restricted? The key reason is that consumption possibilities increase *on the average* but not everyone shares in the gain and some people even lose. Free trade brings benefits to some and costs to others, with total benefits exceeding total costs. It is the uneven distribution of costs and benefits that is the principal source of impediment to achieving more liberal international trade.

Let's return to our example of international trade in cars and grain between Farmland and Mobilia. In Farmland, the benefits from free trade accrue to all the producers of grain and those producers of cars who would not have to bear the costs of adjusting to a smaller car industry. In Mobilia, the benefits from free trade accrue to all the car producers and those grain producers who would not have to bear the costs of adjusting to a smaller grain industry. These costs are transition costs, not permanent costs. The costs of moving to free trade are borne by those Farmland car producers and their employees who have to become grain producers and those Mobilia grain producers and their employees who have to become car producers. The number of people who gain will, in general, be enormous compared with the number who lose. The gain per person will, therefore, be rather small. The loss per person to those who bear the loss will be large. Because the loss that falls on those who bear it is large, it will pay those people to incur considerable expense in order to lobby against free trade. On the other hand, it will not pay those who gain to organize to achieve free trade. The gain from trade for any individual is too small for that individual to spend much time or money on a political organization to achieve free trade. The loss from free trade will be seen as being so great by those bearing that loss that they *will* find it profitable to join a political organization to prevent free trade. Each group is optimizing—weighing benefits against costs and choosing the best action for themselves. The anti–free trade group will, however, undertake a larger quantity of political lobbying than the pro–free trade group.

Compensating Losers

If, in total, the gains from free international trade exceed the losses, why don't those who gain compensate those who lose so that everyone is in favour of free trade? To some degree, such compensation does take place. The losers from freer international trade are compensated indirectly through the normal unemployment compensation arrangements. But only limited attempts are made to compensate those who lose from free international trade. The main reason why full compensation is not attempted is that the costs of identifying all the losers and estimating the value of their losses would be enormous. Also, it would never be clear whether a person who has fallen on hard times is suffering because of free trade or for other reasons, and perhaps reasons largely under the control of the individual. Furthermore, some people who look like losers at one point in time might, in fact, end up gaining. The young autoworker who loses his job in Windsor and becomes a computer assembly worker in Ottawa resents the loss of work and the need to move. But a year or two later, looking back on events, he counts himself fortunate. He's made a move that has increased his income and given him greater job security.

It is because we do not, in general, compensate the losers from free international trade that protectionism is such a popular and permanent feature of our national economic and political life.

There is a second reason why international trade is restricted. Governments receive revenue from tariffs and the governments of developing countries rely on this source of revenue to finance a large part of their expenditures. In these countries, the tariff is a more cost-effective tax than the income tax or the sales tax. It is difficult for these countries to eliminate the tariff.

R E V I E W

■ Trade restrictions aimed at national security goals, stimulating the growth of new industries, and restraining foreign monopoly have little merit.

■ Trade restrictions to save jobs, compensate for low foreign wages, make the economy more diversified, and compensate for costly environmental policies are misguided.

■ The main arguments against trade restrictions are that subsidies and competition policies can achieve domestic goals more efficiently than protection and that protection can trigger a trade war in which all countries lose.

Despite the political pressures for protection, the Canadian and U.S. governments have taken measures designed to secure greater gains from trade between the two countries. Let's take a look at the historical Canada–United States Free Trade Agreement.

Canada–United States Free Trade Agreement

THE CANADA–UNITED STATES FREE TRADE Agreement was signed in October 1987 following two years of intense negotiations and, on the Canadian side of the border, an intense political debate. First, let's look at the terms of the agreement.

Terms of Agreement

The main terms of the Canada–United States Free Trade Agreement are

■ Tariffs to be phased out through 1999
■ Nontariff barriers to be reduced
■ Free trade in energy products, with energy resource sharing in times of national shortage
■ More freedom of trade in services
■ Future negotiations to eliminate subsidies
■ Creation of a dispute-settling mechanism

Removal of Tariffs   Some tariffs were removed on January 1, 1989, when the Free Trade Agreement became effective. Many other tariffs have now been removed, and others will be removed in a series of annual steps through 1999.

Nontariff Barriers   Nontariff barriers such as government procurement policies of buying local products are removed by the agreement. But most quotas, especially those that support agricultural policies in the two countries, remain in place.

Energy Products   Free trade in energy products existed before the Free Trade Agreement but the agreement ratified the intent to maintain that arrangement. The agreement that scarce energy resources will be shared in terms of national shortage became a controversial one. In effect, what the energy sharing clause amounts to is an agreement that governments will not intervene in energy markets to prevent firms from selling their energy to the other country.

Trade in Services   International trade in services has been expanding more quickly than trade in manufactured goods in recent years. The Free Trade Agreement, recognizing this factor and seeking to facilitate further expansion of trade in services between the United States and Canada, incorporates two principles: the *right of establishment* and *national treatment.* The right of establishment means that American firms have the right to set up branches in Canada and Canadian firms have the right to set up operations in the United States. National treatment means that each country will treat the goods and firms and investors of the other country as if they were operating within its own borders.

Future Negotiations on Subsidies In both the United States and Canada, there are many subsidies, especially to agricultural products. The presence of subsidies causes problems and makes it legitimate for the country importing subsidized goods to impose countervailing duties.

Dispute-Settling Mechanism The Free Trade Agreement includes two dispute-settling mechanisms: one to settle disputes relating to all aspects of the agreement and the other to deal with applications of countervailing duties and anti-dumping laws in either country. For example, in 1994, the United States applied for countervailing duties on Canadian exports of durum wheat and on lumber products. In 1996, the United States plans to apply for countervailing duties on Canadian exports of poultry. In each case, the United States accuses Canada of subsidizing these industries unfairly so that Canadian exports are cheaper than U.S. producers can supply them.

Effects of the Free Trade Agreement

Working out the effects of an agreement as complex as the Canada–United States Free Trade Agreement is difficult, and there is no general consensus on what the effects have been. The theory that you have studied in this chapter predicts that the removal of tariffs will produce an increase in the *volume* of international trade. That is, the theory predicts that Canadians will increasingly specialize in those activities at which they have a comparative advantage and Americans will specialize in a different range of activities and that the two countries will exchange a larger volume of goods and services.

As predicted, international trade between Canada and the United States increased during the three years following the agreement. The increase in Canadian exports to the United States between 1989 and 1992 was 17 percent, while the increase between 1986 and 1989 was only 8 percent.

Following the agreement, Canada greatly increased its exports of advertising services, office and telecommunications equipment, paper, and transportation services. And its imports of meat and dairy products, communications services, clothing, furniture, and processed foods and beverages also increased by a large percentage.

These huge changes in exports and imports brought gains from increased specialization and exchange. But they also brought a heavy toll of adjustment. Thousands of jobs were lost in the declining sectors and new jobs were created in the expanding sectors. The amount of job destruction in the years following the Free Trade Agreement was historically high and the unemployment rate rose for three successive years. Only during the Great Depression did the rate of job destruction exceed that in the late 1980s and early 1990s. To what extent this high rate of job destruction was solely caused by the Free Trade Agreement is unclear and controversial. But it is unquestionable that the Free Trade Agreement made a large contribution.

R E V I E W

- Under the Canada–United States Free Trade Agreement, all tariffs on trade between Canada and the United States will be phased out by 1999.
- The agreement has reduced nontariff barriers, freed up trade in energy products and services, and established two dispute-settling mechanisms.
- The agreement has resulted in a huge increase in trade between Canada and the United States.

◆ You've now seen how free international trade enables all nations to gain from increased specialization and trade. By producing the goods and services at which we have a comparative advantage and exchanging some of what we produce with others, we expand our consumption possibilities. Placing impediments on that trade restricts these gains. By opening our country to free international trade, the market for the things that we sell expands and their relative prices rise. The market for the things that we buy also expands and their relative prices fall. All countries gain from free international trade. *Reading Between the Lines* on pp. 924–925 looks at the surge of Canada's international trade as NAFTA swings into high gear.

Policy
WATCH

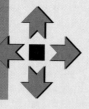

Net Exports Surplus

Essence of
THE STORY

■ Statistics Canada reported that Canada's trade surplus in May was a record $4.1 billion. Exports increased 2.9 percent to $22.4 billion, while imports fell 2.1 percent to $18.3 billion.

■ Also the April surplus was revised up to $3.1 billion from a previously estimated $2.6 billion, making it the second largest ever.

■ The auto sector accounted for most of the May export surge. Car exports were up 11.5 percent and trucks and minivans were up 19.3 percent.

■ The trade surplus reflects the differences between the Canadian and U.S. economies. Exporters are tapping into rapid U.S. growth, but Canadians are reluctant to spend.

■ The trade figures are a reminder that domestic demand is weak.

■ The trade surplus might encourage the Bank of Canada to cut interest rates.

GLOBE AND MAIL, JULY 19, 1996

Trade surplus smashes record

BY BRUCE LITTLE

A stunning increase in Canada's trade surplus reported yesterday could give the Bank of Canada room to reduce interest rates, especially since the U.S. Federal Reserve Board appears to be in no hurry to raise rates south of the border, according to one analyst.

"If I were them I'd do it," Sherry Cooper, chief economist at Nesbitt Burns Inc., said after Statistics Canada reported that a wave of auto exports to the United States lifted Canada's trade surplus to a record $4.1-billion in May as imports sagged for the third consecutive month. ...

Exports increased 2.9 per cent to $22.4-billion in May, while imports fell 2.1 per cent to $18.3-billion, Statscan said. In addition, the April surplus was revised up to $3.1-billion from a previously estimated $2.6-billion, making it the second largest ever. ...

The auto sector accounted for most of the May export surge.

Exports of cars were up 11.5 per cent and trucks, a category that includes minivans, increased 19.3 per cent.

Those gains probably continued into June and July. The big three auto makers have all announced this week that they plan to increase production during the next three months. ...

The big May trade surplus reflects the differences between the Canadian and U.S. economies. Exporters are tapping into rapid growth south of the border, but Canadians have been reluctant to spend their money on either domestic or imported goods.

The downside to the May trade report was its reminder that domestic demand is still weak. Aside from auto products, imports of other consumer goods fell 3.2 per cent as Canadians shunned imported clothing, electronic goods and house furnishings alike.

Economic

A N A L Y S I S

■ Canada's biggest trading partner is the United States. So Canadian exports are strongly influenced by U.S. imports. And U.S. imports are strongly influenced by U.S. real GDP.

■ Figure 1 shows the relationship between U.S. real GDP and Canadian exports. You can see a strong positive relationship between these two variables.

■ You can also see in Fig. 1 that Canadian exports became more responsive to U.S. real GDP during the 1990s, after the Free Trade Agreement came into effect.

■ Canadian imports are determined primarily by Canadian real GDP. Figure 2 shows the relationship between these two variables. You can see a similar pattern to that in Fig. 1. There is a strong positive relationship between Canadian imports and real GDP, and imports became more sensitive to real GDP during the 1990s.

■ Figure 3 shows real GDP growth in Canada and the United States. In 1996, U.S. real GDP growth was running at more than 2 percent a year, while Canadian real GDP growth had slowed to less than 1 percent a year. These relative growth rates contributed to the boom in Canadian exports and the sluggish Canadian imports that created a big trade surplus.

■ The Bank of Canada did cut interest rates during 1996, as the news article suggested was likely. Lower interest rates stimulate spending, which also increases imports and lowers the trade surplus.

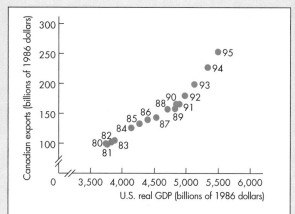

Figure 1 Canadian exports

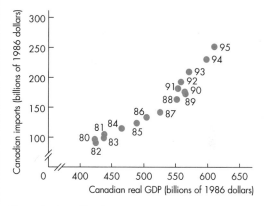

Figure 2 Canadian imports

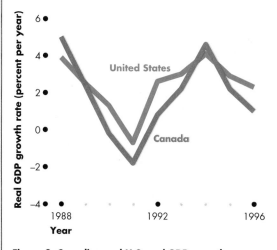

Figure 3 Canadian and U.S. real GDP growth

You're

THE VOTER

■ If you were a member of the Bank of Canada's top policy committee, would you vote for lower interest rates in the situation described in this news article? Why or why not?

S U M M A R Y

Key Points

Patterns and Trends in International Trade
Large flows of trade take place between all countries but the biggest volume of trade is in manufactured goods exchanged among the rich countries. Canada's biggest and fastest growing trading partner is the United States. (pp. 902–905)

Opportunity Cost and Comparative Advantage
When opportunity costs differ between countries, the country with the lowest opportunity cost of producing a good has a comparative advantage in producing that good. Comparative advantage is the source of the gains from international trade. (pp. 905–906)

Gains from Trade   Countries can gain from trade if their opportunity costs differ. Through trade, each country can obtain goods and services at a lower opportunity cost than it could if it produced them all at home. Trading allows consumption to exceed production and enables a country to consume at points outside its production possibility frontier. (pp. 906–910)

Gains from Trade in Reality   Much trade takes the form of exchanging similar goods for each other. Such trade arises because of economies of scale in the face of diversified tastes. (pp. 910–912)

Trade Restrictions   A country can restrict international trade by imposing tariffs or nontariff barriers such as quotas and voluntary export restraints. All trade restrictions raise the domestic price of imported goods, lower the volume of imports, and reduce the total value of imports. They also reduce the total value of exports by the same amount as the reduction in the value of imports. (pp. 912–917)

The Case Against Protection   The arguments that protection is necessary for national security, for infant industries, and to prevent dumping are weak. The arguments that protection saves jobs, allows us to compete with cheap foreign labour, makes the economy diversified and stable, and is needed to offset the costs of environmental policies are fatally flawed. (pp. 918–922)

Canada-United States Free Trade Agreement
The Canada–United States Free Trade Agreement will phase out most tariffs on trade between Canada and the United States by 1999. The agreement has reduced nontariff barriers, brought freer trade in energy products and services, and created two dispute-settling mechanisms. Future negotiations will attempt to reduce subsidies. The reductions in tariffs have increased the volume of trade, which benefits consumers, but have also increased the unemployment rate. (pp. 922–923)

Key Figures

Key Terms

REVIEW QUESTIONS

1. What are Canada's main exports and imports?
2. How does Canada trade services internationally?
3. Which items of international trade have been growing the most quickly in recent years?
4. What is the balance of trade? In what circumstances would Canada be a net exporter?
5. With which countries does Canada do most of its international trade?
6. In 1995, to which country did Canada export the largest amount of goods and services and from which country did Canada import the largest amount of goods and services?
7. Describe how Canada's balance of trade has changed since 1975.
8. What is comparative advantage? Why does it lead to gains from international trade?
9. Explain what the gains from trade are.
10. Explain why international trade brings gains to all countries.
11. Distinguish between comparative advantage and absolute advantage.
12. Explain why all countries have a comparative advantage in something.
13. Explain why, when a country begins to trade, the price received for the good exported rises and the price paid for the good imported falls.
14. Explain why we import and export large quantities of similar goods—such as cars.
15. What are the main ways in which a country restricts international trade?
16. What are the GATT and the WTO? When was each established and what is its role?
17. What is NAFTA? When did it begin and what have its effects been?
18. What are the effects of a tariff?
19. What are the effects of a quota?
20. What are the effects of a voluntary export restraint?
21. What is dumping and what are countervailing duties?
22. Describe the main trends in tariffs and nontariff barriers.
23. What are the main arguments for trade restrictions? Explain the flaw in each argument.
24. Why do countries restrict international trade?
25. What is the Canada–United States Free Trade Agreement? What have its effects been?

CRITICAL THINKING

1. Study *Reading Between the Lines* on pp. 924–925 and the answer the following questions:
   a. How and why are Canadian exports influenced by the state of the U.S. economy?
   b. What changes, if any, have occurred in the relationship between Canadian exports and U.S. real GDP during the 1990s?
   c. To what might these changes be attributed and why?
   d. What are the main influences on Canadian imports?
   e. What changes, if any, have occurred in the relationship between Canadian imports and Canadian real GDP during the 1990s?
   f. To what might these changes be attributed and why?
   g. How has Canada–U.S. trade been influenced by the Canadian and U.S. business cycles during the 1990s?
   h. Why do you think the news article connects the Bank of Canada's interest rate policy to the volume and balance of international trade?
2. "The North American Free Trade Agreement will lead to Canadian jobs being exported to Mexico." Discuss.
3. Sir John A. Macdonald introduced tariffs to increase employment and decrease unemployment. Are there any circumstances under which a tariff might increase employment?
4. The Auto Pact is a unique agreement between Canada and the United States. Are there any other agreements similar to the Auto Pact that might also be successful?

P R O B L E M S

1. Figures 37.4 and 37.5 illustrate Farmland's and Mobilia's production possibilities.
   a. Calculate Farmland's opportunity cost of a car when it produces 2 million cars.
   b. Calculate Mobilia's opportunity cost of a car in when it produces 8 million cars.
   c. With no trade, Farmland produces 2 million cars and Mobilia produces 8 million cars. Which country has a comparative advantage in the production of cars?
   d. If there is no trade between Farmland and Mobilia, how much grain is consumed and how many cars are bought in each country?

2. Suppose that the two countries in problem 1 trade freely.
   a. Which country exports grain?
   b. What adjustments will be made to the amount of each good produced by each country?
   c. What adjustment will be made to the amount of each good consumed by each country?
   d. What can you say about the price of a car under free trade?

3. Compare the total production of each good produced in problems 1 and 2.

4. Compare the situation in problems 1 and 2 with that analysed in the chapter (pp. 905–910). Why does Mobilia export cars in the chapter but import them in problem 2?

5. The following figure depicts the international market for soybeans. Assume that there are only two countries.

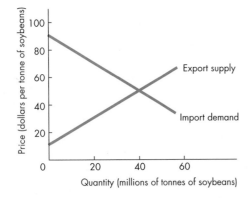

   a. If the two countries did not engage in international trade, what would be the prices of soybeans in the two countries?
   b. What is the world price of soybeans if there is free trade between these countries?
   c. What quantities of soybeans are exported and imported?
   d. What is the balance of trade?

6. If the country in problem 5 that imports soybeans imposes a tariff of $20 a tonne, what is the world price of soybeans and what quantity of soybeans gets traded internationally? What is the price of soybeans in the importing country? Calculate the tariff revenue.

7. The importing country in problem 5(b) imposes a quota of 30 million tonnes on its imports of soybeans.
   a. What is the price of soybeans in the importing country?
   b. What is the revenue from the quota?
   c. Who gets this revenue?

8. The exporting country in problem 5(b) imposes a VER of 30 million tonnes of soybeans.
   a. What is the world price of soybeans?
   b. What is the revenue from exports of the soybean growers in the exporting country?
   c. Which country gains from the VER?

9. Suppose that the exporting country in problem 5(b) subsidizes production by paying its farmers $10 a tonne for soybeans harvested.
   a. What is the price of soybeans in the importing country?
   b. What action might soybean growers in the importing country take? Why?

10. Countries Atlantis and Magic Empire produce only food and balloon rides and have the following production possibility frontiers illustrated in the figures:
    a. If Atlantis produces at point *a*, what is its opportunity cost of a balloon ride?
    b. What are the consumption possibilities of Atlantis?
    c. If Magic Empire produces at point *a'*, what is its opportunity cost of a balloon ride?
    d. What are the consumption possibilities of Magic Empire?

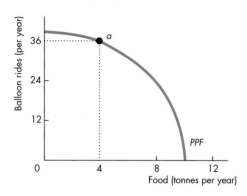

(a) Atlantis

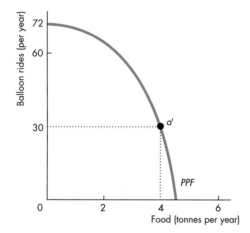

(b) Magic Empire

e. Which country has a comparative advantage in producing food?

11. If Atlantis and Magic Empire in problem 10 enter into a free trade agreement,
    a. How does the price of food in each country change?
    b. Which country exports balloon rides?
    c. Which country exports food?
    d. What are the gains from trade for each country?
    e. Are there any losers as a result of the free trade agreement?

"Free trade, one of the greatest blessings which a government can confer on a people, is in almost every country unpopular."

LORD MACAULAY (1800–1859), *ESSAY ON MITFORD'S HISTORY OF GREECE*

Understanding the Gains from International Trade

THE ISSUES AND IDEAS

Until the mid-eighteenth century, it was generally believed that the purpose of international trade was to keep exports greater than imports and pile up gold. If gold was accumulated, it was believed, the nation would prosper; and if gold was lost through an international deficit, the nation would be drained of money and impoverished. These beliefs are called *mercantilism*, and the *mercantilists* were pamphleteers who advocated with missionary fervour the pursuit of an international surplus. If exports did not exceed imports, the mercantilists wanted imports restricted.

In the 1740s, David Hume explained that as the quantity of money (gold) changes, so also does the price level, and the nation's *real* wealth is unaffected. In the 1770s, Adam Smith argued that import restrictions would reduce the gains from specialization and make a nation poorer, and 30 years later, David Ricardo proved the law of comparative advantage and demonstrated the superiority of free trade. Mercantilism was intellectually bankrupt but remained politically powerful.

Gradually, through the nineteenth century, the mercantilist influence waned, and North America and Western Europe prospered in an environment of increasingly free international trade. But despite remarkable advances in economic understanding, mercantilism never quite died. It had a brief and devastating revival in the 1920s and 1930s when tariff hikes brought about the collapse of international trade and accentuated the Great Depression. It subsided again after World War II with the establishment of the General Agreement on Tariffs and Trade (GATT).

But mercantilism lingers on. Many Canadians fear that NAFTA will bring economic ruin to Canada and this belief is a modern manifestation of mercantilism. It would be interesting to have David Hume, Adam Smith, and David Ricardo commenting on this view. But we know what they would say—the same things that they said to the eighteenth-century mercantilists. And they would still be right today.

THEN . . .

IN THE eighteenth century, when mercantilists and economists were debating the pros and cons of free international exchange, the available transportation technology severely limited the gains from international trade. Sailing ships with tiny cargo holds took close to a month to cross the Atlantic Ocean. But the potential gains were large, and so was the incentive to cut shipping costs. By the 1850s, the clipper ship had been developed, cutting the journey from Halifax to Liverpool to only 12 days. Half a century later, 10,000-ton steamships were sailing between Canada and England in just 4 days. As sailing times and costs declined, the gains from international trade increased and the volume of trade expanded.

THE CONTAINER ship has revolutionized international trade and contributed to its continued expansion. Today, most goods cross the oceans in "containers"—metal boxes—packed into and piled on top of ships like this one. Container technology has cut the cost of ocean shipping by economizing on handling and by making cargoes harder to steal, lowering insurance costs. It is unlikely that there would be much international trade in goods such as television sets and VCRs without this technology. High-value and perishable cargoes such as flowers and fresh foods, as well as urgent courier packages, travel by air. Every day, dozens of cargo-laden 747s fly between major Canadian cities and destinations across the Atlantic and Pacific oceans.

David Ricardo

THE ECONOMISTS: FROM SMITH AND RICARDO TO GATT

David Ricardo (1772–1823) was a highly successful 27-year-old stockbroker when he stumbled on a copy of Adam Smith's *Wealth of Nations* (see p. 65) on a weekend visit to the country. He was immediately hooked and went on to become the most celebrated economist of his age and one of the all-time great economists. One of his many contributions was to develop the principle of comparative advantage, the foundation on which the modern theory of international trade is built. The example that he used to illustrate this principle was the trade between England and Portugal in cloth and wine.

The General Agreement on Tariffs and Trade (GATT) was established as a reaction against the devastation wrought by the beggar-my-neighbour tariffs imposed during the 1930s. But it is also a triumph for the logic first worked out by Smith and Ricardo.

Glossary

Glossary

Absolute advantage A person has an absolute advantage in production if by using the same quantities of inputs that person can produce more than another person; a country has an absolute advantage if its output per unit of inputs of all goods is larger than that of another country.

Adverse selection The tendency for people to enter into agreements in which they can use their private information to their own advantage and to the disadvantage of the less-informed party.

Allocative efficiency The situation that occurs when no resources are wasted—when no one can be made better off without someone else being made worse off. Allocative efficiency is also called *Pareto efficiency.*

Anti-combine law A law that regulates and prohibits certain kinds of market behaviour, such as monopoly and monopolistic practices.

Average cost pricing rule A rule that sets the price equal to average total cost.

Average fixed cost Total fixed cost per unit of output—total fixed cost divided by output.

Average product Average productivity of a factor of production—total product divided by the quantity of the factor employed.

Average revenue The revenue per unit of output sold—total revenue divided by the quantity of the good sold. Average revenue also equals price.

Average total cost Total cost per unit of output.

Average variable cost Total variable cost per unit of output.

Balance of trade The value of exports minus the value of imports.

Barriers to entry Legal or natural impediments that protect a firm from competition from potential new entrants.

Barter The direct exchange of one good or service for another good or service.

Big trade-off The trade-off between inequality and efficiency that is created by the redistribution of income.

Bilateral monopoly A situation in which there is a single buyer (a monopoly) and a single seller (a monopsony).

Black market An illegal trading arrangement in which buyers and sellers do business at a price that is higher than the legally imposed price ceiling.

Bond A legally enforceable debt obligation to pay specified sums of money at specified future dates.

Bond market The market in which the bonds issued by firms and governments are traded.

Budget line The limits to a household's consumption choices.

Bureaucrat A hired official who works in a government department at either the federal, provincial, or local level.

Capital The equipment, buildings, tools, and other manufactured goods that are used in the production of goods and services.

Capital accumulation The growth of capital resources.

Capital gain The income received by selling a stock, bond, or asset for a higher price than the price paid for it.

Capture theory A theory of regulation that states that regulations are supplied to satisfy the demand of producers to maximize producer surplus—to maximize economic profit.

Cartel A group of firms that has entered into a collusive agreement to restrict output so as to increase prices and profits.

Ceteris paribus Other things being equal—all other relevant things remaining the same.

Change in demand A change in buyers' plans that occurs when some influence on these plans other than the price of the good changes. A change in demand is illustrated by a shift of the demand curve.

Change in supply A change in sellers' plans that occurs when some influence on these plans other than the price of the good changes. A change in supply is illustrated by a shift of the supply curve.

Change in the quantity demanded A change in buyers' plans that occurs when the price of a good changes but all other influences on buyers' plans remain the same. A change in the quantity demanded is illustrated by a movement along the demand curve.

Change in the quantity supplied A change in sellers' plans that occurs when the price of a good changes but all other influences on sellers' plans remain the same. A change in the quantity demanded is illustrated by a movement along the supply curve.

Choke price The price at which the quantity demanded of a natural resource is zero.

Coase theorem The proposition that if property rights exist and transactions costs are low, private transactions are efficient—equivalently, there are no externalities.

Collective bargaining A process of negotiation between representatives of employers and unions.

Collusive agreement An agreement between two (or more) producers to restrict output so as to increase prices and profits.

Comparative advantage A person or country has a comparative advantage in an activity if that person or country can perform that activity at a lower opportunity cost than anyone else or any other country.

Complement A good that is used in conjunction with another good.

Constant returns to scale Technological conditions under which a given percentage increase in all the firm's inputs results in the firm's output increasing by the same percentage.

Consumer efficiency A situation that occurs when consumers cannot make themselves better off by reallocating their budget.

Consumer equilibrium A situation in which a consumer has allocated his or her income in the way that, given prices of goods and services, maximizes his or her total utility.

Consumer surplus The value that the consumer places on the good minus the price paid for it.

Contestible market A market structure in which there is one firm (or a small number of firms) and because of freedom of entry and exit, the firm (or firms) faces competition from potential entrants and so it operates as if it were a perfectly competitive firm.

Cooperative equilibrium The outcome of a collusive agreement between players when each player responds rationally to a credible threat from another player to inflict heavy damage if an agreement is broken.

Copyright A government-sanctioned exclusive right granted to the inventor of a good, service, or productive process to produce, use, and sell the invention for a given number of years.

Countervailing duty A tariff that is imposed to enable domestic producers to compete with subsidized foreign producers.

Craft union A group of workers who have a similar range of skills but work for many different firms in many different industries and regions.

Cross elasticity of demand The responsiveness of the demand for a good to the price of a substitute or complement, other things remaining the same. Cross elasticity of demand is calculated as the percentage change in the quantity demanded of a good divided by the percentage change in the price of the substitute or complement.

Cross-section graph A graph that shows the values of an economic variable for different groups in a population at a point in time.

Crown corporation A firm that is publicly owned and operated under government supervision.

Deadweight loss A measure of allocative inefficiency, which is equal to the loss of total surplus (consumer surplus plus producer surplus) that results from producing less than the efficient level of output.

Decreasing returns to scale Technological conditions under which a given percentage increase in all the firm's inputs results in the firm's output increasing by a smaller percentage.

Demand The relationship between the quantity demanded of a good and its price, with all other influences on buyers' plans remaining the same.

Demand is described by a demand schedule and illustrated by a demand curve.

Demand curve A curve that shows the relationship between the quantity demanded of a good and its price, all other influences on buyers' plans remaining the same.

Depreciation The amount of existing capital that wears out in a given period.

Derived demand Demand for an item not for its own sake but for use in the production of goods and services.

Diminishing marginal rate of substitution The general tendency for the marginal rate of substitution of one good for another to diminish as the consumer moves along an indifference curve, increasing the consumption of the good measured on the x-axis and decreasing the consumption of the good measured on the y-axis.

Diminishing marginal returns The tendency for the marginal product of a variable factor eventually to diminish as additional units of the variable factor are employed.

Diminishing marginal utility The decline in marginal utility that occurs as more and more of a good is consumed.

Direct relationship A relationship between two variables that move in the same direction.

Discounting The conversion of a future amount of money to its present value.

Diseconomies of scale Technological conditions under which the long-run average cost increases as output increases.

Dominant strategy equilibrium The outcome of a game in which there is a single best strategy (a dominant strategy) for each player, regardless of the strategy of the other players.

Dumping The sale of an export by a foreign firm for a price that is below its cost of production.

Duopoly A market structure in which two producers of a good or service compete with each other.

Dynamic comparative advantage Comparative advantage that a person or country possesses as a result of having

specialized in a particular activity and then, as a result of learning-by-doing, having become the producer of that activity with the lowest opportunity cost.

Economic depreciation The decrease in the market price of a piece of capital during a given period.

Economic efficiency A situation that occurs when the cost of producing a given output is as low as possible.

Economic growth The expansion of production possibilities that results from capital accumulation and technological change.

Economic information Data on prices, quantities, and qualities of goods and services and factors of production.

Economic model A description of some aspect of the economic world that includes only those features of the world that are needed for the purpose at hand.

Economic profit A firm's total revenue minus its opportunity costs.

Economic rent The income received by the owner of a factor in excess of the amount required to induce that owner to offer the factor for use.

Economic stability The absence of wide fluctuations in the economic growth rate, the level of employment, and average prices.

Economic theory A generalization that summarizes what we think we understand about the economic choices that people make and the performance of industries and entire economies.

Economics The study of how people use their limited resources to try to satisfy unlimited wants.

Economies of scale Technological conditions under which long-run average cost decreases as output increases.

Economies of scope A situation in which average total cost decreases as a result of increasing the number of different goods produced.

Efficient market A market in which the actual price embodies all currently available relevant information.

Elastic demand Demand with a price elasticity greater than 1; other things remaining the same, the percentage change in the quantity demanded of the good exceeds the percentage change in its price.

Elasticity of supply The responsiveness of the quantity supplied of a good to a change in its price, other things remaining the same. Elasticity of supply is calculated as the percentage change in the quantity supplied of a good divided by the percentage change in its price.

Entrepreneurial ability A special type of human resource that organizes the other three factors of production—labour, land, and capital—and makes business decisions, innovates, and bears business risk.

Equilibrium price The price at which the quantity demanded equals the quantity supplied.

Equilibrium quantity The quantity bought and sold at the equilibrium price.

Equity In economics, equity has two meanings: economic justice or fairness and the owner's stake in a business.

Exchange efficiency A situation in which a good or service is exchanged at a price that equals both the marginal social benefit and the marginal social cost of the good or service.

Excise tax A tax on the sale of a good or service. The tax is paid when the good or service is bought.

Excludable good A good is excludable if its benefits can be restricted to the person who has paid for the good.

Exhaustible natural resources Natural resources that can be used only once and that cannot be replaced once used.

Expected utility The average utility arising from all possible outcomes.

Exports The goods and services that we sell to people in other countries.

External benefits Benefits that accrue to members of society other than the buyer of a good.

External costs Costs that are borne by members of society other than the producer of the good.

External diseconomies Factors outside the control of a firm that raise the firm's costs as the industry produces a larger output.

External economies Factors beyond the control of a firm that lower the firm's costs as the industry produces a larger output.

Externality A cost or a benefit arising from an economic transaction that affects people other than those who decide the scale of the activity.

Factors of production The economy's productive resources—land, labour, capital, and entrepreneurial ability.

Farm marketing board A regulatory agency that intervenes in agricultural markets to stabilize the prices of many agricultural products.

Financial intermediary An institution that receives deposits and makes loans.

Firm An institution that hires factors of production and that organizes those factors to produce and sell goods and services.

Fixed cost A cost that is independent of the output level.

Four-firm concentration ratio A measure of market power that is calculated as the sales of the four largest firms in an industry as a percentage of total industry sales.

Free rider A person who consumes a good without paying for it.

Game theory A method of analysing strategic behaviour.

General Agreement on Tariffs and Trade An international agreement designed to limit government intervention to restrict international trade.

Herfindahl–Hirschman Index A measure of market power, which is calculated as the sum of the square of the market share (as a percentage) of each of the largest 50 firms (or all firms if there are fewer than 50 firms) in the market.

Hotelling Principle The proposition that the market for a stock of a natural resource is in equilibrium when the price of the resource is expected to rise at a rate equal to the interest rate on similarly risky assets.

Human capital The skill and knowledge of people, which arises from their education and on-the-job training.

Implicit rental rate The rent that a firm pays to itself for the use of the assets that it owns.

Imports The goods and services that we buy from people in other countries.

Incentive An inducement to take a particular action.

Income effect The change in consumption that results from a change in the consumer's income, other things remaining the same.

Income elasticity of demand The responsiveness of demand to a change in income, other things remaining the same. Income elasticity of demand is calculated as the percentage change in the quantity demanded divided by the percentage change in income.

Increasing marginal returns The tendency for the marginal product of the variable factor to increase as additional units of the variable factor are employed.

Increasing returns to scale Technological conditions under which the percentage increase in a firm's output exceeds the percentage increase in its inputs.

Indifference curve A curve that shows combinations of goods among which the consumer is indifferent.

Industrial union A group of workers who have a variety of skills and job types but who work for the same firm or industry.

Inelastic demand A demand with a price elasticity between 0 and 1; other things remaining the same, the percentage change in the quantity demanded of a good is less than the percentage change in its price.

Infant-industry argument The argument that protection is necessary to enable an infant industry to grow into a mature industry that can compete in world markets.

Inferior good A good for which demand decreases when income increases.

Information cost The cost of acquiring information on prices, quantities, and qualities of goods and services and factors of production—the opportunity cost of economic information.

Intellectual property rights Property rights for discoveries that are owned by creators of knowledge.

Inverse relationship A relationship between two variables that move in opposite directions.

Labour The time and effort that people allocate to producing goods and services.

Labour union An organized group of workers whose purpose is to increase their wages and to influence their other job conditions.

Land All the natural resources used to produce goods and services.

Law of diminishing returns As a firm increases the quantity of a variable factor, given the quantities of other factors (fixed factors), the marginal product of the variable factor eventually diminishes.

Learning-by-doing People can become more productive in an activity (learn) just by repeatedly producing a particular good or service (doing).

Legal monopoly A market structure in which competition and entry is restricted by the granting of a public franchise, licence, patent, or copyright or the firm has acquired ownership of a significant portion of a key resource.

Limit pricing The practice of charging a price below the monopoly profit-maximizing price and producing a quantity greater than that at which marginal revenue equals marginal cost so as to deter entry.

Linear relationship The relationship between two variables that is illustrated by a straight line.

Loan market A market in which households and firms make and receive loans.

Long run A period of time in which the quantities of all inputs can be varied.

Long-run cost The cost of production when a firm uses the economically efficient plant size.

Long-run industry supply curve A curve that shows how the quantity supplied by an industry varies as the market price varies, after all possible changes in plant size and the number of firms in the industry have been made.

Lorenz curve A curve that graphs the cumulative percentage of income or wealth against the cumulative percentage of families or population.

Low-income cutoff The income level, determined separately for different types of families (for example, single persons, couples, one parent), that is selected such that families with incomes below that limit normally spend 54.7 percent or more of their income on food, shelter, and clothing.

Macroeconomics The study of the national economy and the global economy, the way that economic aggregates fluctuate and grow, and the effects of government actions on them.

Marginal benefit The extra benefit received from a small increase in the consumption of a good or service. Marginal benefit is calculated as the increase in total benefit divided by the increase in consumption.

Marginal cost The change in total cost that results from a unit increase in output. Marginal cost is calculated as the increase in total cost divided by the increase in output.

Marginal cost pricing rule The rule that sets price equal to marginal cost.

Marginal product The extra output produced as a result of a small increase in the variable factor. Marginal product is calculated as the increase in total product divided by the increase in the variable factor employed, when the quantities of all other factors are constant.

Marginal rate of substitution The rate at which a person will give up one good in order to get more of another good and at the same time remain indifferent.

Marginal revenue The extra total revenue received from selling one additional unit of the good or service. Marginal revenue is calculated as the change in total revenue divided by the change in quantity sold.

Marginal revenue product The extra total revenue received from employing one more unit of a factor of production while the quantities of all other factors remain the same. Marginal revenue product is calculated as the increase in total revenue divided by the increase in the quantity of the factor.

Marginal social benefit The marginal benefit received by the consumer of a good (marginal private benefit) plus the marginal benefit received by other members of society (external benefit).

Marginal social cost The marginal cost incurred by a producer of a good (marginal private cost) plus the marginal cost imposed on other members of society (external cost).

Marginal utility The change in total utility resulting from a one-unit increase in the quantity of a good consumed.

Marginal utility per dollar spent The marginal utility obtained from the last unit of a good consumed divided by the price of the good.

Market Any arrangement that enables buyers and sellers to get information and to do business with each other.

Market activity People undertake market activity when they buy goods and services in goods markets or sell the services of the factors of production that they own in factor markets.

Market demand The relationship between the total quantity of a good demanded and its price, all other influences on buying plans remaining the same.

Market failure The inability of an unregulated market to achieve, in all circumstances, allocative efficiency.

Median voter theorem The proposition that political parties will pursue policies that appeal most to the median voter.

Merger The combining of the assets of two firms to form a single, new firm.

Microeconomics The study of the decisions of people and businesses, the interactions of those decisions in markets, and the effects of government regulation and taxes on the prices and quantities of goods and services.

Minimum wage law A regulation that makes hiring labour below a specified wage illegal.

Monopolistic competition A market type in which a large number of firms compete with each other by making similar but slightly different products.

Monopoly An industry that produces a good or service for which no close substitute exits, and in which there is one supplier that is protected from competition by a barrier preventing the entry of new firms.

Monopsony A market structure in which there is just a single buyer.

Moral hazard A situation in which one of the parties to an agreement has an incentive, after the agreement is made, to act in a manner that benefits himself or herself at the expense of the other party.

Nash equilibrium The outcome of a game in which player A takes the best possible action given the action of player B and player B takes the best possible action given the action of player A.

Natural monopoly A monopoly that occurs when one firm can supply the entire market at a lower price than two or more firms can.

Natural resources The nonproduced factors of production, which can be exhaustible or nonexhaustible.

Negative income tax A redistribution scheme that gives every family a guaranteed annual income and that decreases the family's benefit at a specified benefit–loss rate as its market income increases.

Negative relationship A relationship between two variables that move in opposite directions.

Net exporter A country whose value of exports exceeds its value of imports—its balance of trade is positive.

Net importer A country whose value of imports exceeds its value of exports—its balance of trade is negative.

Net investment The change in the capital stock in a given period of time. Net investment is calculated as gross investment minus depreciation.

Net present value The present value of the future flow of marginal revenue product generated by capital minus the cost of the capital.

Nonexcludable good A good that it is impossible, or extremely costly, to prevent someone from benefiting from.

Nonexhaustible natural resources Natural resources that can be used repeatedly without depleting what is available for future use.

Nonmarket activity Leisure and nonmarket production activities, including housework, education and training, shopping, cooking, and other activities in the home.

Nonrival good A good that has the characteristic that one person's consumption of it does not decrease the quantity available for another person to consume.

Nontariff barriers Any action other than a tariff that restricts international trade.

Normal good A good for which demand increases as income increases.

Normal profit The return that a firm's owner could obtain in the best alternative business.

Oligopoly A market type in which a small number of producers compete with each other.

Opportunity cost The opportunity cost of an action is the best forgone alternative.

Patent A government-sanctioned exclusive right granted to the inventor of a good, service, or productive process to produce, use, and sell the invention for a given number of years.

Payoff matrix A table that shows the payoffs for every possible action by each player for every possible action by each other player.

Perfect competition A market structure in which there are many firms; each firm sells an identical product; there are many buyers; there are no restrictions on entry into the industry; firms in the industry have no advantage over potential new entrants; and all firms and buyers are completely informed about the price of each firm's product.

Perfectly elastic demand Demand with an infinite price elasticity; the quantity demanded is infinitely responsive to a change in the price.

Perfectly inelastic demand Demand with a price elasticity of zero; the quantity demanded remains constant when the price changes.

Political equilibrium A situation in which the choices of voters, politicians, and bureaucrats are all compatible and in which no one group can improve its position by making a different choice.

Positive relationship A relationship between two variables that move in the same direction.

Poverty A state in which a family's income is too low to be able to buy the quantities of food, shelter, and clothing that are deemed necessary.

Present value The amount of money that, if invested today, will grow to be as large as a given future amount when the interest that it will earn is taken into account.

Price ceiling A regulation that makes it illegal to charge a price higher than a specified level.

Price discrimination The practice of charging some customers a lower price than others for an identical good or of charging an individual customer a lower price on a large purchase than on a small one, even though the cost of servicing all customers is the same.

Price effect The change in consumption that results from a change in the price of a good or service, other things remaining the same.

Price elasticity of demand The responsiveness of the quantity demanded of a good to a change in its price. Price elasticity of demand is measured by the percentage change in the quantity demanded of a good divided by the percentage change in its price.

Price taker A firm that cannot influence the price of the good or service it produces.

Principal–agent problem The problem of devising compensation rules that induce an agent to act in the best interest of a principal.

Principle of minimum differentiation As competitors attempt to appeal to the maximum number of clients or voters, they tend to make themselves identical.

Principle of substitution When the opportunity cost of an activity increases, people substitute other activities that have lower opportunity costs.

Private information Information that is available to one person but is too costly for anyone else to obtain.

Privatization The process of selling publicly owned enterprises to private individuals and firms.

Producer efficiency A situation in which it is not possible to produce more of one good without producing less of some other good.

Producer surplus The price a producer gets for a good or service minus the opportunity cost of producing it.

Product differentiation The making of a product that is slightly different from that of a competing firm.

Production efficiency Production is efficient when it is not possible to produce more of one good without producing less of some other good. Production efficiency occurs only at points *on* the production possibility frontier.

Production function A relationship that shows how the maximum output attainable varies as quantities of all inputs vary.

Production possibility frontier The boundary between those combinations of goods and services that can be produced and those that cannot.

Progressive income tax A tax on income at a marginal rate that increases with the level of income.

Property rights Social arrangements that govern the ownership, use, and disposal of factors of production and goods and services.

Proportional income tax A tax on income that remains at a constant rate, regardless of the level of income.

Protectionism The restriction of international trade.

Public good A good or service that can be consumed simultaneously by everyone and from which no one can be excluded.

Public interest theory A theory of regulation that states that regulations are supplied to satisfy the demand of consumers and producers to maximize total surplus—that is, to attain allocative efficiency.

Quantity demanded The amount of a good or service that consumers plan to buy in a given period of time at a particular price.

Quantity supplied The amount of a good or service that producers plan to sell in a given period of time at a particular price.

Quota A restriction on the quantity of a good that a farm can produce or on the quantity of a good that can be imported.

Rand formula A rule (set out by Mr. Justice Ivan Rand in 1945) that makes it compulsory for all workers to contribute to the union, whether or not they belong to it.

Rank-tournament compensation scheme A scheme in which the payment to a worker depends on the worker's rank in a tournament or game.

Rate of return regulation A regulation that determines a regulated price by setting the price at a level that enables the regulated firm to earn a specified target percent return on its capital.

Rational ignorance The decision not to acquire information because the cost of acquiring the information is greater than the benefit derived from having it.

Real income The quantity of a good that a consumer's income will buy. Real income is the consumer's income expressed in units of goods and is calculated as income divided by the price of the good.

Regressive income tax A tax on income at a marginal rate that falls with the level of income.

Relative price The ratio of the price of one good or service to the price of another good or service. A relative price is an opportunity cost.

Rent ceiling A regulation making it illegal to charge a rent higher than a specified level.

Rent seeking The activity of attempting to create a monopoly.

Reservation price The highest price that the buyer is willing to pay for the good.

Reservation wage The lowest wage rate for which a person will supply labour to the market. The person will not supply labour at a lower wage rate.

Returns to scale The increase in output that results when a firm increases all its inputs by the same percentage.

Risk A situation in which more than one outcome might occur and the probability of each possible outcome can be estimated.

Rival good A good that has the characteristic that one person's consumption of it decreases the consumption available to someone else.

Scarcity The universal state in which wants exceed resources.

Scatter diagram A diagram that plots the value of one economic variable against the value of another.

Search activity The time spent in searching for someone with whom to do business.

Short run The short run in microeconomics has two meanings. For the firm, it is the period of time in which the quantity of at least one input (usually capital) is fixed and the quantities of the other inputs can be varied. For the industry, the short run is the period of time in which each firm has a given plant size and the number of firms in the industry is fixed.

Short-run industry supply curve A curve that shows how the total quantity supplied by the industry varies as the market price varies when the plant size of each firm and the number of firms in the industry remain the same.

Shutdown point The price and output level at which the firm just covers its total variable cost. In the short run, the firm is indifferent between producing the profit-maximizing output and shutting down temporarily. If the firm produces, it makes a loss equal to its total fixed cost.

Signal An action taken outside a market that conveys information that can be used by that market.

Slope The change in the value of the variable measured on the *y*-axis divided by the change in the value of the variable measured on the *x*-axis.

Stock market The market in which the stocks of corporations are traded.

Strategies All the possible actions of each player in a game.

Subsidy A payment made by the government to producers that depends on the level of output.

Substitute A good that can be used in place of another good.

Substitution effect The effect of a change in price on the quantities consumed when the consumer remains indifferent between the original and the new combinations of goods consumed.

Sunk costs The past economic depreciation of a firm's capital (buildings, plant, and equipment).

Supply The relationship between the quantity of a good that producers plan to sell and the price of the good, with all other influences on sellers' plans remaining the same. Supply is described by a supply schedule and illustrated by a supply curve.

Supply curve A curve that shows the relationship between the quantity supplied and the price of a good, all other influences on producers' planned sales remaining the same.

Takeover The purchase of the stock of one firm by another firm.

Tariff A tax that is imposed by the importing country when an imported good crosses its international boundary.

Technological efficiency A situation that occurs when it is not possible to increase output without increasing inputs.

Technological progress The development of new and better ways of producing goods and services and the development of new goods.

Time-series graph A graph that measures time (for example, months or years) on the x-axis and the variable or variables in which we are interested on the y-axis.

Total cost The sum of the costs of all the inputs the firm uses in production.

Total fixed cost The total cost of the fixed inputs.

Total product The total quantity produced by a firm in a given period of time.

Total revenue The value of a firm's sales. Total revenue is calculated as the price of the good multiplied by the quantity of the good sold.

Total revenue test A method of estimating the price elasticity of demand by observing the change in total revenue that results from a change in the price, when all other influences on the quantity sold remain the same.

Total surplus The sum of consumer surplus and producer surplus.

Total utility The total benefit or satisfaction that a person gets from the consumption of goods and services.

Total variable cost The total cost of the variable inputs.

Trade-off A constraint that entails giving up one thing to get something else.

Transactions costs The costs incurred in searching for someone with whom to do business, in reaching an agreement about the price and other aspects of the exchange, and in ensuring that the terms of the agreement are fulfilled.

Transfer earnings The income that an owner of a factor of production requires to induce the owner to supply the factor.

Trend The general direction (rising or falling) in which a variable is moving over the long term.

Uncertainty A situation in which more than one event might occur but we don't know which one will occur.

Unit elastic demand Demand with a price elasticity of 1; other things remaining the same, the percentage change in the quantity demanded equals the percentage change in the price.

Utility The benefit or satisfaction that a person obtains from the consumption of a good or service.

Utility of wealth The amount of utility that a person attaches to a given amount of wealth.

Value The maximum amount that a person is willing to pay for a good.

Variable cost A cost that varies with the output level.

Voluntary export restraint A self-imposed restriction by an exporting country on the volume of its exports of a particular good. Voluntary export restraints are often called VERs.

Wealth The current market value of what a household owns. Wealth is equal to the current market value of the household's past saving plus any inheritances it has derived.

Index

Index

Key concepts and pages where they are defined appear in **boldface**.

Credits

Care has been taken to determine and locate ownership of copyright material used in this text. In the case of any errors or omissions, please advise the publisher.

Cover:
Lighthouse, © Lane Photographics Limited.

Part 1:
Talking with Douglass North, © Bill Stover.

Chapter 1:
Cartoon, Drawing by Modell; © 1985, The New Yorker Magazine, Inc.
Cartoon, Drawing by H. Martin; © 1987, The New Yorker Magazine, Inc.

Chapter 3:
Pin factory, Culver Pictures, Inc.
Woman holding silicon wafer, Bruce Ando/Tony Stone Images.
Adam Smith, Corbis-Bettmann.

Chapter 4:
Steam engine, Courtesy of Stoddart Publishing Co. Limited, from *Canada: The Missing Years.*
Airplanes, Courtesy of Air Canada.
Antoine-Augustin Cournot, © STOCK MONTAGE.
Alfred Marshall, © STOCK MONTAGE.

Chapter 8:
Cartoon, Drawing by Weber; © 1988, The New Yorker Magazine, Inc.

Chapter 11:
Cartoon, Drawing by N. Twohy; © 1985, The New Yorker Magazine, Inc.

Chapter 12:
Cartoon, William Hamilton's cartoon is reprinted courtesy of Chronicle Features, San Francisco, CA.

Chapter 14:
Downtown Montreal 1927, Canadian Pacific Archives, no. 18227.

Cartoon of stacked cars, The Economist, 9/14/91; reprinted by permission of Robert Hunt.
Thomas Robert Malthus, Corbis-Bettmann.
Harold Hotelling, Photography by Wootten-Moulio.

Chapter 17:
Cartoon by Lorenz; © 1986, The New Yorker Magazine, Inc.

Part 9:
Talking with Jacob Frenkel, © Photo Galia.

Chapter 37:
Cartoon, Drawing by M. Stevens; © 1993, The New Yorker Magazine, Inc.
Advertisement for ships sailing to California, Corbis-Bettmann.
Container ship, M. Fife/Superstock.
David Ricardo, Corbis-Bettmann.